SUBJECT INDEX TO BOOKS FOR INTERMEDIATE GRADES

SUBJECT INDEX
TO BOOKS
FOR
INTERMEDIATE
GRADES

THIRD EDITION

COMPILED BY MARY K. EAKIN
STATE COLLEGE OF IOWA

AMERICAN LIBRARY ASSOCIATION
CHICAGO

International Standard Book Number 0-8389-0057-7 (1963)

Library of Congress Catalog Card Number 63-12951

Printed in the United States of America

Seventh Printing, October 1970

PREFACE

This third edition of the *Subject Index to Books for Intermediate Grades*—like the second edition, which was published in 1950—is designed as a reference tool to be used by classroom teachers and librarians in identifying books that have value as teaching materials for Grades 4–6. In selecting the some 1800 books that are indexed, emphasis has been placed on trade books, because trade books contain some of the best informational writing available for children today, and they tend to have greater appeal for children than do most textbooks. Textbooks have been included only when necessary in subject areas where the coverage by trade books was not considered adequate.

Not all of the good material available in trade books for use at the intermediate level could be included. Much good fiction that would be used in an individualized reading program has been omitted, and only those fiction titles included that have a specific subject value or a specific type appeal, i.e., stories with settings in other countries, humorous stories, mystery stories.

New subject headings have been added in the Subject Index to meet the changing needs of classroom teaching, and some older headings have been revised to fit modern terminology. For example, the heading INTERNATIONAL UNDER-STANDING has been added, covering fiction that gives a picture of present-day life in countries other than the United States. The heading CHARACTER EDUCATION has been changed from a main heading to a cross reference to specific aspects of character education, as FEAR—OVERCOMING; RESPONSIBILITY; SELF-CONFI-DENCE. In general, the headings follow the form used in *Children's Catalog* and *Sears List of Subject Headings*. When it was necessary to list subjects not yet included in these two tools, reference was made to standard courses of study for terminology that would most nearly fit classroom needs.

In the List of Books Indexed, publisher, price, and grade level (in parentheses) are given for each title, followed by a simplified Dewey Decimal number or the abbreviation "Fic" for Fiction. Thus the user can quickly distinguish between fiction and nonfiction titles and, for nonfiction, can identify the general area into which a book fits. Collections of short stories are identified by the letters "S C." The numbers are not intended as an aid in cataloging but are given merely as a convenient indication of general subject areas. The prices given were current at the time of compilation but are subject to change. All titles were listed as in print in the 1961 *Books in Print*.

All of the books indexed are recommended titles; there is no indication of first purchase. Order of purchase within any subject area should be based on the needs of the individual library rather than on any general assignment of rank to the books.

In the Subject Index, the grade levels for titles are given in the right-hand column. An asterisk by the grade level indicates that the material is presented in a fictionalized form. Asterisks were not used for titles under headings that are obviously fiction, such as MYSTERY STORIES; FANCIFUL TALES—MODERN; or FOLK TALES (used as a subheading).

The grade levels given are geared to the intermediate grades, Grades 4–6. A book graded as 6 indicates fairly difficult material that could be used with accelerated readers in all three intermediate grades. Books graded 5–6, 4–6, or 4–5 are for the average reader in the intermediate grades, although 5–6 obviously would be somewhat more difficult than 4–6 or 4–5, and 4–5 would be somewhat easier than 4–6 or 5–6. A book graded as 4 would be easier than one graded 4–6 or 4–5.

In listing the books, the author's name has been given as it appears on the title page. In like manner, pseudonyms of famous people have been retained as subject headings. Thus, Johnny Appleseed is listed under APPLESEED, JOHNNY, with a cross reference from Chapman, John. BUFFALO BILL is used as a main heading, with a cross reference from Cody, William Frederick.

In selecting books to be indexed, no attempt was made to index collections of folk and fairy tales or of poetry, since both of these categories are adequately handled in special subject indexes. In a few instances where folk materials are included in collections of stories or in books about other countries, these have been indicated by the subheading FOLK TALES under the names of individual countries. The heading FANCIFUL TALES—MODERN refers to modern stories of fantasy as contrasted with the traditional folk and fairy tales.

It is hoped that this revised edition of *Subject Index to Books for Intermediate Grades* will prove a useful tool in aiding teachers and librarians to make a wide use of books in supplementing and enriching both teaching and individual reading programs.

Mary K. Eakin
State College of Iowa
Cedar Falls, Iowa

LIST OF BOOKS INDEXED

ACKLEY, EDITH F. Dolls To Make for Fun and Profit. Lippincott, 1951. $4.75. (5–6) 649.*

———— Marionettes: Easy To Make! Fun To Use! Lippincott, 1929. $4.50. (5–6) 791.

ADAMS, KATHLEEN, and ATCHINSON, FRANCES E. A Book of Giant Stories. Dodd, 1926. $3. (5–6) S C.

ADAMS, SAMUEL H. The Erie Canal. Random, 1953. $1.95. (5–6) 974.

———— The Pony Express. Random, 1950. $1.95. (4–6) 383.

———— The Santa Fe Trail. Random, 1951. $1.95. (5–6) 978.

ADLER, IRVING. Dust. Day, 1958. $3. (5–6) 551.

———— Fire in Your Life. Day, 1955. $3. (4–6) 536.

———— The Giant Golden Book of Mathematics: Exploring the World of Numbers and Space. Golden Pr., 1960. $3.95. (6) 510.

———— Magic House of Numbers. Day, 1957. $3. (6) 793.

———— Time in Your Life. Day, 1955. $3. (4–6) 529.

———— Tools in Your Life. Day, 1956. $3. (5–6) 621.

———— Tools of Science: From Yardstick to Cyclotron. Day, 1958. $3. (6) 507.

———— Weather in Your Life. Day, 1959. $3. (5–6) 551.

———— and ADLER, RUTH. Things That Spin: From Tops to Atoms. Day, 1960. $2; lib. bdg. $2.19. (5–6) 531.

AGLE, NAN H., and WILSON, ELLEN. Three Boys and the Remarkable Cow. Scribner, 1952. $2.50. (4–5) Fic.

ALBEE, GEORGE S. Three Young Kings. Watts, 1956. $2.75. (4–5) Fic.

ALDEN, RAYMOND M. Why the Chimes Rang, and Other Stories. Bobbs-Merrill, 1945. $3. (4–6) 398.

ALLISON, DOROTHY K. About Helpful Helicopters. Melmont, 1954. $2.50. (4–5) 629.

ALLSTROM, ELIZABETH, ed. Songs along the Way. Abingdon, 1961. $2.50. (4–6) 223.

AMERICAN HERITAGE (periodical). Discoverers of the New World; narrative by Josef Berger in consultation with Lawrence C. Worth. American Heritage, 1960. $3.50. (5–6) 973.

———— Railroads in the Days of Steam; narrative by Albert L. McCready in

*The numbers at the end of the entries are simplified Dewey Decimal numbers.

consultation with Lawrence W. Sagle. American Heritage, 1960. $3.50. (6) 385.

———— The Story of Yankee Whaling; narrative by Irwin Shapiro in consultation with Edouard A. Stackpole. American Heritage, 1959. $3.50. (6) 639.

———— Trappers and Mountain Men; narrative by Evan Jones in consultation with Dale L. Morgan. American Heritage, 1961. $3.50. (6) 973.

AMES, GERALD, and WYLER, ROSE. The First People in the World. Harper, 1958. $2.95; lib. ed. $2.84. (4–5) 573.

ANCKARSVARD, KARIN. Rider by Night. Harcourt, 1960. $3.25. (5–6) Fic.

———— The Robber Ghost. Harcourt, 1961. $3.25. (5–6) Fic.

ANDERSON, ANITA M. Fur Trappers of the Old West. Harper, 1956. $2.20. (5–6) 978.

———— Wild Bill Hickok. Harper, 1956. $2.20. (5–6) 92.

ANDERSON, CLARENCE W. A Filly for Joan. Macmillan, 1960. $3. (4–5) Fic.

———— High Courage. Macmillan, 1941. $3.75. (6) Fic.

———— Salute. Macmillan, 1940. $3.50. (4–6) Fic.

ANDERSON, WILLIAM R. First under the North Pole: The Voyage of the "Nautilus." World, 1959. $2.75. (4–6) 623.

ANDREWS, ROY C. All about Dinosaurs. Random, 1953. $1.95. (4–6) 560.

———— All about Strange Beasts of the Past. Random, 1956. $1.95. (4–6) 560.

———— All about Whales. Random, 1954. $1.95. (5–6) 639.

ANGELO, VALENTI. The Bells of Bleeker Street. Viking, 1949. $2.75. (4–6) Fic.

———— Nino. Viking, 1938. $3. (5–6) Fic.

ANNIXTER, JANE, and ANNIXTER, PAUL. Buffalo Chief. Holiday, 1958. $2.95. (6) Fic.

ANTONACCI, ROBERT J., and BARR, JENE. Baseball for Young Champions. McGraw-Hill, 1956. $2.95. (4–6) 796.

———— Basketball for Young Champions. McGraw-Hill, 1960. $2.95. (5–6) 796.

ARASON, STEINGRIMUR. Smoky Bay: The Story of a Small Boy of Iceland. Macmillan, 1942. $3.50. (4–6) Fic.

ARDIZZONE, EDWARD. Tim to the Rescue. Walck, 1949. $3. (4–5) Fic.

ARMER, LAURA A. Waterless Mountain. Longmans, 1931. $4.95. (5–6) Fic.

ARMSTRONG, RICHARD. Ship Afire! A Story of Adventure at Sea. Day, 1960. $3. (6) Fic.

ARORA, SHIRLEY L. "What Then, Raman?" Follett, 1960. $3.50. (5–6) Fic.

ASIMOV, ISAAC. Breakthroughs in Science. Houghton, 1960. $4. (6) 920.

———— Satellites in Outer Space. Random, 1960. $1.95. (4–5) 629.

———— Words from the Myths. Houghton, 1961. $3. (6) 422.

ASSOCIATION FOR CHILDHOOD EDUCATION. Told under Spacious Skies. Macmillan, 1952. $3.75. (4–6) S C.

———— Told under the Christmas Tree. Macmillan, 1948. $3.50. (4–6) S C.

———— Told under the Stars and Stripes. Macmillan, 1945. $3.50. (4–6) S C.

ATKINSON, MARGARET F., and HILLMAN, MAY. Dancers of the Ballet. Knopf, 1955. $3.75. (6) 793.

ATWATER, RICHARD, and ATWATER, FLORENCE. Mr. Popper's Penguins. Little, 1938. $3.50. (4–6) Fic.

AULAIRE, INGRI D', and AULAIRE, EDGAR P. D'. Benjamin Franklin. Doubleday, 1950. $3. (4–5) 92.

———— Buffalo Bill. Doubleday, 1952. $2.75. (4–5) 92.

———— Children of the Northlights. Viking, 1935. $3.50. (4–5) Fic.

———— Columbus. Doubleday, 1955. $3. (4–5) 92.

———— Leif the Lucky. Doubleday, 1941. $3. (4–5) 92.

———— The Magic Meadow. Doubleday, 1958. $3. (4–6) Fic.

———— Nils. Doubleday, 1948. $3. (4–5) Fic.

———— Pocahontas. Doubleday, 1946. $3. (4–5) 92.

AULT, PHILLIP H. This Is the Desert: The Story of America's Arid Region. Dodd, 1959. $2.95. (5–6) 551.

AVERILL, ESTHER H. Cartier Sails the St. Lawrence. Harper, 1956. $3; lib. bdg. $2.79. (4–6) 92.

———— Daniel Boone. Harper, 1945. $3.50. (4–6) 92.

AYARS, JAMES S. Caboose on the Roof. Abelard-Schuman, 1956. $2.95. (4–5) Fic.

AYER, MARGARET. Getting To Know Thailand. Coward-McCann, 1959. $2.50; lib. bdg. $2.52. (4–6) 959.

BAER, MARIAN E. Sound. Holiday, 1952. $2.50. (4–6) 534.

BAILEY, BERNADINE F. Bolivia. Albert Whitman, 1942. $1. (4–6) 984.

———— Ecuador. Albert Whitman, 1942. $1. (4–6) 986.

———— Greenland. Albert Whitman, 1942. $1. (4–6) 998.

———— Iceland. Albert Whitman, 1942. $1. (4–6) 949.

———— Peru. Albert Whitman, 1942. $1. (4–6) 985.

———— Picture Book of Minnesota. Albert Whitman, 1953. $1.25. (4–6) 977.

———— Picture Book of New Jersey. Albert Whitman, 1951. $1.25. (4–6) 974.

———— Picture Book of Oklahoma. Albert Whitman, 1952. $1.25. (4–6) 976.

———— Picture Book of Tennessee. Albert Whitman, 1952. $1.25. (4–6) 976.

———— Picture Book of Virginia. Albert Whitman, 1951. $1.25. (4–6) 975.

———— Picture Book of Wisconsin. Albert Whitman, 1951. $1.25. (4–6) 977.

———— Venezuela. Albert Whitman, 1942. $1. (4–6) 987.

BAILEY, CAROLYN S. Children of the Handcrafts. Viking, 1935. $3. (5–6) 680.

———— Miss Hickory. Viking, 1946. $3. (4–6) Fic.

———— Pioneer Art in America. Viking, 1944. $3.75. (5–6) 709.

BAKER, ARTHUR O., and others. Your Science World. Junior Scientist. Rand McNally, 1955. $2.80. (6) 500.

BAKER, NINA B. Amerigo Vespucci. Knopf, 1956. $2.50. (5–6) 92.

———— Henry Hudson. Knopf, 1958. $2.50. (4–6) 92.

———— Juan Ponce de León. Knopf, 1957. $2.50. (5–6) 92.

BAKER, ROBERT H. Introducing the Constellations. Viking, 1957. $4. (6) 520.

———— When the Stars Come Out. Viking, 1954. $4. (6) 523.

BALET, JAN B. What Makes an Orchestra. Walck, 1951. $3.75. (4–6) 785.

BANCROFT, JESSIE H. Games. Macmillan, 1937. $8.85; school ed. $6.75. (4–6) 790.

BANNING, NINA L. Pit Pony. Knopf, 1947. $2.50. (4–6) Fic.

BANNON, LAURA M. Billy and the Bear. Houghton, 1949. $2.50. (4–5) Fic.

———— Hat for a Hero: A Tarascan Boy of Mexico. Albert Whitman, 1954. $2.75. (4) Fic.

———— Patty Paints a Picture. Albert Whitman, 1946. $2. (4) Fic.

———— Watchdog. Albert Whitman, 1948. $2.50. (4–5) Fic.

BANTA, RICHARD E. Life in America: The South. Fideler, 1951. $3.28. (5–6) 975.

BARKER, WILL. Winter-sleeping Wildlife. Harper, 1958. $3. lib. bdg. $2.79. (5–6) 591.

BARKSDALE, LENA. The First Thanksgiving. Knopf, 1956. $2.50. (4–5) 394.

———— That Country Called Virginia. Knopf, 1947. $3. (6) 975.

BARNARD, J. DARRELL, and others. Book 6. Macmillan Science-Life Series. Macmillan, 1959. $2.96. (6) 500.

BARNES, NANCY. The Wonderful Year. Messner, 1946. $2.75. (4–6) Fic.

BARNOUW, ADRIAAN J. Land of William of Orange. Lippincott, 1944. $2.95. (4–6) 949.

BARR, GEORGE. More Research Ideas for Young Scientists. McGraw-Hill, 1961. $3. (5–6) 507.

———— Research Ideas for Young Scientists. McGraw-Hill, 1958. $3. (5–6) 507.

———— Young Scientist Takes a Ride: Guide to Outdoor Observations from a Car Window. McGraw-Hill, 1960. $3. (5–6) 629.

BARROWS, HARLAN H., and others. American Continents. Silver Burdett, 1959. $4.88. (5) 910.

———— Old World Lands. Silver Burdett, 1959. $4.88. (6) 910.

———— Our Big World. Silver Burdett, 1959. $3.84. (4) 910.

BARTLETT, RUTH. Insect Engineers: The Story of Ants. Morrow, 1957. $2.75. (4–6) 595.

BATCHELOR, JULIE F. A Cap for Mul Chand. Harcourt, 1950. $2.75. (4–5) Fic.

———— Communication: From Cave Writing to Television. Harcourt, 1953. $2.50. (4–6) 621.

———— Sea Lady. Harcourt, 1956. $2.50. (4–5) Fic.

———— Tim and the Purple Whistle. Harcourt, 1955. $2.50. (4–5) Fic.

———— and DE LYS, CLAUDIA. Superstitious? Here's Why! Harcourt, 1954. $2.50. (5–6) 398.

BAUDOUY, MICHEL AIMÉ. Bruno, King of the Mountain. Harcourt, 1960. $3. (5–6) Fic.

BAUER, HELEN. California Gold Days. Doubleday, 1954. $3. (5–6) 979.

BAUMANN, HANS. The Caves of the Great Hunters. Pantheon, 1954. $3.50. (6) 571.

BEALS, FRANK L. Davy Crockett. Harper, 1956. $2.20. (5–6) 92.

———— Kit Carson. Harper, 1956. $2.20. (5–6) 92.

———— The Rush for Gold. Harper, 1956. $2.20. (5–6) 978.

BEARD, CHARLES A. The Presidents in American History; brought forward since 1948, by William Beard. Messner, 1961. $2.95. (6) 920.

BEATTY, JEROME. Matthew Looney's Voyage to the Earth. W. R. Scott, 1961. $2.75. (4–6) Fic.

BEATY, JOHN Y. The Baby Whale: Sharp Ears. Lippincott, 1938. $3.95. (4) Fic.

BEAUCHAMP, WILBUR L., and others. Discovering Our World, Book 1. Scott, Foresman, 1957. $2.76. (4) 500.

BECHDOLT, JOHN E. Going Up: The Story of Vertical Transportation. Abingdon, 1948. $2.50. (4–6) 621.

BEELER, NELSON F., and BRANLEY, FRANKLYN M. Experiments in Chemistry. Crowell, 1952. $2.95. (5–6) 540.

———— Experiments in Science. Crowell, 1955. $2.95. (4–6) 500.

———— Experiments with Atomics. Crowell, 1954. $2.95. (6) 539.

———— Experiments with Electricity. Crowell, 1949. $2.95. (5–6) 537.

———— Experiments with Light. Crowell, 1957. $2.95. (6) 535.

———— More Experiments in Science. Crowell, 1950. $2.95. (5–6) 507.

BEERY, MARY. Manners Made Easy. McGraw-Hill, 1954. $2.75; text ed. $3.72. (6) 395.

BEHN, HARRY. Roderick. Harcourt, 1961. $2.75. (5–6) Fic.

BEIM, LORRAINE L. Just Plain Maggie. Harcourt, 1950. $2.95. (4–6) Fic.

BELL, THELMA H. Mountain Boy. Viking, 1947. $2.50. (4) Fic.

———— Snow. Viking, 1954. $2.50. (4–6) 551.

BENARY-ISBERT, MARGOT. The Shooting Star. Harcourt, 1954. $2.50. (4–6) Fic.

———— The Wicked Enchantment. Harcourt, 1955. $2.75. (4–6) Fic.

BENDICK, JEANNE. Electronics for Young People. McGraw-Hill, 1960. $3.50. (6) 621.

———— The First Book of Airplanes. Watts, 1958. $1.95. (4–6) 629.

———— The First Book of Automobiles. Watts, 1955. $1.95. (4–6) 629.

———— The First Book of Ships. Watts, 1959. $1.95. (4–6) 387.

———— The First Book of Space Travel. Watts, 1953. $1.95. (4–6) 629.

———— The First Book of Supermarkets. Watts, 1954. $1.95. (4–5) 658.

———— The Good Knight Ghost. Watts, 1956. $2.50. (4–6) Fic.

———— How Much and How Many: The Story of Weights and Measures. McGraw-Hill, 1960. $2.95. (5–6) 389.

———— Television Works Like This. McGraw-Hill, 1959. $2.75. (6) 621.

———— and BERK, BARBARA. The First Book of How To Fix It. Watts, 1961. $1.95. (4–6) 643.

———— and LEVIN, MARCIA. Take a Number: New Ideas + Imagination = More Fun. McGraw-Hill, 1961. $2.50. (4–5) 511.

BENEDICT, DOROTHY P. Pagan the Black. Pantheon, 1960. $3. (5–6) Fic.

BENSON, SALLY. Stories of the Gods and Heroes. Dial, 1940. $3. (5–6) 292.

BENTLEY, PHYLLIS. The Young Brontës. Roy, 1960. $3. (6) 920.

BERGAUST, ERIK. Rockets and Missiles. Putnam, 1957. $2.50; lib. ed. $2.52. (5–6) 629.

_____ Rockets around the World. Putnam, 1958. $2.50; lib. ed. $2.52. (6) 623.

BERGERE, THEA, and BERGERE, RICHARD. From Stones to Skyscrapers: A Book about Architecture. Dodd, 1960. $3.50. (6) 720.

BERRY, ERICK. Men, Moss, and Reindeer: The Challenge of Lapland. Coward-McCann, 1959. $2.95. (5–6) 947.

BETHERS, RAY. Perhaps I'll Be a Railroad Man. Dutton, 1951. $2.95. (5–6) 625.

_____ Story of Rivers. Sterling, 1957. $2.50. (4–5) 551.

BETZ, BETTY. Your Manners Are Showing. Grosset, 1946. $2.95. (6) 395.

BEVANS, MICHAEL H. The Book of Reptiles and Amphibians. Garden City, 1956. $2.95. (4–6) 598.

BIALK, ELISA. Taffy's Foal. Houghton, 1949. $3. (4–5) Fic.

BIANCO, MARGERY W. All about Pets. Macmillan, 1929. $3.25. (5–6) 636.

BIEMILLER, CARL L. Magic Ball from Mars. Morrow, 1953. $2.75. (4–6) Fic.

_____ Starboy. Holt, 1956. $2.50. (4–6) Fic.

BIGLAND, EILEEN. Madame Curie. Criterion, 1957. $3.25. (6) 92.

BILLINGS, HENRY. Diesel-Electric 4030. Viking, 1950. $2.50. (4–6) 385.

BISCHOF, GEORGE P. Atoms at Work. Harcourt, 1951. $2.75. (5–6) 530.

BISHOP, CLAIRE H. All Alone. Viking, 1953. $2.50. (4–6) Fic.

_____ Blue Spring Farm. Viking, 1948. $2.50. (5–6) Fic.

_____ Martin de Porres, Hero. Houghton, 1954. $3.25. (6) 92.

_____ Pancakes—Paris. Viking, 1947. $2.50. (4–6) Fic.

BISHOP, RICHARD W. From Kite to Kitty Hawk. Crowell, 1958. $3. (6) 629.

BIXBY, WILLIAM. The Impossible Journey of Sir Ernest Shackleton. Little, 1960. $3. (5–6) 999.

BLACK, IRMA S. Pete the Parrakeet. Holiday, 1954. $2.50. (4–5) Fic.

BLEEKER, SONIA. The Apache Indians: Raiders of the Southwest. Morrow, 1951. $2.75. (4–6) 970.

_____ The Cherokee: Indians of the Mountains. Morrow, 1952. $2.75. (4–6) 970.

_____ The Chippewa Indians: Rice Gatherers of the Great Lakes. Morrow, 1955. $2.75. (4–6) 970.

_____ The Crow Indians: Hunters of the Northern Plains. Morrow, 1953. $2.75. (4–6) 970.

_____ The Eskimo: Arctic Hunters and Trappers. Morrow, 1959. $2.75. (4–6) 998.

_____ Horsemen of the Western Plateaus: The Nez Percé Indians. Morrow, 1957. $2.75. (4–6) 970.

_____ The Inca: Indians of the Andes. Morrow, 1960. $2.75. (5–6) 985.

———— Indians of the Longhouse: The Story of the Iroquois. Morrow, 1950. $2.75. (4–6) 970.

———— The Maya: Indians of Central America. Morrow, 1961. $2.75. (5–6) 972.

———— The Mission Indians of California. Morrow, 1956. $2.75. (4–6) 970.

———— The Navajo: Herders, Weavers, and Silversmiths. Morrow, 1958. $2.75. (4–6) 970.

———— The Pueblo Indians: Farmers of the Rio Grande. Morrow, 1955. $2.75. (4–6) 970.

———— The Sea Hunters: Indians of the Northwest Coast. Morrow, 1951. $2.75. (4–6) 970.

———— The Seminole Indians. Morrow, 1954. $2.75. (4–6) 970.

BLIVEN, BRUCE. The American Revolution, 1760-1783. Random, 1958. $1.95. (6) 973.

———— The Story of D-Day: June 6, 1944. Random, 1956. $1.95. (5–6) 940.

BLOCH, MARIE H. Dinosaurs. Coward-McCann, 1955. $2.50; lib. bdg. $2.52. (4–6) 568.

———— Marya of Clark Avenue. Coward-McCann, 1957. $2.75. (4–6) Fic.

———— Tunnels. Coward-McCann, 1954. $2.95. (5–6) 624.

BLOCK, IRVIN. The Real Book about Ships. Garden City, 1953. $1.95. (5–6) 623.

BLOUGH, GLENN O. After the Sun Goes Down: The Story of Animals at Night. McGraw-Hill, 1956. $2.95. (4–5) 591.

———— Discovering Dinosaurs. McGraw-Hill, 1960. $2.75; lib. ed. $3.25. (4) 568.

———— Monkey with a Notion. Holt, 1946. $2.75. (4–6) Fic.

———— Not Only for Ducks: The Story of Rain. McGraw-Hill, 1954. $2.95. (4–5) Fic.

———— Tree on the Road to Turntown. McGraw-Hill, 1953. $2.75. (4) Fic.

———— Wait for the Sunshine: The Story of Seasons and Growing Things. McGraw-Hill, 1954. $2.95. (4–5) 580.

———— and CAMPBELL, MARJORIE H. When You Go to the Zoo. McGraw-Hill, 1955. $2.95. (4–6) 591.

BOARDMAN, FON W. Canals. Walck, 1959. $3.50. (6) 386.

———— Castles. Walck, 1957. $3.50. (6) 940.

———— Roads. Walck, 1958. $3.50. (6) 625.

BOND, MICHAEL. A Bear Called Paddington. Houghton, 1960. $2.50. (4–6) Fic.

———— Paddington Helps Out. Houghton, 1961. $2.50. (4–6) Fic.

BONNER, MARY G. Canada and Her Story. Knopf, 1942. $2.75. (5–6) 971.

———— Made in Canada. Knopf, 1943. $2.75. (6) 745.

BONTEMPS, ARNA W. Frederick Douglass: Slave-Fighter-Freeman. Knopf, 1959. $3. (4–6) 92.

BOOZ, ELIZABETH B. M. A Treat in a Trout. Houghton, 1955. $3. (4) Fic.

BOSIGER, E., and GUILCHER, J.-M. A Bird Is Born. Sterling, 1960. $2.50. (4–6) 598.

BOSTON, LUCY M. The Children of Green Knowe. Harcourt, 1955. $2.75. (4–6) Fic.

———— A Stranger at Green Knowe. Harcourt, 1961. $3. (5–6) Fic.

BOTHWELL, JEAN. The Empty Tower. Morrow, 1948. $2.75. (4–5) Fic.

———— The First Book of Roads. Watts, 1955. $1.95. (4–6) 625.

———— Little Boat Boy: A Story of Kashmir. Harcourt, 1945. $3. (4–5) Fic.

———— Thirteenth Stone: A Story of Rajputana. Harcourt, 1946. $3. (5–6) Fic.

BOULTON, RUDYERD. Traveling with the Birds: A Book on Bird Migration. Donohue, 1933. $2.95. (4–6) 598.

BOUTWELL, EDNA. Sailor Tom. World, 1960. $2.95. (4–6) Fic.

BOWERS, GWENDOLYN. Wishing Book Doll. Morrow, 1957. $2.50. (4–5) Fic.

BOWIE, WALTER R. The Bible Story for Boys and Girls: New Testament. Abingdon, 1951. $2.50. (4–6) 225.

———— The Bible Story for Boys and Girls: Old Testament. Abingdon, 1952. $3.50. (4–6) 221.

BOYD-ORR, JOHN. The Wonderful World of Food: The Substance of Life. Garden City, 1958. $2.95. (6) 641.

BOYLSTON, HELEN D. Clara Barton, Founder of the American Red Cross. Random, 1955. $1.95. (4–6) 92.

BRAGDON, ELSPETH. Fairing Weather. Viking, 1955. $2. (4–5) Fic.

BRAGDON, LILLIAN J. The Land and People of France. Lippincott, 1960. $2.95. (6) 944.

———— The Land and People of Switzerland. Lippincott, 1961. $2.95. (5–6) 949.

———— Tell Me the Time, Please. Lippincott, 1946. $2.50. (4–5) 681.

BRANLEY, FRANKLYN M. Exploring by Satellite. Crowell, 1957. $3.50; lib. ed. $3.36. (6) 629.

———— Guide to Outer Space. Home Library, 1960. $1.95. (4–6) 523.

———— The Moon: Earth's Natural Satellite. Crowell, 1960. $3.50. (6) 523.

———— The Nine Planets. Crowell, 1958. $3.50. (6) 523.

———— Solar Energy. Crowell, 1957. $3.50. (6) 621.

BRENNER, BARBARA. Barto Takes the Subway. Knopf, 1961. $2.95. (4) Fic.

BREWSTER, BENJAMIN. The First Book of Baseball. Watts, 1950. $1.95. (4–5) 796.

———— The First Book of Eskimos. Watts, 1952. $1.95. (4–6) 998.

———— The First Book of Indians. Watts, 1950. $1.95. (4–6) 970.

BRIDGES, WILLIAM. Zoo Babies. Morrow, 1953. $2.95; lib. ed. $2.88. (4–6) 591.

———— Zoo Doctor. Morrow, 1957. $2.95. (5–6) 636.

———— Zoo Pets. Morrow, 1955. $2.95. (4–6) 591.

BRIGHT, ROBERT. Richard Brown and the Dragon. Doubleday, 1952. $2.50. (4–5) Fic.

BRINDZE, RUTH. The Gulf Stream. Vanguard, 1945. $3. (4–6) 551.

———— The Story of Gold. Vanguard, 1955. $3. (4–6) 553.

———— The Story of Our Calendar. Vanguard, 1949. $3. (4–6) 529.

———— The Story of the Totem Pole. Vanguard, 1951. $3. (4–6) 970.

———— The Story of the Trade Winds. Vanguard, 1960. $3.50. (4–6) 551.

BRINK, CAROL R. Caddie Woodlawn. Macmillan, 1935. $3. (5–6) Fic.

———— Family Grandstand. Viking, 1952. $2.50. (4–6) Fic.

———— Magical Melons: More Stories about Caddie Woodlawn. Macmillan, 1944. $3.50. (5–6) Fic.

BROCK, EMMA L. Ballet for Mary. Knopf, 1954. $2.75. (4–5) Fic.

———— Drusilla. Macmillan, 1937. $2.50. (4–5) Fic.

———— Here Comes Kristie. Knopf, 1949. $2.75. (4–5) Fic.

———— Plug-Horse Derby. Knopf, 1955. $2.75. (4–5) Fic.

———— Topsy-Turvy Family. Knopf, 1943. $2.50. (4–5) Fic.

BRONSON, WILFRED S. Cats. Harcourt, 1950. $2.95. (4–5) 636.

———— Children of the Sea. Harcourt, 1940. $4.95. (6) 597.

———— Freedom and Plenty: Ours To Save. Harcourt, 1953. $3.50. (4–6) 333.

———— Goats. Harcourt, 1959. $2.95. (4–6) 636.

———— The Grasshopper Book. Harcourt, 1943. $3.25. (4–6) 595.

———— Horns and Antlers. Harcourt, 1942. $3.50. (4–6) 591.

———— Pinto's Journey. Messner, 1948. $2.75. (4–5) Fic.

———— Pollwiggle's Progress. Macmillan, 1932. $3. (4–5) 597.

———— Starlings. Harcourt, 1948. $3.50. (4–6) 598.

———— Wonder World of Ants. Harcourt, 1937. $2.95. (4–6) 595.

BROWN, ABBIE F. In the Days of Giants: A Book of Norse Tales. Houghton, 1902. $2.20. (4–5) 293.

BROWN, CONRAD. Skiing for Beginners: A Complete and Simple Method for Children and Their Parents. Scribner, 1951. $2.95. (4–6) 796.

BROWN, GLADYS E. Tico Bravo, Shark Hunter. Little, 1954. $3. (4–6) Fic.

BROWN, HARRIETT M., and GUADAGNOLO, JOSEPH F. America Is My Country: The Heritage of a Free People. Houghton, 1955. $5; text ed. $3.80. (5–6) 320.

BROWN, JOHN M. Daniel Boone: The Opening of the Wilderness. Random, 1952. $1.95. (6) 92.

BROWN, MARCIA J. Peter Piper's Alphabet. Scribner, 1959. $2.95. (4–5) 821.

BROWN, PALMER. Beyond the Pawpaw Trees: The Story of Anna Lavinia. Harper, 1954. $2.50. (4–6) Fic.

———— The Silver Nutmeg: The Story of Anna Lavinia and Toby. Harper, 1956. $2.50. (4–6) Fic.

BROWN, PAUL. Crazy Quilt: The Story of a Piebald Pony. Scribner, 1934. $2.95. (4–5) Fic.

BROWN, ROSE J. The Land and People of Brazil. Lippincott, 1960. $2.95. (6) 981.

BROWN, VINSON. How To Make a Home Nature Museum. Little, 1954. $3.50. (5–6) 579.

———— How To Make a Miniature Zoo. Little, 1957. $3.50. (5–6) 579.

———— How To Understand Animal Talk. Little, 1958. $3. (6) 591.

BROWNE, C. A. The Story of Our National Ballads; rev. by Willard A. Heaps. Crowell, 1960. $3.50. (5–6) 784.

BRYSON, BERNARDA. The Twenty Miracles of Saint Nicolas. Little, 1960. $4.75. (5–6) 92.

BUCHANAN, FANNIE R., and LUCKENBILL, CHARLES R. How Man Made Music. Follett, 1959. $3.50. (6) 780.

BUCK, FRANK, and FRASER, FERRIN L. Jungle Animals. Random, 1945. $1.95. (5–6) 590.

BUCK, MARGARET W. In Ponds and Streams. Abingdon, 1955. $3; pa. $1.75. (4–6) 574.

———— In Woods and Fields. Abingdon, 1950. $3; pa. $1.75. (4–6) 502.

———— In Yards and Gardens. Abingdon, 1952. $3; pa. $1.75. (4–6) 502.

———— Pets from the Pond. Abingdon, 1958. $3; pa. $1.75. (4–6) 574.

———— Small Pets from Woods and Fields. Abingdon, 1960. $3; pa. $1.75. (4–6) 574.

BUCK, PEARL S. The Big Wave. Day, 1948. $3.25; lib. bdg. $2.97. (4–6) Fic.

———— The Chinese Children Next Door. Day, 1942. $3; lib. bdg. $2.81. (4) Fic.

BUCKLEY, PETER. Luis of Spain. Watts, 1955. $3.50. (4–6) 946.

———— The Spanish Plateau: The Challenge of a Dry Land. Coward-McCann, 1959. $2.95. (6) 946.

BUEHR, WALTER. Bread: The Staff of Life. Morrow, 1959. $2.75; lib. ed. $2.78. (4–6) 641.

———— The Crusaders. Putnam, 1959. $3; lib. ed. $2.81. (5–6) 940.

———— Harbors and Cargoes. Putnam, 1955. $2.75. (5–6) 387.

———— Harvest of the Sea. Morrow, 1955. $2.75; lib. ed. $2.78. (5–6) 639.

———— Knights and Castles and Feudal Life. Putnam, 1957. $2.75; lib. ed. $2.68. (4–6) 940.

———— Meat from Ranch to Table. Morrow, 1956. $2.75. (4–6) 664.

———— Oil . . . Today's Black Magic. Morrow, 1957. $2.78. (4–6) 665.

———— The Story of the Wheel. Putnam, 1960. $2.75; lib. ed. $2.68. (4–6) 600.

———— Through the Locks: Canals Today and Yesterday. Putnam, 1954. $2.75; lib. ed. $2.68. (4–6) 626.

———— Timber! Farming Our Forests. Morrow, 1960. $2.75. (5–6) 634.

———— Treasure: The Story of Money and Its Safeguarding. Putnam, 1955. $2.50; lib. ed. $2.52. (4–6) 332.

———— Underground Riches: The Story of Mining. Morrow, 1958. $2.78. (5–6) 622.

———— World of Marco Polo. Putnam, 1961. $3; lib. ed. $2.81. (5–6) 950.

BUFANO, REMO. Book of Puppetry. Macmillan, 1950. $3.75. (5–6) 791.

BUFF, MARY, and BUFF, CONRAD. The Apple and the Arrow. Houghton, 1951. $4. (4–6) Fic.

———— Big Tree. Viking, 1946. $3.50. (5–6) 582.

———— Dancing Cloud: The Navajo Boy. Viking, 1957. $3. (4–5) 970.

———— Elf Owl. Viking, 1958. $2.75. (4) 598.

———— Hah-Nee of the Cliff Dwellers. Houghton, 1956. $3; school bdg. $3.75. (4–6) Fic.

———— Magic Maize, Houghton, 1953. $3.50. (4–6) Fic.

BULLA, CLYDE R. Eagle Feather. Crowell, 1953. $2.95; lib. bdg. $2.83. (4–5) Fic.

———— Riding the Pony Express. Crowell, 1948. $2.95; lib. bdg. $2.83. (4–5) Fic.

———— Secret Valley. Crowell, 1949. $2.95; lib. bdg. $2.83. (4–5) Fic.

———— Song of St. Francis. Crowell, 1952. $2.95; lib. bdg. $2.83. (4–5) 92.

———— Stories from Favorite Operas. Crowell, 1959. $3.95. (5–6) 782.

BUNCE, WILLIAM. Freight Train. Putnam, 1954. $2.75. (4–6) 625.

BUNYAN, JOHN. Pilgrim's Progress. Lippincott, 1939. $3.95. (5–6) Fic.

BURCH, GLADYS. Modern Composers for Young People. Dodd, 1941. $3. (5–6) 920.

———— and WOLCOTT, JOHN. Famous Composers for Young People. Dodd, 1945. $3. (4–6) 920.

BURCHARD, PETER. Balloons: From Paper Bags to Skyhooks. Macmillan, 1960. $3.75. (4–6) 629.

———— Jed: The Story of a Yankee Soldier and a Southern Boy. Coward-McCann, 1960. $3. (5–6) Fic.

BURGER, CARL. All about Fish. Random, 1960. $1.95. (5–6) 597.

BURGLON, NORA. Children of the Soil: A Story of Scandinavia. Doubleday, 1932. $2.95. (5–6) Fic.

BURNETT, BERNICE. The First Book of Holidays. Watts, 1955. $1.95. (4–6) 394.

BURNETT, FRANCES H. The Secret Garden. Lippincott, 1949. $3.95. (5–6) Fic.

BURNS, WILLIAM A. Horses and Their Ancestors. McGraw-Hill, 1954. $3. (4–5) 636.

———— Man and His Tools. McGraw-Hill, 1956. $3. (5–6) 621.

———— A World Full of Homes. McGraw-Hill, 1953. $3. (4–6) 728.

BURT, OLIVE W. The Cave of the Shouting Silence. Day, 1960. $3.50. (5–6) Fic.

———— Space Monkey: The True Story of Miss Baker. Day, 1960. $2.50. (4–6) 629.

BUSBY, EDITH. Behind the Scenes at the Library. Dodd, 1960. $2.25. (5–6) 025.

BUTLER, EVELYN I., and DALE, GEORGE A. Alaska: The Land and the People. Viking, 1957. $3.50. (6) 979.

BUTTERFIELD, MARGUERITE A. Adventures of Esteban. Scribner, 1956. $2.50. (4–6) Fic.

———— Jaime and His Hen Pollita. Scribner, 1957. $2.50. (4–5) Fic.

BUTTERS, DOROTHY G. Papa Dolphin's Table. Knopf, 1955. $2.25. (4–5) Fic.

BUTTERWORTH, OLIVER. The Trouble with Jenny's Ear. Little, 1960. $3. (4–6) Fic.

CALDER, RITCHIE. The Wonderful World of Medicine. Garden City, 1958. $2.95. (5–6) 610.

CALDWELL, JOHN C. Let's Visit China. Day, 1959. $2.95. (5–6) 951.

———— Let's Visit Formosa, Island Home of Free China. Day, 1956. $2.95. (5–6) 951.

———— Let's Visit India. Day, 1960. $2.95. (4–6) 954.

———— Let's Visit Indonesia. Day, 1960. $2.95. (4–6) 991.

———— Let's Visit Pakistan. Day, 1960. $2.95. (4–6) 954.

———— Let's Visit West Africa. Day, 1959. $2.95. (4–6) 966.

———— and CALDWELL, ELSIE F. Let's Visit Korea. Day, 1959. $2.95. (4–6) 951.

CALHOUN, MARY. Depend on Katie John. Harper, 1961. $2.95; lib. bdg. $2.79. (4–6) Fic.

———— Katie John. Harper, 1960. $2.50; lib. bdg. $2.44. (4–5) Fic.

———— Making the Mississippi Shout. Morrow, 1957. $2.50. (4–6) Fic.

CALL, HUGHIE. Peter's Moose. Viking, 1961. $3. (4–6) Fic.

CAMERON, ELEANOR. The Terrible Churnadryne. Little, 1959. $3. (4–6) Fic.

———— The Wonderful Flight to the Mushroom Planet. Little, 1954. $3. (4–6) Fic.

CAMPION, NARDI R. Patrick Henry: Firebrand of the Revolution. Little, 1961. $3.75. (5–6) 92.

CANFIELD, DOROTHY. Understood Betsy. Holt, 1946. $3. (5–6) Fic.

CARBONNIER, JEANNE. Congo Explorer: Pierre Savorgnan de Brazza, 1852-1905. Scribner, 1960. $3. (5–6) 92.

CARDEN, PRISCILLA. Aldo's Tower. Farrar, 1954. $2.75. (4–6) Fic.

CARLSON, BERNICE W. Act It Out. Abingdon, 1956. $2; pa. $1.35. (4–6) 792.

———— Do It Yourself! Tricks, Stunts, and Skits. Abingdon, 1952. $2.50; pa. $1.60. (4–6) 793.

———— Make It and Use It: Handicraft for Boys and Girls. Abingdon, 1958. $2.50; pa. $1.60. (4–6) 745.

———— Make It Yourself! Handicraft for Boys and Girls. Abingdon, 1950. $2; pa. $1.35. (4–6) 680.

———— The Right Play for You. Abingdon, 1960. $2.50; pa. $1.60. (4–6) 792.

CARLSON, NATALIE S. Alphonse, That Bearded One. Harcourt, 1954. $2.75. (4–6) Fic.

———— Evangeline: Pigeon of Paris. Harcourt, 1960. $2.75. (4–5) Fic.

———— The Family under the Bridge. Harper, 1958. $2.95; lib. bdg. $2.79. (4–5) Fic.

———— The Happy Orpheline. Harper, 1957. $2.95. (4) Fic.

———— Sashes Red and Blue. Harper, 1956. $2.75. (4) S C.

———— The Song of the Lop-eared Mule. Harper, 1961. $2.75; lib. ed. $2.73. (4–5) Fic.

———— The Talking Cat, and Other Stories of French Canada. Harper, 1952. $2.50; lib. bdg. $2.57. (4–6) S C.

———— Wings against the Wind. Harper, 1955. $2.50. (4–6) Fic.

CARR, MARY J. Children of the Covered Wagon: A Story of the Old Oregon Trail. Crowell, 1934. $3.95. (4–6) Fic.

CARROLL, RUTH, and CARROLL, LATROBE. Tough Enough's Indians. Walck, 1960. $2.75. (4–5) Fic.

———— Tough Enough's Pony. Walck, 1957. $2.75. (4–5) Fic.

———— Tough Enough's Trip. Walck, 1956. $2.75. (4–6) Fic.

CASSELL, SYLVIA. Nature Games and Activities. Harper, 1956. $2.50. (4–6) 574.

CAVANNA, BETTY. The First Book of Sea Shells. Watts, 1955. $1.95. (4–6) 594.

———— Lucho of Peru. Watts, 1961. $3.50. (4–6) 985.

CEDER, GEORGIANA D. Ann of Bethany. Abingdon, 1951. $2.50. (4–6) Fic.

———— Ethan, the Shepherd Boy. Abingdon, 1948. $2.50. (4–6) Fic.

———— Joel, the Potter's Son. Abingdon, 1954. $2. (4–6) Fic.

CHANDLER, ANNA C. Story-Lives of Master Artists. Lippincott, 1953. $3.75. (6) 920.

CHAPPELL, WARREN. The Nutcracker. Knopf, 1958. $2.95. (4–5) 785.

CHASE, ALICE E. Famous Paintings: An Introduction to Art for Young People. Platt & Munk, 1951. $3.95. (6) 759.

CHASE, VIRGINIA. The Knight of the Golden Fleece. Little, 1959. $3.50. (6) 92.

CHAUNCY, NAN. Devil's Hill. Watts, 1960. $2.95. (6) Fic.

CHENEY, CORA. The Peg-legged Pirate of Sulu. Knopf, 1960. $2.75. (4–5) Fic.

———— The Rocking Chair Buck. Holt, 1956. $2.25. (4–5) Fic.

CHILD STUDY ASSOCIATION OF AMERICA. Read to Yourself Storybook. Crowell, 1954. $2.50. (4–5) S C.

CHRISMAN, ARTHUR B. Shen of the Sea. Dutton, 1925. $2.95. (5–6) S C.

CHRISTENSEN, GARDELL D. Buffalo Kill. Nelson, 1959. $2.95. (6) Fic.

CHUBB, THOMAS C. The Byzantines. World, 1959. $3.50. (6) 949.

CHURCH, ALFRED J. The Iliad of Homer. Macmillan, 1951. $2.50. (5–6) 883.

———— The Odyssey of Homer. Macmillan, 1951. $2.50. (5–6) 883.

CLARK, ANN N. Little Navajo Bluebird. Viking, 1943. $2.75. (4–6) Fic.

———— Magic Money. Viking, 1950. $2.75. (4–6) Fic.

CLARK, GRAVES G. Thomas Alva Edison. Dutton, 1950. $2.75. (4–6) 92.

CLEARY, BEVERLY. Beezus and Ramona. Morrow, 1955. $2.75. (4–6) Fic.

———— Ellen Tebbits. Morrow, 1951. $2.75. (4–5) Fic.

———— Henry and Beezus. Morrow, 1952. $2.75. (4–6) Fic.

———— Henry and Ribsy. Morrow, 1958. $2.75. (4–6) Fic.

———— Henry and the Paper Route. Morrow, 1957. $2.75. (4–6) Fic.

———— Henry Huggins. Morrow, 1950. $2.75. (4–6) Fic.

———— Otis Spofford. Morrow, 1953. $2.75. (4–5) Fic.

CLEWES, DOROTHY. The Runaway. Coward-McCann, 1957. $2.50. (4–5) Fic.

———— The Secret. Coward-McCann, 1956. $2.75. (4–5) Fic.

CLYMER, ELEANOR L. Trolley Car Family. McKay, 1947. $2.75. (4–6) Fic.

COATSWORTH, ELIZABETH J. Alice-All-By-Herself. Macmillan, 1947. $3.75. (4–6) Fic.

_____ Away Goes Sally. Macmillan, 1947. $3. (4–6) Fic.

_____ The Cat Who Went to Heaven. Macmillan, 1958. $3.50. (4–6) Fic.

_____ The Cave. Viking, 1958. $2.50. (4–6) Fic.

_____ The Fair American. Macmillan, 1940. $3. (4–6) Fic.

_____ First Adventure. Macmillan, 1950. $2.25. (4–5) Fic.

_____ Five Bushel Farm. Macmillan, 1939. $3.50. (4–6) Fic.

_____ The Golden Horseshoe. Macmillan, 1935. $3. (5–6) Fic.

_____ Littlest House. Macmillan, 1940. $3.50. (4) Fic.

_____ The Sod House. Macmillan, 1954. $2.50. (4–5) Fic.

COFFMAN, RAMON P., and GOODMAN, NATHAN G. Famous Authors for Young People. Dodd, 1943. $3. (5–6) 920.

COGGINS, HERBERT L. Busby & Co. McGraw-Hill, 1952. $2.50. (4–5) Fic.

COGGINS, JACK, and PRATT, FLETCHER. Rockets, Satellites, and Space Travel. Random, 1958. $1.95. (6) 629.

COLBERT, EDWIN H. Millions of Years Ago: Prehistoric Life in North America. Crowell, 1958. $2.75. (6) 560.

COLBY, C. B. Bomber Parade: Headliners in Bomber Plane History. Coward-McCann, 1960. $2.50; lib. ed. $2.52. (5–6) 623.

_____ Earthmovers: Giant Machines That Are Changing the Face of the Earth. Coward-McCann, 1955. $2.50; lib. ed. $2.52. (5–6) 625.

_____ First Bow and Arrow: How To Use It Skillfully for Outdoor Fun. Coward-McCann, 1955. $2.50. (4–6) 799.

_____ First Camping Trip. Coward-McCann, 1955. $2.50. (5–6) 796.

_____ First Hunt: With Success and Safety. Coward-McCann, 1957. $2.50. (5–6) 799.

_____ First Rifle: How To Shoot It Straight and Use It Safely. Coward-McCann, 1954. $2.50. (5–6) 799.

_____ Fish and Wildlife: The Story of the Work of the U.S. Fish and Wildlife Service. Coward-McCann, 1955. $2.50; lib. ed. $2.52. (5–6) 353.

_____ Leatherneck: The Training, Weapons, and Equipment of the United States Marine Corps. Coward-McCann, 1957. $2.50; lib. ed. $2.52. (5–6) 359.

_____ Our Space Age Jets; a completely rev. ed. of Our Fighting Jets. Coward-McCann, 1959. $2.50; lib. ed. $2.52. (5–6) 629.

_____ Park Ranger: The Work, Thrills and Equipment of the National Park Rangers. Coward-McCann, 1955. $2.50; lib. ed. $2.52. (5–6) 353.

_____ Plastic Magic: The Material of a Million Uses. Coward-McCann, 1959. $2.50; lib. ed. $2.52. (4–6) 668.

_____ Ships of Our Navy: Carriers, Battleships, Destroyers, & Landing Craft. Coward-McCann, 1953. $2.50; lib. ed. $2.52. (5–6) 359.

_____ Soil Savers: The Work of the Soil Conservation Service of the United States Department of Agriculture. Coward-McCann, 1957. $2.50; lib. ed. $2.52. (4–6) 631.

COLLODI, CARLO. Pinocchio. Lippincott, 1948. $3.50. (4–6) Fic.

COLUM, PADRAIC. The Adventures of Odysseus and The Tale of Troy. Macmillan, 1918. $3.50; school ed. $2.80. (5–6) 883.

———— The Children of Odin. Macmillan, 1920. $3.50. (4–5) 293.

COLVER, ANNE. Secret Castle. Knopf, 1960. $2.50. (4–5) Fic.

COMMAGER, EVAN. Valentine. Harper, 1961. $2.95; lib. bdg. $2.79. (6) Fic.

COMMAGER, HENRY S. The First Book of American History. Watts, 1957. $1.95. (4–6) 973.

———— The Great Declaration. Bobbs-Merrill, 1958. $3.50. (6) 973.

———— and WARD, LYND. America's Robert E. Lee. Houghton, 1951. $3.50; lib. bdg. $4.25. (6) 92.

COMMINS, DOROTHY B. Making an Orchestra. Macmillan, 1931. $3.50. (5–6) 785.

COMSTOCK, ANNA B. Handbook of Nature-Study. Comstock, 1939. $6.75; text ed. $5. (6) 502.

CONSIDINE, BOB. The Panama Canal. Random, 1951. $1.95. (5–6) 986.

COOKE, DAVID C. Better Football for Boys. Dodd, 1958. $2.50. (4–6) 796.

———— How Atomic Submarines Are Made. Dodd, 1957. $1.95. (6) 623.

———— How Automobiles Are Made. Dodd, 1957. $2.25. (5–6) 629.

———— Racing Cars That Made History. Putnam, 1960. $2.50; lib. ed. $2.52. (5–6) 796.

COOKE, DONALD E. Men of Sherwood: New Tales of Robin Hood's Merry Band. Holt, 1961. $3.95. (5–6) Fic.

COOLIDGE, OLIVIA E. Legends of the North. Houghton, 1951. $3.75. (4–6) 293.

COOMBS, CHARLES. Gateway to Space. Morrow, 1960. $3.95. (6) 629.

———— Rockets, Missiles, and Moons. Morrow, 1957. $3.75. (6) 629.

COOPER, ELIZABETH K. Science in Your Own Back Yard. Harcourt, 1958. $3. (5–6) 500.

———— Science on the Shores and Banks. Harcourt, 1960. $3.25. (5–6) 574.

COOPER, LEE. Fun with Spanish. Little, 1960. $3. (4–6) 468.

CORBETT, SCOTT. The Lemonade Trick. Little, 1960. $2.75. (4–6) Fic.

CORBIN, WILLIAM. Golden Mare. Coward-McCann, 1955. $3. (5–6) Fic.

CORMACK, MARIBELLE. The First Book of Stones. Watts, 1950. $1.95. (4–6) 552.

———— The First Book of Trees. Watts, 1951. $1.95. (4–6) 582.

COTTLER, JOSEPH, and JAFFE, HAYM. Heroes of Civilization. Little, 1931. $4.50. (5–6) 920.

COUSINS, MARGARET. Ben Franklin of Old Philadelphia. Random, 1952. $1.95. (4–6) 92.

COY, HAROLD. The Americans. Little, 1958. $4.50. (6) 973.

———— The First Book of Congress. Watts, 1956. $1.95. (6) 328.

———— The First Book of Presidents. Watts, 1952. $1.95. (4–6) 920.

———— The First Book of the Supreme Court. Watts, 1958. $1.95. (5–6) 347.

———— The Real Book about Andrew Jackson. Garden City, 1952. $1.95. (5–6) 92.

CRAWFORD, PHYLLIS. "Hello, the Boat!" Holt, 1938. $3. (5–6) Fic.

CREDLE, ELLIS. Johnny and His Mule. Walck, 1946. $2.25. (4–5) Fic.

CROUSE, ANNA E., and CROUSE, RUSSEL. Alexander Hamilton and Aaron Burr: Their Lives, Their Times, Their Duel. Random, 1958. $1.95. (5–6) 92.

CROUSE, WILLIAM H. Understanding Science. McGraw-Hill, 1956. $3.75. (6) 600.

CROWLEY, MAUDE. Azor and the Blue-eyed Cow: A Christmas Story. Walck, 1956. $2.75. (4–6) Fic.

———— Pringle and the Lavender Goat. Walck, 1960. $2.75. (4–5) Fic.

———— Tor and Azor. Walck, 1955. $2.75. (5–6) Fic.

DAHL, BORGHILD M. The Cloud Shoes. Dutton, 1957. $2.95. (4–6) Fic.

DALGLIESH, ALICE. Adam and the Golden Cock. Scribner, 1959. $2.50. (4–5) Fic.

———— America Begins: The Story of the Finding of the New World. Scribner, 1958. $3. (4–5) 973.

———— America Builds Homes: The Story of the First Colonies. Scribner, 1938. $3. (4) 973.

———— America Travels: The Story of a Hundred Years of Travel in America. Macmillan, 1961. $2.75. (4–6) 380.

———— The Blue Teapot. Macmillan, 1950. $2.75. (4–6) Fic.

———— comp. Christmas: A Book of Stories Old and New. Scribner, 1934. $3. (4–6) 394.

———— The Courage of Sarah Noble. Scribner, 1954. $2.50. (4–5) Fic.

———— The Fourth of July Story. Scribner, 1956. $2.95. (4–6) 973.

———— Ride on the Wind; told from The Spirit of St. Louis by Charles A. Lindbergh. Scribner, 1956. $2.95. (4–5) 629.

DANA, DOROTHEA. Good Bye, Bunny Bangs. Abelard-Schuman, 1956. $2.95. (4–5) Fic.

DARINGER, HELEN F. Adopted Jane. Harcourt, 1947. $2.95. (4–6) Fic.

DARLING, ESTHER B. Baldy of Nome. Knopf, 1947. $2.75. (6) Fic.

DARLING, LOUIS. Chickens and How To Raise Them. Morrow, 1955. $2.75. (4–6) 636.

———— Greenhead. Morrow, 1954. $3. (5–6) 598.

———— Kangaroos and Other Animals with Pockets. Morrow, 1958. $2.75. (4–6) 599.

———— Seals and Walruses. Morrow, 1955. $2.75. (4–6) 599.

DARROW, FLOYD L., and HYLANDER, CLARENCE J. The Boys' Own Book of Great Inventions. Macmillan, 1941. $3.75. (6) 608.

DAUGHERTY, JAMES. Daniel Boone. Viking, 1939. $4. (5–6) 92.

———— The Landing of the Pilgrims. Random, 1950. $1.95. (4–6) 974.

———— Poor Richard. Viking, 1946. $4.50. (6) 92.

DAVIS, NORMAN. Picken's Treasure Hunt. Walck, 1955. $2.75. (4–5) Fic.

DAVIS, RUSSELL G., and ASHABRANNER, BRENT K. The Choctaw Code. McGraw-Hill, 1961. $3. (5–6) Fic.

DAWSON, GRACE S. California: The Story of Our Southwest Corner. Macmillan, 1939. $3.50. (5–6) 979.

DE ANGELI, MARGUERITE L. Bright April. Doubleday, 1946. $2.75. (4–6) Fic.

———— Copper-toed Boots. Doubleday, 1938. $2.75. (4–6) Fic.

———— The Door in the Wall. Doubleday, 1949. $3.50. (4–6) Fic.

———— Elin's Amerika. Doubleday, 1941. $2.95. (4–6) Fic.

———— Henner's Lydia. Doubleday, 1936. $2.75. (4–5) Fic.

———— Jared's Island. Doubleday, 1947. $2.75. (4–6) Fic.

———— The Old Testament. Doubleday, 1960. $6.95. (4–6) 221.

———— Petite Suzanne. Doubleday, 1937. $2.75. (4–6) Fic.

———— Skippack School: Being the Story of Eli Shrawder and of One Christopher Dock, Schoolmaster about the Year 1750. Doubleday, 1939. $1.95. (4–6) Fic.

———— Thee, Hannah! Doubleday, 1940. $2.95. (4–6) Fic.

———— Yonie Wondernose. Doubleday, 1944. $2.75. (4) Fic.

DE JONG, DAVID C. The Seven Sayings of Mr. Jefferson. Parnassus, 1957. $2.75. (4–5) Fic.

DE JONG, DOLA. The Picture Story of Holland. McKay, 1946. $3.95. (4–6) 949.

DE JONG, MEINDERT. Good Luck Duck. Harper, 1950. $2.99. (4–5) Fic.

———— The Little Cow and the Turtle. Harper, 1955. $2.95; lib. bdg. $2.75. (4–6) Fic.

———— Smoke above the Lane. Harper, 1951. $2.50; lib. ed. $2.57. (4–5) Fic.

DE LA MARE, WALTER J., ed. Animal Stories. Scribner, 1940. $4.50. (4–6) S C.

———— Stories from the Bible. Knopf, 1961. $4.95. (5–6) 221.

DE LEEUW, ADELE L. Donny, the Boy Who Made a Home for Animals. Little, 1957. $3. (4–5) Fic.

DE LEEUW, CATEAU. Fear in the Forest. Nelson, 1960. $2.95. (4–6) Fic.

DEUCHER, SYBIL. Edvard Grieg: Boy of the Northland. Dutton, 1946. $3.50. (4–6) 92.

DICKENS, CHARLES. The Magic Fishbone. Vanguard, 1953. $2.95. (4–6) Fic.

DIETZ, DAVID. All about Satellites and Space Ships. Random, 1958. $1.95. (5–6) 629.

DISNEY (WALT) PRODUCTIONS. Walt Disney's Worlds of Nature, by Rutherford Platt and the staff of the Walt Disney Studio. Golden Pr., 1957. $4.95. (4–6) 574.

DISRAELI, ROBERT. New Worlds through the Microscope. Viking, 1960. $4. (6) 578.

DOANE, PELAGIE. A Book of Nature. Walck, 1952. $4. (5–6) 574.

DOBSON, MILLICENT. Hero: The Biggest Cat in the World. Coward-McCann, 1955. $2.50. (4–5) Fic.

DOLBIER, MAURICE. Torten's Christmas Secret. Little, 1954. $3. (4–5) Fic.

DONALDSON, LOIS. Colombia. Albert Whitman, 1944. $1. (4–6) 986.

———— Guiana. Albert Whitman, 1944. $1. (4–6) 988.

———— Newfoundland. Albert Whitman, 1944. $1. (4–6) 971.

_____ Paraguay. Albert Whitman, 1944. $1. (4–6) 989.

_____ Salvador. Albert Whitman, 1943. $1. (4–6) 972.

DOORLY, ELEANOR. The Radium Woman: A Life of Marie Curie. Roy, 1955. $2.75. (5–6) 92.

DORIAN, EDITH, and WILSON, W. N. Hokahey! American Indians Then and Now. McGraw-Hill, 1957. $3.50. (5–6) 970.

DOUGLAS, EMILY T. Appleseed Farm. Abingdon, 1948. $2. (4–6) Fic.

DOW, EMILY R. How To Make Doll Clothes. Coward-McCann, 1953. $2.75. (5–6) 646.

DOWNER, MARION. Discovering Design. Lothrop, 1947. $3.50. (6) 745.

_____ Kites: How To Make and Fly Them. Lothrop, 1959. $3; lib. bdg. $2.89. (4–6) 796.

DRIGGS, HOWARD R. The Pony Express Goes Through: An American Saga Told by Its Heroes. Lippincott, 1935. $4.25. (6) 383.

DU BOIS, WILLIAM P. The Great Geppy. Viking, 1940. $3. (4–5) Fic.

_____ The 3 Policemen; or, Young Bottsford of Farbe Island. Viking, 1960. $3. (4–6) Fic.

_____ The Twenty-one Balloons. Viking, 1947. $3. (5–6) Fic.

DUDLEY, RUTH H. Our American Trees. Crowell, 1956. $2.95. (5–6) 582.

_____ Sea Shells. Crowell, 1953. $2.95. (4–6) 594.

DUGGAN, ALFRED. The Castle Book. Pantheon, 1961. $2.50. (5–6) 728.

DUPUY, TREVOR N. The First Book of Civil War Naval Actions. Watts, 1961. $1.95. (6) 973.

DURELL, ANN. Holly River Secret. Doubleday, 1956. $2.75. (4–6) Fic.

DU SOE, ROBERT C. Three without Fear. Longmans, 1947. $3.25. (4–6) Fic.

DUVOISIN, ROGER A. And There Was America. Knopf, 1938. $3. (4–6) 973.

_____ They Put Out to Sea: The Story of the Map. Knopf, 1943. $3. (4–6) 910.

EARLE, OLIVE L. Crickets. Morrow, 1956. $2.75. (4–6) 595.

_____ Mice at Home and Afield. Morrow, 1957. $2.75. (4–5) 599.

_____ The Octopus. Morrow, 1955. $2.75. (4–6) 594.

_____ Pigs, Tame and Wild. Morrow, 1959. $2.75. (4–6) 636.

_____ State Trees. Morrow, 1960. $2.75; lib. bdg. $2.78. (5–6) 582.

_____ White Patch: A City Sparrow. Morrow, 1958. $2.75. (4–6) 598.

EATON, JEANETTE. America's Own Mark Twain. Morrow, 1958. $3. (6) 92.

_____ That Lively Man, Ben Franklin. Morrow, 1948. $3. (5–6) 92.

_____ Washington, the Nation's First Hero. Morrow, 1951. $2.75. (4–6) 92.

EBERLE, IRMENGARDE. Basketful: The Story of Our Foods. Crowell, 1946. $3.50. (5–6) 641.

_____ Grasses. Walck, 1960. $2.75. (4–6) 633.

_____ Modern Medical Discoveries. Crowell, 1954. $3. (6) 610.

EDELMAN, LILY. Japan in Story and Pictures. Harcourt, 1953. $2.50. (4–6) 952.

EDMONDS, WALTER D. The Matchlock Gun. Dodd, 1941. $2.95. (4–6) Fic.

EDWARDS, CECILE P. Champlain: Father of New France. Abingdon, 1955. $1.75. (4–6) 92.

EECKHOUDT, JEAN P. V. A Butterfly Is Born. Sterling, 1960. $2.50. (4–6) 595.

EISENBERG, PHILIP. Won Kim's Ox. Follett, 1956. $2.95. (4–6) Fic.

ELLIS, HARRY B. The Arabs. World, 1958. $3.50. (6) 953.

ELTING, MARY. The First Book of Nurses. Watts, 1951. $1.95. (4–6) 610.

———— and GOSSETT, MARGARET. Lollypop Factory — and Lots of Others. Doubleday, 1946. $3. (4–5) 670.

———— We Are the Government. Doubleday, 1945. $2.75. (6) 342.

EMBRY, MARGARET J. Blue-nosed Witch. Holiday, 1956. $2.25. (4–5) Fic.

EMETT, FREDERICK R. New World for Nellie. Harcourt, 1952. $2.50. (4–5) Fic.

ENGEMAN, JACK. U.S. Air Force Academy: The Life of a Cadet. Lothrop, 1957. $3.50. (6) 358.

ENRIGHT, ELIZABETH. The Four-Story Mistake. Rinehart, 1942. $3. (4–6) Fic.

———— Gone-Away Lake. Harcourt, 1957. $3. (4–6) Fic.

———— The Saturdays. Rinehart, 1941. $3. (4–6) Fic.

———— Then There Were Five. Rinehart, 1944. $3.25. (4–6) Fic.

———— Thimble Summer. Rinehart, 1938. $3.50. (5–6) Fic.

EPSTEIN, EDNA. The First Book of the United Nations. Watts, 1959. $1.95. (4–6) 341.

EPSTEIN, SAM, and EPSTEIN, BERYL. All about the Desert. Random, 1957. $1.95. (5–6) 551.

———— The First Book of Codes and Ciphers. Watts, 1956. $1.95. (4–6) 652.

———— The First Book of Electricity. Watts, 1953. $1.95. (5–6) 537.

———— The First Book of Glass. Watts, 1955. $1.95. (4–6) 666.

———— The First Book of Hawaii. Watts, 1954. $1.95. (4–6) 996.

———— The First Book of Italy. Watts, 1958. $1.95. (5–6) 945.

———— The First Book of Maps and Globes. Watts, 1959. $1.95. (4–6) 912.

———— The First Book of Mexico. Watts, 1955. $1.95. (4–6) 972.

———— The First Book of Words: Their Family Histories. Watts, 1954. $1.95. (4–6) 422.

———— Prehistoric Animals. Watts, 1956. $3.95. (6) 560.

ESTES, ELEANOR. Ginger Pye. Harcourt, 1951. $3.25. (4–6) Fic.

———— The Hundred Dresses. Harcourt, 1944. $3. (4–6) Fic.

———— The Middle Moffat. Harcourt, 1942. $3.50. (4–6) Fic.

———— The Moffats. Harcourt, 1941. $3.25. (4–6) Fic.

———— Rufus M. Harcourt, 1943. $3.50. (4–6) Fic.

———— The Witch Family. Harcourt, 1960. $3.25. (4–6) Fic.

EVANS, EVA K. Adventure Book of Money. Capitol, 1956. $3.95. (5–6) 737.

———— Adventure Book of Rocks. Capitol, 1955. $3.95. (4–6) 549.

———— All about Us. Capitol, 1947. $3.95. (4–6) 572.

———— People Are Important. Capitol, 1951. $3.95. (4—6) 572.

FALLS, C. B. The First 3000 Years: Ancient Civilizations of the Tigris, Euphrates,

and Nile River Valleys, and the Mediterranean Sea. Viking, 1960. $6. (6) 901.

FARALLA, DANA. The Willow in the Attic. Lippincott, 1960. $3.50. (4) Fic.

FARJEON, ELEANOR. Italian Peepshow. Walck, 1960. $2.75. (4–5) Fic.

_____ Mighty Men. Appleton, 1926. $1.72. (4–6) 904.

_____ The Silver Curlew. Viking, 1953. $2.75. (4–6) Fic.

_____ Ten Saints. Walck, 1936. $4.75. (6) 920.

FAST, HOWARD M. Goethals and the Panama Canal. Messner, 1947. $2.95. (6) 92.

FAULKNER, GEORGENE. Melindy's Happy Summer. Messner, 1949. $2.75. (4–5) Fic.

_____ and BECKER, JOHN. Melindy's Medal. Messner, 1945. $2.75. (4–5) Fic.

FEAGLES, ANITA. Casey: The Utterly Impossible Horse. W. R. Scott, 1960. $2.75. (4–5) Fic.

FENNER, PHYLLIS R., comp. Fools and Funny Fellows. Knopf, 1947. $3. (4–6) S C.

_____ Time To Laugh: Funny Tales from Here and There. Knopf, 1942. $3. (4–6) S C.

FENTON, CARROLL L. Life Long Ago: The Story of Fossils. Day, 1937. $6. (6) 560.

_____ Prehistoric World: Stories of Animal Life in Past Ages. Day, 1954. $3.50. (4–6) 560.

_____ and CARSWELL, EVELYN. Wild Folk in the Desert. Day, 1958. $3.50. (4–6) 574.

_____ and EPSTEIN, ALICE. Cliff Dwellers of Walnut Canyon. Day, 1960. $2.75; lib. bdg. $2.68. (4–5) 970.

_____ and FENTON, MILDRED A. The Land We Live On. Doubleday, 1944. $3. (4–6) 551.

_____ Riches from the Earth. Day, 1953. $3.50. (5–6) 549.

_____ and KITCHEN, HERMINIE B. Plants That Feed Us: The Story of Grains and Vegetables. Day, 1956. $3.25. (4–6) 581.

_____ and PALLAS, DOROTHY C. Birds and Their World. Day, 1954. $3.25. (4–6) 598.

_____ Insects and Their World. Day, 1956. $3.25. (4–6) 595.

_____ Trees and Their World. Day, 1957. $3.25. (5–6) 582.

FENTON, EDWARD. The Phantom of Walkaway Hill. Doubleday, 1961. $2.95. (4–6) Fic.

FERMI, LAURA. The Story of Atomic Energy. Random, 1961. $1.95. (6) 539.

FESSENDEN, KATHARINE. The Old Testament Story: Adam to Jonah. Walck, 1960. $4.75. (4–6) 221.

FICKLEN, BESSIE A. Handbook of Fist Puppets. Lippincott, 1935. $3.50. (4–6) 791.

FIELD, RACHEL. Hitty: Her First Hundred Years. Macmillan, 1929. $3. (5–6) Fic.

FISHER, AILEEN L. Summer of Little Rain. Nelson, 1961. $2.95. (4–6) 591.

FISHER, DOROTHY F. C. And Long Remember: Some Great Americans Who Have Helped Me. McGraw-Hill, 1959. $3.50. (5–6) 920.

———— Our Independence and the Constitution. Random, 1950. $1.95. (4–5) 342.

FISHER, JAMES. The Wonderful World of the Air. Garden City, 1958. $2.95. (5–6) 551.

———— The Wonderful World of the Sea. Garden City, 1957. $2.95. (5–6) 551.

FISHER, LOIS. You and the United Nations. Childrens Pr., 1947. $2. (5–6) 341.

FITCH, FLORENCE M. Allah, the God of Islam: Moslem Life and Worship. Lothrop, 1950. $3. (6) 297.

———— One God: The Ways We Worship Him. Lothrop, 1944. $3. (5–6) 264.

———— Their Search for God: Ways of Worship in the Orient. Lothrop, 1947. $3. (5–6) 290.

FLAKKEBERG, ARDO. The Sea Broke Through. Knopf, 1960. $2.75. (6) Fic.

FLETCHER, DAVID. Confetti for Cortorelli, Pantheon, 1957. $2.75. (5–6) Fic.

FLETCHER, SYDNEY E. The American Indian. Grosset, 1954. $2.95. (5–6) 970.

———— The Big Book of Indians. Grosset, 1950. $1. (4–6) 970.

FLEXNER, HORTENSE. Wishing Window. Lippincott, 1942. $2.25. (4) Fic.

FLOETHE, LOUISE LEE, Triangle X. Harper, 1960. $2. (4) Fic.

FLOHERTY, JOHN J. Aviation from the Ground Up. Lippincott, 1960. $3.75. (6) 629.

———— Our F B I. Lippincott, 1951. $2.95. (6) 351.

FLORY, JANE. Peddler's Summer. Houghton, 1960. $2.75. (4–6) Fic.

FORBES, ESTHER. America's Paul Revere. Houghton, 1946. $2.50. (4–6) 92.

FORBUSH, WILLIAM B., and ALLEN, HARRY R. Book of Games for Home, School, and Playground. Holt, 1954. $3. (4–6) 790.

FORSEE, AYLESA. Louis Agassiz: Pied Piper of Science. Viking, 1958. $4. (6) 92.

FOSTER, GENEVIEVE. Abraham Lincoln. Scribner, 1950. $2.75. (4–6) 92.

———— Abraham Lincoln's World. Scribner, 1949. $4.95. (6) 909.

———— Andrew Jackson. Scribner, 1951. $2.75. (4–6) 92.

———— George Washington's World. Scribner, 1941. $4.95. (6) 909.

———— Theodore Roosevelt. Scribner, 1954. $2.75. (4–6) 92.

———— The World of Captain John Smith, 1580-1631. Scribner, 1959. $4.95. (6) 909.

FOSTER, JOANNA. Pages, Pictures, and Print: A Book in the Making. Harcourt, 1958. $2.95. (6) 655.

FOSTER, VIRGIL E. Close-up of a Honeybee. W. R. Scott, 1960. $3. (4–6) 595.

FOX, WILLIAM, and WELLES, SAMUEL. From Bones to Bodies: A Story of Paleontology. Walck, 1959. $3. (6) 560.

FRANK, R. Ice Island: The Story of Antarctica. Crowell, 1957. $3.75. (6) 999.

FRANKEL, LILLIAN, and FRANKEL, GODFREY. Games for Boys and Girls. Sterling, 1961. $1.25. (4–6) 793.

FRANKLIN, GEORGE C. Monte. Houghton, 1948. $2.75. (4–6) Fic.

_____ Son of Monte. Houghton, 1956. $2.50. (4–6) Fic.

_____ Tricky: The Adventures of a Red Fox. Houghton, 1949. $2.75. (4–6) Fic.

_____ Tuffy. Houghton, 1954. $2.50. (5–6) Fic.

_____ Wild Animals of the Southwest. Houghton, 1950. $3.50. (5–6) 591.

_____ Wild Horses of the Rio Grande. Houghton, 1951. $3.50. (5–6) 978.

FRASCONI, ANTONIO. See and Say: A Picture Book in Four Languages (English, Italian, Spanish, French). Harcourt, 1955. $3; lib. bdg. $3.26. (4–6) 400.

FRAZIER, NETA L. Secret Friend. Longmans, 1956. $2.95. (4–6) Fic.

_____ Somebody Special. Longmans, 1954. $3.25. (4–6) Fic.

FREEMAN, IRA M. All about Electricity. Random, 1957. $1.95. (4–6) 537.

_____ All about the Wonders of Chemistry. Random, 1954. $1.95. (6) 540.

FREEMAN, MAE B. Fun with Ballet. Random, 1952. $1.95. (5–6) 793.

_____ Fun with Cooking. Random, 1947. $1.95. (4–6) 641.

_____ and FREEMAN, IRA M. Fun with Astronomy. Random, 1953. $1.95. (4–6) 520.

_____ Fun with Chemistry. Random, 1944. $1.95. (4–6) 540.

_____ Fun with Figures. Random, 1946. $1.95. (6) 513.

_____ Fun with Science. Random, 1956. $1.95. (5–6) 530.

_____ Fun with Scientific Experiments. Random, 1960. $1.95. (4–6) 507.

_____ Fun with Your Camera. Random, 1955. $1.95. (4–6) 770.

FRENCH, HENRY W. The Lance of Kanana: A Story of Arabia. Lothrop, 1932. $1.75. (6) Fic.

FRIEDMAN, ESTELLE. Digging into Yesterday: The Discovery of Ancient Civilizations. Putnam, 1958. $2.95. (5–6) 913.

FRIEDMAN, FRIEDA. Carol from the Country. Morrow, 1950. $2.75. (4–6) Fic.

_____ Dot for Short. Morrow, 1947. $2.95. (4–5) Fic.

_____ A Sundae with Judy. Morrow, 1949. $2.75. (4–6) Fic.

FRITZ, JEAN. Brady. Coward-McCann, 1960. $3.50. (5–6) Fic.

FROST, FRANCES. Maple Sugar for Windy Foot. McGraw-Hill, 1950. $2.95. (4–6) Fic.

_____ Sleigh Bells for Windy Foot. McGraw-Hill, 1948. $2.95. (4–6) Fic.

_____ Windy Foot at the County Fair. McGraw-Hill, 1947. $2.95. (4–6) Fic.

FRY, ROSALIE K. Bell for Ringelblume. Dutton, 1957. $2.50. (4–5) Fic.

GAER, JOSEPH. Everybody's Weather. Lippincott, 1957. $3.95. (5–6) 551.

GAGE, WILSON. The Secret of Fiery Gorge. World, 1960. $2.95. (4–6) Fic.

_____ A Wild Goose Tale. World, 1961. $2.95. (4–6) Fic.

GALL, ALICE C., and CREW, FLEMING. Flat Tail. Walck, 1935. $3. (4–5) Fic.

_____ Little Black Ant. Walck, 1936. $3. (4–5) Fic.

_____ Ringtail. Walck, 1933. $3. (4–5) Fic.

_____ Wagtail. Walck, 1932. $3. (4–5) Fic.

GALLANT, KATHRYN. The Flute Player of Beppu. Coward-McCann, 1960. $2.75; lib. ed. $2.68. (4) Fic.

GALLANT, ROY A. Exploring Chemistry. Garden City, 1958. $2.95. (6) 540.

———— Exploring Mars. Garden City, 1956. $2.50. (4–6) 523.

———— Exploring the Moon. Garden City, 1955. $2.50. (4–6) 523.

———— Exploring the Planets. Garden City, 1958. $2.95. (5–6) 523.

———— Exploring the Sun. Garden City, 1958. $2.50. (5–6) 523.

———— Exploring the Universe. Garden City, 1956. $2.50. (5–6) 523.

———— Exploring the Weather. Garden City, 1957. $2.50. (5–6) 551.

GALLUP, LUCY. Spinning Wings. Morrow, 1956. $2.75. (5–6) 598.

GALT, TOM. How the United Nations Works. Crowell, 1955. $3. (5–6) 341.

———— Seven Days from Sunday. Crowell, 1956. $3. (6) 529.

———— Volcano. Scribner, 1946. $3.50. (5–6) 551.

GANNETT, RUTH S. Elmer and the Dragon. Random, 1950. $2.95. (4–5) Fic.

———— My Father's Dragon. Random, 1948. $2.95. (4–5) Fic.

GARDNER, MARTIN. Mathematical Puzzles. Crowell, 1961. $2.50. (6) 793.

GARELICK, MAY. Manhattan Island. Crowell, 1957. $2.75. (4–6) 973.

GARNETT, EVE. The Family from One-End Street, and Some of Their Adventures. Vanguard, 1960. $3.50. (6) Fic.

GARRETT, HELEN. Rufous Redtail. Viking, 1947. $2.50. (4–5) Fic.

GARST, SHANNON. Buffalo Bill. Messner, 1948. $2.95. (6) 92.

———— Cowboys and Cattle Trails. Harper, 1960. $2.20. (4) 976.

———— Jim Bridger: Greatest of the Mountain Men. Houghton, 1952. $3.50. (6) 92.

———— Kit Carson: Trail Blazer and Scout. Messner, 1942. $2.95. (6) 92.

———— Sitting Bull: Champion of His People. Messner, 1946. $2.95. (6) 92.

GARTHWAITE, MARION. Mario: A Mexican Boy's Adventures. Doubleday, 1960. $2.50. (4–6) Fic.

GATES, DORIS. Blue Willow. Viking, 1940. $3. (5–6) Fic.

———— Sarah's Idea. Viking, 1938. $2.75. (4–6) Fic.

———— Sensible Kate. Viking, 1943. $3. (4–6) Fic.

GATTI, ATTILIO. Here Is the Veld. Scribner, 1948. $3.95. (6) 968.

———— Saranga, the Pygmy. Scribner, 1939. $2.95. (5–6) 967.

GAUL, ALBRO T. Picture Book of Insects. Lothrop, 1943. $2. (4–6) 595.

———— The Pond Book. Coward-McCann, 1955. $2.75. (4–6) 574.

GEORGE, JEAN. The Hole in the Tree. Dutton, 1957. $2.75. (4–5) 574.

GEORGE, JOHN L., and GEORGE, JEAN. Bubo, the Great Horned Owl. Dutton, 1954. $3.75. (4–6) 598.

———— Vulpes, the Red Fox. Dutton, 1948. $3.50. (6) Fic.

GERALTON, JAMES. The Story of Sound. Harcourt, 1948. $2.50. (5–6) 534.

GIDAL, SONIA, and GIDAL, TIM. Follow the Reindeer. Pantheon, 1959. $3.50. (4–6) 948.

———— My Village in Austria. Pantheon, 1956. $3.50. (4–6) 943.

———— My Village in Greece. Pantheon, 1960. $3.50. (4–6) 949.

———— My Village in Ireland. Pantheon, 1957. $3.50. (4–6) 941.

———— My Village in Israel. Pantheon, 1959. $3.50. (4–6) 956.

———— My Village in Norway. Pantheon, 1958. $3.50. (4–6) 948.

———— My Village in Yugoslavia. Pantheon, 1957. $3.50. (4–6) 949.

———— Sons of the Desert. Pantheon, 1960. $3.50. (5–6) 953.

GILBERT, NAN. Champions Don't Cry. Harper, 1960. $2.95; lib. bdg. $2.79. (5–6) Fic.

GILCHRIST, MARIE E. Story of the Great Lakes. Harper, 1942. $2.95; lib. ed. $2.94. (4–6) 977.

GILLHAM, CHARLES E. Beyond the Clapping Mountains: Eskimo Stories from Alaska. Macmillan, 1943. $3. (4–5) 398.

GILLSÄTER, SVEN, and GILLSÄTER, PIA. Pia's Journey to the Holy Land. Harcourt, 1961. $3.50. (5–6) 956.

GILMORE, HORACE H. Model Boats for Beginners. Harper, 1959. $2.50. (5–6) 623.

———— Model Planes for Beginners. Harper, 1957. $2.25. (5–6) 629.

GLEMSER, BERNARD. All about the Human Body. Random, 1958. $1.95. (5–6) 612.

GODDEN, RUMER. The Doll's House. Viking, 1948. $2.50. (4–5) Fic.

———— Impunity Jane: The Story of a Pocket Doll. Viking, 1954. $2.50. (4–5) Fic.

———— Miss Happiness and Miss Flower. Viking, 1961. $3. (4–5) Fic.

GOETZ, DELIA. The Arctic Tundra. Morrow, 1958. $2.75. (4–6) 998.

———— Deserts. Morrow, 1956. $2.75. (4–6) 551.

———— Grasslands. Morrow, 1959. $2.75. (4–6) 551.

———— Neighbors to the South. Harcourt, 1956. $3.50. (6) 980.

———— Other Young Americans: Latin America's Young People. Morrow, 1948. $3.95. (5–6) 980.

———— Tropical Rain Forests. Morrow, 1957. $2.75. (4–6) 551.

GOLDEN, GRACE B. Made in Iceland. Knopf, 1958. $3. (6) 949.

GOODWIN, HAROLD L. Real Book about Stars. Garden City, 1951. $1.95. (4–6) 520.

GORDON, DOROTHY L. You and Democracy. Dutton, 1951. $2.75. (6) 321.

GOSS, MADELEINE. Beethoven, Master Musician. Holt, 1946. $3.50. (6) 92.

GOTTLIEB, WILLIAM P. Jets and Rockets and How They Work. Garden City, 1959. $2.95. (4–6) 629.

———— Photography with Basic Cameras. Knopf, 1953. $1.75. (4–6) 770.

GOULD, JACK. All about Radio and Television. Random, 1953. $1.95. (5–6) 621.

GRAHAM, ALBERTA P. Christopher Columbus: Discoverer. Abingdon, 1950. $1.75. (4–5) 92.

———— Lafayette: Friend of America. Abingdon, 1952. $1.75. (4–5) 92.

———— La Salle: River Explorer. Abingdon, 1954. $1.75. (4–6) 92.

GRAHAM, EDWARD H., and VAN DERSAL, WILLIAM R. Water for America: The Story of Water Conservation. Walck, 1956. $3.75. (6) 551.

———— Wildlife for America: The Story of Wildlife Conservation. Walck, 1949. $3.75. (6) 333.

GRAHAM, SHIRLEY. Booker T. Washington: Educator of Hand, Head, and Heart. Messner, 1955. $2.95. (6) 92.

———— and LIPSCOMB, GEORGE D. Dr. George Washington Carver: Scientist. Messner, 1944. $2.95; lib. bdg. $2.99. (6) 92.

GRAHAM, VERA M. Treasure in the Covered Wagon: A Story of the Oregon Trail. Lippincott, 1952. $2.95. (4–6) Fic.

GRAHAME, KENNETH. Bertie's Escapade. Lippincott, 1949. $2.50. (4–5) Fic.

———— The Reluctant Dragon. Holiday, 1953. $2.25. (4–6) Fic.

GRANT, BRUCE. The Boy Scout Encyclopedia. Rand McNally, 1952. $2.95. (4–6) 369.

———— Zachary, the Governor's Pig. World, 1960. $2.95. (4–6) Fic.

GRANT, GEORGE H. Boy Overboard! Little, 1961. $3. (5–6) Fic.

GRAY, ALICE. The Adventure Book of Insects. Capitol, 1956. $3.95. (5–6) 595.

GREEN, IVAH E. A Home for Woody. Abelard-Schuman, 1956. $2.50. (4–6) 598.

GUILCHER, JEAN M., and NOAILLES, R. H. A Fruit Is Born. Sterling, 1960. $2.50. (5–6) 581.

GUILLOT, RENÉ. Grishka and the Bear. Criterion, 1959. $2.75. (5–6) Fic.

GUNTHER, JOHN. Julius Caesar. Random, 1959. $1.95. (5–6) 92.

HADER, BERTA H., and HADER, ELMER. Spunky. Macmillan, 1933. $3. (4–6) Fic.

HAHN, EMILY. The First Book of India. Watts, 1955. $1.95. (4–6) 952.

———— The Picture Story of China. McKay, 1946. $3.95. (4–6) 951.

HAINES, MADGE, and MORRILL, LESLIE. Wright Brothers: First To Fly. Abingdon, 1955. $1.75. (4–5) 92.

HALE, LUCRETIA P. The Complete Peterkin Papers. Houghton, 1960. $5. (4–6) Fic.

HALL, ELVAJEAN. The Land and People of Argentina. Lippincott, 1960. $2.95. (6) 982.

HALL, JENNIE. Buried Cities. Macmillan, 1922. $3. (6) 913.

HALL, ROSALYS H. Baker's Man. Lippincott, 1954. $2.50. (4–5) Fic.

HALL-QUEST, OLGA W. How the Pilgrims Came to Plymouth. Dutton, 1946. $2.75. (4–6) 973.

HAMILTON, EDWIN T. Handicraft for Girls. Dodd, 1932. $4. (6) 680.

HAMILTON, ELIZABETH. The First Book of Caves. Watts, 1956. $1.95. (4–6) 551.

HAMILTON, RUSSEL. The First Book of Trains. Watts, 1956. $1.95. (4–5) 625.

HAMMETT, EVELYN A. I, Priscilla. Macmillan, 1960. $3. (5–6) Fic.

HANSEN, HARRY. Old Ironsides: The Fighting "Constitution." Random, 1955. $1.95. (5–6) 973.

HARK, ANN. The Story of the Pennsylvania Dutch. Harper, 1943. $2.95; lib. ed. $2.94. (4–6) 974.

HARPER, WILHELMINA, comp. Easter Chimes: Stories for Easter and the Spring Season. Dutton, 1942. $3. (4–6) 394.

_____ Ghosts and Goblins: Stories for Hallowe'en and Other Times. Dutton, 1936. $3.50. (4–6) 394.

_____ The Harvest Feast: Stories of Thanksgiving Yesterday and Today. Dutton, 1938. $3.75. (4–6) 394.

_____ Merry Christmas to You! Stories for Christmas. Dutton, 1956. $3.50. (4–6) 394.

HARRINGTON, LYN. Ootook: Young Eskimo Girl. Abelard-Schuman, 1956. $2.75. (4–6) 998.

HARRISON, HAL H. Outdoor Adventures. Vanguard, 1951. $3. (4–5) 502.

HARRY, ROBERT R. Island Boy: A Story of Ancient Hawaii. Lothrop, 1956. $3. (4–6) Fic.

HARSHAW, RUTH H., and MACBEAN, DILLA W. What Book Is That? Fun with Books at Home — at School. Macmillan, 1948. $2.75. (4–6) 028.

HARTMAN, GERTRUDE. Builders of the Old World. Little, 1946. $4.50. (6) 909.

_____ In Bible Days. Macmillan, 1948. $4. (6) 220.

_____ Machines and the Men Who Made the World of Industry. Macmillan, 1939. $4. (6) 608.

HAUFF, WILHELM. Dwarf Long-Nose. Random, 1960. $2.95. (4–6) Fic.

HAUSMAN, LEON A. Beginner's Guide to Fresh-Water Life. Putnam, 1950. $2.50. (5–6) 591.

HAVIGHURST, WALTER. The First Book of the Oregon Trail. Watts, 1960. $1.95. (4–6) 978.

_____ Life in America: The Midwest. Fideler, 1951. $3.28. (5–6) 977.

HAVILAND, VIRGINIA. William Penn: Founder and Friend. Abingdon, 1952. $1.75. (4–5) 92.

HAWKES, HESTER. Tami's New House. Coward-McCann, 1955. $2. (4–5) Fic.

HAYES, FLORENCE S. Skid. Houghton, 1948. $3. (5–6) Fic.

HAYS, WILMA P. Christmas on the Mayflower. Coward-McCann, 1956. $2.75; lib. bdg. $2.68. (4–5) Fic.

_____ Easter Fires. Coward-McCann, 1959. $2.75; lib. bdg. $2.68. (4–5) Fic.

_____ Freedom: Reproductions of 26 Significant Documents, from the Declaration of Independence through the United Nations Charter, with a brief historical background of each. Coward-McCann, 1958. $3; lib. bdg. $2.81. (5–6) 973.

_____ Pilgrim Thanksgiving. Coward-McCann, 1955. $2.75; lib. bdg. $2.68. (4–5) 394.

HAYWOOD, CAROLYN. Betsy's Busy Summer. Morrow, 1956. $2.95. (4–5) Fic.

_____ Betsy's Winterhouse. Morrow, 1958. $2.95. (4–5) Fic.

_____ Eddie and His Big Deals. Morrow, 1955. $2.95. (4–5) Fic.

_____ Eddie's Pay Dirt. Morrow, 1953. $2.75. (4–5) Fic.

_____ Penny and Peter. Harcourt, 1946. $2.95. (4) Fic.

HAZELTINE, ALICE I., ed. Hero Tales from Many Lands. Abingdon, 1961. $5.95. (5–6) 398.

———— and SMITH, ELVA S., eds. The Easter Book of Legends and Stories. Lothrop, 1947. $3.50. (4–6) 394.

HECHT, BESSIE M. All about Snakes. Random, 1956. $1.95. (5–6) 598.

HENDRICKSON, WALTER B. Handbook for Space Travelers. Bobbs-Merrill, 1959. $3.95. (5–6) 629.

HENRY, JAN. Tiger's Chance. Harcourt, 1957. $2.75. (4–6) Fic.

HENRY, MARGUERITE. Album of Horses. Rand McNally, 1951. $3.95. (4–6) 636.

———— Always Reddy. McGraw-Hill, 1947. $2.95. (4–6) Fic.

———— Bahamas. Albert Whitman, 1946. $1. (4–6) 972.

———— Benjamin West and His Cat Grimalkin. Bobbs-Merrill, 1947. $3.50. (4–6) 92.

———— Bermuda. Albert Whitman, 1946. $1. (4–6) 972.

———— Black Gold. Rand McNally, 1957. $3.50. (4–6) 798.

———— Brazil. Albert Whitman, 1941. $1. (4–6) 981.

———— British Honduras. Albert Whitman, 1946. $1. (4–6) 972.

———— Dominican Republic. Albert Whitman, 1946. $1. (4–6) 972.

———— Gaudenzia: Pride of the Palio. Rand McNally, 1960. $3.95. (6) 798.

———— Justin Morgan Had a Horse. Rand McNally, 1954. $3.50. (4–6) Fic.

———— King of the Wind. Rand McNally, 1948. $3.50. (5–6) Fic.

———— Misty of Chincoteague. Rand McNally, 1947. $3.50. (4–6) Fic.

———— New Zealand. Albert Whitman, 1946. $1. (4–6) 993.

———— Wagging Tails: An Album of Dogs. Rand McNally, 1955. $2.95. (4–6) 636.

HENRY, ROBERT S. Trains. Bobbs-Merrill, 1949. $4.95. (5–6) 385.

HERMAN, MICHAEL, ed. Folk Dances for All. Barnes, 1947. pa. $1. (4–6) 793.

HEWES, AGNES D. A Boy of the Lost Crusade. Houghton, 1923. $3.50. (6) Fic.

———— Spice Ho! A Story of Discovery. Knopf, 1947. $2.75. (5–6) 910.

HILLYER, VIRGIL M., and HUEY, EDWARD G. A Child's History of Art. Appleton, 1951. $7. (5–6) 709.

———— A Child's History of the World. Appleton, 1947. $6. (5–6) 909.

HINTON, SAM. Exploring under the Sea. Garden City, 1957. $2.50. (5–6) 574.

HOFFINE, LYLA. Jennie's Mandan Bowl. Longmans, 1960. $2.95. (4–6) Fic.

HOFFMAN, PEGGY. Sew Easy! For the Young Beginner. Dutton, 1956. $2.75. (4–6) 646.

HOFSINDE, ROBERT. The Indian and His Horse. Morrow, 1960. $2.75. (4–6) 970.

———— The Indian and the Buffalo. Morrow, 1961. $2.75; lib. ed. $2.78. (4–6) 970.

———— Indian Beadwork. Morrow, 1958. $2.75. (4–6) 746.

———— Indian Picture Writing. Morrow, 1959. $2.75. (4–6) 970.

———— Indian Sign Language. Morrow, 1956. $2.75. (4–6) 419.

———— The Indian's Secret World. Morrow, 1955. $4.50. (5–6) 970.

HOGBEN, LANCELOT T. The Wonderful World of Communication. Garden City, 1959. $2.95. (6) 384.

———— The Wonderful World of Mathematics. Garden City, 1955. $2.95. (6) 510.

HOGEBOOM, AMY. Boats and How To Draw Them. Vanguard, 1950. $2. (4–6) 741.

———— Dogs and How To Draw Them. Vanguard, 1944. $2. (4–5) 741.

———— Familiar Animals and How To Draw Them. Vanguard, 1946. $2. (4–5) 741.

———— Horses and How To Draw Them. Vanguard, 1948. $2. (4–5) 741.

HOGNER, DOROTHY C., and HOGNER, NILS. The Animal Book: American Mammals North of Mexico. Walck, 1942. $5.75. (6) 599.

———— Barnyard Family. Walck, 1948. $4. (5–6) 636.

———— The Cat Family. Walck, 1956. $2.75. (4–5) 599.

———— Earthworms. Crowell, 1953. $2.50; lib. bdg. $2.40. (4–5) 595.

———— Farm Animals and Working and Sporting Breeds of the United States and Canada. Walck, 1945. $5. (6) 636.

———— Frogs and Polliwogs. Crowell, 1956. $2.50; lib. bdg. $2.40. (4–6) 597.

———— Grasshoppers and Crickets. Crowell, 1960. $2.50; lib. bdg. $2.40. (4–5) 595.

———— The Horse Family. Walck, 1953. $3. (4–6) 636.

———— Snails. Crowell, 1958. $2.50; lib. bdg. $2.40. (4–6) 594.

———— Spiders. Crowell, 1955. $2.50; lib. bdg. $2.40. (4–5) 595.

HOKE, JOHN L. The First Book of Snakes. Watts, 1952. $1.95. (4–6) 598.

HOLBERG, RUTH L. John Greenleaf Whittier: Fighting Quaker. Crowell, 1958. $3. (6) 92.

———— Rowena Carey. Doubleday, 1949. $2.75. (4–6) Fic.

HOLBROOK, STEWART H. The Golden Age of Railroads. Random, 1960. $1.95. (5–6) 385.

HOLLAND, JANICE. Christopher Goes to the Castle. Scribner, 1957. $2.95. (4–5) Fic.

———— They Built a City. Scribner, 1953. $2.95. (4–6) 973.

HOLLING, HOLLING C. The Book of Cowboys. Platt & Munk, 1936. $2.95. (5–6) 978.

———— The Book of Indians. Platt & Munk, 1935. $2.95. (4–6) 970.

———— Minn of the Mississippi. Houghton, 1951. $3.75. (5–6) 598.

———— Paddle-to-the-Sea. Houghton, 1941. $3.75. (4–6) Fic.

———— Seabird. Houghton, 1948. $3.75. (5–6) Fic.

———— Tree in the Trail. Houghton, 1942. $3.75. (4–6) Fic.

HOLLOS, CLARA. The Story of Your Coat. International, 1946. $1.75. (4–5) 677.

HONOUR, ALAN. Secrets of Minos: Sir Arthur Evans' Discoveries at Crete. McGraw-Hill, 1961. $3.25. (6) 913.

HOOKER, FORRESTINE C. Star: The Story of an Indian Pony. Doubleday, 1950. $2.50. (5–6) Fic.

HOWARD, ALICE W. Sokar and the Crocodile. Macmillan, 1928. $2.75. (4–5) Fic.

HOWARD, JOAN. The 13th Is Magic. Lothrop, 1950. $3. (4–6) Fic.

HUBBARD, FREEMAN H. The Train That Never Came Back; and Other Railroad Stories. McGraw-Hill, 1952. $2.75. (5–6) S C.

HUDSON, WILLIAM H. A Little Boy Lost. Knopf, 1918. $2.75. (6) Fic.

HUEY, EDWARD G. What Makes the Wheels Go Round: A First-Time Physics. Harcourt, 1952. $3. (6) 530.

HUGHES, LANGSTON. The First Book of Africa. Watts, 1960. $1.95. (5–6) 960.

———— The First Book of Negroes. Watts, 1952. $1.95. (4–6) 326.

———— The First Book of Rhythms. Watts, 1954. $1.95. (4–6) 701.

———— The First Book of the West Indies. Watts, 1956. $1.95. (5–6) 972.

HUME, RUTH F. Florence Nightingale. Random, 1960. $1.95. (6) 92.

HUNT, GEORGE P. The Story of the U.S. Marines. Random, 1951. $1.95. (5–6) 359.

HUNT, LESLIE L. 25 Kites That Fly. Bruce, 1958. $1.25. (5–6) 796.

HUNT, MABEL L. Benjie's Hat. Lippincott, 1938. $3.25. (4–6) Fic.

———— Cupola House. Lippincott, 1961. $3.25. (4–6) Fic.

———— Ladycake Farm. Lippincott. 1952. $2.95. (4–6) Fic.

———— Little Girl with Seven Names. Lippincott, 1936. $2.50. (4–6) Fic.

———— Lucinda: A Little Girl of 1860. Lippincott, 1934. $3.75. (5–6) Fic.

———— Miss Jellytot's Visit. Lippincott, 1955. $2.75. (4–6) Fic.

HUNT, W. BEN. The Golden Book of Indian Crafts and Lore. Golden Pr., 1954. $1.95. (4–6) 970.

HUNTINGTON, HARRIET E. Let's Go to the Desert. Doubleday, 1949. $3. (4–5) 550.

———— Praying Mantis. Doubleday, 1957. $2. (4–5) 595.

———— Tune-up: The Instruments of the Orchestra and Their Players. Doubleday, 1942. $2.75. (4–6) 785.

HUSSEY, LOIS J., and PESSINO, CATHERINE. Collecting Cocoons. Crowell, 1953. $3; lib. bdg. $2.88. (4–6) 595.

HYDE, MARGARET O. Animal Clocks and Compasses: From Animal Migration to Space Travel. McGraw-Hill, 1960. $2.95. (5–6) 591.

———— Plants Today and Tomorrow. McGraw-Hill, 1960. $3. (6) 581.

HYLANDER, CLARENCE J. Animals in Armor. Macmillan, 1958. $3.75. (6) 598.

———— Insects on Parade. Macmillan, 1957. $3.75. (6) 595.

———— Out of Doors in Autumn. Macmillan, 1942. $2.75. (5–6) 502.

———— Out of Doors in Spring. Macmillan, 1942. $3.25. (5–6) 502.

———— Out of Doors in Summer. Macmillan, 1942. $3. (5–6) 502.

———— Out of Doors in Winter. Macmillan, 1943. $2.75. (5–6) 502.

ICENHOWER, JOSEPH B. The First Book of Submarines. Watts, 1957. $1.95. (5–6) 623.

———— The First Book of the Antarctic. Watts, 1956. $1.95. (4–6) 999.

ILIN, M. How the Automobile Learned To Run. International, 1945. $1.95. (4–5) 629.

IRVING, ROBERT. Hurricanes and Twisters. Knopf, 1955. $2.75. (4–6) 551.

_____ Sound and Ultrasonics. Knopf, 1959. $2.75. (6) 534.

ISRAEL, MARION. About Sheep on the Ranch. Melmont, 1958. $2.50. (4) 636.

JACKSON, CAARY. P. Buzzy Plays Midget League Football. Follett, 1956. $2.25. (4–5) Fic.

_____ Spice's Football. Crowell, 1955. $2.50. (4–5) Fic.

JACKSON, DAVID. The Wonderful World of Engineering. Garden City, 1960. $2.95. (6) 620.

JACKSON, JESSE. Call Me Charley. Harper, 1945. $2.50. (5–6) Fic.

JACOBSON, HELEN. The First Book of Mythical Beasts. Watts, 1960. $1.95. (4–6) 398.

_____ and MISCHEL, FLORENCE. The First Book of Letter Writing. Watts, 1957. $1.95. (4–6) 808.

JAEGER, ELLSWORTH. Easy Crafts. Macmillan, 1947. $2.95. (4–6) 680.

JAKEMAN, ALAN. Getting To Know Japan. Coward-McCann, 1960. $2.50; lib. bdg. $2.52. (4–6) 952.

JAMES, WILL. Young Cowboy. Scribner, 1935. $2.95. (4–5) Fic.

JANEWAY, ELIZABETH H. The Vikings. Random, 1951. $1.95. (4–6) 92.

JAUSS, ANNE M. Discovering Nature the Year Round. Dutton, 1955. $2.50. (4–6) 574.

JESSUP, RONALD F. The Wonderful World of Archaeology. Garden City, 1956. $2.95. (5–6) 571.

JEWETT, SOPHIE. God's Troubadour: The Story of Saint Francis of Assisi. Crowell, 1957. $2.75. (6) 92.

JOHNSON, ELIZABETH. The Little Knight. Little, 1957. $2.75. (4–5) Fic.

_____ The Three-in-One Prince. Little, 1961. $2.75. (4–5) Fic.

JOHNSON, GERALD W. America Grows Up. Morrow, 1960. $3.75. (5–6) 973.

_____ America Is Born. Morrow, 1959. $3.95. (5–6) 973.

_____ America Moves Forward. Morrow, 1960. $3.95. (5–6) 973.

JOHNSON, LOIS, ed. Christmas Stories 'round the World. Rand McNally, 1960. $2.95. (4–6) 394.

JOHNSON, MARGARET S. Gay: A Shetland Sheep Dog. Morrow, 1948. $2.50. (4–6) Fic.

_____ and JOHNSON, HELEN LOSSING. Dixie Dobie: A Sable Island Pony. Harcourt, 1945. $2.50. (4–5) Fic.

JOHNSON, SIDDIE J. Cat Hotel. Longmans, 1955. $2.50. (4–6) Fic.

JOHNSON, WILLIAM W. The Birth of Texas. Houghton, 1960. $1.95; lib. ed. $2.80; text ed. $2.24. (5–6) 976.

JONES, ELIZABETH O. Twig. Macmillan, 1942. $3.75. (4–5) Fic.

JONES, JESSIE M. O., comp. A Little Child: The Christmas Miracle Told in Bible Verses. Viking, 1946. $2. (4–6) 232.

JORDAN, NINA R. American Costume Dolls: How To Make and Dress Them. Harcourt, 1941. $3. (5–6) 649.

_____ Holiday Handicraft. Harcourt, 1938. $3.25. (4–6) 680.

———— Homemade Dolls in Foreign Dress. Harcourt, 1939. $3.25. (4–6) 649.

JOSLIN, SESYLE. There Is a Dragon in My Bed: Il y a un Dragon dans Mon Lit; and other useful phrases in French and English for young ladies and gentlemen going abroad or staying at home. Harcourt, 1961. $2.25; lib. bdg. $2.38. (4–5) 448.

JOY, CHARLES R. Desert Caravans: The Challenge of the Changing Sahara. Coward-McCann, 1960. $2.95. (5–6) 966.

———— Getting To Know Israel. Coward-McCann, 1960. $2.50; lib. bdg. $2.52. (4–6) 956.

———— Young People of the Western Mediterranean: Their Stories in Their Own Words. Duell, 1960. $3.50. (6) 940.

JUDSON, CLARA I. Abraham Lincoln: Friend of the People. Follett, 1950. $3.50. (5–6) 92.

———— Andrew Jackson: Frontier Statesman. Follett, 1954. $3.50. (5–6) 92.

———— Benjamin Franklin. Follett, 1957. $3.50. (6) 92.

———— Boat Builder: The Story of Robert Fulton. Scribner, 1947. $2.95. (4–6) 92.

———— City Neighbor: The Story of Jane Addams. Scribner, 1951. $2.95. (6) 92.

———— George Washington: Leader of the People. Follett, 1951. $3.50. (5–6) 92.

———— Lost Violin. Follett, 1947. $3.92. (5–6) Fic.

———— St. Lawrence Seaway. Follett, 1959. $3.95. (6) 627.

———— Soldier Doctor: The Story of William Gorgas. Scribner, 1942. $2.95. (5–6) 92.

———— Theodore Roosevelt: Fighting Patriot. Follett, 1953. $3.50. (5–6) 92.

———— Thomas Jefferson: Champion of the People. Follett, 1952. $3.50. (5–6) 92.

JUPO, FRANK J. Nothing To Wear but Clothes. Dutton, 1953. $2. (4–5) 646.

JUSTUS, MAY. Fiddlers' Fair. Albert Whitman, 1945. $1.25. (4–5) Fic.

———— Sammy. Albert Whitman, 1946. $2. (4–5) Fic.

———— Surprise for Peter Pocket. Holt, 1955. $2.25. (4–6) Fic.

KANE, HENRY B. The Tale of a Meadow. Knopf, 1959. $3. (4–6) 574.

———— The Tale of a Pond. Knopf, 1960. $3. (5–6) 574.

KASTNER, ERICH. Emil and the Detectives. Doubleday, 1930. $2.95. (4–6) Fic.

KAVALER, LUCY. The Wonders of Algae. Day, 1961. $3.50; lib. bdg. $3.29. (6) 589.

KAY, TERENCE. Space Volunteers. Harper, 1960. $2.50. (6) 629.

KEARY, ANNIE, and KEARY, ELIZA. Heroes of Asgard. St. Martin's, 1960. $1; children's ed. $2. (6) 293.

KELLY, ERIC P. The Christmas Nightingale: Three Christmas Stories from Poland. Macmillan, 1932. $2.25. (6) S C.

———— In Clean Hay. Macmillan, 1953. $2; bds. $1.25. (4–6) Fic.

———— The Land of the Polish People. Lippincott, 1943. $2.95. (5–6) 943.

KENNEDY, MARY. Jenny. Lothrop, 1954. $2.75. (4–6) Fic.

KENT, LOUISE A. He Went with Christopher Columbus. Houghton, 1940. $3.50. (6) Fic.

———— He Went with Marco Polo: A Story of Venice and Cathay. Houghton, 1935. $3.50. (6) Fic.

———— He Went with Vasco da Gama. Houghton, 1938. $3.50. (6) Fic.

KENWORTHY, LEONARD S. Profile of Nigeria. Doubleday, 1960. $2.50. (5–6) 966.

KETTELKAMP, LARRY. Drums, Rattles, and Bells. Morrow, 1960. $2.75. (4–6) 789.

———— Kites. Morrow, 1959. $2.75. (4–6) 796.

———— Magic Made Easy. Morrow, 1954. $2.75. (4–6) 793.

———— The Magic of Sound. Morrow, 1956. $2.75; lib. ed. $2.78. (4–6) 534.

———— Singing Strings. Morrow, 1958. lib. ed. $2.78. (4–6) 787.

KIERAN, JOHN. An Introduction to Birds. Garden City, 1950. $2.95. (5–6) 598.

KIERAN, MARGARET, and KIERAN, JOHN. John James Audubon. Random, 1954. $1.95. (5–6) 92.

KIM, YONG-IK. The Happy Days. Little, 1960. $3.50. (5–6) Fic.

KING, MARTHA B. Key to Chicago. Lippincott, 1961. $2.95. (4–6) 977.

KINGMAN, LEE. The Best Christmas. Doubleday, 1949. $1.75. (4–6) Fic.

———— The Magic Christmas Tree. Farrar, 1956. $2.75. (4–5) Fic.

———— The Village Band Mystery. Doubleday, 1956. $2.75. (4–6) Fic.

KINGSLEY, CHARLES. The Heroes: Greek Fairy Tales. Macmillan, 1941. $2.50. (5–6) 292.

KINNEY, HARRISON. The Lonesome Bear. McGraw-Hill, 1949. $2.75. (4–6) Fic.

KIPLING, RUDYARD. Jungle Books. Doubleday, 1948. $5.95, 2 vol. (4–6) Fic.

———— Just So Stories. Doubleday, 1956. $3.95. (4–6) Fic.

KIRKUS, VIRGINIA. The First Book of Gardening. Watts, 1956. $1.95. (4–6) 635.

KISH, GEORGE. Yugoslavia. Holiday, 1952. $2.50. (6) 949.

KJELGAARD, JIM. Boomerang Hunter. Holiday, 1960. $2.95. (5–6) Fic.

KNIGHT, CHARLES R. Life through the Ages. Knopf, 1946. $3. (6) 560.

KNIGHT, CLAYTON. The Big Book of Real Helicopters. Grosset, 1955. $1. (4–5) 629.

KNIGHT, DAVID C. The First Book of Sound: A Basic Guide to the Science of Acoustics. Watts, 1960. $1.95. (5–6) 534.

KNIGHT, ERIC M. Lassie Come-Home. Holt, 1940. $2.95. (6) Fic.

KNOWLTON, WILLIAM. Let's Explore beneath the Sea. Knopf, 1957. $3. (5–6) 797.

KOENIG, RICHARD. The Seven Special Cats. World, 1961. $2.75. (4–5) Fic.

KOHLER, JULILLY H. "Crazy As You Look!" Knopf, 1954. $2.75. (4–6) Fic.

KOMROFF, MANUEL. Mozart. Knopf, 1956. $3. (6) 92.

KRASILOVSKY, PHYLLIS. Benny's Flag. World, 1960. $2.50. (4) 979.

KUBIE, NORA B. The First Book of Archaeology. Watts, 1957. $1.95. (6) 571.

———— The First Book of Israel. Watts, 1953. $1.95. (4–6) 956.

KUWABARA, MINORU, and others. Cut and Paste. Obolensky, 1961. $3.95. (5–6) 745.

LACEY, MARION. Picture Book of Musical Instruments. Lothrop, 1942. $2.75; lib. bdg. $2.73. (5–6) 785.

LADD, ELIZABETH C. Janie. Morrow, 1955. $2.75. (4–5) Fic.

———— The Night of the Hurricane. Morrow, 1956. $2.75. (4–6) Fic.

LAMBERT, ELOISE, and PEI, MARIO. Our Names: Where They Came from and What They Mean. Lothrop, 1960. $3. (6) 929.

LAMPREY, LOUISE. All the Ways of Building. Macmillan, 1933. $5. (6) 720.

LAND, BARBARA, and LAND, MYRICK. The Quest of Isaac Newton. Garden City, 1960. $2.50. (6) 92.

LAND, MYRICK. Jungle Oil: The Search for Venezuela's Hidden Treasure. Coward-McCann, 1957. $2.95. (5–6) 338.

LANDIN, LES. About Atoms for Junior. Melmont, 1961. $2.50. (4) 539.

LANE, CARL D. River Dragon. Little, 1948. $1.75. (4–6) 970.

LANE, FERDINAND C. All about the Insect World. Random, 1956. $1.95. (5–6) 580.

———— All about the Sea. Random, 1953. $1.95. (4–6) 551.

LANG, DON. Strawberry Roan. Walck, 1946. $3. (5–6) Fic.

LANGTON, JANE. The Majesty of Grace. Harper, 1961. $2.95; Harpercrest bdg. $2.84. (4–5) Fic.

LANSING, ALFRED M. Shackleton's Valiant Voyage. McGraw-Hill, 1960. $3.95. (6) 999.

LANSING, ELISABETH C. H. Liza of the Hundredfold. Crowell, 1960. $2.95. (6) Fic.

LAROM, HENRY V. Mountain Pony: A Story of the Wyoming Rockies. Grosset, 1951. $1.75. (6) Fic.

———— Mountain Pony and the Pinto Colt. Grosset, 1954. $1.75. (5–6) Fic.

LARRICK, NANCY. See for Yourself: A First Book of Science Experiments. Dutton, 1952. $2.75. (4–5) 507.

LATHAM, JEAN L. Carry on, Mr. Bowditch. Houghton, 1955. $3.25. (6) 92.

———— Drake: The Man They Called a Pirate. Harper, 1960. $3.50; lib. bdg. $3.19. (6) 92.

———— Young Man in a Hurry: The Story of Cyrus W. Field. Harper, 1958. $2.95. (6) 92.

LATHROP, DOROTHY P. Angel in the Woods. Macmillan, 1947. $3. (4–5) Fic.

———— Let Them Live. Macmillan, 1951. $3.25. (4–6) 333.

LATTIMORE, ELEANOR F. The Chinese Daughter. Morrow, 1960. $2.75. (4–5) Fic.

———— Junior: A Colored Boy of Charleston. Harcourt, 1938. $2.95. (4–5) Fic.

———— Little Pear and His Friends. Harcourt, 1934. $3.25. (4–5) Fic.

———— Molly in the Middle. Morrow, 1956. $2.75. (4) Fic.

———— The Monkey of Crofton. Morrow, 1957. $2.75. (4–5) Fic.

_____ Peachblossom. Harcourt, 1943. $2.95. (4–5) Fic.

_____ The Questions of Lifu: A Story of China. Harcourt, 1942. $2.50. (4–5) Fic.

_____ Willow Tree Village. Morrow, 1955. $2.75. (4–5) Fic.

LAUBER, PATRICIA. All about the Ice Age. Random, 1959. $1.95. (4–6) 551.

_____ Battle against the Sea: How the Dutch Made Holland. Coward-McCann, 1956. $2.95. (5–6) 627.

_____ `Changing the Face of North America: The Challenge of the St. Lawrence Seaway. Coward-McCann, 1959. $2.95. (5–6) 974.

LAUGHLIN, FLORENCE. The Little Left-over Witch. Macmillan, 1960. $2.75. (4–5) Fic.

LAURITZEN, JONREED. The Glitter-eyed Wouser. Little, 1960. $3. (5–6) Fic.

LAVINE, SIGMUND A. Strange Travelers. Little, 1960. $2.95. (5–6) 591.

_____ Wonders of the Anthill. Dodd, 1960. $3. (4–6) 595.

LAWRENCE, MILDRED. The Homemade Year. Harcourt, 1950. $2.95. (5–6) Fic.

_____ Peachtree Island. Harcourt, 1948. $2.75. (4–5) Fic.

_____ Sand in Her Shoes. Harcourt, 1949. $2.95. (4–6) Fic.

LAWSON, MARIE A. Pocahontas and Captain John Smith: The Story of the Virginia Colony. Random, 1950. $1.95. (6) 973.

LAWSON, ROBERT. Edward, Hoppy, and Joe. Knopf, 1952. $3. (4–6) Fic.

_____ Rabbit Hill. Viking, 1944. $3. (4–6) Fic.

_____ They Were Strong and Good. Viking, 1940. $2.75. (4–6) 920.

_____ The Tough Winter. Viking, 1954. $3. (4–6) Fic.

_____ Watchwords of Liberty: A Pageant of American Quotations. Little, 1957. $3.50. (4–6) 973.

LEACH, MARIA. The Thing at the Foot of the Bed, and Other Scary Tales. World, 1959. $2.95. (4–6) S C.

LEAVITT, JEROME E. The True Book of Tools for Building. Childrens Pr., 1955. $2. (4–6) 694.

LEE, TINA. Manners To Grow On: A How-To-Do Book for Boys and Girls. Doubleday, 1955. $2.50. (4–6) 395.

_____ What To Do Now. Doubleday, 1946. $2.75. (4–6) 680.

LEEMING, JOSEPH. The Costume Book. Lippincott, 1938. $4.50. (5–6) 391.

_____ Fun with Boxes. Lippincott, 1937. $3.50. (4–6) 684.

_____ Fun with Clay. Lippincott, 1944. $3.50. (4–6) 738.

_____ Fun with Greeting Cards. Lippincott, 1960. $3. (4–6) 741.

_____ Fun with Paper. Lippincott, 1939. $3.95. (4–5) 745.

_____ Fun with Magic. Lippincott, 1943. $3.50. (5–6) 793.

_____ Fun with Puzzles. Lippincott, 1946. $3.50. (6) 680.

_____ Fun with String. Lippincott, 1939. $3.50. (4–6) 680.

_____ Fun with Wire. Lippincott, 1956. $3.50. (5–6) 745.

LE GRAND. Augustus and the River. Grosset, 1960. $1.50. (4–6) Fic.

_____ Tom Benn and Blackbeard, the Pirate. Abingdon, 1954. $2. (4–5) Fic.

LEMMON, ROBERT S. All about Moths and Butterflies. Random, 1956. $1.95. (5–6) 595.

L'ENGLE, MADELEINE. Meet the Austins. Vanguard, 1960. $3. (5–6) Fic.

LENSKI, LOIS. Bayou Suzette. Lippincott, 1943. $4.50. (5–6) Fic.

———— Blue Ridge Billy. Lippincott, 1946. $4.50. (4–6) Fic.

———— Boom Town Boy. Lippincott, 1948. $4.50. (4–6) Fic.

———— Cotton in My Sack. Lippincott, 1949. $4.50. (4–6) Fic.

———— Flood Friday. Lippincott, 1956. $2.95. (4–6) Fic.

———— Judy's Journey. Lippincott, 1947. $4.50. (4–6) Fic.

———— Peanuts for Billy Ben. Lippincott, 1952. $3.25. (4–5) Fic.

———— Strawberry Girl. Lippincott, 1945. $4.50. (4–6) Fic.

———— We Live in the South. Lippincott, 1952. $2.95. (4–5) Fic.

LENT, HENRY B. "Fly It Away!" Macmillan, 1946. $2.50. (4–6) 629.

———— The Helicopter Book. Macmillan, 1956. $3. (5–6) 629.

———— "I Work on a Newspaper." Macmillan, 1948. $3.75. (5–6) 070.

———— Man Alive in Outer Space: Our Space Surgeons' Greatest Challenge. Macmillan, 1961. $3. (5–6) 616.

———— Men at Work in New England. Putnam, 1956. $2.95. (4–6) 338.

———— Men at Work in the Great Lakes States. Putnam, 1958. $3. (4–6) 338.

LEONARD, JONATHAN N. Exploring Science. World, 1959. $4.95. (6) 500.

LE SUEUR, MERIDEL. Chanticleer of Wilderness Road: A Story of Davy Crockett. Knopf, 1951. $2.75. (5–6) 92.

———— Little Brother of the Wilderness: The Story of Johnny Appleseed. Knopf, 1947. $2.75. (4–5) 92.

LEVINE, MILTON I., and SELIGMANN, JEAN H. A Baby Is Born: The Story of How Life Begins. Golden Pr., 1949. $1.95. (4–5) 612.

LEWELLEN, JOHN. The Earth Satellite: Man's First True Space Adventure. Knopf, 1957. $2.25. (4–6) 629.

———— Helicopters: How They Work. Crowell, 1954. $2.95. (5–6) 629.

———— The Mighty Atom. Knopf, 1955. $2.25. (4–6) 539.

———— You and American Life Lines. Childrens Pr., 1952. $2. (5–6) 385.

LEWIS, LUCIA Z. The First Book of Microbes. Watts, 1955. $1.95. (4–6) 576.

LEWIS, MILDRED D. The Honorable Sword. Houghton, 1960. $2.75. (5–6) Fic.

LEWIS, OSCAR. Hawaii: Gem of the Pacific. Random, 1954. $1.95. (5–6) 996.

LEWIS, ROGER. Stamp Collecting. Knopf, 1952. $1.75. (4–6) 383.

LEWITON, MINA. Faces Looking Up. Harper, 1960. $2.95. (4–6) 372.

LIBERTY, GENE. The First Book of Tools. Watts, 1960. $1.95. (4–5) 680.

LIDE, ALICE A., and JOHANSEN, MARGARET A. Lapland Drum. Abingdon, 1955. $1.50. (4–6) Fic.

LIERS, EMIL E. A Beaver's Story. Viking, 1958. $3. (5–6) 590.

———— An Otter's Story. Viking, 1953. $2.50. (5–6) 599.

LIFE (periodical). The World We Live In; by the editorial staff of *Life* and Lincoln Barnett; text especially adapted by Jane Werner Watson from the orig-

inal version. Golden Pr., 1956. $4.95. (5–6) 574.

LILLIE, AMY M. Book of Three Festivals: Stories for Christmas, Easter and Thanksgiving. Dutton, 1953. $3.25. (4–6) 394.

LINDGREN, ASTRID E. Rasmus and the Vagabond. Viking, 1960. $2.75. (5–6) Fic.

LINDQUIST, JENNIE D. The Golden Name Day. Harper, 1955. $2.75. (4–6) Fic.

_____ The Little Silver House. Harper, 1959. $2.95; lib. bdg. $2.79. (4–6) Fic.

LINDQUIST, WILLIS. Alaska, the Forty-ninth State. McGraw-Hill, 1959. $3. (5–6) 979.

_____ Burma Boy. McGraw-Hill, 1953. $2.75. (4–6) Fic.

LIPKIND, WILLIAM. Boy of the Islands. Harcourt, 1954. $2.75. (4–5) Fic.

_____ Boy with a Harpoon. Harcourt, 1952. $2.75. (4–5) Fic.

LIPPINCOTT, JOSEPH W. Persimmon Jim, the Possum. Lippincott, 1955. $2.50. (4–6) Fic.

_____ Striped Coat, the Skunk. Lippincott, 1954. $2.50. (5–6) Fic.

_____ Wilderness Champion: The Story of a Great Hound. Lippincott, 1944. $3.95. (5–6) Fic.

LITCHFIELD, SARAH. Hello Alaska. Albert Whitman, 1945. $1.50. (4–6) 979.

LIU, BEATRICE. Little Wu and the Watermelons. Follett, 1954. $2.95. (4–6) Fic.

LLOYD, NORRIS. The Desperate Dragons. Hastings, 1960. $2.75. (4–6) Fic.

LOBSENZ, NORMAN M. The First Book of Ghana. Watts, 1960. $1.95. (4–6) 966.

_____ The First Book of West Germany. Watts, 1959. $1.95. (4–6) 943.

LOFTING, HUGH. Doctor Dolittle's Puddleby Adventures. Lippincott, 1952. $4.50. (4–6) Fic.

LONGSWORTH, POLLY. Exploring Caves. Crowell, 1959. $2.95. (6) 551.

LOOMIS, FREDERIC B. Field Book of Common Rocks and Minerals. Putnam, 1948. $3.50. (6) 549.

LORD, BEMAN. Quarterback's Aim. Walck, 1960. $2.75. (4–5) Fic.

LOUDEN, CLAIRE, and LOUDEN, GEORGE. Far into the Night: A Story of Bali. Scribner, 1955. $2.95. (4) Fic.

_____ Rain in the Winds: A Story of India. Scribner, 1953. $2.95. (4–5) 954.

LOVELACE, MAUD H. Betsy-Tacy. Crowell, 1940. $2.50. (4–5) Fic.

LOWNSBERY, ELOISE. The Boy Knight of Reims. Houghton, 1927. $4. (6) Fic.

LUDOVICI, LAURENCE J. The World of the Microscope. Putnam, 1959. $2.95. (5–6) 576.

LUTZ, FRANK E. Field Book of Insects of the United States and Canada. Putnam, 1935. $3.69. (4–6) 595.

LYONS, JOHN H. Stories of Our American Patriotic Songs. Vanguard, 1942. $3.50. (5–6) 784.

McCLOSKEY, ROBERT. Homer Price. Viking, 1951. $2.75. (4–6) Fic.

_____ Time of Wonder. Viking, 1957. $3.50. (4–5) 974.

McCLUNG, ROBERT M. Bufo: The Story of a Toad. Morrow, 1954. $2.75; lib. ed. $2.78. (4–5) 597.

—————— Buzztail: The Story of a Rattlesnake. Morrow, 1958. $2.75; lib. ed. $2.78. (4–6) 598.

—————— Leaper: The Story of an Atlantic Salmon. Morrow, 1957. $2.75. (4–5) 597.

—————— Ruby Throat: The Story of a Humming Bird. Morrow, 1950. $2.75. (4–5) 598.

—————— Shag: Last of the Plains Buffalo. Morrow, 1960. $2.95; lib. ed. $2.88. (4–6) 599.

—————— Spike: The Story of a Whitetail Deer. Morrow, 1952. $2.75; lib. ed. $2.78. (4–5) 591.

—————— Tiger: The Story of a Swallowtail Butterfly. Morrow, 1953. $2.75. (4–5) 595.

—————— Vulcan: The Story of a Bald Eagle. Morrow, 1955. $2.75. (4–5) 598.

—————— Whooping Crane. Morrow, 1959. $2.75. (4–5) 598.

McCoy, Jack. The Big Book of Real Submarines. Grosset, 1955. $1. (4–6) 623.

McCracken, Harold. The Biggest Bear on Earth. Lippincott, 1943. $3.95. (5–6) 591.

—————— Great White Buffalo. Lippincott, 1946. $3.50. (5–6) 970.

—————— Sentinel of the Snow Peaks: A Story of the Alaska Wilderness. Lippincott; 1945. $2.75. (5–6) 599.

—————— Son of the Walrus King. Lippincott, 1944. $3. (5–6) 599.

MacDonald, Betty. Mrs. Piggle-Wiggle's Magic. Lippincott, 1957. $2.95. (4–6) Fic.

Macdonald, George. The Princess and Curdie. Macmillan, 1954. $2.50. (4–6) Fic.

—————— The Princess and the Goblin. Macmillan, 1951. $3. (4–6) Fic.

McGinley, Phyllis. Mince Pie and Mistletoe. Lippincott, 1961. $2.95; lib. bdg. $3.50. (4–6) 821.

—————— The Most Wonderful Doll in the World. Lippincott, 1950. $2.95. (4–5) Fic.

—————— The Plain Princess. Lippincott, 1945. $2.95. (4–6) Fic.

MacGregor, Ellen. Miss Pickerell and the Geiger Counter. McGraw-Hill, 1953. $2.50. (4–6) Fic.

—————— Miss Pickerell Goes to Mars. McGraw-Hill, 1951. $2.50. (4–6) Fic.

—————— Miss Pickerell Goes to the Arctic. McGraw-Hill, 1954. $2.50. (4–6) Fic.

—————— Miss Pickerell Goes Undersea. McGraw-Hill, 1953. $2.50. (4–6) Fic.

McGuire, Edna. A Brave Young Land. Macmillan, 1946. $4.32. (5–6) 973.

—————— Glimpses into the Long Ago. Macmillan, 1945. $3.40. (5–6) 909.

Machetanz, Sara. A Puppy Named Gih. Scribner, 1957. $2.75. (4–5) Fic.

MacKellar, William. The Ghost in the Castle. McKay, 1960. $2.75. (4–6) Fic.

—————— Wee Joseph. McGraw-Hill, 1957. $2.50. (4–5) Fic.

McKenny, Margaret. Trees of the Countryside. Knopf, 1942. $3. (4–6) 582.

McMeekin, Isabella M. The First Book of Horses. Watts, 1949. $1.95. (4–5) 636.

———— Journey Cake. Messner, 1942. $2.75. (5–6) Fic.

———— Kentucky Derby Winner. McKay, 1949. $3. (4–6) Fic.

McNeer, May. The Alaska Gold Rush. Random, 1960. $1.95. (5–6) 979.

———— America's Abraham Lincoln. Houghton, 1957. $3.75; lib. ed. $4.50. (5–6) 92.

———— Armed with Courage. Abingdon, 1957. $2.50. (5–6) 920.

———— The California Gold Rush. Random, 1950. $1.95. (4–6) 979.

———— The Canadian Story. Farrar, 1958. $4.25. (6) 971.

———— Martin Luther. Abingdon, 1953. $3; pa. $1.75. (6) 92.

———— The Mexican Story. Farrar, 1953. $4.25. (6) 972.

———— Story of California. Harper, 1944. $2.95; lib. bdg. $2.94. (4–6) 979.

———— The Story of the Southern Highlands. Harper, 1945. $2.95; lib. ed. $2.94. (4–6) 975.

———— The Story of the Southwest. Harper, 1948. $2.95; lib. ed. $2.94. (4–6) 978.

———— War Chief of the Seminoles. Random, 1954. $1.95. (4–6) 92.

McSpadden, J. Walker. The Book of Holidays. Crowell, 1958. $3.50. (6) 394.

McSwigan, Marie. Snow Treasure. Dutton, 1942. $3. (4–6) Fic.

Maginley, C. J. Historic Models of Early America, and How to Make Them. Harcourt, 1947. $2.75. (6) 680.

———— Make It and Ride It. Harcourt, 1949. $2.50. (5–6) 649.

Malcolmson, David. Yipe: The Story of a Farm Dog. Little, 1955. $3. (4–6) Fic.

Manning, Rosemary. Dragon in Danger. Doubleday, 1960. $2.50. (4–6) Fic.

Manton, Jo. Elizabeth Garrett, M. D. Abelard-Schuman, 1960. $3. (6) 92.

Marcher, Marion W. Monarch Butterfly. Holiday, 1954. $2.50. (4–5) 595.

Markun, Patricia M. The First Book of the Panama Canal. Watts, 1958. $1.95. (5–6) 986.

Marokvia, Mireille, and Marokvia, Artur. Grococo: A French Crow. Lippincott, 1961. $3.50; lib. bdg. $3.95. (4–5) Fic.

Marshall, Dean. Invisible Island. Dutton, 1957. $2.95. (4–6) Fic.

Mason, Bernard S. The Junior Book of Camping and Woodcraft. Ronald, 1943. $4.50. (5–6) 796.

Mason, F. Van Wyck. Winter at Valley Forge. Random, 1953. $1.95. (6) 973.

Mason, George F. Animal Clothing. Morrow, 1955. $2.50. (5–6) 591.

———— Animal Homes. Morrow, 1947. $2.50; lib ed. $2.60. (4–6) 591.

———— Animal Sounds. Morrow, 1948. $2.50. (4–6) 591.

———— Animal Tails. Morrow, 1958. $2.50. (5–6) 591.

———— Animal Tools. Morrow, 1951. $2.50. (5–6) 591.

———— Animal Tracks. Morrow, 1943. $2.50. (4–6) 591.

———— Animal Weapons. Morrow, 1949. $2.50. (4–6) 591.

MASON, MIRIAM E. Hominy and His Blunt-nosed Arrow. Macmillan, 1950. $3. (4–5) Fic.

———— The Middle Sister. Macmillan, 1947. $3. (4) Fic.

———— Susannah: The Pioneer Cow. Macmillan, 1941. $3. (4–5) Fic.

———— Young Mr. Meeker and His Exciting Journey to Oregon. Bobbs-Merrill, 1952. $2.95. (4–5) Fic.

MAY, STELLA B. Let's Read about Brazil. Fideler, 1959. $3.28. (5–6) 981.

MAYNE, WILLIAM. The Blue Boat. Dutton, 1960. $2.95. (4–6) Fic.

MEADOWCROFT, ENID L. M. Abraham Lincoln. Crowell, 1942. $3.50. (6) 92.

———— By Secret Railway. Crowell, 1948. $3.50. (5–6) Fic.

———— By Wagon and Flatboat. Crowell, 1938. $3.50. (4–5) Fic.

———— The First Year. Crowell, 1946. $2.95. (4–6) Fic.

———— The Gift of the River: A History of Ancient Egypt. Crowell, 1937. $3.50. (4–6) 932.

———— Land of the Free. Crowell, 1961. $3.50. (4–5) 973.

———— On Indian Trails with Daniel Boone. Crowell, 1947. $2.95. (4–5) 92.

———— Silver for General Washington. Crowell, 1957. $3.50. (4–6) 636.

MEARS, HELEN. The First Book of Japan. Watts, 1953. $1.95. (4–6) 952.

MEEK, STERNER ST. P. So You're Going To Get a Puppy. Knopf, 1947. $2.75. (6) 636.

MEIGS, CORNELIA. The Covered Bridge. Macmillan, 1936. $3.50. (4–6) Fic.

———— The Dutch Colt. Macmillan, 1952. $2. (6) Fic.

———— The Willow Whistle. Macmillan, 1931. $3. (4–6) Fic.

———— Wind in the Chimney. Macmillan, 1934. $3.50. (5–6) Fic.

MELBO, IRVING R. Our Country's National Parks. Bobbs-Merrill, 1960. 2 vols. $4 ea. (5–6) 973.

MELLIN, JEANNE. Horses across the Ages. Dutton, 1954. $3.75. (4–6) 636.

MEREDITH, NICOLETE. King of the Kerry Fair. Crowell, 1960. $2.50. (4–6) Fic.

MEYER, JEROME S. Machines. World, 1958. $1.75. (4–6) 621.

———— Paper. World, 1960. $3. (6) 676.

———— Picture Book of Astronomy. Lothrop, 1945. $2.75; lib. bdg. $2.73; laminated pa. over bds. $1.95. (4–5) 520.

———— Picture Book of Chemistry. Lothrop, 1950. $2.75. (4–6) 540.

———— Picture Book of Electricity. Lothrop, 1953. $2.75; lib. bdg. $2.73; laminated pa. over bds. $1.95. (5–6) 537.

———— Picture Book of Molecules and Atoms. Lothrop, 1947. $2.75. (5–6) 541.

———— Picture Book of Radio and Television and How They Work. Lothrop, 1951. $2.75; laminated pa. over bds. $1.95. (5–6) 621.

———— Prisms and Lenses. World, 1959. $2.75. (4–6) 535.

MIERS, EARL S. Billy Yank and Johnny Reb: How They Fought and Made Up. Rand McNally, 1959. $3.50. (5–6) 973.

MILHOUS, KATHERINE. Patrick and the Golden Slippers. Scribner, 1951. $2.95. (4–5) Fic.

MILLEN, NINA, comp. Children's Games from Many Lands. Friendship Pr., 1956. $2.95; pa. $1.95. (4–6) 796.

MILLS, LOIS. So Young a Queen. Lothrop, 1961. $3. (6) 92.

MILNE, ALAN A. The World of Pooh: The Complete Winnie-the-Pooh and The House at Pooh Corner. Dutton, 1957. $4.95. (4–5) Fic.

MIRSKY, REBA P. Seven Grandmothers. Follett, 1955. $3.50. (4–6) Fic.

_____ Thirty-one Brothers and Sisters. Follett, 1952. $3.50. (4–6) Fic.

MITCHELL, HELEN, and WILSON, W. N. Ships That Made U. S. History. McGraw-Hill, 1950. $3.75. (6) 973.

MODAK, MANORAMA R. The Land and People of India. Lippincott, 1960. $2.95. (6) 954.

MOE, VIRGINIA, and WINTER, MILO. Animal Inn. Houghton, 1946. $3. (5–6) 591.

MOON, GRACE P. Chi-Wee. Doubleday, 1925. $2.95. (4–6) Fic.

MOORE, LILIAN. The Snake That Went to School. Random, 1957. $1.95. (4) Fic.

MORGAN, ALFRED P. Aquarium Book for Boys and Girls. Scribner, 1959. $3. (5–6) 574.

_____ Boy Electrician. Lothrop, 1948. $3.50. (6) 621.

_____ Boys' Book of Engines, Motors & Turbines. Scribner, 1946. $3. (6) 621.

_____ Boys' Book of Science and Construction. Lothrop, 1951. $3.50. (6) 500.

_____ First Chemistry Book for Boys and Girls. Scribner, 1950. $2.95. (5–6) 540.

_____ A First Electrical Book for Boys. Scribner, 1951. $3.95. (5–6) 621.

MORGAN, ANN H. Field Book of Animals in Winter. Putnam, 1939. $5. (6) 597.

_____ Field Book of Ponds and Streams: An Introduction to the Life of Fresh Water. Putnam, 1930. $5. (6) 591.

MORRIS, RICHARD B. The First Book of the American Revolution. Watts, 1956. $1.95. (4–6) 973.

_____ The First Book of the Constitution. Watts, 1958. $1.95. (5–6) 342.

MORROW, ELIZABETH. A Pint of Judgment: A Christmas Story. Knopf, 1960. $2.50. (4–5) Fic.

MUKERJI, DHAN G. Hari, the Jungle Lad. Dutton, 1924. $2.95. (5–6) Fic.

_____ Kari, the Elephant. Dutton, 1922. $2.95. (5–6) Fic.

MULAC, MARGARET E. The Game Book. Harper, 1946. $3.50. (6) 790.

MUNCH, THEODORE W. What Is a Rocket? Benefic, 1959. $1.60. (4–5) 629.

MURPHEY, ELEANOR A. Nihal. Crowell, 1960. $3; lib. bdg. $2.88. (5–6) Fic.

NANKIVELL, JOICE M. Tales of Christophilos. Houghton, 1954. $2.50. (4–6) Fic.

NASH, MARY. While Mrs. Coverlet Was Away. Little, 1958. $3. (4–5) Fic.

NATHAN, ADELE G. The Building of the First Transcontinental Railroad. Random, 1950. $1.95. (5–6) 385.

_____ and BAKER, W. C. Famous Railroad Stations of the World. Random, 1953. $2.95. (5–6) 385.

NAZAROFF, ALEXANDER. The Land of the Russian People. Lippincott, 1960. $2.95. (6) 947.

NEAL, HARRY E. The Story of the Kite. Vanguard, 1954. $3. (5–6) 796.

NEPHEW, WILLIAM, and CHESTER, MICHAEL. Beyond Mars. Putnam, 1960. $2.75; lib. ed. $2.68. (4–6) 629.

NEUBERGER, RICHARD L. Lewis and Clark Expedition. Random, 1951. $1.95. (4–6) 978.

NEURATH, MARIE. Rockets and Jets. Lothrop, 1960. $2. (4–6) 629.

———— The Wonder World of the Seashore. Lothrop, 1954. $2. (4–6) 574.

NEVIL, SUSAN R. The Picture Story of the Middle East. McKay, 1956. $3.50. (4–6) 956.

NEW YORK HERALD TRIBUNE, HOME INSTITUTE. Young America's Cook Book; rev. by Dorothy Callahan and Alma Smith Payne. Scribner, 1959. $3.95. (4–6) 641.

NEYHART, LOUISE A. Henry's Lincoln. Holiday, 1945. $2.50. (4–6) Fic.

NORLING, JOSEPHINE S., and NORLING, ERNEST. Pogo's Truck Ride: A Story of Motor Freight. Holt, 1954. $2. (4) 629.

NORMAN, GERTRUDE. The First Book of Music. Watts, 1954. $1.95. (4–6) 780.

NORTON, MARY. Bed-Knob and Broomstick. Harcourt, 1957. $3. (4–5) Fic.

———— The Borrowers. Harcourt, 1953. $2.95. (4–6) Fic.

———— The Borrowers Afield. Harcourt, 1955. $2.95. (4–6) Fic.

NOURSE, ALAN E. So You Want To Be a Scientist. Harper, 1960. $3. (6) 506.

OAKES, VANYA. Bamboo Gate: Stories of Children of Modern China. Macmillan, 1946. $2.50. (4–6) Fic.

O'BRIEN, JACK. Silver Chief: Dog of the North. Holt, 1933. $2.95. (6) Fic.

O'DANIEL, JOHN W. The Nation That Refused To Starve: The Challenge of the New Vietnam. Coward-McCann, 1960. $2.95. (6) 959.

O'DELL, SCOTT. Island of the Blue Dolphins. Houghton, 1960. $2.75. (5–6) Fic.

OLCOTT, FRANCES J., ed. Good Stories for Great Birthdays. Houghton, 1922. $4. (4–6) 920.

———— Good Stories for Great Holidays. Houghton, 1944. $4.50. (4–6) 394.

OLDEN, SAM. Getting To Know Nigeria. Coward-McCann, 1960. $2.50; lib. bdg. $2.52. (4–6) 966.

OLDRIN, JOHN. Eight Rings on His Tail. Viking, 1956. $2.50. (4–5) Fic.

OLDS, ELIZABETH. Riding the Rails. Houghton, 1948. $3; lib. bdg. $3.75. (4–5) 385.

OLIVER, RITA N. Rain or Shine: Things To Make. Harcourt, 1954. $2.50. (4–5) 745.

O'NEILL, HESTER. The Picture Story of Alaska. McKay, 1951. $3.95. (4–6) 979.

———— The Picture Story of Denmark. McKay, 1952. $3.50. (4–6) 948.

———— The Picture Story of Hawaii. McKay, 1950. $3.95. (4–6) 996.

———— The Picture Story of Norway. McKay, 1951. $3.50. (4–6) 948.

———— The Picture Story of the Philippines. McKay, 1948. $3.95. (4–6) 991.

ORBAAN, ALBERT. With Banners Flying. Day, 1960. $3.75. (6) 904.

ORTON, HELEN F. The Treasure in the Little Trunk. Lippincott, 1932. $2.75. (4–6) Fic.

OSBORNE, CHESTER G. The First Lake Dwellers. Follett, 1956. $2.75. (4–6) Fic.

OSBORNE, MAURICE M. Ondine: The Story of a Bird Who Was Different. Houghton, 1960. $3; lib. ed. $3.75. (6) Fic.

OSMOND, EDWARD. Animals of the World. Walck, 1956-58. 3 vols. $2.25 ea. (4–6) 591.

 v. 1. Elephants, Camels, Polar Bears, Chimpanzees. 1956.

 v. 2. Kangaroos, Reindeer, Beavers, Whales. 1957.

 v. 3. Llamas, Pandas, Chamois, Lions. 1958.

OTA, KOSHI, and others. Printing for Fun. Obolensky, 1960. $3.95. (4–6) 760.

OTIS, JAMES. Toby Tyler: or, Ten Weeks with a Circus. World, 1947. $2.50. (4–6) Fic.

OWEN, RUTH B. Denmark Caravan. Dodd, 1936. $3. (6) 948.

PACE, MILDRED M. Clara Barton. Scribner, 1941. $2.75. (4–6) 92.

_____ Early American: The Story of Paul Revere. Scribner, 1940. $2.75. (5–6) 92.

_____ Juliette Low. Scribner, 1947. $2.95. (5–6) 92.

PAINE, ALBERT B. The Arkansaw Bear: A Tale of Fanciful Adventure. Harper, 1925. $2.50. (4–6) Fic.

PANNELL, LUCILE, and CAVANAH, FRANCES, eds. Holiday Round Up. Macrae, 1950. $3.95. (4–6)) 394.

PARISH, HELEN A. At the Palace Gates. Viking, 1949. $2.50. (4–6) Fic.

_____ Our Lady of Guadalupe. Viking, 1955. $3. (4–6) Fic.

PARKER, BERTHA M. Animals We Know. Harper, 1952. 48¢. (4–6) 591.

_____ Birds. Harper, 1954. 48¢. (4–6) 598.

_____ Clouds, Rain, and Snow. Harper, 1954. 48¢. (4–6) 551.

_____ Dependent Plants. Harper, 1951. 48¢. (4–6) 589.

_____ The Earth a Great Storehouse. Harper, 1953. 48¢. (4–6) 553.

_____ Electricity. Harper, 1954. 48¢. (4–6) 537.

_____ Fire. Harper, 1949. 48¢. (4–6) 541.

_____ Fishes. Harper, 1955. 48¢. (4–6) 597.

_____ Flowers, Fruits, Seeds. Harper, 1953. 48¢. (4–6) 580.

_____ The Garden and Its Friends. Harper, 1953. 48¢. (4–6) 635.

_____ Garden Indoors. Harper, 1953. 48¢. (4–6) 635.

_____ The Golden Book of Science. Golden Pr., 1956. $3.95. (4–6) 500.

_____ Gravity. Harper, 1954. 48¢. (5–6) 531.

_____ Insects and Their Ways. Harper, 1955. 48¢. (4–6) 595.

_____ Living Things. Harper, 1953. 48¢. (4–6) 574.

_____ Machines. Harper, 1953. 48¢. (4–6) 621.

_____ Magnets. Harper, 1955. 48¢. (4–6) 538.

_____ Plant and Animal Partnerships. Harper, 1953. 48¢. (4–6) 574.

_____ Plant Factories. Harper, 1953. 48¢. (4–6) 580.

_____ Reptiles. Harper, 1954. 48¢. (4–6) 598.

_____ Saving Our Wild Life. Harper, 1952. 48¢. (4–6) 333.

———— The Scientist and His Tools. Harper, 1953. 48¢. (4–6) 500.

———— Seeds and Seed Travels. Harper, 1954. 48¢. (4–6) 581.

———— Sky above Us. Harper, 1955. 48¢. (4–6) 520.

———— Sound. Harper, 1953. 48¢. (4–6) 534.

———— Spiders. Harper, 1955. 48¢. (4–6) 595.

———— Stories Read from the Rocks. Harper, 1955. 48¢. (4–6) 550.

———— Thermometers, Heat, and Cold. Harper, 1954. 48¢. (5–6) 536.

———— Toads and Frogs. Harper, 1955. 48¢. (4–6) 597.

———— Trees. Harper, 1953. 48¢. (4–6) 582.

———— Water. Harper, 1953. 48¢. (4–6) 551.

———— What Things Are Made Of. Harper, 1953. 48¢. (5–6) 540.

———— and DOWNING, M. ELIZABETH. You as a Machine. Harper, 1955. 48¢. (4–6) 612.

———— and PARK, THOMAS. Animal Travels. Harper, 1951. 48¢. (4–6) 591.

PARKER, EDGAR. The Enchantress. Pantheon, 1960. $3.25. (4–5) Fic.

PARKER, FAN. The Russian Alphabet Book. Coward-McCann, 1961. $2.95; lib. ed. $2.81. (6) 491.

PARRISH, ANNE. Floating Island. Harper, 1930. $3.95; lib. bdg. $3.79. (4–6) Fic.

PASCHEL, HERBERT P. The First Book of Color. Watts, 1959. $1.95. (5–6) 535.

PAULI, HERTHA E. Lincoln's Little Correspondent. Doubleday, 1952. $2.50. (4–6) 92.

———— Silent Night: The Story of a Song. Knopf, 1943. $2.75. (4–6) 783.

PAYNE, JOAN B. The Leprechaun of Bayou Luce. Hastings, 1957. $2.75. (4–5) Fic.

PEARE, CATHERINE O. Jules Verne: His Life. Holt, 1956. $2.50. (5–6) 92.

———— Robert Louis Stevenson: His Life. Holt, 1955. $2.50. (4–6) 92.

PEATTIE, RODERICK E. The Law: What It Is and How It Works. Abelard-Schuman, 1952. $2.50. (5–6) 340.

PECK, ANNE M. The Pageant of South American History. Longmans, 1958. $6.50. (6) 980.

PEET, CREIGHTON. The First Book of Bridges. Watts, 1953. $1.95. (4–6) 624.

PEI, MARIO A. All about Language. Lippincott, 1954. $2.95. (6) 400.

PELS, GERTRUDE J. The Care of Water Pets. Crowell, 1955. $2.95; lib. bdg. $2.83. (4–6) 590.

PENNEY, GRACE J. Moki. Houghton, 1960. $2.75. (4–5) Fic.

PERKINS, R. MARLIN. Marlin Perkins' Zooparade. Rand McNally, 1954. $2.95. (5–6) 591.

PETERSHAM, MAUD F., and PETERSHAM, MISKA. America's Stamps: The Story of One Hundred Years of U.S. Postage Stamps. Macmillan, 1947. $5.50. (5–6) 383.

———— David; from the story told in the First Book of Samuel and the First Book of Kings. Macmillan, 1958. $2.50; lib. bdg. $2.13. (4–5) 92.

———— Joseph and His Brothers; from the story told in the book of Genesis. Macmillan, 1958. $2.50; lib. bdg. $2.13. (4–5) 92.

_____ Moses; from the story told in the Old Testament. Macmillan, 1958. $2.50; lib. bdg. $2.13. (4–5) 92.

_____ Ruth; from the story told in the book of Ruth. Macmillan, 1958. $2.50; lib. bdg. $2.13. (4–5) 92.

_____ The Silver Mace: A Story of Williamsburg. Macmillan, 1956. $3.75. (4–5) 975.

_____ Story of the Presidents of the United States of America. Macmillan, 1953. $3.75. (4–6) 920.

PHILLIPS, MARY G. Dragonflies and Damselflies. Crowell, 1960. $2.50. (5–6) 595.

_____ The Makers of Honey. Crowell, 1956. $2.50. (5–6) 595.

PICTURESQUE WORD ORIGINS. Merriam, 1933. $3. (6) 422.

PODENDORF, ILLA. 101 Science Experiments. Childrens Pr., 1960. $4.50. (4–5) 507.

POHLMANN, LILLIAN. Myrtle Albertina's Secret. Coward-McCann, 1956. $2.50. (4–6) Fic.

POLITI, LEO. The Mission Bell. Scribner, 1953. $2.95. (4–6) 92.

POLLAND, MADELEINE. Children of the Red King. Holt, 1961. $3. (5–6) Fic.

POSELL, ELSA Z. This Is an Orchestra. Houghton, 1950. $3; lib. ed. $3.75. (5–6) 785.

POTTER, BEATRIX. The Fairy Caravan. Warne, 1951. $3. (4–5) Fic.

POUGH, FREDERICK H. All about Volcanoes and Earthquakes. Random, 1953. $1.95. (4–6) 551.

PRATT, FLETCHER. The Monitor and the Merrimac. Random, 1951. $1.95. (5–6) 973.

PROKOFIEFF, SERGE. Peter and the Wolf. Knopf, 1940. $3. (4–6) 398.

PROUDFIT, ISABEL B. River-Boy: The Story of Mark Twain. Messner, 1948. $2.95; lib. bdg. $2.99. (6) 92.

_____ The Treasure Hunter: The Story of Robert Louis Stevenson. Messner, 1946. $2.95. (6) 92.

PURDY, CLAIRE L. He Heard America Sing: The Story of Stephen Foster. Messner, 1940. $2.95. (6) 92.

PYNE, MABLE M. Little History of the Wide World. Houghton, 1947. $3.50. (4–5) 909.

QUINN, VERNON. Picture Map Geography of Asia. Lippincott, 1955. $3.50. (4–6) 950.

_____ Picture Map Geography of Canada and Alaska. Lippincott, 1944. $3.50. (4–6) 971.

_____ Picture Map Geography of Mexico, Central America and the West Indies. Lippincott, 1943. $3.50. (5–6) 972.

_____ Picture Map Geography of South America. Lippincott, 1941. $3.50. (5–6) 980.

_____ Picture Map Geography of the Pacific Islands. Lippincott, 1945. $3.50. (4–6) 978.

———— Picture Map Geography of the United States. Lippincott, 1953. $4. (5–6) 973.

RANKIN, CARROLL W. Dandelion Cottage. Holt, 1946. $3. (5–6) Fic.

RANKIN, LOUISE. Daughter of the Mountains. Viking, 1948. $3.25. (5–6) Fic.

RAVIELLI, ANTHONY. Wonders of the Human Body. Viking, 1954. $2.50. (4–6) 611.

RAWLINGS, MARJORIE K. The Secret River. Scribner, 1955. $2.50. (4–5) Fic.

RECK, ALMA K. Clocks Tell the Time. Scribner, 1960. $2.75. (4–6) 681.

RED CROSS. First Aid Textbook for Juniors. Blakiston, 1953. $1. (6) 551.

REED, WILLIAM M. And That's Why. Harcourt, 1932. $2.75. (4) 500.

———— The Earth for Sam; ed. by Paul F. Brandwein. Harcourt, 1960. $4.95. (5–6) 550.

———— Patterns in the Sky: The Story of the Constellations. Morrow, 1951. $3. (5–6) 523.

———— and BRONSON, WILFRID S. The Sea for Sam; ed. by Paul F. Brandwein. Harcourt, 1960. $4.95. (6) 551.

REINFELD, FRED. Chess for Children. Sterling, 1958. $2.50. (5–6) 794.

RENICK, JAMES L., and RENICK, MARION L. David Cheers the Team. Scribner, 1941. $2.95. (4–5) Fic.

———— Steady: A Baseball Story. Scribner, 1942. $2.95. (4–5) Fic.

———— Tommy Carries the Ball. Scribner, 1940. $2.50. (4–6) Fic.

RENICK, MARION L. John's Back Yard Camp. Scribner, 1954. $2.50. (4–5) Fic.

———— Nicky's Football Team. Scribner, 1951. $2.50. (4–5) Fic.

———— Pete's Home Run. Scribner, 1952. $2.50. (4–5) Fic.

———— Seven Simpsons on Six Bikes. Scribner, 1956. $2.50. (4–5) Fic.

———— Shining Shooter. Scribner, 1950. $2.75. (5–6) Fic.

REYNOLDS, BARBARA L. Hamlet and Brownswiggle. Scribner, 1954. $2.95. (4–6) Fic.

———— Pepper. Scribner, 1952. $2.95. (4–6) Fic.

REYNOLDS, QUENTIN J. The Life of Saint Patrick. Random, 1955. $1.95. (5–6) 92.

———— The Wright Brothers: Pioneers of American Aviation. Random, 1950. $1.95. (4–6) 92.

RHOADS, DOROTHY. The Corn Grows Ripe. Viking, 1956. $2.75. (4–6) Fic.

RICH, LOUISE D. The First Book of the Early Settlers. Watts, 1959. $1.95. (4–6) 973.

RIEDMAN, SARAH R. Water for People. Abelard-Schuman, 1960. $3. (6) 551.

RIETVELD, JANE. Nicky's Bugle. Viking, 1947. $2.25. (4–6) Fic.

RIPPER, CHARLES L. Bats. Morrow, 1954. $2.75; lib. ed. $2.78. (4–6) 599.

———— Hawks. Morrow, 1956. $2.75. (5–6) 598.

———— Moles and Shrews. Morrow, 1957. $2.75. (4–6) 599.

———— The Weasel Family. Morrow, 1959. $2.75. (4–5) 599.

RITCHIE, ALICE. The Treasure of Li-Po. Harcourt, 1949. $2.75. (4–6) Fic.

RITCHIE, BARBARA. Ramon Makes a Trade; Los Cambios de Ramon. Parnassus, 1959. $3.25. (4–5) Fic.

ROBERTSON, GLADYS, and GRAHAM, VERA M. Strange Sea Life. Holt, 1950. $3. (5–6) 591.

ROBERTSON, KEITH. Ticktock and Jim. Holt, 1948. $1.75. (4–6) Fic.

ROBINSON, CHARLES A. The First Book of Ancient Egypt. Watts, 1961. $1.95. (4–6) 680.

———— The First Book of Ancient Greece. Watts, 1960. $1.95. (5–6) 938.

ROBINSON, JESSIE. Things To Make from Odds & Ends. Appleton, 1945. $2.50. (4–6) 680.

ROBINSON, WILLIAM W. Beasts of the Tar Pits: Tales of Ancient America. Ward Ritchie, 1961. $2.50. (4–6) 560.

ROGERS, FRANCES. Big Miss Liberty. Lippincott, 1938. $3. (5–6) Fic.

———— and BEARD, ALICE. Heels, Wheels, and Wire: The Story of Messages and Signals. Lippincott, 1953. $3. (5–6) 384.

———— Old Liberty Bell. Lippincott, 1942. $3. (5–6) 974.

ROGERS, MATILDA. The First Book of Cotton. Watts, 1954. $1.95. (5–6) 633.

ROMBAUER, IRMA S. Cookbook for Girls and Boys. Bobbs-Merrill, 1952. $3.95. (6) 641.

ROSS, FRANCES A. The Land and People of Canada. Lippincott, 1960. $2.95. (6) 971.

ROSS, GEORGE E. Know Your Government. Rand McNally, 1960. $2.95; pa. $1.50. (6) 353.

ROSS, NANCY W. Heroines of the Early West. Random, 1960. $1.95. (5–6) 920.

ROTHERY, AGNES E. Central American Roundabout. Dodd, 1944. $3. (6) 972.

———— Scandinavian Roundabout. Dodd, 1946. $3. (5–6) 948.

———— South American Roundabout. Dodd, 1940. $3. (5–6) 980.

ROUNDS, GLEN. The Blind Colt. Holiday, 1960. $2.95. (5–6) Fic.

———— Lone Muskrat. Holiday, 1953. $2.50. (4–6) 599.

———— Stolen Pony. Holiday, 1948. $2.50. (5–6) Fic.

———— Swamp Life. Prentice-Hall, 1957. $3. (5–6) 591.

———— Whitey Ropes and Rides. Holiday, 1956. $2.50. (4–6) Fic.

———— Wildlife at Your Doorstep. Prentice-Hall, 1958. $3. (5–6) 591.

RUCHLIS, HY. The Wonder of Light: A Picture Story of How and Why We See. Harper, 1960. $2.95; lib. bdg. $2.79. (6) 535.

RUSHMORE, HELEN. Cowboy Joe of the Circle S. Harcourt, 1950. $2.50. (4–6) Fic.

———— The Lost Treasure Box. Harcourt, 1949. $2.75. (4–6) Fic.

———— The Shadow of Robbers Roost. World, 1960. $2.95. (4–6) Fic.

RUSKIN, JOHN. The King of the Golden River; or, The Black Brothers. Watts, 1958. $3. (4–6) Fic.

ST. JOHN, ROBERT. Builder of Israel: The Story of Ben-Gurion. Doubleday, 1961. $2.95. (6) 92.

SALOMON, JULIAN H. The Book of Indian Crafts & Indian Lore. Harper, 1928. $4.50; lib. bdg. $3.99. (6) 970.

SALTEN, FELIX. Bambi. Grosset, 1940. $1 and $1.50 eds. (5–6) Fic.

SASEK, MIROSLAV. This Is Edinburgh. Macmillan, 1961. $3. (4–6) 941.

———— This Is London. Macmillan, 1959. $2.95; lib. bdg. $3.51. (4–6) 942.

———— This Is Munich. Macmillan, 1961. $3. (4–6) 943.

———— This Is New York. Macmillan, 1960. $2.95; lib. bdg. $3.51. (4–6) 974.

———— This Is Paris. Macmillan, 1959. $3.50. (4–6) 944.

———— This Is Rome. Macmillan, 1960. $2.95; lib. bdg. $3.51. (4–6) 945.

SAUER, JULIA L. Fog Magic. Viking, 1943. $2.50. (5–6) Fic.

———— The Light at Tern Rock. Viking, 1951. $2.50. (4–6) Fic.

SAWYER, RUTH. The Christmas Anna Angel. Viking, 1944. $2.50. (4–5) Fic.

———— The Enchanted Schoolhouse. Viking, 1956. $2.50. (4–6) Fic.

———— ed. The Long Christmas. Viking, 1941. $3. (4–6) 394.

———— Maggie Rose: Her Birthday Christmas. Harper, 1952. $2.05; lib. bdg. $2.44. (4–6) Fic.

———— This Is the Christmas. Horn Book, 1945. $1.50. (5–6) Fic.

———— This Way to Christmas. Harper, 1944. $2; holiday ed. $2.95. (4–6) Fic.

———— The Year of the Christmas Dragon. Viking, 1960. $2.50. (4–5) Fic.

SAYERS, FRANCES C. Ginny and Custard. Viking, 1951. $2. (4–6) Fic.

———— Tag-along Tooloo. Viking, 1941. $2.50. (4) Fic.

SCHATZ, ALBERT, and RIEDMAN, SARAH R. Story of Microbes. Harper, 1952. $2.75. (6) 589.

SCHAUFFLER, ROBERT H., ed. Christmas. Dodd, 1907. $3.50. (4–6) 394.

SCHEALER, JOHN M. The Sycamore Warrior: A Mystery of Ancient Egypt. Dutton, 1960. $3.50. (6) Fic.

———— This Way to the Stars. Dutton, 1957. $3.25. (6) 523.

SCHEELE, WILLIAM E. Ancient Elephants. World, 1958. $2.75. (4–6) 569.

———— The First Mammals. World, 1955. $4.95. (5–6) 569.

———— The Mound Builders. World, 1960. $2.75. (4–6) 970.

———— Prehistoric Animals. World, 1954. $4.95. (4–6) 560.

SCHEIB, IDA. The First Book of Food. Watts, 1956. $1.95. (4–6) 641.

———— What Happened? The Science Stories behind the News. McKay, 1955. $2.95. (5–6) 500.

SCHIFFER, DON. The First Book of Basketball. Watts, 1959. $1.95. (5–6) 796.

SCHLOAT, G. WARREN. Adventures of a Letter. Scribner, 1949. $2.95. (4–6) 383.

———— Andy's Wonderful Telescope. Scribner, 1958. $2.95. (4–6) 522.

———— The Magic of Water. Scribner, 1955. $2.95. (4–6) 551.

———— Your Wonderful Teeth. Scribner, 1954. $2.95. (4–6) 617.

SCHNEIDER, HERMAN. Everyday Machines and How They Work. McGraw-Hill, 1950. $2.95. (5–6) 643.

———— Everyday Weather and How It Works. McGraw-Hill, 1951. $3. (5–6) 551.

———— and SCHNEIDER, NINA. How Your Body Works. W. R. Scott, 1949. $3.50. (4–6) 612.

———— Let's Look inside Your House. W. R. Scott, 1948. $2.50. (4–6) 600.

———— More Power to You: A Short History of Power from the Windmill to the Atom. W. R. Scott, 1953. $2.75. (4–6) 621.

———— Rocks, Rivers and the Changing Earth: A First Book about Geology. W. R. Scott, 1952. $3.50. (4–6) 550.

———— Science Fun with Milk Cartons. McGraw-Hill, 1953. $2.75. (5–6) 680.

———— Your Telephone and How It Works. McGraw-Hill, 1952. $2.50. (5–6) 621.

SCHNEIDER, LEO. Lifeline: The Story of Your Circulatory System. Harcourt, 1958. $2.95. (6) 612.

———— Space in Your Future. Harcourt, 1961. $3.75. (6) 523.

———— and AMES, MAURICE U. Wings in Your Future: Aviation for Young People. Harcourt, 1955. $2.95. (5–6) 629.

SCHWARTZ, JULIUS. It's Fun To Know Why: Experiments with Things around Us. McGraw-Hill, 1952. $2.75. (4–6) 507.

SCHWIMMER, FRANCISKA. Great Musicians as Children. Doubleday, 1929. $2.75. (4–6) 920.

SCOTT, BARBARA A., and KIRBY, MICHAEL. Skating for Beginners. Knopf, 1953. $3.75. (6) 796.

SCOTT, SALLY. The Brand New Kitten. Harcourt, 1956. $2.25. (4–5) Fic.

———— Chica. Harcourt, 1954. $2.25. (4–6) Fic.

SEAMAN, LOUISE H. Mr. Peck's Pets. Macmillan, 1947. $2. (4–5) Fic.

SEARS, PAUL McC. Barn Swallow. Holiday, 1955. $2. (4–6) 598.

SECHRIST, ELIZABETH H., comp. Christmas Everywhere: A Book of Christmas Customs of Many Lands. Macrae, 1936. $2.95. (6) 394.

———— Heigh-Ho for Halloween! Macrae, 1948. $3.50. (5–6) 394.

———— Red Letter Days: A Book of Holiday Customs. Macrae, 1940. $3.50. (5–6) 394.

———— and WOOLSEY, JANETTE, comps. It's Time for Easter. Macrae, 1961. $3.75. (5–6) 394.

SELDEN, GEORGE. The Cricket in Times Square. Farrar, 1960. $3.50. (4–6) Fic.

SELLEW, CATHARINE F. Adventures with the Giants. Little, 1950. $3.50. (4–6) 292.

———— Adventures with the Gods. Little, 1945. $3.50. (4–6) 292.

SELSAM, MILLICENT E. Birth of an Island. Harper, 1959. $2.75; lib. ed. $2.73. (4–5) 551.

———— How To Grow House Plants. Morrow, 1960. $2.75; lib. ed. $2.78. (4–6) 635.

———— Microbes at Work. Morrow, 1953. $2.75. (5–6) 589.

———— Plants That Heal. Morrow, 1959. $2.75. (6) 581.

———— Plants We Eat. Morrow, 1955. $2.75. (4–6) 581.

———— Play with Seeds. Morrow, 1957. $2.75. (4–6) 581.

———— Play with Trees. Morrow, 1950. $2.75. (4–6) 582.

———— See through the Forest. Harper, 1956. $2.75; lib. bdg. $2.73. (4–6) 574.

———— See through the Jungle. Harper, 1957. $2.75; lib. ed. $2.73. (4–6) 574.

———— See through the Lake. Harper, 1958. $2.75; lib. ed. $2.73. (4–6) 591.

———— Underwater Zoos. Morrow, 1961. $2.75; lib. ed. $2.78. (4–6) 574.

———— and MORROW, BETTY. See through the Sea. Harper, 1955. $2.75; lib. ed. $2.73. (4–6) 591.

SEREDY, KATE. The Good Master. Viking, 1935. $3.50. (5–6) Fic.

———— Philomena. Viking, 1955. $2.75. (4–6) Fic.

———— The Singing Tree. Viking, 1939. $3.50. (5–6) Fic.

———— A Tree for Peter. Viking, 1941. $3.50. (4–6) Fic.

———— The White Stag. Viking, 1937. $3. (6) 398.

SEVERN, BILL, and SEVERN, SUE. Let's Give a Show. Knopf, 1956. $2.75. (4–6) 792.

SEVREY, O. IRENE. The First Book of the Earth. Watts, 1958. $1.95. (5–6) 551.

SEYMOUR, ALTA H. Erik's Christmas Camera. Follett, 1956. $2.75. (4–6) Fic.

———— Kaatje and the Christmas Compass. Follett, 1954. $2.75. (4–6) Fic.

———— The Top o' Christmas Morning: A Story of Ireland. Follett, 1955. $2.75. (4–5) Fic.

SHACKELFORD, JANE D. The Child's Story of the Negro. Associated Pubs., 1938. $3. (5–6) 326.

SHANNON, MONICA. Dobry. Viking, 1934. $3.50. (5–6) Fic.

SHAPIRO, IRWIN. Steamboat Bill and the Captain's Top Hat. Messner, 1943. $2.50. (5–6) Fic.

SHARP, MARGERY. The Rescuers. Little, 1959. $3.50. (4–6) Fic.

SHEEHY, EMMA D. Molly and the Golden Wedding. Holt, 1956. $2.50. (4–5) Fic.

SHERMAN, JANE. The Real Book about Dogs. Garden City, 1951. $1.95. (5–6) 636.

SHIPPEN, KATHERINE B. Lightfoot: The Story of an Indian Boy. Viking, 1950. $2.50. (4–6) Fic.

SHIRER, WILLIAM L. The Rise and Fall of Adolf Hitler. Random, 1961. $1.95. (5–6) 943.

SHURA, MARY F. Simple Spigott. Knopf, 1960. $2.50. (4–5) Fic.

SHUTTLESWORTH, DOROTHY E. Story of Spiders. Garden City, 1959. $2.95. (6) 595.

SICKELS, EVELYN R. That Boy, Johnny! Scribner, 1952. $2.50. (4–6) Fic.

SIMON, CHARLIE M. H. Robin on the Mountain. Dutton, 1953. $2.95. (4–6) Fic.

SINGH, R. LAL, and LOWNSBERY, ELOISE. Gift of the Forest. Longmans, 1942. $4. (5–6) Fic.

SKOLSKY, SYD C. Music Box Book. Dutton, 1946. $2.75. (4–6) 785.

SLEIGH, BARBARA. Carbonel: The King of the Cats. Bobbs-Merrill, 1957. $2.95. (4–6) Fic.

_____ The Kingdom of Carbonel. Bobbs-Merrill, 1960. $3.50. (4–6) Fic.

SLOANE, WILLIAM. British Isles. Holiday, 1946. $2.50. (5–6) 942.

SLOBODKIN, LOUIS. The Adventures of Arab. Macmillan, 1946. $2.75. (4–6) Fic.

_____ The First Book of Drawing. Watts, 1958. $1.95. (5–6) 741.

SMITH, DATUS C. The Land and People of Indonesia. Lippincott, 1961. $2.95. (6) 991.

SMITH, ELVA S., and HAZELTINE, ALICE I., comps. The Christmas Book of Legends & Stories. Lothrop, 1944. $3.95. (5–6) 394.

SMITH, FRANCES C. The First Book of Conservation. Watts, 1954. $1.95. (4–6) 333.

_____ The First Book of Water. Watts, 1959. $1.95. (4–6) 551.

SMITH, IRENE. The Santa Claus Book. Watts, 1948. $2.95. (4–5) 394.

SMITH, J. RUSSELL, and SORENSON, FRANK. Neighbors around the World. Winston, 1952. $3.76. (4) 910.

SMITHER, ETHEL L. Stories of Jesus. Abingdon, 1954. $2. (4–5) 232.

SNOW, DOROTHEA J. Come, Chucky, Come. Houghton, 1952. $2; lib. ed. $2.75. (4–6) Fic.

_____ A Doll for Lily Belle. Houghton, 1960. $2.50; lib. ed. $3.25. (4–5) Fic.

SNYDER, LOUIS L. The First Book of the Soviet Union. Watts, 1959. $1.95. (6) 947.

_____ The First Book of World War I. Watts, 1958. $1.95. (5–6) 940.

_____ The First Book of World War II. Watts, 1958. $1.95. (5–6) 940.

SOONG, MAYING. The Art of Chinese Paper Folding for Young and Old. Harcourt, 1948. $2.95. (4–6) 745.

SOOTIN, LAURA. Let's Go to a Police Station. Putnam, 1957. $1.95; lib. ed. $1.86. (4–5) 352.

_____ Let's Take a Trip to a Newspaper. Putnam, 1956. $1.95; lib. ed. $1.86. (4–6) 070.

SORENSEN, VIRGINIA E. Curious Missie. Harcourt, 1953. $3. (4–6) Fic.

_____ Plain Girl. Harcourt, 1955. $2.75. (4–6) Fic.

SOWERS, PHYLLIS A. Swords and Sails in the Philippines. Albert Whitman, 1944. $2. (5–6) 940.

SPENCER, CORNELIA. Japan. Holiday, 1948. $2.50. (5–6) 952.

_____ The Land of the Chinese People. Lippincott, 1960. $2.95. (6) 951.

_____ Made in China: The Story of China's Expression. Knopf, 1943. $4. (5–6) 951.

SPENCER, PAUL R., and others. The Skills Reading Program. Lyons & Carnahan, 1953. $3.60. 808.

Exploring New Trails. (5)
Finding New Trails. (4)
Traveling New Trails. (6)

SPERLING, WALTER. How To Make Things Out of Paper. Sterling, 1961. $2.50. (5–6) 745.

SPERRY, ARMSTRONG. All about the Arctic and Antarctic. Random, 1957. $1.95. (4–6) 998.

———— All about the Jungle. Random, 1959. $1.95. (5–6) 910.

———— Call It Courage. Macmillan, 1940. $2.75. (5–6) Fic.

———— Captain Cook Explores the South Seas. Random, 1955. $1.95. (5–6) 92.

———— The Rain Forest. Macmillan, 1947. $3.50. (6) Fic.

———— The Voyages of Christopher Columbus. Random, 1950. $1.95. (4–6) 92.

SPICER, DOROTHY G. 46 Days of Christmas: A Cycle of Old World Songs, Legends, and Customs. Coward-McCann, 1960. $3.50. (6) 394.

SPILHAUS, ATHELSTAN F. Weathercraft. Viking, 1958. $2. (6) 551.

SPORTS ILLUSTRATED MAGAZINE. Sports Illustrated Book of Baseball. Lippincott, 1960. $2.95. (6) 976.

SPYKMAN, E. C. Terrible, Horrible Edie. Harcourt, 1960. $3.25. (5–6) Fic.

SPYRI, JOHANNA H. Heidi. World, 1946. $2.50. (4–6) Fic.

STEELE, WILLIAM O. The Buffalo Knife. Harcourt, 1952. $2.50. (4–6) Fic.

———— Daniel Boone's Echo. Harcourt, 1957. $2.50. (4–6) Fic.

———— Davy Crockett's Earthquake. Harcourt, 1956. $2.25. (4–6) Fic.

———— Flaming Arrows. Harcourt, 1957. $2.75. (4–6) Fic.

———— The Spooky Thing. Harcourt, 1960. $2.75. (4–6) Fic.

———— Winter Danger. Harcourt, 1954. $2.50. (4–6) Fic.

STEFANSSON, EVELYN S. B. Here Is Alaska. Scribner, 1959. $3.95. (6) 979.

STEFFERUD, ALFRED. Wonders of Seeds. Harcourt, 1956. $2.75. (5–6) 581.

STEINER, STANLEY. The Last Horse. Macmillan, 1961. $3. (4–5) Fic.

STEINMANN, ELSA. Lia and the Red Carnations. Pantheon, 1960. $3. (6) Fic.

STERLING, DOROTHY. The Story of Caves. Doubleday, 1956. $3. (5–6) 551.

———— The Story of Mosses, Ferns, and Mushrooms. Doubleday, 1955. $2.75. (5–6) 586.

———— Trees and Their Story. Doubleday, 1953. $2.50. (5–6) 582.

STINETORF, LOUISE A. Children of North Africa. Lippincott, 1943. $2.95. (4–6) Fic.

———— Children of South Africa. Lippincott, 1945. $2.95. (4–6) Fic.

STOCKTON, FRANK R. Buccaneers and Pirates of Our Coasts. Macmillan, 1898. $2.75. (6) 910.

STODDARD, EDWARD. The First Book of Magic. Watts, 1953. $1.95. (5–6) 793.

STOLZ, MARY. Belling the Tiger. Harper, 1961. $2.50; lib. bdg. $2.57. (4–5) Fic.

———— A Dog on Barkham Street. Harper, 1960. $2.50; lib. ed. $2.44. (4–6) Fic.

STONG, PHIL. Honk, the Moose. Dodd, 1935. $3. (4–5) Fic.

STOUTENBERG, ADRIEN. Wild Animals of the Far West. Parnassus, 1958. $3.75. (4–6) 599.

STREATFEILD, NOEL. The First Book of England. Watts, 1958. $1.95. (4–6) 942.

_____ The First Book of the Ballet. Watts, 1953. $1.95. (4–6) 793.

_____ New Shoes. Random, 1960. $2.95. (5–6) Fic.

STREET, ALICIA. The Key to London. Lippincott, 1960. $2.95. (5–6) 942.

_____ The Land of the English People. Lippincott, 1946. $2.95. (6) 942.

STUART, JESSE. The Beatinest Boy. McGraw-Hill, 1953. $2.50. (4–6) Fic.

_____ A Penny's Worth of Character. McGraw-Hill, 1954. $2. (4–6) Fic.

_____ The Rightful Owner. McGraw-Hill, 1960. $2.50. (4–6) Fic.

SUCKSDORFF, ASTRID B. Chendru: The Boy and the Tiger. Harcourt, 1960. $3.25. (4–6) 954.

SWAIN, SU ZAN N. Insects in Their World. Garden City, 1955. $2.95. (5–6) 595.

SYME, RONALD. Balboa: Finder of the Pacific. Morrow, 1956. $2.75. (4–6) 92.

_____ Captain Cook: Pacific Explorer. Morrow, 1960. $2.75; lib. ed. $2.78. (4–6) 92.

_____ Cartier: Finder of the St. Lawrence. Morrow, 1958. $2.75. (4–6) 92.

_____ Columbus: Finder of the New World. Morrow, 1952. $2.75; lib. ed. $2.78. (4–6) 92.

_____ De Soto: Finder of the Mississippi. Morrow, 1957. lib. ed. $2.78. (4–5) 92.

_____ Magellan: First around the World. Morrow, 1953. $2.75. (4–6) 92.

TABER, GLADYS. The First Book of Dogs. Watts, 1949. $1.95. (4–5) 591.

TALLANT, ROBERT. Pirate Lafitte and the Battle of New Orleans. Random, 1951. $1.95. (5–6) 92.

TANNEHILL, IVAN R. All about the Weather. Random, 1953. $1.95. (4–6) 551.

TANNENBAUM, BEULAH, and STILLMAN, MYRA. Understanding Maps: Charting the Land, Sea, and Sky. McGraw-Hill, 1957. $3. (5–6) 526.

_____ Understanding Time: The Science of Clocks and Calendars. McGraw-Hill, 1958. $3. (6) 529.

TAPPAN, EVA M. Story of the Greek People. Houghton, 1908. $3.24. (5–6) 938.

_____ When Knights Were Bold. Houghton, 1911. $4. (6) 940.

TARRY, ELLEN, and ETS, MARIE H. My Dog Rinty. Viking, 1946. $2. (4–5) Fic.

TARSHIS, ELIZABETH K. The Village That Learned To Read. Houghton, 1941. $3. (4–6) Fic.

TAVO, GUS. The Buffalo Are Running. Knopf, 1960. $3. (6) Fic.

TAYLOR, ALICE. Iran. Holiday, 1955. $2.50. (6) 955.

TAYLOR, SYDNEY. All-of-a-Kind Family. Follett, 1951. $3.50. (4–6) Fic.

_____ All-of-a-Kind Family Uptown. Follett, 1958. $3.50. (4–6) Fic.

_____ More All-of-a-Kind Family. Follett, 1954. $3.50. (4–6) Fic.

TEALE, EDWIN W. Insect Friends. Dodd, 1955. $3.50. (5–6) 595.

_____ Junior Book of Insects. Dutton, 1953. $3.75. (6) 595.

TENNANT, KYLIE. All the Proud Tribesmen. St. Martin's, 1960. $2.95. (6) Fic.

THARP, LOUISE H. Louis Agassiz: Adventurous Scientist. Little, 1961. $3.75. (5–6) 92.

THURBER, JAMES. The Great Quillow. Harcourt, 1944. $3.25. (4–6) Fic.

_____ Many Moons. Harcourt, 1943. $3.50. (4–5) Fic.

THWAITE, ANN. The House in Turner Square. Harcourt, 1961. $2.95. (6) Fic.

TIBBETS, ALBERT B. The First Book of Bees. Watts, 1952. $1.95. (4–6) 595.

TITUS, EVE. Basil of Baker Street. McGraw-Hill, 1958. $2.75. (4–5) Fic.

TODD, RUTHVEN. Space Cat. Scribner, 1952. $2.50. (4–5) Fic.

———— Space Cat Meets Mars. Scribner, 1957. $2.50. (4–5) Fic.

———— Space Cat Visits Venus. Scribner, 1955. $2.50. (4–5) Fic.

———— Trucks, Tractors, and Trailers. Putnam, 1954. $2.75. (4–6) 629.

TOLBOOM, WANDA N. People of the Snow: Eskimos of Arctic Canada. Coward-McCann, 1956. $2.95. (4–6) 998.

TOR, REGINA. Getting To Know Canada. Coward-McCann, 1957. $2.50; lib. bdg. $2.52. (4–6) 971.

———— Getting To Know Germany. Coward-McCann, 1954. $2.50; lib. bdg. $2.52. (4–6) 943.

———— Getting To Know Korea. Coward-McCann, 1953. $2.50; lib. bdg. $2.52. (4–6) 951.

———— Getting To Know Puerto Rico. Coward-McCann, 1955. $2.50; lib. bdg. $2.52. (4–6) 972.

TOUSEY, SANFORD. Cowboy Tommy. Doubleday, 1932. $2. (4) Fic.

———— Jerry and the Pony Express. Doubleday, 1947. $2.50. (4) Fic.

TREASE, GEOFFREY. Sir Walter Raleigh: Captain & Adventurer. Vanguard, 1950. $3. (5–6) 92.

TREFFINGER, CAROLYN. Li Lun: Lad of Courage. Abingdon, 1947. $2.50. (4–6) Fic.

TRIPP, EDWARD. The New Tuba. Walck, 1955. $2.75. (4–5) Fic.

TUDOR, TASHA. Becky's Birthday. Viking, 1960. $3. (4–5) Fic.

TUNIS, EDWIN. Indians. World, 1959. $4.95. (6) 970.

TURNER, MINA. Town Meeting Means Me. Houghton, 1951. $3. (4–6) 342.

UCHIDA, YOSHIKO. Mik and the Prowler. Harcourt, 1960. $2.95. (4–6) Fic.

———— The Promised Year. Harcourt, 1959. $3. (4–6) Fic.

———— Takao and Grandfather's Sword. Harcourt, 1958. $2.50. (4–6) Fic.

UNDERHILL, RUTH M. Antelope Singer. Coward-McCann, 1961. $3.50. (4–6) Fic.

UNNERSTAD, EDITH. The Journey with Grandmother. Macmillan, 1960. $3. (4–6) Fic.

———— Little O. Macmillan, 1957. $2.50. (4–6) Fic.

———— The Spettecake Holiday. Macmillan, 1958. $3. (4–6) Fic.

URBAHNS, ESTELLE. Little Red Dragon. Dutton, 1947. $2.50. (4–6) Fic.

———— Tangled Web. Dutton, 1943. $2. (5–6) Fic.

URMSTON, MARY. The New Boy. Doubleday, 1950. $2.95. (4–6) Fic.

———— The Seven and Sam. Doubleday, 1955. $2.50. (4–6) Fic.

VANCE, MARGUERITE. The Lees of Arlington: The Story of Mary and Robert E. Lee. Dutton, 1949. $3.25. (5–6) 92.

———— A Star for Hansi. Dutton, 1957. $1.75. (4–5) Fic.

———— While Shepherds Watched. Dutton, 1946. $1.75. (4–6) 232.

_____ Windows for Rosemary. Dutton, 1956. $2.50. (4–6) Fic.

VAN DERSAL, WILLIAM R., and GRAHAM, EDWARD H. The Land Renewed: The Story of Soil Conservation. Walck, 1946. $3.75. (6) 631.

VANDIVERT, RITA. Young Russia: Children of the USSR at Work and Play. Dodd, 1960. $3. (4–6) 301.

VAN METRE, THURMAN W. and VAN METRE, RUSSEL G. Trains, Tracks and Travel. Simmons-Boardman, 1956. $4.95. (5–6) 385.

VAN RIPER, GUERNSEY. Knute Rockne: Young Athlete. Bobbs-Merrill, 1952. $2.25; text ed. $1.96. (4–6) 92.

_____ Lou Gehrig: Boy of the Sand Lots. Bobbs-Merrill, 1949. $2.25; text ed. $1.96. (4–5) 92.

VAN STOCKUM, HILDA. Canadian Summer. Viking, 1948. $2.75. (4–6) Fic.

_____ The Cottage at Bantry Bay. Viking, 1938. $3. (4–6) Fic.

_____ Friendly Gables. Viking, 1960. $2.75. (4–6) Fic.

_____ Pegeen. Viking, 1947. $2.75. (6) Fic.

VAYGOUNY, MARGARITE. Greenland Waters. Macmillan, 1954. $2.25. (4–6) 998.

VOIGHT, VIRGINIA F. Lions in the Barn. Holiday, 1955. $2.25. (4–6) Fic.

WAGNER, RUTH H., and GREEN, IVAH. Put Democracy to Work. Abelard-Schuman, 1961. $3.50. (6) 321.

WALL, GERTRUDE W. Gifts from the Forest. Scribner, 1958. $2.95. (4–6) 634.

_____ Gifts from the Grove. Scribner, 1955. $2.95. (4–6) 634.

WALTRIP, LELA, and WALTRIP, RUFUS. Quiet Boy. Longmans, 1961. $2.95. (4–6) Fic.

_____ White Harvest. Longmans, 1960. $2.95. (4–6) Fic.

WATSON, JANE W. Golden History of the World. Golden Pr., 1955. $5. (5–6) 900.

WEAVER, STELLA. A Poppy in the Corn. Pantheon, 1961. $3.50. (5–6) Fic.

WEBB, ADDISON. Birds in Their Homes. Garden City, 1947. $2.95. (4–6) 598.

WEBBER, IRMA E. S. Thanks to Trees: The Story of Their Use & Conservation. W. R. Scott, 1952. $2.50. (4–5) 582.

WEEKS, SARA. Tales of a Common Pigeon. Houghton, 1960. $2.75. (4–6) Fic.

WEIL, ANN. Animal Families. Childrens Pr., 1956. $2.50. (4) 636.

WEIR, ROSEMARY. Robert's Rescued Railway. Watts, 1960. $2.95. (5–6) Fic.

WEIR, RUTH CROMER. Benjamin Franklin: Printer and Patriot. Abingdon, 1955. $1.75. (4–6) 92.

_____ Leif Ericson: Explorer. Abingdon, 1951. $1.75. (4–6) 92.

WEISGARD, LEONARD. Treasures To See: A Museum Picture-Book. Harcourt, 1956. $3. (4–6) 708.

WEISS, EDNA S. Sally Saucer. Houghton, 1956. $2.50. (4–6) Fic.

WEISS, HARVEY. Paper, Ink and Roller: Print-Making for Beginners. W. R. Scott, 1958. $3.50. (4–6) 761.

_____ Pencil, Pen and Brush: Drawing for Beginners. W. R. Scott, 1961. $3.50. (5–6) 741.

WELLS, ROBERT. What Does an Astronaut Do? Dodd, 1961. $2.50. (6) 629.

WESTON, CHRISTINE. Bhimsa, the Dancing Bear. Scribner, 1945. $2.95. (4–6) Fic.

WHEELER, OPAL. Frederic Chopin: Son of Poland. Dutton, 1948. $3.50. (4–6) 92.

———— Handel at the Court of Kings. Dutton, 1943. $3.75. (4–6) 92.

———— Ludwig Beethoven and the Chiming Tower Bells. Dutton, 1942. $3.75. (4–6) 92.

———— Paganini: Master of Strings. Dutton, 1950. $3.50. (4–6) 92.

———— Robert Schumann and Mascot Ziff. Dutton, 1947. $3.50. (4–6) 92.

———— Stephen Foster and His Little Dog Tray. Dutton, 1955. $3.75. (4–6) 92.

———— and DEUCHER, SYBIL. Edward MacDowell and His Cabin in the Pines. Dutton, 1949. $3.50. (4–6) 92.

———— Franz Schubert and His Merry Friends. Dutton, 1939. $3.50. (4–6) 92.

———— Joseph Haydn: The Merry Little Peasant. Dutton, 1936. $3.75. (4–6) 92.

———— Mozart: The Wonder Boy. Dutton, 1941. $3.50. (4–6) 92.

———— Sebastian Bach: The Boy from Thuringia. Dutton, 1937. $3.50. (4–6) 92.

WHITE, ALICE M. G. and TOBITT, JANET E. Dramatized Ballads. Dutton, 1937. $2.95. (4–6) 793.

WHITE, ANNE H. Junket: The Dog Who Liked Everything "Just So." Viking, 1955. $2.75. (4–6) Fic.

———— The Story of Serapina. Viking, 1951. $2.75. (4–6) Fic.

WHITE, ANNE T. All about Our Changing Rocks. Random, 1955. $1.95. (5–6) 552.

———— Prehistoric America. Random, 1951. $1.95. (4–6) 560.

WHITE, BESSIE F. On Your Own Two Feet. Farrar, 1955. $2.75. (4–6) Fic.

WHITE, E. B. Charlotte's Web. Harper, 1952. $2.95; lib. bdg. $2.79. (4–6) Fic.

WHITNEY, PHYLLIS A. The Mystery of the Haunted Pool. Westminster, 1960. $2.95. (5–6) Fic.

WIBBERLEY, LEONARD. John Treegate's Musket. Farrar, 1959. $2.95. (6) Fic.

———— Peter Treegate's War. Farrar, 1960. $2.95. (6) Fic.

———— Sea Captain from Salem. Farrar, 1961. $2.95. (6) Fic.

WIESE, KURT. Chinese Ink Stick. Doubleday, 1929. $2.75. (4–6) Fic.

WILDE, OSCAR. The Selfish Giant. Kenedy, 1954. $2.50. (4–6) Fic.

WILDER, LAURA I. By the Shores of Silver Lake. Harper, 1953. $2.95; lib. bdg. $2.79. (5–6) Fic.

———— Farmer Boy. Harper, 1953. $2.95; lib. bdg. $2.79. (4–6) Fic.

———— Little House in the Big Woods. Harper, 1953. $2.95; lib. bdg. $2.79. (4–6) Fic.

———— Little House on the Prairie. Harper, 1953. $2.95; lib. bdg. $2.79. (4–6) Fic.

———— Little Town on the Prairie. Harper, 1953. $2.95; lib. bdg. $2.79. (6) Fic.

_____ The Long Winter. Harper, 1953. $2.95; lib. bdg. $2.79. (5–6) Fic.

_____ On the Banks of Plum Creek. Harper, 1953. $2.95; lib. bdg. $2.79. (4–6) Fic.

WILL and NICOLAS. The Two Reds. Harcourt, 1950. $3.50. (4–5) Fic.

WILLIAMS, HENRY L. Stories in Rocks. Holt, 1948. $3. (5–6) 550.

WILLIAMS, URSULA M. Island MacKenzie. Morrow, 1960. $2.95. (5–6) Fic.

WILLIAMSON, MARGARET. The First Book of Birds. Watts, 1951. $1.95. (4–6) 598.

_____ The First Book of Bugs. Watts, 1949. $1.95. (4–5) 595.

WILSON, HAZEL H. Jerry's Charge Account. Little, 1960. $3. (4–6) Fic.

_____ Owen Boys. Abingdon, 1958. $2.50. (5–6) Fic.

WILSON, LEON. This Boy Cody. Watts, 1950. $2.95. (4–6) Fic.

_____ This Boy Cody and His Friends. Watts, 1952. $2.95. (4–6) Fic.

WINTERFELD, HENRY. Castaways in Lilliput. Harcourt, 1960. $3. (5–6) Fic.

WITHERS, CARL, comp. Counting Out. Walck, 1946. $1.75. (4–5) 821.

WITTY, PAUL A., and KOHLER, JULILLY. You and the Constitution of the United States. Childrens Pr., 1948. $2. (5–6) 342.

WOOD, ESTHER. Pedro's Coconut Skates. Longmans, 1938. $2.75. (4–5) Fic.

_____ Silk and Satin Lane. Longmans, 1939. $3. (4–6) Fic.

WOOD, WILLIAM H. The Perils of Pacifico. Watts, 1960. $2.95. (4–6) Fic.

WOOLLEY, CATHERINE. Ellie's Problem Dog. Morrow, 1955. $2.75. (4–6) Fic.

_____ Ginnie and Geneva. Morrow, 1948. $2.75. (4–5) Fic.

_____ Schoolroom Zoo. Morrow, 1950. $2.75. (4–5) Fic.

WRISTON, HILDRETH T. Susan's Secret. Farrar, 1957. $2.75. (4–5) Fic.

WRITERS PROJECT, PENNSYLVANIA. Elementary Science Series. Albert Whitman. 75¢ ea. (5–6)

1. Ladder of Clouds. 1939. 551.
6. Trip on Many Waters. 1940. 551.
9. Warships. 1940. 387.
10. Trains Going By. 1940. 385.
11. Money. 1940. 332.
12. Light of the World. 1940. 520.
14. Gold. 1940. 553.
15. Salmon. 1940. 639.
19. Story of Glass. 1941. 666.
20. Oysters. 1941. 639.
21. Wind, Water, and Air. 1941. 551.
23. Lords of the Old West. 1942. 591.
24. Story of Clay. 1942. 600.
25. Motion Pictures. 1942. 770.
28. Pigeons. 1942. 598.
29. Orchards in All Seasons. 1942. 634.
31. Aluminum. 1943. 669.

33. Cement. 1943. 666.
34. Story of Iron and Steel. 1944. 669.
35. Story of Coal. 1944. 622.
36. Oil and Gas. 1944. 665.
37. Grapes. 1945. 634.
38. Plastics. 1945. 668.
39. Rayon, Nylon, and Glass Fibers. 1945. 677.

WYCKOFF, JEROME. The Story of Geology: Our Changing Earth through the Ages. Golden Pr., 1960. $4.95. (5–6) 550.

WYLER, ROSE. The First Book of Weather. Watts, 1956. $1.95. (4–6) 551.

WYNDHAM, LEE. Susie and the Ballet Family. Dodd, 1955. $2.50. (4–6) Fic.

———— Susie and the Dancing Cat. Dodd, 1954. $2.50. (4–6) Fic.

WYSS, JOHANN D. The Swiss Family Robinson. World, 1947. $2.50. (5–6) Fic.

YASHIMA, MITSU, and YASHIMA, TARO. Plenty To Watch. Viking, 1954. $2.75. (4–5) 952.

YASHIMA, TARO. Crow Boy. Viking, 1955. $3. (4–5) Fic.

———— and MUKU, HATOJU. The Golden Footprints. World, 1960. $2.95. (4–6) Fic.

YATES, ELIZABETH. Mountain Born. Coward-McCann, 1943. $3.50. (5–6) Fic.

———— Once in the Year: A Christmas Story. Coward-McCann, 1947. $2.50. (4–6) Fic.

YATES, RAYMOND F. A Boy and a Battery. Harper, 1959. $2.50. (6) 537.

———— A Boy and a Motor. Harper, 1940. $2.50. (6) 537.

———— Boys' Book of Communications. Harper, 1942. $2.50. (6) 621.

———— Fun with Your Microscope. Appleton, 1943. $2.75. (6) 578.

YOUNG, ELLA. The Unicorn with Silver Shoes. Longmans, 1958. $3.50. (4–6) Fic.

ZAFFO, GEORGE J. The Big Book of Real Airplanes. Grosset, 1951. $1. (5–6) 629.

———— The Big Book of Real Boats and Ships. Grosset, 1951. $1. (4–6) 387.

ZARCHY, HARRY. Let's Make a Lot of Things: Crafts for Home, School, and Camp. Knopf, 1948. $3.25. (5–6) 745.

———— Let's Make More Things. Knopf, 1943. $3.25. (5–6) 680.

———— Let's Make Something. Knopf, 1941. $3.25. (5–6) 680.

ZAREM, LEWIS. New Dimensions of Flight. Dutton, 1959. $4.50. (6) 629.

ZIM, HERBERT S. Alligators and Crocodiles. Morrow, 1952. lib. ed. $2.78. (4–6) 598.

———— The Big Cats. Morrow, 1955. $2.75. (4–6) 599.

———— Dinosaurs. Morrow, 1954. $2.75; lib. ed. $2.78. (4–6) 568.

———— Frogs and Toads. Morrow, 1950. $2.75. (4–6) 597.

———— Great Whales. Morrow, 1951. $2.75; lib. ed. $2.78. (4–6) 599.

———— Homing Pigeons. Morrow, 1949. $2.75; lib. ed. $2.78. (5–6) 636.

———— How Things Grow. Morrow, 1960. $2.75. (4–6) 574.

———— Lightning and Thunder. Morrow, 1952. $2.75. (4–6) 551.

_____ Monkeys. Morrow, 1955. $2.75. (4–6) 599.

_____ Ostriches. Morrow, 1958. $2.75. (4–6) 598.

_____ Our Senses and How They Work. Morrow, 1956. $2.75. (4–6) 152.

_____ Owls. Morrow, 1950. $2.75. (4–6) 598.

_____ Parrakeets. Morrow, 1953. $2.75. (4–6) 636.

_____ Rabbits. Morrow, 1948. lib. ed. $2.78. (4–6) 636.

_____ Snakes. Morrow, 1949. $2.75; lib. ed. $2.78. (4–6) 598.

ZWILGMEYER, DIKKEN. Johnny Blossom. Pilgrim, 1948. $1. (4–6) Fic.

SUBJECT INDEX TO BOOKS
FOR INTERMEDIATE GRADES

ABALONE
Cooper, E. K., Science on the Shores
and Banks, p.69–70   5–6
Dudley, Sea Shells, p.59–69   4–6

ABBEY, EDWIN AUSTIN
Chandler, Story-Lives of Master Artists,
p.238–49   6

ABBEYS: *see* Cathedrals; Monasteries

ABORIGINES: *see* Primitive Man

ABYSSINIA: *see* Ethiopia

ACADIA NATIONAL PARK
Melbo, Our Country's National Parks,
v.1, p.109–21   6

ACCELERATION
Barr, Young Scientist Takes a Ride,
p.99–100   5–6

ACCIDENTS: *see* First Aid; Lifesaving;
Shipwrecks

ACCIDENTS—PREVENTION: *see*
Safety

ACHILLES: *see* Trojan War

ACTING
Enright, Four-Story Mistake, p.90–108,
118–23   *5–6
Estes, Middle Moffat, p.180–206   *4–6

ADAMS, JOHN
Beard, Presidents in American History,
p.13–14, 153–54   6
Coy, First Book of Presidents, p.26
4–6
Foster, G., George Washington's World,
p.12–14, 265–67   6
Olcott, Good Stories for Great Birthdays, p.73–92   4–6
Petersham, Story of the Presidents of
the United States, p.11–13   4–6

ADAMS, JOHN QUINCY
Beard, Presidents in American History,
p.29–30, 156–57   6
Coy, First Book of Presidents, p.31
4–6
Petersham, Story of the Presidents of
the United States, p.21–23   4–6

ADAPTABILITY
Bialk, Taffy's Foal.   *4–5
Bulla, Riding the Pony Express   *4–5
Clewes, Runaway   *4–5
Coatsworth, Away Goes Sally   *4–6
Daringer, Adopted Jane   *4–6
Field, Hitty   *5–6
Friedman, F., Carol from the Country
*4–6
Lawrence, Sand in Her Shoes   *4–6
Lenski, Boom Town Boy   *4–6
Urmston, New Boy   *4–6

ADDAMS, JANE
Judson, City Neighbor   6
McNeer, Armed with Courage, p.57–68
5–6

ADOBE BRICKS
Bleeker, Inca, p.47–48, 57   5–6
Burns, World Full of Homes, p.60–68
4–6

ADOLESCENCE: *see also* Age-Mate Relations
Barnes, Wonderful Year   *4–6

ADOPTED CHILDREN
Haywood, Penny and Peter   *4

ADVENTURE
Ardizzone, Tim to the Rescue   *4–5
Armstrong, Ship Afire!   *6
Beals, Davy Crockett   5–6
_____ Kit Carson   5–6
Brink, Caddie Woodlawn   *6

*The asterisk before the grade levels in the right-hand column represents fictionalized material.

Bulla, Riding the Pony Express   *4–5
Coatsworth, Away Goes Sally   *4–6
Daugherty, Daniel Boone   5–6
———— Poor Richard   6
Du Soe, Three without Fear   *4–6
Enright, Saturdays   *4–6
Field, Hitty   *5–6
Harry, Island Boy   *4–6
Mayne, Blue Boat   *4–6
Renick, M. L., Seven Simpsons on Six
   Bikes   *4–5
Rushmore, Shadow of Robbers Roost
     *6
Seredy, Good Master   *5–6
Sperry, Call It Courage   *5–6
Steele, Flaming Arrows   *4–6

ADVERTISING
Lent, "I Work on a Newspaper," p.125–
37   6

AENEAS: *see also* Trojan War
Farjeon, Mighty Men, p.15–20   4–6
Hazeltine, Hero Tales from Many
   Lands, p.38–50   5–6

AERODYNAMICS: *see* Flight

AERONAUTICS: *see* Aviation

AFGHANISTAN
Quinn, Picture Map Geography of Asia,
   p.49–52   4–6

AFRICA: *see also* Animals—Africa; Bush-
   men; Congo; Nigeria; Nile River;
   Pygmies; Sahara Desert; Somaliland;
   Union of South Africa; Zulus; also
   names of countries, as Egypt; Liberia
Barrows, Old World Lands, p.279–326
     6
Caldwell, Let's Visit West Africa   5–6
Davis, N., Picken's Treasure Hunt
     *4–5
Disney, Worlds of Nature, p.160–75
     4–6
Epstein, S., All about the Desert, p.79–
94   5–6
Gatti, Here Is the Veld   6
———— Saranga, the Pygmy   *5–6
Hughes, First Book of Africa   5–6
Joy, Desert Caravans   5–6
McNeer, Armed with Courage, p.101–
12   5–6
Mirsky, Seven Grandmothers   *4–6

———— Thirty-one Brothers and Sis-
ters   *4–6
Shackelford, Child's Story of the Negro,
   p.1–75   4–5
Sperry, All about the Jungle, p.81–113
     5–6
Stinetorf, Children of North Africa
     *5–6
———— Children of South Africa
     *5–6

AFRICA—EXPLORATION: *see* names
   of explorers, as Livingstone, David

AFRICA—FOLK TALES
Shackelford, Child's Story of the Negro,
   p.48–62, 68–82   4–5

AFRICA—GAMES: *see* Games—Africa

AGAMEMNON, KING OF MYCENAE:
   see Mycenae; Trojan War

AGASSIZ, LOUIS
Forsee, Louis Agassiz   6
Lauber, All about the Ice Age, p.8–20
     4–6
Tharp, Louis Agassiz   5–6
White, A. T., Prehistoric America, p.10–
16, 31–32   4–6

AGE-MATE RELATIONS
Angelo, Bells of Bleeker Street   *4–6
Barnes, Wonderful Year   *4–6
Bragdon, E., Fairing Weather   *4–5
Burnett, F. H., Secret Garden   *5–6
Cleary, Henry and the Paper Route
     *4–5
———— Otis Spofford   *4–6
Clewes, Secret   *4–5
De Leeuw, A. L., Donny   *4–5
Enright, Then There Were Five   *5–6
Estes, Moffats   *4–6
———— Rufus M.   *4–6
Friedman, F., Carol from the Country
     *4–6
———— Dot for Short   *4–5
———— Sundae with Judy   *4–6
Frost, Windy Foot at the County Fair
     *4–6
Gates, Sensible Kate   *4–6
Godden, Miss Happiness and Miss
   Flower   *4–5
Hayes, Skid   *5–6
Haywood, Betsy's Winterhouse   *4–5
———— Eddie and His Big Deals *4–5

———— Eddie's Pay Dirt   *4–5
———— Penny and Peter   *4
Holberg, Rowena Carey   *4–6
Jackson, J., Call Me Charley   *5–6
Kastner, Emil and the Detectives *4–6
McMeekin, Kentucky Derby Winner
                               *4–6
Marshall, Dig for a Treasure   *4–6
———— Invisible Island   *4–6
Renick, M. L., John's Back Yard Camp
                               *4–5
Stolz, Dog on Barkham Street   *5–6
Weaver, Poppy in the Corn   *6

AGRICULTURAL MACHINERY: *see also* McCormick, Cyrus Hall; Threshing
Buehr, Story of the Wheel, p.20–23
                               4–6
Darrow, Boys' Own Book of Great Inventions, p.408–17   6
Eberle, Basketful, p.20–24   4–6
Hartman, Machines, p.193–206   6
Lent, Men at Work in the Great Lakes States, p.78–83, 100–105   4–6
Maginley, Historic Models of Early America, p.103–22   6

AGRICULTURAL PESTS: *see* Fungi; Insects—Injurious; Weeds

AGRICULTURE: *see also* Agricultural Machinery; Animals—Domestic; Cattle; Dairying; Farm Life; Fertilizers; Gardening; Harvesting; Insects—Injurious; Irrigation; Plant Breeding; Plants; Soils; Threshing; also names of agricultural products, as Grain; Tobacco
Barrows, American Continents, p.135–45   5
———— Our Big World   4
Freeman, I. M., All about the Wonders of Chemistry, p.92–101   6

AGRICULTURE—ARGENTINA
Smith, J. R., Neighbors around the World, p.124–26   4

AGRICULTURE—AUSTRIA
Gidal, My Village in Austria   5–6

AGRICULTURE—BRAZIL
May, Let's Read about Brazil, p.51–58
                               4–6

AGRICULTURE—CANADA
Ross, F. A., Land and People of Canada, p.8–11, 39–40, 113–15   6

AGRICULTURE—CHINA
Smith, J. R., Neighbors around the World, p.99–106, 164–68   4

AGRICULTURE—EGYPT—ANCIENT
Hartman, Builders of the Old World, p.46–50   6

AGRICULTURE—ENGLAND
Street, Land of the English People, p.52–59   6

AGRICULTURE—FORMOSA
Caldwell, Let's Visit Formosa, p.22–28
                               5–6

AGRICULTURE—ICELAND
Golden, Made in Iceland, p.60–70   6

AGRICULTURE—INCA
Bleeker, Inca, p.83–98   5–6

AGRICULTURE—INDIA
Caldwell, Let's Visit India, p.85–86
                               4–6
Hahn, First Book of India, p.46–51
                               5–6

AGRICULTURE—INDONESIA
Smith, D. C., Land and People of Indonesia, p.10–13, 45–46, 92–95 6

AGRICULTURE—IRELAND
Gidal, My Village in Ireland   4–6

AGRICULTURE—ISRAEL
Gidal, My Village in Israel   4–6

AGRICULTURE—ITALY
Epstein, S., First Book of Italy, p.6–9
                               5–6

AGRICULTURE—JAPAN
Edelman, Japan in Story and Pictures, p.25–35   4–6

AGRICULTURE—KOREA
Caldwell, Let's Visit Korea, p.52–59
                               5–6

AGRICULTURE—MAYA
Bleeker, Maya, p.36–44   5–6

AGRICULTURE—NETHERLANDS
Lauber, Battle against the Sea, p.14–16, 21–27, 80–85   5–6

AGRICULTURE—NORWAY
Rothery, Scandinavian Roundabout, p.32–41   6

AGRICULTURE—SPAIN
Buckley, Luis of Spain   4–6
———— Spanish Plateau, p.66–68   6

AGRICULTURE—SWITZERLAND
Smith, J. R., Neighbors around the World, p.111–23   4

AGRICULTURE—UNITED STATES
Banta, Life in America: The South, p.45–55   5–6
Elting, We Are the Government, p.54–59   6
Havighurst, Life in America: The Midwest, p.63–76   5–6
Smith, J. R., Neighbors around the World, p.90–98   4
Tor, Getting To Know Puerto Rico, p.32–39   4–6
Writers Project, Wind, Water, and Air, no.21   5–6

AIR: *see also* Aviation; Barometers; Nitrogen; Ventilation
Beauchamp, Discovering Our World, Bk.1, p.48–55   4
Beeler, Experiments in Science, p.22–24   5–6
Branley, Exploring by Satellite, p.24–30   6
Coombs, Rockets, Missiles, and Moons, p.80–95   6
Dietz, All about Satellites and Space Ships, p.6–13   5–6
Fisher, J., Wonderful World of the Air   5–6
Gallant, R. A., Exploring the Weather, p.13–23   5–6
Gottlieb, Jets and Rockets, p.6–12, 28–32   4–6
Huey, What Makes the Wheels Go Round, p.25–35   6
Larrick, See for Yourself, p.7–37   4–5
Life, World We Live In, p.55–71   5–6
Podendorf, 101 Science Experiments, p.16–27   4–5
Reed, And That's Why, p.39–47, 56–65   4–5
———— Earth for Sam, p.9–12   6
Schneider, H., Everyday Weather and

How It Works   5–6
Writers Project, Wind, Water, and Air, no.21   5–6

AIR BRAKES
Henry, R. S., Trains, p.57–60   5–6
Holbrook, Golden Age of Railroads, p.95–97, 99–100   5–6
Van Metre, Trains, Tracks and Travel, p.141–47, 293–95   6

AIR CIRCULATION
Schneider, H., Let's Look inside Your House, p.16–20   4–5

AIR CONDITIONING: *see also* Ventilation
Barnard, Macmillan Science-Life Series, Bk.6, p.17–42   6

AIR FREIGHT
Spencer, P. R., Traveling New Trails, p.433–40   6

AIR LIFT
Floherty, Aviation from the Ground Up, p.85–91   6

AIR MAIL SERVICE
Petersham, America's Stamps, p.129–41   5–6
Rogers, F., Heels, Wheels, and Wire, p.208–18   5–6
Schloat, Adventures of a Letter   4–6

AIR PILOTS: *see* Aviators

AIR PRESSURE: *see also* Barometers; Winds
Beeler, Experiments in Science, p.28–29, 53–55, 101–3   5–6
Comstock, Handbook of Nature Study, p.785–88   6
Schneider, H., Everyday Machines and How They Work, p.29, 32–33   5–6

AIR TRAVEL: *see* Aviation

AIRCRAFT CARRIERS
Bechdolt, Going Up, p.73–74   5–6
Block, Real Book about Ships, p.151–55   5–6
Hogeboom, Boats and How To Draw Them, p.36–39   4–5

AIRPLANES: *see also* Airports; Airships; Aviation; Balloons; Gliders—Aviation; also names of persons, as Wright, Orville, and Wright, Wilbur

Baker, A. O., Your Science World, p.193–205 6

Bendick, First Book of Airplanes 4–6

Bishop, R. W., From Kite to Kitty Hawk 6

Crouse, W. H., Understanding Science, p.152–55 6

Dalgliesh, America Travels, p.121–23 4–6

———— Ride on the Wind 4–5

Darrow, Boys' Own Book of Great Inventions, p.273–300 6

Fisher, J., Wonderful World of the Air, p.44–63 5–6

Haines, Wright Brothers 4–5

Lent, "Fly It Away!" 4–6

———— Men at Work in New England, p.30–33 4–6

Leonard, Exploring Science, p.219–27 6

Morgan, A. P., Boys' Book of Engines, Motors & Turbines, p.129–39 6

Neurath, Rockets and Jets, p.20–27 4–6

Reynolds, Q. J., Wright Brothers 4–6

Zaffo, Big Book of Real Airplanes 4–5

Zarem, New Dimensions of Flight 6

AIRPLANES—IDENTIFICATION

Gilmore, Model Planes for Beginners p.15–19 5–6

AIRPLANES—MILITARY: *see* Aviation —Military

AIRPLANES—MODELS

Gilmore, Model Planes for Beginners 5–6

Maginley, Historic Models of Early America, p.95–102 6

AIRPORTS

Bendick, First Book of Airplanes, p.20–23 4–6

Fisher, J., Wonderful World of the Air, p.60–61 5–6

Jackson, D., Wonderful World of Engineering, p.44–45 6

Schneider, L., Wings in Your Future, p.74–111 5–6

Zaffo, Big Book of Real Airplanes 4–5

AIRSHIPS: *see also* Airplanes; Aviation; Balloons

Darrow, Boys' Own Book of Great Inventions, p.259–73 6

ALABAMA

Banta, Life in America: The South, p.120–25 5–6

Lenski, Judy's Journey, p.1–14 *4–6

Quinn, Picture Map Geography of the United States, p.68–71 4–6

Sorensen, Curious Missie *4–6

ALAMO—SIEGE OF THE: *see also* Crockett, David

Johnson, W. W., Birth of Texas 5–6

Lawson, R., Watchwords of Liberty, p.45–46 4–6

ALASKA: *see also* Aleutian Islands; Eskimos; Mount McKinley National Park

Association for Childhood Education, Told under Spacious Skies, p.313–23 *4–6

Barrows, American Continents, p.228–36 5

———— Our Big World, p.160–64 4

Brindze, Story of the Totem Pole 4–6

Butler, Alaska 6

Darling, E. B., Baldy of Nome *6

Krasilovsky, Benny's Flag 4

Lindquist, W., Alaska, the Forty-ninth State 5–6

Lipkind, Boy with a Harpoon *4–6

Litchfield, Hello Alaska 4–6

McCracken, Biggest Bear on Earth *5–6

———— Sentinal of the Snow Peaks *5–6

Machetanz, Puppy Named Gih *4–5

McNeer, Alaska Gold Rush 5–6

O'Neill, Picture Story of Alaska 4–6

Quinn, Picture Map Geography of Canada and Alaska, p.100–14 4–6

———— Picture Map Geography of the United States, p.192–95 4–6

Stefansson, Here Is Alaska 6

ALASKA—FOLK TALES

Gillham, Beyond the Clapping Mountains 4–6

ALASKA—GAMES: *see* Games—Alaska

ALASKA—HISTORY: *see also* Klondike Gold Rush

Litchfield, Hello Alaska 4–6

ALASKA HIGHWAY

Boardman, Roads, p.111–13 6

Bothwell, First Book of Roads, p.63
5–6

Lindquist, W., Alaska, the Forty-ninth
State, p.51–54   5–6

Smith, J. R., Neighbors around the
World, p.80–83   4

ALBANIANS IN THE UNITED
STATES
Association for Childhood Education,
Told under the Stars and Stripes,
p.249–56   4–6

ALBATROSSES
Hyde, Animal Clocks and Compasses,
p.40–42   5–6

ALBERTA
Quinn, Picture Map Geography of Canada and Alaska, p.66–75   4–6

ALCHEMY: see Chemistry

ALCOHOL
Barnard, Macmillan Science-Life Series,
Bk.6, p.311–16   6
Beeler, Experiments in Chemistry, p.34–
41   5–6

ALCOTT, LOUISA MAY
Coffman, Famous Authors for Young
People, p.101–6   5–6

ALDEN, JOHN
Foster, G., World of Captain John
Smith, p.303–8   6

ALDRIDGE, IRA
Shackelford, Child's Story of the Negro,
p.115–18   4–5

ALEUTIAN ISLANDS
Stefansson, Here Is Alaska, p.123–35
6

ALEXANDER THE GREAT
Duvoisin, They Put Out to Sea, p.28–42
4–6
Falls, First 3000 Years, p.164–76   6
Farjeon, Mighty Men, p.52–66   4–6
Hillyer, Child's History of the World,
p.162–67   5–6

ALFRED THE GREAT
Farjeon, Mighty Men, p.170–78   4–6
Hartman, Builders of the Old World,
p.224–26   6

ALGAE
Barr, More Research Ideas for Young
Scientists, p.108–9   5–6

Branley, Solar Energy, p.63–71   6
Cooper, E. K., Science on the Shores
and Banks, p.46–47, 153–62   5–6
Disraeli, New Worlds through the Mi-
croscope, p.91–101   6
Hyde, Plants Today and Tomorrow,
p.118–28   6
Kavaler, Wonders of Algae   6
Lewis, L. Z., First Book of Microbes,
p.32–33   5–6
Morgan, A. H., Field Book of Ponds
and Streams, p.46–55   6

ALGERIA
Joy, Young People of the Western
Mediterranean, p.73–89   6
Stinetorf, Children of North Africa,
p.95–110, 129–43   *5–6

ALKALOIDS
Hyde, Plants Today and Tomorrow,
p.63–66   6

ALL SAINTS' DAY
Wood, E., Pedro's Coconut Skates,
p.129–58   *4–5

ALLEN, ETHAN
McGuire, Brave Young Land, p.340–42
5–6
Meigs, Covered Bridge, p.36–44, 63–89,
108–17   *4–6

ALLIGATORS: see also Crocodiles; Rep-
tiles
Cooper, E. K., Science on the Shores
and Banks, p.131–32   5–6
Disney, Worlds of Nature, p.151–53
4–6
Hylander, Animals in Armor, p.19–27
6
Lenski, We Live in the South, p.104–28
*4–5
Mason, G. F., Animal Sounds, p.84–87
5–6
Morgan, A. P., Aquarium Book, p.195–
97   5–6
Parker, B. M., Reptiles, p.6–9   4–6
Zim, Alligators and Crocodiles   4

ALLOYS
Darrow, Boys' Own Book of Great
Inventions, p.393–95   6
Writers Project, Aluminum, no.31
5–6

ALPHABETS: *see also* Hieroglyphics; Writing

Brown, M. J., Peter Piper's Alphabet
4–5

Epstein, S., First Book of Words, p.27–28　　　　5–6

Hillyer, Child's History of the World, p.74–78　　　　5–6

Hogben, Wonderful World of Communication, p.12, 16–19　　　6

Kipling, Just So Stories, p.145–67
*4–6

Parker, F., Russian Alphabet Book　6

ALPS

Bishop, C. H., All Alone　　*4–6

Bragdon, L. J., Land and People of Switzerland, p.12, 25–26　　6

Spyri, Heidi　　　*4–6

ALPS—FOLK TALES

Sawyer, Long Christmas, p.123–33
4–6

ALSACE-LORRAINE

Bragdon, L. J., Land and People of France, p.99–103　　　6

ALSACE-LORRAINE—FOLK TALES

Harper, Ghosts and Goblins, p.241–57
4–6

ALUMINUM

Fenton, C. L., Riches from the Earth, p.16–21　　　　5–6

Freeman, I. M., All about the Wonders of Chemistry, p.59–63　　6

Loomis, Field Book of Common Rocks and Minerals, p.73–78　　6

Writers Project, Aluminum, no.31
5–6

AMAZON RIVER

Forsee, Louis Agassiz, p.192–208　6

May, Let's Read about Brazil, p.37–43
4–6

AMAZON VALLEY

Rothery, South American Roundabout, p.191–201　　　　5–6

AMERICA: *see* Canada; Central America; Mexico; South America; United States

AMERICA—DISCOVERY AND EXPLORATION: *see* Discovery Period in America

AMERICAN ART: *see* Art—United States

AMERICAN BALLADS AND SONGS: *see also* Cowboys—Songs; National Songs; Negroes—Songs; Songs—Pioneer Life

Browne, Story of Our National Ballads
5–6

Justus, Sammy　　　*4–5

Lenski, Bayou Suzette　　*5–6

———— Blue Ridge Billy　*5–6

McMeekin, Journey Cake　　*5–6

Simon, Robin on the Mountain, p.81–82
*4–6

AMERICAN BUFFALOES: *see* Bison

AMERICAN COLONIES: *see* Colonial Period in America; United States—History

AMERICAN FLAG: *see* Flags

AMERICAN FOLK TALES: *see* United States—Folk Tales

AMERICAN HISTORY: *see* Civil War in the United States; Colonial Period in America; Discovery Period in America; Spanish-American War, 1898; War of 1812; also names of countries, subhead History, as Mexico—History

AMERICAN INDIAN: *see* Indians of North America; Indians of South America

AMERICAN LIFE: *see* Home Life—United States; also names of national and racial groups in the United States, as Germans in the United States

AMERICAN MUSEUM OF NATURAL HISTORY, NEW YORK

Urmston, New Boy, p.75–106　*4–6

AMERICAN MUSIC: *see* Music—United States

AMERICAN REVOLUTION: *see* Revolutionary War in America

AMERICANIZATION: *see* Brotherhood of Man; Citizenship; Immigration and Emigration

AMISH IN THE UNITED STATES: *see* Mennonites in the United States

AMPHIBIANS: *see also* names of amphibians, as Frogs; Toads

Beauchamp, Discovering Our World, Bk.1, p.31–32   4

Bevans, Book of Reptiles and Amphibians   4–6

Brown, V., How To Make a Home Nature Museum, p.45–48, 85–88, 120–25   5–6

———— How To Make a Miniature Zoo, p.101, 121–40   5–6

Buck, M. W., Small Pets from Woods and Fields, p.20–29   4–6

Cooper, E. K., Science on the Shores and Banks, p.119–30   5–6

Hausman, Beginner's Guide to Fresh-Water Life, p.28–45   6

Lavine, Strange Travelers, p.35–37   5–6

Morgan, A. H., Field Book of Ponds and Streams, p.347–88   6

Parker, B. M., Living Things, p.22–24   4–6

Selsam, Underwater Zoos, p.70–74   4–6

AMUNDSEN, ROALD
Cottler, Heroes of Civilization, p.76–85   6

Frank, Ice Island, p.64–83   6
Rothery, Scandinavian Roundabout, p.77–79   6

AMUSEMENT PARKS
Hader, Spunky, p.82–90   *4–6

AMUSEMENTS: *see also* Boy Scouts; Camping; Circus; Dancing; Dolls; Experiments—Scientific; Fairs; Festivals; Fireworks; Fishing; Games; Handicraft; Holidays; Hunting; Kites; Magic; Motion Pictures; Paper Work; Parties; Picnics; Plays; Puppet Shows; Puzzles; Racing; Radio; Riddles; Shadow Plays; Skating; Sports; Toys; Tricks
Bechdolt, Going Up, p.110–13   5–6

AMUSEMENTS—CHINA
Hahn, Picture Story of China   4–6
Wiese, Chinese Ink Stick, p.149–57   *4–6

AMUSEMENTS—COLONIAL PERIOD IN AMERICA
Coatsworth, Golden Horseshoe, p.39–63   6

AMUSEMENTS—MIDDLE AGES
Tappan, When Knights Were Bold, p.2–3, 93–101, 227–31   6

AMUSEMENTS—PIONEER LIFE
McMeekin, Journey Cake, p.156–62   *5–6

AMUSEMENTS FOR INVALIDS
Forbush, Book of Games, p.267–73   4–6

Mulac, Game Book, p.321–28, 347–57   6

ANATOMY: *see* Physiology

ANCIENT PEOPLES: *see* Alphabets; Civilization; also names of countries, as Assyria; Egypt—Ancient

ANDERSEN, HANS CHRISTIAN
Coffman, Famous Authors for Young People, p.55–61   5–6
Owen, Denmark Caravan, p.26–27; 137–44   5–6

ANDERSON, ELIZABETH GARRETT
Manton, Elizabeth Garrett, M.D.   6

ANDES MOUNTAINS
Bleeker, Inca   5–6
Cavanna, Lucho of Peru   4–6

ANDREA DEL SARTO
Hillyer, Child's History of Art, p.69–70   5–6

ANECDOTES
Meadowcroft, Abraham Lincoln   6
Rombauer, Cookbook for Boys and Girls   6

ANGELICO, FRA
Hillyer, Child's History of Art, p.33–36   5–6

ANGELO, MICHAEL: *see* Michelangelo

ANGLO-EGYPTIAN SUDAN
Stinetorf, Children of North Africa, p.144–57   *5–6

ANGOLA
Stinetorf, Children of South Africa, p.133–45   *5–6

ANIMAL PICTURES: *see* Animals—Pictures

ANIMAL POWER: *see* Force and Energy

ANIMAL SOUNDS
  Brown, V., How To Understand Animal
    Talk   6
  Chrisman, Shen of the Sea   *5–6
  Irving, Sound and Ultrasonics, p.88–97
                                            6
  Mason, G. F., Animal Sounds   5–6
  Parker, B. M., Sound, p.26–27   5–6

ANIMAL TRACKS
  Averill, Daniel Boone, p.40–41   4–6
  Brown, V., How To Make a Home Na-
    ture Museum, p.105–7   5–6
  Hylander, Out of Doors in Winter,
    p.117–23   5–6
  Jaeger, Easy Crafts, p.22–23   4–6
  Mason, G. F., Animal Tracks   4–6

ANIMALS: *see also* Animal Tracks; Bac-
    teria; Birds; Community Life among
    the Animals and Insects; Fishes; Fos-
    sils; Hibernation; Hunting; Insects;
    Interdependence of Plants and Ani-
    mals; Kindness to Animals; Mam-
    mals; Marine Animals; Nature Study;
    Pets; Reptiles; Worms; Zoology
  Barr, Young Scientist Takes a Ride,
    p.123–34   5–6
  Batchelor, Superstitious? Here's Why!,
    p.34–43   6
  Bianco, All about Pets   5–6
  Blough, After the Sun Goes Down   4–5
  ———— When You Go to the Zoo
                                        4–6
  Bridges, Zoo Babies   4–6
  ———— Zoo Pets   4–6
  Buck, M. W., In Ponds and Streams,
    p.66–69   4–6
  ———— In Woods and Fields   4–5
  Cassell, Nature Games and Activities,
    p.36–42   4–6
  De la Mare, Animal Stories   *4–6
  De Leeuw, A., Donny   *4–5
  Fox, From Bones to Bodies   6
  Franklin, Tricky   *4–6
  Gaul, Pond Book   4–6
  George, J., Hole in the Tree   4–5
  Goetz, Tropical Rain Forest, p.16–35
                                        4–6
  Graham, E. H., Wildlife for America
                                        6
  Hamilton, E., First Book of Caves,
    p.26–35   5–6

  Harrison, Outdoor Adventures   4–5
  Hogner, Cat Family   4–5
  Huntington, Let's Go to the Desert,
    p.40–89   4–5
  Jauss, Discovering Nature the Year
    Round   4–6
  Kipling, Jungle Book   *5–6
  Lang, Strawberry Roan   *5–6
  Lathrop, Angel in the Woods   *4–5
  ———— Let Them Live   4–6
  Lawson, R., Rabbit Hill   *4–6
  ———— Tough Winter   *4–6
  Lippincott, Wilderness Champion   *5–6
  Lofting, Doctor Dolittle's Puddleby Ad-
    ventures   *4–6
  Longsworth, Exploring Caves, p.103–21
                                        6
  McCracken, Great White Buffalo   5–6
  Mason, G. F., Animal Tails   5–6
  ———— Animal Tools   5–6
  ———— Animal Tracks   4–6
  Osmond, Animals of the World, v.1,2,3
                                        4–6
  Parker, B. M., Golden Book of Science,
    p.12–29   4–6
  ———— Living Things, p.12–36   4–6
  ———— Saving Our Wild Life, p.2–21
                                        5–6
  Perkins, Marlin Perkins' Zooparade
                                        4–6
  Potter, Fairy Caravan   *4–5
  Rounds, Swamp Life   5–6
  Selsam, See through the Forest   4–6
  ———— See through the Jungle   4–5
  ———— See through the Lake, p.15–44
                                        4–6
  Sterling, Story of Caves, p.66–79   5–6

ANIMALS—AFRICA: *see also* names of
    African animals, as Antelopes; Ba-
    boons; Camels; Elephants; Giraffes;
    Gorillas; Hippopotamus; Leopards;
    Lions; Mandrills; Okapis; Pangolins;
    Rhinoceros; Tigers; Zebras
  Gatti, Saranga, the Pygmy   5–6
  Stinetorf, Children of North Africa
                                      *5–6

ANIMALS—ALASKA
  McCracken, Biggest Bear on Earth
                                        5–6
  ———— Sentinel of the Snow Peaks
                                        5–6

ANIMALS—ARABIA: *see* Camels

ANIMALS—ARCTIC REGIONS: *see also* names of Arctic animals, as Bears (polar); Musk Oxen; Seals (animals); Walrus
McCracken, Son of the Walrus King   6
O'Brien, Silver Chief   *6

ANIMALS—ASIA: *see* Animals—India; also names of Asian animals, as Camels; Elephants; Leopards; Lions; Pandas; Pangolins; Tigers

ANIMALS—AUSTRALIA: *see also* names of Australian animals, as Anteaters; Echidnas; Kangaroos; Lyrebirds
Parker, B. M., Water, p.26–28   5–6

ANIMALS—CARE: *see* Animals—Houses; Dogs—Care and Training; Kindness to Animals; Pets

ANIMALS—CENTRAL AMERICA: *see* names of Central American animals, as Anteaters; Armadillos; Coatis; Jaguars; Manatees

ANIMALS—DESERT
Buff, Elf Owl   4–5
Fenton, C. L., Wild Folk in the Desert   4–6
Goetz, Deserts, p.28–42   4–6
Huntington, Let's Go to the Desert   4–5

ANIMALS—DOMESTIC: *see also* Dairying; Herding; Kindness to Animals; Pets; also names of domestic animals, as Dogs
Hogeboom, Familiar Animals and How To Draw Them   4–5
Hogner, Barnyard Family   5–6
———— Farm Animals   6

ANIMALS—EUROPE: *see* names of European animals, as Deer; Wolves

ANIMALS—EXTINCT: *see* Prehistoric Animals

ANIMALS—FRESH-WATER: *see also* Aquariums; Ponds; also names of fresh-water animals, as Beavers; Crocodiles; Fishes; Frogs; Toads; Turtles
Morgan, A. H., Field Book of Animals in Winter, p.42–142   6

———— Field Book of Ponds and Streams   6

ANIMALS—HABITS AND BEHAVIOR: *see also* Animal Sounds; Animal Tracks; Animals—Houses; Animals—Protection
Moe, Animal Inn   4–6
Salten, Bambi   *5–6
Wyss, Swiss Family Robinson   *6

ANIMALS—HOUSES: *see also* Aquariums; Birdhouses; Birds—Eggs and Nests; Terrariums
Blough, When You Go to the Zoo, p.43–47   4–6
Mason, G. F., Animal Homes   4–6
Zim, Rabbits, p.46–52   4–5

ANIMALS—INDIA: *see also* names of Indian animals, as Antelopes; Elephants; Lions; Rhinoceros; Tigers
Mukerji, Hari, the Jungle Lad   *5–6
Singh, Gift of the Forest   *6

ANIMALS—INDONESIA
Sperry, All about the Jungle, p.63–75   5–6

ANIMALS—MALAY PENINSULA: *see* names of Malay Peninsula animals, as Gibbons; Hornbills; Mouse Deer; Orangutans; Pheasants; Tapirs

ANIMALS—MEXICO: *see* names of Mexican animals, as Armadillos; Crocodiles; Monkeys

ANIMALS—MIGRATION
Hyde, Animal Clocks and Compasses   5–6
Lavine, Strange Travelers   4–6
McCracken, Biggest Bear on Earth, p.27–33   5–6
Morgan, A. H., Field Book of Animals in Winter, p.16–23   6
Parker, B. M., Animal Travels, p.14–16   4–6

ANIMALS—NORTH AMERICA: *see also* names of North American animals, as Antelopes; Badgers; Bears; Beavers; Bison; Coyotes; Deer; Foxes; Moose; Otters; Pikas; Raccoons; Skunks; Weasels; Wolves
Hogner, Animal Book   6

ANIMALS—PANAMA
    Rothery, Central American Roundabout,
        p.169–77   6

ANIMALS—PICTURES
    Buck, F., Jungle Animals   5–6
    Doane, Book of Nature, p.28–29, 72–75
                                                    5–6
    Kieran, M., John James Audubon   5–6

ANIMALS—PREHISTORIC: *see* Prehis-
    toric Animals

ANIMALS—PROTECTION: *see   also*
    Kindness to Animals; Wild Life Con-
    servation
    Hylander, Out of Doors in Winter,
        p.111–15   5–6
    Mason, G. F., Animal Clothing   5–6
    ———— Animal Tails, p.44–51   5–6
    ———— Animal Weapons   5–6

ANIMALS—SOUTH AMERICA: *see al-
    so* names of South American animals,
    as Anteaters; Armadillos; Coatis; Jag-
    uars; Llamas; Manatees; Sloths; Ta-
    pirs
    Hall, E., Land and People of Argentina
                                                    6
    May, Let's Read about Brazil, p.75–83
                                                    4–6
    Rothery, South American Roundabout,
        p.95–101   5–6
    Sperry, All about the Jungle, p.26–40
        (Brazil)   5–6

ANIMALS—SUMATRA: *see* names of
    Sumatran animals, as Elephants; Ti-
    gers; Wild Boars

ANIMALS IN WINTER: *see also* Ani-
    mals—Migration; Birds—Migration;
    Hibernation
    Gall, Flat Tail, p.84–88   *4–6
    ———— Ringtail, p.90–119   *4–5
    Hylander, Out of Doors in Autumn,
        p.114–31   5–6
    Morgan, A. H., Field Book of Animals
        in Winter   6

ANNIVERSARIES: *see* Holidays; also
    names of special days, as Thanks-
    giving Day

ANT COWS: *see* Plant Lice

ANT LIONS
    Comstock, Handbook of Nature Study,
        p.354-56   6
    Parker, B. M., Insects and Their Ways,
        p.18   4–6

ANTAR
    Hazeltine, Hero Tales from Many
        Lands, p.333–46   5–6

ANTARCTIC REGIONS: *see also* Ex-
    plorers; also names of Antarctic ex-
    plorers, as Amundsen, Roald; Wilkes,
    Charles
    Barrows, Old World Lands, p.277–78
                                                    6
    ———— Our Big World, p.126–31   4
    Bixby, Impossible Journey of Sir Ernest
        Shackelton   5–6
    Frank, Ice Island   6
    Icenhower, First Book of the Antarctic
                                                    4–6
    Lansing, A. M., Shackelton's Valiant
        Voyage   6
    Sperry, All about the Arctic and Ant-
        arctic   4–6
    ———— Captain Cook Explores the
        South Seas, p.136–49   5–6

ANTEATERS: *see also* Pangolins
    Parker, B. M., Animals We Know,
        p.28–29   5–6

ANTELOPES
    Bronson, Horns and Antlers, p.126–43
                                                    5–6
    Brown, V., How To Understand Animal
        Talk, p.114–17   6
    Buck, F., Jungle Animals, p.45–49   5–6
    Disney, Worlds of Nature, p.75–77
                                                    4–6
    Lathrop, Let Them Live, p.28–30   4–6
    Mason, G. F., Animal Tracks, p.80–81
                                                    4–6

ANTHROPOLOGY: *see* Archeology; Civ-
    ilization; Language; Prehistoric Man;
    Primitive Man; Races of Man

ANTIBIOTICS
    Hyde, Plants Today and Tomorrow,
        p.67–71   6
    Schatz, Story of Microbes, p.150–54   6

ANTS
    Bartlett, Insect Engineers   4–6

Bronson, Wonder World of Ants   4–6

Comstock, Handbook of Nature Study, p.369–78   6

Disney, Worlds of Nature, p.104–6, 129–40   4–6

Disraeli, New Worlds through the Microscope, p.69–70   6

Eaton, That Lively Man, Ben Franklin, p.108–10   6

Gall, Little Black Ant   *4–5

Gaul, Picture Book of Insects, p.38–39   4–6

Hyde, Animal Clocks and Compasses, p.68–71   5–6

Hylander, Insects on Parade, p.187–93   6

Lane, F. C., All about the Insect World   5–6

Lavine, Strange Travelers, p.12–18   5–6

——— Wonders of the Anthill   4–6

Lutz, Field Book of Insects, p.399–407   4–6

Parker, B. M., Plant and Animal Partnerships, p.5–7, 26–27   5–6

Stinetorf, Children of South Africa, p.80–94   *5–6

Teale, Insect Friends, p.87–90   5–6

——— Junior Book of Insects, p.82–106   6

Williamson, First Book of Bugs, p.29–33   4–5

APACHE INDIANS
Bleeker, Apache Indians   4–6

APES: *see* Baboons; Chimpanzees; Gibbons; Gorillas; Monkeys; Orangutans

APHIDS: *see* Plant Lice

APPALACHIAN MOUNTAINS
Barrows, American Continents, p.73–84   5

APPLE CIDER
Ladd, Janie, p.68–83   *4–5

APPLE TREES
Comstock, Handbook of Nature Study, p.661–70   6

Kane, Tale of a Meadow, p.24–30   4–6

Mason, M. E., Middle Sister   *4–5

APPLES: *see also* Appleseed, Johnny
Douglas, Appleseed Farm   *4–6

Eberle, Basketful, p.105–14   4–6

Hale, Complete Peterkin Papers, p.15–18 (Solomon John Goes for Apples and Cider)   *4–6

Lawrence, Peachtree Island, p.51–77   *4–5

Young, Unicorn with Silver Shoes, p.3–17   *4–6

APPLESEED, JOHNNY
Bailey, C. S., Children of the Handcrafts, p.136–45   5–6

Douglas, Appleseed Farm   *4–6

Le Sueur, Little Brother of the Wilderness   4–5

McMeekin, Journey Cake, p.131–42   *5–6

APPRECIATION OF OTHERS
Canfield, Understood Betsy   *5–6

De Angeli, Jared's Island   *4–6

Hewes, Boy of the Lost Crusade   *6

Jones, E. O., Twig   *4–5

Lawrence, Homemade Year   *4–5

McGinley, Plain Princess   *4–6

Steele, Flaming Arrows   *4–6

APRIL FOOLS' DAY
Burnett, B., First Book of Holidays, p.18–19   4–5

Haywood, Betsy's Winterhouse, p.148–68   *4–5

Jordan, Holiday Handicraft, p.84–89   4–6

Pannell, Holiday Round Up, p.96–107   4–6

Sechrist, Red Letter Days, p.89–95   5–6

APRONS
Robinson, J., Things to Make from Odds & Ends, p.78–80   6

AQUARIUMS: *see also* Fishes; Goldfish; Insects—Aquatic
Barr, More Research Ideas for Young Scientists, p.122–24   5–6

Bianco, All about Pets, p.110–18   5–6

Brown, V., How To Make a Miniature Zoo, p.60–98   5–6

Buck, M. W., Pets from the Pond, p.10–13   4–6

Cooper, E. K., Science on the Shores and Banks   5–6

Hogner, Frogs and Polliwogs, p.53–57   4–5

Hylander, Out of Doors in Winter, p.126–39   5–6

Kane, Tale of a Pond, p.60–66   5–6

Morgan, A. P., Aquarium Book   5–6

Parker, B. M., Garden Indoors, p.29–31   5–6

Pels, Care of Water Pets, p.42–64, 87–92   4–6

Selsam, Underwater Zoos   4–6

ARABIA: *see also* Arabs; Bedouins; Costume—Arabia

Fitch, Allah, the God of Islam   6

French, Lance of Kanana   *6

Quinn, Picture Map Geography of Asia, p.38–44   4–6

ARABIA—HISTORY

Hazeltine, Hero Tales from Many Lands, p.333–46   5–6

ARABIAN NIGHTS

Fitch, Allah, the God of Islam, p.60–62   6

ARABS: *see also* Arabia; Bedouins; Iraq; Islam; Moors; Sahara Desert

Ellis, Arabs   6

Epstein, E., First Book of the United Nations, p.42–43   4–6

Fitch, Allah, the God of Islam   6

Jordan, Homemade Dolls in Foreign Dress, p.173–85   4–6

Kubie, First Book of Archaeology, p.5–9   6

Nevil, Picture Story of the Middle East   4–6

Smith, J. R., Neighbors around the World, p.202–18   4

ARBOR DAY: *see also* Forestry; Trees; also names of trees, as Oak Trees

Burnett, B., First Book of Holidays, p.21–22   4–5

McSpadden, Book of Holidays, p.78–84   6

Olcott, Good Stories for Great Holidays, p.365–85   *4–6

Pannell, Holiday Round Up, p.142–52   *4–6

Sechrist, Red Letter Days, p.96–106   5–6

ARC, JOAN OF: *see* Joan of Arc

ARC LIGHT: *see* Electric Lighting

ARCHEOLOGY: *see also* Alphabets; Bronze Age; Cave Dwellers; Civilization; Cliff Dwellers; Fossils; Indians of North America; Iron Age; Lake Dwellers; Mound Builders; Pottery; Prehistoric Man; Pyramids; Sphinx; Stone Age; Tombs; Tutankhamen

Armer, Waterless Mountain, p.102–5, 173–76   *5–6

Bleeker, Inca, p.46–47, 87, 92   5–6

Friedman, E., Digging into Yesterday   5–6

Hall, J., Buried Cities   5–6

Hazeltine, Easter Book of Legends and Stories, p.295–311   *5–6

Honour, Secrets of Minos   6

Jessup, Wonderful World of Archaeology   5–6

Kubie, First Book of Archaeology   6

Moon, Chi-Wee, p.69–72   *4–6

Schealer, Sycamore Warrior   *6

Stinetorf, Children of North Africa, p.18–21   *5–6

ARCHERY: *see* Bow and Arrow; Robin Hood; Tell, William; Ulysses

ARCHIMEDES

Asimov, Breakthroughs in Science, p.1–8   5–6

ARCHITECTURE: *see also* Bridges; Building Materials; Carpentry; Castles; Cathedrals; Concrete; Heating; Houses; Housing—United States; Skyscrapers; Tombs

Bergere, From Stones to Skyscrapers   6

Fitch, Allah, the God of Islam, p.98–107   6

Hawkes, Tami's New House   *4–5

Hillyer, Child's History of Art, p.277–432   5–6

Spencer, C., Made in China   5–6

Tappan, When Knights Were Bold, p.338–60   6

ARCHITECTURE—BAROQUE

Bergere, From Stones to Skyscrapers, p.64–65   6

ARCHITECTURE—GOTHIC

Bergere, From Stones to Skyscrapers, p.48–55   6

ARCTIC REGIONS: *see also* Alaska; Animals—Arctic Regions; Antarctic Regions; Bering Strait; Eskimos; Explorers; Glaciers; Greenland; Icebergs; also names of Arctic explorers, as Amundsen, Roald

American Heritage, Discoverers of the New World, p.126–33   5–6

Anderson, W. R., First under the North Pole   4–6

Berry, Men, Moss, and Reindeer   5–6

Bleeker, Eskimos   4–6

Disney, Worlds of Nature, p.13–43   4–6

Gidal, Follow the Reindeer   4–6

Goetz, Arctic Tundra   4–6

Lauber, All about the Ice Age, p.128–38   4–6

Life, World We Live In, p.144–59   5–6

McCracken, Son of the Walrus King   6

MacGregor, Miss Pickerell Goes to the Arctic   *4–6

Ross, F. A., Land and People of Canada, p.50–57   6

Rothery, Scandinavian Roundabout, p. 49–81   6

Smith, I., Santa Claus Book   *4–5

Smith, J. R., Neighbors around the World, p.39–48   4

Sperry, All about the Arctic and Antarctic   4–6

Tolboom, People of the Snow   4–6

ARGENTINA
Barrows, American Continents, p.345–51   5

Goetz, Neighbors to the South, p.90–96   5–6

Hall, E., Land and People of Argentina   6

Quinn, Picture Map Geography of South America, p.52–64   4–6

Rothery, South American Roundabout, p.142–57   5–6

Spencer, P. R., Traveling New Trails, p.288–90   6

ARGONAUTS
Benson, Stories of the Gods and Heroes, p.139–49   5–6

Kingsley, Heroes, p.107–246   6

ARITHMETIC: *see also* Barter; Business; Clocks; Engineering; Graphs; Mathematics; Metric System; Money; Numbers; Weights and Measures

Bendick, How Much and How Many   5–6

ARIZONA: *see also* Cliff Dwellers; Colorado River; Grand Canyon National Park; Navaho Indians: Petrified Forests

Armer, Waterless Mountain   *5–6

Quinn, Picture Map Geography of the United States, p.152–55   4–6

ARKANSAS: *see also* Hot Springs National Park

Association for Childhood Education, Told under Spacious Skies, p.181–99   *4–6

Banta, Life in America: The South, p.150–55   5–6

Lenski, Cotton in My Sack   *4–6

Quinn, Picture Map Geography of the United States, p.132–35   4–6

Simon, Robin on the Mountain   *4–6

ARKWRIGHT, SIR RICHARD: *see* Spinning

ARMADILLOS
Hogner, Animal Book, p.32–33   6

Kipling, Just So Stories, p.101–20   *4–6

ARMISTICE DAY: *see* Veterans Day

ARMS AND ARMOR: *see also* Guns; Weapons

Buehr, Knights and Castles and Feudal Life, p.49–58   4–6

Tappan, When Knights Were Bold, p.18–27   6

ARMY LIFE: *see* Soldiers

ARNOLD, BENEDICT
Crouse, A. E., Alexander Hamilton and Aaron Burr, p.41–49, 73–74   6

Foster, G., George Washington's World, p.223–25   6

ARROW: *see* Bow and Arrow

ARSENIC
Loomis, Field Book of Common Rocks and Minerals, p.78–80   6

ART: *see also* Architecture; Art Museums; Artists; Arts and Crafts; Basketry; Block Printing; Color; Costume; Drawing; Embroidery; Engraving; Handicraft; Indians of North America—Art; Jewelry; Leather Work; Motion Pictures; Museums; Paper Work; Photography; Pictures; Pottery; Sculpture; Sewing; Soap Sculpture; Tapestry; Weaving; Wood Carving

Alden, Why the Chimes Rang, p.53–65
*4–6

Bannon, Patty Paints a Picture   *4–5
Downer, Discovering Design   6
Fitch, Allah, the God of Islam, p.92–97
6

Hawkes, Tami's New House   *4–5
Slobodkin, First Book of Drawing   5–6
Weiss, H., Paper, Ink and Roller   4–6
———— Pencil, Pen and Brush   5–6

ART—BABYLONIA
Hillyer, Child's History of Art, p.14–17
5–6

ART—CANADA
Bonner, Made in Canada   5–6

ART—CHINA
Soong, Art of Chinese Paper Folding
4–6
Spencer, C., Land of the Chinese People, p.112–17   6
———— Made in China   5–6

ART—EGYPT
Hillyer, Child's History of Art, p.8–13
5–6
Robinson, C. A., First Book of Ancient Egypt, p.32–35   4–6

ART—ENGLAND: *see also* names of English artists, as Gainsborough, Thomas
Hillyer, Child's History of Art, p.109–21
5–6

ART—FLANDERS
Hillyer, Child's History of Art, p.74–79
5–6

ART—FRANCE: *see also* names of French artists, as Millet, Jean François
Hillyer, Child's History of Art, p.99–108, 122–26   5–6

ART—GERMANY
Hillyer, Child's History of Art, p.85–89
5–6

ART—GREECE
Hillyer, Child's History of Art, p.18–24
5–6

ART—HISTORY
Hillyer, Child's History of Art   5–6

ART—ITALY
Hillyer, Child's History of Art, p.25–73
5–6

ART—JAPAN
Buck, P. S., Big Wave   *6
Hawkes, Tami's New House   *4–5
Kuwabara, Cut and Paste   5–6
Ota, Printing for Fun   4–6
Yashima, T., Golden Footprints *4–6

ART—MEXICO
McNeer, Mexican Story, p.88–91   6

ART—NETHERLANDS: *see also* names of Dutch artists, as Vermeer, Johannes
Barnouw, Land of William of Orange, p.50–60   6
Hillyer, Child's History of Art, p.80–84
5–6

ART—PRIMITIVE MAN: *see also* Cave Drawings
Reed, Earth for Sam, p.216–22   6

ART—SOUTH AMERICA
Goetz, Neighbors to the South, p.123–28   5–6
Peck, Pageant of South American History, p.370–76   6

ART—SPAIN
Hillyer, Child's History of Art, p.93–98
5–6

ART—UNITED STATES
Hillyer, Child's History of Art, p.136–45, 150–56   5–6

ART—VENICE
Hillyer, Child's History of Art, p.63–68
5–6

ART AND HISTORY
Bailey, C. S., Children of the Handcrafts   5–6

ART AND NATURE
Comstock, Handbook of Nature Study, p.17   6

Downer, Discovering Design   6
Hughes, First Book of Rhythms   4–6

ART MUSEUMS
Hillyer, Child's History of Art   5–6
Weisgard, Treasures To See   4–6

ARTHUR, KING
Farjeon, Mighty Men, p.151–58   4–6
Hazeltine, Hero Tales from Many
Lands, p.101–8, 136–46   5–6

ARTHUR, CHESTER ALAN
Beard, Presidents in American History,
p.89–90, 169   6
Coy, First Book of Presidents, p.48
   4–6
Petersham, Story of the Presidents of
the United States, p.51   4–6

ARTIGAS, JOSÉ GERVASIO
Goetz, Neighbors to the South, p.145–
47   5–6

ARTISTS: *see also* Musicians; also names
of artists, as Audubon, John James;
Fulton, Robert; Leonardo da Vinci
Bailey, C. S., Pioneer Art in America,
p.103–28   *5–6
Coatsworth, Away Goes Sally, p.73–80
   *4–6

———— Cat Who Went to Heaven
   *4–6

———— Littlest House, p.124–35 *4–6
Field, Hitty, p.154–58   *5–6
Hartman, Builders of the Old World,
p.340–46   6
Henry, M., Benjamin West and His Cat
Grimalkin   *4–6
Shannon, Dobry   *5–6
Wiese, Chinese Ink Stick, p.17–35
   *4–6

ARTS AND CRAFTS: *see also* Guilds;
Handicraft; also names of special in-
dustries, as Pottery; Stained Glass
Windows; Toys; Weaving
Bailey, C. S., Pioneer Art in America
   *5–6
Bonner, Made in Canada   5–6
Hartman, Builders of the Old World,
p.51–54   6
Lewis, O., Hawaii, p.26–38   5–6
Lownsbery, Boy Knight of Reims   *6
Spencer, C., Land of the Chinese Peo-
ple, p.91–95   6

ASBESTOS
Fenton, C. L., Riches from the Earth,
p.22–25   5–6

ASH TREES
Comstock, Handbook of Nature Study,
p.658–61   6
Cormack, First Book of Trees, p.40
   4–6
McKenny, Trees of the Countryside,
p.42–45   4–6

ASIA: *see also* names of countries, as
India; also names of explorers, as
Polo, Marco
Epstein, S., All about the Desert, p.95–
107   5–6
Quinn, Picture Map Geography of Asia
   4–6

ASIA—GAMES: *see* Games—Asia

ASIA MINOR: *see* Afghanistan; Arabia;
Iran; Iraq; Palestine; Syria; Turkey

ASOKA, KING OF MAGADHA, INDIA
Modak, Land and People of India, p.50–
52   6

ASPHALT
Barr, Young Scientist Takes a Ride,
p.22–23   5–6

ASSEMBLIES: *see* Dancing; Fairs; Festivals; Folk Songs; Holidays; Indians of
North America—Ceremonies; Markets; Pageants; Plays; Safety

ASSES
Hogner, Farm Animals, p.38–39   6

ASSISI, FRANCIS OF: *see* Francis of
Assisi, Saint

ASSYRIA: *see also* Iraq
Falls, First 3000 Years, p.124–34   6
Hillyer, Child's History of the World,
p.94–98   5–6
Kubie, First Book of Archaeology, p.5–
8   6
McGuire, Glimpses into the Long Ago,
p.92–96   5–6
Watson, Golden History of the World,
p.24–25   5–6

ASTEROIDS: *see* Planets—Minor

ASTROLOGY
Kent, He Went with Vasco da Gama
   *6

Tappan, When Knights Were Bold, p.315–17   6

ASTRONAUTS
Kay, Space Volunteers, p.115–22   6
Lent, Man Alive in Outer Space   5–6
Wells, What Does an Astronaut Do?   6

ASTRONOMY: *see also* Aurora Borealis; Calendars; Earth; Eclipses; Meteors; Moon; Navigation; Planetariums; Planets; Seasons; Space Travel; Stars; Sun; Telescopes; Tides; also names of astronomers, as Brahe, Tycho
Adler, Time in Your Life, p.19–34   4–6
Baker, A. O., Your Science World, p.91–118   6
Baker, R. H., Introducing the Constellations   6
———— When the Stars Come Out   6
Barnard, Macmillan Science-Life Series, Bk.6, p.205–19   6
Barr, More Research Ideas for Young Scientists, p.30–46   5–6
Comstock, Handbook of Nature Study, p.815–59   6
Freeman, M. B., Fun with Astronomy   4–6
Gallant, R. A., Exploring the Universe   5–6
Goodwin, Real Book about Stars   4–6
Hartman, Builders of the Old World, p.367–73   6
Life, World We Live In, p.194–211   5–6
Meyer, Picture Book of Astronomy   4–5
Parker, B. M., Sky above Us   4–6
Reed, Patterns in the Sky   5–6
Scheib, What Happened?, p.67–77   5–6
Schloat, Andy's Wonderful Telescope   4–5
Schneider, L., Space in Your Future, p.24–104   6
Tappan, When Knights Were Bold, p.313–14   6

ATEBRIN
Eberle, Modern Medical Discoveries, p.82–87   5–6

ATHENS: *see also* Greece—Ancient

Falls, First 3000 Years, p.157–62   6
Hartman, Builders of the Old World, p.141–58   6

ATHLETES: *see* Gehrig, Lou; Hercules; Rockne, Knute Kenneth

ATHLETICS: *see also* Games; Olympic Games; Sports; also names of sports, as Skating; Skiing; Swimming
Bancroft, Games, p.49–54   4–6
Beeler, More Experiments in Science, p.97–99   5–6

ATLANTIC CABLE: *see also* Field, Cyrus West
Darrow, Boys' Own Book of Great Inventions, p.26–30   6
Hartman, Machines, p.148–58   6
Latham, Young Man in a Hurry   6

ATLANTIC OCEAN: *see* Gulf Stream; Sargasso Sea; also names of explorers, as Columbus, Christopher

ATLANTIC STATES: *see also* Colonial Period in America; New England; also names of states, as New Jersey
Barrows, American Continents, p.55–72   5

ATLAS
Asimov, Words from the Myths, p.29–33   6
Sellew, Adventures with the Gods, p.32–37   4–5
Spencer, P. R., Traveling New Trails, p.207–13   6

ATLASES: *see* Maps

ATMOSPHERE: *see* Air; Weather

ATOMIC BATTERY
Yates, R. F., Boy and a Battery, p.114–19   5–6

ATOMIC ENERGY
Baker, A. O., Your Science World, p.141–50   6
Barnard, Macmillan Science-Life Series, Bk.6, p.301–3   6
Bendick, Electronics for Young People, p.154–72   6
Bischof, Atoms at Work   5–6
Crouse, W. H., Understanding Science, p.13–23   6
Epstein, E., First Book of the United Nations, p.47–49   4–6

Fermi, Story of Atomic Energy   6
Freeman, M. B., Fun with Science, p.59–64   6
Hyde, Plants Today and Tomorrow, p.54–59   6
Lewellen, Mighty Atom   4–6
McCoy, Big Book of Real Submarines   4–6
Morgan, A. P., Boys' Book of Science and Construction, p.453–60   6
Scheib, What Happened?, p.41–55   5–6
Schneider, H., More Power to You, p.106–19   5–6
Zarem, New Dimensions of Flight, p.49–57   6

ATOMIC RESEARCH: *see* Uranium

ATOMS
Adler, Time in Your Life, p.103–11   4–6
_____ Tools of Science   6
Beeler, Experiments with Atomics   6
Gallant, R. A., Exploring Chemistry, p.70–85   6
Landin, About Atoms for Junior   4
Meyer, Picture Book of Molecules and Atoms, p.18–47   5–6
Reed, And That's Why, p.56–65   4–5

ATTILA, KING OF THE HUNS
Farjeon, Mighty Men, p.132–37   4–6
Hazeltine, Hero Tales from Many Lands, p.69–87   5–6
Seredy, White Stag   6

AUCTIONS
Burglon, Children of the Soil, p.238–57   *4–6
Cleary, Henry and Beezus, p.128–47   *4–5
Field, Hitty, p.196–204   *5–6
Mason, M. E., Middle Sister, p.38–45   *4–5
Robertson, K., Ticktock and Jim, p.91–100   *4–6

AUDUBON, JOHN JAMES
Foster, G., Abraham Lincoln's World, p.105–7   6
Kieran, M., John James Audubon   5–6
Spencer, P. R., Finding New Trails, p.413–18   4

AUGUSTUS, EMPEROR OF ROME
Falls, First 3000 Years, p.201–6   6

AURORA BOREALIS
Gallant, R. A., Exploring the Sun, p.45–48   5–6
Morgan, A. P., First Electrical Book for Boys, p.10–12   6

AUSTRALIA: *see also* Animals—Australia; New Guinea; Tasmania
Barrows, Old World Lands, p.267–76   6
_____ Our Big World, p.133–41   4
Bergaust, Rockets around the World, p.36–37   6
Darling, L., Kangaroos and Other Animals with Pockets   4–6
Epstein, S., All about the Desert, p.108–11   5–6
Kjelgaard, Boomerang Hunter   *5–6

AUSTRALIA—HISTORY
Sperry, Captain Cook Explores the South Seas, p.118–21   5–6

AUSTRIA; *see also* Tyrol
Barrows, Old World Lands, p.82–84   6
Fry, Bell for Ringelblume   *4–5
Gidal, My Village in Austria   5–6
Wheeler, Franz Schubert and His Merry Friends   4–6
_____ Mozart, the Wonder Boy   4–6

AUSTRIA—FOLK TALES
Sawyer, Long Christmas, p.71–81   4–6

AUTHORS: *see also* Books; also names of authors, as Alcott, Louisa May; Irving, Washington
Bentley, Young Brontës   6
Coffman, Famous Authors for Young People   5–6

AUTOMATIC PILOTS
Adler, Things That Spin   5–6

AUTOMOBILES: *see also* Ford, Henry; Foreign Cars; Trucks
Barr, Young Scientist Takes a Ride   5–6
Bendick, First Book of Automobiles   4–6
Cooke, D. C., How Automobiles Are Made   5–6
_____ Racing Cars That Made History   5–6
Dalgliesh, America Travels, p.73–80, 115–17   4–6

Darrow, Boys' Own Book of Great Inventions, p.210–21   6
Elting, Lollypop Factory, p.17–19   4–5
Fenner, Time To Laugh, p.67–78   *4–6
Hartman, Machines, p.207–21   6
Huey, What Makes the Wheels Go Round, p.72–76   6
Lent, Men at Work in the Great Lakes States, p.42–49   4–6
Morgan, A. P., First Electrical Book for Boys, p.187–201   6

AUTOMOBILES—HISTORY
Ilin, How the Automobile Learned To Run   4–6

AUTOMOBILES—MODELS
Maginley, Historic Models of Early America, p.87–94   6

AUTOMOBILES—TIRES
Barr, Young Scientist Takes a Ride, p.82–83   5–6
Lent, Men at Work in the Great Lakes States, p.30–33   4–6

AUTOMOBILES—TRAILERS
Burns, World Full of Homes, p.27–29   4–6
Owen, Denmark Caravan   *5–6

AUTUMN: *see also* Seasons
Harrison, Outdoor Adventures, p.86–105   4–5
Hylander, Out of Doors in Autumn   5–6
Kane, Tale of a Pond, p.28–32   5–6

AVALANCHES
Bragdon, L. J., Land and People of Switzerland, p.20–21   6

AVIATION: *see also* Aerodynamics; Air Mail Service; Airplanes; Airports; Airships; Aviators; Balloons; Flight; Gliders—Aviation; Kites; Navigation; Parachutes
Armer, Waterless Mountain, p.67–73   *5–6
Baker, A. O., Your Science World, p.193–213   6
Barrows, Our Big World   4
Darrow, Boys' Own Book of Great Inventions, p.259–305   6
Floherty, Aviation from the Ground Up   6

Hartman, Machines, p.234–44   6
Lent, "Fly It Away!"   4–6
Oakes, Bamboo Gate, p.138–57   *4–6
Schneider, L., Wings in Your Future   5–6

AVIATION—HISTORY: *see* Wright, Orville, and Wright, Wilbur

AVIATION—MILITARY
Colby, Bomber Parade   5–6
Engeman, U. S. Air Force Academy   6

AVIATORS: *see also* names of aviators, as Byrd, Richard Evelyn; Lindbergh, Charles Augustus
Spencer, P. R., Exploring New Trails, p.66–73   5

AVIGNON, FRANCE
Bragdon, L. J., Land and People of France, p.92–93   6

AXES
Schneider, H., Everyday Machines and How They Work, p.77–78   5–6

AZTECS: *see also* Cortez, Hernando; Mexico—History
Epstein, S., First Book of Mexico, p.16–27   5–6
McNeer, Mexican Story   6

BABIES—CARE
Levine, Baby Is Born   4–5
Moon, Chi-Wee, p.169–239   *4–6

BABOONS: *see also* Mandrills; Monkeys
Disney, Worlds of Nature, p.169–70   4–6

BABYLONIA: *see also* Art—Babylonia; Cuneiform Writing; Iraq
Bergere, From Stones to Skyscrapers, p.16–21   6
Falls, First 3000 Years, p.71–80, 134–40   6
Hartman, Builders of the Old World, p.83–98   6
Hillyer, Child's History of the World, p. 99–108   5–6
Lamprey, All the Ways of Building, p.43–52   6
McGuire, Glimpses into the Long Ago, p.77–91   5–6
Watson, Golden History of the World, p.22   5–6

BACH, JOHANN SEBASTIAN
Buchanan, How Man Made Music, p.122–29   6
Burch, Famous Composers for Young People, p.9–17   4–6
Schwimmer, Great Musicians as Children, p.105–10   6
Sechrist, It's Time for Easter, p.111–15   5–6
Wheeler, Sebastian Bach   4–6

BACON, ROGER
Hartman, Builders of the Old World, p.365–67   6

BACON'S REBELLION, 1676: *see also* Colonial Period in America; Virginia —History
Barksdale, That Country Called Virginia, p.43–49   6
Lawson, M. A., Pocahontas and Captain John Smith, p.171–81   6

BACTERIA: *see also* Fungi; Parasites; also names of bacteriologists, as Pasteur, Louis
Comstock, Handbook of Nature Study, p.729–31   6
Freeman, I. M., All about the Wonders of Chemistry, p.81–88, 93–98   6
Lewis, L. Z., First Book of Microbes, p.41–45   5–6
Parker, B. M., Dependent Plants, p.25–29   5–6
———— Plant and Animal Partnerships, p.17–18   5–6
Schatz, Story of Microbes   6

BACTERIOLOGY
Yates, R. F., Fun with Your Microscope, p.138–46   6

BAD LANDS
Rounds, Stolen Pony   *5–6

BADEN-POWELL, ROBERT
Pace, Juliette Low, p.111–16, 123–24   5–6

BADGERS
Barker, Winter-sleeping Wildlife, p.45–49   5–6
Franklin, Wild Animals of the Southwest, p.116–30   5–6
Hogner, Animal Book, p.131–32   6
Mason, G. F., Animal Tracks, p.48–49   4–6

Ripper, Weasel Family, p.60–64   4–5
Stoutenberg, Wild Animals of the Far West, p.37–38   4–6

BAHAMAS
Henry, M., Bahamas   4–6
Quinn, Picture Map Geography of Mexico, Central America and the West Indies, p.81–82   4–6

BAKERS: *see also* Bread; Cooking
Buehr, Bread, p.54–73   4–6
Elting, Lollypop Factory, p.54–66   4–5
Fenner, Fools and Funny Fellows, p.69–76   *4–6
Hall, R. H., Baker's Man   *4–5

BALANCE
Downer, Discovering Design, p.30–35   6

BALANCE OF NATURE: *see also* Aquariums; Beavers; Interdependence of Plants and Animals
Bronson, Horns and Antlers, p.36–39   5–6
Morgan, A. H., Field Book of Ponds and Streams   6
Parker, B. M., Saving Our Wild Life, p.19–21   5–6

BALBOA, VASCO NUÑEZ DE
American Heritage, Discoverers of the New World, p.48–51   5–6
Dalgliesh, America Begins, p.42   4–5
McGuire, Brave Young Land, p.69–74   5–6
Syme, Balboa   4–6

BALDER
Brown, A. F., In the Days of Giants, p.226–42   4–6
Colum, Children of Odin, p.187–99   4–5
Coolidge, Legends of the North, p.62–70   4–6
Keary, Heroes of Asgard   5–6
Sellew, Adventures with the Giants, p.99–122   4–6

BALI
Caldwell, Let's Visit Indonesia, p.40–42, 79–84   4–6
Louden, Far into the Night   4–5
Smith, D. C., Land and People of Indonesia, p.88–89, 103–4   6

BALKAN STATES: *see* Albania; Bulgaria; Greece—Modern; Romania; Yugoslavia

BALL: *see also* Baseball; Basketball; Football; Hockey; Tennis
Bancroft, Games, p.407–654   4–6

BALL-POINT PENS
Schneider, H., Everyday Machines and How They Work, p.14–15   5–6

BALLADS: *see also* American Ballads and Songs; Folk Songs; Songs
Browne, Story of Our National Ballads   5–6
White, A. M. G., Dramatized Ballads   4–6

BALLET
Atkinson, Dancers of the Ballet   6
Brock, Ballet for Mary   *4–5
Freeman, M. B., Fun with Ballet   5–6
Streatfeild, First Book of the Ballet   4–6
Wyndham, Susie and the Ballet Family   *4–6
———— Susie and the Dancing Cat   *4–6

BALLOONS: *see also* Airships; Aviation
Beeler, More Experiments in Science, p.68–72   5–6
Bishop, R. W., From Kite to Kitty Hawk, p.14–55   6
Burchard, Balloons   4–6
Dalgliesh, America Travels, p.57–62   *4–6
Du Bois, Twenty-one Balloons   *6

BALSAM
Rothery, Central American Roundabout, p.56–60   6

BALTIMORE, CECILIUS CALVERT, BARON
Duvoisin, And There Was America, p.70–72   4–6

BALTIMORE ORIOLES
Comstock, Handbook of Nature Study, p.120–23   6
Webb, Birds in Their Homes, p.48–50   4–6

BANANAS
Eberle, Basketful, p.115–20   4–6

Rothery, Central American Roundabout, p.85–94   6
Smith, J. R., Neighbors around the World, p.293–98   4

BANDITS: *see* Crime

BANDS (music)
Buchanan, How Man Made Music, p.89–96   6

BANJO
Kettelkamp, Singing Strings, p.33–36   5–6

BANKING: *see* Money

BANNEKER, BENJAMIN
Shackelford, Child's Story of the Negro, p.83–86   4–5

BARBARIANS: *see also* Attila, King of the Huns
Hartman, Builders of the Old World, p.207–10   6
Hillyer, Child's History of the World, p.219–30   5–6

BARDS: *see also* Minstrels; Troubadours
Buchanan, How Man Made Music, p.15–16, 89   6

BARN SWALLOWS: *see* Swallows

BARNACLES
Cooper, E. K., Science on the Shores and Banks, p.115–16   5–6

BAROMETERS: *see also* Air Pressure
Barr, More Research Ideas for Young Scientists, p.147–49   5–6
Parker, B. M., Scientist and His Tools, p.20–22   5–6
Spilhaus, Weathercraft, p.51–54   6

BARRIE, JAMES MATTHEW
Coffman, Famous Authors for Young People, p.141–45   5–6

BARTER: *see also* Money; Trade
Buehr, Treasure, p.1–3   4–6

BARTHOLDI, AUGUSTE
Rogers, F., Big Miss Liberty   *5–6

BARTÓK, BÉLA
Burch, Modern Composers for Young People, p.163–66   5–6

BARTOLOMMEO, FRA
Hillyer, Child's History of Art, p.54–57   5–6

BARTON, CLARA
Boylston, Clara Barton 4–6
Pace, Clara Barton 5–6

BASEBALL
Antonacci, Baseball for Young Champions 4–6
Bancroft, Games, p.411–12, 437–50, 585–86 4–6
Brewster, First Book of Baseball 5–6
Estes, Rufus M., p.78–104 *4–6
Hayes, Skid, p.11–13, 29–40 *5–6
Lent, Men at Work in New England, p.94–97 (manufacture of baseballs) 4–6
Renick, J. L., Steady *4–5
Renick, M. L., Pete's Home Run (Little League) *4–5
Sports Illustrated Magazine, Sports Illustrated Book of Baseball 6
Van Riper, Lou Gehrig 4–5

BASKETBALL
Antonacci, Basketball for Young Champions 5–6
Bancroft, Games, p.412–14, 450–65 4–6
Estes, Middle Moffat, p.236–67 *4–6
Renick, J. L., David Cheers the Team *4–5
Schiffer, First Book of Basketball 5–6

BASKETRY
Bailey, C. S., Children of the Handcrafts, p.146–55 *5–6
Jaeger, Easy Crafts, p.38–41 4–6

BASUTOLAND
Stinetorf, Children of South Africa, p.67–79 *5–6

BATHS: see Cleanliness

BATIK
Hamilton, E. T., Handicraft for Girls, p.165–77 6

BATS
Barker, Winter-sleeping Wildlife, p.5–10 5–6
Blough, After the Sun Goes Down, p.28–31 4–5
Comstock, Handbook of Nature Study, p.241–45 6
Gall, Ringtail, p.46–53 4–5
Hogner, Animal Book, p.22–31 6

Hyde, Animal Clocks and Compasses, p.98–102 6
Lavine, Strange Travelers, p.79–86 5–6
Longsworth, Exploring Caves, p.58–59, 103–14 6
Mason, G. F., Animal Sounds, p.61–63 5–6
Melbo, Our Country's National Parks, v.1, p.63–65 6
Parker, B. M., Animals We Know, p.11 5–6
Ripper, Bats 5–6
Spencer, P. R., Finding New Trails, p.264–67 4

BATTERIES: see also Atomic Battery; Solar Battery
Crouse, W. H., Understanding Science, p.73–75 6
Huey, What Makes the Wheels Go Round, p.53–56 6
Morgan, A. P., Boy Electrician, p.73–97 6
Schneider, H., More Power to You, p.81–86 5–6

BATTLESHIPS
Block, Real Book about Ships, p.140–46 5–6

BAUCIS AND PHILEMON
Benson, Stories of the Gods and Heroes, p.71–75 5–6
Sellew, Adventures with the Gods, p.95–103 4–5

BAUXITE: see Aluminum

BAY OF FUNDY: see Fundy—Bay of

BAZAARS
Ellis, Arabs, p.76–80, 97–98 6

BEADWORK
Hofsinde, Indian Beadwork 4–6
Hunt, W. B., Golden Book of Indian Crafts and Lore, p.60–71 4–6
Salomon, Book of Indian Crafts & Indian Lore, p.107–27 6

BEARS
Bannon, Billy and the Bear *4–5
Barker, Winter-sleeping Wildlife, p.37–45 5–6
Baudouy, Bruno, King of the Mountain *5–6

Bond, Bear Called Paddington   *4–6
———— Paddington Helps Out   *4–6
Bridges, Zoo Babies, p.11–13   4–6
———— Zoo Pets, p.69–78 (polar)
   4–6
Brown, V., How To Understand Animal
   Talk, p.92–101   6
Buff, Big Tree, p.16–22   5–6
Carlson, N. S., Alphonse, That Bearded
   One   *4–6
Child Study Association, Read to Your-
   self Storybook, p.35–49   *4–5
Colby, First Hunt, p.13   5–6
De la Mare, Animal Stories, p.23–28
   *4–6
Disney, Worlds of Nature, p.64–69
   (black)   4–6
Dolbier, Torten's Christmas Secret
   *4–5
Franklin, Monte   *4–6
———— Son of Monte   *4–6
———— Wild Animals of the South-
   west, p.87–102, 183–96   5–6
Guillot, Griska and the Bear   *5–6
Hogner, Animal Book, p.156–64   6
Kinney, Lonesome Bear   *4–6
Knight, C. R., Life through the Ages,
   p.66–67   6
Lathrop, Let Them Live, p.43–45   4–6
McCracken, Biggest Bear on Earth
   5–6
Mason, G. F., Animal Homes, p.18–23
   4–6
———— Animal Tracks, p.92–95   4–6
Mason, M. E., Susannah, p.128–31
   *4–5
Moon, Chi-Wee, p.73–86, 100–114
   *4–6
Osmond, Animals of the World, v.1
   (polar)   4–6
Paine, Arkansas Bear   *4–6
Parker, B. M., Animals We Know,
   p.16–17   5–6
Perkins, Marlin Perkins' Zooparade,
   p.40–43, 80–83   4–6
Robinson, W. W., Beasts of the Tar
   Pits, p.26–28   5–6
Smith, I., Santa Claus Book, p.79–87
   *4–5
Stoutenberg, Wild Animals of the Far
   West, p.12–17   4–6

Weston, Bhimsa, the Dancing Bear
   *4–6
Wilder, Little House in the Big Woods,
   p.101–16   *4–6

BEASTS OF BURDEN: *see* Animals—
   Domestic; Pack Transportation

BEATTY, CLYDE
   Spencer, P. R., Exploring New Trails,
   p.38–42   5

BEAUTY: *see also* Arts and Crafts; Color;
   Dancing; Kashmir; National Parks;
   Painting; Wild Flowers
   Armer, Waterless Mountain   *5–6
   Lownsbery, Boy Knight of Reims   *6
   Seredy, Tree for Peter   *4–6

BEAUTY CULTURE
   Enright, Saturdays, p.76–102   *4–6

BEAVERS
   Blough, After the Sun Goes Down,
   p.40–45   4–5
   Brown, V., How To Understand Animal
   Talk, p.129–31   6
   Coggins, H. L., Busby and Co.   *4–5
   Disney, Worlds of Nature, p.51–58
   4–6
   Fisher, A. L., Summer of Little Rain
   *4–6
   Franklin, Tuffy   *4–6
   ———— Wild Animals of the South-
   west, p.13–29   5–6
   Gall, Flat Tail   *4–6
   Gaul, Pond Book, p.91–100   4–6
   Hogner, Animal Book, p.55–57   6
   Lathrop, Let Them Live, p.12–15   4–6
   Liers, Beaver's Story   5–6
   Mason, G. F., Animal Homes, p.52–57
   4–6
   ———— Animal Tracks, p.36–37   4–6
   Osmond, Animals of the World, v.2
   4–6
   Stoutenberg, Wild Animals of the Far
   West, p.78–81   4–6

BECQUEREL, HENRI ANTOINE
   Asimov, Breakthroughs in Science,
   p.123–27   5–6
   Fermi, Story of Atomic Energy, p.10–
   12   6

BEDOUINS: *see also* Arabia; Arabs; Sahara Desert

Ellis, Arabs   6
French, Lance of Kanana   *6
Gidal, Sons of the Desert   5–6

BEE WOLF
Hyde, Animal Clocks and Compasses, p.71–75   5–6

BEES: *see also* Honey
Barker, Winter-sleeping Wildlife, p.120–25 (bumblebees)   5–6
Comstock, Handbook of Nature Study, p.384–400   6
De la Mare, Animal Stories, p.180–86   *4–6
Disney, Worlds of Nature, p.115–29   4–6
Foster, V. E., Close-up of a Honeybee   4–6
Hyde, Animal Clocks and Compasses, p.56–68   5–6
Hylander, Insects on Parade, p.173–86   6
Lane, F. C., All about the Insect World, p.66–80   5–6
Lavine, Strange Travelers, p.94–108   5–6
Lutz, Field Book of Insects, p.423–42   4–6
Mason, G. F., Animal Tools, p.34–38   5–6
Parker, B. M., Insects and Their Ways, p.14–17   4–6
Phillips, Makers of Honey   5–6
Teale, Insect Friends, p.13–24   5–6
———— Junior Book of Insects, p.168–82   6
Tibbets, First Book of Bees   4–6
Williamson, First Book of Bugs, p.39, 42–43   4–5

BEET SUGAR: *see also* Sugar
Eberle, Basketful, p.213–17   4–6

BEETHOVEN, LUDWIG VAN
Buchanan, How Man Made Music, p.134–39   6
Burch, Famous Composers for Young People, p.53–61   4–5
Goss, Beethoven   6
Schwimmer, Great Musicians as Children, p.59–66   6
Wheeler, Ludwig Beethoven and the Chiming Tower Bells   4–6

BEETLES: *see also* Ladybugs
Barker, Winter-sleeping Wildlife, p.101–5   5–6
Comstock, Handbook of Nature Study, p.362–66   6
Gaul, Picture Book of Insects, p.16–21   4–6
Hylander, Insects on Parade, p.79–97   6
Lane, F. C., All about the Insect World, p.35–40   5–6
Lutz, Field Book of Insects, p.275–375   4–6
Parker, B. M., Plant and Animal Partnerships, p.8–10   5–6
Teale, Insect Friends, p.25–28, 61   5–6
———— Junior Book of Insects, p.39–54   6
Williamson, First Book of Bugs, p.14–19   4–5

BELGIAN CONGO: *see* Congo

BELGIUM
Barrows, Old World Lands, p.205–9   6

BELL, ALEXANDER GRAHAM: *see also* Telephone
Cottler, Heroes of Civilization, p.211–20   6
Lawson, R., Watchwords of Liberty, p.83–84   4–6

BELLOWS, GEORGE W.
Hillyer, Child's History of Art, p.153–54   5–6

BELLS: *see also* Electric Bells; Liberty Bell
Buchanan, How Man Made Music, p.27–28   6
Huntington, Tune Up   4–6
Kettelkamp, Drums, Rattles, and Bells, p.35–47   4–6
Lacey, Picture Book of Musical Instruments, p.42–43   5–6
Pace, Early American, p.125–33   5–6
Rogers, F., Heels, Wheels, and Wire, p.141–60   5–6

BENGALI
Caldwell, Let's Visit Pakistan, p.91–92   4–6

BEN-GURION, DAVID
St. John, Builder of Israel   6

BEOWULF
Coolidge, Legends of the North, p.159–76   4–6
Farjeon, Mighty Men, p.101–10   4–6
Hazeltine, Hero Tales from Many Lands, p.89–99   5–6
Rothery, Scandinavian Roundabout, p.200–207   6

BERING, VITUS
American Heritage, Discoverers of the New World, p.147–49   5–6
Lindquist, W., Alaska, the Forty-ninth State, p.22–26   5–6

BERING SEA
Kipling, Jungle Book, p.145–83   *5–6

BERING STRAIT
McCracken, Son of the Walrus King   6

BERMUDA
Henry, M., Bermuda   4–6

BERRIES: *see also* Fruit
Hylander, Out of Doors in Autumn, p.74–94   5–6

BESSEMER, HENRY
Asimov, Breakthroughs in Science, p.85–89   5–6
Hartman, Machines, p.111–16   6

BETHUNE, MARY McLEOD
Shackelford, Child's Story of the Negro, p.177–86   4–5

BEVERAGES: *see also* names of beverages, as Chocolate; Coffee
New York Herald Tribune, Young America's Cook Book, p.203–9   4–6
Rombauer, Cookbook for Boys and Girls, p.192–98   6

BHUTAN
Quinn, Picture Map Geography of Asia, p.64–66   4–6

BIBLE—PSALMS
Allstrom, Songs along the Way   4–6

BIBLE STORIES: *see also* Jesus Christ; Jews; also names of Bible characters, as Moses
Bowie, Bible Story for Boys and Girls: New Testament   4–6
——— Bible Story for Boys and Girls: Old Testament   4–6
De Angeli, Old Testament   4–6

De la Mare, Stories from the Bible   5–6
Fessenden, Old Testament Story   4–6
Hartman, In Bible Days   6
Jones, J. M. O., Little Child   4–6
Petersham, David   4–5
——— Joseph and His Brothers   4–5
——— Moses   4–5
——— Ruth   4–5
Sechrist, It's Time for Easter, p.19–20   5–6

BICYCLES
Barnes, Wonderful Year, p.61–82   *4–6
Cleary, Henry and Bezzus, p.128–92   *4–5
Darrow, Boys' Own Book of Great Inventions, p.119–26   6
Enright, Four-Story Mistake, p.43–53   *5–6
Maginley, Historic Models of Early America, p.82–86   6
Renick, M. L., Seven Simpsons on Six Bikes   *4–5
Schneider, H., Everyday Machines and How They Work, p.45–47   5–6

BIG BEND NATIONAL PARK
Melbo, Our Country's National Parks, v.1, p.257–74   6

BIG TREES: *see* Sequoias; Trees

BIGHORNS
Disney, Worlds of Nature, p.46–49   4–6
Franklin, Wild Animals of the Southwest, p.73–84   5–6

BILL: *see* United States—Government

BIOLOGY: *see also* Balance of Nature; Botany; Interdependence of Plants and Animals; Zoology
Barr, More Research Ideas for Young Scientists, p.105–26   5–6
Beauchamp, Discovering Our World, Bk.1   4
Bronson, Pollwiggle's Progress   4–5
Comstock, Handbook of Nature Study   6
Evans, All about Us   4–6
Fenton, C. L., Life Long Ago   6
Morgan, A. H., Field Book of Ponds and Streams   6

Nourse, So You Want To Be a Scientist, p.130–43   5–6

Zim, How Things Grow   4–6

———— Our Senses and How They Work   4–6

BIRD DAY: *see also* Birds

McSpadden, Book of Holidays, p.84   6

Olcott, Good Stories for Great Holidays, p.389–428   *4–6

BIRD SONG: *see* Birds—Songs

BIRDHOUSES

Jaeger, Easy Crafts, p.28–31   4–6

Leeming, Fun with Boxes, p.26–31   4–6

Spencer, P. R., Finding New Trails, p.389–97, 401–2   4

Webb, Birds in Their Homes, p.40–41   4–6

Zarchy, Let's Make Something, p.146–47   5–6

BIRDS: *see also* Audubon, John James; Bird Day; Water Birds; also names of birds, as Robins

Barr, Young Scientist Takes a Ride, p.135–46   5–6

Batchelor, Superstitious? Here's Why!, p.28–33   6

Beauchamp, Discovering Our World, Bk.1, p.24–25   4

Benary-Isbert, Shooting Star   *4–6

Bianco, All about Pets, p.91–109   5–6

Blough, After the Sun Goes Down   4–5

Bosiger, Bird Is Born   5–6

Bronson, Starlings   4–5

Brown, V., How To Make a Home Nature Museum, p.50–51, 96–100   5–6

———— How To Make a Miniature Zoo, p.165–84   5–6

Buck, M. W., In Ponds and Streams, p.54–65   4–6

———— In Yards and Gardens, p.11–23   4–6

———— Small Pets from Woods and Fields, p.66–70   4–6

Cassell, Nature Games and Activities, p.2–16   4–6

Comstock, Handbook of Nature Study, p.27–143   6

Cooper, E. K., Science in Your Own Back Yard, p.133–47   5–6

Disney, Worlds of Nature, p.35–43, 140–42, 156–59   4–6

Earle, White Patch   4–6

Fenton, C. L., Birds and Their World   5–6

———— Life Long Ago, p.216–21, 260–65   6

———— Wild Folk in the Desert, p.78–86   4–6

Fisher, J., Wonderful World of the Air, p.20–25, 27–32   5–6

Fox, From Bones to Bodies, p.33–34, 53–54   6

Gaul, Pond Book   4–6

Gillham, Beyond the Clapping Mountains   *4–6

Graham, E. H., Wildlife for America   6

Harper, Easter Chimes, p.60–67   *4–6

Hazeltine, Easter Book of Legends and Stories, p.159–62, 263–67   *5–6

Hyde, Animal Clocks and Compasses, p.36–55, 144–49   5–6

Hylander, Out of Doors in Spring, p.117–43   5–6

———— Out of Doors in Winter, p.68–104   5–6

Icenhower, First Book of the Antarctic, p.52–56   4–6

Jewett, God's Troubadour, p.51–57   5–6

Kane, Tale of a Meadow, p.11–22   4–6

Kieran, J., Introduction to Birds   5–6

Knight, C. R., Life through the Ages, p.24–25   6

Lavine, Strange Travelers, p.3–4, 8, 58–72   5–6

Lawrence, Peachtree Island, p.164–80   *4–5

Mason, G. F., Animal Clothing, p.38–51   5–6

Moe, Animal Inn, p.119–28   4–6

Morgan, A. H., Field Book of Animals in Winter, p.370–426   6

Parker, B. M., Birds   4–6

———— Golden Book of Science   4–6

———— Living Things, p.24–25   4–6

Robinson, W. W., Beasts of the Tar Pits, p.10–12   5–6

Rounds, Swamp Life   5–6

———— Wildlife at Your Doorstep, p.21–34   5–6

Smith, E. S., Christmas Book of Legends
& Stories, p.249–52   *5–6
Sperry, All about the Arctic and Antarctic, p.84–91   4–6
Webb, Birds in Their Homes   4–6
Williamson, First Book of Birds   4–6

BIRDS—AQUATIC: *see* Water Birds

BIRDS—EGGS AND NESTS
Bronson, Starlings   4–5
Fenton, C. L., Birds and Their World,
p.26–32   5–6
Parker, B. M., Birds, p.22–26   4–6
Webb, Birds in Their Homes   4–6
Williamson, First Book of Birds, p.40–
47   4–6

BIRDS—FEEDING
Hylander, Out of Doors in Winter,
p.99–104   5–6
Jaeger, Easy Crafts, p.28–29   4–6

BIRDS—FLIGHT: *see* Flight

BIRDS—HOUSES: *see* Birdhouses

BIRDS—MIGRATION
Boulton, Traveling with the Birds   4–6
Comstock, Handbook of Nature Study,
p.35–37   6
Fenton, C. L., Birds and Their World,
p.77–84   5–6
Gall, Wagtail, p.98–106   4–6
Garrett, Rufous Redtail, p.66–90, 97–
104   *4–5
Green, Home for Woody, p.53–62   4–6
Hylander, Out of Doors in Autumn,
p.123–31   5–6
Parker, B. M., Animal Travels, p.18–32
     4–6
Spencer, P. R., Finding New Trails,
p.375–85   4
Webb, Birds in Their Homes, p.64–65
     4–6
Williamson, First Book of Birds, p.52–
60   4–6

BIRDS—PICTURES
Doane, Book of Nature, p.26–27, 66–71
     5–6
Webb, Birds in Their Homes   4–6

BIRDS—PROTECTION
Parker, B. M., Birds, p.32   4–6

BIRDS—SONGS
Brown, V., How To Understand Animal
Talk, p.139–66   6
Comstock, Handbook of Nature Study,
p.42–43   6
Mason, G. F., Animal Sounds, p.10–33
     5–6

BIRDS—SOUTH AMERICA: *see also*
names of South American birds, as
Albatrosses; Parrots
Hall, E., Land and People of Argentina,
p.28–29   6

BIRDS IN WINTER
Barker, Winter-sleeping Wildlife, p.59–
64   5–6
Webb, Birds in Their Homes, p.32–33
     4–6

BIRDS OF PARADISE
Buck, F., Jungle Animals, p.22–24   5–6

BIRDS OF PREY: *see also* Eagles;
Hawks; Owls
Hylander, Out of Doors in Autumn,
p.43–57   5–6

BIRDSEYE, CLARENCE
Eberle, Basketful, p.136–39   4–6

BIRTHDAYS: *see also* Holidays; Washington's Birthday
Alden, Why the Chimes Rang   *4–6
Child Study Association of America,
Read to Yourself Storybook, p.95–
113   *4–5
Cleary, Beezus and Ramona, p.131–59
     *4–6
Jordan, Holiday Handicraft, p.209–18
     4–6
Leeming, Fun with Greeting Cards, p.92
     4–6
Milne, World of Pooh, p.70–85   *4–5
Olcott, Good Stories for Great Birthdays   *4–6
Pannell, Holiday Round Up, p.313–25
     4–6
Tudor, Becky's Birthday   *4–5

BISMARCK, OTTO VON
Foster, G., Abraham Lincoln's World,
p.225–27   6

BISON
Annixter, Buffalo Chief   *6
Bleeker, Crow Indians, p.38–58   5–6

Bridges, Zoo Babies, p.91–95   4–6

Christensen, Buffalo Kill   *6

Disney, Worlds of Nature, p.70–74   4–6

Fox, From Bones to Bodies, p.69–77 6

Franklin, Wild Animals of the Southwest, p.30–43   5–6

Hofsinde, Indian and the Buffalo 4–6

Hogner, Animal Book, p.96–100   6

Knight, C. R., Life through the Ages, p.62–63   6

Lavine, Strange Travelers, p.18–24 5–6

McClung, Shag   4–6

McCracken, Great White Buffalo   5–6

Parker, B. M., Saving Our Wild Life, p.5–6   5–6

Perkins, Marlin Perkins' Zooparade, p.88–91   4–6

Robinson, W. W., Beasts of the Tar Pits, p.34–36   5–6

Tavo, Buffalo Are Running   6

Writers Project, Lords of the Old West, no. 23   5–6

BJORNSON, BJORNSTJERNE
Deucher, Edvard Grieg, p.102–15 4–6

BLACKBIRDS: *see also* names of blackbirds, as Cowbirds; Redwings

Parker, B. M., Birds, p.9–11   4–6

Wilder, Little Town on the Prairie, p.86–107   *5–6

BLACKFOOT INDIANS: *see also* Glacier National Park

Hazeltine, Hero Tales from Many Lands, p.448–59   5–6

BLACKSMITHING
Bailey, C. S., Pioneer Art in America, p.13–24   *5–6

BLIMPS: *see* Airships

BLIND
Kelly, Christmas Nightingale, p.51–73   *6

Vance, Windows for Rosemary   *4–6

Wheeler, Handel at the Court of Kings, p.131–35   4–6

Wilder, By the Shores of Silver Lake   *5–6

Zwilgmeyer, Johnny Blossom, p.113–23   *4–6

BLIZZARDS: *see* Storms

BLOCK PRINTING
Hamilton, E. T., Handicraft for Girls, p.40–54   6

Jaeger, Easy Crafts, p.8–9   4–6

Weiss, H., Paper, Ink and Roller, p.49–55   4–6

Zarchy, Let's Make More Things, p.144–47   5–6

BLOOD: *see also* Circulatory System
Barnard, Macmillan Science-Life Series, Bk.6, p.128–41   6

BLOOD TRANSFUSIONS
Eberle, Modern Medical Discoveries, p.88–119   5–6

Schneider, L., Lifeline, p.113–23   6

BLOTTER PRINTING
Jaeger, Easy Crafts, p.10–11   4–6

BLUEBIRDS
Comstock, Handbook of Nature Study, p.62–65   6

BLUEPRINTING
Jaeger, Easy Crafts, p.4–5   4–6

BOAT RACING: *see* Racing

BOATBUILDING: *see* Shipbuilding

BOATS: *see also* Canals; Canoes; Flatboats; Ocean Travel; River Life; Sailing; Ships; Steamboats; Submarines; Tugboats; Warships

Barrows, Our Big World   4

Calhoun, Making the Mississippi Shout   *4–6

Hogeboom, Boats and How To Draw Them   4–5

Lewellen, You and American Life Lines, p.10–27   4–6

Mayne, Blue Boat   *4–6

Stefansson, Here Is Alaska, p.60–64 6

Van Stockum, Cottage at Bantry Bay, p.195–206   *6

Zaffo, Big Book of Real Boats and Ships   4–6

Zwilgmeyer, Johnny Blossom, p.134–43   *4–6

BOATS—MODELS
Gilmore, Model Boats for Beginners   5–6

Maginley, Historic Models of Early America, p.10–11, 46–48, 55–59 6

BOBCATS: *see* Lynxes

BOBWHITES: *see* Quails

BODY—HUMAN: *see* Health; Physiology

BOHEMIA: *see* Czechoslovakia

BOILING: *see* Heat

BOLÍVAR, SIMÓN
  Foster, G., Abraham Lincoln's World, p.15–18   6
  Goetz, Neighbors to the South, p.140–42   5–6
  Olcott, Good Stories for Great Birthdays, p.371–92   *4–6
  Peck, Pageant of South American History, p.231–50, 272–81   6
  Rothery, South American Roundabout, p.216–27   5–6

BOLIVIA
  Bailey, B. F., Bolivia   4–6
  Barrows, American Continents, p.329–31   5
  Goetz, Neighbors to the South, p.73–77   5–6
  Quinn, Picture Map Geography of South America, p.34–42   4–6
  Rothery, South American Roundabout, p.82–94   5–6
  Spencer, P. R., Traveling New Trails, p.308–16   6

BONAPARTE, NAPOLEON: *see* Napoleon I, Emperor of the French

BONES
  Beauchamp, Discovering Our World, Bk. 1, p.70–72   4
  Glemser, All about the Human Body, p.81–92   5–6

BONHOMME RICHARD: *see* Jones, John Paul

BONIFACE, SAINT
  Tappan, When Knights Were Bold, p.197–99   6

BONIFACIO, JOSÉ
  Goetz, Neighbors to the South, p.149–51   5–6

BOOK ENDS
  Zarchy, Let's Make Something, p.56–57   5–6

BOOKBINDING: *see also* Leather Work
  Foster, J., Pages, Pictures, and Print, p.73–86   6
  Zarchy, Let's Make More Things, p.148–53   5–6

BOOKMOBILES
  Sorensen, Curious Missie   *4–6

BOOKS: *see also* Authors; Bookbinding; Libraries; Maps; Paper; Printing
  Bailey, C. S., Children of the Handcrafts, p.95–104   5–6
  Batchelor, Communication, p.34–51   4–6
  Bentley, Young Brontës, p.70–78   6
  Foster, J., Pages, Pictures, and Print   6
  Hale, Complete Peterkin Papers, p.19–26 (The Peterkins Try To Become Wise)   *4–6
  Harshaw, What Book Is That?   4–6
  Hartman, Builders of the Old World, p.265–66, 346–56   6
  Spencer, C., Made in China, p.94–107   5–6

BOOM TOWNS
  Lenski, Boom Town Boy   *4–6

BOONE, DANIEL: *see also* Kentucky
  Averill, Daniel Boone   4–6
  Brown, J. M., Daniel Boone   6
  Daugherty, Daniel Boone   5–6
  Foster, G., George Washington's World, p.10–12, 159–61   6
  McMeekin, Journey Cake, p.205–9   *5–6
  Meadowcroft, On Indian Trails with Daniel Boone   4–5
  Steele, Daniel Boone's Echo   *4–6

BORAX
  Ault, This Is the Desert, p.112–24   5–6
  Fenton, C. L., Riches from the Earth, p.26–29   5–6

BORNEO
  Quinn, Picture Map Geography of the Pacific Islands, p.32–36   5–6

BOSTON
  Association for Childhood Education, Told under Spacious Skies, p.55–64   *4–6
  Faulkner, Melindy's Medal   *4–5
  Wibberley, John Treegate's Musket   *6

BOSTON—HISTORY: *see also* Puritans; Revere, Paul

Eaton, That Lively Man, Ben Franklin, p.11–33   6

Forbes, America's Paul Revere   4–6

BOSTON MASSACRE, 1770: *see also* Revolutionary War in America

Forbes, America's Paul Revere, p.16–19   4–6

Morris, First Book of the American Revolution, p.19–20   4–6

BOSTON TEA PARTY, 1773: *see also* Revolutionary War in America

Commager, H. S., First Book of American History, p.20–21   5–6

Forbes, America's Paul Revere, p.20–24   5–6

Pace, Early American, p.42–62   5–6

BOTANISTS: *see* names of botanists, as Linnaeus

BOTANY: *see also* Algae; Bulbs; Cells; Ferns; Flowers; Fossils; Fruit; Galls (botany); Gardening; Grafting; Grasses; Leaves; Lichens; Microscopes; Mosses; Nature Study; Parasites; Plants; Roots; Seeds; Trees; Vegetables; Weeds; Wild Flowers

Parker, B. M., Flowers, Fruits, Seeds   4–6

Selsam, Play with Trees (experiments)   4–6

BOTTICELLI, ALESSANDRO

Hillyer, Child's History of Art, p.41–45   5–6

BOTTLES

Elting, Lollypop Factory, p.81–88   4–5

Epstein, S., First Book of Glass, p.13   5–6

BOW AND ARROW

Colby, First Bow and Arrow   4–6

———— First Hunt, p.24–25   5–6

Salomon, Book of Indian Crafts & Indian Lore, p.156–76   6

BOWDITCH, NATHANIEL

Latham, Carry on, Mr. Bowditch   6

BOXES

Carlson, B. W., Make It and Use It, p.58–75   4–6

———— Make It Yourself!, p.79–96   4–6

Lee, What To Do Now, p.26–27, 32–33, 56–61   4–6

Leeming, Fun with Boxes   4–6

Sperling, How To Make Things Out of Paper, p.46–52, 86–90   5–6

BOXING

Banning, Pit Pony, p.87–88, 149–61   *4–6

BOY–GIRL RELATIONS

Bulla, Riding the Pony Express   *4–5

Seredy, Good Master   *5–6

BOY SCOUTS

Grant, B., Boy Scout Encyclopedia   5–6

BRADFORD, WILLIAM: *see also* Pilgrim Fathers

Commager, H. S., First Book of American History, p.13–14   4–6

Foster, G., World of Captain John Smith   6

Lawson, R., Watchwords of Liberty, p.3–4   4–6

Olcott, Good Stories for Great Birthdays, p.123–39   *4–6

BRAHE, TYCHO

Foster, G., World of Captain John Smith, p.116–19   6

Gallant, R., Exploring Mars, p.14–18   4–6

Rothery, Scandinavian Roundabout, p.179–80   6

BRAHMS, JOHANNES

Burch, Famous Composers for Young People, p.129–36   4–6

Wheeler, Robert Schumann and Mascot Ziff, p.134–37   4–6

BRAIDING

Leeming, Fun with String, p.117–35   4–6

BRAILLE

Vance, Windows for Rosemary, p.28–31   4–6

BRAIN

Zim, Our Senses and How They Work, p.122–30   4–6

BRAKES: *see* Air Brakes

BRANDING: *see* Ranch Life

BRASS: *see* Copper

BRASS INSTRUMENTS: *see* Wind Instruments; also names of instruments, as Trumpets

BRAVERY: *see* Courage

BRAZIL: *see also* Amazon River; Amazon Valley; Markets—Brazil; Rio de Janeiro
Barrows, American Continents, p.333–43　5
Brown, R. J., Land and People of Brazil　6
Goetz, Neighbors to the South, p.105–12　5–6
Henry, M., Brazil　4–6
May, Let's Read about Brazil　4–6
Quinn, Picture Map Geography of South America, p.79–92　4–6
Rothery, South American Roundabout, p.164–201　5–6
Spencer, P. R., Traveling New Trails, p.290–94　6
Sperry, All about the Jungle, p.15–50　5–6

BRAZIL—HISTORY
Brown, R. J., Land and People of Brazil, p.22–41　6
Peck, Pageant of South American History, p.109–23, 193–213, 305–28　6

BRAZIL—INDUSTRIES
Brown, R. J., Land and People of Brazil　6
May, Let's Read about Brazil, p.84–85　4–6

BREAD: *see also* Bakers; Cooking; Flour; Flour Mills
Buehr, Bread　4–6
Eberle, Basketful, p.24–31　4–6
Scheib, First Book of Food, p.9–14　5–6
Schwartz, It's Fun To Know Why, p.83–92　5–6

BREATHING: *see* Respiration

BRENDAN, SAINT
Hazeltine, Easter Book of Legends and Stories, p.159–62　*5–6

BRICKS: *see also* Adobe Bricks; Clay; Tiles
Burns, World Full of Homes, p.69–72　4–6

Writers Project, Story of Clay, no.24, p.32–36　5–6

BRIDGER, JAMES
Anderson, A. M., Fur Trappers of the Old West　5–6
Garst, Jim Bridger　6
———— Kit Carson　6

BRIDGES: *see also* Avignon, France; Rivers; San Francisco—Bridges
Association for Childhood Education, Told under the Stars and Stripes, p.115–21 (from We're All Americans)　*4–6
Barr, Young Scientist Takes a Ride, p.151–52　5–6
Bethers, Perhaps I'll Be a Railroad Man, p.14–15　5–6
Fenner, Time To Laugh, p.67–73　*4–6
Henry, R. S., Trains, p.27–34　5–6
Hillyer, Child's History of Art, p.413–19　5–6
Jackson, D., Wonderful World of Engineering, p.46–61　6
Peet, First Book of Bridges　5–6
Schneider, H., Science Fun with Milk Cartons, p.14–79　5–6
Van Metre, Trains, Tracks and Travel, p.83–87　6

BRIDGET, SAINT
Farjeon, Ten Saints, p.35–44　6
Sawyer, This Way to Christmas, p.149–57　4–6

BRITISH COLUMBIA
Quinn, Picture Map Geography of Canada and Alaska, p.76–85　4–6

BRITISH HONDURAS
Henry, M., British Honduras　4–6
Quinn, Picture Map Geography of Mexico, Central America and the West Indies, p.27–31　4–6

BRITISH IN AMERICA
Dalgliesh, America Begins, p.36, 55–59, 62–63　4–5
Duvoisin, And There Was America, p.15–17, 41–75　4–6
Ross, F. A., Land and People of Canada, p.69–76　6

BRITISH ISLES: *see also* England; Ireland; Scotland; Wales
Barrows, Old World Lands, p.22–39　6

BRITONS: *see* Vortigern, King of the
Britons

BRITTANY: *see also* Costume—Brittany
Barrows, Old World Lands, p.73–74   6
Bragdon, L. J., Land and People of
France, p.72–75   6

BRITTANY—FOLK TALES
Harper, Ghosts and Goblins, p.219–35
                                            4–6
Hazeltine, Easter Book of Legends and
Stories, p.115–29   5–6
Sawyer, Long Christmas, p.137–50 4–6

BROADCASTING: *see* Radio Broadcasting; Television

BRONTË FAMILY
Bentley, Young Brontës   6

BRONZE AGE
Writers Project, Aluminum, no.31, p.8–
11   5–6

BROOKS
Comstock, Handbook of Nature Study,
p.736–42   6

BROTHERHOOD OF MAN: *see also*
Friendship; Religious Understanding;
also names of national groups in the
United States, as Norwegians in the
United States
De Angeli, Bright April   *4–6
Evans, All about Us   4–6
Jackson, J., Call Me Charley   *5–6
Lillie, Book of Three Festivals, p.45–60,
170–89   *5–6
Oakes, Bamboo Gate, p.102–20   *4–6
Rogers, F., Big Miss Liberty   *5–6
Seredy, Singing Tree   *6
Wagner, Put Democracy to Work, p.77–
84   6

BROWNIES: *see* Girl Scouts

BRUNELLESCHI, FILIPPO
Hillyer, Child's History of Art, p.370–
73   5–6

BRUNHILD: *see* Siegfried

BRYCE CANYON NATIONAL PARK
Melbo, Our Country's National Parks,
v.1, p.231–41   5–6

BRYOZOA
Morgan, A. H., Field Book of Animals
in Winter, p.90–96   6

—————— Field Book of Ponds and
Streams, p.131–38   6

BUCHANAN, JAMES
Beard, Presidents in American History,
p.65–66, 163–64   6
Coy, First Book of Presidents, p.41
                                            4–6
Petersham, Story of the Presidents of
the United States, p.38–39   4–6

BUDDHISM
Caldwell, Let's Visit Pakistan, p.34–35
                                            4–6
Coatsworth, Cat Who Went to Heaven
                                            *4–6
Fitch, Their Search for God, p.110–55
                                            5–6
Modak, Land and People of India,
p.44–56   6
Rankin, L., Daughter of the Mountains,
p.12–26, 53–55   *5–6
Spencer, C., Land of the Chinese Peo-
ple, p.27–29, 31–32, 36–38   6

BUDS: *see* Flowers

BUENOS AIRES
Rothery, South American Roundabout,
p.142–48   5–6

BUFFALO BILL
Aulaire, Buffalo Bill   4
Garst, Buffalo Bill   6
Spencer, P. R., Finding New Trails,
p.235–44   4

BUFFALOES: *see* Bison; Gaurs

BUGLES
Rietveld, Nicky's Bugle   *4–6

BUGS
Hylander, Insects on Parade, p.59–77
                                              6
Lane, F. C., All about the Insect World,
p.62–65   5–6
Teale, Insect Friends, p.63–66   5–6
—————— Junior Book of Insects, p.183–
90   6
Williamson, First Book of Bugs   4–5

BUILDING MATERIALS:
see also Bricks; Cement; Concrete;
Glass; Iron; Lumbering; Minerals;
Steel; Tiles; Wood
Parker, B. M., Earth a Great Store-
house, p.4–8   4–6

BUILDINGS—CONSTRUCTION
Jackson, D., Wonderful World of Engineering, p.24–35   6

BULBS: *see also* Flowers; Gardening; Plants
Parker, B. M., Garden Indoors, p.7–10
                                                5–6

BULGARIA
Barrows, Old World Lands, p.113–14
                                                 6
Shannon, Dobry   *5–6

BULGARIA—FOLK TALES
Shannon, Dobry, p.60–66, 133–38, 157–62   5–6

BULL, OLE BORNEMANN
Deucher, Edvard Grieg, p.42–45, 77–81
                                                4–6

BULLS: *see also* Cattle
Robertson, K., Ticktock and Jim, p.3–11, 42–49, 82–83   *4–6

BUNCHE, RALPH
Shackelford, Child's Story of the Negro, p.208–11   4–5

BUNKER HILL—BATTLE OF, 1775: *see* Revolutionary War in America

BUNYAN, PAUL
Buehr, Timber!, p.43–46   5–6
Fenner, Fools and Funny Fellows, p.96–103   4–6
———— Time To Laugh, p.74–84
                                                4–6

BUOYANCY: *see* Flotation

BURIAL
Bleeker, Inca, p.16, 112–13   5–6

BURLEIGH, HENRY THACKER
Shackelford, Child's Story of the Negro, p.173–75   4–5

BURMA
Barrows, Old World Lands, p.66–67 6
Lindquist, W., Burma Boy   *4–6
Quinn, Picture Map Geography of Asia, p.67–72   4–6

BURMA ROAD
Boardman, Roads, p.112–15   6
Bothwell, First Book of Roads, p.64
                                                5–6
Oakes, Bamboo Gate, p.1–20   *4–6

BURNS, ROBERT
Coffman, Famous Authors for Young People, p.13–17   5–6

BURR, AARON
Crouse, A. E., Alexander Hamilton and Aaron Burr   6

BURROS: *see* Donkeys

BURROWS: *see* Animals—Houses

BURTON, RICHARD FRANCIS
Cottler, Heroes of Civilization, p.54–64
                                                6

BUSHMEN
Gatti, Here Is the Veld, p.10–22   6

BUSINESS: *see also* Advertising; Industries; Mail Service; Manufacturing; Markets; Money; Peddlers; Shopping; Stores; Trade; Typewriters
Hartman, Machines, p.245–60   6

BUSINESS DEPRESSION
Hartman, Machines, p.256–60   6
Langton, Majesty of Grace   *4–5

BUTTER
Canfield, Understood Betsy, p.51–57
                                                *5–6
Eberle, Basketful, p.194–98   4–6

BUTTERFLIES: *see also* Caterpillars; Moths
Barker, Winter-sleeping Wildlife, p.105–7   5–6
Buck, M. W., In Yards and Gardens, p.49–51   4–6
Comstock, Handbook of Nature Study, p.301–10   6
Eeckhoudt, Butterfly Is Born   4–6
Gall, Little Black Ant, p.105–10 *4–5
Gaul, Picture Book of Insects, p.22–23, 26–27   4–6
Hyde, Animal Clocks and Compasses, p.80–84   5–6
Hylander, Insects on Parade, p.99–125
                                                6
Kipling, Just So Stories, p.225–47
                                                *4–6
Lane, F. C., All about the Insect World, p.17–22   5–6
Lavine, Strange Travelers, p.72–78
                                                5–6
Lemmon, All about Moths and Butterflies, p.75–122   5–6

Lutz, Field Book of Insects, p.114–223
4–6
McClung, Tiger 4–5
Marcher, Monarch Butterfly 4–5
Parker, B. M., Insects and Their Ways, p.6–8 4–6
Teale, Insect Friends, p.45–52 5–6
Williamson, First Book of Bugs, p.34–38 4–5

BUYING: *see* Trade

BYRD, RICHARD EVELYN
Frank, Ice Island, p.138–82, 210–13
6

BYZANTINE EMPIRE
Bergere, From Stones to Skyscrapers, p.42–44 6
Bryson, Twenty Miracles of Saint Nicolas 5–6
Chubb, Byzantines 6

CABEZA DE VACA, ÁLVAR NÚÑEZ
American Heritage, Discoverers of the New World, p.90–94 5–6

CABLE CARS
Bechdolt, Going Up, p.87–93 5–6

CABLES: *see also* Atlantic Cable
Rogers, F., Heels, Wheels, and Wire, p.107–20 5–6

CABOT, JOHN
American Heritage, Discoverers of the New World, p.37–41 5–6
Dalgliesh, America Begins, p.36 4–5
Duvoisin, And There Was America, p.15–17 4–6
McGuire, Brave Young Land, p.119–23 5–6

CABRILLO, JUAN RODRIGUEZ
Dawson, California, p.33–38 5–6

CACAO: *see* Chocolate

CACTUS
Buff, Elf Owl, p.7–12 4–5
Disney, Worlds of Nature, p.82–87
4–6
McKenny, Trees of the Countryside, p.62–63 4–6

CADDIS FLY
Comstock, Handbook of Nature Study, p.408–11 6

Cooper, E. K., Science on the Shores and Banks, p.83–86 5–6
Hylander, Insects on Parade, p.158–60
6
Mason, G. F., Animal Homes, p.85–88
4–6

CAESAR, JULIUS
Falls, First 3000 Years, p.199–201 6
Farjeon, Mighty Men, p.92–96 4–6
Gunther, Julius Caesar 6
Hartman, Builders of the Old World, p.189–92 6
Hillyer, Child's History of the World, p.184–90 5–6

CAIRO
Spencer, P. R., Finding New Trails, p.345–53 4

CALCIUM
Loomis, Field Book of Common Rocks and Minerals, p.143–52 6

CALENDARS: *see also* Geological Calendar; Seasons; Time
Adler, Time in Your Life, p.35–41 4–6
Bleeker, Inca, p.121–22, 127–28 5–6
———— Maya, p.108–10 5–6
Brindze, Story of Our Calendar 4–6
Galt, Seven Days from Sunday, p.98–100, 108–11 6
Sechrist, Red Letter Days, p.15–26
5–6
Tannenbaum, Understanding Time, p. 89–107 6

CALIFORNIA: *see also* Fruit Culture; Kings Canyon National Park; Lassen Volcanic National Park; Los Angeles; Motion Pictures; San Francisco; Sequoia National Park; Sequoias; Spanish Missions in California; Yosemite National Park
Association for Childhood Education, Told under Spacious Skies, p.302–12
*4–6
Barrows, American Continents, p.220–26 5
Beals, Rush for Gold 5–6
Bulla, Secret Valley *4–5
Cameron, Terrible Churnadryne *4–6
Dorian, Hokahey!, p.64–72 5–6
Gates, Blue Willow *5–6

———— Sarah's Idea　　　　　　　　*4–6
———— Sensible Kate　　　　　　　　*4–6
McNeer, Story of California　　　　4–6
Pohlmann, Myrtle Albertina's Secret
　　　　　　　　　　　　　　　*4–6
Quinn, Picture Map Geography of the
　United States, p.180–83　　　　4–6
Smith, J. R., Neighbors around the
　World, p.130–42　　　　　　　　4
Uchida, Mik and the Prowler　　*4–6
———— Promised Year　　　　　　*4–6

CALIFORNIA—HISTORY
Bauer, California Gold Days　　　5–6
Beals, Kit Carson　　　　　　　　5–6
———— Rush for Gold　　　　　　5–6
Bleeker, Mission Indians of California
　　　　　　　　　　　　　　　4–6
Bothwell, First Book of Roads, p.62 (El
　Camino Real)　　　　　　　　5–6
Commager, H. S., First Book of Ameri-
　can History, p.35–38　　　　　4–6
Dawson, California　　　　　　　5–6
Driggs, Pony Express Goes Through,
　p.1–14　　　　　　　　　　　6
Havighurst, First Book of the Oregon
　Trail　　　　　　　　　　　　4–6
McNeer, California Gold Rush　　4–6
Politi, Mission Bell　　　　　　　4–6

CALIFORNIA GOLD RUSH
Bauer, California Gold Days　　　5–6
Beals, Rush for Gold　　　　　　5–6
Dawson, California, p.143–52　　5–6
Driggs, Pony Express Goes Through,
　p.8–14　　　　　　　　　　　6
McNeer, California Gold Rush　　4–6
Meadowcroft, Land of the Free, p.89–
　91　　　　　　　　　　　　　4–5

CAMELS
Ault, This Is the Desert, p.78–94　5–6
Kipling, Just So Stories, p.15–27　*4–6
Lavine, Strange Travelers, p.48, 50–52
　　　　　　　　　　　　　　　5–6
Osmond, Animals of the World, v.1　4–6
Parker, B. M., Animals We Know,
　p.18–19　　　　　　　　　　　5–6
Perkins, Marlin Perkins' Zooparade,
　p.58–61　　　　　　　　　　　4–6
Robinson, W. W., Beasts of the Tar Pits,
　p.18–20　　　　　　　　　　　5–6

CAMERAS: *see* Photography

CAMPING: *see also* Automobiles—Trail-
　ers; Boy Scouts; Girl Scouts
Beim, Just Plain Maggie　　　　*4–6
Carlson, B. W., Do It Yourself　4–6
Colby, First Camping Trip　　　5–6
Du Soe, Three without Fear　　*4–6
Marshall, Invisible Island　　　*4–6
Mason, B. S., Junior Book of Camping
　and Woodcraft　　　　　　　5–6
New York Herald Tribune, Young
　America's Cook Book, p.276–84
　　　　　　　　　　　　　　　4–6
Renick, M. L., John's Back Yard Camp
　　　　　　　　　　　　　　　*4–5

CANADA: *see also* Fundy—Bay of; New-
　foundland; Nova Scotia; Quebec; St.
　Lawrence River; Songs—Canada
Barrows, American Continents, p.257–
　78　　　　　　　　　　　　　5
Bergaust, Rockets around the World,
　p.33–35　　　　　　　　　　　6
Bowers, Wishing Book Doll　　*4–5
Carlson, N. S., Alphonse, That Bearded
　One　　　　　　　　　　　　*4–6
Holling, Paddle-to-the-Sea　　*4–6
Lippincott, Wilderness Champion, p.1–
　89, 167–95　　　　　　　　　*5–6
Quinn, Picture Map Geography of Can-
　ada and Alaska　　　　　　　4–6
Ross, F. A., Land and People of Canada
　　　　　　　　　　　　　　　6
Spencer, P. R., Exploring New Trails,
　p.281–327　　　　　　　　　　5
Tor, Getting To Know Canada　4–6
Van Stockum, Canadian Summer　*5–6
———— Friendly Gables　　　　*5–6

CANADA—ART: *see* Art—Canada

CANADA—FOLK TALES
Van Stockum, Canadian Summer,
　p.160–63　　　　　　　　　　5–6

CANADA—GAMES: *see* Games—Can-
　ada

CANADA—GOVERNMENT
Ross, F. A., Land and People of Canada
　　　　　　　　　　　　　　　6

CANADA—HISTORY: *see also* Cartier,
　Jacques; Champlain, Samuel de;
　French and Indian War, 1755-63;
　French in America; La Salle, René
　Robert Cavelier, Sieur de

American Heritage, Discoverers of the New World, p.112–25   5–6
————— Trappers and Mountain Men   6
Averill, Cartier Sails the St. Lawrence   4–6
Bonner, Canada and Her Story   5–6
Graham, A. P., La Salle, River Explorer   4–6
Judson, St. Lawrence Seaway   6
McNeer, Canadian Story   5–6
Ross, F. A., Land and People of Canada, p.58–119   6

CANADA—INDUSTRIES
Ross, F. A., Land and People of Canada, p.29–30   6

CANADA—ROYAL CANADIAN MOUNTED POLICE
Bonner, Canada and Her Story, p.126–48   5–6
McNeer, Alaska Gold Rush   5–6
————— Canadian Story, p.70–74   5–6
O'Brien, Silver Chief   *6
Ross, F. A., Land and People of Canada, p.99–101   6
Spencer, P. R., Exploring New Trails, p.295–304   5

CANALS: *see also* Erie Canal; Irrigation; Netherlands; Panama Canal; St. Lawrence River; Suez Canal
Boardman, Canals   6
Buehr, Through the Locks   5–6
Dalgliesh, America Travels, p.37–44   4–6
Jackson, D., Wonderful World of Engineering, p.76–81   6
Judson, St. Lawrence Seaway   6
Lauber, Changing the Face of North America   5–6
Schneider, H., Science Fun with Milk Cartons, p.112–22   5–6
Spencer, P. R., Traveling New Trails, p.387–405   6

CANARIES
Brown, V., How To Understand Animal Talk, p.47   6
Comstock, Handbook of Nature Study, p.53–57   6

CANDLES
Orton, Treasure in the Little Trunk, p.18–25   *4–6

Robinson, J., Things To Make from Odds & Ends, p.46–47   6
Schneider, H., Everyday Machines and How They Work, p.123–25   5–6
Wilder, Farmer Boy, p.283–84   *4–6

CANDY
Beeler, Experiments in Chemistry, p.30–33   5–6
Elting, Lollypop Factory, p.5–16   4–5
New York Herald Tribune, Young America's Cook Book, p.243–51   4–6
Rombauer, Cookbook for Boys and Girls, p.199–207   6

CANNIBALS
Sperry, Call It Courage, p.45–88   *5–6

CANNING: *see also* Salmon
Lent, Men at Work in the Great Lakes States, p.26–29   4–6
New York Herald Tribune, Young America's Cook Book, p.210–26   4–6
Writers Project, Salmon, no.15, p.35–40   5–6

CANNON: *see* Guns

CANOES
Bleeker, Chippewa Indians, p.36–43   5–6
Holling, Book of Indians, p.103–5   4–6
Tunis, Indians, p.53–56, 140–42   6

CANYONS: *see also* Bryce Canyon National Park; Grand Canyon National Park; Kings Canyon National Park; Zion National Park
Fenton, C. L., Land We Live On, p.42–43   4–6

CAPE PROVINCE
Stinetorf, Children of South Africa, p.24–36, 119–32   *5–6

CAPILLARITY: *see* Surface Tension

CAR LIFT
Barr, Young Scientist Takes a Ride, p.35–36   5–6

CARAVANS: *see also* Camels; Conestoga Wagons; Deserts; Westward Movement
Kent, He Went with Marco Polo   *6
Oakes, Bamboo Gate, p.121–37   *4–6

Potter, Fairy Caravan   *4–5
Rankin, L., Daughter of the Mountains
     *5–6

CARBON: *see also* Chemistry
Huey, What Makes the Wheels Go
     Round, p.53–55   6
Loomis, Field Book of Common Rocks
     and Minerals, p.156–59   6

CARBON DATING
Fermi, Story of Atomic Energy, p.166–
     168   6
Lauber, All about the Ice Age, p.48–51
     4–6

CARBON DIOXIDE
Beeler, Experiments in Science, p.125–
     28   5–6
Morgan, A. P., First Chemistry Book
     for Boys and Girls, p.129–42   5–6
Parker, B. M., What Things Are Made
     Of, p.18–19   5–6

CARCAJOUS: *see* Wolverines

CARDINAL BIRDS
Comstock, Handbook of Nature Study,
     p.127–30   6
Webb, Birds in Their Homes, p.16–17
     4–6

CAREFULNESS: *see* Safety

CARGOES: *see* Trade

CARIBOUS
Bronson, Horns and Antlers, p.113–25
     5–6
Hyde, Animal Clocks and Compasses,
     p.96–97   5–6
Lavine, Strange Travelers, p.30–34
     5–6
Smith, J. R., Neighbors around the
     World, p.52–53   4

CARLSBAD CAVERNS NATIONAL
     PARK
Lavine, Strange Travelers, p.85–86
     5–6
Longsworth, Exploring Caves, p.58–59
     6
Melbo, Our Country's National Parks,
     v.1, p.47–65   6

CARLYLE, THOMAS
Coffman, Famous Authors for Young
     People, p.39–44   5–6

CARNEGIE, ANDREW
Commager, H. S., First Book of Ameri-
     can History, p.56–57   4–6

CARNIVALS: *see* Fairs

CAROLINE ISLANDS
Quinn, Picture Map Geography of the
     Pacific Islands, p.57–61   5–6

CARPENTER, JOHN ALDEN
Burch, Modern Composers for Young
     People, p.145–48   5–6

CARPENTRY: *see also* Animals—Houses;
     Birdhouses; Handicraft; Houses; Log
     Cabins; Tools; Toys; Wood Carving
Leavitt, True Book of Tools for Building
     4–6
Maginley, Make It and Ride It   5–6
Zarchy, Let's Make More Things, p.28–
     29, 32–35   5–6

CARRIAGES
Dalgliesh, America Travels, p.65–70
     *4–6
Maginley, Historic Models of Early
     America, p.23–27   6
Rombauer, Cookbook for Boys and
     Girls, p.202–3   6

CARRIER PIGEONS: *see* Pigeons

CARROLL, LEWIS
Coffman, Famous Authors for Young
     People, p.93–97   5–6

CARSON, KIT
Beals, Kit Carson   5–6
Garst, Kit Carson   6

CARTIER, JACQUES
American Heritage, Discoverers of the
     New World, p.112–19   5–6
Averill, Cartier Sails the St. Lawrence
     4–6
Bonner, Canada and Her Story, p.3–23
     5–6
Duvoisin, And There Was America,
     p.25–26   4–6
McGuire, Brave Young Land, p.139–42
     5–6
Syme, Cartier   4–6

CARTOONS
Lent, "I Work on a Newspaper," p.116–
     24   6
Witty, You and the Constitution of the
     United States   5–6

CARVER, GEORGE WASHINGTON
Asimov, Breakthroughs in Science, p.172–76   5–6
Eberle, Basketful, p.235–39   4–6
Fisher, D. F. C., And Long Remember, p.96–111   6
Graham, S., George Washington Carver   6
McNeer, Armed with Courage, p.41–54   5–6
Shackelford, Child's Story of the Negro, p.137–44   4–5

CARVING: *see* Sculpture; Soap Sculpture; Wood Carving

CASH REGISTERS
Lent, Men at Work in the Great Lakes States, p.106-9   4–6

CASHMERE: *see* Kashmir

CASSOWARIES
Buck, F., Jungle Animals, p.312   5–6

CASTLES: *see also* Middle Ages
Boardman, Castles   6
Buehr, Knights and Castles and Feudal Life, p.26–45   4–6
Duggan, Castle Book   5–6
Hillyer, Child's History of Art, p.340–42   5–6
_____ Child's History of the World, p.272–77   5–6
Holland, Christopher Goes to the Castle   4–5
Owen, Denmark Caravan   5–6
Tappan, When Knights Were Bold, p.52–101   6

CATBIRDS
Comstock, Handbook of Nature Study, p.95–97   6
Webb, Birds in Their Homes, p.15   4–6

CATERPILLARS: *see also* Butterflies; Moths
Gall, Little Black Ant, p.54–60   4–5
Hazeltine, Easter Book of Legends and Stories, p.97–104   *5–6
Hylander, Out of Doors in Spring, p.102–16   5–6
Lemmon, All about Moths and Butterflies, p.16–26   5–6

CATERPILLARS—COLLECTING
Enright, Then There Were Five, p.71–82   *5–6

CATHEDRALS
Hillyer, Child's History of Art, p.347–62   5–6
_____ Child's History of the World, p.304–10   5–6
Lamprey, All the Ways of Building, p.189–202   6
Lownsbery, Boy Knight of Reims   *6
Owen, Denmark Caravan   5–6

CATHERINE II, EMPRESS OF RUSSIA
Foster, G., George Washington's World, p.35–37, 98–101, 271–74, 328–29   6

CATHOLIC CHURCH
Bishop, C. H., Martin de Porres, Hero   6
Epstein, S., First Book of Italy, p.34–36   5–6
Fitch, One God, p.58–97   5–6
Parish, Our Lady of Guadalupe   *4–6

CATHOLICS
Angelo, Bells of Bleeker Street   *4–6

CATHOLICS—HOLIDAYS
Burnett, B., First Book of Holidays, p.57   4–5

CATS: *see also* members of cat family, as Jaguars; Leopards; Lions; Lynxes; Panthers; Tigers
Bannon, Patty Paints a Picture   *4–5
Bianco, All about Pets, p.49–68   5–6
Boutwell, Sailor Tom   *4–6
Bronson, Cats   4–5
Brown, V., How To Understand Animal Talk, p.20–24, 64–73 (wild cat)   6
Carlson, N. S., Talking Cat, p.17–29   *4–6
Coatsworth, Alice-All-By-Herself, p.146–58   *4–6
_____ Cat Who Went to Heaven   *4–6
_____ Littlest House, p.30–42   *4–6
Comstock, Handbook of Nature Study, p.260–66   6
Dalgliesh, Blue Teapot, p.27–38   *4–6
De la Mare, Animal Stories, p.52–57, 59–69, 116–26, 134–42   *4–6
Dobson, Hero   *4–5
Haywood, Betsy's Winterhouse, p.73–108, 128–47   *4–5
Henry, J., Tiger's Chance   *4–6
Henry, M., Benjamin West and His Cat Grimalkin   4–6

————— King of the Wind, p.86–156
*5–6
Hogeboom, Familiar Animals and How
To Draw Them, p.28–31   4–5
Hogner, Animal Book, p.148–56   6
————— Barnyard Family, p.64–66
5–6
————— Cat Family   4–5
————— Farm Animals, p.173–77   6
Howard, J., 13th Is Magic   *4–6
Hyde, Animal Clocks and Compasses,
p.105–9   5–6
Johnson, S. J., Cat Hotel   *4–6
Kipling, Just So Stories, p.197–221
*4–6
Knight, C. R., Life through the Ages,
p.40–41   6
Koenig, Seven Special Cats   *4–5
Mason, G. F., Animal Tracks, p.84–85
4–6
Nash, While Mrs. Coverlet Was Away
*4–5
Robinson, W. W., Beasts of the Tar
Pits, p.22–24 (saber tooth)   5–6
Rombauer, Cookbook for Boys and
Girls, p.72   *6
Sayers, Ginny and Custard   *4–6
Scott, S., Brand New Kitten   *4–5
Seaman, Mr. Peck's Pets, p.46–51
*4–5
Sleigh, Carbonel   *4–6
————— Kingdom of Carbonel   *4–6
Todd, Space Cat   *4–5
————— Space Cat Meets Mars   *4–5
————— Space Cat Visits Venus   *4–5
Uchida, Mik and the Prowler   *4–6
————— Promised Year   *4–6
Weeks, Tales of a Common Pigeon,
p.19–24   *4–6
Weil, Animal Families   4
White, A. H., Story of Serapina   *4–6
Will, Two Reds   *4–5
Williams, U. M., Island MacKenzie
*5–6
Woolley, Ginnie and Geneva, p.55–62,
87–103, 164   *4–5
Wyndham, Susie and the Dancing Cat
*4–6
Zim, Big Cats   5–6

CATTLE: *see also* Cows; Meat Industry;
Milk

Brown, V., How To Understand Animal
Talk, p.28–31   6
Comstock, Handbook of Nature Study,
p.280–86   6
Eberle, Basketful, p.51–71   4–6
Garst, Cowboys and Cattle Trails   4–6
Gatti, Here Is the Veld, p.88–92   6
Hogner, Barnyard Family, p.23–36
5–6
————— Farm Animals, p.40–66   6
Robertson, K., Ticktock and Jim, p.83–
90   *4–6
Wilder, Little House on the Prairie,
p.162–71   *4–6

CAUCASIA
Nazaroff, Land of the Russian People,
p.51–59   6

CAVE DRAWINGS
Andrews, All about Strange Beasts of
the Past, p.133–42   5–6
Baumann, Caves of the Great Hunters
6
Hartman, Builders of the Old World,
p.18–19   6

CAVE DWELLERS
Burns, World Full of Homes, p.31–39
4–6
Hartman, Builders of the Old World,
p.16–26   6
Longsworth, Exploring Caves, p.124–38
6

CAVES: *see also* Carlsbad Caverns Na-
tional Park; Cave Dwellers; Mam-
moth Cave National Park; Wind Cave
National Park
Baumann, Caves of the Great Hunters
6
Hamilton, E., First Book of Caves   5–6
Longsworth, Exploring Caves   6
Sterling, Story of Caves   5–6
White, A. T., All about Our Changing
Rocks, p.94–97   5–6

CELLINI, BENVENUTO
Hillyer, Child's History of Art, p.228–
31   5–6

CELLS: *see also* Biology; Botany; Protozoa
Disraeli, New Worlds through the Microscope, p.85–90   6
Reed, Earth for Sam, p.13–22   6

CEMENT
Schwartz, It's Fun To Know Why, p.31–37   5–6
Writers Project, Cement, no.33   5–6

CENTER OF GRAVITY: *see* Gravitation

CENTIPEDES: *see* Scorpions

CENTRAL AMERICA: *see also* Bananas; British Honduras; Costa Rica; Guatemala; Honduras; Nicaragua; Panama; Salvador
Bleeker, Maya   5–6
Goetz, Neighbors to the South, p.27–51   5–6
Quinn, Picture Map Geography of Mexico, Central America and the West Indies, p.13–77   4–6
Rothery, Central American Roundabout   6

CENTRAL ASIA: *see* Turkestan ·

CENTRAL PLAIN: *see* Great Plains

CENTRIFUGAL FORCE
Adler, Things That Spin   5–6
Schneider, H., Everyday Machines and How They Work, p.176–77   5–6

CEYLON
Barrows, Old World Lands, p.196–99   6
Murphey, Nihal   *5–6
Pace, Juliette Low, p.103   5–6
Quinn, Picture Map Geography of Asia, p.60–61   4–6

CHALDEA: *see* Babylonia; Iraq

CHALIAPIN, FEODOR IVANOVITCH
Schwimmer, Great Musicians as Children, p.131–40   6

CHALK
Williams, H. L., Stories in Rocks, p.55–57   6

CHAMOIS
Osmond, Animals of the World, v.3   4–6

CHAMPLAIN, SAMUEL DE
American Heritage, Discoverers of the New World, p.118–25   5–6
Bonner, Canada and Her Story, p.25–38   5–6
Duvoisin, And There Was America, p.26–31   4–6

Edwards, Champlain   4–6
Foster, G., World of Captain John Smith   6
McGuire, Brave Young Land, p.145–54   5–6

CHANTEYS: *see* Sea Songs

CHAPMAN, JOHN: *see* Appleseed, Johnny

CHARACTER EDUCATION: *see* Adaptability; Cheerfulness; Cleanliness; Consideration of Others; Fear—Overcoming; Generosity; Honesty; Kindness; Obedience; Responsibility; Self-appraisal; Self-confidence; Self-control; Self-reliance

CHARADES
Mulac, Game Book, p.90–91, 93–95   6

CHARCOAL
Beeler, Experiments in Science, p.80–82   5–6

CHARIOTS
Mellin, Horses across the Ages, p.26–32   4–6

CHARLEMAGNE, EMPEROR OF THE WEST
Hartman, Builders of the Old World, p.217–20   6
Hillyer, Child's History of the World, p.257–63   5–6
Tappan, When Knights Were Bold, p.199–203   6

CHARLEMAGNE ROMANCES: *see* Ogier the Dane; Roland

CHEERFULNESS
Alden, Why the Chimes Rang   *4–6

CHEESE
Barrows, Our Big World   4
Eberle, Basketful, p.198–200   4–6
Lent, Men at Work in the Great Lakes States, p.110–13   4–6
Scheib, First Book of Food, p.21–23   5–6
Wilder, Little House in the Big Woods, p.187–92   *4–6

CHEETAHS
Perkins, Marlin Perkins' Zooparade, p.20–23   4–6
Zim, Big Cats, p.47–50   5–6

CHEMICAL GARDENS
Beeler, Experiments in Science, p.92–94   5–6

CHEMISTRY: *see also* Alloys; Atoms; Canning; Coal-Tar Products; Color; Combustion; Dyeing; Experiments—Scientific; Fertilizers; Gases, Liquids, Solids; Helium; Physics; Rayon; Sugar
Barr, More Research Ideas for Young Scientists, p.14–29   5–6
Beeler, Experiments in Chemistry   5–6
Bischof, Atoms at Work   5–6
Freeman, I. M., All about the Wonders of Chemistry   6
Gallant, R. A., Exploring Chemistry   6
Meyer, Picture Book of Chemistry   4–6
Morgan, A. P., Boys' Book of Science and Construction, p.28–92   6
———— First Electrical Book for Boys, p.242–49   6
Nourse, So You Want To Be a Scientist, p.115–29   5–6
Parker, B. M., What Things Are Made Of   5–6
Tappan, When Knights Were Bold, p.322–29   6
Writers Project, Aluminum, no.31, p.13–34   5–6

CHEMISTRY—EXPERIMENTS
Freeman, M. B., Fun with Chemistry   4–6
Morgan, A. P., First Chemistry Book for Boys and Girls   5–6
Podendorf, 101 Science Experiments, p.116–27   4–5

CHEMISTS: *see* names of chemists, as Carver, George Washington

CHEROKEE INDIANS
Bleeker, Cherokee   4–6
Dorian, Hokahey!, p.36–39   5–6
Fletcher, S. E., American Indian, p.89–95   5–6
McNeer, Story of the Southern Highlands   4–6
Melbo, Our Country's National Parks, v.1, p.138–39   6

CHERRY TREES
Guilcher, Fruit Is Born, p.20–24   5–6

CHESS
Reinfeld, Chess for Children   5–6

CHESTNUT TREES
Comstock, Handbook of Nature Study, p.645–50   6
Cormack, First Book of Trees, p.68   4–6
McKenny, Trees of the Countryside, p.40–41   4–6

CHEWINKS: *see* Towhees

CHEYENNE INDIANS
Penney, Moki   *4–5

CHIANG KAI-SHEK
Caldwell, Let's Visit China, p.63–70   5–6

CHICAGO: *see also* Addams, Jane
Bialk, Taffy's Foal   *4–5
Judson, City Neighbor   6
———— Lost Violin   *5–6
King, Key to Chicago   4–6
Lauber, Changing the Face of North America, p.83–88   5–6
Meadowcroft, By Secret Railway   *5–6

CHICAGO—FIRE, 1871
King, Key to Chicago, p.97–103   4–6

CHICAGO—WORLD'S COLUMBIAN EXPOSITION, 1893
Judson, Lost Violin, p.130–31, 199–204 *5–6

CHICKADEES
Comstock, Handbook of Nature Study, p.68–70   6
Webb, Birds in Their Homes, p.39   4–6

CHICKENS: *see also* Poultry
Brown, V., How To Understand Animal Talk, p.37–41   6
Butterfield, Jaime and His Hen Pollita *4–5
Carlson, N. S., Talking Cat, p.43–53   *4–6
Comstock, Handbook of Nature Study, p.47–49   6
De la Mare, Animal Stories, p.47–50   *4–6
Hogeboom, Familiar Animals and How To Draw Them, p.12–15   4–5
Weil, Animal Families   4

CHILD LABOR
Lenski, Judy's Journey   *4–6

CHILDREN'S CRUSADE, 1212
Hewes, Boy of the Lost Crusade   *6
Lillie, Book of Three Festivals, p.88–
109   *5–6

CHILDREN'S DAY
McSpadden, Book of Holidays, p.89–90
6
Sechrist, Red Letter Days, p.137–41
5–6

CHILE
Barrows, American Continents, p.354–
57   5
Goetz, Neighbors to the South, p.83–90
5–6
Quinn, Picture Map Geography of
South America, p.43–51   4–6
Rothery, South American Roundabout,
p.102–19   5–6
Spencer, P. R., Traveling New Trails,
p.294–98   6

CHILE—HISTORY
Peck, Pageant of South American History, p.165–78   6

CHIMES: see Bells

CHIMNEY SWALLOWS: see Swallows

CHIMNEY SWIFTS
Comstock, Handbook of Nature Study,
p.109–15   6
Webb, Birds in Their Homes, p.55   4–6

CHIMPANZEES
Bridges, Zoo Babies, p.57–64   4–6
———— Zoo Doctor, p.49–57   4–6
Osmond, Animals of the World, v.1
4–6
Perkins, Marlin Perkins' Zooparade,
p.52–55   4–6

CHINA: see also Confucianism; Costume
—China; Formosa; Games—China;
Houses—China; Taoism
Barrows, Old World Lands, p.216–20,
222–43   6
———— Our Big World, p.150–56   4
Buck, P. S., Chinese Children Next
Door   *4–5
Caldwell, Let's Visit China   5–6
Chrisman, Shen of the Sea   *5–6
Epstein, E., First Book of the United
Nations, p.38–41 (Communist China)
4–6

Fenner, Fools and Funny Fellows,
p.161–69   *4–6
———— Time To Laugh, p.116–26
*4–6
Hahn, Picture Story of China   4–6
Harper, Ghosts and Goblins, p.58–68
*4–6
Holling, Seabird, p.48–49   *4–6
Jordan, Homemade Dolls in Foreign
Dress, p.186–97   4–6
Kent, He Went with Marco Polo   *6
Kettelkamp, Kites, p.40–43   4–6
Lamprey, All the Ways of Building,
p.140–50   6
Lattimore, Chinese Daughter   *4
———— Little Pear and His Friends
*4–5
———— Peachblossom   *4–5
———— Questions of Lifu   *4–5
———— Willow Tree Village   *4–5
Liu, Little Wu and the Watermelons
*4–5
McGuire, Glimpses into the Long Ago,
p.109–32   5–6
Oakes, Bamboo Gate   *4–6
Quinn, Picture Map Geography of Asia,
p.83–95   4–6
Ritchie, A., Treasure of Li–Po   *4–5
Soong, Art of Chinese Paper Folding
4–6
Spencer, C., Land of the Chinese People
6
———— Made in China   5–6
Treffinger, Li Lun, Lad of Courage
*5–6
Urbahns, Little Red Dragon   *4–6
———— Tangled Web   *5–6
Wiese, Chinese Ink Stick   *4–6
Wood, E., Silk and Satin Lane   *4–5

CHINA—FOLK TALES
Wiese, Chinese Ink Stick, p.10–14   4–6

CHINA—GAMES: see Games—China

CHINA—HISTORY: see also Polo, Marco
Foster, G., Abraham Lincoln's World,
p.147–49, 167–68, 256–61   6
———— George Washington's World,
p.63–66, 338–39   6
Hazeltine, Hero Tales from Many
Lands, p.417–27   5–6
Spencer, C., Land of the Chinese Peo-
ple, p.17–72   6

Watson, Golden History of the World, p.31–33   5–6

CHINA (porcelain): *see* Pottery

CHINESE IN ENGLAND
Boston, Stranger at Green Knowe
    *5–6

CHINESE IN THE UNITED STATES
Association for Childhood Education, Told under the Stars and Stripes, p.91–101   *4–6

CHIPMUNKS
Barker, Winter-sleeping Wildlife, p.28–33   5–6
Buff, Big Tree, p.16–22   5–6
Comstock, Handbook of Nature Study, p.239–41   6
Hogner, Animal Book, p.42–44   6
Mason, G. F., Animal Homes, p.48–51
    4–6
————— Animal Tracks, p.9   4–6

CHIPPEWA INDIANS
Bleeker, Chippewa Indians   5–6

CHIPPING SPARROWS
Webb, Birds in Their Homes, p.28–29
    4–6

CHISHOLM TRAIL
Garst, Cowboys and Cattle Trails, p.123–85   4–6

CHIVALRY: *see also* Crusades; Feudal System; Heroes; Knights; Middle Ages; also names of persons as Arthur, King; Roland
Boardman, Castles, p.27–33   6
Tappan, When Knights Were Bold, p.28–51   6

CHLORINE
Morgan, A. P., First Electrical Book for Boys, p.246–49   6

CHOCOLATE
Bleeker, Inca, p.93–96, 117   5–6
Rothery, Central American Roundabout, p.130–32   6
Scheib, First Book of Food, p.49–50
    5–6
Smith, J. R., Neighbors around the World, p.288–93   4

CHOCTAW INDIANS
Davis, R. G., Choctaw Code   *5–6

CHOPIN, FREDERIC FRANÇOIS
Burch, Famous Composers for Young People, p.70–85   4–6
Schwimmer, Great Musicians as Children, p.34–44   6
Wheeler, Frederic Chopin   4–6
————— Robert Schumann and Mascot Ziff, p.76   4–6

CHRIST: *see* Jesus Christ

CHRISTIANITY: *see also* Jesus Christ
Bunyan, Pilgrim's Progress   *5–6
Galt, Seven Days from Sunday, p.69–75, 87–92   6
Hartman, Builders of the Old World, p.196–99, 238–41   6
————— In Bible Days   6
Hillyer, Child's History of Art, p.25–27
    5–6
————— Child's History of the World, p.215–18, 365–71   5–6

CHRISTMAS: *see also* Toys
Alden, Why the Chimes Rang, p.11–18, 136–46   *4–6
Association for Childhood Education, Told under Spacious Skies, p.55–64
    *4–6
————— Told under the Christmas Tree   *4–6
Bailey, C. S., Miss Hickory, p.68–77
    *4–6
Beeler, Experiments in Science, p.67–68
    5–6
Bloch, Marya of Clark Avenue, p.164–90   *4–6
Bryson, Twenty Miracles of Saint Nicolas   5–6
Burnett, B., First Book of Holidays, p.50–56   4–5
Carlson, B. W., Make It and Use It
    4–6
Cheney, Peg-legged Pirate of Sulu
    *4–5
Crowley, Azor and the Blue-eyed Cow
    *4–6
————— Tor and Azor, p.95–123
    *4–6
Dalgliesh, Blue Teapot, p.63–73   *4–6
————— Christmas   *4–6
Dolbier, Torten's Christmas Secret
    *4–5

Faralla, Willow in the Attic, p.36–57
*4

Fenner, Fools and Funny Fellows, p.48–56 *4–6

Frazier, Secret Friend, p.114–23 *4–6
———— Somebody Special, p.76–99
*4–6

Frost, Sleigh Bells for Windy Foot
*4–6

Grahame, Bertie's Escapade *4–5

Hale, Complete Peterkin Papers, p.66–73 (Peterkins' Christmas Tree) *4–6

Harper, Merry Christmas to You!
*4–6

Hays, Christmas on the Mayflower
*4–5

Haywood, Betsy's Winterhouse, p.33–52
*4–5

Jewett, God's Troubadour, p.89–96
5–6

Johnson, L., Christmas Stories 'round the World *4–6

Jones, J. M. O., Little Child 4–6

Jordan, Holiday Handicraft, p.3–30
4–6

Kingman, Best Christmas *4–6
———— Magic Christmas Tree *4–5

Lathrop, Angel in the Woods *4–5

Lee, What To Do Now, p.80–85 4–6

Leeming, Fun with Greeting Cards, p.69–76 4–6
———— Fun with Wire, p.75–80 5–6

Lillie, Book of Three Festivals, p.11–60
*5–6

Lindquist, J. D., Little Silver House
*4–6

Morrow, Pint of Judgment *4–5

New York Herald Tribune, Young America's Cook Book, p.270–75
4–6

Olcott, Good Stories for Great Holidays, p.299–362 *4–6

Pannell, Holiday Round Up, p.283–312
4–6

Sawyer, Long Christmas *4–6
———— This Way to Christmas *4–6

Schauffler, Christmas 4–6

Sechrist, Red Letter Days, p.205–25
5–6

Smith, E. S., Christmas Book of Legends & Stories *5–6

Smith, I., Santa Claus Book *4–5

Sperling, How To Make Things Out of Paper, p.91–98, 104–7 5–6

Vance, While Shepherds Watched
*4–6

Wheeler, Frederic Chopin, p.24–30
4–6

Yates, E., Once in the Year *4–6

CHRISTMAS—ARMENIA
Spicer, 46 Days of Christmas, p.89–90
6

CHRISTMAS—ASIA
Sechrist, Christmas Everywhere, p.149–57 6

CHRISTMAS—AUSTRALIA
Sechrist, Christmas Everywhere, p.159–61 6

CHRISTMAS—AUSTRIA
Johnson, L., Christmas Stories 'round the World, p.11–17, (Erika's Two Guests) *4–6
Pauli, Silent Night 4–6

CHRISTMAS—BELGIUM
Sechrist, Christmas Everywhere, p.115–21 6
Spicer, 46 Days of Christmas, p.87 6

CHRISTMAS—BULGARIA
Shannon, Dobry, p.139–48 *5–6
Smith, E. S., Christmas Book of Legends & Stories, p.353–61 *5–6
Spicer, 46 Days of Christmas, p.80 6

CHRISTMAS—CANADA
Dalgliesh, Christmas, p.180–88 4–6
De Angeli, Petite Suzanne *4–6
Johnson, L., Christmas Stories 'round the World, p.21–27 (Christmas in Hidden Valley) *4–6

CHRISTMAS—COLONIAL PERIOD IN AMERICA
Bailey, C. S., Children of the Handcrafts, p.75–84 5–6
———— Pioneer Art in America, p.65–77 5–6
De Angeli, Elin's Amerika *4–6
Johnson, L., Christmas Stories 'round the World, p.161–70 (Christmas without Kriss Kringle) *4–6

CHRISTMAS—CUBA
Albee, Three Young Kings *4–5

CHRISTMAS—CUSTOMS
Dalgliesh, America Builds Homes 4–5
McGinley, Mince Pie and Mistletoe
4–6
McSpadden, Book of Holidays, p.176–
86
6
Smith, E. S., Christmas Book of Legends & Stories 5–6

CHRISTMAS—CZECHOSLOVAKIA
Spicer, 46 Days of Christmas, p.45–46
6

CHRISTMAS—ENGLAND
Dalgliesh, Christmas, p.189–211 4–6
Sechrist, Christmas Everywhere, p.67–
85
6
Spicer, 46 Days of Christmas, p.27–29,
48–50, 64–65, 92–93
6

CHRISTMAS—ETHIOPIA
Sechrist, Christmas Everywhere, p.158–
59
6

CHRISTMAS—FRANCE: *see also* Christmas—Provence
Sechrist, Christmas Everywhere, p.63–
66
6
Spicer, 46 Days of Christmas, p.17–18,
41–43
6

CHRISTMAS—GERMANY
Chappell, Nutcracker 4–5
Dalgliesh, Christmas, p.137–46 4–6
Harper, Merry Christmas to You!, p.65–
73, 102–15, 206–20 4–6
Olcott, Good Stories for Great Holidays, p.342–47 4–6
Sawyer, This Way to Christmas, p.51–
60 4–6
Sechrist, Christmas Everywhere, p.97–
100 6
Spicer, 46 Days of Christmas, p.52–53
6
Vance, Star for Hansi *4–5

CHRISTMAS—GYPSIES
Sawyer, This Way to Christmas, p.110–
16 4–6

CHRISTMAS—HUNGARY
Sawyer, Christmas Anna Angel *4–5
Seredy, Good Master, p.186–210 *5–6
Smith, I., Santa Claus Book, p.200–212
*4–5

CHRISTMAS—ICELAND
Arason, Smoky Bay, p.116–31 *5–6

Golden, Made in Iceland, p.137–49 6
Johnson, L., Christmas Stories 'round the World, p.31–37 (Little Red Christmas Tree) *4–6

CHRISTMAS—INDIA
Spicer, 46 Days of Christmas, p.67–69
6

CHRISTMAS—INDIANS OF NORTH AMERICA
Armer, Waterless Mountain, p.60–66
*5–6

CHRISTMAS—IRELAND
Johnson, L., Christmas Stories 'round the World, p.41–49 (Christmas Donkey) *4–6
Sawyer, This Way to Christmas, p.31–
41 (Voyage of the Wee Red Cap)
*4–6
Seymour, Top o' Christmas Morning
*4–5
Spicer, 46 Days of Christmas, p.74–75
6

CHRISTMAS—ISRAEL
Gillsater, Pia's Journey to the Holy Land 4–6

CHRISTMAS—ITALY
Angelo, Nino, p.189–219 *6
Sechrist, Christmas Everywhere, p.137–
48 6
Spicer, 46 Days of Christmas, p.55–56
6

CHRISTMAS—JAPAN
Johnson, L., Christmas Stories 'round the World, p.53–62 (Gift of the Old Pine Tree) *4–6

CHRISTMAS—JORDAN
Johnson, L., Christmas Stories 'round the World, p.65–72 (Small Christmas Pilgrim) *4–6

CHRISTMAS—LATIN AMERICA
Goetz, Other Young Americans, p.210–
18 5–6

CHRISTMAS—LUXEMBOURG
Spicer, 46 Days of Christmas, p.20–21
6

CHRISTMAS—MEXICO
Johnson, L., Christmas Stories 'round the World, p.75–82 (Pinata for Pepita) *4–6

Sawyer, Year of the Christmas Dragon *4–5

Sechrist, Christmas Everywhere, p.28–38   6

CHRISTMAS—NETHERLANDS

Barnouw, Land of William of Orange, p.24–25   6

Dalgliesh, Christmas, p.159–67   4–6

Johnson, L., Christmas Stories 'round the World, p.85–94 (Sinterklaas Eve) *4–6

Sechrist, Christmas Everywhere, p.51–62   6

Seymour, Kaatje and the Christmas Compass *4–6

Smith, I., Santa Claus Book, p.213–22 *4–5

Spicer, 46 Days of Christmas, p.13–15, 35–36, 77–78   6

CHRISTMAS—NORWAY

Deucher, Edvard Grieg, p.102–14   4–6

Johnson, L., Christmas Stories 'round the World, p.97–102 (Best Christmas Nisse) *4–6

Sechrist, Christmas Everywhere, p.108–14   6

Zwilgmeyer, Johnny Blossom, p.68–89 *4–6

CHRISTMAS—PALESTINE

Ceder, Ethan, the Shepherd Boy *4–6

Sechrist, Christmas Everywhere, p.19–27   6

CHRISTMAS—PHILIPPINE ISLANDS

Wood, E., Pedro's Coconut Skates, p.179–91 *4–5

CHRISTMAS—PIONEER LIFE

Bulla, Riding the Pony Express, p.55–61 *4–5

Mason, M. E., Susannah, p.87–95 *4–5

Wilder, By the Shores of Silver Lake, p.175–201 *5–6

———— Farmer Boy, p.312–28 *4–6

———— Little House in the Big Woods, p.59–83 *4–6

———— Little House on the Prairie, p.238–52 *4–6

———— Long Winter, p.168–87, 323–35 *5–6

———— On the Banks of Plum Creek, p.80–96, 245–58 *4–6

CHRISTMAS—PLAYS

Smith, E. S., Christmas Book of Legends & Stories, p.29–36, 90–103, 115–22, 140–47, 202–19   5–6

CHRISTMAS—POLAND

Dalgliesh, Christmas, p.212–24   4–6

Harper, Merry Christmas to You!, p.40–53   4–6

Johnson, L., Christmas Stories 'round the World, p.105–23 (Bell Ringer of Pinsk) *4–6

Kelly, Christmas Nightingale *6

———— In Clean Hay *4–6

Spicer, 46 Days of Christmas, p.38–39   6

CHRISTMAS—PORTUGAL

Spicer, 46 Days of Christmas, p.61–62, 82–83   6

CHRISTMAS—PROVENCE

Dalgliesh, Christmas, p.147–58   4–6

Smith, E. S., Christmas Book of Legends & Stories, p.337–52 *5–6

CHRISTMAS—ROMANIA

Sechrist, Christmas Everywhere, p.130–36   6

Spicer, 46 Days of Christmas, p.71–72   6

CHRISTMAS—SANTA CLAUS

Smith, I., Santa Claus Book *4–5

CHRISTMAS—SERBIA

Sawyer, This Is the Christmas *5–6

Sechrist, Christmas Everywhere, p.39–50   6

CHRISTMAS—SICILY

Johnson, L., Christmas Stories 'round the World, p.127–36 (Buone Natale) *4–6

CHRISTMAS—SOUTH AMERICA

Sechrist, Christmas Everywhere, p.162–64   6

CHRISTMAS—SPAIN

Johnson, L., Christmas Stories 'round the World, p.139–47 (Maria's Christmas Song) *4–6

Sawyer, This Way to Christmas, p.86–98   4–6

Sechrist, Christmas Everywhere, p.86–96   6

Spicer, 46 Days of Christmas, p.58–59, 85   6

CHRISTMAS—SWEDEN

Burglon, Children of the Soil, p.105–54   *4–6

Dalgliesh, Christmas, p.168–79   4–6

Harper, Merry Christmas to You!, p.116–25   4–6

Johnson, L., Christmas Stories 'round the World, p.151–57 (Lucia Bride)   *4–6

Rothery, Scandinavian Roundabout, p.236–48   6

Sechrist, Christmas Everywhere, p.101–7   6

Seymour, Erik's Christmas Camera   *4–6

Smith, I., Santa Claus Book, p.223–34   *4–6

Spicer, 46 Days of Christmas, p.23–25   6

CHRISTMAS—SWITZERLAND

Sechrist, Christmas Everywhere, p.122–29   6

CHRISTMAS—SYRIA

Spicer, 46 Days of Christmas, p.10–11, 31–33   6

CHRISTMAS—UNION OF SOVIET SO-CIALIST REPUBLICS

Smith, E. S., Christmas Book of Legends & Stories, p.258–64   *5–6

CHRISTMAS—UNITED STATES: *see also* Christmas—Colonial Period in America; Christmas—Pioneer Life

Association for Childhood Education, Told under the Stars and Stripes, p.1–12, 47–53, 62–70, 218–38, 315–35   *4–6

Bleeker, Seminole Indians, p.142–49   4–6

Brink, Magical Melons, p.128–44   *5–6

Dalgliesh, Christmas, p.105–34   4–6

Enright, Four-Story Mistake, p.109–17   *5–6

Estes, Middle Moffat, p.147–77   *4–6

Haywood, Penny and Peter, p.139–60   *4

Judson, Lost Violin, p.123–36   *5–6

Ladd, Night of the Hurricane, p.124–35 (Christmas trees)   *4–6

Lawrence, Peachtree Island, p.94–116   *4–5

Lenski, Bayou Suzette, p.124–34   *5–6

Pace, Juliette Low, p.106–10   5–6

Sauer, Light at Tern Rock   *4–6

Sawyer, Maggie Rose   *4–6

Sayers, Tag-along Tooloo, p.32–44   *4

Sechrist, Christmas Everywhere, p.165–76   6

Seredy, Tree for Peter   *4–6

Stuart, Beatinest Boy   *4–6

Tor, Getting To Know Puerto Rico, p.52–54   4–6

CHRISTMAS GREENS: *see* Evergreen Trees

CHRISTOPHER, SAINT

Farjeon, Ten Saints, p.9–15   6

Olcott, Good Stories for Great Holidays, p.305–9   *4–6

Smith, E. S., Christmas Book of Legends & Stories, p.272–76   5–6

CHROMIUM

Loomis, Field Book of Common Rocks and Minerals, p.86–87   6

CHRYSALIS: *see* Butterflies; Caterpillars; Moths; Silkworms

CHUKO LIANG

Hazeltine, Hero Tales from Many Lands, p.417–27   5–6

CHURCH BELLS: *see* Bells

CHURCH MUSIC: *see also* Bach, Johann Sebastian; Handel, Georg Friedrich; Palestrina, Giovanni Pierluigi da

Buchanan, How Man Made Music, 76–79   6

Wheeler, Joseph Haydn, p.31–56   4–6

———— Sebastian Bach, p.68–77   4–6

CICADAS

Gaul, Picture Book of Insects, p.10–11   4–6

Kane, Tale of a Meadow, p.35–37   4–6

Lavine, Strange Travelers, p.87–93   5–6

Parker, B. M., Insects and Their Ways, p.19–20   4–6

Teale, Insect Friends, p.69–72   5–6

CID

Hazeltine, Hero Tales from Many Lands, p.236–51   5–6

CINCINNATI
Meadowcroft, By Wagon and Flatboat, p.162–70 *4–5

CIRCULATORY SYSTEM
Disraeli, New Worlds through the Microscope, p.155–56 6
Glemser, All about the Human Body, p.43–55 5–6
Scheib, What Happened?, p.89–97 5–6
Schneider, H., How Your Body Works, p.28–33, 72–74 4–6
Schneider, L., Lifeline 6

CIRCUS: *see also* Clowns; Zoos; also names of circus animals, as Elephants
Brown, P., Crazy Quilt *4–5
Coatsworth, Alice-All-By-Herself, p.12–24 *4–6
De Angeli, Copper-toed Boots *4–6
Dobson, Hero, p.84–126 *4–5
Du Bois, Great Geppy *4–5
Enright, Saturdays, p.103–18 *4–6
Hader, Spunky, p.30–56, 66–70 *4–6
Lang, Strawberry Roan, p.146–97 *5–6
Mason, M. E., Middle Sister, p.14–19 *4–5
Otis, Toby Tyler *4–6
Robinson, J., Things To Make from Odds & Ends, p.27–28 6
Sayers, Tag-along Tooloo, p.73–87 *4
Severn, Let's Give a Show, p.101–12 4–6
Slobodkin, Adventures of Arab, p.85–94 *4–6
Spencer, P. R., Exploring New Trails, p.3–13, 20–26, 38–42 5
Voight, Lions in the Barn *4–6

CITIES AND TOWNS: *see also* Citizenship; City Planning; Community Life; Hanseatic League; Markets; Rivers; Village Life; also names of cities and towns, as Chicago
Hartman, Machines, p.170–80 6

CITIES AND TOWNS—FORMOSA
Caldwell, Let's Visit Formosa, p.37–41 5–6

CITIES AND TOWNS—GERMANY
Lobsenz, First Book of West Germany, p.8–18 4–6
Sasek, This Is Munich 4–6

CITIES AND TOWNS—INCA
Bleeker, Inca, p.141–42 5–6

CITIES AND TOWNS—KOREA
Caldwell, Let's Visit Korea, p.62–68 5–6

CITIES AND TOWNS—MIDDLE AGES
Tappan, When Knights Were Bold, p. 206–31 6

CITIES AND TOWNS—NETHERLANDS
De Jong, D., Picture Story of Holland 4–6

CITIES AND TOWNS—PHILIPPINE ISLANDS
O'Neill, Picture Story of the Philippines 5–6

CITIES AND TOWNS—POLAND
Kelly, Land of the Polish People, p.38–58 5–6

CITIES AND TOWNS—SWITZERLAND
Bragdon, L. J., Land and People of Switzerland, p.41–108 6

CITIES AND TOWNS—UNITED STATES
Coy, Americans, p.220–28 6
Garelick, Manhattan Island 4–6
Quinn, Picture Map Geography of the United States 4–7
Tor, Getting To Know Puerto Rico, p.15–18 4–6

CITIZENSHIP: *see also* Community Life; Conservation; Election Day; Flags; Government; Immigration and Emigration; Patriotism; Safety; United States—Government; Wild Life Conservation
Brown, H. M., America Is My Country, p.205–23 5–6
Gordon, You and Democracy 6
Lawson, R., They Were Strong and Good 4–6
Oakes, Bamboo Gate, p.82–101 *4–6
Peattie, Law 5–6
Sorensen, Curious Missie *4–6
Spencer, P. R., Finding New Trails, p.302–5 4

CITY LIFE
  Bannon, Patty Paints a Picture   *4–5
  Bendick, First Book of Supermarkets
                                      4–5
  Canfield, Understood Betsy, p.1-20
                                      *5–6
  Clewes, Secret   *4–5
  Friedman, F., Dot for Short   *4–5
  ———— Sundae with Judy   *4–6
  Turner, Town Meeting Means Me   4–6
  Will, Two Reds   *4–5

CITY LIFE—CHINA
  Oakes, Bamboo Gate, p.49–56   *4–6

CITY LIFE—INDIA
  Bothwell, Thirteenth Stone   *5–6

CITY PLANNING: *see also* Airports
  Cousins, Ben Franklin of Old Philadelphia, p.75–86, 174–75   5–6

CIVIL LIBERTIES: *see* Constitution of
  the United States

CIVIL WAR IN THE UNITED STATES:
  see also Costume—Civil War in the
  United States; also names of persons,
  as Grant, Ulysses Simpson; Lee, Rob-
  ert Edward; Lincoln, Abraham
  Boylston, Clara Barton, p.63–130   4–6
  Burchard, Jed   *5–6
  Commager, H. S., First Book of Ameri-
  can History, p.41–51   4–6
  Coy, Americans, p.149–88   6
  Dupuy, First Book of Civil War Naval
  Actions   6
  Foster, G., Abraham Lincoln's World,
  p.266–342   6
  Fritz, Brady   *5–6
  Henry, R. S., Trains, p.44–49   5–6
  Hillyer, Child's History of the World,
  p.446–48   5–6
  Hunt, M. L., Lucinda   *5–6
  Meadowcroft, Abraham Lincoln, p.117–
  84   6
  ———— Land of the Free, p.96–111
                                   4–5
  Miers, Billy Yank and Johnny Reb   5–6
  Pace, Clara Barton, p.20–101   5–6
  ———— Juliette Low, p.1–40   5–6
  Pauli, Lincoln's Little Correspondent
                                   4–6
  Pratt, Monitor and the Merrimac   5–6
  Proudfit, River-Boy, p.143–47   6

CIVILIZATION: *see also* Archeology;
  Community Life; Feudal System; His-
  tory; Incas; Inventions; Machines;
  Manners and Customs; Middle Ages;
  Renaissance; Wheels
  Barrows, Old World Lands, p.1–7   6
  Burns, Man and His Tools   5–6
  Falls, First 3000 Years   6
  Foster, G., Abraham Lincoln's World
                                        6
  ———— George Washington's World
                                        6
  Hartman, Builders of the Old World,
  p.34–39   6
  Osborne, C. G., First Lake Dwellers
                                *4–6
  Pyne, Little History of the Wide World
                                    4–6

CLAMS
  Buck, M. W., In Ponds and Streams,
  p.19   4–6
  ———— Pets from the Pond, p.22–25
                                     4–6
  Cavanna, First Book of Sea Shells, p.8–
  10   4–6
  Cooper, E. K., Science on the Shores
  and Banks, p.76–77   5–6
  Fenton, C. L., Life Long Ago, p.88–92
                                        6

CLARK, GEORGE ROGERS
  Barksdale, That Country Called Vir-
  ginia, p.111–13   6
  Foster, G., George Washington's World,
  p.212–15   6
  McGuire, Brave Young Land, p.372–76
                                    5–6

CLARK, WILLIAM: *see* Lewis and Clark
  Expedition

CLAY, HENRY
  Lawson, R., Watchwords of Liberty,
  p.50–52   4–6

CLAY: *see also* Bricks; Pottery
  Fenton, C. L., Riches from the Earth,
  p.30–34   5–6
  Ota, Printing for Fun, p.18–21   4–6
  Writers Project, Story of Clay, no.24
                                     5–6

CLAY MODELING: *see also* Pottery
  Leeming, Fun with Clay   4–6
  Zarchy, Let's Make Something, p.72–75,
  78–81   5–6

CLAY TABLETS: *see also* Cuneiform Writing
Hartman, Builders of the Old World, p.91–93   6

CLEANLINESS: *see also* Health; Home Economics; Laundry; Soap
Beery, Manners Made Easy, p.63–79 6
Harper, Easter Chimes, p.34–38   *4–6
Mears, First Book of Japan, p.24–25   4–6
Parker, B. M., Water, p.12–13   5–6

CLEMENS, SAMUEL LANGHORNE
Coffman, Famous Authors for Young People, p.109–14   5–6
Eaton, America's Own Mark Twain 6
Proudfit, River-Boy   6
Shapiro, Steamboat Bill and the Captain's Top Hat   *5–6

CLEOPATRA
Gunther, Julius Caesar   6

CLERMONT (ship): *see also* Fulton, Robert
Maginley, Historic Models of Early America, p.49–54   6

CLEVELAND, GROVER
Beard, Presidents in American History, p.93–95, 169–70   6
Coy, First Book of Presidents, p.49   4–6
Petersham, Story of the Presidents of the United States, p.52–53, 55 4–6

CLEVERNESS
Fenner, Time To Laugh, p.44–57 *4–6

CLIFF DWELLERS: *see also* Mesa Verde National Park; Mound Builders
Buff, Hah-Nee of the Cliff Dwellers   *4–6
Fenton, C. L., Cliff Dwellers of Walnut Canyon   4–5
Fletcher, S. E., American Indian, p.39–47   5–6
Holling, Book of Indians, p.81–88 4–6

CLIFF SWALLOWS
Webb, Birds in Their Homes, p.54 4–6

CLIMATE: *see also* Rain; Seasons; Weather
Adler, Dust, p.45–55   5–6
Banta, Life in America: The South, p.33–37   5–6

Bleeker, Inca, p.11–12, 15, 48–51 5–6
Buckley, Spanish Plateau, p.50–58 6
Comstock, Handbook of Nature Study, p.780–807   6
Havighurst, Life in America: The Midwest, p.31–35   5–6
Lane, F. C., All about the Sea, p.135–40   4–6
Selsam, See through the Jungle   4–5
Shackelford, Child's Story of the Negro, p.1–2   4–5
Street, Land of the English People, p.15–18   6

CLINTON, DE WITT: *see* Erie Canal

CLIPPER SHIPS
Hogeboom, Boats and How To Draw Them, p.32–35   4–5
Holling, Seabird, p.34–44   *4–6
Mitchell, Ships That Made U.S. History, p.63–68   6

CLOCKS: *see also* Sundials; Water Clocks
Adler, Time in Your Life   4–6
Bailey, C. S., Children of the Handcrafts, p.33–43   *5–6
Baker, R. H., When the Stars Come Out, p.47–51   6
Dalgliesh, Christmas, p.44–67 *4–6
Lent, Men at Work in New England, p.14–17   4–6
Morgan, A. P., First Electrical Book for Boys, p.253–54   6
Reck, Clocks Tell the Time   4–6
Rogers, F., Heels, Wheels, and Wire, p.146–51   5–6
Schneider, H., Everyday Machines and How They Work, p.68–69, 75–76, 167–72, 180–81   5–6
Tannenbaum, Understanding Time, p.47–88   6

CLOTH: *see* Textiles

CLOTHING: *see also* Costume; Doll Dressmaking; Fibers—Synthetic; Hats; Home Life; Knitting; Shoes; Textiles
Beery, Manners Made Easy, p.95–121   6
Bendick, First Book of Space Travel, p.38–41   5–6
———— How Much and How Many, p.70–80   5–6
Bleeker, Horsemen of the Western Plateaus, p.75–80   4–6

———— Inca　　　　　　　　　5–6

———— Indians of the Longhouse, p.63–68　　　　　　　　　4–6

Brown, R. J., Land and People of Brazil, p.30, 50, 88, 96　　　　6

Caldwell, Let's Visit India, p.75–76　　　　　　　　　　4–6

———— Let's Visit Indonesia, p.48–51　　　　　　　　　4–6

Evans, People Are Important, p.55–60　　　　　　　　　4–5

Fenner, Time To Laugh　　　*4–6

Goetz, Other Young Americans, p.49–65　　　　　　　　　5–6

Hall, E., Land and People of Argentina, p.11, 85–86, 103　　6

Hollos, Story of Your Coat　　4–5

Jakeman, Getting To Know Japan, p.20, 24, 28, 41–42　　　　4–6

Jupo, Nothing To Wear but Clothes　　　　　　　　　　4–5

Kenworthy, Profile of Nigeria, p.30–34　　　　　　　　　5–6

May, Let's Read about Brazil, p.99–102　　　　　　　　　4–6

Spencer, C., Land of the Chinese People, p.10–11, 109　　　　6

Stefansson, Here Is Alaska, p.69–72　　　　　　　　　　6

CLOTHING—COLONIAL PERIOD IN AMERICA

Bailey, C. S., Children of the Handcrafts, p.86–94, 167–78　5–6

CLOUDS: *see also* Weather

Adler, Weather in Your Life, p.64–73　　　　　　　　　5–6

Asimov, Satellites in Outer Space, p.49–51　　　　　　　4–5

Barnard, Macmillan Science-Life Series, Bk.6, p.58–59　　　6

Beeler, Experiments in Science, p.38–39　　　　　　　　5–6

Cooper, E. K., Science in Your Own Back Yard, p.158–63　　5–6

Gallant, R. A., Exploring the Weather, p.34–38　　　　　5–6

Parker, B. M., Clouds, Rain, and Snow, p.10–14　　　　　4–6

Reed, And That's Why, p.3–13　　4–5

Spilhaus, Wethercraft, p.44–50　6

Writers Project, Ladder of Clouds, no.1　　　　　　　　5–6

CLOVER

Comstock, Handbook of Nature Study, p.591–98　　　　　6

CLOWNS: *see also* Circus

Ackley, Dolls To Make, p.66–74　5–6

CLUBS: *see also* Boy Scouts; Girl Scouts

Bishop, C. H., Blue Spring Farm　*5–6

Enright, Saturdays　　　　　*4–6

COACHES: *see* Carriages; Stagecoaches

COAL: *see also* Geology; Mining

Adler, Fire in Your Life, p.116–19　　　　　　　　　4–6

Association for Childhood Education, Told under Spacious Skies, p.105–14　　　　　　　　*4–6

Barrows, American Continents, p.74–76　　　　　　　5

Buehr, Underground Riches, p.71–83　　　　　　　　5–6

Fenton, C. L., Riches from the Earth, p.35–42　　　　　5–6

Hartman, Machines, p.28–33　　6

Loomis, Field Book of Common Rocks and Minerals, p.217–24　6

Parker, B. M., Earth a Great Storehouse, p.15–19　　　　4–6

Schwartz, It's Fun To Know Why, p.21–30　　　　　　5–6

Williams, H. L., Stories in Rocks, p.69–73　　　　　　　6

Writers Project, Story of Coal, no.35　　　　　　　　5–6

COAL AGE

Fenton, C. L., Life Long Ago, p.144–51　　　　　　　6

Reed, Earth for Sam　　　　　6

COAL OIL: *see* Petroleum

COAL-TAR PRODUCTS: *see also* Fibers —Synthetic; Nylon

Writers Project, Story of Coal, no.35, p.42–47　　　　　5–6

COAST GUARD: *see* United States— Coast Guard

COASTING: *see* Skiing; Sleds

COATIS

Fenton, C. L., Wild Folk in the Desert, p.97–98　　　　　4–6

COBB, TY
Spencer, P. R., Traveling New Trails, p.66–72　　6

COBRAS
Buck, F., Jungle Animals, p.32–33　5–6

COCA: *see* Chocolate

COCATOOS: *see* Parrots

COCKROACHES
Bronson, Grasshopper Book, p.108–17　　4–6
Parker, B. M., Plant and Animal Partnerships, p.11–12　　5–6

COCOA: *see* Chocolate

COCONUT PALMS
Barrows, Our Big World, p.147–48　4
Rothery, Central American Roundabout, p.96–98　　6

COCONUTS
Eberle, Basketful, p.247–48　　4–6
Shackelford, Child's Story of the Negro, p.11–12　　4–5
Wood, E., Pedro's Coconut Skates, p.106–16　　*4–5

COCOONS: *see also* Butterflies; Caterpillars; Moths; Silkworms
Hussey, Collecting Cocoons　　4–6

COCOS ISLAND
Rothery, Central American Roundabout, p.142–51　　6

CODES
Epstein, S., First Book of Codes and Ciphers　　4–6

CODY, WILLIAM FREDERICK: *see* Buffalo Bill

COFFEE
Brown, R. J., Land and People of Brazil, p.70–74, 78–79　　6
May, Let's Read about Brazil, p.59–63　　4–6
Rothery, Central American Roundabout, p.63–66　　6
Scheib, First Book of Food, p.46–47　　5–6

COINS: *see* Money

COLD LANDS: *see* Antarctic Regions; Arctic Regions; Eskimos; Greenland; Labrador; Lapland; Norway

COLD STORAGE: *see* Refrigeration

COLLAGE
Kuwabara, Cut and Paste　　5–6

COLLECTING: *see also* Aquariums; Botany; Fossils; Insects—Collecting; Microscopes; Minerals; Postage Stamps; Terrariums
Brown, V., How To Make a Home Nature Museum, p.24–53　　5–6
Cavanna, First Book of Sea Shells, p.32–38　　4–6
Cooper, E. K., Science in Your Own Back Yard　　5–6
Dudley, Sea Shells, p.126–43　　4–6
Evans, Adventure Book of Money, p.55–62　　5–6
Gray, Adventure Book of Insects, p.71–98　　5–6
Hussey, Collecting Cocoons　　4–6
Lewis, R., Stamp Collecting　　4–6
Loomis, Field Book of Common Rocks and Minerals　　6
Morgan, A. H., Field Book of Ponds and Streams, p.26–45　　6
Petersham, America's Stamps　　5–6
Swain, Insects in Their World　　5–6
Teale, Junior Book of Insects　　6

COLOMBIA
Barrows, American Continents, p.313–19　　5
Donaldson, Colombia　　4–6
Goetz, Neighbors to the South, p.64–69　　5–6
Quinn, Picture Map Geography of South America, p.8–17　　4–6
Rothery, South American Roundabout, p.1–15　　6

COLONIAL PERIOD IN AMERICA: *see also* British in America; Costume—Colonial Period in America; Dutch in America; French in America; Germans in America; Pilgrim Fathers; Puritans; Spanish Missions in California; Swedes in America; Thanksgiving Day
Aulaire, Pocahontas　　4–5
Averill, Daniel Boone　　4–6
Bailey, C. S., Children of the Handcrafts　　5–6
Barksdale, That Country Called Virginia, p.7–130　　6

Chase, V., Knight of the Golden Fleece
6

Coatsworth, Golden Horseshoe   *6

Commager, H. S., First Book of American History, p.4–27   4–6

Coy, Americans, p.11–54   6

Dalgliesh, America Builds Homes   4–5

Daugherty, Landing of the Pilgrims
4–6

———— Poor Richard   6

Duvoisin, And There Was America
4–6

Foster, G., World of Captain John Smith   6

Haviland, William Penn   4–6

Hays, Christmas on the Mayflower
*4–5

———— Pilgrim Thanksgiving   *4–5

Johnson, G. W., America Is Born   5–6

Maginley, Historic Models of Early America, p.103–56   6

Meadowcroft, Land of the Free, p.9–43
4–5

Petersham, Silver Mace   4–5

Rich, First Book of the Early Settlers
4–6

Rogers, F., Heels, Wheels, and Wire, p.45–53   5–6

Watson, Golden History of the World, p.107–10   5–6

Weir, R. C., Benjamin Franklin   4–6

COLOR: *see also* Art; Dyeing; Light; Paint; Painting

Beeler, Experiments with Light, p.45–54
6

Foster, J., Pages, Pictures, and Print, p.59–72   6

Land, B., Quest of Isaac Newton, p.7–10   6

Paschel, First Book of Color   5–6

Rogers, F., Heels, Wheels, and Wire, p.185–89   5–6

Ruchlis, Wonder of Light, p.81–98   6

COLORADO: *see also* Mesa Verde National Park; Rocky Mountain National Park

Association for Childhood Education, Told under Spacious Skies, p.243–56
*4–6

Barnes, Wonderful Year   *4–6

Franklin, Son of Monte   *4–6

———— Tuffy   *4–6

Quinn, Picture Map Geography of the United States, p.156–59   4–6

COLORADO RIVER: *see also* Grand Canyon National Park

Ault, This Is the Desert, p.148–59   5–6

COLTER, JOHN

Melbo, Our Country's National Parks, v.1, p.3–4, 6–7   6

COLUMBUS, CHRISTOPHER

American Heritage, Discoverers of the New World, p.17–48   5–6

Aulaire, Columbus   4–5

Baker, N. B., Amerigo Vespucci   5–6

Brindze, Gulf Stream, p.10–17   4–6

Dalgliesh, America Begins, p.19–31
4–5

Dawson, California, p.25–27   5–6

Duvoisin, And There Was America, p.7–14   4–6

———— They Put Out to Sea, p.92–109   4–6

Graham, A. P., Christopher Columbus
4–6

Hartman, Builders of the Old World, p.422–39   6

Hillyer, Child's History of the World, p.337–45   5–6

Kent, He Went with Christopher Columbus   *6

McGuire, Brave Young Land, p.13–43
5–6

Mitchell, Ships That Made U.S. History, p.5–8   6

Sperry, Voyages of Christopher Columbus   4–5

Syme, Columbus   4–6

COLUMBUS DAY

Brown, H. M., America Is My Country, p.197–98   5–6

Burnett, B., First Book of Holidays, p.35–36   4–5

Jordan, Holiday Handicraft, p.140–52
4–6

McSpadden, Book of Holidays, p.138–46   6

Olcott, Good Stories for Great Birthdays, p.1–27   4–6

———— Good Stories for Great Holidays, p.213–29   4–6

Pannell, Holiday Round Up, p.233–38
4–6
Sechrist, Red Letter Days, p.166–73
5–6

COMANCHE INDIANS
Dorian, Hokahey!, p.91–92   5–6
Hooker, Star   *5–6

COMBUSTION: *see also* Fire; Fuel; Heat
Beeler, Experiments in Science, p.43–45
5–6
Crouse, W. H., Understanding Science, p.24–28   6

COMETS: *see also* Astronomy
Baker, R. H., When the Stars Come Out, p.96–99   6
Branley, Guide to Outer Space, p.22–23
4–6
Freeman, M. B., Fun with Astronomy, p.34   4–6
Goodwin, Real Book about Stars, p.67–75   4–6
Land, B., Quest of Isaac Newton, p.31–33   6
Schealer, This Way to the Stars, p.137–43   6
Schneider, L., Space in Your Future, p.87–91   6

COMIC BOOKS
McCloskey, Homer Price, p.34–46
*5–6

COMMERCE: *see* Trade

COMMERCIAL PRODUCTS: *see also* names of commercial products, as Cotton
Rothery, Central American Roundabout, p.238–48   6

COMMUNICATION: *see also* Airplanes; Canals; Express Service; Harbors; Language; Mail Service; Messengers; Newspapers; Pony Express; Radio; Railroads; Records; Roads; Ships; Storytelling; Telegraph; Telephone; Television; Transportation; Writing
Adams, S. H., Pony Express   4–6
Batchelor, Communication   4–6
Buehr, Story of the Wheel, p.16–19,
4–6
Evans, People Are Important, p.11–22
4–5

Hogben, Wonderful World of Communication   6
Jacobson, First Book of Letter Writing
4–6
Latham, Young Man in a Hurry   6
Leonard, Exploring Science, p.190–207
6
Pei, All about Language   6
Yates, R. F., Boys' Book of Communication   6

COMMUNISM: *see also* Union of Soviet Socialist Republics
Caldwell, Let's Visit China, p.72–88
5–6
Smith, D. C., Land and People of Indonesia, p.63–64, 72–74, 84–85, 116–18
6
Snyder, First Book of the Soviet Union
6
Wagner, Put Democracy to Work, p.38–49   6

COMMUNITY LIFE: *see also* Cities and Towns; Dancing; Games; Government; Housing—United States; Mail Service; Maps; Plantation Life; Safety; School Life; Theater; Village Life
Baker, A. O., Your Science World, p.183–90   6
Daringer, Adopted Jane   *4–6
De Angeli, Copper-toed Boots   *4–6
Douglas, Appleseed Farm   *4–6
Elting, Lollypop Factory   4–5
Garelick, Manhattan Island   4–6
Lenski, Flood Friday   *4–6
Osborne, C. G., First Lake Dwellers
*4–6
Sechrist, Heigh-Ho for Halloween!   5–6
Sootin, Let's Go to a Police Station
4–5
———— Let's Take a Trip to a Newspaper   4–6
Streatfeild, New Shoes   *6

COMMUNITY LIFE AMONG THE ANIMALS AND INSECTS: *see also* Ants; Beavers; Bees; Swallows; Termites; Wasps
Bronson, Children of the Sea, p.57–67
6
Morgan, A. H., Field Book of Animals in Winter, p.34–41   6

COMPASS
Barrows, Our Big World, p.4   4
Beauchamp, Discovering Our World, Bk. 1, p.150–54   4
Beeler, More Experiments in Science, p.18–22   5–6
Hillyer, Child's History of the World, p.322–24   5–6
Morgan, A. P., First Electrical Book for Boys, p.25–28   6
Parker, B. M., Magnets, p.18–24   5–6

COMPOSERS: *see* Musicians; also names of composers, as Bach, Johann Sebastian

COMPUTERS
Bendick, Electronics for Young People, p.88–93   6
———— Take a Number, p.48–50   4–5

CONCRETE: *see also* Cement
Writers Project, Cement, no.33   5–6

CONESTOGA WAGONS: *see also* Covered Wagons
Bailey, C. S., Children of the Handcrafts, p.105–14   5–6
Brock, Drusilla, p.14–86   *4–5
Meadowcroft, By Wagon and Flatboat, p.25–27, 35–81   *4–5
Meigs, Wind in the Chimney, p.70–119   *5–6
Orton, Treasure in the Little Trunk   *4–6

CONESTOGA WAGONS—MODELS
Jordan, Holiday Handicraft, p.188–99   4–6
Maginley, Historic Models of Early America, p.28–33   6

CONFUCIANISM
Fitch, Their Search for God, p.52–65   5–6

CONGO
Barrows, Our Big World, p.111–22   4
Carbonnier, Congo Explorer   5–6
Hughes, First Book of Africa, p.15, 19, 23, 58–60   5–6
Jordan, Homemade Dolls in Foreign Dress, p.231–46   4–6
Stinetorf, Children of South Africa, p.37–49   *5–6

CONGRESS: *see* United States—Government

CONIES: *see* Pikas

CONNECTICUT
Batchelor, Tim and the Purple Whistle   *4–5
Dalgliesh, Adam and the Golden Cock   *4–5
———— Courage of Sarah Noble   *4–5
Estes, Middle Moffat   *4–6
———— Rufus M.   *4–6
Hammett, I, Priscilla   *5–6
Hayes, Skid, p.81–216   *5–6
Lenski, Flood Friday   *4–6
Quinn, Picture Map Geography of the United States, p.20–23   4–6

CONSERVATION: *see also* Balance of Nature; Erosion; Floods; Forestry; Hunting; Irrigation; Mining; National Parks; Salmon; Soil Conservation; Wild Life Conservation
Bailey, C. S., Miss Hickory   *4–6
Bethers, Story of Rivers   4–5
Bronson, Freedom and Plenty   4–6
———— Starlings   4–5
Buehr, Timber!, p.54–58   5–6
Colby, Fish and Wildlife   5–6
———— Park Ranger   5–6
———— Soil Savers   4–6
Darling, L., Seals and Walruses   4–6
Dudley, Our American Trees, p.8–9, 130–37   5–6
Fisher, A. L., Summer of Little Rain   *4–6
Franklin, Son of Monte   *4–6
———— Tuffy   *4–6
Gage, Wild Goose Tale   *4–6
Gallup, Spinning Wings   5–6
Gaul, Pond Book   4–6
George, J. L., Bubo   4–6
Graham, E. H., Water for America, p.71–83   6
———— Wildlife for America   6
Green, Home for Woody   4–6
Holling, Minn of the Mississippi   5–6
Lathrop, Let Them Live   4–6
Liers, Beaver's Story   5–6
Lippincott, Persimmon Jim, the Possum   4–6
———— Striped Coat, the Skunk   5–6

McClung, Vulcan 4–5

—— Whooping Crane 4–5

Ripper, Hawks 5–6

Rounds, Swamp Life, p.112–13 5–6

Scheib, What Happened?, p.9–19 5–6

Schloat, Magic of Water 4–6

Selsam, See through the Forest 4–6

Smith, F. C., First Book of Conservation 4–6

—— First Book of Water 4–6

Wall, Gifts from the Forest 4–6

Webber, Thanks to Trees 4–5

CONSIDERATION OF OTHERS

Brink, Caddie Woodlawn *6

—— Magical Melons *5–6

Burnett, F. H., Secret Garden *5–6

Cleary, Otis Spofford *4–6

Collodi, Adventures of Pinocchio *4–6

Daringer, Adopted Jane *4–6

Enright, Saturdays *4–6

Estes, Hundred Dresses *4–6

—— Rufus M. *4–6

Friedman, F., Carol from the Country *4–6

Frost, Windy Foot at the County Fair *4–6

Lenski, Strawberry Girl *4–6

Seredy, Good Master *5–6

Wilson, H. H., Owen Boys *5–6

Woolley, Schoolroom Zoo *4–5

Yashima, T., Crow Boy *4–5

CONSTELLATIONS: *see also* Stars

Baker, R. H., Introducing the Constellations 6

—— When the Stars Come Out, p.30–46 6

Beauchamp, Discovering Our World, Bk.1, p.115–23 4

Comstock, Handbook of Nature Study, p.818–33 6

Goodwin, Real Book about Stars, p.13–18, 125–58 4–6

Jacobson, First Book of Mythical Beasts, p.64–65 4–6

Parker, B. M., Golden Book of Science, p.69–70 4–6

Reed, Patterns in the Sky 5–6

Sellew, Adventures with the Gods, p.86–89 4–5

CONSTITUTION (ship)

Hansen, Old Ironsides 5–6

Mitchell, Ships That Made U.S. History, p.35–39 6

Spencer, P. R., Traveling New Trails, p.14–25 6

CONSTITUTION OF THE UNITED STATES

Brown, H. M., America Is My Country, p.46–55, 229–42 5–6

Fisher, D. F. C., Our Independence and the Constitution 4–5

Foster, G., George Washington's World, p.280–83 6

Hays, Freedom, p.13–14, 17–18 5–6

McGuire, Brave Young Land, p.397–407 5–6

Morris, First Book of the Constitution 5–6

Ross, G. E., Know Your Government, p.60–70 6

Witty, You and the Constitution of the United States 5–6

CONSTITUTIONAL CONVENTION

Eaton, That Lively Man, Ben Franklin, p.243–51 6

CONSTRUCTION WORK: *see* Carpentry; Handicraft; Paper Work

CONTENTMENT

Alden, Why the Chimes Rang *4–6

McGinley, Most Wonderful Doll in the World *4–5

CONTRARINESS

Alden, Why the Chimes Rang, p.41–52 *4–6

Chrisman, Shen of the Sea, p.206–19 *5–6

Fenner, Fools and Funny Fellows, p.57–62 *4–6

CONUNDRUMS: *see* Riddles

CONVENTS: *see* Monasteries

CONVEYORS

Bechdolt, Going Up, p.96–101 5–6

COOK, JAMES

Cottler, Heroes of Civilization, p.34–43 6

Foster, G., George Washington's World, p.48–50, 109–12 6

Frank, Ice Island, p.5–13 6

Lewis, O., Hawaii, p.50–62 5–6

Sperry, Captain Cook Explores the South Seas   5–6

Syme, Captain Cook   5–6

COOK ISLANDS

Quinn, Picture Map Geography of the Pacific Islands, p.104–6   5–6

COOKING: *see also* Bakers; Bread; Candy; Canning; Food; Home Economics; Indians of North America—Food; Kitchens

Beeler, Experiments in Science, p.40–42   5–6

Bendick, How Much and How Many, p.147–48   5–6

Canfield, Understood Betsy, p.93–97   *5–6

Enright, Then There Were Five, p.144–54   *5–6

Freeman, M. B., Fun with Cooking   4–6

Harper, Harvest Feast, p.225–38   4–6

Mason, B. S., Junior Book of Camping and Woodcraft, p.72–101   5–6

New York Herald Tribune, Young America's Cook Book   4–6

Rombauer, Cookbook for Boys and Girls   6

COOLIDGE, CALVIN

Beard, Presidents in American History, p.121–22, 176–77   6

Coy, First Book of Presidents, p.58   4–6

Lawson, R., Watchwords of Liberty, p.105–6   4–6

Petersham, Story of the Presidents of the United States, p.67–68   4–6

COONS: *see* Raccoons

COOPER, PETER: *see* Tom Thumb (locomotive)

COOPERATION: *see also* Community Life; Community Life among the Animals and Insects; Interdependence

Alden, Why the Chimes Rang, p.80–91   *4–6

Bleeker, Inca, p.16, 83–85   5–6

Burglon, Children of the Soil   *4–6

Du Bois, Twenty-one Balloons, p.77–175   *6

Enright, Saturdays   *4–6

———— Then There Were Five *5–6

Hartman, Machines, p.42–47   6

Meigs, Covered Bridge, p.63–103   *4–6

Osborne, C. G., First Lake Dwellers   *4–6

Sorensen, Curious Missie   *4–6

Tarshis, Village That Learned to Read   *4–6

COOPERATIVES

Steinmann, Lia and the Red Carnations   *6

COPENHAGEN

Deucher, Edvard Grieg, p.67–75   4–6

COPERNICUS

Asimov, Breakthroughs in Science, p.17–25   5–6

Cottler, Heroes of Civilization, p.89–97   6

Goodwin, Real Book about Stars, p.36–38, 78   4–6

Schealer, This Way to the Stars, p.26–32   6

Schneider, L., Space in Your Future, p.31–33   6

COPPER

Adler, Fire in Your Life, p.77–80   4–6

Beeler, Experiments in Science, p.76–77   5–6

Fenton, C. L., Riches from the Earth, p.43–48   5–6

Freeman, I. M., All about the Wonders of Chemistry, p.64–66   6

Holling, Book of Indians, p.115–23   4–6

Loomis, Field Book of Common Rocks and Minerals, p.37–47   6

CORAL

Fenton, C. L., Life Long Ago, p.70–75   6

Life, World We Live In, p.114–27   5–6

Reed, Sea for Sam, p.140–44   6

Robertson, G., Strange Sea Life, p.45–49   5–6

Williams, H. L., Stories in Rocks, p.57–59   6

CORIOLANUS, ROMAN LEGENDARY HERO

Farjeon, Mighty Men, p.77–83   4–6

CORK

Elting, Lollypop Factory, p.89–93   4–5

CORMORANTS
Oakes, Bamboo Gate, p.146–57   *4–6

CORN: *see also* Grain; Indians of North America—Food
Bleeker, Indians of the Longhouse, p.40–47   4–6
Comstock, Handbook of Nature Study, p.598–604   6
Eberle, Basketful, p.31–43   4–6
———— Grasses, p.20–29   4–6
Havighurst, Life in America: The Midwest, p.63–69   5–6
Mason, M. E., Hominy and His Blunt-nosed Arrow   *4–5
Rhoads, Corn Grows Ripe   *4–6
Stefferud, Wonders of Seeds, p.77–89   5–6
Wilder, Farmer Boy, p.104–9   *4–6

CORN BELT: *see* North Central States

CORONADO, FRANCISCO VASQUEZ DE
American Heritage, Discoverers of the New World, p.96–105   5–6

COROT, JEAN BAPTISTE CAMILLE
Chandler, Story-Lives of Master Artists, p.187–98   6
Hillyer, Child's History of Art, p.122–24   5–6

CORREGGIO
Hillyer, Child's History of Art, p.71–73   5–6

CORSICA
Joy, Young People of the Western Mediterranean, p.67–72   6

CORTEZ, HERNANDO
American Heritage, Discoverers of the New World, p.72–77   5–6
Dalgliesh, America Begins, p.46–49   4–5
Dawson, California, p.29–31   5–6
Epstein, S., First Book of Mexico, p.24–27   5–6
McGuire, Brave Young Land, p.74–84   5–6
McNeer, Mexican Story, p.18–23   6

COSMIC RAYS
Adler, Tools of Science, p.115–18   6
Coombs, Gateway to Space   6

Gallant, R. A., Exploring the Sun, p.48–51   5–6

COSTA RICA
Brown, G. E., Tico Bravo   *4–6
Clark, A. N., Magic Money   *4–6
Goetz, Neighbors to the South, p.47–51   5–6
Quinn, Picture Map Geography of Mexico, Central America and the West Indies, p.61–67   4–6
Rothery, Central American Roundabout, p.128–51   6

COSTA RICA—FOLK TALES
Rothery, Central American Roundabout, p.207–13   6

COSTUME: *see also* Arms and Armor; Clothing; Hats; Jewelry; Masks for the Face; Motion Pictures; Plays—Production; Shoes
Ackley, Dolls To Make, p.93–107   5–6
———— Marionettes, p.15–22   5–6
Dow, How To Make Doll Clothes, p.74–80   5–6
Ficklen, Handbook of Fist Puppets, p.85–92   4–6
Hamilton, E. T., Handicraft for Girls, p.88–103   4–6
Jordan, American Costume Dolls   5–6
———— Homemade Dolls in Foreign Dress   4–6
Leeming, Costume Book   5–6

COSTUME—ARABIA
Leeming, Costume Book, p.8–10   5–6

COSTUME—AUSTRIA
Leeming, Costume Book, p.10–12   5–6

COSTUME—BRITTANY
Leeming, Costume Book, p.20–22   5–6

COSTUME—CHINA
Leeming, Costume Book, p.12–15   5–6

COSTUME—CIVIL WAR IN THE UNITED STATES
Leeming, Costume Book, p.114–16   5–6

COSTUME—COLONIAL PERIOD IN AMERICA
Leeming, Costume Book, p.105–11   5–6

COSTUME—CZECHOSLOVAKIA
Leeming, Costume Book, p.15–18   5–6

COSTUME—DENMARK
Leeming, Costume Book, p.18–19 5–6

COSTUME—EGYPT—ANCIENT
Leeming, Costume Book, p.74–76 5–6

COSTUME—ENGLAND
Leeming, Costume Book, p.94–97, 112–16 5–6

COSTUME—EUROPE
Leeming, Costume Book, p.94–100 5–6

COSTUME—FRANCE
Leeming, Costume Book, p.20–22 5–6

COSTUME—GERMANY
Leeming, Costume Book, p.22–25 5–6

COSTUME—GREECE—ANCIENT
Leeming, Costume Book, p.78–79 5–6

COSTUME—GREECE—MODERN
Leeming, Costume Book, p.26–28 5–6

COSTUME—HAWAIIAN ISLANDS
Leeming, Costume Book, p.28–29 5–6

COSTUME—HUNGARY
Leeming, Costume Book, p.32–35 5–6

COSTUME—INDIA
Leeming, Costume Book, p.35–37 5–6

COSTUME—INDONESIA
Smith, D. C., Land and People of Indonesia, p.89–91 6

COSTUME—IRELAND
Leeming, Costume Book, p.38–39 5–6

COSTUME—ITALY
Leeming, Costume Book, p.40–42 5–6

COSTUME—JAPAN
Leeming, Costume Book, p.42–45 5–6

COSTUME—LAPPS
Berry, Men, Moss, and Reindeer, p.27–29 5–6

COSTUME—MEXICO
Leeming, Costume Book, p.48–50 5–6

COSTUME—MIDDLE AGES
Leeming, Costume Book, p.82–93 5–6
Tappan, When Knights Were Bold, p.78–85 6

COSTUME—NETHERLANDS
De Jong, D., Picture Story of Holland 4–6
Leeming, Costume Book, p.30–32 5–6

COSTUME—NORWAY
Leeming, Costume Book, p.50–52 5–6

COSTUME—PALESTINE
Leeming, Costume Book, p.76–77 5–6

COSTUME—PIONEER LIFE
Leeming, Costume Book, p.110–11 5–6

COSTUME—POLAND
Leeming, Costume Book, p.52–54 5–6

COSTUME—ROME—ANCIENT
Leeming, Costume Book, p.80–81 5–6

COSTUME—ROMANIA
Leeming, Costume Book, p.54–56 5–6

COSTUME—SCOTLAND
Leeming, Costume Book, p.59–61 5–6
Sasek, This Is Edinburgh, p.17–19 (tartans) 4–6

COSTUME—SPAIN
Leeming, Costume Book, p.62–63 5–6

COSTUME—SWEDEN
Leeming, Costume Book, p.64–66 5–6
Rothery, Scandinavian Roundabout, p.167–68 6

COSTUME—SWITZERLAND
Leeming, Costume Book, p.66–67 5–6

COSTUME—THAILAND
Ayer, Getting To Know Thailand, p.21–23 4–6

COSTUME—TURKEY
Leeming, Costume Book, p.68–70 5–6

COSTUME—UNION OF SOVIET SOCIALIST REPUBLICS
Leeming, Costume Book, p.56–58 5–6

COSTUME—WALES
Leeming, Costume Book, p.70–72 5–6

COSTUME—YUGOSLAVIA
Leeming, Costume Book, p.46–47 5–6

COTTON: *see also* Dyeing; Textiles; Weaving
Association for Childhood Education, Told under the Stars and Stripes, p.122–35 (from Blue Willow) *4–6
Barrows, American Continents, p.102–6 5
Comstock, Handbook of Nature Study, p.604–8 6
Gates, Blue Willow, p.100–108 *4–6

Lenski, Cotton in My Sack   *4–6
Rogers, M., First Book of Cotton   5–6
Smith, J. R., Neighbors around the
   World, p.154–62   4

COTTON GIN: *see* Whitney, Eli

COUGARS: *see* Panthers

COUNTING: *see also* Numbers
Withers, Counting Out   4–5

COURAGE: *see also* Heroes; Lifesaving
Alden, Why the Chimes Rang *4–6
Armstrong, Ship Afire!   *6
Averill, Daniel Boone   4–6
Bannon, Hat for a Hero   *4
Batchelor, Tim and the Purple Whistle
                   *4–5
Beals, Davy Crockett   5–6
———— Kit Carson   5–6
Bothwell, Thirteenth Stone   *5–6
Bronson, Pinto's Journey   *4–5
Bulla, Riding the Pony Express *4–5
Bunyan, Pilgrim's Progress   *5–6
Ceder, Ann of Bethany   *4–6
Chrisman, Shen of the Sea, p.100–114
                   *5–6
Christensen, Buffalo Kill   *6
Dalgliesh, Courage of Sarah Noble
                   *4–5
———— Ride on the Wind   4–5
Du Soe, Three without Fear   *4–6
Edmonds, Matchlock Gun   *4–6
Faulkner, Melindy's Medal   *4–5
French, Lance of Kanana   *6
Hewes, Boy of the Lost Crusade, p.196–
   229   *6
Lindquist, W., Burma Boy   *4–6
McSwigan, Snow Treasure   *5–6
Mason, M. E., Middle Sister *4–5
O'Brien, Silver Chief   *6
Penney, Moki   *4–5
Sperry, Call It Courage   *5–6
Steele, Buffalo Knife   *4–6
Treffinger, Li Lun, Lad of Courage
                   *5–6
Waltrip, Quiet Boy   *4–6
White, B. F., On Your Own Two Feet
                   *4–6
Young, Unicorn with Silver Shoes
                   *4–6

COURTESY: *see* Etiquette; Kindness

COURTS: *see* Government; Law

COVERED WAGONS: *see also* Oregon
   Trail; The West
Dalgliesh, America Travels, p.47–53
                   4–6
Dawson, California, p.118–28   5–6
Graham, V. M., Treasure in the Cov-
   ered Wagon   *4–6
Holling, Tree in the Trail   *4–6
Mason, M. E., Susannah   *4–5
———— Young Mr. Meeker *4–5
Tavo, Buffalo Are Running   *6
Underhill, Antelope Singer   *4–6
Wilder, Little House on the Prairie
                   *4–6

COWBIRDS
Webb, Birds in Their Homes, p.46–47
                   4–6

COWBOYS: *see also* Cattle; Lasso; Ranch
   Life
Brown, R. J., Land and People of Brazil,
   p.87–90   6
Franklin, Wild Horses of the Rio
   Grande   5–6
Garst, Cowboys and Cattle Trails 4–6
Hall, E., Land and People of Argentina,
   p. 82–88   6
Holling, Book of Cowboys   5–6
Leeming, Costume Book, p.116   5–6
Rounds, Whitey Ropes and Rides *4–6
Rushmore, Cowboy Joe of the Circle S
                   *4–5
Spencer, P. R., Finding New Trails,
   p.10–14   4

COWBOYS—SONGS
Buchanan, How Man Made Music,
   p.187–89   6
Eberle, Basketful, p.60–62   4–6
Holling, Book of Cowboys   5–6
Tousey, Cowboy Tommy's Roundup
                   *4–5

COWS: *see also* Butter; Cattle; Cheese;
   Milk
Agle, Three Boys and the Remarkable
   Cow   *4–5
Barr, Young Scientist Takes a Ride,
   p.123–24   5–6
Buehr, Meat from Ranch to Table,
   p.65–76   4–6

Crowley, Azor and the Blue-eyed Cow
*4–6

———— Tor and Azor   *4–6
De Jong, M., Little Cow and the Turtle
*4–6
Eberle, Basketful, p.181–93   4–6
Fry, Bell for Ringelblume   *4–5
Hogeboom, Familiar Animals and How
To Draw Them, p.8–11   4–5
MacGregor, Miss Pickerell and the
Geiger Counter   *4–6
Mason, M. E., Susannah   *4–5
Weil, Animal Families   4

COYOTES
Disney, Worlds of Nature, p.76–80
4–6
Lathrop, Let Them Live, p.34–37   4–6
Mason, G. F., Animal Homes, p.13–17
4–6
———— Animal Sounds, p.72–75   5–6
———— Animal Tracks, p.68–69   4–6
Stoutenberg, Wild Animals of the Far
West, p.42–44   4–6

CRABS: *see also* Hermit Crabs
Bronson, Children of the Sea, p.139–49
6
Cooper, E. K., Science on the Shores
and Banks, p.106–11   5–6
Haywood, Penny and Peter, p.3–21 *4
Hyde, Animal Clocks and Compasses,
p.13–17   5–6
Neurath, Wonder World of the Sea-
shore, p.6–7, 13–16, 20   4–6

CRANES (birds)
Gillham, Beyond the Clapping Moun-
tains, p.76–85   *4–6
McClung, Whooping Crane   4–5

CRATER LAKE NATIONAL PARK
Melbo, Our Country's National Parks,
v.2, p.198–214   6

CRAYFISH
Buck, M. W., Pets from the Pond, p.64–
65   4–6
Comstock, Handbook of Nature Study,
p.425–32   6
Cooper, E. K., Science on the Shores
and Banks, p.116–18   5–6
Kane, Tale of a Pond, p.6, 30, 63, 82–
84   5–6

CREAM: *see* Milk

CREATION
Benson, Stories of the Gods and Heroes,
p.15–43   5–6

CRETE
Falls, First 3000 Years, p.88–91   4–6
Friedman, E., Digging into Yesterday,
p.52–72   5–6
Honour, Secrets of Minos   6
Kubie, First Book of Archaeology, p.50–
52   6
Watson, Golden History of the World,
p.26–28   5–6

CRICKETS
Bronson, Grasshopper Book, p.70–107
4–6
Comstock, Handbook of Nature Study,
p.344–51   6
Earle, Crickets   4–6
Gaul, Picture Book of Insects, p.2–3
4–6
Hogner, Grashoppers and Crickets,
p.41–58   4–5
Irving, Sound and Ultrasonics, p.93–95
6
Mason, G. F., Animal Sounds, p.48–51
5–6
Selden, Cricket in Times Square *4–6
Teale, Insect Friends, p.73–82   5–6
Williamson, First Book of Bugs, p.9–12
4–5

CRIME: *see also* Police
Anckarsvard, Robber Ghost   *5–6
Armer, Waterless Mountain, p.99–102,
170–72, 178–79   *5–6
Cheney, Rocking Chair Buck (poaching)
*4–5
Du Bois, Three Policemen   *4–6
Enright, Then There Were Five, p.89–
97   *5–6
Estes, Ginger Pye   *4–6
Evans, Adventure Book of Money,
p.69–72   5–6
Holbrook, Golden Age of Railroads,
p.129–40   5–6
Larom, Mountain Pony   *6
Lindgren, Rasmus and the Vagabond
*4–6
McCloskey, Homer Price, p.10–29
*5–6
Moon, Chi-Wee, 29–40   *4–6
Oakes, Bamboo Gate, p.121–37 *4–6

O'Brien, Silver Chief   *6
Rounds, Stolen Pony   *5–6
Wood, W. H., Perils of Pacifico   *4–6

CRIMEA
Hume, Florence Nightingale   5–6
McNeer, Armed with Courage, p.9–22
    5–6
Nazaroff, Land of the Russian People,
    p.48–51   6

CROCKETT, DAVID
Beals, Davy Crockett   5–6
Johnson, W. W., Birth of Texas   5–6
Le Sueur, Chanticleer of Wilderness
    Road   5–6
Steele, Davy Crockett's Earthquake
    4–6

CROCODILE BIRDS: see Plovers

CROCODILES
Buck, F., Jungle Animals, p.20–21 5–6
Hylander, Animals in Armor, p.27–29
    6
Parker, B. M., Reptiles, p.6–9   4–6
Zim, Alligators and Crocodiles   4

CROCUSES
Comstock, Handbook of Nature Study,
    p.547–49   6

CROISSANTS—HISTORY
Buehr, Bread, p.26–30   4–6

CROPS: see Agriculture

CROW INDIANS
Bleeker, Crow Indians   5–6

CROWS
Bailey, C. S., Miss Hickory   *4–6
Behn, Roderick   *5–6
Colby, First Hunt, p.17   5–6
Comstock, Handbook of Nature Study,
    p.124–27   6
Field, Hitty, p.20–27   *5–6
Gillham, Beyond the Clapping Moun-
    tains, p.31–43, 51–67   *4–6
Lathrop, Let Them Live, p.64–67 4–6
Marokvia, Grococo   *4–5

CRUELTY: see Kindness to Animals

CRUISERS
Gilmore, Model Boats for Beginners,
    p.48–53   5–6
Hogeboom, Boats and How To Draw
    Them, p.28–31   4–5

CRUSADES: see also Chivalry; Knights;
    Middle Ages
Boardman, Castles, p.32, 35–37, 85 6
Buchanan, How Man Made Music,
    p.164–65   6
Buehr, Crusaders   5–6
Chubb, Byzantines, p.13–22, 107–11
    6
Fitch, Allah, the God of Islam, p.68–73
    6
Harper, Easter Chimes, p.90–103
    *4–6
Hartman, Builders of the Old World,
    p.270–73   6
Hazeltine, Easter Book of Legends and
    Stories, p.330–60   *5–6
Hillyer, Child's History of the World,
    p.292–303   5–6
Jewett, God's Troubadour, p.79–88
    5–6
McGuire, Glimpses into the Long Ago,
    p.309–18   5–6
Tappan, When Knights Were Bold,
    p.137–48   6
Watson, Golden History of the World,
    p.86–89   5–6

CRUSTACEA: see also Barnacles; Crabs;
    Crayfish; Lobsters; Shellfish
Cooper, E. K., Science on the Shores
    and Banks, p.48–49, 104–16 5–6
Hausman, Beginner's Guide to Fresh-
    Water Life, p.78–83   6
Morgan, A. H., Field Book of Animals
    in Winter, p.113–42   6
————— Field Book of Ponds and
    Streams, p.158–74   6
Reed, Sea for Sam, p.157–64   6
Robertson, G., Strange Sea Life, p.54–56
    5–6

CRYSTALS: see also names of crystals,
    as Salt
Adler, Giant Golden Book of Math-
    ematics, p.36–37   6
Beeler, Experiments in Chemistry, p.24–
    29   5–6
Comstock, Handbook of Nature Study,
    p.751–55   6
Disraeli, New Worlds through the Mi-
    croscope, p.164–70   6
Irving, Sound and Ultrasonics, p.115,
    125–27   6

Loomis, Field Book of Common Rocks and Minerals　　6

Morgan, A. P., First Chemistry Book for Boys and Girls, p.36–52　　5–6

CUBA

Albee, Three Young Kings　　*4–5

Goetz, Neighbors to the South, p.9–14　　5–6

Hughes, First Book of the West Indies, p.12–16　　5–6

Judson, Soldier Doctor, p.70–108　　6

Quinn, Picture Map Geography of Mexico, Central America and the West Indies, p.86–92　　4–6

CUBA—GAMES: *see* Games—Cuba

CUCHULAIN

Hazeltine, Hero Tales from Many Lands, p.161–70　　5–6

Van Stockum, Pegeen, p.110–16　　*6

CUCKOOS

Lathrop, Let Them Live, p.74–77　　4–6

Lavine, Strange Travelers, p.67–68　　5–6

CUFFEE, PAUL

Shackelford, Child's Story of the Negro, p.108–13　　4–5

CUNEIFORM WRITING: *see also* Clay Tablets

Kubie, First Book of Archaeology, p.40–42　　6

CURIE, MARIE SKLODOWSKA

Asimov, Breakthroughs in Science, p.154–62　　5–6

Bigland, Madame Curie　　6

Cottler, Heroes of Civilization, p.156–65　　6

Doorly, Radium Woman　　5–6

Fermi, Story of Atomic Energy, p.13–17, 31–33, 155–56　　6

Parker, B. M., Scientist and His Tools, p.2–5　　5–6

CURIOSITY

Alden, Why the Chimes Rang, p.66–79　　*4–6

CURLEWS

Bosiger, Bird Is Born, p.36–43　　5–6

CURRENCY: *see* Money

CURRIER & IVES

Bailey, C. S., Pioneer Art in America, p.168–82　　*5–6

CUSTER, GEORGE ARMSTRONG

Garst, Sitting Bull, p.119–21　　6

CUSTOMS: *see* Festivals; Home Life, name of country; Manners and Customs; School Life, name of country; also names of countries, as Netherlands

CUTTLEFISH

Beaty, Baby Whale, p.28–30, 57–60　　4–6

Bronson, Children of the Sea, p.78–82, 147–50, 253–55　　6

Earle, Octopus　　4–6

Robertson, G., Strange Sea Life, p.95–96　　5–6

CYCLONES: *see* Storms; Winds

CYRUS THE GREAT

Falls, First 3000 Years, p.146–48　　6

CZECHOSLOVAKIA: *see also* Costume —Czechoslovakia

Barrows, Old World Lands, p.107–10　　6

CZECHOSLOVAKIA—FOLK TALES

Fenner, Fools and Funny Fellows, p.87–95　　4–6

CZECHS IN THE UNITED STATES

Association for Childhood Education, Told under the Stars and Stripes, p.1–12, 118–19　　*4–6

Judson, Lost Violin　　*5–6

DADDY LONGLEGS

Comstock, Handbook of Nature Study, p.432–35　　6

DAEDALUS AND ICARUS

Asimov, Words from the Myths, p.143–46　　6

Benson, Stories of the Gods and Heroes, p.181–87　　5–6

Bishop, R. W., From Kite to Kitty Hawk, p.4–8　　6

DAFFODILS

Comstock, Handbook of Nature Study, p.549–52　　6

DAIRYING: *see also* Butter; Cattle; Cheese; Cows; Milk; Netherlands

Barrows, American Continents, p.146–47   5

Eberle, Basketful, p.181–200   4–6

DAKOTA INDIANS

Brewster, First Book of Indians, p.28–36   4–5

McCracken, Great White Buffalo   5–6

DAKOTA TERRITORY

Association for Childhood Education, Told under the Stars and Stripes, p.325–35   *4–6

Meigs, Willow Whistle   *4–6

Wilder, By the Shores of Silver Lake   *5–6

———— Little Town on the Prairie   *5–6

———— Long Winter   *5–6

DAMIEN, FATHER

McNeer, Armed with Courage, p.25–38   5–6

DAMROSCH, WALTER

Schwimmer, Great Musicians as Children, p.141–45   6

DAMS: *see also* Floods; Irrigation; Nile River; Tennessee Valley Authority; Water Power; Water Supply

Buckley, Spanish Plateau, p.84–95   6

Jackson, D., Wonderful World of Engineering, p.82–89   6

Parker, B. M., Water, p.23   5–6

DAMSEL FLIES: *see* Dragonflies

DANCING: *see also* Ballet; Costume; Indians of North America—Dances

Estes, Moffats, p.141–66   *4–6

Herman, Folk Dances for All   4–6

Mulac, Game Book, p.250–57   6

Weston, Bhimsa, the Dancing Bear   *4–6

DANCING—BULGARIA

Herman, Folk Dances for All, p.1–5   4–6

DANCING—COLONIAL PERIOD IN AMERICA

Meigs, Wind in the Chimney, p.36–43   *5–6

DANCING—DENMARK

Herman, Folk Dances for All, p.20–25, 52–53   4–6

DANCING—ESTONIA

Herman, Folk Dances for All, p.84–87   4–6

DANCING—FINLAND

Herman, Folk Dances for All, p.95–99   4–6

DANCING—GERMANY

Herman, Folk Dances for All, p.37–43, 88–92   4–6

DANCING—INDONESIA

Smith, D. C., Land and People of Indonesia, p.101–2   6

DANCING—ISRAEL

Herman, Folk Dances for All, p.10–15   4–6

DANCING—ITALY

Herman, Folk Dances for All, p.75–79   4–6

DANCING—MEXICO

Herman, Folk Dances for All, p.16–19   4–6

DANCING—NORWAY

Herman, Folk Dances for All, p.27–30   4–6

DANCING—PIONEER LIFE

Wilder, Little House in the Big Woods, p.131–55   *4–6

DANCING—POLAND

Herman, Folk Dances for All, p.80–83   4–6

DANCING—SICILY

Herman, Folk Dances for All, p.44–48   4–6

DANCING—SWEDEN

Herman, Folk Dances for All, p.31–36   4–6

DANCING—SWITZERLAND

Herman, Folk Dances for All, p.54–60   4–6

DANCING—THAILAND

Ayer, Getting To Know Thailand, p.18–20   4–6

DANCING—UNION OF SOVIET SOCIALIST REPUBLICS

Herman, Folk Dances for All, p.6–9, 61–65, 70–72   4–6

DANCING—UNITED STATES

Herman, Folk Dances for All, p.66–69   4–6

DANIEL
Bowie, Bible Story for Boys and Girls: Old Testament, p.206–12   4–6

DARE, VIRGINIA
Barksdale, That Country Called Virginia, p.5   6

DARIUS
Falls, First 3000 Years, p.148–54   6

DARK AGES: *see* Barbarians; Middle Ages

DARWIN, CHARLES
Asimov, Breakthroughs in Science, p. 145–53   5–6
Cottler, Heroes of Civilization, p.328–38   6
Ludovici, World of the Microscope, p.14–20   6

DATE LINE: *see* Standard Time

DATES
Eberle, Basketful, p.145–53   4–6

DAVENPORT, THOMAS
Yates, R. F., Boy and a Motor, p.2–5   6

DAVID, KING OF ISRAEL
Adams, K., Book of Giant Stories, p.35–40   *5–6
Bowie, Bible Story for Boys and Girls: Old Testament, p.98–126   4–6
De la Mare, Stories from the Bible, p.395–420   5–6
Falls, First 3000 Years, p.119–21, 123   6
Hartman, In Bible Days, p.99–104   6
Petersham, David   4–5

DAVY, HUMPHRY
Cottler, Heroes of Civilization, p.146–55   6

DAYS: *see also* Calendars; Holidays; also names of special days, as Bird Day; Christmas
Galt, Seven Days from Sunday   6
McSpadden, Book of Holidays, p.436–42   6

DDT
Eberle, Modern Medical Discoveries, p.143–50   5–6

DEAD SEA SCROLLS
Longsworth, Exploring Caves, p.8–10   6

DEATH
Buck, P., Big Wave   *6
White, B. F., On Your Own Two Feet   *4–6

DEBUSSY, ACHILLE CLAUDE
Burch, Famous Composers for Young People, p.165–72   4–6

DECATUR, STEPHEN
Lawson, R., Watchwords of Liberty, p.38   4–6
Mitchell, Ships That Made U.S. History, p.26–30   6
Spencer, P. R., Traveling New Trails, p.33–40   6

DECLARATION OF HUMAN RIGHTS
Wagner, Put Democracy to Work, p.139–46   6

DECLARATION OF INDEPENDENCE: *see also* Fourth of July; Jefferson, Thomas; Revolutionary War in America
Brown, H. M., America Is My Country, p.37–45, 225–27   5–6
Commager, H. S., Great Declaration   6
Dalgliesh, Fourth of July Story   4–6
Fisher, D. F. C., Our Independence and the Constitution   4–5
Foster, G., George Washington's World, p.179–82   6
Hays, Freedom, p.1–4   5–6

DECORATION DAY: *see* Memorial Day

DEER: *see also* Caribous; Moose; Reindeer
Bridges, Zoo Babies, p.28–32, 51–55   4–6
Bronson, Horns and Antlers   5–7
Brown, V., How To Understand Animal Talk, p.103–14   6
Buff, Big Tree, p.38–43   *5–6
Cheney, Rocking Chair Buck   *4–5
Colby, First Hunt, p.14–15   5–6
Disney, Worlds of Nature, p.56–61   4–6
Franklin, Wild Animals of the Southwest, p.154–82   5–6
Hogner, Animal Book, p.107–19   6
Hyde, Animal Clocks and Compasses, p.97–98   5–6
Knight, C. R., Life through the Ages, p.58–59   6

Lathrop, Let Them Live, p.40–42   4–6
McClung, Spike   4
Mason, G. F., Animal Tracks, p.72–75
                                      4–6
Moe, Animal Inn, p.162–74   4–6
Parker, B. M., Animals We Know,
    p.24–26   5–6
Perkins, Marlin Perkins' Zooparade,
    p.84–87   4–6
Salten, Bambi   *5–6
Stoutenberg, Wild Animals of the Far
    West, p.105–13   4–6

DELAWARE
De Angeli, Elin's Amerika   *4–6
Lenski, Judy's Journey, p.171–86   *4–6
Quinn, Picture Map Geography of the
    United States, p.36–39   4–6

DELIUS, FREDERICK
Burch, Modern Composers for Young
    People, p.77–82   5–6

DEMOCRACY: *see also* Government
Brown, H. M., America Is My Country
                                      5–6
Buff, Apple and the Arrow   *4–6
Coy, First Book of Congress   6
Daugherty, Landing of the Pilgrims
                                      4–6
Eaton, That Lively Man, Ben Franklin
                                        6
Elting, We Are the Government   6
Fisher, D. F. C., Our Independence and
    the Constitution   4–5
Fisher, L., You and the United Nations
                                      5–6
Gordon, You and Democracy   6
Hays, Freedom   5–6
Lawson, R., Watchwords of Liberty
                                      4–6
Meadowcroft, By Secret Railway   *5–6
Spencer, C., Made in China, p.67–72
                                      5–6
Turner, Town Meeting Means Me   4–6
Wagner, Put Democracy to Work   6
Witty, You and the Constitution of the
    United States   5–6

DEMOSTHENES
Hartman, Builders of the Old World,
    p.156–58   6

DENMARK: *see also* Copenhagen; Cos-
    tume—Denmark; Dancing—Denmark

Barrows, Old World Lands, p.222–25
                                        6
Hazeltine, Hero Tales from Many
    Lands, p.204–18   5–6
O'Neill, Picture Story of Denmark
                                      4–6
Owen, Denmark Caravan   *5–6

DENMARK—FOLK TALES
Owen, Denmark Caravan   5–6
Parker, B. M., Trees, p.29–30   4–6

DENTISTRY: *see* Teeth

DEPRESSION—BUSINESS: *see* Business
    Depression; Unemployment

DESERTS: *see also* Bedouins; Cactus;
    Camels; Dates; Iraq; Irrigation; Pue-
    blo Indians; Sahara Desert; South-
    west; Yucca
Adler, Weather in Your Life, p.77–80
                                      5–6
Association for Childhood Education,
    Told under the Stars and Stripes,
    p.31–46   *4–6
Ault, This Is the Desert   5–6
Buff, Elf Owl   4–5
Disney, Worlds of Nature, p.82–93
                                      4–6
Ellis, Arabs, p.25–29   6
Epstein, S., All about the Desert 5–6
Fenton, C. L., Land We Live On, p.14–
    17, 48–49   4–6
_____ Wild Folk in the Desert   4–6
French, Lance of Kanana   *6
Gidal, Sons of the Desert   5–6
Goetz, Deserts   4–6
Huntington, Let's Go to the Desert
                                      4–5
Joy, Desert Caravans   5–6
Life, World We Live In, p.128–43   5–6
Moon, Chi-Wee   *4–6
Nevil, Picture Story of the Middle East
                                      4–6
Spencer, P. R., Finding New Trails,
    p.337–43   4

DESIGN: *see also* Art; Indians of North
    America—Art
Downer, Discovering Design   6
Jaeger, Easy Crafts, p.64–65   4–6

DE SOTO, HERNANDO
American Heritage, Discoverers of the
    New World, p.104–11   5–6

Duvoisin, And There Was America, p.20–24   4–6
Syme, De Soto   4–5

DESTROYERS
Lent, Men at Work in New England, p.34–41   4–6

DETECTIVE STORIES: *see* Crime

DETERGENTS: *see also* Soap
Beeler, Experiments in Chemistry, p.122–26   5–6

DEWEY, GEORGE
Lawson, R., Watchwords of Liberty, p.92–94   4–6
Mitchell, Ships That Made U.S. History, p.77–80   6

DIAMONDS
Barrows, Old World Lands, p.44   6
Batchelor, Superstitious? Here's Why!, p.70–71   6
Du Bois, Twenty-one Balloons, p.69–108   *6
May, Let's Read about Brazil, p.71–72   4–6
Rothery, South American Roundabout, p.185–87   5–6

DIAZ, BARTHOLOMEW
Duvoisin, They Put Out to Sea, p.88–91   4–6
Hartman, Builders of the Old World, p.411–13   6

DICKENS, CHARLES
Coffman, Famous Authors for Young People, p.73–82   5–6
Foster, G., Abraham Lincoln's World, p.102–4   6

DICTAPHONES
Lent, Men at Work in New England, p.106–11   4–6
Parker, B. M., Sound, p.22–23   5–6

DICTIONARIES
Picturesque Word Origins   6

DIESEL ENGINES
Barnard, Macmillan Science-Life Series, Bk.6, p.293–94   6
Billings, Diesel-Electric 4030, p.45–72   5–6
Darrow, Boys' Own Book of Great Inventions, p.153–55   6

McCoy, Big Book of Real Submarines   4–6
Morgan, A. P., Boys' Book of Engines, Motors & Turbines, p.140–46   6
Schneider, H., More Power to You, p.57–58   5–6
Van Metre, Trains, Tracks and Travel, p.224–28   6

DIGESTION
Glemser, All about the Human Body, p.25–32   5–6
Ravielli, Wonders of the Human Body, p.110–17   5–6
Schneider, H., How Your Body Works, p.11–21   4–6

DINGOES
Kjelgaard, Boomerang Hunter   *5–6

DINOSAURS: *see* Prehistoric Animals; Reptiles

DIOMEDE ISLANDS
Stefansson, Here Is Alaska, p.107–11   6

DIRECTION FINDING
Barr, Young Scientist Takes a Ride, p.103–9   5–6
Barrows, Our Big World, p.16–17   4

DIRIGIBLES: *see* Airships

DISCOVERIES IN GEOGRAPHY: *see also* Antarctic Regions; Arctic Regions; Discovery Period in America; Explorers; Trade—Middle Ages; also names of explorers, as Diaz, Bartholomew; Gama, Vasco da; Polo, Marco
Duvoisin, They Put Out to Sea   4–6

DISCOVERIES IN SCIENCE: *see also* Electricity; Fossils; Industries; Inventions; Machines; Medicine; Science; also names of various inventions, as Telegraph; also names of scientists, as Galileo
Asimov, Breakthroughs in Science   6
Bigland, Madame Curie   6

DISCOVERY PERIOD IN AMERICA: *see also* Colonial Period in America; Explorers; Northmen; also names of explorers, as Columbus, Christopher
American Heritage, Discoverers of the New World   5–6

Baker, N. B., Amerigo Vespucci   5–6
———— Juan Ponce de León   5–6
Bonner, Canada and Her Story   5–6
Dalgliesh, America Begins   4–5
Dawson, California   5–6
Duvoisin, And There Was America
    4–6
Hartman, Builders of the Old World,
    p.419–47   6
Hillyer, Child's History of the World,
    p.337–58   5–6
Janeway, Vikings   4–6
McGuire, Brave Young Land   5–6
Meadowcroft, Land of the Free, p.1–7
    4–5
Peck, Pageant of South American His-
    tory, p.67–123   6
Trease, Sir Walter Raleigh   5–6

DISEASES: *see also* Antibiotics; Bacteria;
    Health; Medicine
Baker, A. O., Your Science World,
    p.163–69   6
Bleeker, Inca, p.117–20   5–6
Calder, Wonderful World of Medicine
    5–6
Ludovici, World of the Microscope,
    p.23–31   6
Schatz, Story of Microbes, p.126–32   6

DISTANCE ESTIMATION
Barr, Young Scientist Takes a Ride,
    p.89–93   5–6

DIVING
Knowlton, Let's Explore beneath the
    Sea   5–6
MacGregor, Miss Pickerell Goes Under-
    sea   *4–6
Scheib, What Happened?, p.99–109
    5–6

DIX, DOROTHEA
Fisher, D. F. C., And Long Remember,
    p.72–83   6

DOCTORS: *see also* Medicine; Medicine
    Man; Veterinarians; also names of
    doctors, as Gorgas, William Craw-
    ford
Carr, Children of the Covered Wagon,
    p.165–91   *4–6
Eberle, Modern Medical Discoveries
    5–6
Manton, Elizabeth Garrett, M.D.   6

DODDER
Parker, B. M., Dependent Plants, p.30–
    31   5–6

DODGE, MARY MAPES
Coffman, Famous Authors for Young
    People, p.85–89   5–6

DODGSON, CHARLES LUTWIDGE:
    see Carroll, Lewis

DOG RACING: *see* Racing

DOGS: *see also* St. Bernard Pass
Bannon, Watchdog   *4–5
Bianco, All about Pets, p.31–48   5–6
Brown, V., How To Understand Animal
    Talk, p.11–20, 73–88   6
Carlson, N. S., Talking Cat, p.30–42
    *4–6
Carroll, Tough Enough's Indians   *4–5
———— Tough Enough's Pony   *4–5
———— Tough Enough's Trip   *4–6
Child Study Association of America,
    Read to Yourself Storybook, p.114–
    35, 220–35   *4–5
Cleary, Henry and Beezus   *4–5
———— Henry and Ribsy   *4–6
———— Henry Huggins   *4–5
Comstock, Handbook of Nature Study,
    p.254–60   6
Darling, E. B., Baldy of Nome   *6
De la Mare, Animal Stories, p.111–14
    *4–6
Enright, Saturdays, p.61–70   *4–6
Estes, Ginger Pye   *4–6
Fenton, E., Phantom of Walkaway Hill
    *4–6
Fox, From Bones to Bodies, p.24–25
    6
Franklin, Wild Animals of the South-
    west, p.197–214   5–6
Haywood, Penny and Peter, p.42–80,
    94–109   *4
Henry, M., Always Reddy   *4–6
———— Wagging Tails   4–6
Hogeboom, Dogs and How To Draw
    Them   4–5
Hogner, Animal Book, p.139–48   6
———— Barnyard Family, p.56–63
    5–6
———— Farm Animals, p.107–72   6
Hyde, Animal Clocks and Compasses,
    p.108–9   5–6
Icenhower, First Book of the Antarctic,
    p.48–49   4–6

Jackson, C. P., Spice's Football   *4–5
Johnson, M. S., Gay   *4–6
Knight, C. R., Life through the Ages, p.38–39   6
Knight, E. M., Lassie Come-Home   *6
Lindquist, W., Alaska, p.70–81   5–6
Lippincott, Wilderness Champion   5–6
Machetanz, Puppy Named Gih   *4–5
MacKellar, Wee Joseph   *4–5
Malcolmson, Yipe   *4–6
Mason, G. F., Animal Tracks, p.60–61   4–6
Norling, Pogo's Truck Ride   *4
O'Brien, Silver Chief   *6
Rankin, L., Daughter of the Mountains   *5–6
Robertson, K., Ticktock and Jim, p.86–90, 110–15   *4–6
Rounds, Stolen Pony   *5–6
Seaman, Mr. Peck's Pets, p.9–25, 73–80   *4–5
Sherman, Real Book about Dogs   5–6
Spencer, P. R., Finding New Trails, p.33–76   4
Sperry, All about the Arctic and Antarctic, p.96–101   4–6
Stefansson, Here Is Alaska, p.64–69   6
Stolz, Dog on Barkham Street   *5–6
Stuart, Rightful Owner   *4–6
Taber, First Book of Dogs   4–5
Tarry, My Dog Rinty   *4–5
Urmston, New Boy   *4–6
Weil, Animal Families   4
White, A. H., Junket   *4–6
Woolley, Ellie's Problem Dog   *4–6

DOGS—CARE AND TRAINING
Johnson, M. S., Gay, p.53–69   *4–6
Meek, So You're Going To Get a Puppy   4–6
Sherman, Real Book About Dogs, p.21–102   5–6

DOGWOOD
Comstock, Handbook of Nature Study, p.680–82   6
McKenny, Trees of the Countryside, p.50–51   4–6

DOLL DRESSMAKING
Ackley, Dolls To Make   5–6
Dow, How To Make Doll Clothes   5–6
Hoffmann, Sew Easy!, p.69–79   4–6

DOLL FESTIVAL
Jakeman, Getting To Know Japan, p.20–21   4–6

DOLL FURNITURE
Carlson, B. W., Make It Yourself!, p.94–96   4–6
Lee, What To Do Now, p.32–47   4–6
Oliver, Rain or Shine, p.24–29   4–5
Soong, Art of Chinese Paper Folding, p.58–62, 119–32   4–6
Zarchy, Let's Make More Things, p.46–49   5–6

DOLLS
Ackley, Dolls To Make   5–6
Bailey, C. S., Miss Hickory   *4–6
Bowers, Wishing Book Doll   *4–5
Brock, Drusilla   *4–5
Carlson, B. W., Make It and Use It   4–6
Elting, Lollypop Factory, p.42–53   4–5
Field, Hitty   *5–6
Godden, Doll's House   *4–6
———— Impunity Jane   *4–5
———— Miss Happiness and Miss Flower   *4–5
Jordan, American Costume Dolls   5–6
———— Homemade Dolls in Foreign Dress   4–6
Lee, What To Do Now, p.18–19, 28–31   4–6
McGinley, Most Wonderful Doll in the World   *4–5
Parrish, Floating Island   *4–6
Snow, Doll for Lily Belle   *4–5

DOLPHINS
Andrews, All about Whales, p.133–44   5–6
Bronson, Children of the Sea   6
Hogner, Animal Book, p.185–94   6
Hyde, Animal Clocks and Compasses, p.102–3   5–6

DOMESTIC ANIMALS: *see* Animals—Domestic; Kindness to Animals; Pets; also names of animals, as Cats

DOMESTIC SCIENCE: *see* Home Economics

DOMINIC, SAINT
Tappan, When Knights Were Bold, p.188–93   6

DOMINICAN REPUBLIC

Goetz, Neighbors to the South, p.19–21
5–6

Henry, M., Dominican Republic   4–6

Hughes, First Book of the West Indies,
p.22–23   5–6

Quinn, Picture Map Geography of Mexico, Central America and the West Indies, p.97–99   4–6

DONKEYS

Association for Childhood Education, Told under the Stars and Stripes, p.186–95   *4–6

Bronson, Pinto's Journey   *4–5

De la Mare, Animal Stories, p.203–11
*4–6

Fenton, C. L., Wild Folk in the Desert, p.123–26   4–6

Gates, Sarah's Idea   *4–6

Henry, M., Album of Horses, p.98–101
5–6

Hogeboom, Familiar Animals and How To Draw Them, p.32–35   4–5

Hogner, Barnyard Family, p.17–19
5–6

———— Horse Family, p.29–31   4–6

Stinetorf, Children of North Africa, p.44–57   *5–6

Vance, While Shepherds Watched
*4–6

Weil, Animal Families   4

DOPPLER'S PRINCIPLE

Barr, Young Scientist Takes a Ride, p.79–80   5–6

DOUGLAS, STEPHEN ARNOLD

Neyhart, Henry's Lincoln   *4–6

DOUGLASS, FREDERICK

Bontemps, Frederick Douglass   4–6

Shackelford, Child's Story of the Negro, p.120–24   4–5

DOVES: *see* Mourning Doves; Pigeons

DRAGONFLIES

Barker, Winter-sleeping Wildlife, p.116–20   5–6

Comstock, Handbook of Nature Study, p.401–8   6

Cooper, E. K., Science on the Shores and Banks, p.42, 52–53   5–6

Gaul, Picture Book of Insects, p.8–9
4–6

Hylander, Insects on Parade, p.160–63
6

Kane, Tale of a Pond   5–6

Lane, F. C., All About the Insect World, p.50–53   5–6

Parker, B. M., Insects and Their Ways, p.10–11   4–6

Phillips, Dragonflies and Damselflies
5–6

Teale, Insect Friends, p.35–38   5–6

———— Junior Book of Insects, p.140–48   6

DRAGONS

Bright, Richard Brown and the Dragon
*4–5

Gannett, Elmer and the Dragon   *4–5

———— My Father's Dragon   *4–5

Grahame, Reluctant Dragon   *4–6

Jacobson, First Book of Mythical Beasts, p.10–27   4–6

Lloyd, Desperate Dragons   *4–6

Manning, Dragon in Danger   *4–6

Sawyer, Year of the Christmas Dragon
*4–5

Spencer, C., Made in China, p.21–27
5–6

DRAGS: *see* Travois

DRAKE, FRANCIS

American Heritage, Discoverers of the New World, p.144–49   5–6

Dalgliesh, America Begins, p.55–56
4–5

Dawson, California, p.42–44   5–6

Duvoisin, And There Was America, p.41–43   4–6

Foster, G., World of Captain John Smith, p.5–11, 37, 56, 291–92   6

Latham, Drake   6

DRAMATICS: *see* Ballet; Costume; Dancing; Fairs; Festivals; Games; Motion Pictures; Operas; Pageants; Pantomimes; Plays; Shadow Plays; Singing Games; Theater; also names of subjects, subhead Plays, as Christmas—Plays

DRAWING: *see also* Cartoons; Design

Hogeboom, Boats and How To Draw Them   4–5

———— Dogs and How To Draw Them   4–5

_____ Familiar Animals and How To Draw Them   4–5

_____ Horses and How To Draw Them   4–6

Slobodkin, First Book of Drawing   5–6

Wiess, H., Pencil, Pen and Brush   5–6

DRIED FRUITS: *see* Dates; Prunes; Raisins

DRINKS: *see* Beverages

DRIVING: *see* Automobiles

DROSOPHILA
Hyde, Animal Clocks and Compasses, p.139–43   5–6

DROUGHT: *see also* Dust Storms; Erosion; Irrigation; Soil Conservation
Buff, Hah-Nee of the Cliff Dwellers   *4–6

DRUGS: *see* Medicine; Narcotics

DRUMS
Buchanan, How Man Made Music, p.21–25   6
Huntington, Tune Up   4–6
Kettelkamp, Drums, Rattles, and Bells, p.11–26   4–6
Lacey, Picture Book of Musical Instruments, p.36–39   5–6
Rogers, F., Heels, Wheels, and Wire, p.132–41   5–6

DRY LANDS: *see* Deserts; Drought

DUCKS: *see also* Poultry
Brown, V., How To Understand Animal Talk, p.45–46   6
Darling, L., Greenhead   5–6
De Jong, M., Good Luck Duck   *4–5
Fox, From Bones to Bodies, p.59–61   6
Green, Home for Woody (wood duck)   4–6
Kane, Tale of a Meadow, p.28–30   4–6
Lathrop, Let Them Live, p.24–27   4–6
Weil, Animal Families   4

DUNBAR, PAUL LAWRENCE
Shackelford, Child's Story of the Negro, p.151–57   4–5

DUNIWAY, ABIGAIL SCOTT
Ross, N. W., Heroines of the Early West, p.156–78   5–6

DÜRER, ALBRECHT
Chandler, Story-Lives of Master Artists, p.41–53   6
Hillyer, Child's History of Art, p.85–87   5–6

DUST
Adler, Dust   5–6
Disraeli, New Worlds through the Microscope, p.157–58   6

DUST STORMS
Van Dersal, Land Renewed, p.24–29   6

DUTCH EAST INDIES: *see* East Indies

DUTCH IN AMERICA: *see also* Hudson, Henry
Bailey, C. S., Pioneer Art in America, p.78–89   *5–6
Dalgliesh, America Builds Homes   4–5
Duvoisin, And There Was America, p.37–40   4–6
Edmonds, Matchlock Gun   *4–6
McGinley, Mince Pie and Mistletoe   4–6
Rich, First Book of the Early Settlers, p.46–62   4–6

DVOŘÁK, ANTON
Burch, Modern Composers for Young People, p.17–24   5–6
Judson, Lost Violin, p.195–98   *5–6
Schwimmer, Great Musicians as Children, p.223–30   6

DWARFS
Brown, A. F., In the Days of Giants, p.80–97   4–6
Hauff, Dwarf Long-Nose   *4–6

DWELLINGS: *see* Eskimos—Dwellings; Houses; Indians of North America—Dwellings

DYEING
Bailey, C. S., Pioneer Art in America, p.155–67   *5–6
Beeler, Experiments in Chemistry, p.127–33   5–6
Hollos, Story of Your Coat   4–5

DYNAMOS: *see also* Electric Motors; Faraday, Michael
Darrow, Boys' Own Book of Great Inventions, p.182–89   6
Hartman, Machines, p.93–97   6
Land, B., Quest of Isaac Newton, p.17–31   6

Morgan, A. P., Boy Electrician, p.322–
36   6
———— First Electrical Book for Boys,
p.154–64   6
Yates, R. F., Boy and a Motor, p.14–18
         6

EAGLES
Buff, Big Tree, p.52–61   *5–6
McClung, Vulcan   4–5

EAR
Glemser, All about the Human Body,
p.114–17   5–6
Irving, Sound and Ultrasonics, p.98–108
         6
Knight, D. C., First Book of Sound,
p.18–19   5–6
Parker, B. M., Sound, p.28–34   5–6
Zim, Our Senses and How They Work,
p.59–86   4–6

EARNING MONEY: see Money—Acquisition and Use

EARTH see also Antarctic Regions; Arc-
tic Regions; Earthquakes; Geography;
Geology; Maps; Minerals; Ocean;
Volcanoes
Baker, A. O., Your Science World,
p.37–49   6
Beauchamp, Discovering Our World,
Bk.1, p.91–103   4
Bethers, Story of Rivers   4–5
Branley, Nine Planets, p.37–43   6
Brindze, Gulf Stream   4–6
Freeman, M. B., Fun with Astronomy,
p.3–4   4–6
Gallant, R. A., Exploring the Planets,
p.41–50   5–6
Leonard, Exploring Science, p.17–21   6
Life, World We Live In, p.9–19   5–6
Nourse, So You Want To Be a Scientist,
p.144–53   5–6
Parker, B. M., Earth a Great Store-
house   4–6
Reed, Earth for Sam   6
Schealer, This Way to the Stars, p.33–
46   6
Schneider, L., Space in Your Future,
p.11–23   6
Sevrey, First Book of the Earth   5–6
Williams, H. L., Stories in Rocks   6

EARTHQUAKES: see also Geology
Pough, All about Volcanoes and Earthquakes, p.103–47   4–6

Sevrey, First Book of the Earth, p.27–
28   5–6
Steele, Davy Crockett's Earthquake
         *4–6
Wyckoff, Story of Geology, p.132–37
         5–6

EAST INDIES: see also Borneo; Java;
Malay Peninsula; Sumatra
American Heritage, Discoverers of the
New World, p.12–18   5–6
Barnouw, Land of William of Orange,
p.63–66   6
Quinn, Picture Map Geography of the
Pacific Islands, p.32–44   5–6

EASTER
Adams, K., Book of Giant Stories,
p.198–205 (Selfish Giant)   *5–6
Alden, Why the Chimes Rang, p.30–40
         *4–6
Benary-Isbert, Wicked Enchantment
         *4–6
Bloch, Marya of Clark Avenue, p.39–56
         *4–6
Burnett, B., First Book of Holidays,
p.13–17   4–5
Faralla, Willow in the Attic, p.59–71
         *4
Fitch, One God, p.90–96   5–6
Harper, Easter Chimes   *4–6
Hays, Easter Fires   *4–5
Hazeltine, Easter Book of Legends and
Stories   *5–6
Jordan, Holiday Handicraft, p.90–109
         4–6
Leeming, Fun with Greeting Cards, p.83
         4–6
Lillie, Book of Three Festivals, p.63–
126   *5–6
Lovelace, Betsy-Tacy, p.56–64   *4–5
McSpadden, Book of Holidays, p.62–68
         6
Nankivell, Tales of Christophilos, p.56–
66   *4–6
Olcott, Good Stories for Great Holi-
days, p.71–85   *4–6
Pannell, Holiday Round Up, p.113–26
         4–6
Sechrist, It's Time for Easter   5–6
———— Red Letter Days, p.77–88
         5–6
Wilde, Selfish Giant   *4–6

EASTER—CZECHOSLOVAKIA
Harper, Easter Chimes, p.207–15
*4–6
Hazeltine, Easter Book of Legends and
Stories, p.210–26   *5–6

EASTER—HUNGARY
Harper, Easter Chimes, p.108–17   *4–6
Hazeltine, Easter Book of Legends and
Stories, p.234–43   *5–6
Seredy, Good Master, p.51–60   *5–6

EASTER—ITALY
Angelo, Nino, p.111–31   *6
Harper, Easter Chimes, p.162–74   *4–6
Hazeltine, Easter Book of Legends and
Stories, p.227–33, 244–60   *5–6

EASTER—MAJORCA
Butterfield, Jaime and His Hen Pollita,
p.103–21   *4–5

EASTER—NORWAY
Harper, Easter Chimes, p.135–45   *4–6

EASTER—PLAYS
Hazeltine, Easter Book of Legends and
Stories, p.15–23, 172–83, 381–84
*5–6

EASTER ISLAND
Quinn, Picture Map Geography of the
Pacific Islands, p.121–22   5–6

ECHIDNAS
Asimov, Words from the Myths, p.114–
18   6

ECHOES
Hyde, Animal Clocks and Compasses,
p.102–3   5–6
Irving, Sound and Ultrasonics, p.81–83
6
Kettelkamp, Magic of Sound, p.37–45
4–6
Knight, D. C., First Book of Sound,
p.46–53   5–6
Lavine, Strange Travelers, p.81–82
5–6
Parker, B. M., Sound, p.13   5–6
Steele, Daniel Boone's Echo   *4–6

ECLIPSES: *see also* Astronomy; Moon;
Sun
Baker, R. H., When the Stars Come
Out, p.78–84   6
Branley, Moon, p.33–42   6
Estes, Middle Moffat, p.207–35   *4–6

Freeman, M. B., Fun with Astronomy,
p.44–45   4–6
Gallant, R. A., Exploring the Moon,
p.62–63   4–6
Goodwin, Real Book about Stars, p.52–
57   4–6
Schneider, L., Space in Your Future,
p.246–49   6

ECONOMIC DIFFERENCES—UNDER-
STANDING
Angelo, Bells of Bleeker Street   *4–6
Carlson, N. S., Family under the Bridge
*4–5
Daringer, Adopted Jane   *4–6
Friedman, F., Dot for Short   *4–5
Garnett, Family from One-End Street
*6
Kennedy, Jenny   *4–6
Langton, Majesty of Grace   *4–5
Lenski, Cotton in My Sack   *4–6
———— We Live in the South   *4–5
McNeer, Armed with Courage   5–6
Renick, M. L., Shining Shooter   *4–6
Thwaite, House in Turner Square   *6

ECONOMICS
Bendick, First Book of Supermarkets
4–5
Wilson, H. H., Jerry's Charge Account
*4–6

ECUADOR
Bailey, B. F., Ecuador   4–6
Barrows, American Continents, p.323–
24   5
Goetz, Neighbors to the South, p.69–
73   5–6
Quinn, Picture Map Geography of
South America, p.18–22   4–6
Rothery, South American Roundabout,
p.34–43   5–6

EDISON, THOMAS ALVA: *see also*
Electric Lighting; Phonograph
Asimov, Breakthroughs in Science, p.
128–36   5–6
Clark, G. G., Thomas Alva Edison
4–6
Cottler, Heroes of Civilization, p.220–
29   6
Hartman, Machines, p.181–92   6
Lawson, R., Watchwords of Liberty,
p.84–86   4–6
Parker, B. M., Fire, p.21–22   4–6

Spencer, P. R., Finding New Trails, p.215–20   4

EDITING: *see* Journalism

EDUCATION—AFRICA
Gatti, Here Is the Veld, p.146–50   6

EDUCATION—ALASKA
Stefansson, Here Is Alaska, p.84–90   6

EDUCATION—CHINA
Oakes, Bamboo Gate, p.21–39, 102–20
                                                      *4–6

EDUCATION—COLONIAL PERIOD
IN AMERICA
Coatsworth, Golden Horseshoe, p.27–38
                                                        *6
Judson, Boat Builder, p.1–19   5–6

EDUCATION—ENGLAND
Streatfeild, First Book of England, p.36–
37   4–6
Street, Land of the English People,
p.49–51   6

EDUCATION—ESKIMOS
Stefansson, Here Is Alaska, p.84–90   6

EDUCATION—INCA
Bleeker, Inca, p.69–79   5–6

EDUCATION—INDIA
Caldwell, Let's Visit India, p.77–78
                                                      4–6

EDUCATION—KOREA
Tor, Getting To Know Korea, p.32, 36–
37   4–6

EDUCATION—MEXICO
Tarshis, Village That Learned To Read
                                                      *4–6

EDUCATION—MIDDLE AGES
Hartman, Builders of the Old World,
p.357–60   6
Tappan, When Knights Were Bold, p.1–
17, 97–99, 224–26, 276–88   6

EDUCATION—NORWAY
Rothery, Scandinavian Roundabout, p.
42–48   6

EDUCATION—SWEDEN
Rothery, Scandinavian Roundabout, p.
147–49, 160–62   6

EDUCATION—UNITED STATES
Banta, Life in America: The South,
p.73–79   5–6
Coy, Americans   6
Graham, S., Booker T. Washington 6

_____ Dr. George Washington Carver
                                                        6
Havighurst, Life in America: The Mid-
west, p.77–78   5–6

EELS
Gall, Wagtail, p.80–97   4–6
Hyde, Animal Clocks and Compasses,
p.10, 31–35   5–6
Lavine, Strange Travelers, p.123–28
                                                      5–6
Morgan, A. P., Aquarium Book, p.116–
19   5–6
Parker, B. M., Animal Travels, p.10–12
                                                        4–6
_____ Fishes, p.23–26   4–6
Robertson, G., Strange Sea Life, p.75–
79   5–6

EGGS: *see* Birds—Eggs and Nests; Cooking; Food; Poultry

EGRETS
Lathrop, Let Them Live, p.16–19   4–6

EGYPT—ANCIENT: *see also* Art—
Egypt; Costume—Egypt—Ancient;
Hieroglyphics; Joseph; Nile River;
Pyramids; Sahara Desert; Sphinx; also
names of cities, as Cairo
Bergere, From Stones to Skyscrapers,
p.8–15   6
Falls, First 3000 Years, p.42–48, 84–87,
94–99   6
Friedman, E., Digging into Yesterday,
p.52–72   5–6
Galt, Seven Days from Sunday, p.108–
11   6
Hartman, Builders of the Old World,
p.44–77   6
_____ In Bible Days, p.41–57   6
Hillyer, Child's History of the World,
p.30–41   5–6
Howard, A. W., Sokar and the Croco-
dile   *4–5
Kubie, First Book of Archaeology,
p.14–19, 44–47   6
Lamprey, All the Ways of Building,
p.21–42   6
McGuire, Glimpses into the Long Ago,
p.39–72   5–6
Meadowcroft, Gift of the River   5–6
Petersham, Moses   4–5
Robinson, C. A., First Book of Ancient
Egypt   4–6

Schealer, Sycamore Warrior   *6
Writers Project, Cement, no.33, p.12–
15   5–6

EGYPT—FOLK TALES
Stinetorf, Children of North Africa,
p.24–33, 38–43   *5–6

EGYPT—HISTORY
Meadowcroft, Gift of the River   5–6
Stinetorf, Children of North Africa,
p.16–20   *5–6
Watson, Golden History of the World,
p.14–17   5–6

EGYPT—MODERN: *see also* Sahara
Desert; Suez Canal
Barrows, Old World Lands, p.290–97 6
——— Our Big World, p.96–108   4
Epstein, E., First Book of the United
Nations, p.16–18   4–6
Nevil, Picture Story of the Middle East
4–6
Stinetorf, Children of North Africa,
p.11–43, 58–75   *5–6

EHRLICH, PAUL
Asimov, Breakthroughs in Science, p.
137–44   5–6

EIGHT IMMORTALS
Fitch, Their Search for God, p.71   5–6

EINSTEIN, ALBERT
Asimov, Breakthroughs in Science, p.
163–71   5–6
Cottler, Heroes of Civilization, p.166–
76   6

EISENHOWER, DWIGHT DAVID
Beard, Presidents in American History,
p.143–47, 180–81   6
Petersham, Story of the Presidents of
the United States, p.76–78   4–6

ELAND
Perkins, Marlin Perkins' Zooparade,
p.66–67   4–6

ELECTION DAY
Burnett, B., First Book of Holidays,
p.44–45   4–5
McSpadden, Book of Holidays, p.156–
60   6

ELECTRIC APPLIANCES
Schneider, H., Everyday Machines and
How They Work   5–6

——— Let's Look inside Your House,
p.23–39   4–5

ELECTRIC BATTERIES: *see also* Elec-
tricity
Darrow, Boys' Own Book of Great In-
ventions, p.155–66   6
Morgan, A. P., First Electrical Book for
Boys, p.39–52, 193–96   6
Parker, B. M., Electricity, p.8–9   5–6
Yates, R. F., Boy and a Battery   5–6

ELECTRIC BELLS
Morgan, A. P., First Electrical Book
for Boys, p.84–88   6
Parker, B. M., Electricity, p.10–13 5–6
Schneider, H., Everyday Machines and
How They Work, p.65–68   5–6

ELECTRIC CURRENTS
Adler, Tools of Science, p.55–62, 96–97
6
Crouse, W. H., Understanding Science,
p.58–69, 76–78   6
Huey, What Makes the Wheels Go
Round, p.49–52   6
Parker, B. M., Electricity, p.18–20
5–6

ELECTRIC EYE: *see* Photoelectric Cells

ELECTRIC FUSES
Yates, R. F., Boy and a Battery, p.75–
80   5–6

ELECTRIC HEATING
Morgan, A. P., First Electrical Book
for Boys, p.101–12   6
Yates, R. F., Boy and a Battery, p.102–
6   5–6

ELECTRIC LIGHTING: *see also* Edison,
Thomas Alva
Clark, G. G., Thomas Alva Edison,
p.108–21   4–6
Epstein, S., First Book of Glass, p.52–
54   5–6
Morgan, A. P., First Electrical Book for
Boys, p.132–53   6
Parker, B. M., Electricity, p.21–22 5–6
Schneider, H., Everyday Machines and
How They Work, p.60–64   5–6

ELECTRIC MOTORS
Freeman, I. M., All About Electricity,
p.50–56   5–6
Morgan, A. P., Boy Electrician, p.301–
21   6

_____ Boys' Book of Engines, Motors & Turbines, p.147–63   6

Schneider, H., Everyday Machines and How They Work, p.68–70, 135–39, 174–76, 179–81   .5–6

_____ More Power to You, p.78–81   5–6

Yates, R. F., Boy and a Battery, p.94–101   5–6

_____ Boy and a Motor   6

ELECTRIC POLE
Barr, Young Scientist Takes a Ride, p.64–65   5–6

ELECTRIC POWER
Barnard, Macmillan Science-Life Series, Bk.6, p.304–8   6

Morgan, A. P., Boys' Book of Engines, Motors & Turbines, p.47–53   6

Schneider, H., Everyday Machines and How They Work, p.65–70   5–6

ELECTRIC POWER TRANSMISSION
Barr, Young Scientist Takes a Ride, p.57–61   5–6

Morgan, A. P., First Electrical Book for Boys, p.178–86   6

ELECTRIC RAILROADS: *see also* Subways
Morgan, A. P., Boy Electrician, p.337–51   6

Parker, B. M., Electricity, p.28–29   5–6

Van Metre, Trains, Tracks and Travel, p.168–200   6

ELECTRICITY: *see also* Dynamos; Lightning; Magnetism; Physics; Radio; Telegraph; Telephone; X Rays; also headings beginning with Electric or Electro-, and names of scientists, as Edison, Thomas Alva; Faraday, Michael

Baker, A. O., Your Science World, p.123–37   6

Barr, More Research Ideas for Young Scientists, p.47–62   5–6

Beeler, Experiments in Science, p.13–15   5–6

_____ Experiments with Electricity   5–6

Bendick, First Book of How To Fix It, p.24–30   4–6

_____ How Much and How Many, p.96–98   5–6

Crouse, W. H., Understanding Science, p.56–65   6

Darrow, Boys' Own Book of Great Inventions, p.155–91   6

Eaton, That Lively Man, Ben Franklin, p.91–4, 100–108   6

Epstein, S., First Book of Electricity   5–6

Freeman, I. M., All about Electricity   5–6

Freeman, M. B., Fun with Science, p.47–52   6

Hartman, Machines, p.83–97   6

Huey, What Makes the Wheels Go Round, p.42–60   6

Meyer, Picture Book of Electricity   5–6

Morgan, A. P., Boy Electrician   6

_____ Boys' Book of Engines, Motors & Turbines, p.27–37   6

_____ Boys' Book of Science and Construction, p.331–401   6

_____ First Electrical Book for Boys   6

Parker, B. M., Electricity   5–6

_____ Golden Book of Science   4–6

Podendorf, 101 Science Experiments, p.44–57   4–5

Reed, And That's Why, p.48–55, 75–85   4–5

Scheib, What Happened?, p.29–39   5–6

Schneider, H., More Power to You, p.64–90   5–6

Weir, R. C., Benjamin Franklin, p.89–98   4–6

Yates, R. F., Boy and a Battery   5–6

ELECTROCHEMISTRY
Beeler, Experiments in Chemistry, p.10–17   5–6

Yates, R. F., Boy and a Battery, p.68–74   5–6

ELECTROMAGNETISM
Adler, Tools of Science, p.57–59   6

Barr, Research Ideas for Young Scientists, p.12–24   5–6

Beeler, Experiments with Electricity, p.60–72   5–6

Crouse, W. H., Understanding Science, p.102–4   6

Darrow, Boys' Own Book of Great Inventions, p.168–75   6

Freeman, I. M., All About Electricity, p.42–49   5–6

Huey, What Makes the Wheels Go Round, p.137–42   6

Irving, Sound and Ultrasonics, p.111–14   6

Land, B., Quest of Isaac Newton, p.48–49   6

Morgan, A. P., Boy Electrician, p.98–105   6

———— First Electrical Book for Boys, p.53–65   6

Parker, B. M., Electricity, p.16–17   5–6

———— Magnets, p.26–36   5–6

Schneider, H., Everyday Machines and How They Work, p.65–70   5–6

———— More Power to You, p.68–70, 75–77   5–6

Yates, R. F., Boy and a Battery, p.32–62   5–6

ELECTRONICS

Bendick, Electronics for Young People   6

Buchanan, How Man Made Music, p.170–79   6

Butterworth, Trouble with Jenny's Ear   *4–6

ELECTROPLATING

Morgan, A. P., First Electrical Book for Boys, p.248–49   6

ELECTROSTATICS

Beeler, More Experiments in Science, p.11–17   5–6

Morgan, A. P., Boy Electrician, p.34–72   6

ELEPHANTS: *see also* Mammoths

Bothwell, Empty Tower, p.140–46   *4–5

Bridges, Zoo Babies, p.42–50   4–6

———— Zoo Doctor, p.34–47   4–6

———— Zoo Pets, p.22–29   4–6

Buck, F., Jungle Animals, p.5–8   5–6

Disney, Worlds of Nature, p.170–73   4–6

Fox, From Bones to Bodies, p.16–21   6

Gatti, Saranga, the Pygmy   5–6

Kipling, Jungle Book, p.223–61   *5–6

———— Just So Stories, p.63–81   *4–6

Knight, C. R., Life through the Ages, p.32–37   6

Lindquist, W., Burma Boy   *4–6

Mukerji, Hari, the Jungle Lad   *5–6

———— Kari, the Elephant   *4–6

Osmond, Animals of the World, v.1   4–6

Parker, B. M., Animals We Know, p.26–27   5–6

Perkins, Marlin Perkins' Zooparade, p.12–15   4–6

Scheele, Ancient Elephants   4–6

Shackelford, Child's Story of the Negro, p.14–19   4–5

Spencer, P. R., Exploring New Trails, p.3–13   5

Weston, Bhimsa, the Dancing Bear, p.72–79   *4–6

ELEVATORS

Bechdolt, Going Up   5–6

Morgan, A. P., First Electrical Book for Boys, p.255–57   6

Schneider, H., Science Fun with Milk Cartons, p.125–28, 131–35   5–6

ELGAR, EDWARD WILLIAM

Burch, Modern Composers for Young People, p.63–73   5–6

ELIZABETH, QUEEN OF ENGLAND: *see also* England—History

Foster, G., World of Captain John Smith   6

Hillyer, Child's History of the World, p.372–83   5–6

ELK: *see* Deer

ELM TREES

Comstock, Handbook of Nature Study, p.634–38   6

Cormack, First Book of Trees, p.16   4–6

McKenny, Trees of the Countryside, p.20–21   4–6

EMANCIPATION DAY

Shackelford, Child's Story of the Negro, p.126–28   4–5

EMANCIPATION PROCLAMATION

Hays, Freedom, p.29–30   5–6

EMBROIDERY: *see also* Beadwork; Sewing

Bailey, C. S., Children of the Handcrafts, p.11–21   5–6

EMBRYOLOGY: *see* Reproduction

EMIGRATION: *see* Immigration and Emigration

EMMETT, DANIEL DECATUR
Buchanan, How Man Made Music, p.196–200   6
Lyons, Stories of Our American Patriotic Songs, p.39–45   5–6

ENCYCLOPEDIAS
Spencer, P. R., Exploring New Trails, p.175–80   5

ENERGY: *see* Force and Energy

ENGINEERING: *see also* Air Conditioning; Architecture; Aviation; Bridges; Building Materials; Canals; Dams; Engines; Harbors; Irrigation; Lighthouses; Machines; Mechanics; Mining; Radio; Railroads; Rivers; Roads; Steam Engines; Tools; Tunnels; Ventilation; Water Supply
Bendick, How Much and How Many, p.81–88   5–6
Henry, R., Trains   5–6
Jackson, D., Wonderful World of Engineering   6

ENGINES: *see also* Diesel Engines; Electric Motors; Gas and Oil Engines; Locomotives; Steam Engines
Darrow, Boys' Own Book of Great Inventions, p.127–91   6
Huey, What Makes the Wheels Go Round, p.61–68, 72–78   6
Morgan, A. P., Boys' Book of Engines, Motors & Turbines   6

ENGLAND: *see also* Art—England; British Isles; Costume—England; Games—England; London
Bentley, Young Brontës   6
Bergaust, Rockets around the World, p.30–33   6
Boardman, Canals, p.47–61   6
Bond, Paddington Helps Out   *4–6
Boston, Children of Green Knowe   *4–6
Epstein, E., First Book of the United Nations, p.16–17   4–6
Garnett, Family from One-End Street   *6

Godden, Miss Happiness and Miss Flower   *4–5
Knight, E. M., Lassie Come-Home   *6
Mayne, Blue Boat   *4–6
Norton, Borrowers   *4–6
Pace, Juliette Low, p.78–91, 121–24   5–6
Sleigh, Carbonel   *4–6
Streatfeild, First Book of England   4–6
———— New Shoes   *6
Street, Land of the English People   6
Weaver, Poppy in the Corn   *6

ENGLAND—ARMY
Kipling, Jungle Book, p.265–97   *5–6

ENGLAND—FOLK TALES: *see also* Arthur, King; Robin Hood
Harper, Ghosts and Goblins, p.77–79, 112–17, 187–93, 269–71   4–6

ENGLAND—GOVERNMENT
Hartman, Builders of the Old World, p.295–325   6
Streatfeild, First Book of England, p.16–21   4–6

ENGLAND—HISTORY: *see also* Magna Charta; also names of persons, as Alfred the Great
Farjeon, Mighty Men, p.122–30, 139–58, 170–78, 194–211   4–6
Foster, G., Abraham Lincoln's World   4–6
———— George Washington's World   6
Hartman, Builders of the Old World, p.221–26   6
Hazeltine, Hero Tales from Many Lands, p.89–134   5–6
Hillyer, Child's History of the World, p.264–68, 284–91, 311–15, 369–94   5–6
Latham, Drake   6
McGuire, Glimpses into the Long Ago, p.265–71   5–6
Manton, Elizabeth Garrett, M.D.   6
Sawyer, Long Christmas, p.191–200   *4–6
Sloane, British Isles   5–6
Sperry, Captain Cook Explores the South Seas   5–6
Street, Land of the English People, p.68–122   6
Trease, Sir Walter Raleigh   5–6

ENGLAND—INDUSTRIES
Street, Land of the English People, p.60–67, 101–5   6
Writers Project, Cement, no.33, p.18–21   5–6

ENGLAND—13TH CENTURY
De Angeli, Door in the Wall   *4–6

ENGLAND—18TH CENTURY
Henry, M., King of the Wind, p.95–173   *5–6

ENGLISH BALLADS: *see* Ballads

ENGLISH IN THE UNITED STATES
Association for Childhood Education, Told under the Stars and Stripes, p.13–30   *4–6

ENGLISH LITERATURE: *see also* Authors; Ballads; Books; also names of authors, as Dickens, Charles
Bunyan, Pilgrim's Progress   *5–6
Kipling, Jungle Book   *5–6

ENGRAVING
Lent, "I Work on a Newspaper," p.50–55   6
Weiss, H., Paper, Ink and Roller, p.62–63   4–6

ENTERTAINMENTS: *see* Amusements; Dancing; Festivals; Games; Holidays; Pageants; Parties; Plays

ENTOMOLOGY: *see* Insects

EPICS: *see also* names of epics, as Beowulf
Modak, Land and People of India, p.33–43   6

ERICSON, LEIF
Aulaire, Leif the Lucky   4–5
Duvoisin, And There Was America, p.3–6   4–6
Janeway, Vikings   4–6
Rothery, Scandinavian Roundabout, p.5–12   6
Weir, R. C., Leif Ericson, Explorer   4–5

ERICSSON, JOHN
Pratt, Monitor and Merrimac   5–6
Rothery, Scandinavian Roundabout, p.190–91   6

ERIE CANAL
Adams, S. H., Erie Canal   5–6

Barrows, American Continents, p.34–35   5
Boardman, Canals, p.9–25   6
Buehr, Through the Locks, p.34–42   5–6
Orton, Treasure in the Little Trunk, p.173–93   *4–6

ERITREA
Epstein, E., First Book of the United Nations, p.67–68   4–6

ERMINE: *see* Weasels

EROSION: *see also* Dams; Glaciers; Soil Conservation
Beeler, More Experiments in Science, p.103–7   5–6
Colby, Soil Savers   4–6
Comstock, Handbook of Nature Study, p.766–70   6
Cooper, E. K., Science in Your Own Back Yard, p.55–57   5–6
Graham, E. H., Water for America, p.67–69   6
Schneider, H., Rocks, Rivers & the Changing Earth, p.23–30   4–6
Van Dersal, Land Renewed   6
Writers Project, Wind, Water, and Air, no.21   5–6
Wyckoff, Story of Geology, p.48–63   5–6

ESCALATORS
Bechdolt, Going Up, p.102–7   5–6

ESKIMOS: *see also* Alaska; Arctic Regions; Greenland; Labrador
Association for Childhood Education, Told under Spacious Skies, p.313–23   *4–6
Bleeker, Eskimo   4–6
Brewster, First Book of Eskimos   4–6
Butler, Alaska, p.63–96   6
Fletcher, S. E., American Indian, p.110–15   5–6
Harrington, Ootook   4–6
Jordan, Homemade Dolls in Foreign Dress, p.38–49   4–6
Lindquist, W., Alaska, p.92–97   5–6
Lipkind, Boy with a Harpoon   *4–6
Machetanz, Puppy Named Gih   *4–5
McNeer, Canadian Story, p.82–84   5–6
O'Neill, Picture Story of Alaska   4–6

Smith, J. R., Neighbors around the World, p.30–48   4

Sperry, All about the Arctic and Antarctic   4–6

Stefansson, Here Is Alaska, p.47–80   6

Tolboom, People of the Snow   4–6

ESKIMOS—DWELLINGS

Bleeker, Eskimo, p.22–38   4–6

Smith, J. R., Neighbors around the World, p.32–34   4

Stefansson, Here Is Alaska, p.56–58, 98–104   6

ESKIMOS—FOLK TALES

Gillham, Beyond the Clapping Mountains   4–6

ESKIMOS—HUNTING: *see* Hunting—Arctic Regions

ESKIMOS—MANNERS AND CUSTOMS

Bleeker, Eskimo, p.114–40   4–6

ESTHER, QUEEN

Bowie, Bible Story for Boys and Girls: Old Testament, p.183–91   4–6

Farjeon, Mighty Men, p.29–36   4–6

ETHIOPIA

Barrows, Old World Lands, p.313–14   6

ETIQUETTE: *see also* Manners and Customs; Table Etiquette

Beery, Manners Made Easy   6

Betz, Your Manners Are Showing   6

Daringer, Adopted Jane, p.19–21   *4–6

Jacobson, First Book of Letter Writing, p.14–23   4–6

Lee, Manners To Grow On   4–5

Pei, All about Language, p.72–80   6

Rombauer, Cookbook for Boys and Girls, p.107   6

EUPHRATES RIVER: *see* Babylonia; Iraq

EUROPE: *see also* Costume—Europe; also names of European countries, as France

Barrows, Old World Lands   6

Watson, Golden History of the World, p.41, 73–75   5–6

EUROPE—GAMES: *see* Games—Europe

EUROPEAN WAR, 1914-18: *see* World War, 1914-18

EVANS, SIR ARTHUR

Honour, Secrets of Minos   6

EVAPORATED MILK: *see* Milk

EVAPORATION: *see also* Clouds; Water

Huey, What Makes the Wheels Go Round, p.106–9   6

Reed, And That's Why   4–5

Schneider, H., Everyday Machines and How They Work, p.140–45   5–6

EVERGLADES NATIONAL PARK

Melbo, Our Country's National Parks, v.1, p.167–88   6

EVERGREEN TREES

Hylander, Out of Doors in Winter, p.9–35   5–6

EVOLUTION: *see also* Darwin, Charles; Prehistoric Man

Epstein, S., Prehistoric Animals, p.37–44   6

Fisher, J., Wonderful World of the Air, p.16–27   5–6

Ludovici, World of the Microscope, p.17–20   6

EXCURSIONS: *see* Field Trips

EXPERIMENTS—SCIENTIFIC

Baer, Sound   4–6

Beeler, Experiments in Science   5–6

———— More Experiments in Science   5–6

Darrow, Boys' Own Book of Great Inventions   6

Freeman, M. B., Fun with Science   6

———— Fun with Scientific Experiments   5–6

Geralton, Story of Sound   5–6

Larrick, See for Yourself   4–5

Morgan, A. P., First Electrical Book for Boys   6

Parker, B. M., Electricity   5–6

———— Sound   5–6

———— What Things Are Made Of   5–6

Podendorf, 101 Science Experiments   4–5

Schneider, H., Everyday Weather and How It Works   5–6

———— Let's Look inside Your House   4–5

———— Science Fun with Milk Cartons　5–6

Schneider, L., Space in Your Future　6

Schwartz, It's Fun To Know Why　5–6

Yates, R. F., Boy and a Battery　5–6

———— Boy and a Motor　6

———— Fun with Your Microscope　6

EXPLORERS: *see also* British in America; Discoveries in Geography; Discovery Period in America; Dutch in America; French in America; Geography; Lewis and Clark Expedition; Northmen; Spaniards in America; also names of explorers, as Columbus, Christopher

Bleeker, Eskimo, p.141–55　4–6

Duvoisin, And There Was America　4–6

———— They Put Out to Sea　4–6

Icenhower, First Book of the Antarctic, p.25–29, 35–40　4–6

Sperry, Captain Cook Explores the South Seas　5–6

EXPORTS: *see* Trade

EXPRESS SERVICE: *see also* Pony Express

Spencer, P. R., Traveling New Trails, p.420–30　6

EXTINCT ANIMALS: *see* Fossils; Prehistoric Animals

EYE: *see also* Light

Barr, More Research Ideas for Young Scientists, p.132–35　5–6

Beauchamp, Discovering Our World, Bk.1, p.83–85　4

Crouse, W. H., Understanding Science, p.115–19　6

Glemser, All about the Human Body, p.117–21　5–6

Scheib, What Happened?, p.79–87　5–6

Spencer, P. R., Exploring New Trails, p.350–56　5

———— Finding New Trails, p.367–71　4

Zim, Our Senses and How They Work, p.5–58　4–6

FACTORIES: *see* Manufacturing

FACTORY SYSTEM: *see also* Industrial Revolution

Hartman, Machines, p.35–47　6

FAIRIES

Batchelor, Superstitious? Here's Why!, p.124–29　6

Jones, E. O., Twig　*4–5

FAIRS: *see also* Bazaars; Chicago—World's Columbian Exposition, 1893; Costume; Markets

De Jong, M., Good Luck Duck　*4–5

Mulac, Game Book, p.258–74　6

FAIRS—ANGLO-EGYPTIAN SUDAN

Stinetorf, Children of North Africa, p.44–57　*5–6

FAIRS—FRANCE

Hazeltine, Easter Book of Legends and Stories, p.285–94　*5–6

FAIRS—GERMANY

Tor, Getting To Know Germany, p.37–38　4–6

FAIRS—HUNGARY

Seredy, Good Master, p.108–25　*5–6

FAIRS—INDIA

Bothwell, Empty Tower, p.117–50　*4–5

———— Thirteenth Stone, p.3–130　*5–6

FAIRS—IRELAND

Meredith, King of the Kerry Fair　*4–6

Van Stockum, Cottage at Bantry Bay, p.207–32　*6

FAIRS—ITALY

Angelo, Nino, p.154–88　*6

FAIRS—LAPLAND

Berry, Men, Moss, and Reindeer, p.77–84　5–6

FAIRS—MIDDLE AGES

Tappan, When Knights Were Bold, p.252–62　6

FAIRS—SWEDEN

Burglon, Children of the Soil, p.223–37　*4–6

FAIRS—UNITED STATES

Agle, Three Boys and the Remarkable Cow　*4–5

Brock, Plug-Horse Derby　*4–5

Canfield, Understood Betsy, p.160-84
*5-6

Coatsworth, Alice-All-By-Herself, p.46-57 *4-6

Enright, Then There Were Five, p.204-28 *5-6

———— Thimble Summer, p.95-119
*5-6

Frost, Windy Foot at the County Fair
*4-6

Gates, Blue Willow, p.44-61 *5-6

Wilder, Farmer Boy, p.252-74 *4-6

FAIRS—WALES

Banning, Pit Pony, p.61-75 *4-6

FALLA, MANUEL DE

Burch, Modern Composers for Young People, p.151-54 5-6

FALLING STARS: *see* Meteors

FAMILY LIFE: *see* Home Life

FAMILY RELATIONS: *see also* Home Life

Angelo, Bells of Bleeker Street *4-6

Armer, Waterless Mountain *5-6

Barnes, Wonderful Year *4-6

Beim, Just Plain Maggie *4-6

Bothwell, Little Boat Boy *4-5

Brink, Caddie Woodlawn *6

———— Family Grandstand *4-6

———— Magical Melons *5-6

Brock, Ballet for Mary *4-5

———— Topsy-Turvy Family *4-5

Calhoun, Katie John *4-5

Clymer, Trolley Car Family *4-6

Coatsworth, Away Goes Sally *4-6

De Angeli, Bright April *4-6

———— Copper-toed Boots *4-6

———— Elin's Amerika *4-6

Durell, Holly River Secret *5-6

Enright, Saturdays *4-6

Estes, Ginger Pye *4-6

———— Middle Moffat *4-6

———— Moffats *4-6

———— Rufus M. *4-6

Fenton, E., Phantom of Walkaway Hill
*4-6

Flory, Peddler's Summer *4-6

Frazier, Somebody Special *4-6

Friedman, F., Dot for Short *4-5

———— Sundae with Judy *4-6

Frost, Maple Sugar for Windy Foot
*4-6

———— Windy Foot at the County Fair *4-6

Gage, Secret of Fiery Gorge *4-6

Garnett, Family from One-End Street
*6

Gilbert, Champions Don't Cry *5-6

Haywood, Penny and Peter *4

Holberg, Rowena Carey *4-6

Hunt, M. L., Cupola House *4-6

———— Ladycake Farm *4-6

———— Miss Jellytot's Visit *4-6

Kingman, Best Christmas *4-6

Langton, Majesty of Grace *4-5

Lattimore, Molly in the Middle *4-5

Lawrence, Sand in Her Shoes *4-6

L'Engle, Meet the Austins *5-6

Lenski, Boom Town Boy *4-6

———— Cotton in My Sack *4-6

Liu, Little Wu and the Watermelons
*4-5

McGinley, Plain Princess *4-6

McMeekin, Kentucky Derby Winner
*4-6

Marshall, Invisible Island *4-6

Renick, M. L., Seven Simpsons on Six Bikes *4-5

Rushmore, Lost Treasure Box *4-6

Sawyer, Maggie Rose *4-6

Sayers, Ginny and Custard *4-6

———— Tag-along Tooloo *4

Seredy, Singing Tree *6

Sheehy, Molly and the Golden Wedding *4-5

Sickels, That Boy, Johnny! *4-6

Streatfeild, New Shoes *6

Taylor, S., All-of-a-Kind Family *4-6

———— More All-of-a-Kind Family
*4-6

Uchida, Takao and Grandfather's Sword
*4-6

Unnerstad, Little O *4-6

Van Stockum, Canadian Summer *5-6

———— Cottage at Bantry Bay *6

———— Friendly Gables *5-6

———— Pegeen *6

Wilson, H. H., Jerry's Charge Account
*4-6

Wilson, L., This Boy Cody *4-6

———— This Boy Cody and His Friends *4-6

Woolley, Ellie's Problem Dog *4-6

Wyss, Swiss Family Robinson *6

Yates, E., Mountain Born *5-6

FAMINE: *see also* Floods
Buff, Hah-Nee of the Cliff Dwellers
*4-6
Rawlings, Secret River   *4-5

FANCIFUL TALES—MODERN
Bailey, C. S., Miss Hickory   4-6
Benary-Isbert, Wicked Enchantment
4-6
Bendick, Good Knight Ghost   4-6
Bond, Bear Called Paddington   4-6
———— Paddington Helps Out   4-6
Boston, Children of Green Knowe
4-6
Brown, Palmer, Beyond the Pawpaw
Trees   4-6
———— Silver Nutmeg   4-6
Butterworth, Trouble with Jenny's Ear
4-6
Coatsworth, Cat Who Went to Heaven
4-6
Collodi, Adventures of Pinocchio   4-6
Corbett, Lemonade Trick   4-6
Dahl, Cloud Shoes   4-6
De la Mare, Animal Stories   4-6
Dickens, Magic Fishbone   4-6
Embry, Blue-nosed Witch   4-5
Emett, New World for Nellie   4-5
Estes, Witch Family   4-6
Farjeon, Silver Curlew   4-6
Gannett, My Father's Dragon   4-5
Grahame, Reluctant Dragon   4-6
Henry, J., Tiger's Chance   4-6
Howard, J., 13th Is Magic   4-6
Hudson, Little Boy Lost   5-6
Johnson, E., Little Knight   4-6
Jones, E. O., Twig   4-5
Laughlin, Little Left-over Witch   4-5
Le Grand, Tom Benn and Blackbeard,
the Pirate   4-5
Lofting, Doctor Dolittle's Puddleby Ad-
ventures   4-6
Macdonald, G., Princess and Curdie
4-6
———— Princess and the Goblin   4-6
McGinley, Plain Princess   4-6
Norton, Bed-Knob and Broomstick
4-5
———— Borrowers   4-6
———— Borrowers Afield   4-6
Paine, Arkansas Bear   4-6
Parker, E., Enchantress   4-5
Parrish, Floating Island   4-6

Payne, Leprechaun of Bayou Luce   4-5
Rawlings, Secret River   4-5
Ritchie, A., Treasure of Li-Po   4-5
Ruskin, King of the Golden River   4-6
Sauer, Fog Magic   5-6
Sawyer, Enchanted Schoolhouse   4-6
Selden, Cricket in Times Square   4-6
Shura, Simple Spigott   4-5
Sleigh, Carbonel   4-6
———— Kingdom of Carbonel   4-6
Thurber, Great Quillow   4-6
———— Many Moons   4-5
White, A. H., Story of Serapina   4-6
White, E. B., Charlotte's Web   4-6
Wilde, Selfish Giant   4-6
Winterfeld, Castaways in Lilliput   5-6
Young, Unicorn with Silver Shoes
4-6

FAR EAST: *see* Orient

FARADAY, MICHAEL
Asimov, Breakthroughs in Science, p.
67-75   5-6
Darrow, Boys' Own Book of Great In-
ventions, p.175-79   6
Hartman, Machines, p.90-96   6
Morgan, A. P., First Electrical Book
for Boys, p.156-60   6
Yates, R. F., Boy and a Motor, p.6-8
6

FARM ANIMALS: *see* Animals—Domestic; Dairying; also names of animals,
as Horses

FARM LIFE: *see also* Agriculture; Cattle;
Dairying; Harvesting; Plantation Life;
Ranch Life
Blough, Not Only for Ducks   *4-5

FARM LIFE—CHINA
Liu, Little Wu and the Watermelons
*4-5
Spencer, C., Land of the Chinese People, p.86-91   6

FARM LIFE—FRANCE
Bishop, C. H., All Alone   *4-6

FARM LIFE—HUNGARY
Seredy, Good Master   *5-6
———— Singing Tree   *6

FARM LIFE—ICELAND
Arason, Smoky Bay   *5-6

FARM LIFE—INDONESIA
Caldwell, Let's Visit Indonesia, p.57–64
4–6

FARM LIFE—JAPAN
Buck, P. S., Big Wave   *6

FARM LIFE—SWEDEN
Burglon, Children of the Soil   *4–6
Unnerstad, Spettecake Holiday   *4–6

FARM LIFE—UNITED STATES
Barnes, Wonderful Year   *4–6
Bishop, C. H., Blue Spring Farm   *5–6
Brock, Plug-Horse Derby   *4–5
Canfield, Understood Betsy, p.21–213
*5–6
Coatsworth, Away Goes Sally   *4–6
Daringer, Adopted Jane, p.138–95
*4–6
De Angeli, Copper-toed Boots   *4–6
———— Henner's Lydia   *4–5
———— Yonie Wondernose   *4–5
De Jong, M., Little Cow and the Tur-
tle   *4–6
Enright, Then There Were Five   *5–6
———— Thimble Summer   *5–6
Faulkner, Melindy's Happy Summer
*4–5
Frost, Maple Sugar for Windy Foot
*4–6
———— Sleigh Bells for Windy Foot
*4–6
———— Windy Foot at the County
Fair   *4–6
Hunt, M. L., Benjie's Hat   *4–6
———— Ladycake Farm   *4–6
Lang, Strawberry Roan, p.60–116
*5–6
Lawrence, Homemade Year   *4–5
———— Peachtree Island   *4–5
Lenski, Boom Town Boy, p.1–40, 170–
75   *4–6
———— Judy's Journey   *4–6
———— Peanuts for Billy Ben   *4–5
———— Strawberry Girl   *4–6
Malcolmson, Yipe   *4–6
Meigs, Covered Bridge   *4–6
Robertson, K., Ticktock and Jim   *4–6
Rushmore, Lost Treasure Box   *4–6
Tudor, Becky's Birthday   *4–5
Weiss, E. S., Sally Saucer   *4–6
White, A. H., Junket   *4–6
White, E. B., Charlotte's Web   *4–6
Wilder, Farmer Boy   *4–6

FARM MACHINERY: *see* Agricultural
Machinery

FARRAGUT, DAVID GLASGOW
Dupuy, First Book of Civil War Naval
Actions, p.33–38, 56–60, 87–90   6
Fisher, D. F. C., And Long Remem-
ber, p.68–71   6
Lawson, R., Watchwords of Liberty,
p.59–60   4–6
Mitchell, Ships That Made U.S. History,
p.73–76   6

FASHION: *see* Clothing; Costume

FATHER-SON RELATIONS
Bulla, Riding the Pony Express   *4–5
MacKellar, Wee Joseph   *4–5
Steele, Winter Danger   *4–6

FATHER'S DAY
Burnett, B., First Book of Holidays,
p.28   4–5
Leeming, Fun with Greeting Cards, p.91
4–6
McSpadden, Book of Holidays, p.89   6
Pannell, Holiday Round Up, p.201–4
4–6

FATS: *see* Oils and Fats

FEAR—OVERCOMING
Buck, P. S., Big Wave   *6
De Leeuw, Fear in the Forest   *4–6
Jewett, God's Troubadour, p.58–65
5–6
Mason, M. E., Middle Sister   *4–5
Woolley, Schoolroom Zoo   *4–5

FEASTS: *see* Festivals

FEDERAL BUREAU OF INVESTIGA-
TION
Floherty, Our F.B.I.   6

FENCE—ELECTRIC
Barr, Young Scientist Takes a Ride,
p.66–67   5–6

FENIAN SAGA: *see* Finn Mac Cool

FENNEC
Perkins, Marlin Perkins' Zooparade,
p.68–71   4–6

FERMENTATION: *see* Bacteria; Wine;
Yeast

FERNS
Comstock, Handbook of Nature Study,
p.693–706   6

Hylander, Out of Doors in Spring, p.84–86, 91–101　　5–6

Sterling, Story of Mosses, Ferns, and Mushrooms, p.106–55　　5–6

FERRETS
Hogner, Farm Animals, p.186　　6

FERRIES
Buehr, Harbors and Cargoes, p.60–61　　5–6

Gilmore, Model Boats for Beginners, p.59–63　　5–6

Orton, Treasure in the Little Trunk, p.49–51　　*4–6

FERTILE CRESCENT
Hartman, Builders of the Old World, p.82–83　　6

FERTILIZERS
Freeman, I. M., All about the Wonders of Chemistry, p.93–100　　6

FESTIVALS: *see also* Costume; Fairs; Games; Holidays; Indians of North America—Ceremonies; Pageants; Theater; also names of special days, as Thanksgiving Day
Ceder, Joel, the Potter's Son, p.25–33　　*4–6

Fitch, Their Search for God　　5–6

Neal, Story of the Kite, p.46–51　　5–6

FESTIVALS—BRAZIL
May, Let's Read about Brazil, p.114–17　　4–6

FESTIVALS—CHINA
Caldwell, Let's Visit China, p.52–54　　5–6

Spencer, C., Made in China, p.231–39　　5–6

Wiese, Chinese Ink Stick, p.143–46　　*4–6

FESTIVALS—FORMOSA
Caldwell, Let's Visit Formosa, p.60–62　　5–6

FESTIVALS—GERMANY
Lobsenz, First Book of West Germany, p.31–42　　4–6

Tor, Getting To Know Germany, p.19–21　　4–6

FESTIVALS—GUATEMALA
Rothery, Central American Roundabout, p.29–40　　6

FESTIVALS—INCA
Bleeker, Inca, p.121–29　　5–6

FESTIVALS—INDIA
Bothwell, Empty Tower, p.23–32　　*4–5

FESTIVALS—ITALY
Fletcher, D. M., Confetti for Cortorelli　　*4–6

FESTIVALS—JAPAN
Mears, First Book of Japan, p.50, 52–57　　4–6

FESTIVALS—JEWS
Fitch, One God, p.40–55　　5–6
Taylor, S., All-of-a-Kind Family　　*4–6

FESTIVALS—LATIN AMERICA
Goetz, Other Young Americans, p.197–230　　5–6

FESTIVALS—MAYA
Bleeker, Maya, p.120–35　　5–6

FESTIVALS—MEXICO
Bannon, Watchdog　　*4–5
Tarshis, Village That Learned To Read, p.22–29　　*4–6

FESTIVALS—NEW ORLEANS
Lenski, Bayou Suzette, p.135–47　　*5–6

FESTIVALS—NICARAGUA
Rothery, Central American Roundabout, p.114–22　　6

FESTIVALS—PHILIPPINE ISLANDS
O'Neill, Picture Story of the Philippines　　5–6

FESTIVALS—SPAIN
Buckley, Luis of Spain, p.67–87　　4–6

FESTIVALS—SWEDISH
De Angeli, Elin's Amerika　　*4–6
Lindquist, J. D., Golden Name Day　　*4–6

FESTIVALS—YUGOSLAVIA
Gidal, My Village in Yugoslavia, p.28–33　　4–6

FEUDAL SYSTEM: *see also* Chivalry; Europe; Middle Ages
Boardman, Castles, p.27–33, 89, 97　　6
Buehr, Knights and Castles and Feudal Life, p.7–25, 57–71　　4–6
Hartman, Builders of the Old World, p.246–61　　6

Tappan, When Knights Were Bold, p.102–22   6

Watson, Golden History of the World, p.82–85   5–6

FIBERGLASS

Epstein, S., First Book of Glass, p.58–61   5–6

Writers Project, Rayon, Nylon, and Glass Fibers, no.39, p.41–46   5–6

FIBERS: *see* names of fibers, as Asbestos; Cotton; Paper; Rayon; Wool

FIBERS—SYNTHETIC

Writers Project, Rayon, Nylon, and Glass Fibers, no.39   5–6

FIELD, CYRUS WEST: *see also* Atlantic Cable

Latham, Young Man in a Hurry   6

FIELD SPARROWS

Webb, Birds in Their Homes, p.21–22   4–6

FIELD TRIPS

Comstock, Handbook of Nature Study, p.13–15   6

FIESTAS: *see* Festivals

FIJI ISLANDS

Quinn, Picture Map Geography of the Pacific Islands, p.88–93   5–6

FILLMORE, MILLARD

Beard, Presidents in American History, p.57–58, 162   6

Coy, First Book of Presidents, p.39   4–6

Petersham, Story of the Presidents of the United States, p.36   4–6

FINDING DIRECTIONS: *see* Direction Finding

FINGER PLAYS

Mulac, Game Book, p.211–20   6

FINLAND: *see also* Dancing—Finland

Barrows, Old World Lands, p.262–64   6

Hazeltine, Hero Tales from Many Lands, p.317–31   5–6

FINLAND—FOLK TALES

Fenner, Fools and Funny Fellows, p.57–62, 115–26   4–6

———— Time To Laugh, p.17–35   4–6

Sawyer, Long Christmas, p.63–67   4–6

FINN MAC COOL

Hazeltine, Hero Tales from Many Lands, p.185–202   5–6

FINNS IN THE UNITED STATES

Association for Childhood Education, Told under the Stars and Stripes, p.282–94   *4–6

Kingman, Best Christmas   *4–6

———— Village Band Mystery   *4–5

FIRE: *see also* Combustion; Fire Departments; Fires; Forest Fires; Fuel; Heat; Heating; Prairie Fires; Safety

Adler, Fire in Your Life   4–6

Burns, Man and His Tools, p.70–93   5–6

Crouse, W. H., Understanding Science, p.24–28   6

Huey, What Makes the Wheels Go Round, p.117–21   6

Orton, Treasure in the Little Trunk, p.13–17   *4–6

Parker, B. M., Fire   4–6

Reed, And That's Why, p.56–65   4–5

Salomon, Book of Indian Crafts & Indian Lore, p.239–47   6

Schneider, H., Everyday Machines and How They Work, p.121–28   5–6

FIRE DEPARTMENTS: *see also* Fire Prevention; Fires

Bechdolt, Going Up, p.108–9   5–6

Eaton, That Lively Man, Ben Franklin, p.78–80   6

Parker, B. M., Fire, p.27–30   4–6

Spencer, P. R., Finding New Trails, p.91–102   4

FIRE EXTINCTION

Beeler, More Experiments in Science, p.153–57   5–6

Parker, B. M., Fire, p.22–27   4–6

FIRE PREVENTION

Barnard, Macmillan Science-Life Series, Bk.6, p.31   6

Beeler, Experiments in Science, p.86–88, 95–97   5–6

FIREARMS: *see* Guns

FIREFLIES

Comstock, Handbook of Nature Study, p.367–69   6

Parker, B. M., Insects and Their Ways, p.24–25   4–6

Teale, Insect Friends, p.59–60   5–6

FIREPLACES

Schneider, H., Everyday Machines and How They Work, p.130–31   5–6

FIRES: *see also* Chicago—Fire, 1871; Fire Departments; Fire Prevention; Forest Fires; Prairie Fires

Coatsworth, Fair American   *5–6

Colby, First Camping Trip, p.24–27   5–6

De Angeli, Yonie Wondernose   *4–5

Enright, Saturdays, p.145–57   *4–6

———— Then There Were Five, p.121–34   *5–6

Kohler, "Crazy As You Look!", p.85–102   *4–6

Mason, B. S., Junior Book of Camping and Woodcraft, p.46–71   5–6

Oakes, Bamboo Gate, p.55–58   *4–6

Orton, Treasure in the Little Trunk, p.165–72   *4–6

Parker, B. M., Fire, p.9–20   4–6

Robertson, K., Ticktock and Jim, p.208–18   *4–6

Rogers, F., Heels, Wheels, and Wire, p.168–71   5–6

Rounds, Stolen Pony, p.127–42   *5–6

Spencer, P. R., Exploring New Trails, p.331–36   5

Van Stockum, Canadian Summer, p.168–75   *5–6

FIREWORKS

Parker, B. M., Fire, p.32–34   4–6

FIRST AID: *see also* Lifesaving

Baker, A. O., Your Science World, p.176–81   6

Lenski, Judy's Journey, p.87–89, 141–44, 191–93   *4–6

O'Brien, Silver Chief, p.87–90   *6

Red Cross, First Aid Textbook for Juniors   6

Spencer, P. R., Finding New Trails, p.359–65   4

FISH: *see* Fishes

FISH AS FOOD: *see also* Fisheries

Scheib, First Book of Food, p.32–35   5–6

FISH HAWKS: *see* Hawks

FISHERIES: *see also* Fishes; Fishing; Grand Banks; Nets; Pearl Fisheries; Salmon; Sponge Fisheries; Whaling

Barrows, American Continents, p.46–48   5

Buehr, Harvest of the Sea   5–6

Burger, All about Fish, p.92–108   5–6

Duvoisin, And There Was America, p.17, 25–26   4–6

Eberle, Basketful, p.85–104   4–6

FISHERIES—ALASKA

Stefansson, Here Is Alaska, p.155–59   6

FISHERIES—CANADA

Dalgliesh, Blue Teapot, p.53–60   *4–6

FISHERIES—CHINA

Wiese, Chinese Ink Stick, p.57–59   *4–6

FISHERIES—COSTA RICA

Brown, G. E., Tico Bravo, Shark Hunter   *4–6

FISHERIES—GRAND BANKS

Buehr, Harvest of the Sea, p.32–42   5–6

FISHERIES—ICELAND

Golden, Made in Iceland, p.76–87   6

FISHERIES—JAPAN

Jakeman, Getting To Know Japan, p.51–52   4–6

FISHERIES—NORWAY: *see also* Lofoten Islands

Gidal, My Village in Norway   4–6

Rothery, Scandinavian Roundabout, p.21–31   6

FISHERIES—THAILAND

Ayer, Getting To Know Thailand, p.46–48   4–6

FISHERIES—UNITED STATES

Association for Childhood Education, Told under the Stars and Stripes, p.239–48   *4–6

Lenski, We Live in the South, p.74–103   *4–5

Lent, Men at Work in New England, p.22–29   4–6

FISHERMEN

Buck, P. S., Big Wave   *6

Carlson, N. S., Wings against the Wind   *4–6

FISHERS (animals): *see* Martens

FISHES: *see also* Aquariums; Fisheries; Fishing; Marine Animals; also names of fishes, as Eels; Salmon

Barker, Winter-sleeping Wildlife, p.86–92 5–6

Beauchamp, Discovering Our World, Bk.1, p.30–31 4

Brindze, Gulf Stream, p.47–54 4–6

Bronson, Children of the Sea, p.25–28, 38–56, 69–82, 103–13 6

Brown, V., How To Understand Animal Talk, p.177–78 6

Buck, M. W., In Ponds and Streams, p.30–41 4–6

———— Pets from the Pond, p.28–43 4–6

Burger, All about Fish 5–6

Cassell, Nature Games and Activities, p.56–64 4–6

Comstock, Handbook of Nature Study, p.144–69 6

Cooper, E. K., Science on the Shores and Banks, p.141–52 5–6

Doane, Book of Nature, p.78–79 5–6

Gaul, Pond Book 4–6

Hausman, Beginner's Guide to Fresh-Water Life, p.46–65 6

Lavine, Strange Travelers, p.24–29, 102–5, 119–22, 137–39 5–6

McClung, Leaper 4–5

Mason, G. F., Animal Homes, p.83–87 4–6

———— Animal Weapons, p.48–59 5–6

Morgan, A. H., Field Book of Animals in Winter, p.319–30 6

———— Field Book of Ponds and Streams, p.324–46 6

Morgan, A. P., Aquarium Book 5–6

Parker, B. M., Fishes 4–6

———— Golden Book of Science, p.18–19, 24 4–6

———— Living Things, p.19–20 4–6

Pels, Care of Water Pets, p.1–27, 65–86, 93–98 4–6

Reed, Earth for Sam, p.62–70 6

———— Sea for Sam, p.180–209 6

Robertson, G., Strange Sea Life, p.3–17 5–6

Selsam, See through the Sea 4–6

———— Underwater Zoos, p.19–26, 63–70 4–6

FISHES—MIGRATION: *see also* Salmon

Parker, B. M., Fishes, p.27–28 4–6

FISHES—TROPICAL

Morgan, A. P., Aquarium Book, p.67–97 5–6

FISHING: *see also* Fisheries; Fishes; Nets; Whaling

Bendick, First Book of Ships, p.22–25 4–6

Booz, Treat in a Trout *4

Burger, All about Fish, p.125–32 5–6

Cleary, Henry and Ribsy, p.144–70 *4–6

Coatsworth, Alice-All-By-Herself, p.123–33 *4–6

Du Bois, Three Policemen *4–6

Du Soe, Three without Fear, p.54–57 *4–6

Harrington, Ootook, p.11–16 4–6

Lattimore, Little Pear and His Friends, p.54–62 *4–5

Lawrence, Peachtree Island, p.82–97 *4–5

Wilder, On the Banks of Plum Creek, p.133–39 *4–6

Zwilgmeyer, Johnny Blossom, p.1–30 *4–6

FISHING INDUSTRY: *see* Fisheries

FLAG DAY

Brown, H. M., America Is My Country, p.195–96 5–6

Burnett, B., First Book of Holidays, p.29–30 4–5

Jordan, Holiday Handicraft, p.126–30 4–6

McSpadden, Book of Holidays, p.98–104 6

Olcott, Good Stories for Great Holidays, p.137–56 *4–6

Pannell, Holiday Round Up, p.195–200 4–6

Sechrist, Red Letter Days, p.148–57 5–6

FLAGS: *see also* Signaling

Bailey, C. S., Children of the Handcrafts, p.115–25 *5–6

Brown, H. M., America Is My Country, p.13–19 5–6

Krasilovsky, Benny's Flag 4

Rothery, Central American Roundabout, p.225–37 6

FLAMINGOS
Disney, Worlds of Nature, p.155–57
                                                                        4–6
FLASHLIGHTS
Parker, B. M., Electricity, p.14–15   5–6
FLATBOATS
Steele, Buffalo Knife   *4–6
FLEAS
Gaul, Picture Book of Insects, p.30–31
                                                                        4–6
FLEMING, ALEXANDER
Ludovici, World of the Microscope,
    p.116–20   6
FLICKERS
Webb, Birds in Their Homes, p.36–37
                                                                        4–6
FLIES
Comstock, Handbook of Nature Study,
    p.358–61   6
Gaul, Picture Book of Insects, p.32–35
                                                                        4–6
Hylander, Insects on Parade, p.151–58
                                                                         6
Lutz, Field Book of Insects, p.224–74
                                                                        4–6
Mason, G. F., Animal Tools, p.39–43
                                                                        5–6
Teale, Junior Book of Insects, p.196–
    202   6
Williamson, First Book of Bugs, p.20–
    23   4–5
FLIGHT: *see also* Aerodynamics; Air-
    planes; Airships; Aviation; Balloons;
    Birds—Migration; Kites
Bronson, Starlings   4–5
Burchard, Balloons   4–6
Crouse, W. H., Understanding Science,
    p.156–60   6
Gilmore, Model Planes for Beginners,
    p.10–14   5–6
Schneider, L., Wings in Your Future
                                                                        5–6
FLOODS: *see also* Noah; Rivers
Association for Childhood Education,
    Told under Spacious Skies, p.115–27
                                                                       *4–6
Chrisman, Shen of the Sea, p.16–31
                                                                       *5–6
Flakkeberg, Sea Broke Through   *6
Frost, Maple Sugar for Windy Foot,
    p.105–45   *4–6

George, J. L., Vulpes, the Red Fox,
    p.103–13   6
Graham, E. H., Water for America,
    p.87–91   6
Hubbard, Train That Never Came
    Back, p.111–27   5–6
Lansing, E. C. H., Liza of the Hundred-
    fold   *5–6
Lauber, Battle against the Sea   5–6
Le Grand, Augustus and the River
                                                                       *4–6
Lenski, Bayou Suzette, p.149–80   *5–6
———— Flood Friday   *4–6
Liers, Beaver's Story, p.76–87   5–6
Mukerji, Hari, the Jungle Lad, p.23–26
                                                                       *5–6
Sellew, Adventures with the Gods, p.50–
    53   4–5
Van Dersal, Land Renewed, p.22–23
                                                                         6
FLORENCE, ITALY
Epstein, S., First Book of Italy, p.38–41
                                                                        5–6
FLORIDA: *see also* Fruit Culture
Association for Childhood Education,
    Told under Spacious Skies, p.136–52
                                                                       *4–6
Baker, N. B., Juan Ponce de León   5–6
Banta, Life in America: The South,
    p.114–19   5–6
Bleeker, Seminole Indians   4–6
Cheney, Rocking Chair Buck   *4–5
Kennedy, Jenny   *4–6
Lawrence, Sand in Her Shoes   *4–6
Lenski, Judy's Journey, p.15–122, 200–
    212   *4–6
———— Strawberry Girl   *4–6
———— We Live in the South   *4–5
Lippincott, Wilderness Champion, p.
    134–67   *5–6
McNeer, War Chief of the Seminoles
                                                                        5–6
Quinn, Picture Map Geography of the
    United States, p.64–67   4–6
Rawlings, Secret River   *4–5
FLOTATION
Beeler, Experiments in Science, p.58–
    60, 76–79   5–6
FLOUR: *see also* Bread; Corn; Grain;
    Wheat
Beeler, Experiments in Chemistry, p.42–
    47   5–6

FLOUR MILLS
Buehr, Bread, p.45–53   4–6
Lent, Men at Work in the Great Lakes
    States, p.34–37   4–6
Shannon, Dobry, p.53–60   *5–6

FLOWERS: *see also* Botany; Bulbs; Gar-
    dening; Interdependence of Plants and
    Animals; Leaves; May Day; Plant
    Breeding; Plants; Seed Dispersal;
    Seeds; Weeds; Wild Flowers
Brown, V., How To Make a Home Na-
    ture Museum, p.132–41   5–6
Buck, M. W., In Yards and Gardens,
    p.29–34   4–6
Coatsworth, Alice-All-By-Herself, p.99–
    110   *4–6
Comstock, Handbook of Nature Study,
    p.546–90   6
Cooper, E. K., Science in Your Own
    Back Yard, p.68–78   5–6
Doane, Book of Nature, p.20–23, 54–
    56   5–6
Hylander, Out of Doors in Spring, p.11–
    14   5–6
———— Out of Doors in Summer,
    p.51–72   5–6
Kirkus, First Book of Gardening, p.25–
    29   4–6
Parker, B. M., Flowers, Fruits, Seeds,
    p.8–21   4–6
———— Garden and Its Friends, p.5–
    10   4–6
Selsam, Plants We Eat, p.57–62   4–6
Steinmann, Lia and the Red Carnations
     *6
Uchida, Promised Year   *4–6

FLOWERS—ARTIFICIAL
Jordan, Holiday Handicraft, p.116–18
     4–6

FLUTES
Buchanan, How Man Made Music,
    p.50–52   6
Gallant, K., Flute Player of Beppu   *4
Huntington, Tune Up   4–6
Lacey, Picture Book of Musical Instru-
    ments, p.12–13   5–6
Zarchy, Let's Make Something, p.48–
    50   5–6

FLYING: *see* Aviation; Birds; Daedalus
    and Icarus; Flight; Perseus; Space
    Travel

FLYING FOXES: *see* Bats

FLYING SQUIRRELS
Blough, After the Sun Goes Down,
    p.21–25   4–5
Moe, Animal Inn, p.28–34   4–6

FLYTRAPS
Parker, B. M., Garden Indoors, p.25–
    28   5–6

FOG: *see also* Evaporation
Parker, B. M., Clouds, Rain, and Snow,
    p.15–17   4–6
Sauer, Fog Magic   *5–6

FOLK COSTUMES: *see* Costume

FOLK DANCING: *see* Dancing

FOLK SONGS: *see also* American Bal-
    lads and Songs; Ballads; Dancing;
    National Songs; Singing Games;
    Songs; also names of composers of
    songs, as Foster, Stephen Collins
Buchanan, How Man Made Music,
    p.16, 82–83   6

FOOD: *see also* Agriculture; Bakers; Bev-
    erages; Canning; Cooking; Digestion;
    Farm Life; Fruit; Grain; Indians
    of North America—Food; Markets;
    Meat Industry; Nutrition; Nuts; Poul-
    try; Table Etiquette; Vegetables; also
    names of special foods, as Bread;
    Milk
Barnard, Macmillan Science–Life Series,
    Bk.6, p.115–28   6
Batchelor, Superstitious? Here's Why!,
    p.9–18   6
Beauchamp, Discovering Our World,
    Bk.1, p.76–80   4
Bleeker, Apache Indians, p.26–37   4–6
———— Mission Indians of California,
    p.31–48   4–6
———— Sea Hunters, p.84–110   5–6
Boyd-Orr, Wonderful World of Food
     6
Buehr, Meat from Ranch to Table   4–6
Carlson, B. W., Make It and Use It,
    p.76–81   4–6
Eberle, Basketful   4–6
Evans, People Are Important, p.35–48
     4–5
Fenton, C. L., Plants That Feed Us
     5–6

Freeman, I. M., All about the Wonders of Chemistry, p.67–80   6

Gallant, R. A., Exploring Chemistry, p.110–16   6

Graham, S., Dr. George Washington Carver, p.237–42   6

Kavaler, Wonders of Algae, p.41–44   6

Lent, Man Alive in Outer Space, p.82–89   5–6

Parker, B. M., Plant Factories   5–7

Rombauer, Cookbook for Boys and Girls   6

Scheib, First Book of Food   5–6

Selsam, Plants We Eat   4–6

Tor, Getting To Know Korea, p.16–19   4–6

———— Getting To Know Puerto Rico, p.32–35   4–6

FOOD—BRAZIL

Brown, R. J., Land and People of Brazil, p.16, 51, 89–90, 95–96, 115–17   6

May, Let's Read about Brazil, p.94–98   4–6

FOOD—CHINA

Spencer, C., Land of the Chinese People, p.11–12, 14–15, 104–6   6

———— Made in China, p.199–214   5–6

FOOD—COLONIAL PERIOD IN AMERICA

Buehr, Meat from Ranch to Table, p.33–37   4–6

FOOD—ENGLAND

Street, Land of the English People, p.47–48   6

FOOD—FRANCE

Bishop, C. H., Pancakes—Paris   *4–6

FOOD—FROZEN

Eberle, Basketful, p.136–39   4–6

New York Herald Tribune, Young America's Cook Book, p.227–42   4–6

Scheib, First Book of Food, p.56–57   5–6

FOOD—INCA

Bleeker, Inca, p.51–53   5–6

FOOD—INDIA

Caldwell, Let's Visit India, p.71–73   4–6

FOOD—ITALY

Angelo, Nino, p.21–45, 120–24, 201–4   *6

Hazeltine, Easter Book of Legends and Stories, p.244–45, 250–55   *5–6

FOOD—JAPAN

Buck, P. S., Big Wave, p.13, 17–18   *6

Jakeman, Getting To Know Japan, p.22, 28–31, 37   4–6

FOOD—KOREA

Tor, Getting To Know Korea, p.16–19   4–6

FOOD—MAYA

Bleeker, Maya, p.48–55   5–6

FOOD—MEXICO

Tarshis, Village That Learned To Read, p.58–60   *4–6

FOOD—MIDDLE AGES

Buehr, Meat from Ranch to Table, p.24–31   4–6

Tappan, When Knights Were Bold, p.86–92   6

FOOD—PIONEER LIFE

Wilder, By the Shores of Silver Lake   *5–6

———— Farmer Boy   *4–6

———— Little House in the Big Woods   *4–6

———— Long Winter   *5–6

FOOD—SOUTH AMERICA

Hall, E., Land and People of Argentina, p.95–96, 101–3   6

FOOD—SPAIN

Buckley, Luis of Spain   4–6

FOOD—SWEDEN

Burglon, Children of the Soil, p.15–32   *4–6

FOOD—THAILAND

Ayer, Getting To Know Thailand, p.38–40   4–6

FOOD—TIBET

Rankin, L., Daughter of the Mountains, p.28–29   *5–6

FOOD AND DRUG ADMINISTRATION: *see* Food Laws

FOOD CONSERVATION: *see* Canning; Refrigeration

FOOD LAWS
Elting, We Are the Government, p.72–74   6

FOOD SUPPLY: *see also* Agriculture; Foods; Markets; Meat Industry
Barnard, Macmillan Science-Life Series, Bk.6, p.238–63   6

FOOTBALL
Bancroft, Games, p.535–36, 592–600, 606–11   4–6
Cooke, D. C., Better Football for Boys   5–6
Jackson, C. P., Buzzy Plays Midget League Football   *4–5
———— Spice's Football   *4–5
Lord, Quarterback's Aim   *4–5
Renick, J. L., Tommy Carries the Ball   *4–6
Renick, M. L., Nicky's Football Team   *4–5
Van Riper, Knute Rockne   4–6

FORCE AND ENERGY: *see also* Acceleration; Machines; Power Mechanics
Beeler, More Experiments in Science, p.100–102   5–6
Branley, Solar Energy   6
Leonard, Exploring Science, p.249–77   6

FORD, HENRY
Hartman, Machines, p.213–17   6

FOREIGN CARS
Bendick, First Book of Automobiles, p.48–49   4–6

FOREST FIRES
Adler, Fire in Your Life, p.102–4   4–6
Bronson, Pollwiggle's Progress, p.102–6   4–5
Buehr, Timber!, p.60–70   5–6
Buff, Big Tree, p.46–49   5–6
Carroll, Tough Enough's Indians   *4–5
Child Study Association of America, Read to Yourself Storybook, p.87–94   *4–5
Colby, Park Ranger, p.14–16   5–6
Fenton, C. L., Land We Live On, p.78–81   4–6
Gall, Flat Tail, p.15–24   4–6
Holling, Paddle-to-the-Sea   *4–6
Hubbard, Train That Never Came Back, p.7–23   5–6

McClung, Spike, p.35–43   4
Smith, J. R., Neighbors around the World, p.76–78   4

FORESTRY: *see also* Amazon Valley; Arbor Day; Congo; Conservation; Petrified Forests; Sequoias; Trees; Wood
Barr, Young Scientist Takes a Ride, p.121–22   5–6
Barrows, American Continents, p.148–49   5
Buehr, Timber!   5–6
Dudley, Our American Trees   5–6
Elting, We Are the Government, p.60–61   6
Goetz, Tropical Rain Forests   4–6
Life, World We Live In, p.178–92   5–6
Parker, B. M., Trees, p.31–34   4–6
Selsam, See through the Forest   4–6
Wall, Gifts from the Forest   4–6

FORMOSA
Caldwell, Let's Visit China, p.11–14, 90–93   5–6
———— Let's Visit Formosa   5–6
Quinn, Picture Map Geography of Asia, p.96–98   4–6

FORMOSA—GOVERNMENT
Caldwell, Let's Visit Formosa, p.46–48   5–6

FORMOSA—HISTORY
Caldwell, Let's Visit Formosa, p.13–19   5–6

FORMOSA—INDUSTRIES
Caldwell, Let's Visit Formosa, p.42–46   5–6

FOSSILS: *see also* Geology; Mammoths; Prehistoric Animals
Andrews, All about Dinosaurs, p.27–34   4–6
———— All about Strange Beasts of the Past, p.15–27   4–6
Blough, Discovering Dinosaurs, p.20–33   4–5
Colbert, Millions of Years Ago, p.3–5   6
Comstock, Handbook of Nature Study, p.756–57   6
Cooper, E. K., Science in Your Own Back Yard, p.40–48   5–6
Fenton, C. L., Life Long Ago   6

———— Prehistoric World   4–6
Lauber, All about the Ice Age, p.42–51
                                              4–6
Loomis, Field Book of Common Rocks
    and Minerals, p.266   6
Parker, B. M., Stories Read from the
    Rocks   4–6
———— Water, p.33–34   5–6
Reed, Earth for Sam   6
Sevrey, First Book of the Earth, p.55–
    59   5–6
White, A. T., All about Our Changing
    Rocks, p.110–22, 127–29   5–6
Williams, H. L., Stories in Rocks,
    p.100–105   6
Wyckoff, Story of Geology, p.166–75
                                              5–6

FOSTER, STEPHEN COLLINS
Bailey, C. S., Pioneer Art in America,
    p.183–94   *5–6
Buchanan, How Man Made Music,
    p.187   6
Burch, Famous Composers for Young
    People, p.121–27   4–6
Purdy, He Heard America Sing   6
Wheeler, Stephen Foster and His Little
    Dog Tray   4–6

FOSTER PARENTS, ADJUSTMENT TO
Lattimore, Chinese Daughter   *4
Rushmore, Lost Treasure Box   *4–6

FOURTH OF JULY: *see also* Declaration
    of Independence
Bailey, C. S., Children of the Hand-
    crafts, p.179–88   *5–6
Brown, H. M., America Is My Country,
    p.187–89   5–6
Burnett, B., First Book of Holidays,
    p.31–33   *4–5
Crawford, "Hello, the Boat!", p.210–27
                                              *6
Dalgliesh, Fourth of July Story   4–6
Estes, Rufus M., p.212–32   *4–6
Frazier, Secret Friend, p.47–60   *4–6
Hale, Complete Peterkin Papers, p.102–
    12 (The Peterkins Celebrate the 4th
    of July)   *4–6
Jordan, Holiday Handicraft, p.131–39
                                              4–6
Judson, Boat Builder, p.35–42   5–6
Langton, Majesty of Grace, p.87–104
                                              *4–5

McSpadden, Book of Holidays, p.106–
    13   6
Olcott, Good Stories for Great Holi-
    days, p.159–75   *4–6
Pannell, Holiday Round Up, p.205–18
                                              *4–6
Sechrist, Red Letter Days, p.158–65
                                              5–6
Wilder, Farmer Boy, p.173–89   *4–6
———— Little Town on the Prairie,
    p.63–85   *5–6

FOWLS: *see* Poultry

FOX HUNTING
George, J. L., Vulpes, the Red Fox,
    p.36–46, 48–51, 117–20, 139–68,
    180–84   *6

FOXES
Colby, First Hunt, p.7   5–6
Comstock, Handbook of Nature Study,
    p.251–53   6
De la Mare, Animal Stories, p.81–86
                                              *4–6
Franklin, Tricky   *4–6
———— Wild Animals of the South-
    west, p.1–12   5–6
George, J. L., Vulpes, the Red Fox   *6
Gillham, Beyond the Clapping Moun-
    tains, p.99–105, 117–20   *4–6
Hogner, Animal Book, p.144–48   6
Kane, Tale of a Meadow, p.94–96   4–6
Lathrop, Let Them Live, p.50–53   4–6
Mason, G. F., Animal Tracks, p.64–65
                                              4–6
Moe, Animal Inn, p.35–41   4–6
Stoutenberg, Wild Animals of the Far
    West, p.38–42   4–6
Yashima, T., Golden Footprints   *4–6

FRANCE
Barrows, Old World Lands, p.52–62   6
Baudouy, Bruno, King of the Mountain
                                              *5–6
Baumann, Caves of the Great Hunters
                                              6
Bishop, C. H., Pancakes—Paris   *4–6
Booz, Treat in a Trout   *4
Bragdon, L. J., Land and People of
    France   6
Carlson, N. S., Evangeline, Pigeon of
    Paris   *4–5
———— Happy Orpheline   *4

———— Wings against the Wind
*4–6

Epstein, E., First Book of the United
Nations, p.16–17   4–6

Jordan, Homemade Dolls in Foreign
Dress, p.119–32   4–6

Joy, Young People of the Western Mediterranean, p.55–72   6

Marokvia, Grococo   *4–5

Peare, Jules Verne   5–6

FRANCE—FOLK TALES: *see also* Brittany—Folk Tales; Roland
Sawyer, Long Christmas, p.99–107
4–6

FRANCE—HISTORY: *see also* French
and Indian War, 1755–63; French in
America; French Revolution, 1789–
99; also names of persons, as Joan of
Arc
Bergaust, Rockets around the World,
p.22–29   6

Bragdon, L. J., Land and People of
France, p.17–63   6

Flexner, Wishing Window   *4

Foster, G., Abraham Lincoln's World
6

———— George Washington's World
6

Hazeltine, Hero Tales from Many
Lands, p.220–34   5–6

Hillyer, Child's History of the World,
p.395–401   5–6

Lownsbery, Boy Knight of Reims   *6

McGuire, Glimpses into the Long Ago,
p.258–64   5–6

FRANCIS OF ASSISI, SAINT
Bulla, Song of St. Francis   4–5

Farjeon, Ten Saints, p.99–124   6

Hartman, Builders of the Old World,
p.267–69   6

Jewett, God's Troubadour   5–6

Lillie, Book of Three Festivals, p.28–44
*5–6

Smith, E. S., Christmas Book of Legends & Stories, p.327–31   5–6

Tappan, When Knights Were Bold,
p.183–88   6

Van Stockum, Cottage at Bantry Bay,
p.94–97   *6

FRANKLIN, BENJAMIN
Aulaire, Benjamin Franklin   4–6

Barksdale, That Country Called Virginia, p.100   6

Brindze, Gulf Stream, p.26–32   4–6

Cousins, Ben Franklin of Old Philadelphia   5–6

Daugherty, Poor Richard   6

Eaton, That Lively Man, Ben Franklin
6

Fisher, D. F. C., And Long Remember,
p.38–47   6

Foster, G., George Washington's World,
p.21–25, 56–58, 186–88   6

Hartman, Machines, p.83–86   6

Judson, Benjamin Franklin   6

Lawson, R., Watchwords of Liberty,
p.8–9   4–6

Olcott, Good Stories for Great Birthdays, p.163–72   *4–6

Weir, R. C., Benjamin Franklin   4–6

Wibberley, Sea Captain from Salem
*6

FREDERICK THE GREAT
Foster, G., George Washington's World,
p.31–33, 77–78, 93–95, 124–25, 270–
71   6

Hillyer, Child's History of the World,
p.407–11   5–6

FREEZING: *see also* Refrigeration
Beeler, Experiments in Science, p.19-21,
25–27   5–6

FREIGHT
Bechdolt, Going Up, p.70–72   5–6

Henry, R. S., Trains   5–6

Norling, Pogo's Truck Ride   4

FREIGHT CARS: *see* Railroads—Freight
Cars

FREIGHT TERMINALS
Bethers, Perhaps I'll be a Railroad
Man, p.24–25   5–6

Van Metre, Trains, Tracks and Travel,
p.387–412   6

FRÉMONT, JOHN CHARLES
Dawson, California, p.132–36   5–6

Garst, Kit Carson   6

FRENCH, DANIEL CHESTER
Hillyer, Child's History of Art, p.262–
64   5–6

FRENCH AND INDIAN WAR, 1755-
63: *see also* Colonial Period in America

Barksdale, That Country Called Virginia, p.90–96   6
Daugherty, Poor Richard, p.71–77   6
Eaton, That Lively Man, Ben Franklin, p.111–42   6
Edmonds, Matchlock Gun   *4–6
Foster, G., George Washington's World, p.71–76   6
Meadowcroft, Land of the Free, p.38–42   4–5

FRENCH CANADIANS: *see also* Quebec
Carlson, N. S., Alphonse, That Bearded One   *4–6
———— Sashes Red and Blue   *4–6
———— Talking Cat   *4–6
De Angeli, Petite Suzanne   *4–6
McNeer, Canadian Story   5–6
Ross, F. A., Land and People of Canada, p.6–11   6
Spencer, P. R., Exploring New Trails, p.306–14   5
Van Stockum, Canadian Summer   *5–6

FRENCH IN AMERICA: *see also* French and Indian War, 1755–63; Quebec; also names of French explorers, as Cartier, Jacques
American Heritage, Trappers and Mountain Men   6
Bonner, Canada and Her Story, p.3–45   5–6
Dalgliesh, America Begins, p.50–51, 60–61   4–5
Duvoisin, And There Was America, p.25–36   4–6
Graham, A. P., La Salle, River Explorer   4–6
Ross, F. A., Land and People of Canada, p.58–68   6

FRENCH IN THE UNITED STATES
Bishop, C. H., Blue Spring Farm   *5–6

FRENCH REVOLUTION, 1789-99; *see also* France—History; Napoleon I, Emperor of the French
Bragdon, L. J., Land and People of France, p.53–57   6
Coatsworth, Fair American   *5–6
Foster, G., George Washington's World, p.290–326   6
Hillyer, Child's History of the World, p.420–27   5–6

FRENCH WEST AFRICA
Stinetorf, Children of North Africa, p.177–90   *5–6

FREQUENCY MODULATION: *see* Radio

FRESH-WATER ANIMALS: *see* Animals —Fresh-Water

FRICTION
Adler, Things That Spin   5–6
Huey, What Makes the Wheels Go Round, p.122–25   6
Parker, B. M., Machines, p.32–34   5–6

FRIENDLINESS: *see* Kindness

FRIENDLY ISLANDS
Quinn, Picture Map Geography of the Pacific Islands, p.102–4   5–6

FRIENDS—SOCIETY OF: *see also* Penn, William
Association for Childhood Education, Told under the Stars and Stripes, p.71–82   *4–6
De Angeli, Jared's Island   *4–6
———— Thee, Hannah!   *4–6
Field, Hitty, p.109–30   *5–6
Fitch, One God, p.132–33   5–6
Haviland, William Penn   4–6
Henry, M., Benjamin West and His Cat Grimalkin   4–6
———— King of the Wind, p.92–103   *5–6
Holberg, John Greenleaf Whittier   6
Hunt, M. L., Benjie's Hat   *4–6
———— Little Girl with Seven Names   *4–6
———— Lucinda   *5–6
Leeming, Costume Book, p.106   5–6

FRIENDSHIP
Barnes, Wonderful Year   *4–6
Beim, Just Plain Maggie   *4–6
Calhoun, Katie John   *4–5
Cleary, Ellen Tebbits   *4–5
Clewes, Runaway   *4–5
Corbett, Lemonade Trick   *4–6
Daringer, Adopted Jane   *4–6
Durell, Holly River Secret   *4–6
Estes, Hundred Dresses   *4–6
Evans, All about Us, p.73–82   4–6
Frazier, Secret Friend   *4–6
Friedman, F., Carol from the Country   *4–6

Gates, Blue Willow *5-6
Kohler, "Crazy As You Look!" *4-6
Lenski, Bayou Suzette *5-6
Lovelace, Betsy-Tacy *4-5
Meadowcroft, By Secret Railway *5-6
Weiss, E. S., Sally Saucer *4-6
Will, Two Reds *4-5

FRIGATE BIRDS
Disney, Worlds of Nature, p.157–59
4-6

FRITHIOF
Hazeltine, Hero Tales from Many
Lands, p.306–15 5-6

FROGS: see also Toads
Bailey, C. S., Miss Hickory, p.93–99
*4-6
Barker, Winter-sleeping Wildlife, p.83–
85 5-6
Barr, More Research Ideas for Young
Scientists, p.105–7 5-6
Bevans, Book of Reptiles and Amphib-
ians, p.52–56 4-6
Blough, After the Sun Goes Down,
p.37–39 4-5
Bronson, Pollwiggle's Progress 4-5
Brown, V., How To Understand Ani-
mal Talk, p.175–76 6
Buck, M. W., In Ponds and Streams,
p.47–49 4-6
———— Pets from the Pond, p.44–51
4-6
Comstock, Handbook of Nature Study,
p.177–87 6
Cooper, E. K., Science on the Shores
and Banks, p.120–29 5-6
Gall, Wagtail 4-6
Gaul, Pond Book 4-6
George, J. L., Vulpes, the Red Fox, p.15
*6
Hogner, Frogs and Polliwogs 4-5
Hyde, Animal Clocks and Compasses,
p.135–38 5-6
Hylander, Out of Doors in Spring, p.29–
38, 49–57 5-6
Kane, Tale of a Pond 5-6
Lavine, Strange Travelers, p.39–40 (tad-
poles) 5-6
Mason, G. F., Animal Sounds, p.54–58
5-6
Moe, Animal Inn, p.139–41 4-6
Morgan, A. H., Field Book of Animals
in Winter, p.352–60 6

———— Field Book of Ponds and
Streams, p.368–88 6
Morgan, A. P., Aquarium Book, p.129–
69 5-6
Parker, B. M., Toads and Frogs 4-6
Pels, Care of Water Pets, p.27–30 4-6
Zim, Frogs and Toads 4-6

FRONTIER LIFE: see Pioneer Life

FRONTIERSMEN: see names of frontiersmen, as Boone, Daniel

FROZEN FOOD: see Food—Frozen

FRUIT: see also Berries; Canning; Fruit
Culture; also names of fruits, as Ap-
ples
Eberle, Basketful, p.105–53 4-6
Guilcher, Fruit Is Born 5-6
Parker, B. M., Flowers, Fruits, Seeds,
p.22–24 4-6
Scheib, First Book of Food, p.40–42
5-6
Selsam, Plants We Eat, p.63–107 4-6
Wall, Gifts from the Grove 4-6

FRUIT CULTURE
Dawson, California, p.185–91 5-6
Smith, J. R., Neighbors around the
World, p.130–42 4
Writers Project, Orchards in All Sea-
sons, no.29 5-6

FUEL: see also Coal; Petroleum
Dudley, Our American Trees, p.68–73
5-6
Kavaler, Wonders of Algae, p.78–80 6

FULTON, ROBERT: see also Steamboats
Cottler, Heroes of Civilization, p.190–
200 6
Hartman, Machines, p.64–68 6
Judson, Boat Builder 5-6

FUNDY—BAY OF
Dalgliesh, Blue Teapot *4-6

FUNGI: see also Cheese; Molds; Mushrooms; Yeast
Comstock, Handbook of Nature Study,
p.714–29 6
Disraeli, New Worlds through the Microscope, p.102–10 6
Hylander, Out of Doors in Summer,
p.91–106 5-6
Jaeger, Easy Crafts, p.14–19 4-6
Parker, B. M., Plant and Animal Partnerships, p.19–25 5-6

FUR-BEARING ANIMALS: *see* names of animals, as Weasels

FUR TRADE: *see also* Canada—History; French in America; Hunting; Trapping
American Heritage, Trappers and Mountain Men   6
Anderson, A. M., Fur Trappers of the Old West   5–6
Bonner, Canada and Her Story, p.59–84, 100–104   5–6
Dalgliesh, America Begins, p.50–51   4–5
Duvoisin, And There Was America, p.25–40   4–6

FURNACES: *see also* Fuel; Heating
Adler, Fire in Your Life, p.82–85 (blast furnace)   4–6
Branley, Solar Energy, p.72–80   6
Enright, Saturdays, p.130–39   *4–6
Schneider, H., Everyday Machines and How They Work, p.131–39   5–6

FURNITURE: *see also* Clocks; Doll Furniture; Mirrors; Wood Carving
Bendick, First Book of How To Fix It, p.56–60   4–6
Leeming, Fun with Boxes   4–6
Lent, Men at Work in the Great Lakes States, p.70–73   4–6
Maginley, Historic Models of Early America, p.123–40   6

FUSES—ELECTRIC: *see* Electric Fuses

GAINSBOROUGH, THOMAS
Chandler, Story-Lives of Master Artists, p.163–76   6

GALILEO
Asimov, Breakthroughs in Science, p.31–40   5–6
Cottler, Heroes of Civilization, p.98–107   6
Foster, G., World of Captain John Smith, p.126–30, 243–46, 250–53, 376–79   6
Goodwin, Real Book About Stars, p.98–99   4–6
Parker, B. M., Scientist and His Tools, p.6–8   5–6

GALLS (botany)
Comstock, Handbook of Nature Study, p.335–38   6

Lutz, Field Book of Insects, p.443–57   4–6

GALVANISM: *see* Electricity

GAMA, VASCO DA
Cottler, Heroes of Civilization, p.13–23   6
Duvoisin, They Put Out to Sea, p.111–33   4–6
Hewes, Spice Ho!, p.62–75   5–6
Kent, He Went with Vasco da Gama   *6
McGuire, Brave Young Land, p.48–50   5–6

GAMES: *see also* Amusements; Athletics; Baseball; Basketball; Dancing; Festivals; Football; Indians of North America—Games; Olympic Games; Puzzles; Racing; Singing Games; Sports; Toys; Tricks
Adler, Magic House of Numbers   6
Bancroft, Games   4–6
Bendick, First Book of Automobiles, p.56–57   4–6
Carlson, B. W., Act It Out, p.14–25   4–6
Cassell, Nature Games and Activities   4–6
Forbush, Book of Games   4–6
Frankel, Games for Boys and Girls   4–6
Gardner, Mathematical Puzzles, p.54–64   6
Goetz, Other Young Americans, p.167–96   5–6
Harshaw, What Book Is That?   4–6
Leeming, Fun with Boxes   4–6
——— Fun with String, p.135–59   4–6
Mulac, Game Book   6
Parker, B. M., Living Things, p.28–35   4–6
Renick, M. L., Shining Shooter, p.215–18   *4–6
Sechrist, Heigh-Ho for Halloween!, p.199–223   5–6
Zarchy, Let's Make Something, p.44–45, 154–55   5–6

GAMES—AFRICA
Millen, Children's Games from Many Lands, p.5–28   4–6

GAMES—ALASKA
Millen, Children's Games from Many
Lands, p.133–36   4–6

GAMES—ASIA
Millen, Children's Games from Many
Lands, p.29–86   4–6

GAMES—BRAZIL
Millen, Children's Games from Many
Lands, p.119–23   4–6

GAMES—CANADA
Millen, Children's Games from Many
Lands, p.136–46   4–6

GAMES—CHINA
Millen, Children's Games from Many
Lands, p.36–44   4–6
Wood, E., Silk and Satin Lane, p.81–
83   *4–5

GAMES—CUBA
Millen, Children's Games from Many
Lands, p.88–93   4–6

GAMES—CZECHOSLOVAKIA
Millen, Children's Games from Many
Lands, p.185   4–6

GAMES—ENGLAND
Millen, Children's Games from Many
Lands, p.187–89   4–6

GAMES—EUROPE
Millen, Children's Games from Many
Lands, p.183–210   4–6

GAMES—INDIA
Millen, Children's Games from Many
Lands, p.44–55   4–6

GAMES—JAPAN
Millen, Children's Games from Many
Lands, p.61–69   4–6

GAMES—KOREA
Millen, Children's Games from Many
Lands, p.70–73   4–6

GAMES—LATIN AMERICA
Millen, Children's Games from Many
Lands, p.87–131, 159–61   4–6

GAMES—MEXICO
Millen, Children's Games from Many
Lands, p.100–106   4–6

GAMES—NICARAGUA
Millen, Children's Games from Many
Lands, p.107–9   4–6

GAMES—NORWAY
Millen, Children's Games from Many
Lands, p.200   4–6

GAMES—OTHER LANDS
Bancroft, Games   4–6

GAMES—PERSIA
Millen, Children's Games from Many
Lands, p.55–60   4–6

GAMES—PHILIPPINE ISLANDS
Millen, Children's Games from Many
Lands, p.82–86   4–6

GAMES—PUERTO RICO
Millen, Children's Games from Many
Lands, p.93–98   4–6

GAMES—UNION OF SOVIET SOCIAL-
IST REPUBLICS
Millen, Children's Games from Many
Lands, p.202–4   4–6

GANDHI, MOHANDAS K.
Caldwell, Let's Visit India, p.54–58, 65–
66   4–6
———— Let's Visit Pakistan, p.56–57
                                         4–6
McNeer, Armed with Courage, p.85–98
                                         5–6
Modak, Land and People of India, p.74–
80, 87   6

GANGES RIVER
Caldwell, Let's Visit India, p.83–84
                                         4–6

GARDEN FLOWERS: *see* Flowers; Gardening

GARDEN PESTS: *see* Insects—Injurious

GARDENING: *see also* Botany; Bulbs;
Flowers; Fruit; Fruit Culture; Graft-
ing; Indians of North America—
Food; Insects—Injurious; Plant Breed-
ing; Plants; Seeds; Vegetables; Weeds
Armer, Waterless Mountain, p.194–96,
200–201   *5–6
Bailey, C. S., Children of the Hand-
crafts, p.55–64   *5–6
Beeler, More Experiments in Science,
p.46–50   5–6
Estes, Rufus M., p.188–211   *4–6
Kirkus, First Book of Gardening   4–6
Parker, B. M., Garden and Its Friends
                                         4–6
———— Garden Indoors   5–6

Spencer, C., Made in China, p.108–16
                                             5–6
Tappan, When Knights Were Bold,
  p.217–19   6

GARDENS—MINIATURE
  Hamilton, E. T., Handicraft for Girls,
    p.153–64   6

GARFIELD, JAMES ABRAM
  Beard, Presidents in American History,
    p.85–86, 168   6
  Coy, First Book of Presidents, p.47
                                             4–6
  Petersham, Story of the Presidents of
    the United States, p.50   4–6

GAS AND OIL ENGINES
  Barnard, Macmillan Science-Life Series,
    Bk.6, p.291–92   6
  Darrow, Boys' Own Book of Great In-
    ventions, p.140–53   6
  Morgan, A. P., Boys' Book of Engines,
    Motors & Turbines, p.101–28   6
  Schneider, H., More Power to You,
    p.49–56   5–6

GAS STATIONS
  Spencer, P. R., Finding New Trails,
    p.103–10   4

GASES, LIQUIDS, SOLIDS: *see also* Air;
  Airships; Balloons; Chemistry; Nat-
  ural Gas; Water; also names of gases,
  as Nitrogen
  Freeman, M. B., Fun with Science,
    p.19–24   6
  Morgan, A. P., Boys' Book of Science
    and Construction, p.151–98   6

GASOLINE: *see* Petroleum

GASOLINE ENGINES: *see* Gas and Oil
  Engines

GASPÉ PENINSULA: *see* Quebec

GAUCHOS: *see* Cowboys

GAURS
  Buck, F., Jungle Animals, p.33   5–6

GEESE: *see also* Poultry
  Comstock, Handbook of Nature Study,
    p.130–35   6
  Gage, Wild Goose Tale   *4–6
  Gillham, Beyond the Clapping Moun-
    tains, p.1–16   *4–6
  Kane, Tale of a Pond   5–6
  Weil, Animal Families   4

GEHRIG, LOU
  Spencer, P. R., Traveling New Trails,
    p.78–83   6
  Van Riper, Lou Gehrig   4–5

GEIGER COUNTERS
  Beeler, Experiments with Atomics,
    p.66–76   6
  MacGregor, Miss Pickerell and the
    Geiger Counter   *4–6

GEMS: *see* names of gems, as Diamonds

GENEALOGY
  Lawson, R., They Were Strong and
    Good   4–6

GENEROSITY
  Alden, Why the Chimes Rang   *4–6
  Enright, Then There Were Five   *5–6
  Hazeltine, Easter Book of Legends and
    Stories, p.210–33   *5–6
  Liu, Little Wu and the Watermelons
                                             *4–5
  Sawyer, This Way to Christmas   *4–6

GEOGRAPHY: *see also* Antarctic Regions; Arctic Regions; Climate; Discoveries in Geography; Discovery
  Period in America; Earth; Explorers;
  Industries; Maps; Rivers; Tropics;
  also names of places, as Brazil
  Fenton, C. L., Land We Live On   4–6

GEOLOGICAL CALENDAR
  Sevrey, First Book of the Earth, p.60–
    61   5–6
  White, A. T., Prehistoric America,
    p.169–78   4–6
  Williams, H. L., Stories in Rocks, p.106–
    23   6
  Wyckoff, Story of Geology, p.174–75
                                             5–6

GEOLOGY: *see also* Coal; Coral; Earth;
  Earthquakes; Evolution; Fossils; Gla-
  ciers; Metals; Minerals; Mining;
  Mountains; Natural Gas; Ocean; Pe-
  troleum; Rock Records; Rocks; Salt;
  Soils; Volcanoes
  Evans, Adventure Book of Rocks   4–6
  Fenton, C. L., Land We Live On   4–6
  ———— Life Long Ago   6
  Forsee, Louis Agassiz   6
  Land, M., Jungle Oil, p.33–43, 72–74
                                             5–6

Melbo, Our Country's National Parks, v.1, v.2   6

Parker, B. M., Stories Read from the Rocks   4–6

Reed, Earth for Sam   6

Schneider, H., Rocks, Rivers & the Changing Earth   4–6

Sevrey, First Book of the Earth   5–6

Sterling, Story of Caves   5–6

Tharp, Louis Agassiz   5–6

White, A. T., All about Our Changing Rocks   5–6

———— Prehistoric America   4–6

Williams, H. L., Stories in Rocks   6

Wyckoff, Story of Geology   5–6

GEORGE III, KING OF ENGLAND

Foster, G., George Washington's World, p.55, 85–86, 116–22, 183–84, 265–67   6

GEORGIA

Banta, Life in America: The South, p.108–13   5–6

Commager, E., Valentine   *6

Hayes, Skid, p.1–62   *5–6

Lenski, Judy's Journey, p.123–38   *4–6

———— We Live in the South   *4–5

Pace, Juliette Low   5–6

Quinn, Picture Map Geography of the United States, p.60–63   4–6

GERANIUMS

Comstock, Handbook of Nature Study, p.585–87   6

GERMANS IN AMERICA

Dalgliesh, America Builds Homes   4–5

GERMANS IN THE UNITED STATES

Association for Childhood Education, Told under the Stars and Stripes, p.159–71, 218–38   *4–6

Coatsworth, Sod House   *4–5

Hark, Story of the Pennsylvania Dutch   4–6

GERMANY: *see also* Art—Germany; Costume—Germany; Dancing—Germany

Barrows, Old World Lands, p.70–81   6

Kastner, Emil and the Detectives   *4–6

Lobsenz, First Book of West Germany   4–6

Sasek, This Is Munich   4–6

Shirer, Rise and Fall of Adolf Hitler   5–6

Tor, Getting To Know Germany   4–6

Wheeler, Robert Schumann and Mascot Ziff   4–6

———— Sebastian Bach   4–6

GERMANY—FOLK TALES: *see also* Nibelungenlied; Siegfried

Fenner, Fools and Funny Fellows, p.82–86, 154–60   4–6

Harper, Ghosts and Goblins, p.133–37   4–6

GERMANY—HISTORY: *see also* Barbarians; Gutenberg, Johannes; Hanseatic League

Hazeltine, Hero Tales from Many Lands, p.253–68   5–6

Lobsenz, First Book of West Germany, p.1–7   4–6

McNeer, Martin Luther   6

Tor, Getting To Know Germany, p.7–10   4–6

GERMS: *see* Bacteria

GERSHWIN, GEORGE

Buchanan, How Man Made Music, p.110–11, 193   6

Burch, Modern Composers for Young People, p.193–202   5–6

Schwimmer, Great Musicians as Children, p.231–38   6

GESSAR KHAN

Hazeltine, Hero Tales from Many Lands, p.401–15   5–6

GEYSERS: *see also* Yellowstone National Park

Pough, All about Volcanoes and Earthquakes, p.95–102   4–6

Williams, H. L., Stories in Rocks, p.52–53   6

GHANA

Caldwell, Let's Visit West Africa, p.51–59   5–6

Hughes, First Book of Africa, p.62–69   5–6

Lobsenz, First Book of Ghana   4–6

GHIBERTI, LORENZO

Hillyer, Child's History of Art, p.211–14   5–6

GHOSTS

Bendick, Good Knight Ghost   *4–6

Carlson, N. S., Talking Cat, p.66–76
*4–6

Driggs, Pony Express Goes Through,
p.79–85   6

Fenner, Time To Laugh, p.127–49
*4–6

Hazeltine, Easter Book of Legends and
Stories, p.115–29   *5–6

Leach, Thing at the Foot of the Bed
*4–6

MacKellar, Ghost in the Castle   *4–6

Shura, Simple Spigott   *4–5

GIANT PANDAS
Buck, F., Jungle Animals, p.34–35
5–6

GIANTS: *see also* Bunyan, Paul; David,
King of Israel; Tall Tales
Adams, K., Book of Giant Stories
*5–6

Brown, A. F., In the Days of Giants
4–6

Colum, Children of Odin   4–5

Keary, Heroes of Asgard   5–6

Sellew, Adventures with the Giants
4–6

Smith, I., Santa Claus Book, p.163–71
*4–5

Thurber, Great Quillow   *4–6

GIBBONS
Bridges, Zoo Babies, p.81–88   4–6

Buck, F., Jungle Animals, p.16   5–6

GIBRALTAR, ROCK OF
Barrows, Old World Lands, p.10, 12   6

Joy, Young People of the Western Mediterranean, p.139–51   6

GIFTS: *see* Handicraft

GILBERT AND ELLICE ISLANDS
Quinn, Picture Map Geography of the
Pacific Islands, p.72–75   5–6

GIOTTO
Chandler, Story-Lives of Master Artists,
p.1–14   6

Hillyer, Child's History of Art, p.28–32
5–6

Jewett, God's Troubadour   5–6

GIRAFFES
Buck, F., Jungle Animals, p.42–43
5–6

Disney, Worlds of Nature, p.166–67
4–6

Parker, B. M., Animals We Know,
p.22–23   5–6

Perkins, Marlin Perkins' Zooparade,
p.72–75   4–6

GIRL-BOY RELATIONS: *see* Boy-Girl
Relations

GIRL SCOUTS
De Angeli, Bright April   *4–6

Pace, Juliette Low, p.111–86   5–6

GLACIAL EPOCH
Epstein, S., Prehistoric Animals, p.172–
92   6

Lauber, All about the Ice Age   4–6

Longsworth, Exploring Caves, p.130–38,
140–44   6

Parker, B. M., Stories Read from the
Rocks, p.28–34   4–6

Williams, H. L., Stories in Rocks, p.93–
97   6

Writers Project, Cement, no.33, p.12–
13   5–6

GLACIER NATIONAL PARK
Melbo, Our Country's National Parks,
v.2, p.110–33   6

GLACIERS: *see also* Icebergs
Bragdon, L. J., Land and People of
Switzerland, p.18–20   6

Fenton, C. L., Land We Live On, p.50–
55   4–6

Forsee, Louis Agassiz   6

Lauber, All about the Ice Age   4–6

Melbo, Our Country's National Parks,
v.1, v.2   6

Reed, Earth for Sam   6

Sevrey, First Book of the Earth, p.52–
54   5–6

White, A. T., All about Our Changing
Rocks, p.26–30   5–6

Wyckoff, Story of Geology, p.92–101
5–6

GLASS: *see also* Mirrors; Stained Glass
Windows
Adler, Fire in Your Life, p.71–74   4–6

Bailey, C. S., Pioneer Art in America,
p.143–54   *5–6

Elting, Lollypop Factory, p.81–88   4–5

Epstein, S., First Book of Glass   5–6

Lent, Men at Work in the Great Lakes
States, p.38–41   4–6

Schwartz, It's Fun To Know Why, p.38–53   5–6

Writers Project, Story of Glass, no.19   5–6

GLIDERS—AVIATION
Bishop, R. W., From Kite to Kitty Hawk, p.81–86   6
Fisher, J., Wonderful World of the Air, p.23–27   5–6
Haines, Wright Brothers, p.97–115   4–5
Reynolds, Q. J., Wright Brothers, p.128–61   4–6

GLOBES
Epstein, S., First Book of Maps and Globes, p.42–46   4–6
Jordan, Holiday Handicraft, p.149–52   4–6

GLOUCESTER, MASSACHUSETTS
Association for Childhood Education, Told under the Stars and Stripes, p.239–48   *4–6

GLOWWORMS: *see* Fireflies

GLUCK, CHRISTOPH WILLIBALD VON
Burch, Famous Composers for Young People, p.27–32   4–6

G-MEN: *see* Federal Bureau of Investigation

GOATS
Association for Childhood Education, Told under the Stars and Stripes, p.62–70   *4–6
Bothwell, Empty Tower   *4–5
Bronson, Goats   4–5
Comstock, Handbook of Nature, p.266–70   6
Crowley, Pringle and the Lavender Goat   *4–5
Disney, Worlds of Nature, p.50–51 (mountain goats)   4–6
Fenner, Time To Laugh, p.127–49   *4–6
Franklin, Wild Animals of the Southwest, p.131–43   5–6
Hogeboom, Familiar Animals and How To Draw Them, p.16–19   4–5
Hogner, Barnyard Family, p.43–47   5–6
———— Farm Animals, p.87–92   6

Lenski, Judy's Journey   *4–6
Mason, G. F., Animal Tracks, p.76–77   4–6
Meredith, King of the Kerry Fair   *4–6
Moon, Chi-Wee, p.14–28   *4–6
Weil, Animal Families   4

GODDARD, ROBERT HUTCHINGS
Asimov, Breakthroughs in Science, p.190–93   5–6

GOETHALS, GEORGE WASHINGTON
Considine, Panama Canal   5–6
Fast, Goethals and the Panama Canal   6

GOETHE, JOHANN WOLFGANG VON
Foster, G., George Washington's World, p.95–97   6

GOLD: *see also* California Gold Rush; Klondike Gold Rush; Mining; Money
Barrows, American Continents, p.191–96   5
Bauer, California Gold Days   5–6
Beals, Rush for Gold   5–6
Bleeker, Inca, p.101–2 (crafts)   5–6
Brindze, Story of Gold   4–6
Buehr, Underground Riches, p.57–70   5–6
Bulla, Secret Valley   *4–5
Fenton, C. L., Riches from the Earth, p.131–35   5–6
Gatti, Here Is the Veld, p.111–22   6
Golden, Made in Iceland, p.109–16   6
Loomis, Field Book of Common Rocks and Minerals, p.29–32   6
McNeer, Alaska Gold Rush   5–6
———— California Gold Rush   4–6
———— Canadian Story, p.79–82   5–6
Writers Project, Gold, no.14   5–6

GOLDEN FLEECE: *see* Argonauts

GOLDFINCHES
Comstock, Handbook of Nature Study, p.53–57   6
Webb, Birds in Their Homes, p.25   4–6

GOLDFISH
Comstock, Handbook of Nature Study, p.144–48   6
Morgan, A. P., Aquarium Book, p.15–35   5–6
Parker, B. M., Fishes, p.3–7   4–6

GOLF
Bancroft, Games, p.536–40   4–6

GOODYEAR, CHARLES: *see also* Rubber
Hartman, Machines, p.122–25   6

GOONEY BIRDS
Hyde, Animal Clocks and Compasses, p.40–42   5–6

GOPHERS
Hogner, Animal Book, p.59–62   6

GORGAS, WILLIAM CRAWFORD
Cottler, Heroes of Civilization, p.307–18   6
Judson, Soldier Doctor   6
Markun, First Book of the Panama Canal, p.33–35   5–6

GORILLAS
Boston, Stranger at Green Knowe   *5–6
Bridges, Zoo Babies, p.14–21   4–6
――――― Zoo Doctor, p.116–26   4–6
――――― Zoo Pets, p.88–95   4–6
Buck, F., Jungle Animals, p.54–55   5–6
Knight, C. R., Life through the Ages, p.64–65   6
Perkins, Marlin Perkins' Zooparade, p.36–39   4–6
Spencer, P. R., Finding New Trails, p.274–86   4

GOTHS: *see* Barbarians; Germany—History

GOUNOD, CHARLES FRANÇOIS
Schwimmer, Great Musicians as Children, p.99–104   6

GOVERNMENT: *see also* Citizenship; Constitution of the United States; Declaration of Independence; Democracy; Election Day; Justice; Law; Patriotism; Police; Safety; Slavery; also names of countries, subhead Government, as United States—Government
Hillyer, Child's History of the World, p.114–23   5–6
Turner, Town Meeting Means Me   4–6

GOVERNMENT—ROME—ANCIENT
Hartman, Builders of the Old World, p.171–73   6

GRACCHI
Hartman, Builders of the Old World, p.186–87   6

GRAFTING
Writers Project, Grapes, no.37, p.18–21   5–6

GRAIL: *see* Arthur, King

GRAIN: *see also* Corn; Rice; Wheat
Petersham, Ruth   4–5
Selsam, Plants We Eat, p.108–23   4–6

GRAND BANKS
Brindze, Gulf Stream, p.22–25   4–6

GRAND CANYON NATIONAL PARK
Melbo, Our Country's National Parks, v.1, p.205–30   6

GRAND TETON NATIONAL PARK
Melbo, Our Country's National Parks, v.2, p.94–109   6

GRANT, ULYSSES SIMPSON
Beard, Presidents in American History, p.77–78, 166–67   6
Coy, First Book of Presidents, p.45   4–6
Dupuy, First Book of Civil War Naval Actions, p.25–28, 63–66   6
Fisher, D. F. C., And Long Remember, p.90–95   6
Foster, G., Abraham Lincoln's World, p.115–17   6
Lawson, R., Watchwords of Liberty, p.62–64, 79–80   4–6
Meadowcroft, Land of the Free, p.107–10   4–5
Petersham, Story of the Presidents of the United States, p.46–47   4–6

GRAPEFRUIT
Wall, Gifts from the Grove   4–6

GRAPES: *see also* Wine
Writers Project, Grapes, no.37   5–6

GRAPHS
Hartman, Machines, p.243, 257, 259, 272   6

GRASSES
Cooper, E. K., Science in Your Own Back Yard, p.58–67   5–6
Eberle, Grasses   4–6

GRASSHOPPERS: *see also* Cicadas; Katydids

Barker, Winter-sleeping Wildlife, p.110–
13   5–6
Bronson, Grasshopper Book   4–6
Comstock, Handbook of Nature Study,
p.338–43   6
Gaul, Picture Book of Insects, p.4–5
                                          4–6
Hogner, Grasshoppers and Crickets,
p.1–40   4–5
Hyde, Animal Clocks and Compasses,
p.10–11, 84–87   5–6
Hylander, Insects on Parade, p.47–57
                                            6
Mason, M. E., Middle Sister, p.88–99
                                          *4–5
Parker, B. M., Insects and Their Ways,
p.8–10   4–6
Teale, Insect Friends, p.83–86   5–6
Wilder, On the Banks of Plum Creek,
p.61–66, 192–212, 259–67   *4–6

GRASSLANDS: *see also* Prairies
Goetz, Grasslands   4–6
Smith, J. R., Neighbors around the
World, p.228–36   4

GRAVITATION: *see also* Astronomy;
Physics
Adler, Tools of Science, p.23–29   6
Beeler, Experiments in Science, p.10–
12   5–6
Freeman, M. B., Fun with Scientific
Experiments, p.2–3   5–6
Huey, What Makes the Wheels Go
Round, p.89–94   6
Kay, Space Volunteers, p.19–27   6
Land, B., Quest of Isaac Newton   6
Meyer, Picture Book of Astronomy,
p.4–6   4–5
Parker, B. M., Gravity   5–6
Schneider, L., Space in Your Future,
p.40–42, 45–49   6

GRAZING: *see* Grasslands; Herding;
Ranch Life; Shepherd Life

GREAT BRITAIN: *see* England

GREAT LAKES: *see also* French in
America
Bleeker, Chippewa Indians   5–6
Gilchrist, Story of the Great Lakes
                                          4–6
Holling, Paddle-to-the-Sea   *4–6
Lauber, Changing the Face of North
America   5–6

Mitchell, Ships That Made U.S. History,
p.86–89   6
GREAT PLAINS: *see also* North Central
States; Prairies; Ranch Life
Barrows, American Continents, p.165–
80   5
Bleeker, Crow Indians   5–6
Dorian, Hokahey!, p.86–96   5–6
Fenton, C. L., Land We Live On, p.10–
11   4–6
McClung, Shag: Last of the Plains Buf-
falo   4–6
GREAT SMOKY MOUNTAINS
Credle, Johnny and His Mule   *4–5
McNeer, Story of the Southern High-
lands   4–6
GREAT SMOKY MOUNTAINS NA-
TIONAL PARK
Melbo, Our Country's National Parks,
v.1, p.136–55   6
GREAT WALL OF CHINA: *see* Wall of
China
GRECO, EL
Chandler, Story-Lives of Master Artists,
p.80–88   6
GREECE—ANCIENT: *see also* Art—
Greece; Athens; Costume—Greece—
Ancient; Crete; Mycenae; Myths—
Greece and Rome; Olympia; Olympic
Games
Bergere, From Stones to Skyscrapers,
p.22–31   6
Falls, First 3000 Years, p.110–14, 143–
46, 153–67   6
Friedman, E., Digging into Yesterday,
p.52–72   5–6
Hartman, Builders of the Old World,
p.21–59   6
Hillyer, Child's History of the World,
p.79–88, 124–61   5–6
Honour, Secrets of Minos   6
Lamprey, All the Ways of Building,
p.64–77   6
McGuire, Glimpses into the Long Ago,
p.155–87   5–6
Robinson, C. A., First Book of Ancient
Greece   5–6
Rogers, F., Heels, Wheels, and Wire,
p.22–25   5–6
Tappan, Story of the Greek People
                                          5–6

Watson, Golden History of the World, p.42–51   5–6

GREECE—ANCIENT—HISTORY: *see also* Trojan War; also names of persons, as Pericles
Church, Iliad for Boys and Girls   5–6
Colum, Adventures of Odysseus   5–6
Hazeltine, Hero Tales from Many Lands, p.13–34, 52–67   5–6

GREECE—MODERN: *see also* Costume—Greece—Modern
Barrows, Old World Lands, p.100–101   6
———— Our Big World, p.86–89   4
Gidal, My Village in Greece   4–6
Nankivell, Tales of Christophilos   *4–6

GREEDINESS
Gillham, Beyond the Clapping Mountains, p.51–67   *4–6
Harper, Harvest Feast, p.261–85   *4–6
Renick, J. L., Steady   *4–5
Shannon, Dobry, p.133–38   *5–6

GREENLAND: *see also* Glaciers
Bailey, B. F., Greenland   4–6
O'Neill, Picture Story of Denmark   4–6
Vaygouny, Greenland Waters   4–6

GREETING CARDS
Freeman, M. B., Fun with Your Camera, p.48–49   4–6
Leeming, Fun with Greeting Cards   4–6
Robinson, J., Things To Make from Odds & Ends, p.15–17   6
Zarchy, Let's Make More Things, p.124–25   5–6

GRENFELL, WILFRED THOMASON
McNeer, Armed with Courage, p.71–82   5–6

GRETTIR THE STRONG
Hazeltine, Hero Tales from Many Lands, p.279–95   5–6

GRIEG, EDVARD HAGERUP
Burch, Famous Composers for Young People, p.147–54   4–6
Deucher, Edvard Grieg   4–6
Schwimmer, Great Musicians as Children, p.76–83   6

GRIFFES, CHARLES TOMLINSON
Burch, Modern Composers for Young People, p.179–81   5–6

GRIFFINS
Jacobson, First Book of Mythical Beasts, p.35–36   4–6

GROCERY STORES
Fenner, Time To Laugh, p.36–43   *4–6

GROUND-HOG DAY
Bailey, C. S., Miss Hickory, p.78–84   *4–6

GROUND HOGS: *see* Woodchucks

GROUND SQUIRRELS
Barker, Winter-sleeping Wildlife, p.23–28   5–6
Fenton, C. L., Wild Folk in the Desert, p.59–63   4–6
Hogner, Animal Book, p.44–50   6

GROUP ACCEPTANCE
Beim, Just Plain Maggie   *4–6
Cleary, Otis Spofford   *4–6
Crowley, Tor and Azor   *4–6
Urmston, New Boy   *4–6

GROUP ORGANIZATION: *see* Community Life; Community Life among the Animals and Insects

GROUSE
Colby, First Hunt, p.19   5–6
Mason, G. F., Animal Sounds, p.41–47   5–6

GROWING UP
Barnes, Wonderful Year   *4–6
Brink, Caddie Woodlawn, p.233–42   *6
Fritz, Brady   *5–6
Gage, Wild Goose Tale   *4–6
Holberg, Rowena Carey   *4–6
Lipkind, Boy of the Islands   *4–5
McGinley, Most Wonderful Doll in the World   *4–5
Rushmore, Cowboy Joe of the Circle S   *4–5
Sauer, Fog Magic   *5–6
Sperry, Call It Courage   *5–6
Uchida, Takao and Grandfather's Sword   *4–6
Van Stockum, Pegeen   *6

GROWTH: *see* Biology

GRUBER, FRANZ XAVIER
Pauli, Silent Night   4–6

GRUNIONS
Hyde, Animal Clocks and Compasses, p.17–21   5–6

Lavine, Strange Travelers, p.137–39
5–6

GUAM
Quinn, Picture Map Geography of the
Pacific Islands, p.64–67   5–6

GUANO
Rothery, South American Roundabout,
p.73–77   5–6

GUATEMALA: see also Mayas
Barrows, American Continents, p.302–4
5
Buff, Magic Maize   *4–6
Goetz, Neighbors to the South, p.33–
38   5–6
Quinn, Picture Map Geography of Mex-
ico, Central America and the West
Indies, p.17–26   4–6
Rothery, Central American Roundabout,
p.11–51   6

GUATEMALA—FOLK TALES
Rothery, Central American Roundabout,
p.195–99   6

GUATEMALA—INDUSTRIES
Rothery, Central American Roundabout,
p.41–51   6

GUIANA
Donaldson, Guiana   4–6
Quinn, Picture Map Geography of
South America, p.105–12   4–6

GUIDO
Buchanan, How Man Made Music,
p.78–81   6

GUILDS
Buchanan, How Man Made Music,
p.91–92   6
Lownsbery, Boy Knight of Reims   *6
Tappan, When Knights Were Bold,
p.232–46   6

GUINEA PIGS
Bianco, All about Pets, p.81–90   5–6
Hogner, Farm Animals, p.184   6

GUITARS
Kettelkamp, Singing Strings, p.28–31
5–6

GULF STREAM
Brindze, Gulf Stream   4–6

GULLS
Carlson, N. S., Wings against the Wind
*4–6

Gillham, Beyond the Clapping Moun-
tains, p.17–30   *4–6
Holling, Seabird, p.8–11   *4–6
Lathrop, Let Them Live, p.71–73   4–6

GUNPOWDER
Chrisman, Shen of the Sea, p.129–43
*5–6
Hillyer, Child's History of the World,
p.324–26   5–6
Pace, Early American, p.106–13   5–6

GUNS: see also Arms and Armor; Hunt-
ing
Bendick, How Much and How Many,
p.155–59   5–6
Colby, First Hunt, p.20–23   5–6
———— First Rifle   5–6
Edmonds, Matchlock Gun   *4–6
Holling, Book of Cowboys, p.111
5–6
Judson, Boat Builder, p.28–34   5–6
Lent, Men at Work in New England,
p.78–81   4–6

GUNSMITHING: see Blacksmithing

GUSTAVUS I, OR GUSTAVUS VASA,
KING OF SWEDEN
Rothery, Scandinavian Roundabout,
p.170–72   6

GUTENBERG, JOHANNES
Asimov, Breakthroughs in Science, p.9–
16   5–6
Cottler, Heroes of Civilization, p.179–
89   6
Hartman, Builders of the Old World,
p.349–55   6

GYPSIES
Ackley, Dolls To Make, p.75–79   5–6
Angelo, Nino, p.154–88   *6
Carlson, N. S., Family under the Bridge
*4–5
Seredy, Good Master, p.145–64   *5–6
Shannon, Dobry, p.49–52, 91–95   *5–6

GYROCOMPASS
Adler, Things That Spin   5–6

GYROSCOPES
Adler, Things That Spin   5–6
Morgan, A. P., Boys' Book of Science
and Construction, p.127–37   6

HABIT: see also Animals—Habits and
Behavior

Evans, All about Us, p.41–60   4–6

HACIENDAS: *see* Ranch Life

HAIR
Mason, G. F., Animal Clothing, p.13–37   5–6

HAITI
Goetz, Neighbors to the South, p.14–19   5–6
Hughes, First Book of the West Indies, p.17–21   5–6
Quinn, Picture Map Geography of Mexico, Central America and the West Indies, p.93–97   4–6

HALE, NATHAN
Fisher, D. F. C., And Long Remember, p.62–67   6
Lawson, R., Watchwords of Liberty, p.20   4–6

HALL, CHARLES MARTIN
Writers Project, Aluminum, no.31, p.16–30, 41–42   5–6

HALLOWEEN: *see also* Ghosts; Superstition; Witchcraft
Burnett, B., First Book of Holidays, p.38–42   4–5
Embry, Blue-nosed Witch   *4–6
Estes, Moffats, p.119–40   *4–6
Harper, Ghosts and Goblins   *4–6
Jordan, Holiday Handicraft, p.153–76   4–6
Laughlin, Little Left-over Witch   *4–5
McSpadden, Book of Holidays, p.148–53   6
Olcott, Good Stories for Great Holidays, p.233–65   *4–6
Pannell, Holiday Round Up, p.239–56   *4–6
Sechrist, Heigh-Ho for Halloween!   5–6
———— Red Letter Days, p.174–87   5–6
Urmston, New Boy, p.107–42   *4–6

HALLOWEEN—PLAYS
Sechrist, Heigh-Ho for Halloween!, p.83–196   5–6

HALS, FRANS
Chandler, Story-Lives of Master Artists, p.98–109   6

HAMILTON, ALEXANDER
Crouse, A. E., Alexander Hamilton and Aaron Burr   6
Foster, G., George Washington's World, p.151–53, 302–9   6
Olcott, Good Stories for Great Birthdays, p.153–61   4–6

HAMMERS
Burns, Man and His Tools, p.33–42   5–6
Leavitt, True Book of Tools for Building, p.20–23   4–6
Lent, Men at Work in New England, p.70–73   4–6

HAMMURABI, KING OF BABYLONIA
Falls, First 3000 Years, p.76–80   6

HAMPTON—VIRGINIA NORMAL AND AGRICULTURAL INSTITUTE
Graham, S., Booker T. Washington   6

HAMSTERS
Reynolds, B. L., Hamlet and Brownswiggle   *4–6

HANCOCK, JOHN
Foster, G., George Washington's World, p.15–18   6

HAND PUPPETS
Ficklen, Handbook of Fist Puppets   4–6

HANDBALL
Bancroft, Games, p.541–46   4–6

HANDEL, GEORG FRIEDRICH
Buchanan, How Man Made Music, p.111–14, 116–22   6
Burch, Famous Composers for Young People, p.19–25   4–6
Schwimmer, Great Musicians as Children, p.172–79   6
Sechrist, It's Time for Easter, p.105–10   5–6
Wheeler, Handel at the Court of Kings   4–6

HANDICAPPED: *see also* Blind
Burnett, F. H., Secret Garden   *5–6
Corbin, Golden Mare (chronic heart trouble)   *4–6
De Angeli, Door in the Wall (polio)   *4–6
Foster, G., Theodore Roosevelt   4–6
Goss, Beethoven (deafness)   6

Judson, Theodore Roosevelt   5–6

Lenski, We Live in the South, p.50–73
(heart trouble)   *4–5

Lipkind, Boy of the Islands   *4–5

Peare, Robert Louis Stevenson   4–6

Underhill, Antelope Singer   *4–6

Vance, Windows for Rosemary (blindness)   *4–6

Wheeler, Ludwig Beethoven and the Chiming Tower Bells   4–6

Whitney, Mystery of the Haunted Pool   5–6

HANDICRAFT: *see also* Basketry; Birdhouses; Bookbinding; Boxes; Clay Modeling; Dolls; Metalwork; Models; Paper Work; Pottery; Puppet Shows; Rugs; Sewing; Shadow Plays; Soap Sculpture; Tools; Toys; Twine; Weaving; Wood Carving; Woodcraft

Bailey, C. S., Pioneer Art in America   5–6

Bleeker, Pueblo Indians, p.59–78   4–6

Carlson, B. W., Make It and Use It   4–6

———— Make It Yourself   4–6

Hamilton, E. T., Handicraft for Girls   6

Jaeger, Easy Crafts   4–6

Jordan, Holiday Handicraft   4–6

———— Homemade Dolls in Foreign Dress   4–6

Lee, What To Do Now   4–6

Leeming, Fun with Greeting Cards   4–6

———— Fun with Wire   5–6

McNeer, Story of the Southern Highlands   4–6

Maginley, Make It and Ride It   5–6

Robinson, J., Things To Make from Odds & Ends   6

Salomon, Book of Indian Crafts & Indian Lore   6

Unnerstad, Journey with Grandmother   *4–6

Zarchy, Let's Make a Lot of Things   5–6

———— Let's Make More Things   5–6

———— Let's Make Something   5–6

HANDICRAFT—HISTORY

Bailey, C. S., Children of the Handcrafts   5–6

HANNIBAL

Falls, First 3000 Years, p.188–91   6

Farjeon, Mighty Men, p.85–90   4–6

HANNO, CARTHAGINIAN NAVIGATOR

Duvoisin, They Put Out to Sea, p.10–17   4–6

HANSEATIC LEAGUE

Tappan, When Knights Were Bold, p.268–75   6

HANUKKAH

Pannell, Holiday Round Up, p.275–82   4–6

Taylor, S., More All-of-a-Kind Family, p.55–71   *4–6

HARBORS: *see also* Pilots; also names of harbors, as Rio de Janeiro

Buehr, Harbors and Cargoes   5–6

Coatsworth, Fair American   *5–6

Dawson, California, p.179–81   5–6

Jackson, D., Wonderful World of Engineering, p.70–75   6

HARDING, WARREN GAMALIEL

Beard, Presidents in American History, p.117–19, 175–76   6

Coy, First Book of Presidents, p.57   4–6

Petersham, Story of the Presidents of the United States, p.65–66   4–6

HARES: *see also* Rabbits

Brown, V., How To Understand Animal Talk, p.119–20   6

HARPS

Buchanan, How Man Made Music, p.61–67   6

Huntington, Tune Up   4–6

Kettelkamp, Singing Strings, p.6–13   5–6

Lacey, Picture Book of Musical Instruments, p.48–49   5–6

Leeming, Fun with Boxes, p.102   4–6

HARRIS, JOEL CHANDLER

Coffman, Famous Authors for Young People, p.117–22   5–6

HARRISON, BENJAMIN

Beard, Presidents in American History, p.97–98, 170–71   6

Coy, First Book of Presidents, p.50   4–6

Petersham, Story of the Presidents of the United States, p.54–55　　4–6

HARRISON, WILLIAM HENRY
Beard, Presidents in American History, p.41–42, 159　　6
Coy, First Book of Presidents, p.35　　4–6
Petersham, Story of the Presidents of the United States, p.29　　4–6

HARVESTING: *see also* Agricultural Machinery; McCormick, Cyrus Hall
Wilder, Farmer Boy, p.228–51　　*4–6
———— Little House in the Big Woods, p.199–228　　*4–6

HARVEY, WILLIAM
Asimov, Breakthroughs in Science, p. 26–30　　5–6
Cottler, Heroes of Civilization, p.251–59　　6

HATS: *see also* Costume; Indians of North America—Costume
Association for Childhood Education, Told under the Stars and Stripes, p.71–82　　*4–6
Bailey, C. S., Children of the Handcrafts, p.86–94　　*5–6
Hunt, M. L., Benjie's Hat　　*4–6
Lent, Men at Work in New England, p.42–45　　4–6

HAWAII NATIONAL PARK
Melbo, Our Country's National Parks, v.2, p.234–54　　6

HAWAIIAN ISLANDS: *see also* Costume —Hawaiian Islands
Barrows, American Continents, p.236–41　　5
Epstein, S., First Book of Hawaii　　4–6
Harry, Island Boy　　*4–6
Lewis, O., Hawaii　　5–6
Lipkind, Boy of the Islands　　*4–5
O'Neill, Picture Story of Hawaii　　4–6
Quinn, Picture Map Geography of the Pacific Islands, p.8–20　　5–6
———— Picture Map Geography of the United States, p.196–200　　4–6

HAWAIIAN LANGUAGE
Epstein, S., First Book of Hawaii, p.36–38, 64　　4–6
Lewis, O., Hawaii, p.173–75　　5–6
O'Neill, Picture Story of Hawaii　　4–6

HAWKS
Comstock, Handbook of Nature Study, p.104–9　　6
Garrett, Rufous Redtail　　*4–5
Hylander, Out of Doors in Autumn, p.47–52　　5–6
Lathrop, Let Them Live, p.54–57　　4–6
Ripper, Hawks　　5–6

HAWKS—EGGS AND NESTS
Garrett, Rufous Redtail, p.131–41　　*4–5

HAWTHORNE, NATHANIEL
Coffman, Famous Authors for Young People, p.47–52　　5–6

HAY: *see* Grasses

HAYDN, FRANZ JOSEPH
Buchanan, How Man Made Music, p.129–33　　6
Burch, Famous Composers for Young People, p.33–41　　4–6
Goss, Beethoven, p.105–24　　6
Schwimmer, Great Musicians as Children, p.92–98　　6
Wheeler, Joseph Haydn　　4–6

HAYES, RUTHERFORD BIRCHARD
Beard, Presidents in American History, p.81–82, 167–68　　6
Coy, First Book of Presidents, p.46　　4–6
Petersham, Story of the Presidents of the United States, p.48–49　　4–6

HEADLIGHT
Barr, Young Scientist Takes a Ride, p.41–42　　5–6

HEALTH: *see also* Babies—Care; Bacteria; Diseases; First Aid; Food; Milk; Narcotics; Nursing; Nutrition; Physiology; Teeth; Ventilation
Beauchamp, Discovering Our World, Bk.1, p.157–79　　4
Eberle, Modern Medical Discoveries　　5–6
Lewis, L. Z., First Book of Microbes　　5–6
Parker, B. M., You as a Machine　　5–6
Ravielli, Wonders of the Human Body　　5–6
Schloat, Your Wonderful Teeth　　4–6
Wall, Gifts from the Grove　　4–6

Zim, Our Senses and How They Work
4–6

HEART

Glemser, All about the Human Body,
p.43–55   5–6

HEAT: *see also* Combustion; Fire; Heating; Physics; Steam; Sun; Thermometers

Beeler, Experiments in Chemistry, p.97–
101   5–6

——— Experiments in Science, p.51–
52, 56–57, 73–75   5–6

Bendick, How Much and How Many,
p.99–100   5–6

Freeman, M. B., Fun with Science,
p.41–46   6

Morgan, A. P., Boys' Book of Science
and Construction, p.231–79   6

Parker, B. M., Thermometers, Heat, and
Cold   5–6

Podendorf, 101 Science Experiments,
p.74–85   4–5

Schneider, H., Everyday Machines and
How They Work, p.58–62, 122–23
5–6

HEATING: *see also* Coal; Electric Heating; Fuel; Heat; Petroleum; Steam;
Stoves; Ventilation; Wood

Barnard, Macmillan Science-Life Series,
Bk.6, p.28–30   6

Beeler, More Experiments in Science,
p.83–86   5–6

Branley, Solar Energy   6

Eaton, That Lively Man, Ben Franklin,
p.87–91   6

Schneider, H., Everyday Machines and
How They Work, p.129–39   5–6

——— Let's Look inside Your House,
p.13–21   4–5

HEBREWS: *see* Jews

HECTOR: *see* Trojan War

HELICOPTERS

Allison, About Helpful Helicopters
4–5

Beeler, More Experiments in Science,
p.73–77   5–6

Bendick, First Book of Airplanes, p.42–
45   4–6

Colby, Leatherneck, p.39–43   5–6

Floherty, Aviation from the Ground
Up, p.92–102   6

Knight, C., Big Book of Real Helicopters   4–6

Lent, Helicopter Book   5–6

Lewellen, Helicopters   6

Schneider, L., Wings in Your Future,
p.51–61   5–6

Zaffo, Big Book of Real Airplanes   4–5

HELIOGRAPH

Rogers, F., Heels, Wheels, and Wire,
p.184–85   5–6

HELIUM

Writers Project, Oil and Gas, no.36,
p.47   5–6

HELPFULNESS

Alden, Why the Chimes Rang, p.106–22
*4–6

HEMLOCK TREES

Comstock, Handbook of Nature Study,
p.679–80   6

Cormack, First Book of Trees, p.55
4–6

Dudley, Our American Trees, p.81–83
5–6

McKenny, Trees of the Countryside,
p.14–15   4–6

HENRY, JOHN: *see* John Henry

HENRY, JOSEPH

Asimov, Breakthroughs in Science, p.
76–84   5–6

HENRY, PATRICK

Barksdale, That Country Called Virginia, p.100–101, 105–6, 110   6

Campion, Patrick Henry   5–6

Fisher, D. F. C., And Long Remember,
p.56–61   6

Lawson, R., Watchwords of Liberty,
p.6–7   4–6

Olcott, Good Stories for Great Birthdays, p.315–23   4–6

HENRY, PRINCE OF PORTUGAL

Duvoisin, They Put Out to Sea, p.81–88
4–6

Hartman, Builders of the Old World,
p.407–11   6

Hewes, Spice Ho!, p.43–52   5–6

HENRY THE NAVIGATOR: *see* Henry,
Prince of Portugal

HENS: *see* Chickens; Poultry

HERACLES: *see* Hercules

HERBS
Coatsworth, Alice-All-By-Herself, p.58–
65   *4–6
De Angeli, Elin's Amerika   *4–6
Hunt, M. L., Lucinda, p.38–48   *5–6
Lenski, Blue Ridge Billy, p.50–58
                                       *5–6

HERCULES
Asimov, Words from the Myths, p.168–
76   6
Benson, Stories of the Gods and Heroes,
p.157–69   5–6
Sellew, Adventures with the Gods, p.32–
43   4–5

HERDING: *see also* Lapland; Navaho
Indians; Pueblo Indians; Reindeer;
Shepherd Life
Barrows, Our Big World   4

HERDING—SWITZERLAND
Spyri, Heidi   *4–6

HERMIT CRABS
Cooper, E. K., Science on the Shores
and Banks, p.108–9   5–6
Lavine, Strange Travelers, p.53–57
                                        5–6
Parker, B. M., Plant and Animal Part-
nerships, p.13–15   5–6

HERMITS
Tappan, When Knights Were Bold,
p.175–81   6

HEROES: *see also* Argonauts; Courage;
Discoveries in Geography; Epics; Ex-
plorers; Fire Departments; Lifesaving;
Missionaries; Myths; Patriotism; Tro-
jan War; also names of heroes, as
Beowulf; Perseus; Ulysses
Hall, J., Buried Cities, p.1–15   5–6
Hazeltine, Hero Tales from Many Lands
                                        5–6
Seredy, White Stag   6

HEROINES: *see* names of women, as
Joan of Arc

HERRING
Coatsworth, Alice-All-By-Herself, p.160–
69   *4–6

HERRING GULLS: *see* Gulls

HIBERNATION
Barker, Winter-sleeping Wildlife   5–6
Barr, More Research Ideas for Young
Scientists, p.105–7   5–6
Bronson, Pollwiggle's Progress, p.46–48
                                        4–5
Gall, Wagtail, p.107–31   4–6
Hyde, Animal Clocks and Compasses,
p.77–79, 110–14   5–6
Hylander, Out of Doors in Autumn,
p.116–22   5–6
———— Out of Doors in Winter,
p.105–11   5–6
Morgan, A. H., Field Book of Animals
in Winter, p.24–33   6

HICKOK, JAMES BUTLER (WILD
BILL)
Anderson, A. M., Wild Bill Hickok
                                        5–6
Garst, Buffalo Bill   6

HICKORY TREES
Comstock, Handbook of Nature Study,
p.643–45   6
Cormack, First Book of Trees, p.27–28
                                        4–6
Dudley, Our American Trees, p.71–72
                                        5–6
McKenny, Trees of the Countryside,
p.26–27   4–6

HIEROGLYPHICS: *see also* Alphabets;
Picture Writing; Rosetta Stone
Hartman, Builders of the Old World,
p.54–57   6
Hillyer, Child's History of the World,
p.30–35   5–6
Kubie, First Book of Archaeology,
p.38–39   6
Meadowcroft, Gift of the River, p.19–
23   5–6

HIGH VOLTAGE LINE: *see* Electric
Power Transmission

HIGHWAYS: *see* Roads

HIKING
Mulac, Game Book, p.236–45   6

HINDUISM: *see also* Ganges River
Caldwell, Let's Visit India, p.37–41, 79–
81   4–6
Fitch, Allah, the God of Islam, p.119–
28   6

_____ Their Search for God, p.11–51   5–6

Jordan, Homemade Dolls in Foreign Dress, p.198–210   4–6

HIPPOPOTAMUS

Bridges, Zoo Pets, p.30–44   4–6

Earle, Pigs, Tame and Wild, p.59–61   4–6

Parker, B. M., Animals We Know, p.23–24   5–6

HISTORY: *see also* Archeology; Ballads; Civilization; Crusades; Discoveries in Geography; Feudal System; Government; Heroes; Middle Ages; Slavery; Wheels; also names of countries, subhead History, as United States—History, and names of wars, as Civil War in the United States

Hillyer, Child's History of the World   5–6

Picturesque Word Origins   6

Pyne, Little History of the Wide World   4–6

HISTORY AND ART: *see* Art and History

HISTORY AND SCIENCE: *see* Fossils; Races of Man; Rock Records

HITLER, ADOLF

Shirer, Rise and Fall of Adolf Hitler   5–6

HITTITES

Falls, First 3000 Years, p.79–84   6

HOBBIES: *see also* Airplanes—Models; Aquariums; Athletics; Birdhouses; Clay Modeling; Collecting; Cooking; Dancing; Dolls; Drawing; Experiments—Scientific; Fishing; Games; Gardening; Handicraft; Insects—Collecting; Kites; Magic; Models; Music; Nature Study; Photography; Postage Stamps; Puppet Shows; Puzzles; Railroads—Models; Sewing; Ships—Models; Soap Sculpture; Sports; Weaving; Wood Carving

Baker, R. H., When the Stars Come Out   6

Brown, V., How To Make a Home Nature Museum   5–6

_____ How To Make a Miniature Zoo   5–6

Carlson, B. W., Make It Yourself   4–6

Cassell, Nature Games and Activities   4–6

Cormack, First Book of Stones   4–6

Darling, L., Chickens   4–6

Evans, Adventure Book of Money   5–6

_____ Adventure Book of Rocks   4–6

Freeman, M. B., Fun with Chemistry   4–6

_____ Fun with Science   6

Goodwin, Real Book about Stars   4–6

Gray, Adventure Book of Insects   5–6

Hoffmann, Sew Easy!   4–6

Hogeboom, Dogs and How To Draw Them   4–5

Hogner, Earthworms   4–6

Hussey, Collecting Cocoons   4–6

Kettelkamp, Magic Made Easy   4–6

Kirkus, First Book of Gardening   4–6

Leavitt, True Book of Tools for Building   4–6

Leeming, Fun with Clay   4–6

_____ Real Book about Magic   5–6

Neal, Story of the Kite   5–6

Petersham, America's Stamps   5–6

Schneider, H., Everyday Weather and How It Works   5–6

Selsam, How To Grow House Plants   5–6

Stoddard, First Book of Magic   5–6

Weiss, H., Pencil, Pen and Brush   5–6

Zim, Homing Pigeons   5–6

HOCKEY

Bancroft, Games, p.414–17, 511–12, 524–33, 549–54   4–6

HOGS: *see* Pigs

HOLBEIN, HANS, THE YOUNGER

Hillyer, Child's History of Art, p.87–89   5–6

HOLIDAYS: *see also* April Fools' Day; Arbor Day; Christmas; Columbus Day; Easter; Fairs; Festivals; Flag Day; Fourth of July; Halloween; Labor Day; Lincoln's Birthday; May Day; Memorial Day; New Year's Day; Saint Patrick's Day; Thanksgiving Day; Valentine's Day; Veterans Day; Washington's Birthday

Carlson, B. W., Make It Yourself   4–6

Galt, Seven Days from Sunday, p.202–8
    6
Jordan, Holiday Handicraft   4–6
McSpadden, Book of Holidays   6
Olcott, Good Stories for Great Holidays
    *4–6
Pannell, Holiday Round Up   4–6
Sechrist, Red Letter Days   5–6
Tor, Getting To Know Puerto Rico,
    p.49–54   4–6

HOLIDAYS—CHINA
Spencer, C., Land of the Chinese People, p.90–91   6

HOLIDAYS—ENGLAND
McSpadden, Book of Holidays, p.188–95   6

HOLIDAYS—FRANCE
McSpadden, Book of Holidays, p.195–200   6

HOLIDAYS—GERMANY
McSpadden, Book of Holidays, p.200–206   6

HOLIDAYS—INDIA
Hahn, First Book of India, p.44–45
    5–6
McSpadden, Book of Holidays, p.214–19   6
Modak, Land and People of India, p.14–15, 121–22   6

HOLIDAYS—ISLAM
McSpadden, Book of Holidays, p.219–22   6

HOLIDAYS—ISRAEL
Kubie, First Book of Israel, p.36–39
    4–6

HOLIDAYS—ITALY
McSpadden, Book of Holidays, p.201–10   6

HOLIDAYS—JAPAN
McSpadden, Book of Holidays, p.210–14   6

HOLIDAYS—JEWS
Burnett, B., First Book of Holidays, p.58–61   4–5
McSpadden, Book of Holidays, p.124–36   6
Pannell, Holiday Round Up, p.108–12, 225–32, 275–82   4–6

HOLIDAYS—LATIN AMERICA
Hall, E., Land and People of Argentina, p.113–16   6
McSpadden, Book of Holidays, p.52–59
    6
May, Let's Read about Brazil, p.118–22
    4–6

HOLIDAYS—MEXICO
Epstein, S., First Book of Mexico, p.30–31, 35–43   5–6

HOLIDAYS—NETHERLANDS
De Jong, D., Picture Story of Holland
    4–6

HOLIDAYS—SWEDEN
Rothery, Scandinavian Roundabout, p.168–70   6

HOLLAND: *see* Netherlands

HOLY LAND: *see* Palestine

HOME ECONOMICS: *see also* Babies—Care; Cooking; Food; Fuel; Furniture; Heating; Laundry; Lighting; Plumbing; Sewing; Ventilation
Hoffmann, Sew Easy!   4–6
Schneider, H., Everyday Machines and How They Work   5–6

HOME LIFE: *see also* Babies—Care; City Life; Farm Life; Houses; Safety at Home
Beery, Manners Made Easy, p.17–30
    6
Goetz, Other Young Americans, p.19–48   5–6

HOME LIFE—AFRICA
Mirsky, Seven Grandmothers   *4–6
———— Thirty-one Brothers and Sisters   *4–6

HOME LIFE—BRAZIL
Brown, R. J., Land and People of Brazil, p.112–15   6

HOME LIFE—BULGARIA
Shannon, Dobry   *5–6

HOME LIFE—CHINA
Hahn, Picture Story of China   4–6
Lattimore, Little Pear and His Friends
    *4–5
Spencer, C., Land of the Chinese People, p.79–86   6
Wood, E., Silk and Satin Lane   *4–5

HOME LIFE—COLONIAL PERIOD IN AMERICA
Coy, Americans, p.36–45   6
Pace, Early American, p.35–41   5–6

HOME LIFE—ENGLAND
Street, Land of the English People, p.42–49   6

HOME LIFE—ESKIMOS
Bleeker, Eskimos, p.39–64   4–6
Harrington, Ootook   4–6

HOME LIFE—INDIA
Bothwell, Little Boat Boy   *4–5
Modak, Land and People of India, p.114–21   6
Singh, Gift of the Forest   6

HOME LIFE—INDIANS OF NORTH AMERICA
Bleeker, Apache Indians, p.18–44   4–6
———— Indians of the Longhouse, p.68–74   4–6
———— Pueblo Indians, p.9–24   4–6
Clark, A. N., Little Navajo Bluebird
                                               4–6
Holling, Book of Indians   4–6

HOME LIFE—IRELAND
Van Stockum, Pegeen   *6

HOME LIFE—ITALY
Angelo, Nino   *6

HOME LIFE—JAPAN
Edelman, Japan in Story and Pictures, p.14–24   4–6
Mears, First Book of Japan, p.10–21, 26–27   4–6
Spencer, C., Japan, p.10–13   5–6

HOME LIFE—KOREA
Caldwell, Let's Visit Korea, p.44–52
                                               5–6

HOME LIFE—MEXICO
Galt, Volcano   5–6
Tarshis, Village That Learned To Read
                                              *4–6

HOME LIFE—NEGROES
De Angeli, Bright April   *4–6
Faulkner, Melindy's Medal   *4–5
Hayes, Skid   *5–6
Hunt, M. L., Ladycake Farm   *4–6

HOME LIFE—PHILIPPINE ISLANDS
Wood, E., Pedro's Coconut Skates
                                              *4–5

HOME LIFE—POLAND
Wheeler, Frederic Chopin   4–6

HOME LIFE—SWEDEN
Rothery, Scandinavian Roundabout, p. 227–35   6

HOME LIFE—THAILAND
Ayer, Getting To Know Thailand, p.35–37   4–6

HOME LIFE—UNITED STATES: *see also* Citizenship; Education—United States; Home Life—Colonial Period in America; Home Life—Negroes; Migrant Labor; School Life—United States; United States—History; Village Life—United States; also names of states and cities of the United States
Canfield, Understood Betsy   *5–6
Credle, Johnny and His Mule   *4–5
Enright, Four-Story Mistake   *5–6
———— Then There Were Five   *5–6
Estes, Middle Moffat   *4–6
———— Moffats   *4–6
———— Rufus M.   *4–6
Friedman, F., Dot for Short   *4–5
Judson, Lost Violin   *5–6
Lawrence, Peachtree Island   *4–5
Lawson, R., They Were Strong and Good   4–6
Lenski, Blue Ridge Billy   *5–6
———— Boom Town Boy   *5–6
McCloskey, Homer Price   *5–6
Meadowcroft, By Secret Railway
                                              *5–6
Wilson, H. H., Owen Boys   *5–6
Woolley, Ginnie and Geneva   *4–5

HOMER, WINSLOW
Chandler, Story-Lives of Master Artists, p.223–37   6

HONDURAS
Barrows, American Continents, p.304–5
                                               5
Goetz, Neighbors to the South, p.28–33
                                               5–6
Quinn, Picture Map Geography of Mexico, Central America and the West Indies, p.32–41   4–6
Rothery, Central American Roundabout, p.77–99   6

HONDURAS—FOLK TALES
Rothery, Central American Roundabout,
p.201–5   6

HONESTY
Angelo, Bells of Bleeker Street   *4–6
Gallant, K., Flute Player of Beppu   *4
Harper, Easter Chimes, p.22–33   *4–6
Knight, E. M., Lassie Come-Home,
p.61–69, 224–39   *6
Oakes, Bamboo Gate, p.47–50   *4–6
Stuart, Penny's Worth of Character
*4–6
Wiese, Chinese Ink Stick, p.89–100
*4–6

HONEY
Eberle, Basketful, p.220–27   4–6
Stinetorf, Children of South Africa,
p.119–32   *5–6
Stuart, Beatinest Boy, p.79–92   *4–6
Wilder, Little House in the Big Woods,
p.193–98   *4–6

HONG KONG
Barrows, Old World Lands, p.220–22
6
———— Our Big World, p.151–54   4

HONOR
Davis, R. G., Choctaw Code   *5–6

HOOVER, HERBERT CLARK
Beard, Presidents in American History,
p.125–27, 177–78   6
Coy, First Book of Presidents, p.59
4–6
Petersham, Story of the Presidents of
the United States, p.69–70   4–6

HOOVER, JOHN EDGAR
Floherty, Our F.B.I.   6

HOPI INDIANS
Bailey, C. S., Pioneer Art in America,
p.195–207   *5–6

HORNBILLS
Buck, F., Jungle Animals, p.14–15
5–6

HORNBOOKS
Maginley, Historic Models of Early
America, p.126–27   6

HORNED LARKS
Webb, Birds in Their Homes, p.34
4–6

HORNED TOADS: *see* Lizards

HORNETS
Kane, Tale of a Meadow, p.31–34   4–6

HORNS (musical instrument)
Buchanan, How Man Made Music,
p.36–48   6

HORSEMANSHIP: *see* Riding

HORSERACING
Anderson, C. W., Filly for Joan   *4–5
———— High Courage   *4–6
———— Salute   *4–5
Brock, Plug-Horse Derby   *4–5
Frost, Windy Foot at the County Fair
*4–6
Henry, M., Black Gold   *4–6
———— Gaudenzia   6
———— King of the Wind   *5–6
Lang, Strawberry Roan   *5–6
McMeekin, Kentucky Derby Winner
*4–6

HORSES
Anckarsvard, Rider by Night   *5–6
Anderson, C. W., Filly for Joan   *4–5
———— High Courage   *4–6
———— Salute   *4–5
Andrews, All about Strange Beasts of
the Past, p.98–112   5–6
Banning, Pit Pony   *4–6
Benedict, Pagan the Black   *5–6
Bialk, Taffy's Foal   *4–5
Bothwell, Thirteenth Stone   *5–6
Brock, Here Comes Kristie   *4–5
———— Plug-Horse Derby   *4–5
Brown, Paul, Crazy Quilt   *4–5
Brown, V., How To Understand Animal
Talk, p.25–28   6
Buff, Dancing Cloud, p.27–34   *4–5
Burns, Horses and Their Ancestors
4–5
Carlson, N. S., Sashes Red and Blue,
p.53–64   *4–6
Carroll, Tough Enough's Pony   *4–5
Child Study Association of America,
Read to Yourself Storybook, p.87–
94, 143–53   *4–5
Comstock, Handbook of Nature Study,
p.274–80   6
Corbin, Golden Mare   *4–6
Dalgliesh, America Travels, p.65–70
*4–6
Driggs, Pony Express Goes Through,
p.62–69   *6
Du Bois, Great Geppy   *4–5

Feagles, Casey   *4–5
Fox, From Bones to Bodies, p.28–30,
    46–48   6
Franklin, Wild Horses of the Rio
    Grande   *5–6
Frost, Maple Sugar for Windy Foot
                                          *4–6
_____ Sleigh Bells for Windy Foot
                                          *4–6
_____ Windy Foot at the County
    Fair   *4–6
Hader, Spunky   *4–6
Henry, M., Album of Horses   5–6
_____ Black Gold   *4–6
_____ Justin Morgan Had a Horse
                                          *4–6
_____ King of the Wind   *5–6
_____ Misty of Chincoteague   *4–6
Hofsinde, Indian and His Horse   4–6
Hogeboom, Familiar Animals and How
    To Draw Them, p.4–7   4–5
_____ Horses and How To Draw
    Them   4–6
Hogner, Barnyard Family, p.7–22
                                            5–6
_____ Farm Animals, p.11–39   6
_____ Horse Family   4–6
Holberg, Rowena Carey   *4–6
Holling, Book of Cowboys   5–6
Hooker, Star   *5–6
James, Young Cowboy   *4–5
Johnson, M. S., Dixie Dobie   *4–5
Knight, C. R., Life through the Ages,
    p.46–51   6
Lang, Strawberry Roan   *5–6
Larom, Mountain Pony   *6
_____ Mountain Pony and the Pinto
    Colt   *5–6
Lavine, Strange Travelers, p.48–50
                                            5–6
McMeekin, First Book of Horses   4–5
_____ Kentucky Derby Winner
                                          *4–6
Meigs, Dutch Colt   *4–6
Mellin, Horses across the Ages   4–6
Reed, Earth for Sam, p.160–63   6
Robertson, K., Ticktock and Jim   *4–6
Robinson, W. W., Beasts of the Tar
    Pits, p.38–40   5–6
Rounds, Blind Colt   *5–6
_____ Stolen Pony   *5–6
Scott, S., Chica   *4–6

Seaman, Mr. Peck's Pets, p.26–33, 81–
    91   *4–5
Slobodkin, Adventures of Arab   *4–6
Spencer, P. R., Exploring New Trails,
    p.20–26   5
Steiner, Last Horse   *4–5
Tousey, Jerry and the Pony Express
                                          *4–5
Urmston, Seven and Sam   *4–6
Weil, Animal Families   4
Zwilgmeyer, Johnny Blossom, p.124–33
                                            4–6

HORSETAILS
Comstock, Handbook of Nature Study,
    p.706–9   6

HOSPICE OF SAINT BERNARD: *see*
St. Bernard Pass

HOSPITALERS: *see* Malta—Knights of

HOSPITALS: *see* Nursing

HOT LANDS: *see* Africa; Amazon Val-
    ley; Congo; Deserts; Jungles; Pacific
    Islands; Sahara Desert; Tropics

HOT SPRINGS NATIONAL PARK
Melbo, Our Country's National Parks,
    v.1, 93–99   6

HOUDINI
Spencer, P. R., Exploring New Trails,
    p.207–17   5

HOURGLASSES
Adler, Time in Your Life, p.58   4–6
Reck, Clocks Tell the Time, p.16–17
                                            4–6
Tannenbaum, Understanding Time, p.
    40–46   6

HOUSEBOATS
Burns, World Full of Homes, p.21–23
                                            4–6
Le Grand, Augustus and the River
                                          *4–6
Schneider, H., Science Fun with Milk
    Cartons, p.123–24   5–6

HOUSEKEEPING: *see* Home Economics

HOUSES: *see also* Animals—Houses;
    Architecture; Automobiles—Trailers;
    Birdhouses;   Eskimos—Dwellings;
    Home Life; Indians of North Amer-
    ica—Dwellings; Lake Dwellers; Light-
    ing; Log Cabins; Safety at Home

Bleeker, Inca, p.44–65　5–6
Burns, World Full of Homes　4–6
Coatsworth, Five Bushel Farm　*4–5
———— Littlest House　*4–6
Dalgliesh, America Builds Homes
　4–5
Evans, People Are Important, p.49–55
　4–5
Hall, E., Land and People of Argentina,
　p.84, 90, 92, 112–13　6
Hillyer, Child's History of Art, p.401–7
　5–6
Hunt, M. L., Cupola House　*4–6
———— Ladycake Farm　*4–6
Jakeman, Getting To Know Japan,
　p.24–26　4–6
Kenworthy, Profile of Nigeria, p.23–29
　5–6
Lindquist, J. D., Little Silver House
　*4–6
Rothery, Central American Roundabout,
　p.20–28　6
Schneider, H., Let's Look inside Your
　House　4–5
Simon, Robin on the Mountain　*4–6
Tor, Getting To Know Puerto Rico,
　p.26–30　4–6
Wilder, Little House on the Prairie
　*4–6
———— On the Banks of Plum Creek,
　p.8–17, 107–17　*4–6
Wood, E., Pedro's Coconut Skates,
　p.129–91　*4–5

HOUSES—CHINA: *see also* River Life—
　China
Spencer, C., Land of the Chinese Peo-
　ple, p.10, 12, 14　6
Wiese, Chinese Ink Stick, p.120–25
　*4–6

HOUSES—MAYA
Bleeker, Maya, p.44–48　5–6

HOUSES—PRIMITIVE MAN
Bergere, From Stones to Skyscrapers,
　p.6–7　6
Fenton, C. L., Cliff Dwellers of Walnut
　Canyon, p.13–19　4–5
Osborne, C. G., First Lake Dwellers
　*4–6

HOUSES—THAILAND
Ayer, Getting To Know Thailand, p.32–
　38　4–6

HOUSING—FRANCE
Carlson, N. S., Family under the Bridge
　*4–5

HOUSING—INDONESIA
Smith, D. C., Land and People of
　Indonesia, p.87–89　6

HOUSING—ITALY
Carden, Aldo's Tower　*4–6

HOUSING—UNITED STATES: *see also*
　Automobiles—Trailers; City Plan-
　ning; Engineering; Skyscrapers
Butters, Papa Dolphin's Table　*4–5
Faulkner, Melindy's Medal　*4–5
McCloskey, Homer Price, p.126–49
　*5–6
Seredy, Tree for Peter　*4–6

HOUSTON, SAMUEL
Foster, G., Abraham Lincoln's World,
　p.25–27　6
Johnson, W. W., Birth of Texas　5–6

HOWE, ELIAS: *see also* Sewing Machines
Hartman, Machines, p.130–36　6

HOWE, JULIA WARD
Lyons, Stories of Our American Pa-
　triotic Songs, p.59–65　5–6

HUBAY, JENO
Schwimmer, Great Musicians as Chil-
　dren, p.214–18　6

HUDSON, HENRY
American Heritage, Discoverers of the
　New World, p.130–33　5–6
Baker, N. B., Henry Hudson　4–6
Bonner, Canada and Her Story, p.55–
　58　5–6
Duvoisin, And There Was America,
　p.37–40　4–6
Mitchell, Ships That Made U.S. History,
　p.13–16　6

HUDSON'S BAY COMPANY
Spencer, P. R., Exploring New Trails,
　p.281–89　5

HULL HOUSE, CHICAGO: *see also* Ad-
　dams, Jane
Judson, City Neighbor　6
———— Lost Violin, p.92–97　*5–6

HUMAN BODY: *see* Health; Physiology;
　also parts of body, as Eye

HUMIDITY

Barnard, Macmillan Science-Life Series, Bk.6, p.19–23   6

Barr, More Research Ideas for Young Scientists, p.66–68   5–6

Beeler, Experiments in Science, p.110–12   5–6

Spilhous, Weathercraft, p.34–43   6

HUMMINGBIRDS

Bridges, Zoo Pets, p.52–58   4–6

Brown, V., How To Understand Animal Talk, p.151–52   6

Comstock, Handbook of Nature Study, p.115–17   6

McClung, Ruby Throat   4–5

Webb, Birds in Their Homes, p.4–7   4–6

HUMOROUS STORIES: see also Tall Tales

Agle, Three Boys and the Remarkable Cow   *4–5

Ardizzone, Tim to the Rescue   *4–5

Atwater, Mr. Popper's Penguins   *4–5

Beatty, Matthew Looney's Voyage to the Earth   *4–6

Benary-Isbert, Wicked Enchantment   *4–6

Bendick, Good Knight Ghost   *4–6

Bond, Bear Called Paddington   *4–6

———— Paddington Helps Out   *4–6

Brink, Family Grandstand   *4–6

Brock, Ballet for Mary   *4–5

———— Plug-Horse Derby   *4–5

———— Topsy Turvy Family   *4–5

Butters, Papa Dolphin's Table   *4–5

Butterworth, Trouble with Jenny's Ear   *4–6

Carlson, N. S., Alphonse, That Bearded One   *4–6

———— Talking Cat   *4–6

Carroll, Tough Enough's Trip   *4–6

Cleary, Beezus and Ramona   *4–6

———— Henry and Beezus   *4–5

———— Henry and Ribsy   *4–6

———— Henry and the Paper Route   *4–5

———— Henry Huggins   *4–5

Coggins, H. L., Busby & Co.   *4–5

Collodi, Adventures of Pinocchio   *4–6

Crowley, Azor and the Blue-eyed Cow   *4–6

Daugherty, Poor Richard   6

De Jong, D. C., Seven Sayings of Mr. Jefferson   *4–5

De Jong, M., Good Luck Duck   *4–5

———— Little Cow and the Turtle   *4–6

———— Smoke above the Lane   *4–5

Dickens, Magic Fishbone   *4–6

Dolbier, Torten's Christmas Secret   *4–5

Du Bois, Great Geppy   *4–5

———— Three Policemen   *4–6

Enright, Saturdays   *4–6

Estes, Ginger Pye   *4–6

———— Middle Moffat   *4–6

———— Moffats   *4–6

———— Rufus M.   *4–6

Faulkner, Melindy's Medal   *4–5

Feagles, Casey   *4–5

Fenner, Fools and Funny Fellows   *4–6

———— Time To Laugh   *4–6

Garnett, Family from One-End Street   *6

Grahame, Bertie's Escapade   *4–5

———— Reluctant Dragon   *4–6

Hale, Complete Peterkin Papers   *4–6

Haywood, Betsy's Busy Summer   *4–5

———— Eddie and His Big Deals   *4–5

———— Penny and Peter   *4

Hunt, M. L., Miss Jellytot's Visit   *4–6

Johnson, E., Little Knight   *4–5

———— Three-in-One Prince   *4–5

Jones, E. O., Twig   *4–5

Justus, Surprise for Peter Pocket   *4–6

Kastner, Emil and the Detectives   *4–6

Kinney, Lonesome Bear   *4–6

Lattimore, Monkey of Crofton   *4–5

Le Grand, Tom Benn and Blackbeard, the Pirate   *4–5

Lofting, Doctor Dolittle's Puddleby Adventures   *4–6

McCloskey, Homer Price   *5–6

MacDonald, Mrs. Piggle-Wiggle's Magic   *4–5

MacGregor, Miss Pickerell and the Geiger Counter   *4–6

———— Miss Pickerell Goes to Mars   *4–6

———— Miss Pickerell Goes to the Arctic   *4–6

———— Miss Pickerell Goes Undersea   *4–6
Milne, World of Pooh   *4–5
Nash, While Mrs. Coverlet Was Away   *4–5
Parker, E., Enchantress   *4–5
Payne, Leprechaun of Bayou Luce   *4–5
Reynolds, B. L., Pepper   *4–6
Sayers, Tag-along Tooloo   *4
Seredy, Good Master   *5–6
Steele, Daniel Boone's Echo   *4–6
———— Davy Crockett's Earthquake   *4–6
———— Spooky Thing   *4–6
Stong, Honk, the Moose   *4–5
Tripp, New Tuba   *4–5
Unnerstad, Little O   *4–6
Van Stockum, Canadian Summer   *5–6
White, A. H., Junket   *4–6
———— Story of Serapina   *4–6
White, E. B., Charlotte's Web   *4–6
Wilson, L., This Boy Cody   *4–6
———— This Boy Cody and His Friends   *4–6
Wood, W. H., Perils of Pacifico   *4–6
Young, Unicorn with Silver Shoes   *4–6

HUMPERDINCK, ENGELBERT
Burch, Modern Composers for Young People, p.55-59   5–6

HUNDRED YEARS' WAR, 1337-1453
Hillyer, Child's History of the World, p.327–32   5–6

HUNGARY: *see also* Costume—Hungary
Barrows, Old World Lands, p.110–11   6
Hazeltine, Hero Tales from Many Lands, p.69–87   5–6
Sawyer, Christmas Anna Angel   *4–5
Seredy, Good Master   *5–6
———— Philomena   *4–6
———— Singing Tree   *6

HUNGARY—FOLK TALES
Harper, Ghosts and Goblins, p.258-68   4–6
Seredy, Good Master, p.79–85, 173–82   5–6
———— White Stag   6

HUNS: *see* Attila, King of the Huns

HUNTING: *see also* Boone, Daniel; Crockett, David; Fishing; Fox Hunting; Guns; Indians of North America—Hunting; Trapping
Carr, Children of the Covered Wagon, p.105–20   *4–6
Colby, First Bow and Arrow, p.38–39   4–6
———— First Hunt   5–6
———— First Rifle, p.32–33   5–6
Crawford, "Hello the Boat!", p.102–10   *6
George, J. L., Vulpes, the Red Fox   *6
Henry, M., Always Reddy   *4–6
Lippincott, Wilderness Champion   *5–6
McMeekin, Journey Cake, p.165–82   *5–6

HUNTING—AFRICA
Gatti, Saranga, the Pygmy   5–6
Stinetorf, Children of South Africa, p.11–23, 95–106   *5–6

HUNTING—ARCTIC REGIONS
Bleeker, Eskimos, p.96–113   4–6
Lipkind, Boy with a Harpoon   *4–6
McCracken, Son of the Walrus King, p.72–77, 115–19, 125–28   6
Smith, J. R., Neighbors around the World, p.37–43   4
Tolboom, People of the Snow, p.35–47   4–6

HUNTING—INDIA
Mukerji, Hari, the Jungle Lad   *5–6
———— Kari, the Elephant, p.91–104   *4–6

HURRICANES: *see* Storms

HUYGENS, CHRISTIAN
Cottler, Heroes of Civilization, p.108–16   6

HYDRAS
Cooper, E. K., Science on the Shores and Banks, p.50–52   5–6
Hausman, Beginner's Guide to Fresh-Water Life, p.108–9   6
Morgan, A. H., Field Book of Animals in Winter, p.60–68   6
———— Field Book of Ponds and Streams, p.112–18   6

HYDRAULIC ENGINEERING: *see* Engineering; Water Power

HYDROGEN: *see* Chemistry

HYDROIDS

Parker, B. M., Plant and Animal Partnerships, p.13–15   5–6

HYDROMETERS

Barr, More Research Ideas for Young
Scientists, p.87–88   5–6

Beeler, Experiments in Science, p.26–
27   5–6

HYGIENE: *see* Health

I AM AN AMERICAN DAY

Pannell, Holiday Round Up, p.170–81
4–6

IBERIAN PENINSULA: *see* Portugal;
Spain

ICE CREAM

Elting, Lollypop Factory, p.33–39   4–5

ICE SHEETS: *see* Glaciers

ICEBERGS: *see* also Arctic Regions;
Glaciers

Beaty, Baby Whale, p.63–67   4–6

Reed, Sea for Sam, p.84–93   6

ICELAND: *see also* Northmen

Arason, Smoky Bay   *5–6

Bailey, B. F., Iceland   4–6

Barrows, Our Big World, p.21–25   4

Golden, Made in Iceland   6

Hazeltine, Hero Tales from Many
Lands, p.279–315   5–6

ICELAND—GOVERNMENT

Golden, Made in Iceland, p.34–40   6

ICELANDIC LITERATURE: *see* Grettir
the Strong; Myths—Northmen; Njal;
Sagas

IDAHO

Quinn, Picture Map Geography of the
United States, p.172–75   4–6

ILLINOIS

Havighurst, Life in America: The Midwest, p.104–9   5–6

Lang, Strawberry Roan, p.60–197
*5–6

Lent, Men at Work in the Great Lakes
States, p.12–15, 100–105   4–6

Neyhart, Henry's Lincoln   *4–6

Quinn, Picture Map Geography of the
United States, p.92–95   4–6

ILLUMINATION: *see* Lighting

IMAGINATION

Gannett, Elmer and the Dragon   *4–5

———— My Father's Dragon   *4–5

Howard, J., 13th Is Magic   *4–6

Jones, E. O., Twig   *4–5

Kennedy, Jenny   *4–6

Mayne, Blue Boat   *4–6

Norton, Borrowers   *4–6

Sauer, Fog Magic   *5–6

Slobodkin, Adventures of Arab   *4–6

IMMIGRATION AND EMIGRATION:
see also Citizenship; also names of
various national groups in the United
States, as Germans in the United
States; Mexicans in the United States

Arason, Smoky Bay   *5–6

IMPORTS: *see* Trade

IMPRESSIONISM (art)

Hillyer, Child's History of Art, p.127–31
5–6

INCAS: *see also* Peru; Pizarro, Francisco

Bleeker, Inca   5–6

Boardman, Roads, p.40–48   6

Cavanna, Lucho of Peru   4–6

Friedman, E., Digging into Yesterday,
p.102–26   5–6

Peck, Pageant of South American History, p.30–63   6

INCLINED PLANES

Liberty, First Book of Tools, p.31–33
5–6

Parker, B. M., Machines, p.8–9   5–6

INDEPENDENCE—DECLARATION
OF: *see* Declaration of Independence

INDEPENDENCE DAY: *see* Fourth of
July

INDIA: *see also* Animals—India; Buddhism; Burma; Ceylon; Costume—
India; Ganges River; Hinduism; Indus River; Kashmir; Taj Mahal

Arora, "What Then, Raman?"   *5–6

Barrows, Old World Lands, p.186–95
6

———— Our Big World, p.142–48   4

Batchelor, Cap for Mul Chand   *4–5

Bothwell, Empty Tower   *4–5

———— Little Boat Boy   *4–5

———— Thirteenth Stone   *5–6

Branley, Solar Energy, p.81–86   6

Caldwell, Let's Visit India   4–6

———— Let's Visit Indonesia, p.46–48
4–6

———— Let's Visit Pakistan   4–6

Field, Hitty, p.81–92   *5–6

Hahn, First Book of India   5–6

Kipling, Jungle Book   *5–6

Louden, Rain in the Winds   4–5

McGuire, Glimpses into the Long Ago,
p.141–48   5–6

McNeer, Armed with Courage   5–6

Modak, Land and People of India   6

Mukerji, Hari, the Jungle Lad   *5–6

———— Kari, the Elephant   *4–6

Pace, Juliette Low, p.104–6   5–6

Quinn, Picture Map Geography of Asia,
p.53–58   4–6

Rankin, L., Daughter of the Mountains
*5–6

Singh, Gift of the Forest   *6

Smith, J. R., Neighbors around the
World, p.238–50   4

Sucksdorff, Chendru   4–6

Weston, Bhimsa, the Dancing Bear
*4–6

INDIA—FOLK TALES: *see also* Ramayana

Fenner, Fools and Funny Fellows, p.26–
36, 63–68, 104–14   4–6

INDIA—HISTORY

Foster, G., Abraham Lincoln's World,
p.145–46, 253–55   6

Hahn, First Book of India, p.14–21
5–6

Hazeltine, Hero Tales from Many
Lands, p.363–99   5–6

Modak, Land and People of India,
p.29–30   6

INDIAN LITERATURE

Modak, Land and People of India, p.24,
29–30, 33–43, 54–56   6

INDIANA

Douglas, Appleseed Farm   *4–6

Havighurst, Life in America: The Midwest, p.98–103   5–6

Hunt, M. L., Little Girl with Seven
Names   *4–6

———— Lucinda   *5–6

Lent, Men at Work in the Great Lakes
States, p.20–25, 38–41, 50–53, 62–65,
74–77   4–6

Quinn, Picture Map Geography of the
United States, p.88–91   4–6

INDIANS OF NORTH AMERICA: *see
also* Cliff Dwellers; Eskimos; Mound
Builders; Totem Poles; Travois; United States—History; Wampum; West;
also names of Indians, as Pocahontas; Sacajawea; also names of tribes,
as Hopi Indians

Association for Childhood Education,
Told under the Stars and Stripes,
p.31–46, 295–314   *4–6

Aulaire, Pocahontas   4–5

Bleeker, Sea Hunters   5–6

Bonner, Canada and Her Story   5–6

Brewster, First Book of Indians   4–5

Brindze, Story of the Totem Pole   4–6

Brink, Caddie Woodlawn, p.111–63
*6

Brock, Drusilla, p.98–120   *4–5

Bronson, Pinto's Journey   *4–5

Bulla, Riding the Pony Express   *4–5

Butler, Alaska, p.108–41   6

Carr, Children of the Covered Wagon
*4–6

Carroll, Tough Enough's Indians   *4–5

Coatsworth, Five Bushel Farm, p.128–
40   *4–5

———— Golden Horseshoe   *6

Dalgliesh, America Begins, p.7–9   4–5

Daugherty, Daniel Boone   5–6

Dawson, California, p.3–22   5–6

De Angeli, Jared's Island, p.56–76
*4–6

De Leeuw, C., Fear in the Forest   *4–6

Dorian, Hokahey!   5–6

Douglas, Appleseed Farm   *4–6

Driggs, Pony Express Goes Through,
p.62–78, 86–103   *6

Duvoisin, And There Was America
4–6

Edmonds, Matchlock Gun   *4–6

Fletcher, S. E., American Indian   5–6

———— Big Book of Indians   4–6

Garst, Kit Carson   6

Harper, Harvest Feast   *4–6

Hays, Easter Fires   *4–5

Hoffine, Jennie's Mandan Bowl   *4–6

Hofsinde, Indian and His Horse   4–6

———— Indian and the Buffalo   4–6

———— Indian Beadwork   4–6

———— Indian Picture Writing   5–6

_____ Indian Sign Language   4–6
_____ Indian's Secret World   5–6
Holling, Book of Indians   4–6
_____ Tree in the Trail   *4–6
Hunt, W. B., Golden Book of Indian
  Crafts and Lore   4–6
Jaeger, Easy Crafts   4–6
Jordan, Homemade Dolls in Foreign
  Dress, p.74–83   4–6
Kent, He Went with Christopher Co-
  lumbus   *6
Lane, C. D., River Dragon   *4–6
Lenski, Bayou Suzette   *5–6
Lillie, Book of Three Festivals, p.146–
  68   *5–6
McMeekin, Journey Cake, p.204–22
    *5–6
McNeer, Alaska Gold Rush   5–6
_____ Canadian Story   5–6
_____ Story of the Southwest   4–6
Meadowcroft, By Wagon and Flatboat,
  p.91–98, 146–61   *4–5
_____ First Year   *4–6
Meigs, Willow Whistle   *4–6
O'Dell, Island of the Blue Dolphins
    *6
Orton, Treasure in the Little Trunk,
  p.146–52   *4–6
Pace, Juliette Low, p.14–28   5–6
Robinson, J., Things To Make from
  Odds & Ends, p.36   4–6
Salomon, Book of Indian Crafts & In-
  dian Lore   6
Spencer, P. R., Finding New Trails,
  p.3–8   4
Tunis, Indians   6
Wilder, Little House on the Prairie
    *4–6

INDIANS OF NORTH AMERICA—
  AGRICULTURE
Bleeker, Pueblo Indians, p.25–41   4–6

INDIANS OF NORTH AMERICA—
  ART
Armer, Waterless Mountain, p.184–88
    *5–6
Bonner, Made in Canada, p.3–31   5–6
Brindze, Story of the Totem Pole   4–6
Leeming, Fun with Clay, p.39–40   4–6
Salomon, Book of Indian Crafts & In-
  dian Lore, p.107–29   6
Steiner, Last Horse   *4–5

INDIANS OF NORTH AMERICA—
  CEREMONIES
Armer, Waterless Mountain, p.37–42,
  49–52, 74–81, 111–13, 180–93   *5–6
Salomon, Book of Indian Crafts & In-
  dian Lore, p.331–64   6

INDIANS OF NORTH AMERICA—
  COSTUME
Hofsinde, Indian Beadwork   4–6
_____ Indian's Secret World, p.69–
  82   5–6
Holling, Book of Indians, p.19–23   4–6
Hunt, W. B., Golden Book of Indian
  Crafts and Lore   4–6
Jaeger, Easy Crafts, p.66–73   4–6
Jordan, American Costume Dolls, p.66–
  67   5–6
Leeming, Costume Book, p.102–4   5–6
McCracken, Great White Buffalo   5–6
Salomon, Book of Indian Crafts & In-
  dian Lore, p.34–129   6
Tunis, Indians, p.44–51, 63–64, 76, 95–
  98, 109, 116–17, 146–49   6

INDIANS OF NORTH AMERICA—
  DANCES
Armer, Waterless Mountain, p.208–12
    *5–6
Bleeker, Seminole Indians, p.84–91
    4–6
Hofsinde, Indian and the Buffalo, p.66–
  83   4–6
Hunt, W. B., Golden Book of Indian
  Crafts and Lore, p.84–92   4–6
Salomon, Book of Indian Crafts & In-
  dian Lore, p.284–364   6

INDIANS OF NORTH AMERICA—
  DWELLINGS
Bleeker, Navajo, p.11–45   4–6
Buff, Dancing Cloud, p.8–11   4–5
Burns, World Full of Homes, p.93–97
    4–6
Hofsinde, Indian's Secret World, p.7–
  16   5–6
Holling, Book of Indians, p.17–19, 46–
  49, 76–80, 100–101   4–6
Hunt, W. B., Golden Book of Indian
  Crafts and Lore, p.102–7   4–6
Salomon, Book of Indian Crafts & In-
  dian Lore, p.130–55   6
Tunis, Indians, p.32–34, 65–66, 84–85,
  91–94, 115–16, 136–38   6

INDIANS OF NORTH AMERICA—
FISHING
Bleeker, Sea Hunters, p.9–29　　5–6
Tunis, Indians, p.40–41, 142–44　6

INDIANS OF NORTH AMERICA—
FOLK TALES
Armer, Waterless Mountain, p.44–46,
109–10, 135–36, 140–42, 184–86
5–6
Bonner, Made in Canada, p.96–107
5–6
Harper, Ghosts and Goblins, p.25–36,
156–64, 182–86　　　　　　4–6
Moon, Chi-Wee, p.119–31, 205–15
4–6

INDIANS OF NORTH AMERICA—
FOOD
Buff, Dancing Cloud, p.44–50　4–5
Hofsinde, Indian and the Buffalo, p.44–
49　　　　　　　　　　　　4–6
McCracken, Great White Buffalo　5–6
Salomon, Book of Indian Crafts & In-
dian Lore, p.247–60　　　　　6
Tunis, Indians, p.42–43, 98–99, 108–9,
118–20　　　　　　　　　　6

INDIANS OF NORTH AMERICA—
GAMES
Bleeker, Cherokee, p.89–110　　4–6
Millen, Children's Games from Many
Lands, p.146, 161–82　　　　4–6
Salomon, Book of Indian Crafts & In-
dian Lore, p.261–83　　　　　6
Shippen, Lightfoot, p.107–14　*4–6
Tunis, Indians, p.56–57, 68–69, 79–82,
104–5　　　　　　　　　　　6

INDIANS OF NORTH AMERICA—
HUNTING
Bleeker, Cherokee, p.47–64　　4–6
Holling, Book of Indians, p.26–34, 51–
60, 67–70　　　　　　　　　4–6
McCracken, Great White Buffalo, p.77–
83　　　　　　　　　　　　5–6
Smith, J. R., Neighbors around the
World, p.62–67　　　　　　　4
Tunis, Indians, p.34–39, 76, 145–46　6
Writers Project, Lords of the Old West,
no.23, p.33–44　　　　　　5–6

INDIANS OF NORTH AMERICA—
MUSEUMS
Armer, Waterless Mountain, p.138–43
*5–6

INDIANS OF NORTH AMERICA—
MUSIC: *see also* Drums
Armer, Waterless Mountain, p.196–99
*5–6
Buchanan, How Man Made Music,
p.17–18, 181–83　　　　　　6
Salomon, Book of Indian Crafts & In-
dian Lore, p.218–38　　　　　6

INDIANS OF NORTH AMERICA—
NAMES
Salomon, Book of Indian Crafts & In-
dian Lore, p.379–404　　　　6

INDIANS OF NORTH AMERICA—
POTTERY
Moon, Chi-Wee, p.1–13, 136–52　*4–6

INDIANS OF NORTH AMERICA—
RELIGION: *see also* Indians of
North America—Ceremonies; Indians
of North America—Dances; Indians
of North America—Folk Tales
Armer, Waterless Mountain　　*5–6
Hofsinde, Indian's Secret World　5–6

INDIANS OF NORTH AMERICA—
SIGN LANGUAGE
Hofsinde, Indian Sign Language　4–6
Salomon, Book of Indian Crafts & In-
dian Lore, p.384–403　　　　6
Tunis, Indians, p.20–22, 105–6　6

INDIANS OF NORTH AMERICA—
WARS: *see also* French and Indian
War, 1755–63; Indians of North
America—Costume; Pontiac's Con-
spiracy, 1763
Bleeker, Cherokee, p.112–16　　4–6
Hooker, Star　　　　　　　　*5–6
Meadowcroft, On Indian Trails with
Daniel Boone, p.53–60, 64–97, 101–9,
117–19, 122–23　　　　　　4–5
Salomon, Book of Indian Crafts & In-
dian Lore, p.177–99　　　　　6

INDIANS OF SOUTH AMERICA: *see
also* Amazon Valley; Incas
Brown, R. J., Land and People of Brazil, p.28–31　　　　　　　　6
Hall, E., Land and People of Argentina
6
May, Let's Read about Brazil　4–6

INDIANS OF SOUTH AMERICA—
FOLK TALES: *see* South America—
Folk Tales

INDIVIDUALITY, EXPRESSING
Frazier, Somebody Special   *4–6

INDO-CHINA
Quinn, Picture Map Geography of Asia,
p.80–82   4–6

INDONESIA: *see also* East Indies
Barrows, Old World Lands, p.205–7 6
Caldwell, Let's Visit Indonesia   4–6
Epstein, E., First Book of the United
Nations, p.27–28   4–6
Smith, D. C., Land and People of In-
donesia   6
Sperry, All about the Jungle, p.53–78
                                   5–6

INDONESIA—HISTORY
Smith, D. C., Land and People of Indonesia, p.24–50   6

INDUCTION COILS
Morgan, A. P., Boy Electrician, p.195–
219   6
———— First Electrical Book for Boys,
p.174–77   6

INDUS RIVER
Caldwell, Let's Visit India, p.89–90
                                   4–6
Watson, Golden History of the World,
p.29–30   5–6

INDUSTRIAL ARTS: *see* Arts and Crafts;
Handicraft; Industries

INDUSTRIAL REVOLUTION: *see also*
Guilds; Inventions; Machines; Tex-
tiles
Hartman, Machines   6
Street, Land of the English People,
p.101–5   6
Watson, Golden History of the World,
p.133–37   5–6

INDUSTRIES: *see also* names of industries, as Agriculture; Lumbering; also
names of countries, subhead Industries, as United States—Industries
Banta, Life in America: The South,
p.61–63   5–6
Barrows, American Continents, p.42–46
                                   5
Burns, Man and His Tools   5–6
Havighurst, Life in America: The Midwest, p.45–55   5–6
King, Key to Chicago, p.27–33   4–6

Lent, Men at Work in New England
                                   4–6
———— Men at Work in the Great
Lakes States   4–6
Leonard, Exploring Science, p.172–77
                                   6
Rogers, M., First Book of Cotton   5–6
Wall, Gifts of the Grove   4–6

INDUSTRY (diligence)
Collodi, Adventures of Pinocchio   *4–6
Otis, Toby Tyler   *4–6

INERTIA
Barr, Young Scientist Takes a Ride,
p.17–19, 52   5–6
Freeman, M. B., Fun with Scientific
Experiments, p.4–5, 14   5–6
Huey, What Makes the Wheels Go
Round, p.110–16   6

INFANTS: *see* Babies—Care

INFECTION: *see* Bacteria

INGENUITY
Atwater, Mr. Popper's Penguins   *4–5
Bishop, C. H., Pancakes—Paris   *4–6
Coatsworth, Away Goes Sally   *4–6
Daugherty, Poor Richard   6
Du Soe, Three without Fear   *4–6
Henry, M., Benjamin West and His
Cat Grimalkin   4–6

INK
Beeler, Experiments in Chemistry,
p.102–7   5–6
———— Experiments in Science, p.1–3
                                   5–6
Epstein, S., First Book of Codes and
Ciphers, p.44–48   4–6
Spencer, C., Made in China, p.215–20
                                   5–6
Weiss, H., Paper, Ink and Roller   4–6

INLAND NAVIGATION: *see* Canals;
Lakes; Rivers

INSECT AQUARIUMS: *see* Insects—Collecting

INSECT GALLS: *see* Galls (botany)

INSECTS: *see also* Caterpillars; Interdependence of Plants and Animals;
Parasites; Seed Dispersal; also names
of insects, as Butterflies; Flies
Barr, Research Ideas for Young Scientists, p.83–94   5–6

Beauchamp, Discovering Our World, Bk. 1, p.33–36   4

Beeler, More Experiments in Science, p.60–63   5–6

Blough, After the Sun Goes Down, p.32–36   4–5

Brown, V., How To Make a Home Nature Museum, p.37–45, 77–85, 181–83   5–6

———— How To Make a Miniature Zoo, p.21–59   5–6

———— How To Understand Animal Talk, p.179–90   6

Buck, M. W., In Yards and Gardens, p.39–48   4–6

———— Small Pets from Woods and Fields, p.44–56   4–6

Cassell, Nature Games and Activities, p.70–76   4–6

Comstock, Handbook of Nature Study, p.294–415   6

Cooper, E. K., Science in Your Own Back Yard, p.111–22   5–6

———— Science on the Shores and Banks, p.23–44   5–6

Disraeli, New Worlds through the Microscope, p.23–68   6

Doane, Book of Nature, p.30–31, 76–77, 100–101   5–6

Earle, Crickets   4–6

Fenton, C. L., Insects and Their World   4–6

Gaul, Picture Book of Insects   4–6

Gray, Adventure Book of Insects   5–6

Hausman, Beginner's Guide to Fresh-Water Life, p.66–77   6

Hylander, Insects on Parade   6

Kane, Tale of a Meadow, p.31–40   4–6

Lane, F. C., All about the Insect World   5–6

Lathrop, Let Them Live, p.78–80   4–6

Lavine, Strange Travelers   5–6

Lutz, Field Book of Insects   4–6

Mason, G. F., Animal Clothing, p.78–91   5–6

———— Animal Homes, p.68–81   4–6

———— Animal Sounds, p.48–53   5–6

———— Animal Weapons, p.80–89   5–6

Parker, B. M., Golden Book of Science, p.25–27   4–6

———— Insects and Their Ways   4–6

Smith, F. C., First Book of Conservation, p.12–16   4–6

Swain, Insects in Their World   5–6

Teale, Insect Friends   5–6

———— Junior Book of Insects   6

Williamson, First Book of Bugs   4–5

INSECTS—AQUATIC

Buck, M. W., In Ponds and Streams, p.21–29   4–6

———— Pets from the Pond, p.66–70   4–6

Comstock, Handbook of Nature Study, p.400–415   6

Lutz, Field Book of Insects   4–6

Morgan, A. H., Field Book of Animals in Winter, p.256–78   6

———— Field Book of Ponds and Streams, p.179–300   6

Teale, Junior Book of Insects, p.149–56   6

INSECTS—COLLECTING

Hussey, Collecting Cocoons   4–6

Jaeger, Easy Crafts, p.24–25   4–6

Lutz, Field Book of Insects, p.7–24   4–6

Zarchy, Let's Make More Things, p.130–39   5–6

INSECTS—INJURIOUS: *see also* names of injurious insects, as Flies; Plant Lice

Lutz, Field Book of Insects   4–6

INSECTS—PROTECTION

Parker, B. M., Insects and Their Ways, p.31–33   4–6

INSECTS IN WINTER

Barker, Winter-sleeping Wildlife, p.100–125   5–6

Morgan, A. H., Field Book of Animals in Winter, p.143–278   6

INSTINCT

Knight, E. M., Lassie Come-Home   *6

INTERCULTURAL UNDERSTANDING

Armer, Waterless Mountain   *5–6

Association for Childhood Education, Told under the Stars and Stripes   *4–6

Bleeker, Apache Indians   4–6

———— Chippewa Indians   5–6

———— Crow Indians   5–6

_____ Horsemen of the Western Plateaus   4–6
_____ Indians of the Longhouse
                                       4–6
_____ Mission Indians of California
                                       4–6
_____ Pueblo Indians   4–6
_____ Sea Hunters   5–6
Bloch, Marya of Clark Avenue   *4–6
Brewster, First Book of Eskimos 4–6
_____ First Book of Indians   4–5
Brindze, Story of the Totem Pole 4–6
Bronson, Starlings   4–5
Bulla, Eagle Feather   *4–5
Burnett, B., First Book of Holidays
                                       4–5
Dalgliesh, Courage of Sarah Noble
                                      *4–5
Davis, R. G., Choctaw Code   *5–6
De Angeli, Bright April   *4–6
Dorian, Hokahey!   5–6
Epstein, S., First Book of Hawaii 4–6
Evans, All about Us   4–6
_____ People Are Important   4–5
Faukner, Melindy's Happy Summer
                                      *4–5
_____ Melindy's Medal   *4–5
Friedman, F., Sundae with Judy *4–6
Hayes, Skid   *5–6
Hughes, First Book of Negroes   4–6
Hunt, M. L., Ladycake Farm   *4–6
Jackson, J., Call Me Charley   *5–6
Kingman, Village Band Mystery   *4–5
Lattimore, Chinese Daughter   *4
Lenski, We Live in the South   *4–5
Lillie, Book of Three Festivals 5–6
Meadowcroft, By Secret Railway *5–6
Meigs, Willow Whistle   *4–6
Pannell, Holiday Round Up   4–6
Shippen, Lightfoot   *4–6
Sorensen, Plain Girl   *4–6
Taylor, S., All-of-a-Kind Family *4–6
_____ All-of-a-Kind Family Uptown
                                      *4–6
_____ More All-of-a-Kind Family
                                      *4–6
Uchida, Promised Year   *4–6
Underhill, Antelope Singer   *4–6

INTERDEPENDENCE: *see also* Brotherhood of Man; Community Life; Cooperation; Industrial Revolution; International Understanding; Trade

Hartman, Machines, p.261–69   6

INTERDEPENDENCE OF PLANTS AND ANIMALS: *see also* Community Life among the Animals and Insects; Ponds
Comstock, Handbook of Nature Study, p.457–58   6
Fisher, A. L., Summer of Little Rain
                                       4–6
Hussey, Collecting Cocoons, p.68 (yucca moth)   4–6
Parker, B. M., Plant and Animal Partnerships   5–6
Smith, F. C., First Book of Conservation   4–6

INTERGROUP UNDERSTANDING
De Angeli, Henner's Lydia   *4–5
_____ Thee Hannah!   *4–6
Lenski, Judy's Journey   *4–6
_____ Peanuts for Billy Ben *4–5
Sawyer, This Way to Christmas   *4–6

INTERNATIONAL DATE LINE: *see* Standard Time

INTERNATIONAL FRIENDSHIP: *see* Brotherhood of Man; Intercultural Understanding

INTERNATIONAL RADIO CODE
Yates, R. F., Boys' Book of Communications, p.31–46   6

INTERNATIONAL UNDERSTANDING: *see also* Brotherhood of Man; Pan Americanism; War
Batchelor, Cap for Mul Chand (India)
                                      *4–5
Bishop, C. H., Pancakes—Paris   *4–6
Bothwell, Empty Tower (India)   *4–5
_____ Little Boat Boy (India) *4–5
Bowers, Wishing Book Doll (Canada)
                                      *4–5
Brown, G. E., Tico Bravo, Shark Hunter (Costa Rica)   *4–6
Buckley, Luis of Spain   4–6
Buff, Magic Maize (Guatemala)   *4–6
Burglon, Children of the Soil (Sweden)
                                      *4–6
Butterfield, Adventures of Esteban (Majorca)   *4–6
_____ Jaime and His Hen Pollita (Majorca)   *4–5
Carden, Aldo's Tower (Italy)   *4–6

Clark, A. N., Magic Money (Costa Rica) *4–6

Eisenberg, Won Kim's Ox (Korea) *4–6

French, Lance of Kanana (Arabia) *6

Fry, Bell for Ringelblume (Austria) *4–5

Hawkes, Tami's New House (Japan) *4–5

Kim, Happy Days (Korea) *5–6

Lattimore, Peachblossom (China) *4–5

———— Willow Tree Village (China) *4–5

Lide, Lapland Drum *4–6

Liu, Little Wu and the Watermelons (China) *4–5

Mirsky, Seven Grandmothers (West Africa) *4–6

———— Thirty-one Brothers and Sisters (West Africa) *4–6

Rankin, L., Daughter of the Mountains (Tibet) *4–6

Rhoads, Corn Grows Ripe (Yucatan) *4–6

Seredy, Good Master (Hungary) *5–6

———— Singing Tree (Hungary) *6

Seymour, Erik's Christmas Camera (Sweden) *4–6

———— Kaatje and the Christmas Compass (Holland) *4–6

———— Top o' Christmas Morning (Ireland) *4–5

INTERRELIGIOUS UNDERSTANDING

Angelo, Bells of Bleeker Street *4–6

Fitch, One God 5–6

———— Their Search for God 5–6

Rankin, L., Daughter of the Mountains *5–6

INVENTIONS: *see also* Industrial Revolution; Inventors; also names of inventions, as Telegraph

Clark, G. G., Thomas Alva Edison 4–6

Cousins, Ben Franklin of Old Philadelphia 5–6

Darrow, Boys' Own Book of Great Inventions 6

Du Bois, Twenty-one Balloons, p.98–180 *6

Hartman, Machines 6

Judson, Boat Builder 5–6

Spencer, C., Made in China, p.156–66 5–6

INVENTORS: *see also* Inventions; also names of inventors, as Franklin, Benjamin; Fulton, Robert; Stephenson, George

Rothery, Scandinavian Roundabout, p.189–97 6

IOWA

Association for Childhood Education, Told under Spacious Skies, p.217–29 *4–6

———— Told under the Stars and Stripes, p.159–71 *4–6

Havighurst, Life in America: The Midwest, p.124–29 5–6

Lane, C. D., River Dragon *4–6

Quinn, Picture Map Geography of the United States, p.116–19 5–6

IRAN: *see also* Persia

Hazeltine, Hero Tales from Many Lands, p.348–61 5–6

Nevil, Picture Story of the Middle East 4–6

Quinn, Picture Map Geography of Asia, p.45–48 4–6

Taylor, A., Iran 6

IRAQ: *see also* Babylonia

Falls, First 3000 Years, p.65–70 6

Friedman, E., Digging into Yesterday, p.73–101 5–6

Quinn, Picture Map Geography of Asia, p.34–37 4–6

IRELAND: *see also* Costume—Ireland; Songs—Ireland

Gidal, My Village in Ireland 4–6

Meredith, King of the Kerry Fair *4–6

Polland, Children of the Red King *6

Sawyer, Enchanted Schoolhouse *4–6

———— Long Christmas, p.173–87 *4–6

Seymour, Top o' Christmas Morning *4–5

Van Stockum, Cottage at Bantry Bay *6

———— Pegeen *6

Williams, U. M., Island MacKenzie *5–6

IRELAND—FOLK TALES: *see also* Brendan, Saint; Cuchulain; Finn Mac Cool; Patrick, Saint

Fenner, Fools and Funny Fellows, p.170–82   4–6

———— Time To Laugh, p.3–16, 58–66, 217–40   4–6

Harper, Ghosts and Goblins, p.165–81
                                          4–6

Sawyer, Long Christmas, p.47–60, 111–20 (Voyage of the Wee Red Cap)
                                          4–6

Smith, E. S., Christmas Book of Legends & Stories, p.277–79   5–6

IRELAND—HISTORY

Farjeon, Mighty Men, p.112–20   4–6

Hazeltine, Hero Tales from Many Lands, p.161–202   5–6

Reynolds, Q. J., Life of Saint Patrick
                                          5–6

IRIS

Comstock, Handbook of Nature Study, p.571–74   6

IRISH IN THE UNITED STATES

Association for Childhood Education, Told under the Stars and Stripes, p.119–20   *4–6

IRISH POETRY

Van Stockum, Cottage at Bantry Bay, p.154–252   *6

IRON

Buehr, Underground Riches, p.84–90
                                          5–8

Fenton, C. L., Riches from the Earth, p.71–79   5–6

Hartman, Machines, p.24–32   6

Land, M., Jungle Oil, p.72–84   5–6

Lent, Men at Work in the Great Lakes States, p.16–19   4–6

Loomis, Field Book of Common Rocks and Minerals, p.47–59   6

Schwartz, It's Fun To Know Why, p.11–20   5–7

Williams, H. L., Stories in Rocks, p.66–69   6

Writers Project, Story of Iron and Steel, no.34   5–6

IRON AGE: *see also* Prehistoric Man

Writers Project, Aluminum, no.31, p.11
                                          5–6

IRONWORK

Bailey, C. S., Pioneer Art in America, p.13–24   *5–6

Zarchy, Let's Make a Lot of Things, p.88–97   5–6

IROQUOIAN INDIANS

Bleeker, Indians of the Longhouse   4–6

Dorian, Hokahey!, p.17–27   5–6

Fletcher, S. E., American Indian, p.64–74, 127–29   5–6

Shippen, Lightfoot   *4–6

Tunis, Indians, p.58–69   6

IRRIGATION: *see also* Dams; Rice; Water Wheels; Windmills

Bleeker, Inca, p.87–88   5–6

Buckley, Luis of Spain, p.12–17   4–6

Dawson, California, p.182–94   5–6

Fenton, C. L., Land We Live On, p.86–87   4–6

Meadowcroft, Gift of the River, p.15–17   5–6

Parker, B. M., Water, p.21–22   5–6

Stinetorf, Children of North Africa, p.23–25   *5–6

Van Dersal, Land Renewed, p.74–75
                                          6

Wall, Gifts from the Grove, p.32–34
                                          4–6

IRVING, WASHINGTON

Coffman, Famous Authors for Young People, p.31–35   5–6

ISLAM: *see also* Holidays—Islam

Caldwell, Let's Visit India, p.47–50
                                          4–6

———— Let's Visit Indonesia, p.27–30
                                          4–6

———— Let's Visit Pakistan, p.37–39, 74–75   4–6

Fitch, Allah, the God of Islam   6

Hartman, Builders of the Old World, p.211–15   6

Hillyer, Child's History of the World, p.242–56   5–6

McGuire, Glimpses into the Long Ago, p.255–57   5–6

ISLANDS: *see also* Coral; also names of islands, as Cuba; and groups of islands, as Pribilof Islands

Association for Childhood Education, Told under Spacious Skies, p.1–20
                                          *4–6

Bragdon, E., Fairing Weather   *4–5
Du Bois, Three Policemen   *4–6
Field, Hitty, p.60–80   *5–6
Gidal, My Village in Norway   4–6
Henry M., Misty of Chincoteague   *4–6
Loudon, Far into the Night   *4–5
Marshall, Invisible Island   *4–6
Meadowcroft, Gift of the River, p.111–17   5–6
Parrish, Floating Island   *4–6
Selsam, Birth of an Island   4–5
Smith, D. C., Land and People of Indonesia   6
Tor, Getting To Know Puerto Rico   4–6
Wyss, Swiss Family Robinson   *6

ISLANDS OF THE PACIFIC: *see* Pacific Islands

ISLE ROYALE NATIONAL PARK
Melbo, Our Country's National Parks, v.1, p.156–66   6

ISRAEL: *see also* Palestine
Barrows, Old World Lands, p.167–70   6
Epstein, E., First Book of the United Nations, p.16–18, 42–43   4–6
Gidal, My Village in Israel   4–6
Gillsater, Pia's Journey to the Holy Land   4–6
Joy, Getting To Know Israel   4–6
Kubie, First Book of Israel   4–6
Nevill, Picture Story of the Middle East   4–6
Quinn, Picture Map Geography of Asia, p.29–32   4–6
St. John, Builder of Israel   6

ISRAEL—GOVERNMENT
Kubie, First Book of Israel, p.47   4–6

ITALIANS IN THE UNITED STATES
Angelo, Bells of Bleeker Street   *4–6
Association for Childhood Education, Told under the Stars and Stripes, p.196–217   *4–6

ITALY: *see also* Art—Italy; Costume—Italy; Dancing—Italy; also names of cities, as Venice; also names of mountains, as Vesuvius, Mount
Angelo, Nino   *6
Barrows, Old World Lands, p.95–100   6

———— Our Big World, p.81–85   4
Bergaust, Rockets around the World, p.45   6
Carden, Aldo's Tower   *4–6
Epstein, S., First Book of Italy   5–6
Farjeon, Italian Peepshow   *4–5
Henry, M., Gaudenzia   6
Jewett, God's Troubadour   5–6
Jordan, Homemade Dolls in Foreign Dress, p.144–56   4–6
Joy, Young People of the Western Mediterranean, p.43–54   6
Steinmann, Lia and the Red Carnations   *6
Wheeler, Paganini   4–6

ITALY—FOLK TALES
Harper, Ghosts and Goblins, p.80–87   4–6
Hazeltine, Easter Book of Legends and Stories, p.322–60   5–6

ITALY—HISTORY: *see also* Rome—Ancient—History
Falls, First 3000 Years, p.117–19   6
Foster, G., Abraham Lincoln's World, p.123–26, 247–52   6

ITALY—INDUSTRIES
Epstein, S., First Book of Italy, p.10–12   5–6

ITHACA
Church, Odyssey for Boys and Girls   4–6

JACK O'LANTERNS: *see* Halloween; Pumpkins

JACKSON, ANDREW
Beard, Presidents in American History, p.33–35, 157–58   6
Coy, First Book of Presidents, p.32–33   4–6
———— Real Book about Andrew Jackson   5–6
Foster, G., Abraham Lincoln's World, p.41–44, 129–33   6
———— Andrew Jackson   4–6
Judson, Andrew Jackson   5–6
Lawson, R., Watchwords of Liberty, p.44–45   4–6
Olcott, Good Stories for Great Birthdays, p.279–302   4–6
Petersham, Story of the Presidents of the United States, p.24–26   4–6

Spencer, P. R., Finding New Trails, p.223–32   4

JACKSON, THOMAS JONATHAN (STONEWALL)
Lawson, R., Watchwords of Liberty, p.55–56   4–6

JADE
Spencer, C., Made in China, p.28–34   5–6

JADWIGA
Mills, So Young a Queen   6

JAGUARS
Stoutenberg, Wild Animals of the Far West, p.51–52   4–6
Zim, Big Cats, p.51–53   5–6

JAMAICA
Hughes, First Book of the West Indies, p.47–52   5–6
Quinn, Picture Map Geography of Mexico, Central America and the West Indies, p.82–85   4–6

JAMESTOWN, VIRGINIA: *see also* Smith, John
Barksdale, That Country Called Virginia, p.7–51   6
Lawson, M. A., Pocahontas and Captain John Smith   6
Rich, First Book of Early Settlers, p.5–20   4–6

JAPAN: *see also* Buddhism; Costume—Japan; Festivals—Japan; Formosa; Games—Japan; Korea; Pottery—Japan; Rice; Shintoism
Barrows, Old World Lands, p.250–64   6
———— Our Big World, p.155–60   4
Bergaust, Rockets around the World, p.42–44   6
Buck, P. S., Big Wave   *6
Coatsworth, Cat Who Went to Heaven   *4–6
Edelman, Japan in Story and Pictures   4–6
Gallant, K., Flute Player of Beppu   *4
Godden, Miss Happiness and Miss Flower   *4–5
Hawks, Tami's New House   *4–5
Jakeman, Getting To Know Japan   4–6

Jordan, Homemade Dolls in Foreign Dress, p.211–30   4–6
Kettelkamp, Kites, p.38–40   4–6
Kuwabara, Cut and Paste   5–6
Lewis, M. D., Honorable Sword   *5–6
Mears, First Book of Japan   4–6
Ota, Printing for Fun   4–6
Quinn, Picture Map Geography of Asia, p.118–22   4–6
Spencer, C., Japan   5–6
Uchida, Takao and Grandfather's Sword   *4–6
Yashima, M., Plenty To Watch   4–5
Yashima, T., Crow Boy   *4–5
———— Golden Footprints   *4–6

JAPAN—HISTORY
Foster, G., Abraham Lincoln's World, p.178–80, 272–77   6
———— George Washington's World, p.147–49   6
Hazeltine, Hero Tales from Many Lands, p.429–46   5–6
McGuire, Glimpses into the Long Ago, p.133–40   5–6
Mears, First Book of Japan, p.34–36   4–6
Spencer, C., Japan, p.4–10, 14–15, 20–24   5–6

JAPANESE IN THE UNITED STATES
Association for Childhood Education, Told under the Stars and Stripes, p.172–85   *4–6
Uchida, Mik and the Prowler   *4–6

JASON: *see* Argonauts

JAVA
Caldwell, Let's Visit Indonesia, p.20–22   4–6
Quinn, Picture Map Geography of the Pacific Islands, p.40–41   5–6
Smith, D. C., Land and People of Indonesia   6

JAZZ
Buchanan, How Man Made Music, p.201–13   6

JEFFERSON, THOMAS
Barksdale, That Country Called Virginia, p.115–20, 124–36   6
Beard, Presidents in American History, p.17–19, 154   6
Coy, First Book of Presidents, p.27–28   4–6

Fisher, D. F. C., And Long Remember, p.26–37   6

Foster, G., George Washington's World, p.89–92, 251–53, 259–61, 304–9   6

Judson, Thomas Jefferson   6

Lawson, R., Watchwords of Liberty, p.10–12   4–6

Olcott, Good Stories for Great Birthdays, p.303–13   4–6

Petersham, Story of the Presidents of the United States, p.14–16   4–6

JELLYFISH

Doane, Book of Nature, p.104–5   5–6

Fenton, C. L., Life Long Ago, p.41–45   6

Hausman, Beginner's Guide to Fresh-Water Life, p.108–9   6

Neurath, Wonder World of the Seashore, p.28–29   4–6

Reed, Sea for Sam, p.132–37   6

Robertson, G., Strange Sea Life, p.28–34   5–6

JENNER, EDWARD

Asimov, Breakthroughs in Science, p.90–98   5–6

Cottler, Heroes of Civilization, p.269–77   6

Ludovici, World of the Microscope, p.39–42   6

JERUSALEM

Fitch, Allah, the God of Islam, p.130–34   6

Hazeltine, Easter Book of Legends and Stories, p.268–84   *5–6

JESTERS: *see* Clowns

JESUS CHRIST: *see also* Christmas; Easter

Ceder, Joel, the Potter's Son   *4–6

Fitch, One God, p.56–57   5–6

Hartman, In Bible Days, p.135–82   6

Hillyer, Child's History of the World, p.197–202   5–6

Jones, J. M. O., Little Child   4–6

Lillie, Book of Three Festivals, p.11–27, 63–87, 131–45   *5–6

Smith, E. S., Christmas Book of Legends & Stories   5–6

Smither, Stories of Jesus   4–5

JET PROPULSION

Beeler, Experiments in Science, p.98–100   5–6

Colby, Our Space Age Jets   5–6

Coombs, Rockets, Missiles, and Moons, p.64–68   6

Crouse, W. H., Understanding Science, p.161–70   6

Dalgliesh, America Travels, p.127–34   4–6

Fisher, J., Wonderful World of the Air, p.56–63   5–6

Floherty, Aviation from the Ground Up, p.103–32   6

Gottlieb, Jets and Rockets and How They Work   4–6

Lewellen, Helicopters, p.64–66, 122–27   6

Neurath, Rockets and Jets   4–6

Schneider, H., More Power to You, p.93–97   5–6

Schneider, L., Wings in Your Future, p.30–50   5–6

Zaffo, Big Book of Real Airplanes   4–5

Zarem, New Dimensions of Flight, p.42–48   6

JEWELRY: *see also* Beadwork; Diamonds; Jade; Precious Stones; Silversmithing

Hamilton, E. T., Handicraft for Girls, p.188–220   6

Lee, What To Do Now, p.72–75   4–6

Leeming, Fun with Wire, p.60–69   5–6

Lent, Men at Work in New England, p.52–55   4–6

Zarchy, Let's Make a Lot of Things, p.42–87   5–6

———— Let's Make Something   5–6

JEWS: *see also* Ben-Gurion, David; David, King of Israel; Holidays—Jews; Israel; Jerusalem; Joseph; Moses; Palestine; Solomon, King

Burnett, B., First Book of Holidays, p.58–61   4–5

Falls, First 3000 Years, p.104–7, 119–24   6

Fitch, One God, p.12–55   5–6

Galt, Seven Days from Sunday, p.24–26, 86–92   6

Gidal, My Village in Israel   4–6

Hartman, Builders of the Old World, p.99–106   6

———— In Bible Days   6

Hillyer, Child's History of the World, p.49–55, 70–73   5–6

Kent, He Went with Vasco da Gama, p.150–55   *6

Kubie, First Book of Israel   4–6

Watson, Golden History of the World, p.21–22   5–6

JEWS IN THE UNITED STATES
Taylor, S., All-of-a-Kind Family   *4–6
———— All-of-a-Kind Family Uptown   *4–6
———— More All-of-a-Kind Family   *4–6

JOAN OF ARC
Bragdon, L. J., Land and People of France, p.38–42   6
Lownsbery, Boy Knight of Reims, p.265–324   *6

JOHN, KING OF ENGLAND
Hillyer, Child's History of the World, p.311–15   5–6

JOHN HENRY
Hubbard, Train That Never Came Back, p.24–40   5–6

JOHNNY APPLESEED: see Appleseed, Johnny

JOHNSON, ANDREW
Beard, Presidents in American History, p.73–74, 165–66   6
Coy, First Book of Presidents, p.44   4–6
Petersham, Story of the Presidents of the United States, p.44–45   4–6

JOKES: see Tricks

JOLLIET, LOUIS
American Heritage, Discoverers of the New World, p.135–40   5–6

JONES, CASEY
Hubbard, Train That Never Came Back, p.87–98   5–6

JONES, JOHN PAUL
Fisher, D. F. C., And Long Remember, p.48–55   6
Foster, G., George Washington's World, p.153–55, 203–4, 217–18   6
Lawson, R., Watchwords of Liberty, p.23–26   4–6
Mitchell, Ships That Made U.S. History, p.21–25   6
Olcott, Good Stories for Great Birthdays, p.357–70   4–6

Spencer, P. R., Traveling New Trails, p.3–12   6

JOSEPH
Bowie, Bible Stories for Boys and Girls: Old Testament, p.33–46   4–6
De la Mare, Stories from the Bible, p.61–130   5–6
Hartman, In Bible Days, p.33–38   6
Petersham, Joseph and His Brothers   4–5

JOURNALISM: see also Cartoons; Newspapers; Reporters
Eaton, That Lively Man, Ben Franklin   6
Lent, "I Work on a Newspaper," p.75–78   6
Proudfit, River-Boy, p.173–203   6
Spencer, P. R., Traveling New Trails, p.477–85   6

JUÁREZ, BENITO PABLO
Goetz, Neighbors to the South, p.161–63   5–6
McNeer, Mexican Story, p.56–58   6

JUDO
Jakeman, Getting To Know Japan, p.39–40   4–6

JUGOSLAVIA: see Yugoslavia

JUNCOS
Webb, Birds in Their Homes, p.35   4–6

JUNGLES: see also Amazon Valley; Congo; Pacific Islands; Tropics
Davis, N., Picken's Treasure Hunt   *4–5
Gatti, Saranga, the Pygmy   *5–6
Kipling, Jungle Book   *5–6
Life, World We Live In, p.160–77   5–6
Lindquist, W., Burma Boy   *4–6
Mukerji, Hari, the Jungle Lad   *5–6
———— Kari, the Elephant   *4–6
Selsam, See through the Jungle   4–5
Singh, Gift of the Forest   *6
Smith, J. R., Neighbors around the World, p.254–85   4
Sperry, All about the Jungle   5–6
———— Rain Forest   *6
Weston, Bhimsa, the Dancing Bear, p.100–110   *4–6

JUPITER (planet)
Branley, Nine Planets, p.51–55   6

Gallant, R. A., Exploring the Planets, p.74–87   5–6

Goodwin, Real Book about Stars, p.95–101   4–6

Hendrickson, Handbook for Space Travelers, p.229–32   5–6

Schneider, L., Space in Your Future, p.93–97   6

JUSTICE: *see* Law

KANGAROOS

Darling, L., Kangaroos   4–6

Fox, From Bones to Bodies, p.62–63   6

Kipling, Just So Stories, p.85–97   *4–6

Osmond, Animals of the World, p.2   4–6

Parker, B. M., Animals We Know, p.34–35   5–6

Perkins, Marlin Perkins' Zooparade, p.24–27   4–6

KANSAS

Coatsworth, Sod House   *4–5

Quinn, Picture Map Geography of the United States, p.128–31   4–6

Wilder, Little House on the Prairie   *4–6

KARNAK, TEMPLE OF

Hillyer, Child's History of Art, p.285–87   5–6

KASHMIR

Bothwell, Little Boat Boy   *4–5

KATYDIDS

Bronson, Grasshopper Book, p.70–92   4–6

Comstock, Handbook of Nature Study, p.343–44   6

KENNEDY, JOHN FITZGERALD

Beard, Presidents in American History, p.149–50, 182   6

KENTUCKY: *see also* Mammoth Cave National Park

Banta, Life in America: The South, p.138–43   5–6

Commager, H. S., First Book of American History, p.29–31   4–6

Kohler, "Crazy As You Look!"   *4–6

Lansing, E. C. H., Liza of the Hundred-fold   *5–6

McMeekin, Journey Cake   *5–6

Meadowcroft, On Indian Trails with Daniel Boone   4–5

Quinn, Picture Map Geography of the United States, p.80–83   4–6

Stuart, Penny's Worth of Character   *4–6

KENYA

Barrows, Old World Lands, p.315–16   6

Hughes, First Book of Africa   5–6

Stinetorf, Children of South Africa, p.80–94   *5–6

KEROSENE: *see* Petroleum

KEY, FRANCIS SCOTT

Lawson, R., Watchwords of Liberty, p.36–37   4–6

Lyons, Stories of Our American Patriotic Songs, p.9–16   5–6

KIENZL, WILHELM

Schwimmer, Great Musicians as Children, p.219–22   6

KINDNESS

Alden, Why the Chimes Rang   *4–6

Estes, Hundred Dresses   *4–6

Jewett, God's Troubadour   5–6

Moon, Chi-Wee, p.115–18, 153–68   *4–6

Zwilgmeyer, Johnny Blossom   *4–6

KINDNESS TO ANIMALS

Anderson, C. W., Salute   *4–5

Darling, E. B., Baldy of Nome   *6

Henry, M., King of the Wind   *5–6

Le Sueur, Little Brother of the Wilderness   4–5

Meigs, Wind in the Chimney, p.70–101   *5–6

Moe, Animal Inn   4–6

Mukerji, Kari, the Elephant, p.11–14   *4–6

KINGFISHERS

Comstock, Handbook of Nature Study, p.97–100   6

Gall, Ringtail, p.34–38   4–5

Sellew, Adventures with the Gods, p.90–94   4–5

Webb, Birds in Their Homes, p.44–45   4–6

KINGS CANYON NATIONAL PARK

Melbo, Our Country's National Parks, v.2, p.50–72   6

KIPLING, RUDYARD
Coffman, Famous Authors for Young People, p.149–53   5–6

KITCHENS
New York Herald Tribune, Young America's Cook Book   4–6

KITES
Chrisman, Shen of the Sea, p.189–205   *5–6
Downer, Kites   4–6
Hunt, L. L., 25 Kites That Fly   5–6
Judson, Benjamin Franklin, p.98–110   6
Kettelkamp, Kites   4–6
Neal, Story of the Kite   5–6
Sperling, How To Make Things out of Paper, p.53–55   5–6
Zarchy, Let's Make More Things, p.40–41   5–6

KLONDIKE GOLD RUSH
Lindquist, W., Alaska, p.36–47   5–6

KNIGHTS: *see also* Chivalry; Feudal System; Middle Ages; also names of knights, as Roland
Alden, Why the Chimes Rang, p.19–29   *4–6
Boardman, Castles, p.28–33   6
Buehr, Knights and Castles and Feudal Life, p.46–52   4–6
Hillyer, Child's History of the World, p.278–83   5–6
Holland, Christopher Goes to the Castle   *4–5
Johnson, E., Little Knight   *4–5
Lownsbery, Boy Knight of Reims, p.251–64   *6
Mellin, Horses across the Ages, p.32–40   4–6
Tappan, When Knights Were Bold, p.1–27   6

KNIGHTS OF THE ROUND TABLE: *see* Arthur, King

KNITTING
Leeming, Fun with String, p.87–88   4–6

KNIVES
Burns, Man and His Tools, p.22–32   5–6

KNOTS AND SPLICES
Leeming, Fun with String, p.30–83   4–6

KOCH, ROBERT
Cottler, Heroes of Civilization, p.287–95   6
Ludovici, World of the Microscope, p.67–72   6

KORAN
Caldwell, Let's Visit Pakistan, p.36–37   4–6

KOREA
Barrows, Old World Lands, p.246–49   6
Caldwell, Let's Visit Korea   5–6
Eisenberg, Won Kim's Ox   *4–6
Epstein, E., First Book of the United Nations, p.32–33   4–6
Hunt, G. P., Story of the U.S. Marines, p.3–15, 81–83   5–6
Kim, Happy Days   *5–6
Quinn, Picture Map Geography of Asia, p.111–17   4–6
Tor, Getting To Know Korea   4–6

KOREA—GOVERNMENT
Caldwell, Let's Visit Korea, p.83–86   5–6

KOREA—HISTORY
Caldwell, Let's Visit Korea, p.20–33   5–6

KUBLAI KHAN: *see also* Polo, Marco
Kent, He Went with Marco Polo, p.139–93   *6
Spencer, C., Land of the Chinese People, p.39–44   6

LABOR DAY
Burnett, B., First Book of Holidays, p.34   4–5
McSpadden, Book of Holidays, p.116–22   6
Olcott, Good Stories for Great Holidays, p.179–210   *4–6
Pannell, Holiday Round Up, p.219–24   4–6

LABORATORIES: *see* United States—Bureau of Standards

LABRADOR: *see also* Grenfell, Wilfred Thomason
McNeer, Armed with Courage   5–6

LACEWINGS
Comstock, Handbook of Nature Study, p.356–58   6

LACQUER
Spencer, C., Made in China, p.44–50
                                                               5–6

LADDERS
Bechdolt, Going Up, p.11–12, 108–9
                                                               5–6

LADYBUGS
Comstock, Handbook of Nature Study, p.364–66   6
Hyde, Animal Clocks and Compasses, p.78–80   5–6
Parker, B. M., Insects and Their Ways, p.22–24   4–6

LAFAYETTE, MARQUIS DE
Barksdale, That Country Called Virginia, p.115–16, 142–43   6
Eaton, That Lively Man, Ben Franklin, p.203–4, 219–22   6
Foster, G., George Washington's World, p.131–34, 192–94, 205–8, 215–16, 219–20, 275–76   6
Graham, A. P., Lafayette   4–5
Olcott, Good Stories for Great Birthdays, p.411–24   4–6

LAFITTE, JEAN
Lenski, Bayou Suzette, p.44–56   *5–6
Tallant, Pirate Lafitte and the Battle of New Orleans   5–6

LAKE DWELLERS
Bragdon, L. J., Land and People of Switzerland, p.30–31, 48   6
Burns, World Full of Homes, p.43–48
                                                               4–6
Hartman, Builders of the Old World, p.33   6
Osborne, C. G., First Lake Dwellers
                                                              *4–6

LAKES: *see also* Great Lakes; Lake Dwellers
Selsam, See through the Lake   4–6
Wyckoff, Story of Geology, p.70–77
                                                               5–6

LAMBS: *see* Sheep

LAMPREYS
Morgan, A. H., Field Book of Ponds and Streams, p.324–46   6

LAMPS
Bailey, C. S., Pioneer Art in America, p.52–64   *5–6
Barr, Young Scientist Takes a Ride, p.42–43 (incandescent)   5–6
Zarchy, Let's Make Something, p.32–33, 108–9   5–6

LANCELOT OF THE LAKE: *see* Arthur, King

LAND: *see also* Earth
Tannenbaum, Understanding Maps, p.29–44   5–6

LANGMUIR, IRVING
Asimov, Breakthroughs in Science, p.177–80   5–6

LANGUAGE: *see also* Alphabets; Words; Writing
Caldwell, Let's Visit India, p.78–82
                                                               4–6
Epstein, S., First Book of Words, p.8–22
                                                               5–6
Hogben, Wonderful World of Communication, p.56–57   6
Kubie, First Book of Israel, p.35   4–6
Pei, All about Language   6
Picturesque Word Origins   6

LANGUAGE—ARABIC
Ellis, Arabs, p.44–50, 66–69   6

LANGUAGE—ESKIMO
Stefansson, Here Is Alaska, p.55–56, 74–78, 98–99   6

LANGUAGE—FRENCH
Frasconi, See and Say   4–6
Joslin, There Is a Dragon in My Bed
                                                               4–5

LANGUAGE—INDONESIAN
Smith, D. C., Land and People of Indonesia, p.14–15, 107–11   6

LANGUAGE—ITALIAN
Frasconi, See and Say   4–6

LANGUAGE—KOREAN
Caldwell, Let's Visit Korea, p.71–74
                                                               5–6

LANGUAGE—SPANISH
Cooper, L., Fun with Spanish   4–6
Frasconi, See and Say   4–6
Ritchie, B., Ramon Makes a Trade
                                                               4–5

LANGUAGE—UNION OF SOVIET SO-
CIALIST REPUBLICS
Parker, F., Russian Alphabet Book   6

LANTERNS
Rogers, F., Heels, Wheels, and Wire,
p.180–84   5–6

LAPLAND
Lide, Lapland Drum   *4–6

LAPPS
Aulaire, Children of the Northlights
                                  *4–5
Berry, Men, Moss, and Reindeer   5–6
Gidal, Follow the Reindeer   4–6
Rothery, Scandinavian Roundabout,
p.55–61, 160–64   6

LARIAT: see Lasso

LARKS: see Horned Larks; Meadow
Larks

LA SALLE, RENÉ ROBERT CAVE-
LIER, SIEUR DE
American Heritage, Discoverers of the
New World, p.139–43   5–6
Duvoisin, And There Was America,
p.32–36   4–6
Graham, A. P., La Salle   4–6

LASSEN   VOLCANIC   NATIONAL
PARK
Melbo, Our Country's National Parks,
v.2, p.181–97   6

LASSO
Leeming, Fun with String, p.101–3
                                  4–6

LATEX
Freeman, I. M., All about the Wonders
of Chemistry, p.119–21   6

LATIN AMERICA: see also Central
America; Mexico; South America;
West Indies
Barrows, American Continents, p.281–
357   5
Goetz, Neighbors to the South   5–6
———— Other Young Americans   5–6

LATIN AMERICA—GAMES: see Games
—Latin America

LATITUDE: see Geography; Maps; Navigation

LAUNDRY
Bond, Paddington Helps Out, p.93–110
(laundromat)   *4–6
Crawford, "Hello, the Boat!", p.117–23
                                  *6

LAVA: see also Volcanoes
Disney, Worlds of Nature, p.100–101
                                  4–6

LAVOISIER, ANTOINE-LAURENT
Asimov, Breakthroughs in Science, p.
58–66   5–6
Cottler, Heroes of Civilization, p.128–
37   6

LAW: see also Citizenship; Crime; Federal
Bureau of Investigation; Govern-
ment; Hammurabi, King of Baby-
lonia; Justice; Police; also names of
countries, subhead Government, as
United States—Government
Coy, First Book of the Supreme Court
                                  5–6
Elting, We Are the Government   6
Hillyer, Child's History of the World,
p.114–18   5–6
Meadowcroft, Abraham Lincoln, p.79–
87   6
Peattie, Law   5–6
Tappan, When Knights Were Bold,
p.47–51   6

LAWRENCE, ERNEST ORLANDO
Asimov, Breakthroughs in Science, p.
186–89   5–6

LEAD
Fenton, C. L., Riches from the Earth,
p.80–82   5–6
Loomis, Field Book of Common Rocks
and Minerals, p.59–63   6

LEAD PENCILS: see Pencils

LEADERSHIP
Armstrong, Ship Afire!   *6
Behn, Roderick   *5–6

LEAF MINERS
Comstock, Handbook of Nature Study,
p.329–32   6

LEAF ROLLERS
Comstock, Handbook of Nature Study,
p.332–34   6

LEATHER WORK
Hamilton, E. T., Handicraft for Girls,
p.237–52   6

Jaeger, Easy Crafts, p.106–11   4–6
Zarchy, Let's Make a Lot of Things,
    p.38–41, 120–47   5–6

LEAVES: *see also* Botany; Flowers; Trees
Disraeli, New Worlds through the Mi-
    croscope, p.117–21   6
Hylander, Out of Doors in Autumn,
    p.12–14, 105–12   5–6
———— Out of Doors in Summer,
    p.9–28   5–6
Selsam, Plants We Eat, p.44–56   4–6

LEBANON
Quinn, Picture Map Geography of Asia,
    p.24–28   4–6

LEE, ROBERT EDWARD
Commager, H. S., America's Robert E.
    Lee   6
———— First Book of American His-
    tory, p.47–51   4–6
Fisher, D. F. C., And Long Remember,
    p.84–89   6
Foster, G., Abraham Lincoln's World,
    p.71–73   6
Lawson, R., Watchwords of Liberty,
    p.70–71   4–6
Meadowcroft, Land of the Free, p.103–
    10   4–5
Pannell, Holiday Round Up, p.39–44
                                      4–6
Vance, Lees of Arlington   5–6

LEECHES
Cooper, E. K., Science on the Shores
    and Banks, p.98–99   5–6
Morgan, A. H., Field Book of Animals
    in Winter, p.102–12   6
———— Field Book of Ponds and
    Streams, p.148–57   6

LEEUWENHOEK, ANTON VAN
Asimov, Breakthroughs in Science, p.
    41–44   5–6
Cottler, Heroes of Civilization, p.260–
    68   6
Schatz, Story of Microbes, p.47–52   6

LEEWARD ISLANDS
Quinn, Picture Map Geography of Mex-
    ico, Central America and the West
    Indies, p.109–11   4–6

LEGENDS: *see also* Arthur, King; Bal-
    lads; Beowulf; Christmas; Cuchulain;
    Folk Songs; Indians of North Amer-

ica—Folk Tales; Myths; Nibelungen-
    lied; Sagas; Trojan War; also names
    of legendary heroes, as Ogier the
    Dane; Robin Hood; Roland; Tell,
    William
Berger, All about Fish, p.22–28   5–6
Coolidge, Legends of the North   4–6
Seredy, White Stag   6
Smith, E. S., Christmas Book of Leg-
    ends & Stories   5–6

LEGISLATURE: *see* United States—Gov-
    ernment

LEIF THE LUCKY: *see* Ericson, Leif

LEMMINGS
Disney, Worlds of Nature, p.31–36
                                      4–6
Hogner, Animal Book, p.72–74   6
Hyde, Animal Clocks and Compasses,
    p.105–8   5–6
Lavine, Strange Travelers, p.41–47
                                      5–6
Parker, B. M., Animal Travels, p.5–6
                                      4–6
Rothery, Scandinavian Roundabout, p.
    61–62   6

LEMONS
Wall, Gifts from the Grove   4–6

LENIN, NIKOLAI
Nazaroff, Land of the Russian People,
    p.142–47   6

LENINGRAD
Nazaroff, Land of the Russian People,
    p.35–42   6

LENSES: *see also* Microscopes; Tele-
    scopes
Beeler, Experiments with Light, p.55–
    73   6
Epstein, S., First Book of Glass, p.47–
    52   5–6
Freeman, M. B., Fun with Your Cam-
    era, p.8–9   4–6
Meyer, Prisms and Lenses   6
Ruchlis, Wonder of Light, p.127–40
                                       6
Schneider, L., Space in Your Future,
    p.136–41   6

LEONARDO DA VINCI
Bishop, R. W., From Kite to Kitty
    Hawk, p.9–13   6
Chandler, Story-Lives of Master Artists,
    p.27–40   6

Hillyer, Child's History of Art, p.57–62
5–6

LEOPARDS: *see also* Jaguars
Buck, F., Jungle Animals, p.29–30   5–6
Kipling, Just So Stories, p.43–59   *4–6
Zim, Big Cats, p.41–46   5–6

LEPRECHAUNS
Payne, Leprechaun of Bayou Luce
*4–5

LEPROSY
McNeer, Armed with Courage, p.34–38
5–6

LETTER WRITING
Beery, Manners Made Easy, p.250–63
6
Betz, Your Manners Are Showing, p.48–
51   6
Jacobson, First Book of Letter Writing
4–6

LEVERS
Bechdolt, Going Up, p.15–18   5–6
Liberty, First Book of Tools, p.28–30
5–6
Meyer, Machines, p.39–47   4–6
Parker, B. M., Machines, p.10–15
5–6

LEWIS AND CLARK EXPEDITION:
see also Sacajawea
Havighurst, First Book of the Oregon
Trail, p.1–9   4–6
Neuberger, Lewis and Clark Expedition
4–6

LEYDEN—SIEGE OF, 1573–74
Barnouw, Land of William of Orange,
p.34–36   6

LIBERIA
Barrows, Old World Lands, p.305–6
6
Caldwell, Let's Visit West Africa, p.40–
50   5–6
Hughes, First Book of Africa, p.47, 63–
64   5–6
Steintorf, Children of North Africa,
p.162–76   *5–6

LIBERTY—STATUE OF
Hillyer, Child's History of Art, p.246–
48, 388   5–6
Rogers, F., Big Miss Liberty   *5–6

LIBERTY BELL
Rogers, F., Old Liberty Bell   5–6

LIBRARIES: *see also* Authors; Bookmo-
biles; Books
Busby, Behind the Scenes in the Li-
brary   5–6
Estes, Rufus M., p.3–30   *4–6
Judson, Benjamin Franklin, p.74–85   6
Lent, "I Work on a Newspaper," p.112–
15   6
Spencer, P. R., Traveling New Trails,
p.195–205   6
Taylor, S., All-of-a-Kind Family, p.11–
24   *4–6

LIBYA
Epstein, E., First Book of the United
Nations, p.67–68   4–6

LICE: *see* Plant Lice

LICHENS: *see also* Mosses
Barr, More Research Ideas for Young
Scientists, p.18, 108–10   5–6
Doane, Book of Nature, p.64–65   5–6
Parker, B. M., Plant and Animal Part-
nerships, p.19–21   5–6

LIFE: *see* Biology; Evolution

LIFESAVING
Brink, Magical Melons, p.179–93
*5–6
Seredy, Good Master, p.137–44   *5–6
Unnerstad, Spettecake Holiday, p.191–
200   *4–6

LIGHT: *see also* Aurora Borealis; Color;
Eye; Lighting; Lightning; Mirrors;
Photography; Physics; Rainbow; Sun;
X rays
Adler, Dust, p.31–44   5–6
Baker, A. O., Your Science World,
p.71–87   6
Barr, More Research Ideas for Young
Scientists, p.132–40   5–6
——— Research Ideas for Young
Scientists, p.44–50   5–6
Beeler, Experiments in Science, p.7–9,
129–32   5–6
——— Experiments with Light   6
Bendick, How Much and How Many,
p.98–99   5–6
Crouse, W. H., Understanding Science,
p.111–19   6
Freeman, I. M., All about Electricity,
p.114–26   5–6
Freeman, M. B., Fun with Science,
p.53–58   6

Huey, What Makes the Wheels Go Round, p.135–42   6

Land, B., Quest of Isaac Newton   6

Meyer, Prisms and Lenses   6

Morgan, A. P., Boys' Book of Science and Construction, p.280–329   6

Paschel, First Book of Color   5–6

Podendorf, 101 Science Experiments, p.96–105   4–5

Ruchlis, Wonder of Light   6

Schneider, L., Space in Your Future, p.154–58, 165–66   6

LIGHTHOUSES

Burns, World Full of Homes, p.23–24   4–6

Rogers, F., Heels, Wheels, and Wire, p.172–79   5–6

Sauer, Light at Tern Rock   *4–6

LIGHTING: *see also* Candles; Electric Lighting; Lamps; Lighthouses; Natural Gas; Petroleum

Darrow, Boys' Own Book of Great Inventions, p.309–19   6

Morgan, A. P., Boy Electrician, p.352–67   6

LIGHTNING

Morgan, A. P., First Electrical Book for Boys, p.8–10   6

Reed, And That's Why, p.48–55   4–5

Zim, Lightning and Thunder   4–5

LILIENTHAL, OTTO

Hartman, Machines, p.235–37   6

LIMESTONE

Cooper, E. K., Science in Your Own Back Yard, p.34–36   5–6

Fenton, C. L., Riches from the Earth, p.84–90   5–6

Lent, Men at Work in the Great Lakes States, p.50–53   4–6

LIMPETS

Cooper, E. K., Science on the Shores and Banks, p.68–71   5–6

Dudley, Sea Shells, p.1–12   4–6

LINCOLN, ABRAHAM

Beard, Presidents in American History, p.69–71, 164–65   6

Coy, First Book of Presidents, p.42–43   4–6

Fisher, D. F. C., And Long Remember, p.14–19   6

Foster, G., Abraham Lincoln's World   6

Judson, Abraham Lincoln   6

Lawson, R., Watchwords of Liberty, p.65–69   4–6

McNeer, America's Abraham Lincoln   5–6

Meadowcroft, Abraham Lincoln   6

———— By Secret Railway   *5–6

Neyhart, Henry's Lincoln   *4–6

Pauli, Lincoln's Little Correspondent   4–6

Petersham, Story of the Presidents of the United States, p.40–43   4–6

LINCOLN'S BIRTHDAY

Brown, H. M., America Is My Country, p.189–91   5–6

Burnett, B., First Book of Holidays, p.7   4–5

Jordan, Holiday Handicraft, p.38–49   4–6

McSpadden, Book of Holidays, p.12–23   6

Olcott, Good Stories for Great Birthdays, p.173–87   4–6

———— Good Stories for Great Holidays, p.27–38   4–6

Pannell, Holiday Round Up, p.45–62   4–6

Sechrist, Red Letter Days, p.41–50   5–6

LIND, JENNY

Association for Childhood Education, Told under the Stars and Stripes, p.150–58   *4–6

Wheeler, Robert Schumann and Mascot Ziff, p.134   4–6

LINDBERGH, CHARLES AUGUSTUS

Dalgliesh, Ride on the Wind   4–5

LINNAEUS

Rothery, Scandinavian Roundabout, p.163–64   6

LINOLEUM-BLOCK PRINTING: *see* Block Printing

LIONS

Bridges, Zoo Doctor, p.80–86   4–6

Buck, F., Jungle Animals, p.53   5–6

Mason, G. F., Animal Tracks, p.90–91   4–6

Osmond, Animals of the World, v.3   4–6

Parker, B. M., Animals We Know, p.20–21   5–6

Perkins, Marlin Perkins' Zooparade, p.16–19   4–6

Robinson, W. W., Beasts of the Tar Pits, p.42–44   5–6

Voight, Lions in the Barn   *4–6

Zim, Big Cats, p.27–34   5–6

LIPPI, FILIPPO
Chandler, Story-Lives of Master Artists, p.15–26   6

LIQUIDS: *see* Gases, Liquids, Solids

LISTER, JOSEPH
Cottler, Heroes of Civilization, p.296–306   6

LISZT, FRANZ
Burch, Famous Composers for Young People, p.95–102   4–5

Deucher, Edvard Grieg, p.117–24   4–6

Schwimmer, Great Musicians as Children, p.84–91   6

Wheeler, Robert Schumann and Mascot Ziff, p.79–83, 134   4–6

LITERATURE: *see* Authors; English Literature

LITERATURE—MIDDLE AGES
Tappan, When Knights Were Bold, p.289–311   6

LITERATURE AND HISTORY: *see also* Legends
Bragdon, L. J., Land and People of France   6

LITERATURE AND SCIENCE: *see* Constellations

LIVING THINGS: *see* Biology

LIVINGSTONE, DAVID
Cottler, Heroes of Civilization, p.65–75   6

Hughes, First Book of Africa, p.14–19, 23, 33   5–6

LIZARDS
Bevans, Book of Reptiles and Amphibians, p.33–40   4–6

Brown, V., How To Understand Animal Talk, p.169–71   6

Comstock, Handbook of Nature Study, p.210–13   6

Cooper, E. K., Science on the Shores and Banks, p.132–33   5–6

Fenton, C. L., Life Long Ago, p.204–9   6

———— Wild Folk in the Desert, p.87–92, 117–22   4–6

Harper, Easter Chimes, p.52–59   *4–6

Huntington, Let's Go to the Desert, p.40–53   4–5

Hylander, Animals in Armor, p.87–121   6

Parker, B. M., Reptiles, p.11–15   4–6

LLAMAS
Bleeker, Inca, p.36–39   5–6

Osmond, Animals of the World, v.3, p.3–31   4–6

LOBSTERS
Cooper, E. K., Science on the Shores and Banks, p.113–15   5–6

LOCKS (canals)
Boardman, Canals   6

Buehr, Through the Locks   5–6

LOCKS AND KEYS
Schneider, H., Everyday Machines and How They Work, p.86–95   5–6

LOCOMOTIVES: *see also* Air Brakes; Diesel Engines; Jones, Casey; Railroads; Steam Engines; Streamlined Trains; Tom Thumb (locomotive)
Bethers, Perhaps I'll Be a Railroad Man, p.30–39   5–6

Hartman, Machines, p.72–82   6

Henry, R. S., Trains   5–6

Huey, What Makes the Wheels Go Round, p.61–65   6

Van Metre, Trains, Tracks and Travel, p.113–67   6

Writers Project, Trains Going By, no.10, p.12–22   5–6

LOCOMOTIVES—MODELS: *see* Railroads—Models

LOCUSTS: *see* Cicadas; Grasshoppers

LOFOTEN ISLANDS: *see also* Fisheries—Norway
Rothery, Scandinavian Roundabout, p.25–28   6

LOG CABINS
Burns, World Full of Homes, p.88–90   4–6

Crawford, "Hello, the Boat!", p.180–82   *6

Orton, Treasure in the Little Trunk, p.109–14   *4–6

LOG CABINS—MODELS
Jordan, Holiday Handicraft, p.40–46   4–6
Maginley, Historic Models of Early America, p.141–44   6

LONDON, JACK
Coffman, Famous Authors for Young People, p.157–62   5–6

LONDON
Aulaire, Pocahontas   4–5
Bond, Bear Called Paddington   *4–6
Eaton, That Lively Man, Ben Franklin, p.130–75   6
Fenner, Time To Laugh, p.175–91   *4–6
Harper, Easter Chimes, p.22–33   *4–6
Sasek, This Is London   4–6
Sleigh, Kingdom of Carbonel   *4–6
Street, Key to London   5–6
Thwaite, House in Turner Square   *6

LONGFELLOW, HENRY WADSWORTH
Coffman, Famous Authors for Young People, p.65–70   5–6

LONGITUDE: *see* Geography; Maps; Navigation

LOOMS: *see* Weaving

LOONS
Mason, G. F., Animal Sounds, p.30–33   5–6

LORENZINI, CARLO
Collodi, Adventures of Pinocchio, p.ix–xiii   4–6

LOS ALAMOS
Fermi, Story of Atomic Energy, p.118–28, 130   6

LOS ANGELES
Sayers, Ginny and Custard   *4–6
Schloat, Adventures of a Letter, p.10–22   4–6

LOUIS XV, KING OF FRANCE
Foster, G., George Washington's World, p.38–40   6
Henry, M., King of the Wind, p.68–76   *5–6

LOUISIANA: *see also* New Orleans
Banta, Life in America: The South, p.132–36   5–6
Lenski, Bayou Suzette   *5–6
Quinn, Picture Map Geography of the United States, p.136–39   4–6

LOW, JULIETTE GORDON
Pace, Juliette Low   5–6

LOWLANDS: *see* Belgium; Netherlands; Scotland

LOYALTY: *see also* Patriotism
Bothwell, Thirteenth Stone   *5–6
Ceder, Ethan, the Shepherd Boy   *4–6
Daringer, Adopted Jane   *4–6
Petersham, Ruth   4–5

LOYOLA, SISTER MARY
Ross, N. W., Heroines of the Early West, p.126–55   5–6

LULLABIES
Wheeler, Franz Schubert, p.40–41   4–6

LUMBERING: *see also* Forestry; Trees; Wood
Blough, Tree on the Road to Turntown   *4–5
Buehr, Timber!   5–6
Buff, Big Tree, p.74–79   5–6
Dudley, Our American Trees, p.48–67   5–6
Holling, Paddle-to-the-Sea   *4–6
Smith, J. R., Neighbors around the World, p.78–79   4
Wall, Gifts from the Forest   4–6

LUNGFISHES
Shackelford, Child's Story of the Negro, p.7–9   4–5

LUTE
Kettelkamp, Singing Strings, p.26–28   5–6

LUTHER, MARTIN
Buchanan, How Man Made Music, p.161–63   6
Hartman, Builders of the Old World, p.334–36   6
McNeer, Martin Luther   6

LYNXES
Franklin, Wild Animals of the Southwest, p.58–72   5–6
Mason, G. F., Animal Tracks, p.86–89   4–6

Stoutenberg, Wild Animals of the Far
West, p.48–49   4–6

LYREBIRDS
Buck, F., Jungle Animals, p.56   5–6

MACAWS: *see* Parrots

McCORMICK, CYRUS HALL: *see also*
Agricultural Machinery
Hartman, Machines, p.199–203   6

MacDOWELL, EDWARD ALEXANDER
Buchanan, How Man Made Music,
p.17, 190–91   6
Burch, Famous Composers for Young
People, p.155–63   4–6
Schwimmer, Great Musicians as Chil-
dren, p.28–33   6
Spencer, P. R., Exploring New Trails,
p.231–46   5
Wheeler, Edward MacDowell and His
Cabin in the Pines   4–6

MACHINES: *see also* Agricultural Ma-
chinery; Clocks; Dairying; Electric
Motors; Engines; Factory System;
Force and Energy; Inclined Planes;
Industrial Revolution; Inventions;
Levers; Locomotives; Manufacturing;
Mechanics; Mining; Power Mechan-
ics; Printing; Pulleys; Sewing Ma-
chines; Spinning; Steam Engines;
Tools; Water Wheels; Weaving;
Wheels; Windmills
Adler, Tools in Your Life, p.79–98
                                 5–6
Barnard, Macmillan Science-Life Series,
Bk.6, p.287–95   6
Buehr, Harbors and Cargoes, p.19–22,
36–43   5–6
Burns, Man and His Tools   5–6
Colby, Earthmovers   5–6
Hartman, Machines   6
Lent, Men at Work in New England,
p.90–93   4–6
Leonard, Exploring Science, p.178–89
                                  6
Meyer, Machines   5–6
Parker, B. M., Machines   5–6
Podendorf, 101 Science Experiments,
p.108–13   4–5
Schneider, H., Everyday Machines and
How They Work   5–6

McKINLEY, WILLIAM
Beard, Presidents in American History,
p.101–3, 171–72   6
Coy, First Book of Presidents, p.51
                                 4–6
Petersham, Story of the Presidents of
the United States, p.56–57   4–6

MADISON, JAMES
Beard, Presidents in American History,
p.21–22, 155   6
Coy, First Book of Presidents, p.29
                                 4–6
Petersham, Story of the Presidents of
the United States, p.17–18   4–6

MAGELLAN, FERDINAND
American Heritage, Discoverers of the
New World, p.53–63   5–6
Cottler, Heroes of Civilization, p.24–33
                                  6
Dalgliesh, America Begins, p.44–45
                                 4–5
Duvoisin, They Put Out to Sea, p.136–
71   4–6
Hall, E., Land and People of Argentina,
p.58–62   6
Hewes, Spice Ho!, p.85–120   5–6
Syme, Magellan   4–6

MAGIC: *see also* Puzzles; Superstition;
Tricks; Witchcraft; also names of
countries, subhead Folk Tales, as
Spain—Folk Tales
Corbett, Lemonade Trick   *4–6
Howard, J., 13th Is Magic   *4–6
Jones, E. O., Twig   *4–5
Kent, He Went with Marco Polo, p.160–
64   *6
Kettelkamp, Magic Made Easy   4–6
Leeming, Real Book about Magic
                                 5–6
MacDonald, Mrs. Piggle-Wiggle's Magic
                                 *4–5
Renick, M. L., Shining Shooter   *4–6
Severn, Let's Give a Show, p.3–29
                                 4–6
Stoddard, First Book of Magic   5–6

MAGNA CHARTA
Hartman, Builders of the Old World,
p.298–303   6

MAGNESIUM
Fenton, C. L., Riches from the Earth,
p.91–92   5–6

MAGNETISM: *see also* Compass; Electricity; Electromagnetism; Physics

Asimov, Satellites in Outer Space, p.42–45   4–5

Barr, More Research Ideas for Young Scientists, p.47   5–6

Beauchamp, Discovering Our World, Bk.1, p.139–54   4

Comstock, Handbook of Nature Study, p.776–79   6

Freeman, I. M., All about Electricity, p.35–41   5–6

Huey, What Makes the Wheels Go Round, p.36–41   6

Meyer, Picture Book of Electricity   5–6

Morgan, A. P., Boy Electrician, p.13–33   6

———— Boys' Book of Science and Construction, p.340–49   6

———— First Electrical Book for Boys, p.24–38   6

Parker, B. M., Magnets   5–6

Podendorf, 101 Science Experiments, p.30–41   4–5

Schneider, H., Everyday Machines and How They Work, p.67–70   5–6

Wyckoff, Story of Geology, p.152–56   5–6

Yates, R. F., Boy and a Motor, p.18–29   6

MAHABHARATA

Modak, Land and People of India, p.38–43   6

MAHOGANY

Rothery, Central American Roundabout, p.94–96   6

MAID OF ORLEANS: *see* Joan of Arc

MAIL SERVICE: *see also* Air Mail Service; Pony Express; Postage Stamps

De Angeli, Bright April, p.37–41   *4–6

Eaton, That Lively Man, Ben Franklin, p.66, 86, 113–14   6

Elting, We Are the Government, p.41–45   6

Petersham, America's Stamps   5–6

Rogers, F., Heels, Wheels, and Wire, p.15–60, 85–86   5–6

Schloat, Adventures of a Letter   4–6

Van Metre, Trains, Tracks and Travel, p.325–29   6

MAINE: *see also* Acadia National Park

Coatsworth, Alice-All-By-Herself   *4–6

———— Away Goes Sally   *4–6

———— Five Bushel Farm   *4–5

Ladd, Janie   *4–5

———— Night of the Hurricane   *4–6

McCloskey, Time of Wonder   *4–5

Quinn, Picture Map Geography of the United States, p.1–3   4–6

Wilson, H. H., Owen Boys   *5–6

MAJORCA

Butterfield, Adventures of Esteban   *4–6

———— Jaime and His Hen Pollita   *4–5

Joy, Young People of the Western Mediterranean, p.118–23   6

MAKAH INDIANS

Brewster, First Book of Indians, p.36–43   4–5

MALARIA

Selsam, Plants That Heal, p.37–42   6

Wilder, Little House on the Prairie, p.182–98   *4–6

MALAY PENINSULA

Quinn, Picture Map Geography of Asia, p.76–79   4–6

MALTA

Joy, Young People of the Western Mediterranean, p.23–32   6

MALTA—KNIGHTS OF

Tappan, When Knights Were Bold, p.149–54   6

MAMMALS: *see also* Animals; Zoology; also names of mammals, as Bats; Dogs

Andrews, All about Strange Beasts of the Past, p.28–39   5–6

Beauchamp, Discovering Our World, Bk.1, p.21–23   4

Brown, V., How To Make a Miniature Zoo, p.142–64   5–6

Buck, M. W., In Yards and Gardens, p.62–69   4–6

———— Small Pets from Woods and Fields, p.60–65   4–6

Hogner, Animal Book   6

Hylander, Out of Doors in Summer, p.29–50   5–6

———— Out of Doors in Winter, p.105–23   5–6

Life, World We Live In, p.86–97   5–6

Morgan, A. H., Field Book of Animals in Winter, p.427–80   6

Parker, B. M., Animals We Know, p.8–35   5–6

Scheele, First Mammals   6

MAMMOTH CAVE NATIONAL PARK

Melbo, Our Country's National Parks, v.1, p.66–81   6

MAMMOTHS: *see also* Elephants; Fossils; Prehistoric Animals

Andrews, All about Strange Beasts of the Past, p.65–77   5–6

Fenton, C. L., Life Long Ago, p.253–59   6

Reed, Earth for Sam, p.206–9   6

Robinson, W. W., Beasts of the Tar Pits, p.6–8   5–6

MAN—PREHISTORIC: *see* Prehistoric Man

MAN—PRIMITIVE: *see* Primitive Man

MAN O' WAR

Henry, M., King of the Wind, p.11–17   *5–6

MAN-O'-WAR BIRDS: *see* Frigate Birds

MANATEES

Hogner, Animal Book, p.179–80   6

MANAWYDDAN

Hazeltine, Hero Tales from Many Lands, p.149–59   5–6

MANCHURIA

Quinn, Picture Map Geography of Asia, p.107–10   4–6

MANDRILLS

Buck, F., Jungle Animals, p.19–20   5–6

MANITOBA

Quinn, Picture Map Geography of Canada and Alaska, p.49–57   4–6

MANNERS AND CUSTOMS: *see also* Amusements; Archeology; Chivalry; Costume; Etiquette; Fairs; Festivals; Holidays; Sports; Table Etiquette; also names of countries, as France

Evans, All about Us, p.41–60   4–6

Goetz, Other Young Americans, p.66–111   5–6

Spencer, P. R., Exploring New Trails, p.259–63, 265–76   5

MANTIS

Barker, Winter-sleeping Wildlife, p.113–16   5–6

Bronson, Grasshopper Book, p.124–27   4–6

Gaul, Picture Book of Insects, p.6–7   4–6

Huntington, Praying Mantis   4–5

Hyde, Animal Clocks and Compasses, p.77–78   5–6

Lane, F. C., All about the Insect World, p.54–58   5–6

Parker, B. M., Insects and Their Ways, p.13–14   4–6

Teale, Insect Friends, p.29–34   5–6

MANUAL TRAINING: *see* Carpentry; Handicraft; Wood Carving

MANUFACTURING: *see also* Canning; Factory System; Industrial Revolution; also names of products, as Glass, and names of countries, subhead Industries, as United States—Industries

Elting, Lollypop Factory and Lots of Others   4–5

Lent, Men at Work in New England   4–6

———— Men at Work in the Great Lakes States   4–6

MANX SHEARWATER

Hyde, Animal Clocks and Compasses, p.43–44   5–6

MAPLE SUGAR

Bleeker, Indians of the Longhouse, p.29–39   4–6

Canfield, Understood Betsy, p.110–16   *5–6

Eberle, Basketful, p.217–20   4–6

Frost, Maple Sugar for Windy Foot   *4–6

Lent, Men at Work in New England, p.46–51   4–6

Shippen, Lightfoot, p.44–53   *4–6

Wilder, Farmer Boy, p.109–13   *4–6

———— Little House in the Big Woods, p.117–30   *4–6

MAPLE TREES

Comstock, Handbook of Nature Study, p.628–34   6

Cormack, First Book of Trees, p.72–76　4–6

Dudley, Our American Trees, p.57–60　5–6

McKenny, Trees of the Countryside, p.10–13　4–6

MAPS: *see also* City Planning; also names of countries and continents

Baker, N. B., Amerigo Vespucci　5–6

Barr, Young Scientist Takes a Ride, p.88–89　5–6

Barrows, American Continents, p.4–22　5

———— Our Big World, p.1–15　4

Brindze, Gulf Stream, p.26–29　4–6

Duvoisin, They Put Out to Sea　4–6

Epstein, S., First Book of Maps and Globes, p.2–41　4–6

Falls, First 3000 Years　6

Spencer, P. R., Traveling New Trails, p.333–40　6

Tannenbaum, Understanding Maps　5–6

MAPS—GEOLOGIC

Reed, Earth for Sam　6

MARBLES

Renick, M. L., Shining Shooter　*4–6

Waltrip, Quiet Boy　*4–6

MARCONI, GUGLIELMO

Cottler, Heroes of Civilization, p.230–38　6

Hartman, Machines, p.223–28　6

MARDI GRAS

Sayers, Tag-along Tooloo, p.47–59　*4

MARIANA ISLANDS

Quinn, Picture Map Geography of the Pacific Islands, p.62–67　5–6

MARIE ANTOINETTE, QUEEN OF FRANCE

Coatsworth, Alice-All-By-Herself, p.87–97　*4–6

Foster, G., George Washington's World, p.127–30, 189–91, 262–64, 267–69　6

MARINE ANIMALS: *see also* Animals —Fresh-Water; Coral; Fishes; also names of animals, as Lobsters

Baker, A. O., Your Science World, p.7–25　6

Barnard, Macmillan Science-Life Series, Bk.6, p.275–83　6

Beaty, Baby Whale　4–6

Doane, Book of Nature, p.100–103　5–6

Fenton, C. L., Life Long Ago　6

Fisher, J., Wonderful World of the Sea　5–6

Hinton, Exploring under the Sea　5–6

Jacobson, First Book of Mythical Beasts, p.46–47, 60　4–6

Lane, F. C., All about the Sea　4–6

Life, World We Live In, p.98–113　5–6

Robertson, G., Strange Sea Life　5–6

Selsam, See through the Sea　4–6

MARINE CORPS: *see* United States— Marine Corps

MARINE PLANTS: *see also* Algae

Doane, Book of Nature, p.104–5　5–6

Reed, Sea for Sam, p.107–14　6

MARINER'S COMPASS: *see* Compass

MARIONETTES: *see* Puppet Shows

MARKETS—AZTEC

McNeer, Mexican Story, p.10–12　6

MARKETS—BRAZIL

May, Let's Read about Brazil, p.89–93　4–6

MARKETS—CHINA

Oakes, Bamboo Gate, p.60–81　*4–6

MARKETS—COSTA RICA

Clark, A. N., Magic Money, p.98–108　*4–6

MARKETS—GUATEMALA

Buff, Magic Maize, p.38–48　*4–6

MARKETS—INCA

Bleeker, Inca, p.30–34　5–6

MARKETS—MEXICO

Ritchie, B., Ramon Makes a Trade　*4–5

Tarshis, Village That Learned To Read, p.52–81　*4–6

MARKETS—PHILIPPINE ISLANDS

O'Neill, Picture Story of the Philippines　5–6

Wood, E., Pedro's Coconut Skates, p.37–51　*4–5

MARKETS—SWEDEN
Burglon, Children of the Soil, p.15–28
                                    *4–6

MARKETS—UNITED STATES
De Angeli, Henner's Lydia   *4–5
Sasek, This Is New York, p.24–27
                                    4–6

MARMOTS: *see* Prairie Dogs; Woodchucks

MARQUESAS ISLANDS
Quinn, Picture Map Geography of the
Pacific Islands, p.114–18   5–6

MARQUETTE, JACQUES: *see also* Jol-
liet, Louis
American Heritage, Discoverers of the
New World, p.136–37   5–6

MARS (planet)
Branley, Nine Planets, p.44–50   6
Gallant, R. A., Exploring Mars   4–6
———— Exploring the Planets, p.55–65
                                    5–6
Goodwin, Real Book about Stars, p.83–
90   4–6
Hendrickson, Handbook for Space Trav-
elers, p.173–78, 212–23   5–6
MacGregor, Miss Pickerell Goes to
Mars   *4–6
Schealer, This Way to the Stars, p.100–
113   6
Schneider, L., Space in Your Future,
p.81–86   6
Todd, Space Cat Meets Mars   *4–5

MARSH WRENS
Webb, Birds in Their Homes, p.53
                                    4–6

MARSHALL, JOHN, CHIEF JUSTICE
Olcott, Good Stories for Great Birthdays, p.425–49   4–6

MARSHALL ISLANDS
Quinn, Picture Map Geography of the
Pacific Islands, p.68–72   5–6

MARSUPIALS
Darling, L., Kangaroos   4–6

MARTENS
Hogner, Animal Book, p.128–30   6
Mason, G. F., Animal Tracks, p.38–39,
42–43   4–6
Ripper, Weasel Family, p.48–52   4–5
Stoutenberg, Wild Animals of the Far
West, p.21–23   4–6

MARTI, JOSÉ JULIAN
Goetz, Neighbors to the South, p.154–
55   5–6

MARTIN DE PORRES
Bishop, C. H., Martin de Porres, Hero
                                     6

MARYLAND
Anderson, C. W., High Courage   *4–6
Quinn, Picture Map Geography of the
United States, p.40–43   4–6

MASKS: *see also* Costume; Halloween
Hamilton, E. T., Handicraft for Girls,
p.104–15   6
Jaeger, Easy Crafts, p.80–85   4–6
Leeming, Fun with Paper, p.79–82
                                    4–5
Robinson, J., Things To Make from
Odds & Ends, p.9–11   4–6
Zarchy, Let's Make Something, p.74–
77, 94–95   5–6

MASONRY: *see* Bricks; Bridges; Cement; Concrete; Dams; Stonemasonry

MASSACHUSETTS: *see also* Boston;
Plymouth
Crowley, Pringle and the Lavender Goat
                                    *4–5
Quinn, Picture Map Geography of the
United States, p.12–15   4–6

MASSACHUSETTS BAY COLONY: *see*
Puritans

MATHEMATICS: *see also* Graphs; Num-
bers; Weights and Measures
Adler, Giant Golden Book of Math-
ematics   6
Bendick, How Much and How Many
                                    5–6
Freeman, M. B., Fun with Figures 6
Gardner, Mathematical Puzzles   6
Hogben, Wonderful World of Math-
ematics   6
Latham, Carry on, Mr. Bowditch   6
Leeming, Fun with Puzzles   6
Nourse, So You Want To Be a Scien-
tist, p.98–114   5–6
Schneider, L., Space in Your Future,
p.192–201   6

MATZELINGER, JAN E.
Shackelford, Child's Story of the Negro, p.163–67   4–5

MAURY, MATTHEW FONTAINE
Brindze, Story of the Trade Winds,
p.38–49   4–6

MAXIMILIAN, EMPEROR OF MEX-
ICO
McNeer, Mexican Story, p.51–55   6

MAY DAY
Burnett, B., First Book of Holidays,
p.23–24   4–5
Gates, Blue Willow, p.164–71   *5–6
Haywood, Betsy's Winterhouse, p.169–
92   *4–5
Jordan, Holiday Handicraft, p.110–15
4–6
McSpadden, Book of Holidays, p.70–76
6
Olcott, Good Stories for Great Holidays,
p.89–118   *4–6
Pannell, Holiday Round Up, p.153–
59   4–6
Sechrist, Red Letter Days, p.118–31
5–6

MAY DAY—MIDDLE AGES
Lownsbery, Boy Knight of Reims, p.73–
82   *6

MAYAS
Bleeker, Maya   5–6
Dorian, Hokahey!, p.33–35   5–6
Fletcher, S. E., American Indian, p.26–
38   5–6
Friedman, E., Digging into Yesterday,
p.20–35   5–6
Rhoads, Corn Grows Ripe   *4–6
Watson, Golden History of the World,
p.34–36   5–6

MAYAS—FOLK TALES
Harper, Ghosts and Goblins, p.105–11
4–6

MAYFLOWER (ship): *see also* Pilgrim
Fathers; Plymouth
Hall-Quest, How the Pilgrims Came to
Plymouth, p.51–75   4–6
Mitchell, Ships That Made U.S. History,
p.17–20   6

MEADOW LARKS
Comstock, Handbook of Nature Study,
p.80–82   6
Webb, Birds in Their Homes, p.20–22
4–6

MEADOWS
Doane, Book of Nature   5–6
Kane, Tale of a Meadow   4–6

MEASURES: *see* Weights and Measures

MEAT INDUSTRY: *see also* Cattle;
Ranch Life; Sheep
Buehr, Meat from Ranch to Table,
p.38–64   4–6
Eberle, Basketful, p.51–78   4–6
Lent, Men at Work in the Great Lakes
States, p.12–15, 74–77   4–6
Scheib, First Book of Food, p.24–28
5–6

MECHANICS: *see also* Engineering;
Force and Energy; Gases, Liquids,
Solids; Machines; Power Mechanics
Morgan, A. P., Boys' Book of Science
and Construction, p.93–150   6

MEDICINE: *see also* Antibiotics; Bac-
teria; Diseases; Doctors; Health;
Herbs; Nursing; Physiology
Bendick, How Much and How Many,
p.149–51   5–6
Calder, Wonderful World of Medicine
5–6
Dietz, All about Satellites and Space
Ships, p.90–97   5–6
Eberle, Modern Medical Discoveries
5–6
Fermi, Story of Atomic Energy, p.168–
72   6
Freeman, I. M., All about the Wonders
of Chemistry, p.81–91   6
Hyde, Plants Today and Tomorrow,
p.58–75   6
Judson, Soldier Doctor, p.70–129   6
Kavaler, Wonders of Algae, p.18–20,
69–70   6
Leonard, Exploring Science, p.233–48
6
Ludovici, World of the Microscope   6
McNeer, Armed with Courage, p.9–38,
71–82, 101–12   5–6
Selsam, Plants That Heal   6
Spencer, C., Made in China, p.85–93
5–6
Tappan, When Knights Were Bold,
p.316–22   6

MEDICINE MAN
Selsam, Plants That Heal   6

MEDIEVAL HISTORY: *see* Middle Ages

MEDITERRANEAN LANDS: *see also* names of countries, ancient and modern, bordering the Mediterranean Sea, as Italy; Phoenicia
Bragdon, L. J., Land and People of France, p.95–97   6
Joy, Young People of the Western Mediterranean   6
Smith, J. R., Neighbors around the World, p.143–50   4

MELANESIA: *see* Pacific Islands

MEMORIAL DAY
Brown, H. M., America Is My Country, p.193–95   5–6
Burnett, B., First Book of Holidays, p.27   4–5
McSpadden, Book of Holidays, p.92–96   6
Olcott, Good Stories for Great Holidays, p.137–56   4–6
Pannell, Holiday Round Up, p.182–94   4–6
Sechrist, Red Letter Days, p.142–47   5–6

MENDEL, GREGOR JOHANN
Asimov, Breakthroughs in Science, p. 107–10   5–6
Cottler, Heroes of Civilization, p.339–47   6

MENDELSSOHN-BARTHOLDY, FELIX
Burch, Famous Composers for Young People, p.71–78   4–6
Schwimmer, Great Musicians as Children, p.194–206   6
Wheeler, Robert Schumann and Mascot Ziff, p.75–78, 81, 102, 110   4–6

MENELAUS: *see also* Trojan War
Hazeltine, Hero Tales from Many Lands, p.13–25   5–6

MENNONITES IN THE UNITED STATES
Association for Childhood Education, Told under the Stars and Stripes, p.54–61   *4–6
De Angeli, Henner's Lydia   *4–5
———— Skippack School   *4–6
———— Yonie Wondernose   *4–5
Sorensen, Plain Girl   *4–6

MERCHANTS: *see* Business; Stores; Trade

MERCURY (metal)
Fenton, C. L., Riches from the Earth, p.95–98   5–6
Loomis, Field Book of Common Rocks and Minerals, p.90–92   6
Schneider, H., Everyday Machines and How They Work, p.147–49   5–6

MERCURY (myth)
Sellew, Adventures with the Gods, p.11–31   4–5

MERCURY (planet)
Branley, Nine Planets, p.22–28   6
Gallant, R. A., Exploring the Planets, p.24–31   5–6
Goodwin, Real Book about Stars, p.76–79   4–6
Hendrickson, Handbook for Space Travelers, p.200–204   5–6
Schealer, This Way to the Stars, p.89–93   6
Schneider, L., Space in Your Future, p.64–66   6

MERRY-GO-ROUND
Slobodkin, Adventures of Arab   *4–6

MESA VERDE NATIONAL PARK
Melbo, Our Country's National Parks, v.1, p.257–74   6

MESOPOTAMIA: *see* Iraq

MESSENGERS
French, Lance of Kanana   *6
Hewes, Boy of the Lost Crusade, p.196–229   *6

METALLURGY: *see also* Alloys; Metals; also names of metals, as Steel
Darrow, Boys' Own Book of Great Inventions, p.379–407   6

METALS: *see also* Minerals; Mining; also names of metals, as Copper; Gold
Adler, Fire in Your Life, p.75–90   4–6
Parker, B. M., Earth a Great Storehouse, p.24–33   4–6

METALWORK: *see also* Handicraft; Jewelry; Silversmithing; Steel; Tinware
Hamilton, E. T., Handicraft for Girls, p.188–236   6
Lent, Men at Work in New England, p.82–85   4–6
Zarchy, Let's Make a Lot of Things, p.15–31, 88–103   5–6

METCHNIKOFF, ELIE
Cottler, Heroes of Civilization, p.319–27 6

METEOROLOGY: *see* Weather Forecasting

METEORS
Asimov, Satellites in Outer Space, p.26–29 4–5
Baker, R. H., When the Stars Come Out, p.85–96 6
Branley, Exploring by Satellite, p.32–34 6
Comstock, Handbook of Nature Study, p.839–40 6
Enright, Then There Were Five, p.88–89 *5–6
Goodwin, Real Book about Stars, p.62, 70–75 4–6
Loomis, Field Book of Common Rocks and Minerals, p.262–66 6

METRIC SYSTEM
Bendick, How Much and How Many, p.160–67 5–6

MEXICANS IN THE UNITED STATES
Association for Childhood Education, Told under the Stars and Stripes, p.47–53, 83–90, 186–95 *4–6
Gates, Blue Willow *5–6

MEXICO: *see also* Costume—Mexico; Yucatan
Bannon, Hat for a Hero *4
———— Watchdog *4–5
Barrows, American Continents, p.288–301 5
Du Soe, Three without Fear *4–6
Epstein, S., First Book of Mexico 5–6
Galt, Volcano 5–6
Garthwaite, Mario *4–6
Goetz, Neighbors to the South, p.22–26 5–6
Jordan, Homemade Dolls in Foreign Dress, p.50–73 4–6
Parish, Our Lady of Guadalupe *4–6
Quinn, Picture Map Geography of Mexico, Central America and the West Indies, p.3–12 4–6
Ritchie, B., Ramon Makes a Trade *4–5
Rombauer, Cookbook for Boys and Girls, p.128–30 6

Sawyer, Year of the Christmas Dragon *4–5
Spencer, P. R., Traveling New Trails, p.233–76 6
Tarshis, Village That Learned To Read *4–6
Tripp, New Tuba *4–5

MEXICO—GAMES: *see* Games—Mexico

MEXICO—HISTORY: *see also* Alamo—Siege of the; Aztecs; California—History; Juárez, Benito Pablo; Mayas; also names of explorers, as Cortez, Hernando
American Heritage, Discoverers of the New World, p.70–77, 94–96 5–6
Foster, G., Abraham Lincoln's World, p.84–87, 194–99, 298–301 6
McNeer, Mexican Story 6

MEXICO—LANGUAGE
Epstein, S., First Book of Mexico, p.60–62 5–6

MIAMI WOODLAND INDIANS
Mason, M. E., Hominy and His Blunt-nosed Arrow *4–5

MICA
Fenton, C. L., Riches from the Earth, p.99–105 5–6
Loomis, Field Book of Common Rocks and Minerals, p.128–41 6

MICE
Barker, Winter-sleeping Wildlife, p.33–37 (jumping mouse) 5–6
Bianco, All about Pets, p.11–22 5–6
Comstock, Handbook of Nature Study, p.224–28 6
Earle, Mice at Home and Afield 4–5
Hogner, Animal Book, p.62–64, 67–70, 75–78, 208 6
Mason, G. F., Animal Homes, p.39–43 4–6
———— Animal Sounds, p.59–60 5–6
———— Animal Tracks, p.10–13, 20–21 4–6
Moe, Animal Inn, p.142–54 4–6
Sharp, Rescuers *4–6
Smith, I., Santa Claus Book, p.136–44 *4–5
Stolz, Belling the Tiger *4–5
Titus, Basil of Baker Street *4–5

Weeks, Tales of a Common Pigeon, p.35–42   *4–6

MICHELANGELO
Angelo, Nino, p.209–12   *6
Chandler, Story-Lives of Master Artists, p.54–66   6
Hillyer, Child's History of Art, p.52–56, 225–27   5–6

MICHIGAN
De Angeli, Copper-toed Boots   *4–6
Frazier, Secret Friend   *4–6
———— Somebody Special   *4–6
Havighurst, Life in America: The Midwest, p.116–23   5–6
Lent, Men at Work in the Great Lakes States, p.42–49, 70–73, 88–99   4–6
Quinn, Picture Map Geography of the United States, p.96–99   4–6

MICROBES
Lewis, L. Z., First Book of Microbes   5–6
Ludovici, World of the Microscope   6
Schatz, Story of Microbes   6
Selsam, Microbes at Work   5–6

MICRONESIA: *see* Pacific Islands

MICROPHONE
Yates, R. F., Boy and a Battery, p.81–88   5–6

MICROPHOTOGRAPHY
Yates, R. F., Fun with Your Microscope, p.94–118   6

MICROSCOPES
Beeler, Experiments in Science, p.133–38   5–6
Disraeli, New Worlds through the Microscope   6
Ludovici, World of the Microscope   6
Parker, B. M., Scientist and His Tools, p.22–24   5–6
Yates, R. F., Fun with Your Microscope   6
Zarchy, Let's Make Something, p.54–55   5–6

MIDAS, KING
Benson, Stories of the Gods and Heroes, p.65–70   5–6

MIDDLE AGES: *see also* Arthur, King; Castles; Chivalry; Costume—Middle Ages; Crusades; Fairs—Middle Ages; Feudal System; Guilds; Hanseatic League; Knights; Legends; Renaissance; also names of persons, as Charlemagne, Emperor of the West; Polo, Marco; Robin Hood
Boardman, Castles   6
Cooke, D. E., Men of Sherwood   *5–6
Duvoisin, They Put Out to Sea, p.53–61   4–6
Hartman, Builders of the Old World, p.207–325   6
Hillyer, Child's History of the World, p.231–35   5–6
Jewett, God's Troubadour   5–6
Lamprey, All the Ways of Building, p.151–63   6
Lownsbery, Boy Knight of Reims   *6
McGuire, Glimpses into the Long Ago, p.279–303   5–6
Street, Land of the English People, p.74–81   6
Tappan, When Knights Were Bold,   6
Watson, Golden History of the World, p.90–94   5–6

MIDDLE ATLANTIC STATES: *see* Atlantic States; also names of states, as New Jersey

MIDDLE EAST
Caldwell, Let's Visit Indonesia, p.27–29   4–6
Gidal, Sons of the Desert   5–6
Nevil, Picture Story of the Middle East   4–6

MIDDLE WEST: *see* North Central States

MIDSUMMER EVE
Seymour, Erik's Christmas Camera, p.43–67   *4–6

MIGRANT LABOR
Association for Childhood Education, Told under Spacious Skies, p.83–90, 122–35   *4–6
———— Told under the Stars and Stripes, p.200–216, 302–12   *4–6
Garthwaite, Mario   *4–6
Gates, Blue Willow   *5–6
Lenski, Judy's Journey   *4–6
Simon, Robin on the Mountain   *4–6
Waltrip, White Harvest   *4–6

MIGRATION: *see* Animals—Migration; Birds—Migration; Herding; Immigra-

tion and Emigration; Nomads; Prehistoric Man; Salmon

MILK: *see also* Butter; Cheese; Cows; Dairying; Nutrition

Beeler, Experiments in Chemistry, p.48–53   5–6

Eberle, Basketful, p.181–94   4–6

Morgan, A. P., First Chemistry Book for Boys and Girls, p.98–102   5–6

Scheib, First Book of Food, p.15–21   5–6

MILK—PASTEURIZATION

Elting, Lollypop Factory and Lots of Others, p.31–32   4–5

MILKY WAY

Baker, R. H., Introducing the Constellations, p.88–103   6

———— When the Stars Come Out, p.41–45, 152–58, 177   6

Branley, Guide to Outer Space, p.28–29   4–6

Dietz, All about Satellites and Space Ships, p.154–59   5–6

Freeman, M. B., Fun with Astronomy, p.50–51   4–6

Schneider, L., Space in Your Future, p.111–14   6

MILLERS: *see* Flour Mills

MILLET, JEAN FRANÇOIS

Chandler, Story-Lives of Master Artists, p.199–211   6

Hillyer, Child's History of Art, p.124–26   5–6

MINERALS: *see also* Crystals; Geology; Metals; Mining; Rocks; also names of minerals, as Coal; Salt

Buehr, Underground Riches, p.11–20   5–6

Comstock, Handbook of Nature Study, p.743–59   6

Cormack, First Book of Stones   4–6

Evans, Adventure Book of Rocks   4–6

Loomis, Field Book of Common Rocks and Minerals   6

May, Let's Read about Brazil, p.64–69   4–6

Schneider, H., Rocks, Rivers & the Changing Earth, p.49–59   4–6

Williams, H. L., Stories in Rocks   6

Wyckoff, Story of Geology, p.144–51   5–6

MINING: *see also* Aluminum; Asbestos; Coal; Copper; Diamonds; Geology; Gold; Iron; Lead; Metals; Minerals; Nickel; Petroleum; Salt; Silver; Tin

Association for Childhood Education, Told under the Stars and Stripes, p.282–94   *4–6

Banning, Pit Pony   *4–6

Bleeker, Inca, p.99–100, 138–40   5–6

Buehr, Underground Riches   5–6

Dawson, California, p.146–52   5–6

Hader, Spunky, p.20–28   *4–6

Hartman, Machines, p.24–34   6

McCracken, Sentinel of the Snow Peaks   5–6

Macdonald, G., Princess and Curdie   *4–6

———— Princess and the Goblin   *4–6

Pohlmann, Myrtle Albertina's Secret   *4–6

Smith, J. R., Neighbors around the World, p.74–76   4

Writers Project, Aluminum, no.31, p.23–24   5–6

———— Story of Coal, no.35, p.20–42   5–6

MINKS

Mason, G. F., Animal Tracks, p.44–45   4–6

Ripper, Weasel Family, p.30–38   4–5

Stoutenberg, Wild Animals of the Far West, p.27–28   4–6

MINNESOTA

Association for Childhood Education, Told under the Stars and Stripes, p.150–58   *4–6

Bailey, B. F., Picture Book of Minnesota   4–6

Brock, Drusilla, p.49–120   *4–5

———— Topsy-Turvy Family   *4–5

Havighurst, Life in America: The Midwest, p.136–40   5–6

Lent, Men at Work in the Great Lakes States, p.16–19, 26–29, 34–37, 114–17   4–6

Mason, M. E., Middle Sister   *4–5

Quinn, Picture Map Geography of the United States, p.104–7   4–6

Stong, Honk, the Moose   *4–5

Wilder, On the Banks of Plum Creek   *4–6

MINORITIES: *see* Brotherhood of Man

MINSTREL SHOWS: *see* Foster, Stephen Collins

MINSTRELS: *see also* Bards; Troubadours
Jewett, God's Troubadour   5–6
Smith, E. S., Christmas Book of Legends & Stories, p.311–20   *5–6

MIRACLE PLAYS
Tappan, When Knights Were Bold, p.238–44   6

MIRAGE
Ruchlis, Wonder of Light, p.61–66   6

MIRANDA, FRANCISCO DE
Olcott, Good Stories for Great Birthdays, p.325–46   4–6

MIRRORS: *see also* Periscopes
Beeler, Experiments in Science, p.46–47   5–6
Epstein, S., First Book of Glass, p.44–46   5–6
Ruchlis, Wonder of Light, p.33–50   6

MISSILES
Bergaust, Rockets and Missiles   5–6
Coombs, Gateway to Space   6
———— Rockets, Missiles and Moons, p.104–84   6
Zaffo, Big Book of Real Airplanes   4–5
Zarem, New Dimensions of Flight, p.67–137   6

MISSION INDIANS
Bleeker, Mission Indians of California   4–6

MISSIONARIES: *see also* Marquette, Jacques; Patrick, Saint; Spanish Missions in California
Tappan, When Knights Were Bold, p.193–205   6

MISSISSIPPI
Banta, Life in America: The South, p.127–31   5–6
Burchard, Jed   *5–6
Quinn, Picture Map Geography of the United States, p.72–75   4–6

MISSISSIPPI RIVER: *see also* De Soto, Hernando; La Salle, René Robert Cavelier, Sieur de; Marquette, Jacques; New Orleans

American Heritage, Discoverers of the New World, p.134–43   5–6
Calhoun, Making the Mississippi Shout   *4–6
Dupuy, First Book of Civil War Naval Actions, p.23–38, 56–66   6
Graham, A. P., La Salle   4–6
Holling, Minn of the Mississippi   5–6
Le Grand, Augustus and the River   *4–6
Proudfit, River-Boy, p.107–39   6
Shapiro, Steamboat Bill and the Captain's Top Hat   *5–6
Syme, De Soto   4–5
Writers Project, Trip on Many Waters, no.6, p.15–48   5–6

MISSOURI
Havighurst, Life in America; The Midwest, p.110–15   5–6
Quinn, Picture Map Geography of the United States, p.124–27   4–6
Robertson, K., Ticktock and Jim   *4–6

MOCKINGBIRDS
Comstock, Handbook of Nature Study, p.91–94   6
Webb, Birds in Their Homes, p.19   4–6

MODELS: *see also* Airplanes—Models; Railroads—Models; Ships—Models; Toys
Brown, V., How To Make a Home Nature Museum, p.104–49   5–6
Jordan, Holiday Handicraft, p.40–46, 140–52, 177–80, 188–99   4–6
Leeming, Fun with Clay, p.45–51   4–6
———— Fun with Paper   4–5
Maginley, Historic Models of Early America   6
Morgan, A. P., Boys' Book of Engines, Motors & Turbines, p.172–260   6
Schneider, H., Science Fun with Milk Cartons   5–6

MODERN HISTORY: *see* History; also names of countries, subhead History, as England—History

MOHAMMED
Caldwell, Let's Visit Pakistan, p.36–37   4–6
Ellis, Arabs, p.34–44, 51–52   6
Watson, Golden History of the World, p.76–78   5–6

MOHAMMEDANISM: *see* Islam

MOLDS: *see also* Penicillin
Lewis, L. Z., First Book of Microbes, p.34–37   5–6
Parker, B. M., Dependent Plants, p.18–21   5–6

MOLECULES: *see also* Chemistry
Beeler, More Experiments in Science, p.139–42   5–6
Bischof, Atoms at Work   5–6
Crouse, W. H., Understanding Science, p.29–31   6
Freeman, I. M., All about the Wonders of Chemistry, p.23–32   6
Huey, What Makes the Wheels Go Round, p.101–9   6
Meyer, Picture Book of Molecules and Atoms, p.8–18   5–6

MOLES (animals)
Fox, From Bones to Bodies, p.56–57   6
Hogner, Animal Book, p.16–21   6
Mason, G. F., Animal Homes, p.34–38   4–6
Parker, B. M., Animals We Know, p.10   5–6
Ripper, Moles and Shrews, p.3–38   4–6

MOLLUSKS: *see* Shellfish

MOLOKAI ISLAND
McNeer, Armed with Courage, p.25–38   5–6
Proudfit, Treasure Hunter, p.180–82   6

MONASTERIES: *see also* St. Bernard Pass
Buchanan, How Man Made Music, p.75–77   6
Buehr, Knights and Castles and Feudal Life, p.13–16   4–6
Hartman, Builders of the Old World, p.262–69   6
Hillyer, Child's History of the World, p.236–41   5–6
Tappan, When Knights Were Bold, p.154–74   6
Wheeler, Sebastian Bach, p.33–56   4–6

MONEY: *see also* Business; Gold; Silver; Wampum
Batchelor, Superstitious? Here's Why!, p.52–55   6
Bendick, How Much and How Many, p.53–65   5–6
Buehr, Treasure   4–6

Evans, Adventure Book of Money   5–6
Foster, G., George Washington's World, p.231–33   6
Hillyer, Child's History of the World, p.105   5–6
Weir, R. C., Benjamin Franklin, p.9–17   4–6
Writers Project, Money, no.11   5–6

MONEY—ACQUISITION AND USE
Ackley, Dolls To Make for Fun and Profit   5–6
Clark, A. N., Magic Money   *4–6
Cleary, Henry and Beezus, p.39–74   *4–5
Crawford, "Hello, the Boat!," p.165   *6
Hunt, M. L., Cupola House   *4–6
Langton, Majesty of Grace, p.105–20   *4–5
Lattimore, Junior   *4–5
Lenski, Boom Town Boy   *4–6
Snow, Doll for Lily Belle   *4–5
Tarry, My Dog Rinty   *4–5
Wilson, H. H., Jerry's Charge Account   *4–6
Zim, Homing Pigeons   5–6
———— Rabbits   4–5

MONGOLIA
Barrows, Old World Lands, p.244–46   6
Buehr, World of Marco Polo, p.17–25   5–8
Quinn, Picture Map Geography of Asia, p.103–6   4–6
Watson, Golden History of the World, p.95–96   5–6

MONGOOSES
Kipling, Jungle Book, p.187–219   *5–6

MONKEYS: *see also* Baboons
Blough, Monkey with a Notion   *4–6
Bridges, Zoo Pets, p.9–21   4–6
Burt, Space Monkey   4–6
Fox, From Bones to Bodies, p.63–64   6
Kipling, Jungle Book, p.49–104   *5–6
Lattimore, Monkey of Crofton   *4–5
Otis, Toby Tyler   *4–6
Parker, B. M., Animals We Know, p.12–13   5–6
Perkins, Marlin Perkins' Zooparade, p.55–57   4–6

Rombauer, Cookbook for Boys and Girls, p.41   *6

Stinetorf, Children of South Africa, p.50–66   *5–6

Zim, Monkeys   4–5

MONROE, JAMES

Beard, Presidents in American History, p.25–26, 155–56   6

Coy, First Book of Presidents, p.30   4–6

Lawson, R., Watchwords of Liberty, p.39–40   4–6

Petersham, Story of the Presidents of the United States, p.19–20   4–6

MONROE DOCTRINE

Hays, Freedom, p.27–28   5–6

MONTANA: *see also* Glacier National Park

Call, Peter's Moose   *4–6

Quinn, Picture Map Geography of the United States, p.168–71 ·   4–6

MONTEZUMA II, EMPEROR OF MEXICO: *see also* Aztecs; Cortez, Hernando

American Heritage, Discoverers of the New World, p.73–77   5–6

McNeer, Mexican Story, p.14–16   6

MONUMENTS: *see* Archeology; Pyramids; Tombs

MOON: *see also* Astronomy; Eclipses; Tides

Baker, R. H., When the Stars Come Out, p.60–72   6

Beatty, Matthew Looney's Voyage to the Earth   *4–6

Beauchamp, Discovering Our World, Bk.1, p.124–29   4

Branley, Exploring by Satellite, p.2–5   6

——— Guide to Outer Space, p.8–10   4–6

——— Moon   6

Chrisman, Shen of the Sea, p.144–58   *5–6

Comstock, Handbook of Nature Study, p.855–59   6

Freeman, M. B., Fun with Astronomy, p.12–22   4–6

Gallant, R. A., Exploring the Moon   4–6

——— Exploring the Planets, p.51–54   5–6

Goodwin, Real Book about Stars, p.39, 49–66   4–6

Hendrickson, Handbook for Space Travelers   5–6

Land, B., Quest of Isaac Newton, p.13–24   6

Leonard, Exploring Science, p.107–16   6

Meyer, Picture Book of Astronomy, p.13–18   4–5

Schealer, This Way to the Stars, p.64–80   6

Schneider, L., Space in Your Future, p.77–80   6

Spencer, P. R., Finding New Trails, p.317–20   4

Thurber, Many Moons   *4–5

MOORS: *see also* Arabs; Islam; Morocco; Spain—Folk Tales

Hartman, Builders of the Old World, p.211–16   6

MOOSE

Bronson, Horns and Antlers, p.99–112   5–6

Call, Peter's Moose   *4–6

Mason, G. F., Animal Sounds, p.76–81   5–6

——— Animal Tracks, p.70–71   4–6

Perkins, Marlin Perkins' Zooparade, p.62–65   4–6

Stong, Honk, the Moose   *4–5

MORMONS

Burt, Cave of the Shouting Silence   *5–6

MOROCCO

Henry, M., King of the Wind, p.19–67   *5–6

Joy, Young People of the Western Mediterranean, p.90–106   6

Stinetorf, Children of North Africa, p.111–28, 144–61   *5–6

MORSE, SAMUEL FINLEY BREESE: *see also* Telegraph

Cottler, Heroes of Civilization, p.201–10   6

Hartman, Machines, p.138–47   6

Lawson, R., Watchwords of Liberty, p.81–82   4–6

MORSE CODE
Epstein, S., First Book of Codes and
Ciphers, p.29–30   4–6

MOSCOW
Nazaroff, Land of the Russian People,
p.25–34   6

MOSES
Bowie, Bible Stories for Boys and Girls:
Old Testament, p.47–66   4–6
De la Mare, Stories from the Bible,
p.133–227   5–6
Petersham, Moses   4–5

MOSLEMS: *see* Islam; Mohammed

MOSQUITOES: *see also* Malaria
Comstock, Handbook of Nature Study,
p.411–15   6
Lane, F. C., All about the Insect World,
p.113–19   5–6
Mason, G. F., Animal Tools, p.44–48
5–6
Oakes, Bamboo Gate, p.30–39   *4–6
Parker, B. M., Insects and Their Ways,
p.12–13   4–6

MOSSES
Comstock, Handbook of Nature Study,
p.709–14   6
Disraeli, New Worlds through the Mi-
croscope, p.111–12   6
Hylander, Out of Doors in Spring,
p.84–91   5–6
Morgan, A. H., Field Book of Ponds
and Streams, p.58–66   6
Sterling, Story of Mosses, Ferns, and
Mushrooms, p.25–40   5–6

MOTHER'S DAY
Burnett, B., First Book of Holidays,
p.25–26   4–5
Friedman, F., Dot for Short, p.70–90
*4–5
Jordan, Holiday Handicraft, p.116–25
4–6
Leeming, Fun with Greeting Cards,
p.89–90   4–6
McSpadden, Book of Holidays, p.86–89
6
Olcott, Good Stories for Great Holidays,
p.121–33   4–6
Pannell, Holiday Round Up, p.160–69
4–6
Sechrist, Red Letter Days, p.132–37
5–6

MOTHS: *see also* Butterflies; Caterpillars;
Silkworms
Barker, Winter-sleeping Wildlife, p.107–
10   5–6
Buck, M. W., In Yards and Gardens,
p.52–53   4–6
Comstock, Handbook of Nature Study,
p.310–29   6
Gall, Little Black Ant, p.90–94
4–5
Gaul, Picture Book of Insects, p.28–29
4–6
Hussey, Collecting Cocoons   4–6
Hyde, Animal Clocks and Compasses,
p.83–84   5–6
Hylander, Insects on Parade, p.127–49
6
Lane, F. C., All about the Insect World,
p.23–30   5–6
Lemmon, All about Moths and Butter-
flies   5–6
Lutz, Field Book of Insects, p.114–223
4–6
Parker, B. M., Insects and Their Ways,
p.4–6   4–6
Teale, Insect Friends, p.53–58   5–6
Williamson, First Book of Bugs, p.34–
38   4–5

MOTION: *see also* Sound
Freeman, M. B., Fun with Science,
p.11–18   6
Land, B., Quest of Isaac Newton, p.29–
31, 36–37   6

MOTION PICTURES
Armer, Waterless Mountain, p.144–47
*5–6
Beeler, Experiments in Science, p.36–37
5–6
Crouse, W. H., Understanding Science,
p.129–38   6
Darrow, Boys' Own Book of Great In-
ventions, p.339–53   6
Dawson, California, p.199–200   5–6
Hogben, Wonderful World of Commu-
nication, p.40–47   6
Writers Project, Motion Pictures, no.25
5–6
Zim, Our Senses and How They Work,
p.50–57   4–6

MOTOR CARS: *see* Automobiles

MOTORBOATS
Gilmore, Model Boats for Beginners, p.44–47   5–6
Lent, Men at Work in the Great Lakes States, p.84–87   4–6

MOTORS: *see* Electric Motors; Gas and Oil Engines; Machines; Water Wheels

MOUND BUILDERS
Dorian, Hokahey!, p.32–35   5–6
Fletcher, S. E., American Indian, p.57–63   5–6
Holling, Minn of the Mississippi, p.46–47   5–6
Scheele, Mound Builders   4–6

MOUNT McKINLEY NATIONAL PARK
Lindquist, W., Alaska, p.79–81   5–6
Melbo, Our Country's National Parks, v.2, p.157–78   6

MOUNT RAINIER NATIONAL PARK
Melbo, Our Country's National Parks, v.2, 215–33   6

MOUNT VERNON
Foster, G., George Washington's World, p.246–50   6

MOUNTAIN LAUREL
Comstock, Handbook of Nature Study, p.689–92   6

MOUNTAIN LIFE—INDIA
Rankin, L., Daughter of the Mountains
                                       *5–6

MOUNTAIN LIFE—SOUTH
Carroll, Tough Enough's Indians
                                       *4–5
Child Study Association of America, Read to Yourself Storybook, p.10–24
                                       *4–5
Credle, Johnny and His Mule   *4–5
Justus, Surprise for Peter Pocket
                                       *4–6
Lansing, E. C. H., Liza of the Hundredfold   *5–6
Lenski, Blue Ridge Billy   *5–6
Simon, Robin on the Mountain   *4–6
Snow, Come, Chucky, Come   *4–6
———— Doll for Lily Belle   *4–5
Stuart, Beatinest Boy   *4–6

MOUNTAIN LIONS: *see* Panthers

MOUNTAIN SHEEP: *see* Bighorns; Sheep

MOUNTAINS: *see also* Alaska; Geology; Peru; Switzerland; Volcanoes; also names of mountains, as Alps
Association for Childhood Education, Told under the Stars and Stripes, p.295–314   *4–6
Bragdon, L. J., Land and People of Switzerland, p.18–29   6
Disney, Worlds of Nature, p.44–69
                                       4–6
Fenton, C. L., Land We Live On, p.28–31   4–6
Leonard, Exploring Science, p.41–55   6
Life, World We Live In, p.40–45 5–6
Melbo, Our Country's National Parks, v.1, v.2   6
Reed, Earth for Sam   6
Wyckoff, Story of Geology, p.125–31
                                       5–6

MOURNING DOVES
Webb, Birds in Their Homes, p.18   4–6

MOUSE DEER
Buck, F., Jungle Animals, p.41   5–6

MOVING PICTURES: *see* Motion Pictures

MOZAMBIQUE
Stinetorf, Children of South Africa, p.95–106   *5–6

MOZART, WOLFGANG AMADEUS
Burch, Famous Composers for Young People, p.43–52   4–6
Komroff, Mozart   6
Schwimmer, Great Musicians as Children, p.20–27   6
Wheeler, Mozart   4–6

MULES
Carlson, N. S., Song of the Lop-eared Mule   *4–5
Credle, Johnny and His Mule   *4–5
Henry M., Album of Horses, p.102–5
                                       5–6
Hogner, Horse Family, p.27–29   4–6

MUMMERS
Milhous, Patrick and the Golden Slippers   *4–5

MURILLO
Hillyer, Child's History of Art, p.97–98
                                       5–6

MUSCLES
Beauchamp, Discovering Our World, Bk.1, p.73–75   4
Glemser, All about the Human Body, p.93–99   5–6
Ravielli, Wonders of the Human Body, p.58–81   5–6
Zim, Our Senses and How They Work, p.109–12   4–6

MUSEUMS: *see also* American Museum of Natural History, New York; Art Museums; Collecting; Indians of North America—Museums; Insects—Collecting; Trailside Museum of Natural History, Thatcher Woods
Bendick, Good Knight Ghost   *4–6
Brown, V., How To Make a Home Nature Museum   5–6
Robinson, W. W., Beasts of the Tar Pits, p.3–4, 45–49   5–6

MUSHROOMS: *see also* Fungi
Beeler, More Experiments in Science, p.56–59   5–6
Parker, B. M., Dependent Plants, p.5–17   5–6
Sterling, Story of Mosses, Ferns, and Mushrooms, p.56–96   5–6

MUSIC: *see also* American Ballads and Songs; Bards; Bells; Folk Songs; Indians of North America—Music; Minstrels; Musical Instruments; Musicians; National Songs; Negroes—Songs; Operas; Orchestras; Songs
Adler, Time in Your Life, p.117–20   4–6
Alden, Why the Chimes Rang, p.80–91   *4–6
Association for Childhood Education, Told under the Stars and Stripes, p.270–81   *4–6
Bailey, C. S., Pioneer Art in America, p.90–102   *5–6
Bishop, C. H., Blue Spring Farm   *5–6
Bulla, Stories of Favorite Operas   5–6
Chappell, Nutcracker   4–5
Enright, Four-Story Mistake, p.123–32   *5–6
Estes, Middle Moffat, p.27–59   *4–6
Faulkner, Melindy's Medal   *4–5
Goss, Beethoven   6
Hughes, First Book of Rhythms, p.29–33   4–6

Irving, Sound and Ultrasonics, p.64–74   6
Justus, Fiddlers' Fair   *4–5
Kettelkamp, Singing Strings   5–6
Komroff, Mozart   6
Lenski, Blue Ridge Billy   *5–6
McNeer, Story of the Southern Highlands   4–6
Norman, First Book of Music   4–6
Sawyer, Long Christmas, p.35–43   *4–6
Skolsky, Music Box Book   *4–6

MUSIC—AFRICA
Shackelford, Child's Story of the Negro, p.32–35, 103–6   5–6

MUSIC—BOHEMIA: *see* Dvořák, Anton

MUSIC—CANADA: *see* Songs—Canada

MUSIC—CHINA
Spencer, C., Made in China, p.35–43   5–6

MUSIC—ENGLAND: *see* Songs—England; also names of English musicians, as Elgar, Edward William; Smyth, Ethel Mary; Vaughan-Williams, Ralph

MUSIC—FINLAND: *see* Sibelius, Jean

MUSIC—FRANCE: *see* names of French musicians, as Debussy, Achille Claude; Gounod, Charles François; Ravel, Maurice

MUSIC—GERMANY: *see* Songs—Germany; also names of German musicians, as Bach, Johann Sebastian; Beethoven, Ludwig van; Brahms, Johannes

MUSIC—HISTORY
Buchanan, How Man Made Music   6
Hillyer, Child's History of the World, p.435–42   5–6
Wheeler, Edward MacDowell and His Cabin in the Pines   4–6
——— Mozart   4–6
——— Paganini   4–6

MUSIC—HUNGARY: *see* Bartók, Béla; Hubay, Jeno; Liszt, Franz; Zichy, Geza

MUSIC—INDONESIA
Smith, D. C., Land and People of Indonesia, p.96–101   6

MUSIC—ITALY: *see* names of Italian musicians, as Palestrina, Giovanni Pierluigi da; Respighi, Ottorino; Stradivari, Antonio; Verdi, Giuseppe

MUSIC—MIDDLE AGES: *see* Minstrels; Troubadours

MUSIC—NORWAY: *see* Bull, Ole Bornemann; Grieg, Edvard Hagerup

MUSIC—PIONEER LIFE: *see* Songs—Pioneer Life

MUSIC—POLAND: *see also* names of Polish musicians, as Chopin, Frederic François
  Kelly, Land of the Polish People, p.18–28   5–6

MUSIC—PRIMITIVE MAN
  Buchanan, How Man Made Music, p.13–17, 74   6

MUSIC—SWEDEN: *see* Lind, Jenny; Songs—Sweden

MUSIC—UNITED STATES: *see also* American Ballads and Songs; National Songs; also names of individual musicians, as Carpenter, John Alden; Foster, Stephen Collins; Gershwin, George
  Buchanan, How Man Made Music, p.180–95   6
  Lyons, Stories of Our American Patriotic Songs   5–6

MUSIC AND ANIMALS
  Mukerji, Kari, the Elephant, p.91–95   *4–6

MUSIC AND LITERATURE: *see also* Orpheus
  Prokofieff, Peter and the Wolf   4–6
  Wheeler, Franz Schubert and His Merry Friends   4–6

MUSICAL INSTRUMENTS: *see also* Indians of North America—Music; Orchestras; also names of musical instruments, as Drums
  Baer, Sound   4–6
  Balet, What Makes an Orchestra   5–6
  Geralton, Story of Sound, p.59–67   5–6
  Huntington, Tune Up   4–6
  Jaeger, Easy Crafts, p.90–91   4–6
  Kettelkamp, Drums, Rattles, and Bells
                                         4–6

Knight, D. C., First Book of Sound, p.44–45   5–6
Lacey, Picture Book of Musical Instruments   5–6
Lent, Men at Work in the Great Lakes States, p.62–65   4–6
Parker, B. M., Sound, p.18–21   5–6
Schneider, H., Everyday Machines and How They Work, p.96–120   5–6
Tappan, When Knights Were Bold, p.358–59   6

MUSICAL INTERVALS AND SCALES
  Buchanan, How Man Made Music, p.72–75, 79–86   6

MUSICAL TERMS
  Buchanan, How Man Made Music, p.218–21   6

MUSICIANS: *see also* names of musicians, as Wagner, Richard
  Burch, Famous Composers for Young People   4–6
  ———— Modern Composers for Young People   5–6
  Schwimmer, Great Musicians as Children   6

MUSK OXEN: *see also* Nunivak Island
  Disney, Worlds of Nature, p.15–19
                                         4–6

MUSKRATS
  Comstock, Handbook of Nature Study, p.219–23   6
  Gall, Flat Tail, p.40–45   *4–6
  ———— Ringtail, p.56–57, 64–79
                                       *4–5
  Hogner, Animal Book, p.70–72   6
  Mason, G. F., Animal Homes, p.59–61
                                         4–6
  ———— Animal Tracks, p.34–35
                                         4–6
  Rounds, Lone Muskrat   5–6

MUSORGSKI, MODEST PETROVICH
  Burch, Modern Composers for Young People, p.3–13   5–6

MUSSELS: *see* Shellfish

MYCENAE: *see also* Greece—Ancient
  Hall, J., Buried Cities, p.159–99   5–6

MYSTERY STORIES
  Anckarsvard, Rider by Night   5–6
  ———— Robber Ghost   5–6
  Bothwell, Thirteenth Stone   5–6

Cheney, Rocking Chair Buck 4–5
Colver, Secret Castle 4–5
Du Bois, Great Geppy 4–5
———— Three Policemen 4–6
Durell, Holly River Secret 4–6
Fenton, E., Phantom of Walkaway Hill 4–6
Gage, Secret of Fiery Gorge 4–6
Judson, Lost Violin 5–6
Kastner, Emil and the Detectives 4–6
Kingman, Village Band Mystery 4–5
Ladd, Janie 4–5
Larom, Mountain Pony 6
———— Mountain Pony and the Pinto Colt 5–6
Lawrence, Sand in Her Shoes 4–6
Pohlmann, Myrtle Albertina's Secret 4–6
Schealer, Sycamore Warrior 6
Titus, Basil of Baker Street 4–5
Uchida, Mik and the Prowler 4–6
Urmston, Seven and Sam 4–6
Whitney, Mystery of the Haunted Pool 5–6

MYTHS—GREECE AND ROME: *see also* Constellations; Planets; also names of mythical characters, as Argonauts; Daedalus and Icarus; Hercules; Pegasus; Perseus; Prometheus; Theseus
Benson, Stories of the Gods and Heroes 5–6
Hillyer, Child's History of the World, p.56–63 5–6
Jacobson, First Book of Mythical Beasts 4–6
Kingsley, Heroes 6
Reed, Patterns in the Sky 5–6
Sellew, Adventures with the Gods 4–5
Tappan, Story of the Greek People, p.1–23 5–6

MYTHS—INCA
Bleeker, Inca, p.93–94, 149–50 5–6

MYTHS—NORTHMEN
Brown, A. F., In the Days of Giants 4–6
Colum, Children of Odin 4–5
Keary, Heroes of Asgard 5–6
Rothery, Scandinavian Roundabout, p. 97–110 6
Sellew, Adventures with the Giants 4–6

NAMES: *see also* Indians of North America—Names
Evans, People Are Important, p.23–34 4–5
Lambert, Our Names 6
Pei, All about Language, p.62–71 6

NANSEN, FRIDTJOF
Rothery, Scandinavian Roundabout, p. 73–75, 84 6

NAPOLEON I, EMPEROR OF THE FRENCH
Bragdon, L. J., Land and People of France, p.58–63 6
Foster, G., Abraham Lincoln's World, p.5–10, 36–38, 45–48, 56–60 6
———— George Washington's World, p.221, 330–37 6
Hillyer, Child's History of the World, p.428–34 5–6

NAPOLEON III, EMPEROR OF THE FRENCH
Foster, G., Abraham Lincon's World, p.220–24 6

NARCOTICS
Gatti, Saranga, the Pygmy 5–6

NASTURTIUMS
Comstock, Handbook of Nature Study, p.566–68 6

NATIONAL PARKS: *see also* names of national parks, as Yellowstone National Park
Colby, Park Ranger 5–6
Melbo, Our Country's National Parks, v.1, v.2 6

NATIONAL SONGS: *see also* Folk Songs; Key, Francis Scott; Songs
Brown, H. M., America Is My Country, p.174–85 5–6
Browne, Story of Our National Ballads 5–6
Hays, Freedom 5–6
Lyons, Stories of Our American Patriotic Songs 5–6

NATURAL GAS
Fenton, C. L., Riches from the Earth, p.113–18 5–6
Parker, B. M., Earth a Great Storehouse, p.23–24 4–6
Writers Project, Oil and Gas, no.36, p.44–47 5–6

NATURAL RESOURCES: *see also* Conservation; Fisheries; Forestry; Minerals; Mining; National Parks; Water Power; Water Supply

Bronson, Freedom and Plenty 4–6
Fenton, C. L., Land We Live On 4–6
Land, M., Jungle Oil 5–6
Street, Land of the English People, p.60–67 6

NATURALISTS: *see* Scientists; also names of naturalists, as Audubon, John James

NATURE STUDY: *see also* Animals; Aquariums; Birdhouses; Birds; Botany; Flowers; Fossils; Gardening; Geology; Insects; Microscopes; Minerals; Ocean; Plants; Reptiles; Science; Seashore; Soils; Trees; Water; Zoology

Blough, After the Sun Goes Down 4–5
———— Not Only for Ducks *4–5
———— Tree on the Road to Turntown *4–5
———— Wait for the Sunshine 4–5
Buck, M. W., In Ponds and Streams 4–6
———— In Woods and Fields 4–5
———— In Yards and Gardens 4–6
Comstock, Handbook of Nature Study 6
De Angeli, Bright April *4–6
Gaul, Pond Book 4–6
George, J., Hole in the Tree 4–5
Goetz, Deserts 4–6
Hudson, Little Boy Lost *5–6
Huntington, Let's Go to the Desert 4–5
Hylander, Out of Doors in Autumn 5–6
———— Out of Doors in Spring 5–6
Tappan, When Knights Were Bold, p.329–33 6

NAVAHO INDIANS

Armer, Waterless Mountain *5–6
Association for Childhood Education, Told under Spacious Skies, p.287–94 *4–6
———— Told under the Stars and Stripes, p.295–314 *4–6
Bleeker, Navajo 4–6
Brewster, First Book of Indians, p.63–65 4–5

Buff, Dancing Cloud 4–5
Bulla, Eagle Feather *4–5
Clark, A. N., Little Navajo Bluebird 4–6
Coatsworth, Cave *4–6
Dorian, Hokahey!, p.100–106 5–6
Fletcher, S. E., American Indian, p.116–22 5–6
Moon, Chi-Wee *4–6
Steiner, Last Horse *4–5
Waltrip, Quiet Boy *4–6

NAVAL BATTLES: *see also* Submarines; United States—Navy; Warships
Dupuy, First Book of Civil War Naval Actions 6

NAVAL OBSERVATORY, WASHINGTON, D.C.: *see* Navigation; Standard Time

NAVIGATION: *see also* Boats; Canals; Canoes; Compass; Harbors; Lighthouses; Maps; Maury, Matthew Fontaine; Ocean Travel; Sailing; Shipbuilding; Ships; Shipwrecks; Signaling; Steamboats; Submarines; Tides; Tugboats; Winds
Bendick, How Much and How Many, p.119–29 5–6
Block, Real Book about Ships, p.81–96 5–6
Epstein, S., First Book of Maps and Globes, p.36–37, 50–51 4–6
Latham, Carry on, Mr. Bowditch 6
Tannenbaum, Understanding Maps, p.82–88 5–6

NAVY—UNITED STATES: *see* United States—Navy

NEAR EAST: *see* Middle East

NEBRASKA
Bulla, Riding the Pony Express *4–5
Quinn, Picture Map Geography of the United States, p.120–23 4–6

NEBULAE
Baker, R. H., When the Stars Come Out, p.163–67 6
Goodwin, Real Book about Stars, p.31–32, 153–54 4–6

NEEDLEWORK: *see also* Beadwork; Embroidery; Knitting; Sewing; Tapestry
Golden, Made in Iceland, p.123–29 6

NEGRITOS: *see* Malay Peninsula; Pygmies

NEGRO ART: *see* Tanner, Henry Ossawa

NEGROES: *see also* Emancipation Day; Slavery; also names of Negroes, as Washington, Booker Taliaferro
Association for Childhood Education, Told under Spacious Skies, p.88–104　　*4–6
———— Told under the Stars and Stripes, p.62–70, 270–81　　*4–6
Bishop, C. H., Martin de Porres, Hero　　6
Bontemps, Frederick Douglass　　4–6
Bronson, Children of the Sea, p.119–264　　*6
De Angeli, Bright April　　*4–6
Faulkner, Melindy's Happy Summer　　*4–5
———— Melindy's Medal　　*4–5
Graham, S., Booker T. Washington　　6
———— Dr. George Washington Carver　　6
Hayes, Skid　　*5–6
Hughes, First Book of Negroes　　4–6
Hunt, M. L., Ladycake Farm　　*4–6
Jackson, J., Call Me Charley　　*5–6
Kohler, "Crazy As You Look!"　　*4–6
Lang, Strawberry Roan　　*5–6
Lattimore, Junior　　*4–5
Lenski, Peanuts for Billy Ben　　*4–5
———— We Live in the South, p.50–73　　*4–5
Lillie, Book of Three Festivals, p.170–89　　*5–6
McMeekin, Journey Cake　　*5–6
McNeer, Armed with Courage, p.41–54　　5–6
Meadowcroft, By Secret Railway　　*5–6
Shackelford, Child's Story of the Negro　　4–5
Tarry, My Dog Rinty　　*4–5

NEGROES—FOLK TALES: *see also* John Henry
Shackelford, Child's Story of the Negro, p.38–46, 94–97　　4–5

NEGROES—SONGS: *see also* Emmett, Daniel Decatur
Buchanan, How Man Made Music, p.184–85　　6
Purdy, He Heard America Sing　　6

Wheeler, Stephen Foster and His Little Dog Tray　　4–6

NEHRU, JAWAHARLAL
Modak, Land and People of India, p.80–82　　6

NEIGHBORLINESS
Ayars, Caboose on the Roof　　*4–5
Bishop, C. H., All Alone　　*4–6
Clymer, Trolley Car Family　　*4–6
Douglas, Appleseed Farm　　*4–6
Friedman, F., Sundae with Judy　　*4–6
Lenski, Flood Friday　　*4–6
Meigs, Covered Bridge　　*4–6
Reynolds, B. L., Pepper　　*4–6
Sawyer, Maggie Rose　　*4–6
———— This Way to Christmas　　*4–6
Shackelford, Child's Story of the Negro, p.47–49　　4–5
Van Stockum, Canadian Summer　　*5–6

NEPAL
Quinn, Picture Map Geography of Asia, p.62–64　　4–6

NEPTUNE (planet)
Branley, Nine Planets, p.66–69　　6
Gallant, R. A., Exploring the Planets, p.108–13　　5–6
Goodwin, Real Book about Stars, p.105–8　　4–6

NERVOUS SYSTEM
Zim, Our Senses and How They Work, p.114–32　　4–6

NETHERLANDS: *see also* Art—Netherlands; Borneo; Costume—Netherlands; East Indies; Java; New Guinea; Tulips
Barnouw, Land of William of Orange　　6
Barrows, Old World Lands, p.62–69　　6
———— Our Big World, p.45–59　　4
De Jong, D., Picture Story of Holland　　4–6
Epstein, E., First Book of the United Nations, p.27–28　　4–6
Flakkeberg, Sea Broke Through　　*6
Jordan, Homemade Dolls in Foreign Dress, p.95–107　　4–6
Lauber, Battle against the Sea　　5–6
Seymour, Kaatje and the Christmas Compass　　*4–6

NETHERLANDS—GOVERNMENT
Barnouw, Land of William of Orange,
p.26–49   6

NETHERLANDS—HISTORY
Barnouw, Land of William of Orange
                                 6
Hall-Quest, How the Pilgrims Came to
Plymouth, p.27–37   4–6

NETHERLANDS INDIES: *see* East Indies

NETS
Leeming, Fun with String, p.81–83
                                4–6

NEVADA
Proudfit, River-Boy, p.162–82   6
Quinn, Picture Map Geography of the
United States, p.176–79   4–6

NEW AMSTERDAM: *see* Dutch in America

NEW BRUNSWICK
Quinn, Picture Map Geography of Canada and Alaska, p.21–27   4–6

NEW CALEDONIA
Quinn, Picture Map Geography of the
Pacific Islands, p.97–101   5–6

NEW ENGLAND
Barrows, American Continents, p.39–54
                                 5
Coatsworth, Away Goes Sally   *4–6
——— Littlest House   *4–6
Dalgliesh, America Travels, p.3–12
                                *4–6
Field, Hitty, p.3–36   *5–6
Frost, Maple Sugar for Windy Foot
                                *4–6
Lang, Strawberry Roan, p.9–59, 198–
218   *5–6

NEW ENGLAND—HISTORY: *see also*
Colonial Period in America; Pilgrim
Fathers; Puritans; also names of the
New England states
Dalgliesh, America Builds Homes   4–5
McGinley, Mince Pie and Mistletoe
                                4–6

NEW ENGLAND—INDUSTRIES
Lent, Men at Work in New England
                                4–6

NEW GUINEA: *see also* Birds of Paradise; Cassowaries

Quinn, Picture Map Geography of the
Pacific Islands, p.45–52   5–6
Sperry, Rain Forest   *6

NEW HAMPSHIRE
Association for Childhood Education,
Told under Spacious Skies, p.35–43
                                *4–6
Lindquist, J. D., Golden Name Day
                                *4–6
Quinn, Picture Map Geography of the
United States, p.4–7   4–6
Yates, E., Mountain Born   *5–6

NEW HEBRIDES
Quinn, Picture Map Geography of the
Pacific Islands, p.94–97   5–6

NEW JERSEY
Bailey, B. F., Picture Book of New Jer-
sey   4–6
De Angeli, Jared's Island   *4–6
Durell, Holly River Secret   *4–6
Lenski, Judy's Journey, p.187–99 *4–6
Quinn, Picture Map Geography of the
United States, p.28–31   4–6

NEW MEXICO: *see also* Carlsbad Cav-
erns National Park; Cliff Dwellers;
Navaho Indians; Pueblo Indians
Bronson, Pinto's Journey   *4–5
Quinn, Picture Map Geography of the
United States, p.148–51   4–6

NEW ORLEANS
Field, Hitty, p.156–66   *5–6
Tallant, Pirate Lafitte and the Battle of
New Orleans   5–6

NEW YEAR'S DAY
Alden, Why the Chimes Rang, p.92–105
                                *4–6
Burnett, B., First Book of Holidays,
p.4–6   4–5
Field, Hitty, p.142–46   *5–6
Haywood, Betsy's Winterhouse, p.53–72
                                *4–5
Jordan, Holiday Handicraft, p.31–37
                                4–6
Leeming, Fun with Greeting Cards,
p.76–77   4–6
McSpadden, Book of Holidays, p.2–9
                                 6
Milhous, Patrick and the Golden Slip-
pers   *4–5

Olcott, Good Stories for Great Holidays, p.3–24   4–6

Pannell, Holiday Round Up, p.19–38   4–6

Sechrist, Red Letter Days, p.27–40   5–6

NEW YEAR'S DAY—BULGARIA
Shannon, Dobry, p.149–63   *5–6

NEW YEAR'S DAY—CHINA
Lattimore, Little Pear and His Friends, p.81–103   *4–5
Wiese, Chinese Ink Stick, p.177–80   *4–6

NEW YEAR'S DAY—ITALY
Angelo, Nino, p.220–38   *6

NEW YORK CITY: *see also* Liberty—Statue of
Angelo, Bells of Bleeker Street   *4–6
Association for Childhood Education, Told under Spacious Skies, p.65–104   *4–6
————— Told under the Stars and Stripes, p.196–217, 270–81   *4–6
Brenner, Barto Takes the Subway   *4
Dalgliesh, America Travels, p.57–62   *4–6
Enright, Saturdays   *4–6
Friedman, F., Carol from the Country   *4–6
————— Dot for Short   *4–5
————— Sundae with Judy   *4–6
Garelick, Manhattan Island   4–6
Koenig, Seven Special Cats   *4–5
Sasek, This Is New York   4–6
Selden, Cricket in Times Square   *4–6
Tarry, My Dog Rinty   *4–5
Taylor, S., All-of-a-Kind Family   *4–6
————— All-of-a-Kind Family Uptown   *4–6
————— More All-of-a-Kind Family   *4–6

NEW YORK STATE
Barrows, American Continents, p.57–64   5
Dalgliesh, America Travels, p.27–33   *4–6
Edmonds, Matchlock Gun   *4–6
Orton, Treasure in the Little Trunk   *4–6
Quinn, Picture Map Geography of the United States, p.24–27   4–6

Wilder, Farmer Boy   *4–6

NEW ZEALAND
Barrows, Old World Lands, p.276–77   6
Henry, M., New Zealand   4–6

NEWFOUNDLAND
Donaldson, Newfoundland   4–6

NEWSPAPERS: *see also* Advertising; Journalism
Lawrence, Sand in Her Shoes   *4–6
Lent, "I Work on a Newspaper"   6
Scheib, What Happened?   5–6
Sootin, Let's Take a Trip to a Newspaper   4–6

NEWTON, ISAAC
Asimov, Breakthroughs in Science, p.45–53   5–6
Cottler, Heroes of Civilization, p.117–27   6
Land, B., Quest of Isaac Newton   6

NEWTS
Comstock, Handbook of Nature Study, p.187–92   6
Hylander, Out of Doors in Spring, p.43–45   5–6
Morgan, A. P., Aquarium Book, p.188–93   5–6
Parker, B. M., Toads and Frogs, p.33–35   4–6
Pels, Care of Water Pets, p.40–41   4–6

NEZ PERCÉ INDIANS
Bleeker, Horsemen of the Western Plateaus   4–6

NIASI
Hazeltine, Hero Tales from Many Lands, p.174–83   5–6

NIBELUNGENLIED
Coolidge, Legends of the North, p.77–136   4–6

NICARAGUA
Barrows, American Continents, p.305–6   5
Goetz, Neighbors to the South, p.41–47   5–6
Quinn, Picture Map Geography of Mexico, Central America and the West Indies, p.51–60   4–6
Rothery, Central American Roundabout, p.100–127   6

NICARAGUA—FOLK TALES
Rothery, Central American Roundabout, p.206–7   6

NICARAGUA—GAMES: *see* Games—Nicaragua

NICHOLAS, SAINT: *see also* Christmas —Santa Claus
Bryson, Twenty Miracles of Saint Nicolas   5–6
Farjeon, Ten Saints, p.89–96   6

NICKEL
Fenton, C. L., Riches from the Earth, p.106–12   5–6
Loomis, Field Book of Common Rocks and Minerals, p.82–84   6

NIGERIA
Barrows, Old World Lands, p.306–8   6
Caldwell, Let's Visit West Africa, p.60– 66   5–6
Kenworthy, Profile of Nigeria   5–6
Olden, Getting To Know Nigeria   4–6

NIGHTINGALE, FLORENCE
Foster, G., Abraham Lincoln's World, p.240–42   6
Hume, Florence Nightingale   5–6
McNeer, Armed with Courage, p.9–22
                                           5–6

NILE RIVER: *see also* Crocodiles; Egypt —Modern
Meadowcroft, Gift of the River   5–6

NITROGEN: *see also* Chemistry
Freeman, I. M., All about the Wonders of Chemistry, p.93–96   6
Parker, B. M., What Things Are Made Of, p.20–21   5–6

NJAL
Hazeltine, Hero Tales from Many Lands, p.297–304   5–6

NOAH
De la Mare, Stories from the Bible, p.41–57   5–6

NOMADS: *see also* Arabs; Automobiles— Trailers; Barbarians; Bedouins; Eskimos; Gypsies; Herding; Lapland; Malay Peninsula; Migrant Labor; Mongolia; Northmen; Sahara Desert; Shepherd Life; Siouan Indians; Turkestan; Westward Movement
Gidal, Follow the Reindeer   4–6

Lamprey, All the Ways of Building, p.12–20   6
Smith, J. R., Neighbors around the World, p.174–84, 202–18   4
Taylor, A., Iran, p.9–11   6

NONSENSE RHYMES
Withers, Counting Out   4–5

NORMAN CONQUEST
Polland, Children of the Red King   *6

NORMANDY
Bragdon, L. J., Land and People of France, p.64–71   6

NORMANDY—FOLK TALES
Smith, E. S., Christmas Book of Legends & Stories, p.311–20   5–6

NORSE MYTHS: *see* Myths—Northmen

NORSEMEN: *see* Northmen

NORTH CAROLINA: *see also* Great Smoky Mountains National Park
Association for Childhood Education, Told under the Stars and Stripes, p.71–82   *4–6
Banta, Life in America: The South, p.96–100   5–6
Bell, Mountain Boy   *4
Carroll, Tough Enough's Pony   *4–5
———— Tough Enough's Trip   *4–6
Gage, Secret of Fiery Gorge   *4–6
Hazeltine, Easter Book of Legends and Stories, p.361–74   *5–6
Hunt, M. L., Benjie's Hat   *4–6
Lenski, Blue Ridge Billy   *5–6
Quinn, Picture Map Geography of the United States, p.52–55   4–6

NORTH CENTRAL STATES
Barrows, American Continents, p.125– 64   5
Havighurst, Life in America: The Midwest   5–6

NORTH DAKOTA
Quinn, Picture Map Geography of the United States, p.108–11   4–6

NORTH POLE: *see* Arctic Regions

NORTHERN LIGHTS: *see* Aurora Borealis

NORTHMEN: *see also* Myths—Northmen; Sagas; Viking Ships; also names of Northmen, as Ericson, Leif; Sigurd

Aulaire, Leif the Lucky   4–5
Dalgliesh, America Begins, p.10–12
                                    4–5
Golden, Made in Iceland, p.18–26   6
Hartman, Builders of the Old World,
    p.227–31   6
Janeway, Vikings   4–6
Rothery, Scandinavian Roundabout, p.
    3–20   6
Watson, Golden History of the World,
    p.79–81   5–6
Weir, R. C., Leif Ericson   4–5

NORTHWEST PASSAGE: *see* Arctic
    Regions; Hudson, Henry

NORWAY: *see also* Costume—Norway;
    Dancing—Norway; Lofoten Islands;
    also names of Norwegians, as Grieg,
    Edvard Hagerup
Barrows, Our Big World, p.29–42   4
Dahl, Cloud Shoes   *4–6
Gidal, Follow the Reindeer   4–6
———— My Village in Norway   4–6
McSwigan, Snow Treasure   *5–6
O'Neill, Picture Story of Norway   4–6
Rothery, Scandinavian Roundabout, p.
    13–131   6
White, B. F., On Your Own Two Feet
                                    *4–6

NORWAY—FOLK TALES
Fenner, Fools and Funny Fellows,
    p.127–30   4–6
———— Time To Laugh, p.168–74
                                    4–6

NORWEGIAN LITERATURE
Zwilgmeyer, Johnny Blossom   *4–6

NORWEGIANS IN THE UNITED
    STATES
Association for Childhood Education,
    Told under the Stars and Stripes,
    p.325–35   *4–6
Aulaire, Nils   *4–5
Crowley, Tor and Azor   *5–6
Rothery, Scandinavian Roundabout, p.
    111–19   6

NOSE
Zim, Our Senses and How They Work,
    p.97–107   4–6

NOVA SCOTIA
Johnson, M. S., Dixie Dobie   *4–5

Quinn, Picture Map Geography of Can-
    ada and Alaska, p.7–15   4–6
Sauer, Fog Magic   *5–6

NUMBERS
Adler, Giant Golden Book of Mathe-
    matics, p.12–13, 39–47   6
———— Magic House of Numbers   6
Batchelor, Superstitious? Here's Why!,
    p.44–51   6
Bendick, Take a Number   4–5
Carlson, B. W., Do It Yourself!, p.19–
    20   4–6
Epstein, S., First Book of Codes and
    Ciphers, p.16–19   4–6
Hillyer, Child's History of the World,
    p.250–51   5–6
Hogben, Wonderful World of Mathe-
    matics, p.44–51   6
Leeming, Real Book about Magic, p.58–
    68   5–6
Mulac, Game Book, p.112–20   6
Stoddard, First Book of Magic, p.48–50
                                    5–6

NUNIVAK ISLAND
Stefansson, Here Is Alaska, p.116–23
                                    6

NUREMBERG: *see* Dürer, Albrecht

NURSING: *see also* Babies—Care; Bar-
    ton, Clara; First Aid; Health; Medi-
    cine; Nightingale, Florence; Red
    Cross
Elting, First Book of Nurses   4–5
Hume, Florence Nightingale   5–6
McNeer, Armed with Courage, p.9–22
                                    5–6

NUTHATCHES
Comstock, Handbook of Nature Study,
    p.65–68   6
Webb, Birds in Their Homes, p.38–39
                                    4–6

NUTRITION
Beauchamp, Discovering Our World,
    Bk.1, p.166–68   4

NUTS
Eberle, Basketful, p.240–48   4–6
Robinson, J., Things To Make from
    Odds & Ends, p.38–41   4–6

NYLON
Colby, Plastic Magic, p.10   6
Freeman, I. M., All about the Wonders
    of Chemistry, p.109   6

Writers Project, Rayon, Nylon, and Glass Fibers, no.39, p.29–34   5–6

OAK TREES
Blough, Tree on the Road to Turntown
    *4–5
Comstock, Handbook of Nature Study, p.638–42   6
Cormack, First Book of Trees, p.32–37
    4–6
Dudley, Our American Trees, p.61–64, 126–27   5–6
McKenny, Trees of the Countryside, p.4–7   4–6

OBEDIENCE
Bulla, Riding the Pony Express   *4–5
Chrisman, Shen of the Sea, p.65–78
    *5–6
Meadowcroft, By Wagon and Flatboat, p.153–61   *4–5

OBSERVATORIES
Baker, R. H., When the Stars Come Out, p.138–50   6
Benary-Isbert, Shooting Star   *4–6
Schneider, L., Space in Your Future, p.119–202   6

OCCUPATIONS: *see* names of occupations, as Agriculture

OCEAN: *see also* Gulf Stream; Icebergs; Marine Animals; Maury, Matthew Fontaine; Navigation; Ships; Shipwrecks; Storms; Tides; Water
Barnard, Macmillan Science-Life Series, Bk.6, p.267–83   6
Beaty, Baby Whale   4–6
Fisher, J., Wonderful World of the Sea
    5–6
Hinton, Exploring under the Sea   5–6
Knowlton, Let's Explore beneath the Sea   5–6
Lane, F. C., All about the Sea   4–6
Life, World We Live In, p.20–36   5–6
Reed, And That's Why, p.66–74   4–5
——— Sea for Sam   6
Schneider, H., Rocks, Rivers & the Changing Earth, p.95–106   4–6

OCEAN LIFE: *see* Fisheries; Fishes; Marine Animals; Marine Plants; Seashore; Shellfish; Sponges; also names of animals, as Walrus

OCEAN TRAVEL: *see also* Sailing; Steamboats
Rogers, F., Heels, Wheels, and Wire, p.85–93   5–6

OCELOTS
Zim, Big Cats, p.59–60   5–6

OCTOPUS: *see* Cuttlefish

ODYSSEUS: *see* Ulysses

OGIER THE DANE
Farjeon, Mighty Men, p.160–68   4–6
Hazeltine, Hero Tales from Many Lands, p.204–18   5–6

OGLETHORPE, JAMES EDWARD
Harper, Easter Chimes, p.22–33   *4–6

O'HIGGINS, BERNARDO
Goetz, Neighbors to the South, p.143–44   5–6
Olcott, Good Stories for Great Birthdays, p.393–409   4–6
Spencer, P. R., Traveling New Trails, p.324–29   6

OHIO
Association for Childhood Education, Told under Spacious Skies, p.170–80
    *4–6
Dalgliesh, America Travels, p.37–44
    *4–6
Havighurst, Life in America: The Midwest, p.92–97   5–6
Lent, Men at Work in the Great Lakes States, p.30–33, 58–61, 106–9   4–6
Quinn, Picture Map Geography of the United States, p.84–87   4–6
Scheele, Mound Builders   4–6

OHIO RIVER
Crawford, "Hello, the Boat!"   *6
Meadowcroft, By Wagon and Flatboat, p.87–161   *4–5

OIL INDUSTRY: *see* Petroleum

OILS AND FATS
Beeler, Experiments in Chemistry, p.59–63   5–6
Eberle, Basketful, p.228–39   4–6

OKAPIS
Buck, F., Jungle Animals, p.38–39
    5–6

OKLAHOMA: *see also* Platt National Park

Bailey, B. F., Picture Book of Oklahoma 4–6

Davis, R. G., Choctaw Code (Indian Territory) *5–6

Dorian, Hokahey!, p.36–39　　5–6

Lenski, Boom Town Boy　　*4–6

Quinn, Picture Map Geography of the United States, p.144–47　4–6

Rushmore, Shadow of Robbers Roost *6

OLAF I (TRYGVESSON), KING OF NORWAY

Farjeon, Mighty Men, p.180–92　4–6

OLD IRONSIDES: *see* Constitution (ship)

OLDER-YOUNGER CHILD RELATIONS

Cleary, Beezus and Ramona　*4–6

Lattimore, Molly in the Middle *4–5

Sayers, Tag-along Tooloo　　*4

OLIVES

Angelo, Nino, p.132–41　　*6

Eberle, Basketful, p.228–32　4–6

OLYMPIA

Hall, J., Buried Cities, p.94–157　5–6

OLYMPIC GAMES

Hall, J., Buried Cities, p.94–122　5–6

Hartman, Builders of the Old World, p.133–36　　6

Hillyer, Child's History of the World, p.84–88　5–6

OLYMPIC NATIONAL PARK

Melbo, Our Country's National Parks, v.2, p.134–56　6

ONTARIO

Quinn, Picture Map Geography of Canada and Alaska, p.39–48　4–6

OPALS

Batchelor, Superstitious? Here's Why!, p.69–70　6

OPERAS: *see also* names of composers, as Gluck, Christoph Willibald von; Verdi, Giuseppe; Wagner, Richard

Buchanan, How Man Made Music, p.102–3, 107–11　6

Bulla, Stories of Favorite Operas　5–6

Enright, Saturdays, p.50–57　*4–6

OPOSSUMS

Blough, After the Sun Goes Down, p.26–27　4–5

Hogner, Animal Book, p.92–94　6

Lawson, R., Edward, Hoppy, and Joe *4–6

Lippincott, Persimmon Jim, the Possum　4–6

Mason, G. F., Animal Tracks, p.52–53 4–6

Moe, Animal Inn, p.19–27　　4–6

ORANGES

Eberle, Basketful, p.121–27　4–6

Lenski, We Live in the South, p.104–28 *4–5

Wall, Gifts from the Grove　4–6

ORANGUTANS

Bridges, Zoo Babies, p.33–41　4–6

Buck, F., Jungle Animals, p.17–19 5–6

Perkins, Marlin Perkins' Zooparade, p.92–95　4–6

ORATORIO

Buchanan, How Man Made Music, p.102–7　6

ORATORY: *see* names of orators, as Demosthenes; Henry, Patrick

ORBIT

Adler, Things That Spin　5–6

ORCHARDS: *see* Appleseed, Johnny; Fruit Culture

ORCHESTRAS: *see also* Musical Instruments; also names of orchestral leaders, as Damrosch, Walter

Balet, What Makes an Orchestra 5–6

Buchanan, How Man Made Music, p.95–101, 109　6

Commins, Making an Orchestra 5–6

Posell, This Is an Orchestra 5–6

ORCHIDS

Parker, B. M., Plant and Animal Partnerships, p.22–25　5–6

OREGON: *see also* Crater Lake National Park

Association for Childhood Education, Told under Spacious Skies, p.295–301 *4–6

Quinn, Picture Map Geography of the United States, p.184–87　4–6

OREGON—HISTORY

Foster, G., Abraham Lincoln's World, p.162–64　6

OREGON TRAIL
  Carr, Children of the Covered Wagon
    *4–6
  Graham, V. M., Treasure in the Covered Wagon   *4–6
  Havighurst, First Book of the Oregon Trail   4–6
  Mason, M. E., Young Mr. Meeker
    *4–5
  Tavo, Buffalo Are Running   *6

ORGAN-GRINDERS
  Weeks, Tales of a Common Pigeon, p.25–34   *4–6

ORGANS
  Angelo, Nino, p.213–19   *6
  Buchanan, How Man Made Music, p.57–58, 172–73 (electronic)   6
  Graham, V. M., Treasure in the Covered Wagon   *4–6
  Huntington, Tune Up   4–6

ORIENT: *see also* Kublai Khan; also names of countries, as China; Japan; also names of products, as Rice
  Hartman, Builders of the Old World, p.379–413   6

ORIOLES: *see* Baltimore Orioles

ORPHANS
  Carlson, N. S., Happy Orpheline   *4
  Commager, E., Valentine   *6
  Daringer, Adopted Jane   *4–6
  De Angeli, Jared's Island   *4–6
  Enright, Then There Were Five   *5–6
  Gates, Sensible Kate   *4–6
  Kennedy, Jenny   *4–6
  Kim, Happy Days   *5–6
  Ladd, Night of the Hurricane   *4–6
  Lawrence, Peachtree Island   *4–5
  L'Engle, Meet the Austins   *5–6
  Lindgren, Rasmus and the Vagabond
    *4–6
  Otis, Toby Tyler   *4–6
  Urbahns, Little Red Dragon   *4–6
  Van Stockum, Pegeen   *6
  Weaver, Poppy in the Corn   *6
  Woolley, Ginnie and Geneva, p.35–68, 132–48, 157–91   *4–5

ORPHEUS
  Benson, Stories of the Gods and Heroes, p.205–10   5–6

OSCEOLA (Indian chief)
  Bleeker, Seminole Indians   4–6
  McNeer, War Chief of the Seminoles
    5–6

OSTRICHES
  Stinetorf, Children of South Africa, p.67–79   *5–6
  Zim, Ostriches   4–5

OTIS, ELISHA GRAVES
  Bechdolt, Going Up, p.45–51   5–6

OTTERS
  Franklin, Tuffy, p.32–47   *4–6
  Hogner, Animal Book, p.132–35   6
  Liers, Otter's Story   5–6
  Lindquist, W., Alaska, p.22–29 (sea otter)   5–6
  Mason, G. F., Animal Tracks, p.50–51
    4–6
  Perkins, Marlin Perkins' Zooparade, p.44–47   4–6
  Ripper, Weasel Family, p.38–47   4–5
  Stoutenberg, Wild Animals of the Far West, p.30–33   4–6

OUTDOOR LIFE
  Bailey, C. S., Miss Hickory   *4–6
  Coatsworth, Alice-All-By-Herself
    *4–6
  Enright, Gone-Away Lake   *4–6
  Franklin, Monte   *4–6
  George, J. L., Vulpes, the Red Fox   *6

OUTLAWS: *see also* Robin Hood
  O'Brien, Silver Chief   *6

OVENBIRDS
  Webb, Birds in Their Homes, p.27   4–6

OVERLAND JOURNEYS TO THE PACIFIC: *see* Lewis and Clark Expedition; also names of routes or trails, as Oregon Trail

OWLS
  Blough, After the Sun Goes Down, p.14–20   4–5
  Bosiger, Bird Is Born, p.59–65   5–6
  Buff, Big Tree, p.31–35   *5–6
  ———— Elf Owl   4–5
  Comstock, Handbook of Nature Study, p.100–103   6
  Fenton, C. L., Wild Folk in the Desert, p.105–10   4–6
  George, J. L., Bubo, the Great Horned Owl   4–6

———— Vulpes, the Red Fox, p.21–24
*6

Gillham, Beyond the Clapping Mountains, p.44–50 *4–6

Hylander, Out of Doors in Autumn, p.53–57 5–6

Kane, Tale of a Meadow 4–6

Lathrop, Let Them Live, p.46–49 4–6

Mason, G. F., Animal Sounds, p.33–37
5–6

Moe, Animal Inn, p.42–51, 79–88 4–6

Spencer, P. R., Finding New Trails, p.405–10 4

Zim, Owls 4–6

OXCARTS (models)
Schneider, H., Science Fun with Milk Cartons, p.80–84 5–6

OXEN
Eisenberg, Won Kim's Ox *4–6

OXYGEN: *see also* Chemistry
Cooper, E. K., Science on the Shores and Banks, p.25–26, 144–45 5–6

Parker, B. M., What Things Are Made Of, p.16–17 5–6

Schneider, H., Everyday Machines and How They Work, p.121–23 5–6

OYSTERS
Cavanna, First Book of Sea Shells, p.11–13 4–6

Cooper, E. K., Science on the Shores and Banks, p.75–76, 85–86 5–6

Fenton, C. L., Life Long Ago, p.114–16
6

Writers Project, Oysters, no.20 5–6

PACIFIC ISLANDS: *see also* names of islands, as Bali; Java; Sumatra; also groups of islands, as East Indies; Hawaiian Islands
Du Bois, Twenty-one Balloons, p.61–168 *6

Proudfit, Treasure Hunter, p.165–200
6

Quinn, Picture Map Geography of the Pacific Islands 5–6

Sperry, Call It Courage *5–6

———— Captain Cook Explores the South Seas 5–6

Tennant, All the Proud Tribesmen *6

PACIFIC OCEAN: *see also* Pacific Islands
Syme, Captain Cook 5–6

———— Magellan 4–6

PACK RATS
Armer, Waterless Mountain, p.53–59
*5–6

Buff, Big Tree, p.64–70 *5–6

Fenton, C. L., Wild Folk in the Desert, p.111–16 4–6

Huntington, Let's Go to the Desert, p.64–69 4–5

PACK TRANSPORTATION
Meigs, Wind in the Chimney, p.70–119
*5–6

PAGANINI, NICOLO
Wheeler, Paganini 4–6

PAGEANTS: *see also* Costume; Fairs; Festivals; Plays
Carlson, B. W., Act It Out, p.85–92
4–6

Salomon, Book of Indian Crafts & Indian Lore, p.365–78 6

Tappan, When Knights Were Bold, p.360–65 6

PAINE, THOMAS
Lawson, R., Watchwords of Liberty, p.22–23 4–6

PAINT: *see also* Color
Beeler, Experiments in Chemistry, p.90–96 5–6

PAINTING: *see also* Art; Artists; Color; Design; Pictures
Bendick, First Book of How To Fix It, p.36–40 4–6

Haywood, Penny and Peter, p.22–41
*4

Hillyer, Child's History of Art, p.3–156
5–6

Robinson, J., Things To Make from Odds & Ends, p.29–31 4–6

Spencer, C., Made in China, p.135–42
5–6

PAINTINGS: *see* Pictures

PAIUTE INDIANS
Underhill, Antelope Singer *4–6

PAKISTAN
Barrows, Old World Lands, p.182–86
6

Caldwell, Let's Visit Pakistan 4–6

Fitch, Allah, the God of Islam, p.119–29 6

Quinn, Picture Map Geography of Asia, p.59–60   4–6

PALEONTOLOGY: *see* Fossils; Prehistoric Animals

PALESTINE: *see also* Israel
Ceder, Ann of Bethany   *4–6
———— Ethan, the Shepherd Boy   *4–6
———— Joel, the Potter's Son   *4–6
Epstein, E., First Book of the United Nations, p.42–43   4–6
Fitch, Allah, the God of Islam, p.131–35   6
Hewes, Boy of the Lost Crusade   *6
Lillie, Book of Three Festivals, p.11–27, 63–87, 131–45   *5–6
Quinn, Picture Map Geography of Asia, p.29–32   4–6

PALESTINE—HISTORY
Hartman, In Bible Days   6
McGuire, Glimpses into the Long Ago, p.96–100   5–6

PALESTRINA, GIOVANNI PIERLUIGI DA
Burch, Famous Composers for Young People, p.1–7   4–6

PALM TREES
Stinetorf, Children of North Africa, p.25–33   *5–6

PALOLO
Lavine, Strange Travelers, p.135–37   5–6

PAN AMERICAN DAY
Burnett, B., First Book of Holidays, p.20   4–5
McSpadden, Book of Holidays, p.52–59   6
Pannell, Holiday Round Up, p.127–41   4–6
Sechrist, Red Letter Days, p.107–17   5–6

PAN AMERICAN HIGHWAY
Boardman, Roads, p.130–37   6
Bothwell, First Book of Roads, p.63   5–6
Hall, E., Land and People of Argentina, p.13–15   6

PAN AMERICANISM
Goetz, Neighbors to the South, p.136–39   5–6

Peck, Pageant of South American History, p.381–86   6

PANAMA
American Heritage, Discoverers of the New World, p.47–50   5–6
Goetz, Neighbors to the South, p.52–58   5–6
Quinn, Picture Map Geography of Mexico, Central America and the West Indies, p.68–77   4–6
Rothery, Central American Roundabout, p.152–94   6
———— South American Roundabout, p.26–33   5–6
Syme, Balboa   4–6

PANAMA CANAL
Boardman, Canals, p.115–33   6
Buehr, Through the Locks, p.23–28, 58–62   5–6
Considine, Panama Canal   5–6
Fast, Goethals and the Panama Canal   6
Goetz, Neighbors to the South, p.43–44, 57–58   5–6
Judson, Soldier Doctor, p.109–41   6
Markun, First Book of the Panama Canal   5–6
Rothery, Central American Roundabout, p.154–64   6
———— South American Roundabout, p.16–25   5–6
Spencer, P. R., Exploring New Trails, p.412–18   5

PANCHATANTRA
Fitch, Their Search for God, p.34   5–6

PANDAS: *see also* Giant Pandas
Bridges, Zoo Babies, p.22–27   4–6
———— Zoo Doctor, p.59–67   4–6
Osmond, Animals of the World, v.3   4–6

PANDORA
Benson, Stories of the Gods and Heroes, p.29–34   5–6
Sellew, Adventures with the Gods, p.44–49   4–5

PANGOLINS: *see also* Anteaters
Buck, F., Jungle Animals, p.10–11   5–6

PANSIES
Comstock, Handbook of Nature Study, p.555–58   6

PANTHERS: *see also* Jaguars; Leopards
Disney, Worlds of Nature, p.61–63
4–6
Franklin, Wild Animals of the Southwest, p.44–57 5–6
Lathrop, Let Them Live, p.38–39 4–6
Stoutenberg, Wild Animals of the Far West, p.46–48 4–6
Wilder, Little House on the Prairie, p.253–62 *4–6
Zim, Big Cats, p.54–58 5–6

PANTOMIMES: *see also* Pageants; Plays; Puppet Shows; Shadow Plays
Carlson, B. W., Act It Out, p.19–37 4–6
Mulac, Game Book, p.91–93 6

PAPER: *see also* Books; Paper Work
Bailey, C. S., Pioneer Art in America, p.78–89 5–6
Beeler, More Experiments in Science, p.147–52 5–6
Crawford, "Hello, the Boat!", p.97–99 *6
Disraeli, New Worlds through the Microscope, p.171–72 6
Dudley, Our American Trees, p.74–79 5–6
Lent, "I Work on a Newspaper," p.62–74 6
———— Men at Work in New England, p.66–69 4–6
———— Men at Work in the Great Lakes States, p.66–69 4–6
Meyer, Paper 6
Rogers, F., Heels, Wheels, and Wire, p.37–39 5–6
Schwartz, It's Fun To Know Why, p.107–19 5–6

PAPER MONEY: *see* Money

PAPER WORK
Carlson, B. W., Make It and Use It, p.15–48 4–6
———— Make It Yourself!, p.18–73 4–6
Hamilton, E. T., Handicraft for Girls, p.14–21, 31–39 6
Kuwabara, Cut and Paste 5–6
Lee, What To Do Now, p.8–17, 34–55 4–6
Leeming, Fun with Paper 4–5

Robinson, J., Things To Make from Odds & Ends, p.1–28 4–6
Soong, Art of Chinese Paper Folding 4–6
Sperling, How To Make Things Out of Paper 5–6
Weiss, H., Paper, Ink and Roller 4–6
Zarchy, Let's Make More Things, p.44–45 5–6
———— Let's Make Something, p.13, 82–85, 94–95 5–6

PARACHUTES
Bishop, R. W., From Kite to Kitty Hawk, p.58–73 6
Neurath, Rockets and Jets, p.28–29 4–6

PARADES
Estes, Middle Moffat, p.294–317 *4–6
Milhous, Patrick and the Golden Slippers *4–5

PARAGUAY
Donaldson, Paraguay 4–6
Goetz, Neighbors to the South, p.96–101 5–6
Quinn, Picture Map Geography of South America, p.73–78 4–6
Rothery, South American Roundabout, p.127–41 5–6

PARAKEETS
Black, Pete the Parrakeet *4–5
Brown, V., How To Understand Animal Talk, p.47–48 6
Renick, M. L., John's Back Yard Camp *4–5
Zim, Parrakeets 4–6

PARASITES: *see also* Bacteria
Parker, B. M., Dependent Plants 5–6

PARIS
Bishop, C. H., Pancakes—Paris *4–6
Bragdon, L. J., Land and People of France, p.104–10 6
Carlson, N. S., Family under the Bridge *4–5
Eaton, That Lively Man, Ben Franklin, p.198–236 6
Hazeltine, Easter Book of Legends and Stories, p.263–67, 285–94 *5–6
Sasek, This Is Paris 4–6

PARROTS
Coatsworth, Alice-All-By-Herself, p. 171–80 *4–6

De Jong, D. C., Seven Sayings of Mr. Jefferson   *4–5

PARTHENON
Hillyer, Child's History of Art, p.294–99   5–6

PARTIES: *see also* Amusements; Costume; Dancing; Games; Picnics
Carlson, B. W., Do It Yourself!   4–6
Coatsworth, Littlest House, p.138–51   *4–6
Forbush, Book of Games, p.280–83, 320–22   4–6
Hamilton, E. T., Handicraft for Girls, p.55–103, 116–30   6
Jordan, Holiday Handicraft   4–6
Mulac, Game Book, p.1–51   6
New York Herald Tribune, Young America's Cook Book, p.267–69   4–6
Oliver, Rain or Shine   4–5
Sechrist, Heigh-Ho for Halloween!, p.227–34   5–6
Soong, Art of Chinese Paper Folding, p.83–87   4–6
Stoddard, First Book of Magic   5–6

PARTIES—PIONEER LIFE
Wilder, On the Banks of Plum Creek, p.160–76   *4–6

PARTRIDGES: *see* Quails

PASSENGER PIGEONS
Parker, B. M., Saving Our Wild Life, p.3–4   5–6

PASSOVER
Pannell, Holiday Round Up, p.108–12   4–6

PASTEUR, LOUIS
Asimov, Breakthroughs in Science, p.99–106   5–6
Cottler, Heroes of Civilization, p.278–86   6
Ludovici, World of the Microscope, p.43–61   6
Parker, B. M., Scientist and His Tools, p.9–11   5–6
Schatz, Story of Microbes, p.54–58   6
Writers Project, Grapes, no.37, p.40–43   5–6

PASTEURIZATION: *see* Dairying; Milk —Pasteurization

PASTORAL LIFE: *see* Shepherd Life

PATRICK, SAINT: *see also* Saint Patrick's Day
Farjeon, Ten Saints, p.45–62   6
Hazeltine, Easter Book of Legends and Stories, p.149–58   *5–6
Reynolds, Q. J., Life of Saint Patrick   5–6
Tappan, When Knights Were Bold, p.193–95   6

PATRIOTIC SONGS: *see* American Ballads and Songs; National Songs; Songs

PATRIOTISM: *see also* Democracy; Loyalty
French, Lance of Kanana   *6
Parish, At the Palace Gates   *4–6

PEACHES
Lawrence, Peachtree Island, p.181–218   *4–5

PEACOCKS
Haywood, Eddie and His Big Deals, p.103–50   *4–5

PEANUTS
Eberle, Basketful, p.235–39   4–6
Lenski, Peanuts for Billy Ben   *4–5

PEARL FISHERIES
Writers Project, Oysters, no.20, p.18–24   5–6

PEARLS
Batchelor, Superstitious? Here's Why!, p.72–73   6

PEARY, ROBERT EDWIN
Rothery, Scandinavian Roundabout, p.75–76   6

PECANS
Dudley, Our American Trees, p.90–95   5–6

PECCARIES
Earle, Pigs, Tame and Wild, p.40–45   4–6
Fenton, C. L., Wild Folk in the Desert, p.72–77   4–6
Mason, G. F., Animal Tracks, p.82–83   4–6

PEDDLERS
Bailey, C. S., Pioneer Art in America, p.90–102   *5–6
Batchelor, Tim and the Purple Whistle   *4–5
Coatsworth, Away Goes Sally, p.102–13   *4–6

Flory, Peddler's Summer   *4–6
Hader, Spunky, p.72–81   *4–6
Knight, E. M., Lassie Come-Home, p.185–215   *6
Orton, Treasure in the Little Trunk, p.153–57   *4–6
Wilder, Farmer Boy, p.133–40   *4–6

PEDRO II, EMPEROR OF BRAZIL
Brown, R. J., Land and People of Brazil, p.36–38   6
Olcott, Good Stories for Great Birthdays, p.109–22   4–6
Peck, Pageant of South American History, p.318–28   6

PEER GYNT
Deucher, Edvard Grieg, p.125–27   4–6

PEGASUS
Sellew, Adventures with the Gods, p.104–12   4–5

PELICANS
Lathrop, Let Them Live, p.71–73   4–6

PENCILS
Bailey, C. S., Children of the Handcrafts, p.126–35   *5–6
Elting, Lollypop Factory and Lots of Others, p.20–30   4–5
Schneider, H., Everyday Machines and How They Work, p.49–50   5–6

PENDULUMS
Adler, Things That Spin   5–6
———— Tools of Science, p.23–32   6
Beeler, Experiments in Science, p.61–63   5–6
Reck, Clocks Tell the Time, p.24–25   4–6
Schneider, H., Everyday Machines and How They Work, p.167–70   5–6

PENGUINS
Atwater, Mr. Popper's Penguins *4–5
Bridges, Zoo Pets, p.79–87   4–6
Fox, From Bones to Bodies, p.53–54 6
Frank, Ice Island, p.195–99   6
Hyde, Animal Clocks and Compasses, p.42–43   5–6
Icenhower, First Book of the Antarctic, p.52–55   4–6
Mason, G. F., Animal Sounds, p.39–40   5–6
Rombauer, Cookbook for Boys and Girls, p.59   6

PENICILLIN
Eberle, Modern Medical Discoveries, p.1–49   5–6
Ludovici, World of the Microscope, p.118–21   6

PENMANSHIP: *see* Writing

PENN, WILLIAM
Dalgliesh, America Builds Homes 4–5
Duvoisin, And There Was America, p.72–74   4–6
Haviland, William Penn   4–6
Olcott, Good Stories for Great Birthdays, p.29–42   4–6

PENNSYLVANIA
Association for Childhood Education, Told under Spacious Skies, p.105–27   *4–6
———— Told under the Stars and Stripes, p.54–61, 218–38 *4–6
Bishop, C. H., Blue Spring Farm *5–6
De Angeli, Henner's Lydia   *4–5
———— Skippack School   *4–6
———— Yonie Wondernose   *4–5
Flory, Peddler's Summer   *4–6
Hark, Story of the Pennsylvania Dutch   4–6
Haviland, William Penn   4–6
Henry, M., Benjamin West and His Cat Grimalkin   4–6
Lawrence, Homemade Year   *4–5
Meigs, Dutch Colt   *4–6
———— Wind in the Chimney *5–6
Quinn, Picture Map Geography of the United States, p.32–35   4–6
Sheehy, Molly and the Golden Wedding   *4–5

PENS
Crawford, "Hello, the Boat!", p.187–88   *6
Wiese, Chinese Ink Stick   *4–6

PERCUSSION INSTRUMENTS: *see also* Drums
Balet, What Makes an Orchestra, p.26–35   5–6
Buchanan, How Man Made Music, p.20–35   6
Commins, Making an Orchestra, p.18–24   5–6
Huntington, Tune Up   4–6
Kettelkamp, Drums, Rattles, and Bells, p.9–10   4–6

Lacey, Picture Book of Musical Instruments, p.35–51   5–6

Norman, First Book of Music, p.56–57
4–6

Posell, This Is an Orchestra, p.51–65
5–6

PERENNIALS: *see* Flowers

PERICLES

Hartman, Builders of the Old World, p.150–53   6

PERISCOPES: *see also* Submarines

Beeler, Experiments in Science, p.104–6
5–6

Lee, What To Do Now, p.78   4–6

Zarchy, Let's Make Something, p.58–59
5–6

PERIWINKLES

Cooper, E. K., Science on the Shores and Banks, p.64–65   5–6

PERKIN, WILLIAM HENRY

Asimov, Breakthroughs in Science, p. 111–19   5–6

PERRY, OLIVER HAZARD

Foster, G., Abraham Lincoln's World, p.39–40   6

Lawson, R., Watchwords of Liberty, p.33–35   4–6

Mitchell, Ships That Made U.S. History, p.40–44   6

PERSEUS

Asimov, Words from the Myths, p.149–55   6

Benson, Stories of the Gods and Heroes, p.125–35   5–6

Kingsley, Heroes, p.1–102   6

Sellew, Adventures with the Gods, p.69–85   4–5

PERSEVERANCE

Batchelor, Cap for Mul Chand   *4–5

Brock, Topsy-Turvy Family   *4–5

Bunyan, Pilgrim's Progress   *5–6

Considine, Panama Canal   5–6

Dalgliesh, Ride on the Wind   4–5

Henry, M., Benjamin West and His Cat Grimalkin   4–6

Lenski, Judy's Journey   *4–6

McSwigan, Snow Treasure   *5–6

Rankin, L., Daughter of the Mountains
*5–6

Renick, M. L., Nicky's Football Team
*4–5

_____ Pete's Home Run   *4–5

Reynolds, Q. J., Wright Brothers   4–6

Sawyer, Maggie Rose   *4–6

Van Riper, Lou Gehrig   4–5

Wilson, L., This Boy Cody and His Friends   *4–6

PERSIA—GAMES: *see* Games—Persia

PERSIA—HISTORY: *see also* Xerxes the Great, King of Persia

Falls, First 3000 Years, p.144–57, 168–76   6

Hartman, Builders of the Old World, p.111–15   6

Hillyer, Child's History of the World, p.124–42   5–6

PERU

Bailey, B. F., Peru   4–6

Barrows, American Continents, p.325–28   5

Cavanna, Lucho of Peru   4–6

Friedman, E., Digging into Yesterday, p.102–26   5–6

Goetz, Neighbors to the South, p.77–83
5–6

Jordan, Homemade Dolls in Foreign Dress, p.84–94   4–6

Parish, At the Palace Gates   *4–6

Quinn, Picture Map Geography of South America, p.23–33   4–6

Rothery, South American Roundabout, p.44–81   5–6

PERU—HISTORY: *see also* Incas; Pizarro, Francisco

American Heritage, Discoverers of the New World, p.77–81   5–6

Bishop, C. H., Martin de Porres, Hero
6

Peck, Pageant of South American History, p.67–90, 143–53, 267–81   6

PESTS (insect): *see* Insects—Injurious

PET SHOPS

Blough, Monkey with a Notion   *4–6

PETER THE GREAT, CZAR OF RUSSIA

Hillyer, Child's History of the World, p.402–6   5–6

Nazaroff, Land of the Russian People, p.108–17   6

PETRIFIED FORESTS: *see also* Yellowstone National Park

Disney, Worlds of Nature, p.84–85
  4–6
Fenton, C. L., Life Long Ago, p.248 6
Reed, Earth for Sam, p.48–49 6

PETROLEUM: *see also* Coal-Tar Products; Natural Gas
Adler, Fire in Your Life, p.94–96, 119–24 4–6
Barr, Young Scientist Takes a Ride, p.11–12, 30–37, 148 5–6
Buehr, Oil . . . Today's Black Magic 5–6
Dawson, California, p.175–79 5–6
Fenton, C. L., Riches from the Earth, p.113–18 5–6
Freeman, I. M., All about the Wonders of Chemistry, p.33–39 6
Hartman, Machines, p.98–107 6
Land, M., Jungle Oil 5–6
Lenski, Boom Town Boy *4–6
Loomis, Field Book of Common Rocks and Minerals, p.224–29 6
Morgan, A. P., Boys' Book of Engines, Motors & Turbines, p.78–100 6
Parker, B. M., Earth a Great Storehouse, p.20–22 4–6
Reed, And That's Why, p.86–94 4–5
———— Earth for Sam, p.135 6
Schneider, H., More Power to You, p.58–62 5–6
Williams, H. L., Stories in Rocks, p.73–76 6
Writers Project, Oil and Gas, no.36 5–6

PETS: *see also* Animals—Domestic; Animals—Houses; Kindness to Animals; also names of animals, as Cats; Dogs
Black, Pete the Parrakeet *4–5
Buck, M. W., Small Pets from Woods and Fields 4–6
Burger, All about Fish, p.109–24 5–6
Carroll, Tough Enough's Trip *4–6
Coatsworth, Away Goes Sally, p.82–88 *4–6
Mason, M. E., Susannah, p.101–18 *4–5
Rothery, Central American Roundabout, p.125–27 6
Seaman, Mr. Peck's Pets *4–5
Taber, First Book of Dogs 4–5
Woolley, Schoolroom Zoo *4–5
Zim, Monkeys 4–5

———— Parrakeets 4–6
PETS—CARE
Bianco, All about Pets 5–6
Zim, Rabbits, p.31–63 4–5

PETUNIAS
Comstock, Handbook of Nature Study, p.581–84 6

PHAËTHON
Sellew, Adventures with the Gods, p.54–61 4–5

PHARAOHS: *see* Egypt—Ancient

PHEASANTS
Buck, F., Jungle Animals, p.24–25 5–6
Colby, First Hunt, p.18 5–6

PHIDIAS
Hillyer, Child's History of Art, p.181–85 5–6

PHILADELPHIA
De Angeli, Thee, Hannah! *4–6
Meigs, Dutch Colt *4–6
Milhous, Patrick and the Golden Slippers *4–5

PHILANTHROPISTS: *see* names of philanthropists, as Carnegie, Andrew

PHILIPPINE ISLANDS
Barrows, Old World Lands, p.201–5 6
Cheney, Peg-legged Pirate of Sulu *4–5
O'Neill, Picture Story of the Philippines 5–6
Quinn, Picture Map Geography of the Pacific Islands, p.21–31 5–6
Sowers, Swords and Sails in the Philippines *5–6
Wood, E., Pedro's Coconut Skates *4–5

PHILIPPINE ISLANDS—GAMES: *see* Games—Philippine Islands

PHILIPPINE ISLANDS—INDUSTRIES
O'Neill, Picture Story of the Philippines 5–6

PHILLIP, JOHN WOODWARD
Fisher, D. F. C., And Long Remember, p.112–18 6

PHIPS, WILLIAM
Chase, V., Knight of the Golden Fleece 6

PHOENICIA
Falls, First 3000 Years, p.113–16   6
Hartman, Builders of the Old World, p.106–11   6
Hillyer, Child's History of the World, p.74–78   5–6
McGuire, Glimpses into the Long Ago, p.101–4   5–6

PHOENIX
Jacobson, First Book of Mythical Beasts, p.33–34   4–6

PHONOGRAPH: *see also* Edison, Thomas Alva
Buchanan, How Man Made Music, p.173–77   6
Crouse, W. H., Understanding Science, p.87–92   6
Irving, Sound and Ultrasonics, p.113–16   6
Schneider, H., Everyday Machines and How They Work, p.119–20, 176   5–6
Wood, E., Pedro's Coconut Skates, p.37–84   *4–5

PHOSPHORUS
Loomis, Field Book of Common Rocks and Minerals, p.159–61   6

PHOTOELECTRIC CELLS
Asimov, Satellites in Outer Space, p.50–54   4–5

PHOTOGRAPHY: *see also* Microphotography; Motion Pictures; Telephotography
Beeler, Experiments in Science, p.70–72, 116–18   5–6
Bendick, How Much and How Many, p.152–54   5–6
Crouse, W. H., Understanding Science, p.122–28   6
Darrow, Boys' Own Book of Great Inventions, p.331–53   6
Freeman, M. B., Fun with Your Camera   4–6
Gottlieb, Photography with Basic Cameras   4–6
Hamilton, E. T., Handicraft for Girls, p.178–87   6
Morgan, A. P., Boys' Book of Science and Construction, p.303–13   6
Pohlmann, Myrtle Albertina's Secret   *4–6

Seymour, Eric's Christmas Camera   *4–6
Teale, Junior Book of Insects, p.131–39   6

PHOTOSYNTHESIS
Barr, Young Scientist Takes a Ride, p.112–13   5–6
Branley, Solar Energy, p.57–71   6

PHYFE, DUNCAN
Bailey, C. S., Children of the Handcrafts, p.65–74   5–6

PHYSICAL GEOGRAPHY: *see* Caves; Climate; Clouds; Deserts; Earth; Earthquakes; Geography; Geology; Glaciers; Icebergs; Islands; Lakes; Mountains; Ocean; Prairies; Rain; Rivers; Seashore; Storms; Tides; Tropics; Volcanoes; Water; Weather; Winds

PHYSICIANS: *see* Doctors

PHYSICS: *see also* Aerodynamics; Air; Barometers; Chemistry; Electricity; Experiments—Scientific; Gases, Liquids, Solids; Gravitation; Heat; Light; Magnetism; Mechanics; Radium; Sound; Thermometers
Freeman, M. B., Fun with Science   6
Nourse, So You Want To Be a Scientist, p.115–29   5–6

PHYSIOLOGY: *see also* Eye; Health; Medicine
Baker, A. O., Your Science World, p.155–61   6
Barr, More Research Ideas for Young Scientists, p.90–104   5–6
———— Research Ideas for Young Scientists, p.54–63   5–6
Beauchamp, Discovering Our World, Bk.1, p.67–88   4
Calder, Wonderful World of Medicine   5–6
Glemser, All about the Human Body   5–6
Parker, B. M., Golden Book of Science, p.42–49   4–6
———— You as a Machine   5–6
Ravielli, Wonders of the Human Body   5–6
Schneider, H., How Your Body Works   4–6

PIANOS

Buchanan, How Man Made Music, p.29–30, 171–72 (electronic)   6

Estes, Rufus M., p.57–77   *4–6

Hale, Complete Peterkin Papers, p.13–14 (About Elizabeth Eliza's Piano)   *4–6

Huntington, Tune Up   4–6

Lacey, Picture Book of Musical Instruments, p.50–51   5–6

PICNICS

Coatsworth, Alice-All-By-Herself, p.26–33   *4–6

Enright, Saturdays, p.119–29   *4–6

Jaeger, Easy Crafts, p.128–29   4–6

Lattimore, Molly in the Middle, p.16–28   *4–5

Lovelace, Betsy-Tacy, p.15–20   *4–5

Mulac, Game Book, p.275–97   6

New York Herald Tribune, Young America's Cook Book, p.285–94   4–6

Rombauer, Cookbook for Boys and Girls, p.208–14   6

Woolley, Ginnie and Geneva, p.102–16   *4–5

PICTOGRAPHS: *see* Graphs; Picture Writing

PICTURE TRANSMISSION: *see* Telephotography; Television

PICTURE WRITING: *see also* Hieroglyphics

Epstein, S., First Book of Words, p.23–26   5–6

Hofsinde, Indian Picture Writing   5–6

————— Indian's Secret World, p.41–46   5–6

Hogben, Wonderful World of Communication, p.11, 28   6

Kipling, Just So Stories, p.123–41   *4–6

Rogers, F., Heels, Wheels, and Wire, p.9–11   5–6

Salomon, Book of Indian Crafts & Indian Lore, p.393, 396   6

PICTURES: *see also* Art; Art Museums; Artists; Motion Pictures; Painting; Photography

Chase, A. E., Famous Paintings   6

Downer, Discovering Design, p.80–103   6

Fessenden, Old Testament Story   4–6

Weisgard, Treasures To See   4–6

PIERCE, FRANKLIN

Beard, Presidents in American History, p.61–62, 162–63   6

Coy, First Book of Presidents, p.40   4–6

Petersham, Story of the Presidents of the United States, p.37   4–6

PIERS: *see* Harbors

PIGEONS: *see also* Passenger Pigeons

Carlson, N. S., Evangeline   *4–5

Comstock, Handbook of Nature Study, p.50–53   6

Hyde, Animal Clocks and Compasses, p.48–49   5–6

Rogers, F., Heels, Wheels, and Wire, p.198–208   5–6

Spencer, P. R., Traveling New Trails, p.463–74   6

Weeks, Tales of a Common Pigeon   *4–6

Writers Project, Pigeons, no.28   5–6

Zim, Homing Pigeons   5–6

PIGMIES: *see* Pygmies

PIGS

Barr, Young Scientist Takes a Ride, p.125–26   5–6

Buehr, Meat from Ranch to Table, p.80–85   4–6

Carlson, N. S., Sashes Red and Blue, p.1–9   *4–6

Comstock, Handbook of Nature Study, p.286–93   6

De la Mare, Animal Stories, p.16–19   *4–6

Earle, Pigs, Tame and Wild   4–6

Eberle, Basketful, p.76–78   4–6

Grahame, Bertie's Escapade   *4–5

Grant, B., Zachary, the Governor's Pig   *4–6

Hogeboom, Familiar Animals and How To Draw Them, p.20–23   4–5

Hogner, Barnyard Family, p.48–55   5–6

————— Farm Animals, p.93–106   6

Robertson, K., Ticktock and Jim, p.71–76   *4–6

Weil, Animal Families   4

White, E. B., Charlotte's Web   *4–6

PIKAS
Hogner, Animal Book, p.90–91   6
Stoutenberg, Wild Animals of the Far
West, p.95   4–6

PILGRIM FATHERS: *see also* Colonial
Period in America; Plymouth; Puritans; Thanksgiving Day
Coatsworth, First Adventure   *4–5
Dalgliesh, America Builds Homes   4–5
Daugherty, Landing of the Pilgrims
   4–6
Duvoisin, And There Was America,
p.57–65   4–6
Hall-Quest, How the Pilgrims Came to
Plymouth   4–6
Harper, Harvest Feast, p.29–121   4–6
Hays, Christmas on the Mayflower
   *4–5
Meadowcroft, First Year   *4–6

PILGRIMAGES: *see* Crusades

PILOTS: *see also* Aviators
Buehr, Harbors and Cargoes, p.65–67
   5–6

PINE TREES
Comstock, Handbook of Nature Study,
p.670–75   6
Cormack, First Book of Trees, p.43–50
   4–6
Dudley, Our American Trees, p.4–7,
52–55, 128–29   5–6
McKenny, Trees of the Countryside,
p.2–3, 8–9   4–6

PINWHEELS
Soong, Art of Chinese Paper Folding,
p.18–22   4–6
Sperling, How To Make Things Out of
Paper, p.112–18   5–6

PIONEER LIFE: *see also* Colonial Period
in America; Costume—Pioneer Life;
Lewis and Clark Expedition; Log
Cabins; Oregon Trail; Prairies; Ranch
Life; Sante Fe Trail; West; Westward
Movement; also names of pioneers,
as Boone, Daniel; Carson, Kit; Crockett, David
Bailey, C. S., Pioneer Art in America
   *5–6
Beals, Davy Crockett   5–6
Brink, Caddie Woodlawn   *6
———— Magical Melons   *5–6
Brock, Topsy-Turvy Family   *4–5

Bulla, Riding the Pony Express   4–5
Coatsworth, Away Goes Sally   *4–6
———— Five Bushel Farm   *4–5
Commager, H. S., First Book of American History, p.29–37   4–6
Dalgliesh, Courage of Sarah Noble
   *4–5
Daugherty, Daniel Boone   5–6
De Leeuw, C., Fear in the Forest   *4–6
Douglas, Appleseed Farm   *4–6
Edmonds, Matchlock Gun   *4–6
Enright, Thimble Summer, p.17–27
   *5–6
Hammett, I, Priscilla   *5–6
Hark, Story of the Pennsylvania Dutch
   4–6
Harper, Harvest Feast, p.124–48   *4–6
Judson, Andrew Jackson   5–6
Le Sueur, Little Brother of the Wilderness   4–5
McMeekin, Journey Cake   *5–6
McNeer, Story of the Southern Highlands   4–6
Mason, M. E., Middle Sister   *4–5
———— Susannah   *4–5
———— Young Mr. Meeker   *4–5
Meadowcroft, Abraham Lincoln, p.1–87
   6
Meigs, Willow Whistle   *4–6
Purdy, He Heard America Sing   6
Rietveld, Nicky's Bugle   *4–6
Steele, Buffalo Knife   *4–6
———— Winter Danger   *4–6
Wilder, By the Shores of Silver Lake
   *5–6
———— Little House in the Big Woods
   *4–6
———— Little Town on the Prairie
   *5–6
———— Long Winter   *5–6

PIPES (musical)
Buchanan, How Man Made Music,
p.49–54   6

PIRATES: *see also* Cocos Island
Cheney, Peg-legged Pirate of Sulu
   *4–5
Hughes, First Book of the West Indies,
p.7–11   5–6
Le Grand, Tom Benn and Blackbeard,
the Pirate   *4–5
Stockton, Buccaneers and Pirates of Our
Coasts   6

Tallant, Pirate Lafitte and the Battle of New Orleans   5–6

PITCAIRN ISLAND
Quinn, Picture Map Geography of the Pacific Islands, p.119–21   5–6

PITCH (musical)
Geralton, Story of Sound, p.7   5–6

PITT, WILLIAM, EARL OF CHATHAM, 1708–78
Olcott, Good Stories for Great Birthdays, p.93–107   4–6

PITTSBURGH
Crawford, "Hello, the Boat!", p.1–32
                                       *6
Meadowcroft, By Wagon and Flatboat, p.82–90   *4–5

PIZARRO, FRANCISCO
American Heritage, Discoverers of the New World, p.77–81   5–6
Bleeker, Inca, p.130–31, 135–38, 145–46   5–6
Peck, Pageant of South American History, p.69–90   6
Rothery, South American Roundabout, p.44–50   5–6

PLAGUES
Bronson, Grasshopper Book, p.39–55
                                      4–6

PLAINS: *see* Great Plains

PLAINS INDIANS
Annixter, Buffalo Chief   *6
Burns, World Full of Homes, p.11–13
                                     4–6
Christensen, Buffalo Kill   *6
Tunis, Indians, p.89–106   6

PLANETARIUMS
Baker, R. H., When the Stars Come Out, p.51–56   6
Goodwin, Real Book about Stars, p.162–64   4–6
Jaeger, Easy Crafts, p.20–21   4–6

PLANETS—MAJOR
Baker, R. H., When the Stars Come Out, p.99–111   6
Beauchamp, Discovering Our World, Bk.1, p.130–35   4
Bendick, First Book of Space Travel, p.53–59   5–6

Branley, Guide to Outer Space, p.12–21
                                      4–6
_____ Nine Planets   6
Freeman, M. B., Fun with Astronomy, p.30–32   4–6
Gallant, R. A., Exploring the Planets
                                     5–6
Goodwin, Real Book about Stars, p.12, 34–108   4–6
Leonard, Exploring Science, p.117–35
                                      6
Meyer, Picture Book of Astronomy, p.18–30   4–5
Schneider, L., Space in Your Future, p.29–37   6

PLANETS—MINOR
Baker, A. O., When the Stars Come Out, p.113–15   6
Gallant, R. A., Exploring the Planets, p.66–73   5–6
Schealer, This Way to the Stars, p.114–18   6

PLANKTON
Cooper, E. K., Science on the Shores and Banks, p.48–49   5–6
Kavaler, Wonders of Algae, p.65–76
                                      6

PLANT BREEDING: *see also* Grafting
Eberle, Basketful, p.173–80   4–6

PLANT LICE
Comstock, Handbook of Nature Study, p.351–54   6
Gaul, Picture Book of Insects, p.12–13
                                     4–6
Parker, B. M., Insects and Their Ways, p.21–22   4–6
_____ Plant and Animal Partnerships, p.5–7   5–6

PLANTATION LIFE: *see also* Negroes; Rubber; Slavery; South; Tobacco
Coatsworth, Golden Horseshoe   *6
Dalgliesh, America Builds Homes   4
Shackelford, Child's Story of the Negro, p.88–106   4–5

PLANTING: *see* Agriculture; Gardening

PLANTS: *see also* Botany; Bulbs; Ferns; Flowers; Fruit; Fungi; Galls (botany); Gardening; Grasses; Herbs; Leaves; Marine Plants; Mosses; Nature Study; Parasites; Roots; Seeds;

Trees; Vegetables; Weeds; Wild Flowers

Barr, Research Ideas for Young Scientists, p.95–108   5–6

Beauchamp, Discovering Our World, Bk.1, p.38–43   4

Beeler, More Experiments in Science, p.33–40   5–6

Buck, M. W., In Ponds and Streams, p.11–16   4–6

———— In Woods and Fields   4–5

———— In Yards and Gardens   4–6

———— Pets from the Pond, p.14–21   4–6

———— Small Pets from Woods and Fields, p.12–19   4–6

Cassell, Nature Games and Activities, p.44–54   4–6

Comstock, Handbook of Nature Study, p.453–731   6

Cooper, E. K., Science on the Shores and Banks, p.46–48, 153–72   5–6

Doane, Book of Nature, p.24–25, 58–59, 96–97   5–6

Fenton, C. L., Plants That Feed Us   5–6

Gaul, Pond Book   4–6

Goetz, Deserts, p.16–27   4–6

Guilcher, Fruit Is Born   5–6

Harrison, Outdoor Adventure   4–5

Huntington, Let's Go to the Desert, p.6–39   4–5

Hyde, Plants Today and Tomorrow   6

Jauss, Discovering Nature the Year Round   4–6

Kirkus, First Book of Gardening   4–6

Morgan, A. H., Field Book of Ponds and Streams   6

Morgan, A. P., Aquarium Book for Boys and Girls, p.42–46   5–6

Parker, B. M., Golden Book of Science, p.30–41   4–6

———— Living Things, p.6–11   4–6

———— Plant and Animal Partnerships, p.16–35   5–6

———— Plant Factories   5–6

———— Saving Our Wild Life, p.22–25   5–6

Podendorf, 101 Science Experiments, p.130–45   4–5

Selsam, How To Grow House Plants   5–6

———— Plants That Heal   6

———— Plants We Eat   4–6

———— Play with Seeds   4–6

———— See through the Forest   4–6

———— See through the Lake, p.6–12   4–6

———— Underwater Zoos, p.47–48, 60–62, 87–89   4–6

Sperry, All about the Jungle, p.57–62 (Indonesia)   5–6

PLANTS—FERTILIZATION: *see* Interdependence of Plants and Animals; Seed Dispersal

PLANTS IN WINTER

Hylander, Out of Doors in Autumn, p.95–113   5–6

Parker, B. M., Garden Indoors   5–6

PLASTICS

Beeler, Experiments in Science, p.64–66   5–6

Colby, Plastic Magic   6

Freeman, I. M., All about the Wonders of Chemistry, p.110–16   6

Lent, Men at Work in the Great Lakes States, p.96–99   4–6

Writers Project, Plastics, no.38   5–6

PLATINUM

Loomis, Field Book of Common Rocks and Minerals, p.95–96   6

PLATT NATIONAL PARK

Melbo, Our Country's National Parks, v.1, p.100–106   6

PLAY: *see* Amusements; Athletics; Games; Sports; Toys

PLAYS: *see also* Christmas—Plays; Miracle Plays; Motion Pictures; Operas; Pageants; Pantomimes; Puppet Shows; Shadow Plays

Carlson, B. W., Act It Out   4–6

———— Right Play for You   4–6

PLAYS—PRODUCTION: *see also* Costume

Ackley, Marionettes   5–6

Severn, Let's Give a Show, p.118–78   4–6

White, A. M. G., Dramatized Ballads   4–6

PLOVERS

Hyde, Animal Clocks and Compasses, p.37–38   5–6

Lavine, Strange Travelers, p.68–72
5–6
Webb, Birds in Their Homes, p.59, 62–63   4–6

PLUMBING
Bendick, First Book of How To Fix It, p.51–55   4–6

PLUTO (planet)
Branley, Nine Planets, p.70–73   6
Gallant, R. A., Exploring the Planets, p.114–19   5–6
Goodwin, Real Book about Stars, p.105–8   4–6

PLUTONIUM
Fermi, Story of Atomic Energy, p.98–100   6

PLYMOUTH: *see also* Pilgrim Fathers
Hall-Quest, How the Pilgrims Came to Plymouth, p.109–15   4–6
Rich, First Book of the Early Settlers, p.21–45   4–6

POCAHONTAS
Aulaire, Pocahontas   4–5
Barksdale, That Country Called Virginia, p.24–28   6
Dalgliesh, America Builds Homes   4–5
Lawson, M. A., Pocahontas and Captain John Smith   6

POETRY—CHINESE
Spencer, C., Made in China, p.143–49
5–6

POETS
Brown, A. F., In the Days of Giants, p.21–34   4–6

POISONS
Selsam, Plants That Heal, p.68–81   6

POLAND: *see also* Costume—Poland
Alden, Why the Chimes Rang, p.19–29
*4–6
Barrows, Old World Lands, p.103–5   6
Kelly, Christmas Nightingale   *6
———— Land of the Polish People
5–6
Wheeler, Frederic Chopin   4–6

POLAND—HISTORY
Kelly, Land of the Polish People, p.1–17
5–6
Mills, So Young a Queen   6

POLAR BEARS: *see* Bears

POLAR EXPEDITIONS: *see* Antarctic Regions; Arctic Regions; also names of explorers, as Amundsen, Roald

POLAR LIGHTS: *see* Aurora Borealis

POLAR REGIONS: *see* Antarctic Regions; Arctic Regions; Eskimos; Greenland; Iceland; Lapland

POLECATS: *see also* Skunks
Moe, Animal Inn, p.52–59   4–6

POLES IN THE UNITED STATES
Association for Childhood Education, Told under the Stars and Stripes, p.136–49   *4–6
Estes, Hundred Dresses   *4–6
Hazeltine, Easter Book of Legends and Stories, p.199–209   *5–6

POLICE: *see also* Canada—Royal Canadian Mounted Police
Enright, Saturdays, p.114–18   *4–6
Estes, Moffats, p.24–52   *4–6
Sootin, Let's Go to a Police Station
4–5
Spencer, P. R., Finding New Trails, p.81–90   4

POLITENESS: *see* Etiquette

POLITICS: *see* Government; also names of countries, subhead Government, as United States—Government

POLK, JAMES KNOX
Beard, Presidents in American History, p.49–50, 160–61   6
Coy, First Book of Presidents, p.37
4–6
Petersham, Story of the Presidents of the United States, p.32–33   4–6

POLLEN
Disraeli, New Worlds through the Microscope, p.126–37   6

POLLINATION: *see also* Botany; Interdependence of Plants and Animals; Plants
Cooper, E. K., Science in Your Own Back Yard, p.71–73   5–6
Parker, B. M., Plant and Animal Partnerships, p.30–33   5–6

POLO, MARCO
Buehr, World of Marco Polo   5–6
Cottler, Heroes of Civilization, p.3–12
6

Dalgliesh, America Begins, p.16–17
4–5
Duvoisin, They Put Out to Sea, p.62–
80   4–6
Hartman, Builders of the Old World,
p.393–403   6
Hillyer, Child's History of the World,
p.316–21   5–6
Kent, He Went with Marco Polo   *6
Spencer, C., Land of the Chinese People, p.42–44   6

POLYNESIA: *see* Pacific Islands

POMPEII
Hall, J., Buried Cities, p.1–93   5–6
Pough, All about Volcanoes and Earth-
quakes, p.3–12   4–6

PONCE DE LEÓN, JUAN
American Heritage, Discoverers of the
New World, p.64–69   5–6
Baker, N. B., Juan Ponce de León   5–6
Dalgliesh, America Begins, p.40–41
4–5
Duvoisin, And There Was America,
p.19–20   4–6
Hazeltine, Easter Book of Legends and
Stories, p.167–71   *5–6

PONCE DE LEÓN, JUAN—PLAYS
Hazeltine, Easter Book of Legends and
Stories, p.172–83   5–6

POND LILIES: *see* Water Lilies

PONDS: *see also* Animals—Fresh-Water;
Beetles; Insects—Aquatic
Bronson, Pollwiggle's Progress   4–5
Buck, M. W., Pets from the Pond   4–6
Gaul, Pond Book   4–6
Hylander, Out of Doors in Spring, p.28–
57   5–6
Kane, Tale of a Pond   5–6
Morgan, A. H., Field Book of Ponds
and Streams   6

PONTIAC'S CONSPIRACY, 1763
Foster, G., George Washington's World,
p.83–84   6

PONY EXPRESS
Adams, S. H., Pony Express   4–6
Bulla, Riding the Pony Express   *4–5
Driggs, Pony Express Goes Through
6
Garst, Buffalo Bill   6

Mellin, Horses across the Ages, p.68–
72   4–6
Petersham, America's Stamps, p.20–21
5–6
Rogers, F., Heels, Wheels, and Wire,
p.53–60   5–6
Tousey, Jerry and the Pony Express
*4–5

POPLAR TREES
Comstock, Handbook of Nature Study,
p.655–58   6
McKenny, Trees of the Countryside,
p.56–57   4–6

POPPIES
Comstock, Handbook of Nature Study,
p.560–65   6

PORCELAIN: *see* Pottery

PORCUPINES
Brown, V., How To Understand Animal
Talk, p.135–36   6
Franklin, Wild Animals of the South-
west, p.144–53   5–6
Gall, Flat Tail, p.100–108   *4–6
Hogner, Animal Book, p.58–59   6
Mason, G. F., Animal Tracks, p.58–59
4–6
———— Animal Weapons, p.76–79
5–6
Spencer, P. R., Finding New Trails,
p.259–62   4
Stoutenberg, Wild Animals of the Far
West, p.92–93   4–6

PORPOISES: *see* Dolphins

PORTS: *see* Harbors

PORTUGAL
Barrows, Old World Lands, p.92–93
6
Joy, Young People of the Western Mediterranean, p.124–38   6
Kent, He Went with Vasco da Gama
*6

PORTUGUESE IN SOUTH AMERICA
Brown, R. J., Land and People of Bra-
zil, p.22–41   6
May, Let's Read about Brazil   4–6

PORTUGUESE IN THE UNITED
STATES
Association for Childhood Education,
Told under the Stars and Stripes,
p.239–48   *4–6

POSTAGE STAMPS
Hillyer, Child's History of Art, p.239–41
5–6
Lewis, R., Stamp Collecting   4–6
Petersham, America's Stamps   5–6
Rothery, Central American Round-
about, p.214–24   6

POSTAL SERVICE: *see* Mail Service

POSTIMPRESSIONISM (art)
Hillyer, Child's History of Art, p.132–
35   5–6

POSTURE
Beery, Manners Made Easy, p.50–62
6

POTATOES
Bleeker, Inca, p.92–93   5–6
Eberle, Basketful, p.165–68   4–6
Hyde, Animals Clocks and Compasses,
p.130–32   5–6
Lent, Men at Work in New England,
p.102–5   4–6

POTTERY: *see also* Clay Modeling; In-
dians of North America—Pottery;
Tiles
Bailey, C. S., Pioneer Art in America,
p.195–207   *5–6
Ceder, Joel, the Potter's Son   *4–6
Chrisman, Shen of the Sea, p.220–34
*5–6
Gates, Blue Willow   *5–6
Hamilton, E. T., Handicraft for Girls,
p.14–21, 131–52   6
Hark, Story of the Pennsylvania Dutch
4–6
Hillyer, Child's History of Art, p.201–3
5–6
Hoffine, Jennie's Mandan Bowl   *4–6
Jaeger, Easy Crafts, p.50–63   4–6
Leeming, Fun with Clay   4–6
Stinetorf, Children of North Africa,
p.44–57   *5–6
Urbahns, Little Red Dragon   *4–6
————— Tangled Web   *5–6
Writers Project, Story of Clay, no.24,
p.36–46   5–6
Zarchy, Let's Make a Lot of Things,
p.32–38, 104–19   5–6

POTTERY—CANADA
Bonner, Made in Canada, p.65–75   5–6

POTTERY—CHINA
Spencer, C., Made in China, p.3–9,
150–55   5–6
POTTERY—INCA
Bleeker, Inca, p.96, 102–6   5–6
POTTERY—JAPAN
Uchida, Takao and Grandfather's Sword
*4–6
POTTOS
Bridges, Zoo Doctor, p.68–79   4–6
POULTRY: *see also* Chickens; Ducks;
Geese; Pigeons; Turkeys
Darling, L., Chickens   4–6
Eberle, Basketful, p.79–85   4–6
Scheib, First Book of Food, p.29–31
5–6
POWELL, JOHN WESLEY
Melbo, Our Country's National Parks,
v.1, p.209–12, 232   6
POWER MECHANICS
Schneider, H., More Power to You
5–6
POWHATAN: *see* Pocahontas; Smith,
John; Virginia—History
PRAIRIE CHICKENS: *see* Grouse
PRAIRIE DOGS
Barker, Winter-sleeping Wildlife, p.18–
23   5–6
Carr, Children of the Covered Wagon,
p.121–23   *4–6
Hogner, Animal Book, p.50–52   6
Mason, G. F., Animal Homes, p.30–34
4–6
PRAIRIE FIRES
Brink, Caddie Woodlawn, p.214–18
*6
Wilder, Little House on the Prairie,
p.274–85   *4–6
————— On the Banks of Plum Creek,
p.268–75   *4–6
PRAIRIE SCHOONERS: *see* Covered
Wagons
PRAIRIES: *see also* Iowa; Westward
Movement
Disney, Worlds of Nature, p.70–81
4–6
Fenton, C. L., Land We Live On, p.12–
13   4–6

Goetz, Grasslands, p.8–33   4–6
Wilder, By the Shores of Silver Lake,
    *5–6
———— Little House on the Prairie
    *4–6
———— Long Winter   *5–6

PRAYERS
Fitch, One God   5–6

PRECIOUS STONES: *see also* names of
precious stones, as Diamonds
Loomis, Field Book of Common Rocks
and Minerals, p.121–25   6

PREHISTORIC ANIMALS: *see also* Fos-
sils; Mammoths
Andrews, All about Dinosaurs   4–6
———— All about Strange Beasts of
the Past   5–6
Baker, A. O., Your Science World,
p.53–61   6
Bloch, Dinosaurs   4–6
Blough, Discovering Dinosaurs   4–5
Burger, All about Fish, p.18–21   5–6
Burns, Horses and Their Ancestors
    4–5
Cameron, Terrible Churnadryne   *4–6
Colbert, Millions of Years Ago   6
Epstein, S., Prehistoric Animals   6
Fenton, C. L., Life Long Ago   6
———— Prehistoric World   4–6
Fisher, J., Wonderful World of the Air,
p.14–23   5–6
Fox, From Bones to Bodies, p.30–31,
65–66, 90–91   6
Hall, E., Land and People of Argentina,
p.29–30   6
Knight, C. R., Life through the Ages   6
Leonard, Exploring Science, p.22–29
    6
Life, World We Live In, p.72–97   5–6
Parker, B. M., Reptiles, p.34–35   4–6
Reed, Earth for Sam   6
Robinson, W. W., Beasts of the Tar Pits
    5–6
Scheele, Ancient Elephants   4–6
———— First Mammals   6
———— Prehistoric Animals   6
Spencer, P. R., Finding New Trails,
p.288–95   4
White, A. T., All about Our Changing
Rocks, p.122–26   5–6
———— Prehistoric America   4–6

Williams, H. L., Stories in Rocks,
p.108–22   6
Zim, Dinosaurs   5–6

PREHISTORIC MAN: *see also* Archeol-
ogy; Bronze Age; Cave Drawings;
Cave Dwellers; Cliff Dwellers; Evolu-
tion; Fire; Geology; Lake Dwellers;
Races of Man; Stone Age
Adler, Tools in Your Life, p.30–54
    5–6
Ames, First People in the World   4–5
Batchelor, Communication, p.7–16
    4–6
Baumann, Caves of the Great Hunters
    6
Burns, Man and His Tools   5–6
Colbert, Millions of Years Ago, p.121–
50   6
Hartman, Builders of the Old World,
p.3–33   6
Hillyer, Child's History of the World,
p.10–15   5–6
Lamprey, All the Ways of Building,
p.1–11   6
Leonard, Exploring Science, p.149–54
    6
Liberty, First Book of Tools, p.11–13,
38–52   5–6
McGuire, Glimpses into the Long Ago,
p.1–31   5–6
Osborne, C. G., First Lake Dwellers
    *4–6
Pyne, Little History of the Wide World
    4–6
Reed, Earth for Sam   6
Sterling, Story of Caves, p.82–99   5–6
Tunis, Indians, p.15–19   6
Watson, Golden History of the World,
p.10–13   5–6
White, A. T., Prehistoric America   4–6

PRESIDENTS—UNITED STATES: *see
also* United States—Government;
United States—History; also names
of presidents, as Adams, John
Beard, Presidents in American History
    6
Brown, H. M., America Is My Country,
p.60–69   5–6
Coy, First Book of Presidents   4–6
Petersham, Story of the Presidents of
the United States   4–6

Ross, G. E., Know Your Government, p.71   6

PRIBILOF ISLANDS
Lindquist, W., Alaska, p.84–86   5–6
Spencer, P. R., Finding New Trails, p.269–73   4
Stefansson, Here Is Alaska, p.112–15   6

PRIDE IN BACKGROUND AND HER-ITAGE
Aulaire, Nils   *4–5
Hoffine, Jennie's Mandan Bowl   *4–6
Parish, At the Palace Gates   *4–6

PRIMITIVE MAN: *see also* Art—Primitive Man; Barbarians; Cannibals; Cave Drawings; Congo; Houses—Primitive Man; Music—Primitive Man; Pacific Islands; Prehistoric Man; Pygmies
Jupo, Nothing To Wear but Clothes   4–5

PRINCE EDWARD ISLAND
Quinn, Picture Map Geography of Canada and Alaska, p.16–20   4–6

PRINCESSES: *see also* names of various countries, subhead Folk Tales, as Spain—Folk Tales
Johnson, E., Three-in-One Prince   *4–5
Macdonald, G., Princess and Curdie   *4–6
———— Princess and the Goblin   *4–6
Thurber, Many Moons   *4–5

PRINTING: *see also* Books; Franklin, Benjamin; Gutenberg, Johannes; Ink; Paper
Bailey, C. S., Children of the Handcrafts, p.181–88   *5–6
Bendick, How Much and How Many, p.89–94   5–6
Chrisman, Shen of the Sea, p.1–15   *5–6
Darrow, Boys' Own Book of Great Inventions, p.3–15   6
Daugherty, Poor Richard   6
Eaton, That Lively Man, Ben Franklin, p.11–99   6
Fenner, Time To Laugh, p.116–26   *4–6
Foster, J., Pages, Pictures, and Print   6

Hark, Story of the Pennsylvania Dutch   4–6
Haywood, Eddie and His Big Deals   *4–5
Hillyer, Child's History of the World, p.333–35   5–6
Hogben, Wonderful World of Communication, p.24–37   6
Lent, "I Work on a Newspaper," p.62–74   6
Ota, Printing for Fun   4–6
Proudfit, River-Boy, p.71–100   6
Spencer, C., Land of the Chinese People, p.36–38   6
Spencer, P. R., Finding New Trails, p.194–96   4
Weiss, H., Paper, Ink and Roller   4–6

PRISMS
Land, B., Quest of Isaac Newton, p.7–11   6
Meyer, Prisms and Lenses   6

PRISONS
Henry, M., King of the Wind, p.111–23   *5–6
Kent, He Went with Vasco da Gama, p.66–74, 197–211   *6
Sharp, Rescuers   *4–6

PROGRESS, ACCEPTANCE OF AND ADJUSTMENT TO
Buff, Magic Maize   *4–6
Burns, Man and His Tools   5–6
Eisenberg, Won Kim's Ox   *4–6
Holling, Seabird   *4–6
Lane, C. D., River Dragon   *4–6
Steiner, Last Horse   *4–5
Tennant, All the Proud Tribesmen   *6
Waltrip, Quiet Boy   *4–6

PROKOFIEV, SERGE
Burch, Modern Composers for Young People, p.185–89   5–6

PROMETHEUS
Asimov, Words from the Myths, p.122–25   6
Sellew, Adventures with the Gods, p.1–10, 32–37   4–5

PROSERPINA
Benson, Stories of the Gods and Heroes, p.76–86   5–6
Sellew, Adventures with the Gods, p.62–68   4–5

PROTECTION: *see* Animals—Protection; Birds—Protection; Insects—Protection; Safety

PROTESTANTISM
Fitch, One God, p.98–135   5–6
McNeer, Martin Luther   6

PROTOZOA
Cooper, E. K., Science on the Shores and Banks, p.47–48   5–6
Disraeli, New Worlds through the Microscope, p.81–84   6
Morgan, A. H., Field Book of Ponds and Streams, p.55–57   6
Parker, B. M., Plant and Animal Partnerships, p.11–12   5–6
Reed, Sea for Sam, p.114–20   6

PROVENCE
Bragdon, L. J., Land and People of France, p.91–97   6

PRUNES
Gates, Sarah's Idea, p.60–77, 95–108   *4–6

PTARMIGANS
Gillham, Beyond the Clapping Mountains, p.86–98   *4–6

PUBLIC UTILITIES: *see* Electric Railroads; Railroads; Water Supply

PUEBLO INDIANS: *see also* Cliff Dwellers; Hopi Indians; Indians of North America
Bleeker, Pueblo Indians   4–6
Burns, World Full of Homes, p.64–68   4–6
Dorian, Hokahey!, p.42–52   5–6
Fletcher, S. E., American Indian, p.39–56   5–6
Holling, Book of Indians, p.73–96   4–6
Moon, Chi-Wee   *4–6
Spencer, P. R., Exploring New Trails, p.92–102   5

PUERTO RICANS
Brenner, Barto Takes the Subway   *4

PUERTO RICO
Baker, N. B., Juan Ponce de León   5–6
Barrows, American Continents, p.241–44   5
Hughes, First Book of the West Indies, p.24–25   5–6

Quinn, Picture Map Geography of Mexico, Central America and the West Indies, p.100–105   4–6
Spencer, P. R., Exploring New Trails, p.418–21   5
Tor, Getting To Know Puerto Rico   4–6

PUERTO RICO—GAMES: *see* Games—Puerto Rico

PULLEYS
Bechdolt, Going Up, p.25–30   5–6
Liberty, First Book of Tools, p.26–27   5–6
Parker, B. M., Machines, p.16–19   5–6
Schneider, H., Everyday Machines and How They Work, p.38–39   5–6

PULLMANS: *see* Railroads—Sleeping Cars

PUMAS: *see* Panthers

PUMPKINS
Comstock, Handbook of Nature Study, p.611–17   6

PUMPS: *see* Water Supply

PUNISHMENT—COLONIAL PERIOD IN AMERICA
Maginley, Historic Models of Early America, p.148–56   6

PUPPET SHOWS
Ackley, Marionettes   5–6
Bufano, Remo Bufano's Book of Puppetry   5–6
Carlson, B. W., Act It Out, p.93–154   4–6
Ficklen, Handbook of Fist Puppets   4–6
Lee, What To Do Now, p.61–65   4–6
Mulac, Game Book, p.107–8   6
Robinson, J., Things To Make from Odds & Ends, p.2–4   4–6
Severn, Let's Give a Show, p.35–69   4–6
Zarchy, Let's Make More Things, p.42–43, 45   5–6
———— Let's Make Something, p.86–93   5–6

PUPPET SHOWS—POLAND
Dalgliesh, Christmas, p.212–24   4–6
Harper, Merry Christmas to You!, p.40–53   *4–6

Kelly, Christmas Nightingale, p.51–73
                                    *6

————— In Clean Hay   *4–6

PUPPETS
Collodi, Adventures of Pinocchio *4–6
Haywood, Betsy's Winterhouse, p.148–
68   *4–5

PUPPETS—HISTORY
Bufano, Remo Bufano's Book of Puppetry, p.1–9   5–6

PURE FOOD AND DRUG LAWS: *see*
Food Laws

PURIM
Taylor, S., All-of-a-Kind Family, p.91–
103   *4–6

PURITANS: *see also* Colonial Period in
America; Pilgrim Fathers
Dalgliesh, America Builds Homes 4–5
Duvoisin, And There Was America,
p.65–69   4–6
Jordan, American Costume Dolls, p.55–
65, 68–69   5–6
Leeming, Costume Book, p.100–102
                              5–6

PUSSY WILLOWS
Dudley, Our American Trees, p.112–
13   5–6

PUTNAM, ISRAEL
Lawson, R., Watchwords of Liberty,
p.16–18   4–6
Olcott, Good Stories for Great Birthdays, p.141–45   4–6

PUZZLES: *see also* Riddles; Tricks
Adler, Magic House of Numbers, p.55–
67   6
Bendick, Take a Number, p.56–61 4–5
Gardner, Mathematical Puzzles   6
Leeming, Fun with Paper, p.121–33
                              4–5

————— Fun with Puzzles   6
Mulac, Game Book, p.112–37   6

PYGMIES
Adams, K., Book of Giant Stories,
p.100–133   5–6
Gatti, Saranga, the Pygmy   *5–6
Mirsky, Thirty-one Brothers and Sisters,
p.162–71   *4–6
Sperry, All about the Jungle, p.105–10
                              5–6

————— Rain Forest, p.158–88   *6
Stinetorf, Children of South Africa,
p.37–49   *5–6

PYRAMIDS
Falls, First 3000 Years, p.57–65   6
Hartman, Builders of the Old World,
p.71–74   6
Hillyer, Child's History of Art, p.278–
83   5–6
Lamprey, All the Ways of Building,
p.21–31   6
Meadowcroft, Gift of the River, p.35–
43   5–6
Robinson, C. A., First Book of Ancient
Egypt, p.27–31   4–6
Stinetorf, Children of North Africa,
p.11–20   *5–6

PYTHEAS
Duvoisin, They Put Out to Sea, p.18–27
                              4–6

PYTHONS
Buck, F., Jungle Animals, p.38–40
                              5–6

QUAILS
Colby, First Hunt, p.16   5–6
Fenton, C. L., Wild Folk in the Desert,
p.43–45   4–6

QUAKERS: *see* Friends—Society of

QUARRYING: *see also* Rocks
Lent, Men at Work in New England,
p.98–101   4–6
————— Men at Work in the Great
Lakes States, p.52   4–6

QUARTZ
Fenton, C. L., Riches from the Earth,
p.55–56   5–6

QUEBEC: *see also* French Canadians
Quinn, Picture Map Geography of Canada and Alaska, p.28–38   4–6

QUEBEC—SIEGE OF, 1759
Bonner, Canada and Her Story, p.88–93
                              5–6

QUEENS: *see* names of queens, as Elizabeth, Queen of England

QUILTS
Bailey, C. S., Children of the Hand-
crafts, p.156–66   *5–6
Coatsworth, Five Bushel Farm, p.47–56
                              *4–5

Dalgliesh, Blue Teapot, p.5–23   *4–6
Meigs, Wind in the Chimney, p.120–36
                                   *5–6

RABBITS: *see also* Pikas
Bianco, All about Pets, p.69–80   5–6
Brown, V., How To Understand Animal
    Talk, p.34–37, 118–19   6
Clewes, Secret   *4–5
Colby, First Hunt, p.10–11   5–6
Comstock, Handbook of Nature Study,
    p.215–19   6
Dana, Good Bye, Bunny Bangs   *4–5
Fenton, C. L., Wild Folk in the Desert,
    p.46–51   4–6
Harper, Easter Chimes, p.176–81
                                   *4–6
Hogner, Animal Book, p.82–90   6
————— Barnyard .Family, p.67–71
                                   5–6
————— Farm Animals, p.178–84   6
Lawrence, Peachtree Island, p.133–46
                                   *4–5
Lawson, R., Edward, Hoppy, and Joe
                                   *4–6
————— Rabbit Hill   *4–6
Mason, G. F., Animal Tracks, p.28–33
                                   4–6
Moe, Animal Inn, p.1–6, 67–74   4–6
Weil, Animal Families   4
Zim, Rabbits   4–5

RABIES: *see* Pasteur, Louis

RACCOONS
Barker, Winter-sleeping Wildlife, p.49–
    52   5–6
Colby, First Hunt, p.12   5–6
Comstock, Handbook of Nature Study,
    p.247–50   6
Fenton, C. L., Wild Folk in the Desert,
    p.93–97   4–6
Gall, Flat Tail, p.50–52   *4–6
————— Ringtail   *4–5
Hogner, Animal Book, p.135–38   6
Mason, G. F., Animal Tracks, p.56–57
                                   4–6
Mason, M. E., Susannah, p.87–95, 106–
    8   *4–5
Moe, Animal Inn, p.109–18   4–6
Oldrin, Eight Rings on His Tail   *4–5
Reynolds, B. L., Pepper   *4–6
Seaman, Mr. Peck's Pets, p.52–61
                                   *4–5

Stoutenberg, Wild Animals of the Far
    West, p.18–19   4–6

RACES OF MAN: *see also* Archeology;
    Civilization;   Costume;   Language;
    Manners and Customs; Prehistoric
    Man; also names of races, as Indians
    of North America
Evans, All about Us   4–6

RACING: *see also* Games; Horseracing
Bothwell, Little Boat Boy, p.204–27
                                   *4–5
Cooke, D. C., Racing Cars That Made
    History   5–6
Darling, E. B., Baldy of Nome (dog)
                                   *6
French, Lance of Kanana, p.76–85 *6

RADAR
Crouse, W. H., Understanding Science,
    p.148–51   6
Huey, What Makes the Wheels Go
    Round, p.161–62   6
Morgan, A. P., First Electrical Book
    for Boys, p.236–41   6

RADIO: *see also* Marconi, Guglielmo
Adler, Tools of Science, p.60–61, 92–
    100   6
Barr, Young Scientist Takes a Ride,
    p.57–59 (static)   5–6
Butterworth, Trouble with Jenny's Ear
                                   *4–6
Crouse, W. H., Understanding Science,
    p.93, 102–10   6
Darrow, Boys' Own Book of Great In-
    ventions, p.98–116   6
Freeman, I. M., All about Electricity,
    p.106–13   5–6
Gould, All about Radio and Television,
    p.53–83, 106–39   5–6
Hartman, Machines, p.222–33   6
Huey, What Makes the Wheels Go
    Round, p.155–60   6
Meyer, Picture Book of Radio and Tele-
    vision, p.7–24   5–6
Morgan, A. P., Boy Electrician, p.240–
    69   6
————— First Electrical Book for Boys,
    p.222–23, 226–30   6
Rogers, F., Heels, Wheels, and Wire,
    p.219–32   5–6
Yates, R. F., Boys' Book of Communi-
    cations   6

RADIO BROADCASTING
Enright, Four-Story Mistake, p.118–23
*5–6
Harshaw, What Book Is That?   4–6
Spencer, P. R., Traveling New Trails,
p.487–91   6

RADIOACTIVITY
Crouse, W. H., Understanding Science,
p.187–88   6

RADIUM
Bigland, Madame Curie   6
Doorly, Radium Woman   5–6
Fermi, Story of Atomic Energy   6
Loomis, Field Book of Common Rocks
and Minerals, p.89–90   6
Parker, B. M., Earth a Great Store-
house, p.33–34   4–6
Ross, F. A., Land and People of Can-
ada, p.54–57   6
Williams, H. L., Stories in Rocks, p.90–
91   6

RAFFIA WORK: *see* Basketry

RAILROADS: *see also* Diesel Engines;
Electric Railroads; Freight; Loco-
motives; Steam Engines; Streamlined
Trains; Subways; Transcontinental
Railway; Tunnels; also names of rail-
road men, as Stephenson, George
American Heritage, Railroads in the
Days of Steam   6
Ayars, Caboose on the Roof   *4–5
Bechdolt, Going Up, p.82–95   5–6
Bethers, Perhaps I'll Be a Railroad Man
5–6
Billings, Diesel-Electric 4030   5–6
Dalgliesh, America Travels, p.29–33
*4–6
Darrow, Boys' Own Book of Great In-
ventions, p.192–209   6
Emett, New World for Nellie   *4–5
Foster, G., Abraham Lincoln's World,
p.118–20   6
Hamilton, R., First Book of Trains
4–5
Henry, R. S., Trains   5–6
Holbrook, Golden Age of Railroads
5–6
Hubbard, Train That Never Came Back
5–6
Lewellen, You and American Life Lines,
p.28–45   4–6

Olds, Riding the Rails   4–5
Rogers, F., Heels, Wheels, and Wire,
p.68–84   5–6
Van Metre, Trains, Tracks and Travel
6
Weir, R., Robert's Rescued Railway
(narrow gauge)   *5–6
Wilder, By the Shores of Silver Lake,
p.15–27   *5–6
Writers Project, Trains Going By, no.10
5–6

RAILROADS—FREIGHT CARS
Bethers, Perhaps I'll Be a Railroad Man,
p.22–23   5–6
Bunce, Freight Train   4–6
Hamilton, R., First Book of Trains,
p.11–16   4–5
Spencer, P. R., Traveling New Roads,
p.408–17   6
Van Metre, Trains, Tracks and Travel,
p.254–84   6

RAILROADS—MODELS
Maginley, Historic Models of Early
America, p.60–74   6
Schneider, H., Science Fun with Milk
Cartons, p.104–11   5–6

RAILROADS—RAILS
Van Metre, Trains, Tracks and Travel,
p.57–112   6

RAILROADS—SIGNALING
Henry, R. S., Trains, p.49–51   5–6
Olds, Riding the Rails, p.30–31   4–5
Van Metre, Trains, Tracks and Travel,
p.454–76   6

RAILROADS—SLEEPING CARS
Holbrook, Golden Age of Railroads,
p.83–89   5–6
Van Metre, Trains, Tracks and Travel,
p.305–16   6

RAILROADS—TERMINALS
Nathan, Famous Railroad Stations of
the World   5–6
Van Metre, Trains, Tracks and Travel,
p.359–85   6

RAIN: *see also* Floods; Snow; Storms;
Weather
Adler, Weather in Your Life, p.57–88
5–6
Blough, Not Only for Ducks   *4–5

Chrisman, Shen of the Sea, p.173–88
*5–6
Fenner, Time To Laugh, p.74–84 *4–6
Graham, E. H., Water for America,
p.13–17 6
Parker, B. M., Clouds, Rain, and Snow,
p.3–5 4–6
Reed, And That's Why, p.41–44 4–5

RAINBOW
Huey, What Makes the Wheels Go
Round, p.143–45 6
Land, B., Quest of Isaac Newton, p.44–
45 6
Parker, B. M., Clouds, Rain, and Snow,
p.32–34 4–6

RAISINS
Writers Project, Grapes, no.37, p.32–37
5–6

RALEIGH, WALTER
Barksdale, That Country Called Vir-
ginia, p.4–7 6
Duvoisin, And There Was America,
p.42–46 4–6
Foster, G., World of Captain John
Smith 6
Trease, Sir Walter Raleigh 5–6

RAMAYANA
Fitch, Their Search for God, p.32–34
5–6
Hazeltine, Hero Tales from Many
Lands, p.382–99 5–6
Modak, Land and People of India,
p.34–38 6

RANCH LIFE: *see also* Australia; Cattle;
Grasslands; Prairies; Sheep; Shepherd
Life; West
Benedict, Pagan the Black *5–6
Eberle, Basketful, p.51–71 4–6
Floethe, Triangle X *4
Franklin, Wild Horses of the Rio
Grande, p.7–25 5–6
Garst, Cowboys and Cattle Trails
4–6
Gates, Sarah's Idea *4–6
Hall, E., Land and People of Argentina,
p.20–21, 88–91 6
Harper, Harvest Feast, p.153–68 *4–6
Holling, Book of Cowboys 5–6
Israel, About Sheep on the Ranch 4
James, Young Cowboy *4–6
Larom, Mountain Pony *6

———— Mountain Pony and the Pinto
Colt *5–6
Lauritzen, Glitter-eyed Wouser *5–6
McMeekin, First Book of Horses, p.6–
16 4–5
Rounds, Stolen Pony *5–6
———— Whitey Ropes and Rides
*4–6
Rushmore, Cowboy Joe of the Circle S
*4–5
Scott, S., Chica *4–6
Smith, J. R., Neighbors around the
World, p.186–98 4
Tousey, Cowboy Tommy *4–5

RANGE FINDERS
Beeler, Experiments in Science, p.116–
18 5–6

RANGERS: *see also* Forestry
Colby, Park Rangers 5–6
Spencer, P. R., Exploring New Trails,
p.56–62 5

RAPHAEL
Chandler, Story-Lives of Master Artists,
p.67–79 6
Hillyer, Child's History of Art, p.48–51
5–6

RATS: *see also* Pack Rats
Bianco, All about Pets, p.23–30 5–6
Brown, V., How To Understand Animal
Talk, p.121–28 6
Cleary, Otis Spofford, p.64–97 (white
rats) *4–6
Fenner, Time To Laugh, p.175–91
*4–6
Fenton, C. L., Wild Folk in the Desert,
p.99–104 4–6
Fox, From Bones to Bodies, p.16–21
6
Hogner, Animal Book, p.64–67, 78–81,
207–8 6
Huntington, Let's Go to the Desert,
p.70–73 (kangaroo rats) 4–5
Mason, G. F., Animal Tracks, p.16–19,
22–23 4–6
Moe, Animal Inn, p.72–74 4–6

RATTLES: *see* Percussion Instruments

RAVEL, MAURICE
Burch, Modern Composers for Young
People, p.137–41 5–6

RAWLINSON, HENRY CRESWICKE
Cottler, Heroes of Civilization, p.44–53
6

RAYON
Freeman, I. M., All about the Wonders of Chemistry, p.107–9   6
Writers Project, Rayon, Nylon, and Glass Fibers, no.39   5–6

RECIPES: *see* Cooking

RECONSTRUCTION: *see* Civil War in the United States; Johnson, Andrew; Negroes; United States—History

RECORDS: *see also* Alphabets; Archeology; Books; Cave Drawings; Clay Tablets; Communication; Fossils; Hieroglyphics; Language; Motion Pictures; Newspapers; Numbers; Paper; Pens; Picture Writing; Printing; Rock Records; Wampum; Writing
Peck, Pageant of South American History, p.54–55   6

RECREATION: *see* Amusements; Art; Athletics; Camping; Circus; Clubs; Dancing; Games; Handicraft; Hobbies; Music; National Parks; Parties; Sports; Tourist Trade—United States; Toys

RED CROSS
Boylston, Clara Barton   4–6
Bragdon, L. J., Land and People of Switzerland, p.57–58   6
Pace, Clara Barton, p.102–25   5–6

REDHEADED WOODPECKERS
Webb, Birds in Their Homes, p.38
4–6

REDWINGS
Comstock, Handbook of Nature Study, p.117–19   6
Webb, Birds in Their Homes, p.52
4–6

REDWOOD TREES: *see* Sequoias

REFLECTION (of light): *see* Light; Mirrors

REFLECTION (of sound)
Geralton, Story of Sound, p.37–42
5–6

REFORESTATION: *see* Forestry

REFRACTION
Geralton, Story of Sound, p.42–45
5–6
Ruchlis, Wonder of Light, p.52–66   6

REFRIGERATION: *see also* Food—Frozen
Schweib, What Happened?, p.57–65
5–6
Schneider, H., Everyday Machines and How They Work, p.140–45   5–6
Van Metre, Trains, Tracks and Travel, p.259–65   6

REINDEER: *see* Lapland
Berry, Men, Moss, and Reindeer   5–6
Bronson, Horns and Antlers, p.113–25
5–6
Butler, Alaska, p.97–107   6
Gidal, Follow the Reindeer   4–6
Hogner, Farm Animals, p.185   6
Lide, Lapland Drum   *4–6
Osmond, Animals of the World, v.2
4–6
Smith, J. R., Neighbors around the World, p.53–58   4

REJECTION, FACING AND OVERCOMING
Daringer, Adopted Jane   *4–6
Hayes, Skid   *5–6

RELATIVITY: *see* Einstein, Albert; Physics

RELIGION: *see also* Bible Stories; Buddhism; Christianity; Francis of Assisi, Saint; Hinduism; Interreligious Understanding; Islam; Jesus Christ; Jews; Missionaries; Myths; Saint Brendan; Saint Patrick; Tombs
Fitch, One God   5–6
———— Their Search for God   5–6
Hark, Story of the Pennsylvania Dutch
4–6
Hartman, Builders of the Old World, p.332–40   6
Hillyer, Child's History of the World, p.109–13   5–6
Smither, Stories of Jesus   4–5

RELIGION—CHINA
Hahn, Picture Story of China   4–6

RELIGION—EGYPT—ANCIENT
Hartman, Builders of the Old World, p.59–65   6

Meadowcroft, Gift of the River, p.163–68   5–6

RELIGION—INDIA
Modak, Land and People of India   6

RELIGION—MIDDLE AGES
Tappan, When Knights Were Bold, p.154–205   6

RELIGIOUS FESTIVALS: *see* Festivals; also names of festivals, as Christmas; Easter; Hanukkah

RELIGIOUS UNDERSTANDING
Hall-Quest, How the Pilgrims Came to Plymouth, p.17–20   4–6
Lillie, Book of Three Festivals   5–6

REMBRANDT
Chandler, Story-Lives of Master Artists, p.135–48   6

REMINGTON, FREDERIC
Hillyer, Child's History of Art, p.150–52   5–6
Spencer, P. R., Exploring New Trails, p.250–54   5

RENAISSANCE: *see also* Art; Compass; Discoveries in Geography; Gunpowder; Luther, Martin; Middle Ages; Polo, Marco; Printing
Bergere, From Stones to Skyscrapers, p.56–63   6
Bragdon, L. J., Land and People of France, p.43–47   6
Epstein, S., First Book of Italy, p.42–47   5–6
Hartman, Builders of the Old World, p.330–73   6
Hillyer, Child's History of Art, p.37–40   5–6
———— Child's History of the World, p.359–64   5–6
McGuire, Glimpses into the Long Ago, p.343–60   5–6
Watson, Golden History of the World, p.97–101   5–6

REPORTERS
Lent, "I Work on a Newspaper," p.9–42   6

REPRODUCTION: *see also* Cells
Darling, L., Chickens   4–6
Glemser, All about the Human Body, p.123–32   5–6

Levine, Baby Is Born   4–5
Zim, How Things Grow   4–6

REPTILES: *see also* Alligators; Crocodiles; Lizards; Snakes; Turtles
Beauchamp, Discovering Our World, Bk.1, p.26–29   4
Bevans, Book of Reptiles and Amphibians   4–6
Brown, V., How To Make a Miniature Zoo, p.101–8, 121–40   5–6
Buck, M. W., Small Pets from Woods and Fields, p.30–40   4–6
Comstock, Handbook of Nature Study, p.193–213   6
Cooper, E. K., Science in Your Own Back Yard, p.152–54   5–6
———— Science on the Shores and Banks, p.131–39   5–6
Doane, Book of Nature, p.30–31, 78–79   5–6
Fenton, C. L., Life Long Ago, p.164–74, 198–215   6
Hausman, Beginner's Guide to Fresh-Water Life, p.16–27   6
Hylander, Animals in Armor   6
———— Out of Doors in Summer, p.73–90   5–6
Knight, C. R., Life through the Ages, p.30–31   6
Morgan, A. H., Field Book of Ponds and Streams, p.389–406   6
Parker, B. M., Living Things, p.30–32   4–6
———— Reptiles   4–6
Reed, Earth for Sam, p.103–50   6
Robertson, G., Strange Sea Life, p.80–86   5–6
Zim, Snakes   5–6

RESERVOIRS: *see* Irrigation; Water Supply

RESOURCEFULNESS
Brock, Topsy-Turvy Family   *4–5
Du Soe, Three without Fear   *4–6
Thurber, Many Moons   *4–5
Wyss, Swiss Family Robinson   *6

RESPECT FOR PROPERTY
Sechrist, Heigh-Ho for Halloween!, p.235–40   5–6

RESPIGHI, OTTORINO
Burch, Modern Composers for Young People, p.157–59   5–6

RESPIRATION

Beauchamp, Discovering Our World, Bk.1, p.80–81   4

Glemser, All about the Human Body, p.57–68   5–6

RESPONSIBILITY

Batchelor, Tim and the Purple Whistle   *4–5

Brown, G. E., Tico Bravo, Shark Hunter   *4–6

De Angeli, Yonie Wondernose   *4–5

Fritz, Brady   *5–6

Johnson, S. J., Cat Hotel   *4–6

Kim, Happy Days   *5–6

Lansing, E. C. H., Liza of the Hundred-fold   *5–6

Mason, M. E., Hominy and His Blunt-nosed Arrow   *4–5

Meigs, Covered Bridge   *4–6

Renick, M. L., John's Back Yard Camp   *4–5

Reynolds, B. L., Hamlet and Brown-swiggle   *4–6

Sickels, That Boy, Johnny!   *4–6

Unnerstad, Journey with Grandmother   *4–6

REVERE, PAUL

Bailey, C. S., Children of the Hand-crafts, p.44–54   5–6

Forbes, America's Paul Revere   4–6

Pace, Early American   5–6

REVOLUTIONARY WAR IN AMERICA: *see also* Declaration of Independence; United States—History; also names of persons, as Revere, Paul

Barksdale, That Country Called Virginia, p.97–122   6

Bliven, American Revolution, 1760-1783   6

Campion, Patrick Henry   5–6

Commager, H. S., First Book of American History, p.17–27   4–6

Cousins, Ben Franklin of Old Philadelphia, p.124–59   5–6

Coy, Americans, p.57–79   6

Dalgliesh, Adam and the Golden Cock   *4–5

Daugherty, Poor Richard, p.91–142   6

Eaton, That Lively Man, Ben Franklin, p.185–230   6

Fisher, D. F. C., Our Independence and the Constitution   4–5

Forbes, America's Paul Revere   4–6

Foster, G., George Washington's World, p.162–233   6

Graham, A. P., Lafayette, p.28–95   4–5

Hillyer, Child's History of the World, p.412–19   5–6

Johnson, G. W., America Is Born, p.196–246   5–6

Jordan, American Costume Dolls, p.70–100   5–6

Judson, George Washington   5–6

McGuire, Brave Young Land, p.351–82   5–6

Mason, F. V., Winter at Valley Forge   6

Meadowcroft, Land of the Free, p.45–65   4–5

———— Silver for General Washington   *5–6

Morris, First Book of the American Revolution   4–6

Rogers, F., Old Liberty Bell   5–6

Wibberley, John Treegate's Musket   *6

———— Peter Treegate's War   *6

———— Sea Captain from Salem   *6

REYNOLDS, JOSHUA

Chandler, Story-Lives of Master Artists, p.163–76   6

RHEIMS CATHEDRAL: *see also* Joan of Arc

Lownsbery, Boy Knight of Reims   *6

RHINOCEROS

Andrews, All about Strange Beasts of the Past, p.56–63   5–6

Buck, F., Jungle Animals, p.12–13   5–6

Fox, From Bones to Bodies, p.63–64   6

Kipling, Just So Stories, p.29–39   *4–6

Knight, C. R., Life through the Ages, p.54–57   6

Perkins, Marlin Perkins' Zooparade, p.32–35   4–6

RHODE ISLAND: *see also* Williams, Roger

Quinn, Picture Map Geography of the United States, p.16–19   4–6

RHODES, CECIL
Hughes, First Book of Africa, p.19–21, 23   5–6

RHODESIA
Stinetorf, Children of South Africa, p.146–75   *5–6

RHYTHM
Adler, Time in Your Life   4–6
Buchanan, How Man Made Music, p.14, 81–82   6
Downer, Discovering Design, p.42–47   6
Hughes, First Book of Rhythms   4–6

RICE
Ayer, Getting To Know Thailand, p.40–45   4–6
Eberle, Basketful, p.43–50   4–6
——— Grasses, p.34–40   4–6
O'Neill, Picture Story of the Philippines   5–6
Treffinger, Li Lun, Lad of Courage   *5–6

RICKENBACKER, EDWARD VERNON
Spencer, P. R., Traveling New Trails, p.454–59   6

RIDDLES: see also Tricks
Harshaw, What Book Is That?   4–6
Wilson, L., This Boy Cody, p.132–98   *4–6

RIDING: see also Horses; Hunting; Stagecoaches
Coatsworth, Golden Horseshoe, p.119–29   *6
Seredy, Good Master, p.39–48, 63–70, 87–107   *5–6

RIFLES: see Guns

RIMSKI-KORSAKOV, NIKOLAI ANDREEVICH
Burch, Modern Composers for Young People, p.27–52   5–6

RIO DE JANEIRO
Brown, R. J., Land and People of Brazil, p.42–58   6
May, Let's Read about Brazil, p.31–36   4–6
Rothery, South American Roundabout, p.171–87   5–6

RIVER LIFE
Meadowcroft, Abraham Lincoln, p.34–52   6
Purdy, He Heard America Sing, p.51–63, 144–63   6

RIVER LIFE—CHINA
Oakes, Bamboo Gate, p.138–57   *4–6
Spencer, C., Land of the Chinese People, p.15–16   6
Wiese, Chinese Ink Stick, p.63–83   *4–6

RIVER LIFE—INDIA
Bothwell, Little Boat Boy   *4–5

RIVER PILOTS
Proudfit, River-Boy, p.107–39   6

RIVERS: see also Dams; Floods; Water Power; Water Supply; also names of rivers, as Mississippi River
Bethers, Story of Rivers   4–5
Fenton, C. L., Land We Live On, p.40–41   4–6
Schneider, H., Rocks, Rivers & the Changing Earth, p.5–22   4–6
Sevrey, First Book of the Earth, p.39–41   5–6
Writers Project, Trip on Many Waters, no.6   5–6
Wyckoff, Story of Geology, p.78–91   5–6

ROAD RUNNERS
Disney, Worlds of Nature, p.89–90   4–6
Du Soe, Three without Fear, p.44–181   *4–6
Fenton, C. L., Wild Folk in the Desert, p.40–43   4–6

ROADS: see also Alaska Highway; Engineering; Railroads
Barr, Young Scientist Takes a Ride, p.20–23   5–6
Bleeker, Inca, p.27–43   5–6
Boardman, Roads   6
Bothwell, First Book of Roads   5–6
Jackson, D., Wonderful World of Engineering, p.36–43   6
Lent, Men at Work in New England, p.86–89   4–6
Orton, Treasure in the Little Trunk, p.43–48, 64–71, 91–101 *4–6
Spencer, P. R., Traveling New Trails, p.342–67   6

ROBIN HOOD
Cooke, D. E., Men of Sherwood
*5–6
Leeming, Costume Book, p.90–92   5–6

ROBINS
Comstock, Handbook of Nature Study, p.57–62   6
Gall, Wagtail, p.43–52   4–6
Parker, B. M., Birds, p.14–21   4–6
Webb, Birds in Their Homes, p.8–12
4–6
Weil, Animal Families   4

ROCK RECORDS: *see also* Fossils; Geology; Hieroglyphics; Picture Writing
Williams, H. L., Stories in Rocks   6

ROCKETS: *see also* Space Travel
Bendick, First Book of Space Travel, p.20–29   5–6
Bergaust, Rockets and Missiles   5–6
———— Rockets around the World   6
Coggins, J., Rockets, Satellites, and Space Travel, p.7–24   6
Coombs, Gateway to Space   6
———— Rockets, Missiles, and Moons, p.15–103   6
Crouse, W. H., Understanding Science, p.171–78   6
Dietz, All about Satellites and Space Ships   5–6
Fisher, J., Wonderful World of the Air, p.62–68   5–6
Gottlieb, Jets and Rockets and How They Work, p.48–55   4–6
Hendrickson, Handbook for Space Travelers   5–6
Munch, What Is a Rocket?   4–5
Neurath, Rockets and Jets   4–6
Schneider, H., More Power to You, p.98–101   5–6
Schneider, L., Space in Your Future, p.206–10, 218–21   6
Zaffo, Big Book of Real Airplanes
4–5

ROCKNE, KNUTE KENNETH
Van Riper, Knute Rockne   4–6

ROCKS: *see also* Geology; Minerals
Adler, Time in Your Life, p.94–101
4–6
Comstock, Handbook of Nature Study, p.743–59   6

Cooper, E. K., Science in Your Own Back Yard, p.33–39   5–6
Cormack, First Book of Stones   4–6
Epstein, S., Prehistoric Animals, p.5–13
6
Evans, Adventure Book of Rocks
4–6
Fenton, C. L., Land We Live On, p.32–33   4–6
Loomis, Field Book of Common Rocks and Minerals   6
Parker, B. M., Stories Read from the Rocks, p.15–28   4–6
Schneider, H., Rocks, Rivers & the Changing Earth   4–6
Sevrey, First Book of the Earth, p.16–21
5–6
White, A. T., All about Our Changing Rocks   5–6
Williams, H. L., Stories in Rocks   6
Wyckoff, Story of Geology, p.24–29, 102–9, 139–43   5–6

ROCKY MOUNTAIN NATIONAL PARK
Melbo, Our Country's National Parks, v.2, p.75–93   6

RODENTS: *see also* names of rodents, as Rats
Hogner, Animal Book, p.34–81   6
Parker, B. M., Animals We Know, p.30–33   5–6

RODEOS
Holling, Book of Cowboys, p.118–20
5–6
Spencer, P. R., Finding New Trails, p.16–21   4

ROENTGEN, WILHELM CONRAD
Asimov, Breakthroughs in Science, p.120–27   5–6

ROGERS, WILL
Spencer, P. R., Exploring New Trails, p.218–29   5

ROLAND
Hazeltine, Hero Tales from Many Lands, p.220–34   5–6

ROMANCES: *see* Arthur, King; Legends

ROMANIA
Barrows, Old World Lands, p.111–12
6

ROME

Epstein, S., First Book of Italy, p.27–33
5–6

Sasek, This Is Rome   4–6

ROME—ANCIENT: *see also* Costume—
Rome—Ancient

Bergere, From Stones to Skyscrapers,
p.32–41   6

Falls, First 3000 Years, p.184–211   6

Gunther, Julius Caesar   6

Hartman, Builders of the Old World,
p.165–201   6

Hillyer, Child's History of the World,
p.89–93, 119–23, 168–218   5–6

Lamprey, All the Ways of Building,
p.78–91   6

McGuire, Glimpses into the Long Ago,
p.193–238   5–6

Rogers, F., Heels, Wheels, and Wire,
p.28–34   5–6

Watson, Golden History of the World,
p.52–67   5–6

Writers Project, Cement, no.33, p.15–16
5–6

ROME—ANCIENT—HISTORY

Hazeltine, Hero Tales from Many
Lands, p.38–50   5–6

ROMULUS AND REMUS

Farjeon, Mighty Men, p.68–75   4–6

Hartman, Builders of the Old World,
p.165–68   6

ROOSEVELT, FRANKLIN DELANO

Beard, Presidents in American History,
p.129–34, 178–79   6

Coy, First Book of Presidents, p.60–61
4–6

Lawson, R., Watchwords of Liberty,
p.107   4–6

Petersham, Story of the Presidents of
the United States, p.71–73   4–6

ROOSEVELT, THEODORE

Beard, Presidents in American History,
p.105–6, 172–73   6

Coy, First Book of Presidents, p.52–53
4–6

Foster, G., Theodore Roosevelt   4–6

Judson, Theodore Roosevelt   5–6

Lawson, R., Watchwords of Liberty,
p.96–99   4–6

Olcott, Good Stories for Great Birthdays, p.43–71   4–6

Petersham, Story of the Presidents of
the United States, p.58–60   4–6

ROOTS

Disney, Worlds of Nature, p.102–3
4–6

Disraeli, New Worlds through the Microscope, p.122–25   6

Hyde, Plants Today and Tomorrow,
p.19–23   6

Selsam, Plants We Eat, p.18–30
4–6

ROPE

Lent, Men at Work in New England,
p.112–15   4–6

ROSE-BREASTED GROSBEAKS

Webb, Birds in Their Homes, p.16
4–6

ROSETTA STONE

Kubie, First Book of Archaeology,
p.38–39   6

Meadowcroft, Gift of the River, p.7–9
5–6

Robinson, C. A., First Book of Ancient
Egypt, p.37–39   4–6

ROTIFERA

Morgan, A. H., Field Book of Animals
in Winter, p.79–89   6

——— Field Book of Ponds and
Streams, p.127–30   6

ROUMANIA: *see* Romania

ROUND TABLE: *see* Arthur, King

ROUNDUPS: *see* Rodeos

ROUTES OF TRADE: *see* Trade

ROWING: *see* Boats; Canoes; Sports

**ROYAL CANADIAN MOUNTED PO-
LICE**: *see* Canada—Royal Canadian
Mounted Police

RUBBER: *see also* Goodyear, Charles

Freeman, I. M., All about the Wonders
of Chemistry, p.117–28   6

Hartman, Machines, p.121–29   6

May, Let's Read about Brazil, p.45–50
4–6

Rothery, South American Roundabout,
p.194–99   5–6

Schwartz, It's Fun To Know Why, p.54–
61   5–6

Smith, J. R., Neighbors around the
World, p.286–88   4

RUBENS, PETER PAUL
Chandler, Story-Lives of Master Artists,
p.89–97 6

RUFFED GROUSE: *see* Grouse

RUGS: *see also* Weaving
Bailey, C. S., Pioneer Art in America,
p.155–67 5–6
Hamilton, E. T., Handicraft for Girls,
p.22–30 6
Leeming, Fun with String, p.84–87
4–6

RURAL COMMUNITIES: *see* Village
Life

RURAL-URBAN CONTRASTS
Blough, Not Only for Ducks *4–5
Clewes, Runaway *4–5
Frost, Sleigh Bells for Windy Foot
*4–6

RUSSIA: *see* Union of Soviet Socialist
Republics

RUSSIAN REVOLUTION, 1917
Nazaroff, Land of the Russian People,
p.141–47 6

RUSSIANS IN THE UNITED STATES
Association for Childhood Education,
Told under the Stars and Stripes,
p.257–69 *4–6

RUSTUM
Hazeltine, Hero Tales From Many
Lands, p.348–61 5–6

RUTH
Bowie, Bible Story for Boys and Girls:
Old Testament, p.83–87 4–6
Petersham, Ruth 4–5

RUTHERFORD, ERNEST
Asimov, Breakthroughs in Science, p.
181–89 5–6

SABBATH
Pannell, Holiday Round Up, p.326–29
4–6

SACAJAWEA
Havighurst, First Book of the Oregon
Trail, p.3–8 4–6
Ross, N. W., Heroines of the Early
West, p.34–51 5–6

SAFETY: *see also* Air Brakes; Fire Departments; Fire Prevention; First Aid;
Lighthouses; Otis, Elisha Graves;

Police; Radio; Railroads—Signaling;
United States—Coast Guard
Baker, A. O., Your Science World,
p.137, 173–75 6
Barnard, Macmillan Science-Life Series,
Bk.6, p.167–70, 183 6
Beauchamp, Discovering Our World,
Bk.1, p.174–79 4
Bendick, First Book of How To Fix It,
p.16–17, 23 4–6
Colby, First Bow and Arrow, p.40–41
4–6
———— First Camping Trip, p.6–10,
27, 36–39 5–6
———— First Hunt, p.26–27, 48 5–6
———— First Rifle, p.31, 47 5–6
Downer, Kites, p.52 4–6
Hamilton, E., First Book of Caves,
p.55–58 5–6
Knowlton, Let's Explore beneath the
Sea, p.54–60 5–6
Leavitt, True Book of Tools for Build-
ing, p.40–41 4–6
Longsworth, Exploring Caves 6
Mason, B. S., Junior Book of Camp-
ing and Woodcraft 5–6
Red Cross, First Aid Textbook for Jun-
iors, p.129–39 6
Renick, M. L., Seven Simpsons on Six
Bikes, p.122 *4–5
Spencer, P. R., Exploring New Trails,
p.331–58 5
Zim, Lightning and Thunder 4–5

SAFETY AT HOME
Schneider, H., Let's Look inside Your
House, p.35–37 4–5
Spencer, P. R., Exploring New Trails,
p.337–47 5

SAGAS: *see also* Cuchulain; Epics; Eric-
son, Leif; Grettir the Strong; Myths—
Northmen; Siegfried; Sigurd
Golden, Made in Iceland, p.41–51 6

SAHARA DESERT
Barrows, Old World Lands, p.286–90
6
———— Our Big World, p.91–95 4
Joy, Desert Caravans 5–6
Smith, J. R., Neighbors around the
World, p.219–21 4

SAILING: *see also* Boats; Clipper Ships;
Navigation; Ships

American Heritage, Story of Yankee
Whaling 5–6
Ardizzone, Tim to the Rescue *4–5
Block, Real Book about Ships, p.73–80
5–6
Boutwell, Sailor Tom *4–6
Coatsworth, Fair American, p.47–130
*5–6
Dalgliesh, America Travels, p.15–23,
90–92 4–6
Latham, Drake 6

SAILORS: *see also* Jones, John Paul
Coatsworth, Littlest House, p.108–22
*4–6

ST. BERNARD PASS
Bragdon, L. J., Land and People of
Switzerland, p.27–28 6

SAINT BRENDAN: *see* Brendan, Saint

SAINT DOMINIC: *see* Dominic, Saint

SAINT FRANCIS OF ASSISI: *see* Francis of Assisi, Saint

SAINT-GAUDENS, AUGUSTUS
Hillyer, Child's History of Art, p.257–
61 5–6

SAINT JOHN OF JERUSALEM,
KNIGHTS OF: *see* Malta—Knights
of

ST. LAWRENCE RIVER
American Heritage, Discoverers of the
New World, p.118–20 5–6
Averill, Cartier Sails the St. Lawrence
4–6
Boardman, Canals, p.110–14 6
Holling, Paddle-to-the-Sea 4–6
Judson, St. Lawrence Seaway 6
Lauber, Changing the Face of North
America 5–6
Lent, Men at Work in the Great Lakes
States, p.54–57 4–6
McNeer, Canadian Story 5–6
Syme, Cartier 4–6

SAINT NICHOLAS: *see* Nicholas, Saint

SAINT PATRICK'S DAY: *see also* Patrick, Saint
Burnett, B., First Book of Holidays,
p.11–12 4–5
Jordan, Holiday Handicraft, p.78–83
4–6

McSpadden, Book of Holidays, p.44–49
6
Pannell, Holiday Round Up, p.86–95
4–6
Sechrist, Red Letter Days, p.67–76
5–6

SALAMANDERS
Bevans, Book of Reptiles and Amphib-
ians, p.59–62 4–6
Buck, M. W., In Ponds and Streams,
p.42–45 4–6
———— Pets from the Pond, p.52–57
4–6
Comstock, Handbook of Nature Study,
p.190–91 6
Cooper, E. K., Science on the Shores
and Banks, p.129–30 5–6
Fox, From Bones to Bodies, p.36–37
6
Lavine, Strange, Travelers, p.35, 37–40
5–6
Moe, Animal Inn, p.75–78 4–6
Morgan, A. H., Field Book of Animals
in Winter, p.331–48 6
———— Field Book of Ponds and
Streams, p.352–66 6
Morgan, A. P., Aquarium Book, p.193–
95 5–6
Parker, B. M., Toads and Frogs, p.33–
35 4–6
Pels, Care of Water Pets, p.40–41 4–6

SALMON
Barrows, American Continents, p.216–
18 5
Holling, Book of Indians, p.98–99 4–6
Hyde, Animal Clocks and Compasses,
p.23–31, 125–26 5–6
Lavine, Strange Travelers, p.128–35
5–6
Lindquist, W., Alaska, p.58–60 5–6
McClung, Leaper 4–5
Parker, B. M., Animal Travels, p.7–10
4–6
Writers Project, Salmon, no.15 5–6

SALT
Beeler, Experiments in Chemistry, p.10–
17 5–6
Comstock, Handbook of Nature Study,
p.753–54 6
Fenton, C. L., Riches from the Earth,
p.119–23 5–6

Orton, Treasure in the Little Trunk, p.125–31   *4–6

Parker, B. M., Earth a Great Storehouse, p.10–13   4–6

Reed, And That's Why, p.66–74   4–5

———— Earth for Sam, p.60–61, 107–9   6

Rothery, Central American Roundabout, p.133–34   6

Scheib, First Book of Food, p.50–51   5–6

Schwartz, It's Fun To Know Why, p.75–82   5–6

Williams, H. L., Stories in Rocks, p.76–78   6

SALVADOR

Donaldson, Salvador   4–6

Goetz, Neighbors to the South, p.38–41   5–6

Quinn, Picture Map Geography of Mexico, Central America and the West Indies, p.42–50   4–6

Rothery, Central American Roundabout, p.52–76   6

SALVADOR—FOLK TALES

Rothery, Central American Roundabout, p.199–201   6

SAMOAN ISLANDS

Quinn, Picture Map Geography of the Pacific Islands, p.81–87   5–6

SAND

Fenton, C. L., Riches from the Earth, p.124–28   5–6

Parker, B. M., Earth a Great Storehouse, p.9–10   4–6

SAND DOLLARS: *see* Sea Urchins

SANDGLASSES: *see* Hourglasses

SANDPIPERS

Osborne, M. M., Ondine   *4–6

Webb, Birds in Their Homes, p.60   4–6

SANDSTORMS

Armer, Waterless Mountain, p.88–90   *5–6

SAN FRANCISCO

Proudfit, River-Boy, p.183–88   6

SAN FRANCISCO—BRIDGES

Dawson, California, p.196–97   5–6

SAN MARTÍN, JOSÉ DE

Goetz, Neighbors to the South, p.142–43   5–6

Olcott, Good Stories for Great Birthdays, p.235–78   *4–6

Peck, Pageant of South American History, p.251–73   6

SANTA ANNA, ANTONIO LÓPEZ DE

McNeer, Mexican Story, p.46–48   6

SANTA CLAUS: *see* Christmas—Santa Claus

SANTA FE TRAIL

Adams, S. H., Santa Fe Trail   5–6

Garst, Kit Carson   6

Holling, Tree in the Trail   4–6

SANTA MARÍA (ship): *see* Columbus, Christopher

SANTA SOPHIA MOSQUE

Chubb, Byzantines, p.31–34   6

Hillyer, Child's History of Art, p.326–30   5–6

SANTO DOMINGO: *see* Dominican Republic

SÃO PAULO

Brown, R. J., Land and People of Brazil, p.65–79   6

SARGASSO SEA

Lavine, Strange Travelers, p.122–23   5–6

SARGENT, JOHN SINGER

Hillyer, Child's History of Art, p.149   5–6

SARTO, ANDREA DEL: *see* Andrea del Sarto

SASKATCHEWAN

Quinn, Picture Map Geography of Canada and Alaska, p.58–65   4–6

SATELLITES

Adler, Things That Spin   5–6

Asimov, Satellites in Outer Space   4–5

Branley, Exploring by Satellite   6

Coggins, J., Rockets, Satellites, and Space Travel, p.25–34   6

Coombs, Gateway to Space, p.121–48   6

———— Rockets, Missiles, and Moons, p.185–243   6

Dietz, All about Satellites and Space Ships 5–6

Hendrickson, Handbook for Space Travelers, p.94–106 5–6

Lewellen, Earth Satellite 4–6

Schneider, L., Space in Your Future, p.210–12, 221–22 6

Zarem, New Dimensions of Flight, p.164–72 6

SATURN (planet)
Branley, Nine Planets, p.56–59 6

Gallant, R. A., Exploring the Planets, p.88–101 5–6

Goodwin, Real Book about Stars, p.101–4 4–6

Hendrickson, Handbook for Space Travelers, p.233–37 5–6

Schneider, L., Space in Your Future, p.97–100 6

SAVAGE ISLANDS: *see* Cook Islands

SAVANNAH (ship)
Rogers, F., Heels, Wheels, and Wire, p.89–93 5–6

SAVANNAS: *see* Grasslands

SAVORGNAN DE BRAZZA, PIERRE
Carbonnier, Congo Explorer 5–6

SAWS
Burns, Man and His Tools, p.48–51 5–6

Leavitt, True Book of Tools for Building, p.12–19 4–6

SCALES (music): *see* Musical Intervals and Scales

SCANDINAVIA: *see also* Denmark; Iceland; Lemmings; Northmen; Norway; Sweden
Barrows, Old World Lands, p.40–51 6

Hazeltine, Hero Tales of Many Lands, p.270–77 5–6

SCARECROWS
Smith, I., Santa Claus Book, p.173–83 4–5

SCARFACE, BLACKFOOT INDIAN
Hazeltine, Hero Tales of Many Lands, p.448–59 5–6

SCARLET TANAGERS
Webb, Birds in Their Homes, p.17 4–6

SCHLIEMANN, HEINRICH
Friedman, E., Digging into Yesterday, p.128–49 5–6

SCHOENBERG, ARNOLD
Burch, Modern Composers for Young People, p.129–33 5–6

SCHOOL LIFE: *see also* Education
Beery, Manners Made Easy, p.31–49 6

Goetz, Neighbors to the South, p.129–36 5–6

————— Other Young Americans, p.112–43 5–6

SCHOOL LIFE—ARGENTINA
Hall, E., Land and People of Argentina, p.106–13 6

SCHOOL LIFE—AUSTRIA
Wheeler, Franz Schubert and His Merry Friends, p.30–94 4–6

SCHOOL LIFE—BEDOUIN
Gidal, Sons of the Desert, p.14–16 5–6

SCHOOL LIFE—BRAZIL
May, Let's Read about Brazil, p.110–13 4–6

SCHOOL LIFE—CANADA
Bonner, Canada and Her Story, p.114–16 5–6

De Angeli, Petite Suzanne *4–6

SCHOOL LIFE—CHINA
Hahn, Picture Story of China 4–6

Lattimore, Peachblossom, p.56–79 *4–5

Oakes, Bamboo Gate, p.21–39 *4–6

Spencer, C., Land of the Chinese People, p.106–8 6

Wiese, Chinese Ink Stick, p.183–93 *4–6

SCHOOL LIFE—COLONIAL PERIOD IN AMERICA
De Angeli, Jared's Island, p.82–84 *4–6

————— Skippack School *4–6

SCHOOL LIFE—DENMARK
Lewiton, Faces Looking Up, p.108–19 4–6

SCHOOL LIFE—EGYPT—MODERN
Lewiton, Faces Looking Up, p.44–56 4–6

SCHOOL LIFE—ENGLAND
Bentley, Young Brontës, p.39–52, 79–93
6
Lewiton, Faces Looking Up, p.57–71
4–6
Thwaite, House in Turner Square   *6

SCHOOL LIFE—FORMOSA
Caldwell, Let's Visit Formosa, p.53–56
5–6

SCHOOL LIFE—FRANCE
Lewiton, Faces Looking Up, p.85–98
4–6

SCHOOL LIFE—GERMANY
Lobsenz, First Book of West Germany,
p.25–26   4–6
Tor, Getting To Know Germany, p.55–
57   4–6

SCHOOL LIFE—GHANA
Lobsenz, First Book of Ghana, p.42–47
4–6

SCHOOL LIFE—GREECE—MODERN
Lewiton, Faces Looking Up, p.132–41
4–6

SCHOOL LIFE—INDIA
Arora, "What Then, Raman?"   *5–6
Bothwell, Empty Tower   *4–5
Lewiton, Faces Looking Up, p.72–84
4–6

SCHOOL LIFE—INDONESIA
Caldwell, Let's Visit Indonesia, p.64–68
4–6

SCHOOL LIFE—IRAN
Lewiton, Faces Looking Up, p.5–14
4–6

SCHOOL LIFE—IRELAND
Van Stockum, Cottage at Bantry Bay,
p.85–104   *6
———— Pegeen, p.103–36   *6

SCHOOL LIFE—ISRAEL
Lewiton, Faces Looking Up, p.99–107
4–6

SCHOOL LIFE—ITALY
Epstein, S., First Book of Italy, p.24–25
5–6

SCHOOL LIFE—JAPAN
Edelman, Japan in Story and Pictures,
p.6–13   4–6
Jakeman, Getting To Know Japan,
p.38–39   4–6

Lewiton, Faces Looking Up, p.15–29
4–6
Mears, First Book of Japan, p.44–48
4–6
Spencer, C., Japan, p.13–14   5–6
Yashima, T., Crow Boy   *4–5

SCHOOL LIFE—KOREA
Caldwell, Let's Visit Korea, p.69–75
5–6
Kim, Happy Days   *5–6

SCHOOL LIFE—MEXICO
Epstein, S., First Book of Mexico, p.12–
13   5–6

SCHOOL LIFE—NIGERIA
Kenworthy, Profile of Nigeria, p.62–66
5–6
Lewiton, Faces Looking Up, p.142–53
4–6

SCHOOL LIFE—NORWAY
Zwilgmeyer, Johnny Blossom, p.31–40
*4–6

SCHOOL LIFE—PHILIPPINE ISLANDS
Lewiton, Faces Looking Up, p.30–43
4–6
O'Neill, Picture Story of the Philippines
5–6

SCHOOL LIFE—PIONEER
Brink, Caddie Woodlawn, p.59–70, 97–
106, 211–18   *6
Flory, Peddler's Summer   *4–6
Meadowcroft, By Wagon and Flatboat,
p.7–13   *4–5
Meigs, Willow Whistle, p.63–69, 116–44
*4–6
———— Wind in the Chimney, p.18–
22   *5–6
Wilder, Farmer Boy, p.1–12   *4–6
———— Little Town on the Prairie,
p.124–36, 145–84, 267–97   *5–6
———— On the Banks of Plum Creek,
p.140–52   *4–6

SCHOOL LIFE—PUERTO RICO
Tor, Getting To Know Puerto Rico,
p.41–44   4–6

SCHOOL LIFE—SWEDEN
Burglon, Children of the Soil   *4–6

SCHOOL LIFE—UNION OF SOVIET
SOCIALIST REPUBLICS
Lewiton, Faces Looking Up, p.120–31
4–6

SCHOOL LIFE—UNITED STATES

Association for Childhood Education, Told under the Stars and Stripes, p.13–30, 91–101, 136–49, 159–71, 249–69 *4–6

Bloch, Marya of Clark Avenue *4–6

Calhoun, Depend on Katie John *4–6

Call, Peter's Moose *4–6

Canfield, Understood Betsy, p.63–86 *5–6

Cleary, Ellen Tebbits *4–5

———— Otis Spofford *4–6

De Angeli, Copper-toed Boots *4–6

Estes, Hundred Dresses *4–6

———— Moffats, p.53–80 *4–6

———— Rufus M., p.33–56, 183–89 *4–6

Frazier, Somebody Special, p.31–40 *4–6

Friedman, F., Dot for Short *4–5

Gates, Blue Willow, p.85–99 *5–6

———— Sensible Kate, p.55–72 *4–6

Hayes, Skid, p.1–27, 104–23, 157–216 *5–6

Hunt, M. L., Lucinda, p.91–97, 112–19 *5–6

Jackson, J., Call Me Charley *5–6

Lenski, Cotton in My Sack, p.31–41 *4–6

———— Judy's Journey *4–6

Lovelace, Betsy-Tacy, p.30–39 *4–5

Moore, Snake That Went to School *4

Pace, Juliette Low, p.47–77 5–6

Purdy, He Heard America Sing, p.107–29 6

Sawyer, Enchanted Schoolhouse, p.67–128 *4–6

Simon, Robin on the Mountain, p.105–12 *4–6

Sorensen, Curious Missie *4–6

———— Plain Girl *4–6

Urmston, New Boy *4–6

Woolley, Ginnie and Geneva *4–5

SCHUBERT, FRANZ PETER

Burch, Famous Composers for Young People, p.63–69 4–6

Schwimmer, Great Musicians as Children, p.45–53 6

Wheeler, Franz Schubert and His Merry Friends 4–6

———— Robert Schumann and Mascot Ziff, p.79–80 4–6

SCHUMANN, CLARA WIECK

Schwimmer, Great Musicians as Children, p.67–75 6

Wheeler, Robert Schumann and Mascot Ziff 4–6

SCHUMANN, ROBERT ALEXANDER

Burch, Famous Composers for Young People, p.87–94 4–6

Wheeler, Robert Schumann and Mascot Ziff 4–6

SCHWEITZER, ALBERT

Hughes, First Book of Africa, p.23–24 5–6

McNeer, Armed with Courage, p.101–12 5–6

SCIENCE: *see also* Aerodynamics; Astronomy; Biology; Botany; Chemistry; Electricity; Evolution; Experiments—Scientific; Geology; Inventions; Machines; Medicine; Metallurgy; Minerals; Nature Study; Physics; Physiology; Races of Man; Scientists; Weather Forecasting; Zoology

Adler, Tools of Science 6

Bendick, How Much and How Many, p.95–159 5–6

Carlson, B. W., Do It Yourself!, p.27–34 4–6

Crouse, W. H., Understanding Science 6

Kettelkamp, Magic of Sound 4–6

Larrick, See for Yourself 4–5

Leonard, Exploring Science 6

Neurath, Rockets and Jets 4–6

Nourse, So You Want To Be a Scientist 5–6

Parker, B. M., Golden Book of Science 4–6

Scheib, What Happened? 5–6

Tappan, When Knights Were Bold, p.312–37 6

SCIENCE FICTION

Beatty, Matthew Looney's Voyage to the Earth *4–6

Biemiller, Magic Ball from Mars *4–6

———— Starboy *4–6

Cameron, Wonderful Flight to the Mushroom Planet *4–6

MacGregor, Miss Pickerell Goes to Mars   *4–6
Peare, Jules Verne   5–6
Todd, Space Cat   *4–5
———— Space Cat Meets Mars   *4–5
———— Space Cat Visits Venus   *4–5

SCIENTIFIC EXPEDITIONS: *see also* Antarctic Regions; Arctic Regions
Sperry, Rain Forest   *6

SCIENTIFIC EXPERIMENTS: *see* Experiments—Scientific

SCIENTIFIC METHOD
Barnard, Macmillan Science-Life Series, Bk.6, p.3–14   6
Leonard, Exploring Science, p.155–61   6
Parker, B. M., Scientist and His Tools, p.15–18   5–6

SCIENTISTS: *see also* Doctors; Explorers; Inventors; also names of scientists, as Darwin, Charles
Barr, Research Ideas for Young Scientists   5–6
McNeer, Armed with Courage, p.41–54   5–6
Nourse, So You Want To Be a Scientist   5–6
Parker, B. M., Scientist and His Tools   5–6

SCORPIONS
Huntington, Let's Go to the Desert, p.54–59   4–5

SCOTLAND: *see also* Costume—Scotland
Jordan, Homemade Dolls in Foreign Dress, p.108–18   4–6
MacKellar, Ghost in the Castle   *4–6
———— Wee Joseph   *4–5
Pace, Juliette Low, p.111–21   5–6
Peare, Robert Louis Stevenson   4–6
Proudfit, Treasure Hunter   6
Sasek, This Is Edinburgh   4–6

SCOTLAND—FOLK TALES
Harper, Ghosts and Goblins, p.69–76, 205–7   4–6

SCOTT, ROBERT FALCON
Frank, Ice Island, p.37–48, 84–108   6

SCOTT, WALTER
Coffman, Famous Authors for Young People, p.21–27   5–6

SCREWS
Meyer, Machines, p.49–55   4–6
Parker, B. M., Machines, p.24–25   5–6
Schneider, H., Everyday Machines and How They Work, p.48–49, 135–36   5–6

SCRIABIN, ALEXANDER NIKOLAIE-VITCH: *see* Skriabin, Aleksandr Nikolaevich

SCULPTORS: *see* names of sculptors, as Michelangelo; Saint-Gaudens, Augustus

SCULPTURE: *see also* Clay Modeling; Soap Sculpture; Wood Carving; also names of special works, as Liberty—Statue of
Hillyer, Child's History of Art, p.159–273   5–6
Holling, Seabird, p.14–15   *4–6
Lownsbery, Boy Knight of Reims   *6
Spencer, C., Made in China, p.130–34   5–6
Weisgard, Treasures To See   4–6

SEA: *see also* Fishing; Pirates; Sailing; Shipwrecks; Whaling
Armstrong, Ship Afire!   *6
Boutwell, Sailor Tom   *4–6
Coatsworth, Fair American   *5–6
Grant, G. H., Boy Overboard   *5–6
Holling, Seabird   *4–6
Kent, He Went with Christopher Columbus   *6
———— He Went with Vasco da Gama   *6
Sauer, Fog Magic   *5–6
Syme, Captain Cook   5–6
Tannenbaum, Understanding Maps, p.45–88   5–6
Wibberley, Sea Captain from Salem   *6
Wyckoff, Story of Geology, p.158–65   5–6

SEA ANEMONES
Cooper, E. K., Science on the Shores and Banks, p.177–79   5–6
Neurath, Wonder World of the Seashore, p.12   4–6
Reed, Sea for Sam, p.137–40   6
Robertson, G., Strange Sea Life, p.40–44   5–6

SEA ANIMALS: *see* Marine Animals

SEA BIRDS: *see* Water Birds

SEA COWS: *see* Manatees

SEA FIGHTS: *see* Naval Battles

SEA FOOD: *see* Fisheries; Oysters; Shellfish

SEA GULLS: *see* Gulls

SEA LIFE: *see* Marine Animals; Marine Plants

SEA LIONS: *see also* Seals (animals)
  Bridges, Zoo Pets, p.59–68   4–6
  Brown, V., How To Understand Animal Talk, p.88–92   6
  Fox, From Bones to Bodies, p.54–55   6
  Perkins, Marlin Perkins' Zooparade, p.76–79   4–6

SEA OTTERS: *see* Otters

SEA SONGS
  Coatsworth, Five Bushel Farm, p.118–19   *4–5

SEA URCHINS
  Cooper, E. K., Science on the Shores and Banks, p.90–91   5–6
  Dudley, Sea Shells, p.97–107   4–6
  Robertson, G., Strange Sea Life, p.24–28   5–6

SEA WORMS
  Hyde, Animal Clocks and Compasses, p.20–21   5–6
  Reed, Sea for Sam, p.145–48   6

SEALS (animals): *see also* Pribilof Islands
  Brown, V., How To Understand Animal Talk, p.88–92   6
  Darling, L., Seals and Walruses   4–6
  Disney, Worlds of Nature, p.23–29 (Alaskan fur seals)   4–6
  Hogner, Animal Book, p.166–78   6
  Hyde, Animal Clocks and Compasses, p.10, 89–92   5–6
  Icenhower, First Book of the Antarctic, p.61–63   4–6
  Lathrop, Let Them Live, p.20–23   4–6
  Lavine, Strange Travelers, p.113–18   5–6
  Stoutenberg, Wild Animals of the Far West, p.52–57   4–6

SEAMANSHIP: *see* Navigation

SEASHORE: *see also* Ocean

Bronson, Children of the Sea, p.119–264   *6
Carroll, Tough Enough's Pony   *4–5
_____ Tough Enough's Trip   *4–6
Hylander, Out of Doors in Summer, p.107–29   5–6
Neurath, Wonder World of the Seashore   4–6
Schneider, H., Rocks, Rivers & the Changing Earth, p.85–91   4–6
Spykman, Terrible, Horrible Edie   *5–6

SEASHORE BIRDS: *see* Water Birds

SEASONS: *see also* Animals in Winter; Autumn; Calendars; Spring; Summer; Weather; Winter
  Adler, Things That Spin, p.38–41 5–6
  Beauchamp, Discovering Our World, Bk.1, p.104–9   4
  Blough, Wait for the Sunshine   4–5
  Buck, M. W., In Woods and Fields   4–5
  Disney, Worlds of Nature, p.95–98   4–6
  Doane, Book of Nature   5–6
  Freeman, M. B., Fun with Astronomy, p.6–9   4–6
  Gaul, Pond Book   4–6
  Jauss, Discovering Nature the Year Round   4–6
  Mason, M. E., Susannah   *4–5
  Rounds, Wildlife at Your Doorstep   5–6
  Schneider, L., Space in Your Future, p.72–76   6
  Wilder, Farmer Boy   *4–6

SEAWEEDS: *see* Algae; Marine Plants

SECESSION: *see* Civil War in the United States

SECRETS
  Burnett, F. H., Secret Garden   *5–6

SECURITY
  Ceder, Ethan, the Shepherd Boy   *4–6
  Lenski, Judy's Journey   *4–6
  Sayers, Ginny and Custard   *4–6
  _____ Tag-along Tooloo   *4

SEED DISPERSAL
  Hylander, Out of Doors in Autumn, p.58–73   5–6

Parker, B. M., Plant and Animal Partnerships, p.34   5–6

———— Seeds and Seed Travels   4–6

SEEDS: *see also* Botany; Gardening; Plants

Beeler, Experiments in Science, p.16–18, 48–50   5–6

Cooper, E. K., Science in Your Own Back Yard, p.79–90   5–6

Disraeli, New Worlds through the Microscope, p.129–37   6

Parker, B. M., Flowers, Fruits, Seeds, p.25–26   4–6

———— Seeds and Seed Travels   4–6

Selsam, Play with Seeds   4–6

Stefferud, Wonders of Seeds   5–6

SELF-APPRAISAL

Faulkner, Melindy's Happy Summer   *4–5

Friedman, F., Sundae with Judy   *4–6

SELF-CONFIDENCE

Bell, Mountain Boy   *4

Bloch, Marya of Clark Avenue   *4–6

De Angeli, Yonie Wondernose   *4–5

Stolz, Dog on Barkham Street   *5–6

SELF-CONTROL

Burnett, F. H., Secret Garden   *5–6

Fritz, Brady   *5–6

Gilbert, Champions Don't Cry   *5–6

Jackson, C. P., Buzzy Plays Midget League Football   *4–5

Lenski, Judy's Journey   *4–6

Otis, Toby Tyler   *4–6

Seredy, Good Master   *5–6

Young, Unicorn with Silver Shoes   *4–6

SELF-EXPRESSION

Enright, Four-Story Mistake   *5–6

Ota, Printing for Fun   4–6

SELF-RELIANCE

Brink, Magical Melons   *5–6

Canfield, Understood Betsy   *5–6

Daugherty, Poor Richard   6

Enright, Four-Story Mistake   *5–6

———— Then There Were Five   *5–6

McGinley, Plain Princess   *4–6

O'Dell, Island of the Blue Dolphins   *6

SEMAPHORE CODE

Rogers, F., Heels, Wheels, and Wire, p.189–94   5–6

SEMINOLE INDIANS

Bleeker, Seminole Indians   4–6

McNeer, War Chief of the Seminoles   5–6

SENECA INDIANS

Brewster, First Book of Indians, p.18–28   4–5

SENSES

Cooper, E. K., Science in Your Own Back Yard, p.10–13   5–6

Schneider, H., How Your Body Works, p.82–115   4–6

Zim, Our Senses and How They Work   4–6

SEQUOIA NATIONAL PARK

Melbo, Our Country's National Parks, v.2, p.29–49   6

SEQUOIAS

Buff, Big Tree   5–6

Cormack, First Book of Trees, p.62–63   4–6

Dudley, Our American Trees, p.97–104   5–6

Parker, B. M., Saving Our Wild Life, p.22–23   5–6

SEQUOYA

Bleeker, Cherokee, p.111–30   4–6

Fletcher, S. E., American Indian, p.90–94   5–6

SERRA, JUNÍPERO

Dawson, California, p.43–72   5–6

Foster, G., George Washington's World, p.28–30, 155–59   6

Politi, Mission Bell   4–6

SERVICE TO OTHERS

Bishop, C. H., Martin de Porres, Hero   6

Bothwell, Empty Tower   *4–5

Bulla, Song of St. Francis   4–5

Clark, A. N., Magic Money   *4–6

Daugherty, Poor Richard   6

Ladd, Night of the Hurricane   *4–6

McNeer, Armed with Courage   5–6

Reynolds, Q. J., Life of Saint Patrick   5–6

SETTLEMENTS—SOCIAL: *see* Social Settlements

SEVEN YEARS' WAR, 1756–63

Foster, G., George Washington's World, p.77–95   6

SEWING: *see also* Beadwork; Embroidery; Sewing Machines; Tapestry
Ackley, Dolls To Make   5–6
    ——— Marionettes   5–6
Canfield, Understood Betsy, p.128–47
     *5–6
Dow, How To Make Doll Clothes
     5–6
Hoffmann, Sew Easy!   4–6
Lee, What To Do Now, p.20–25   4–6
Robinson, J., Things To Make from Odds & Ends, p.55–85   4–6

SEWING MACHINES: *see also* Howe, Elias
Lent, Men at Work in New England, p.116–19 (industrial)   4–6

SEX EDUCATION: *see* Reproduction

SEX ROLES—ACCEPTANCE OF
Brink, Caddie Woodlawn   *6
Johnson, E., Little Knight   *4–5
Lansing, E., Liza of the Hundredfold
     *5–6
Mirsky, Thirty-one Brothers and Sisters
     *4–6
Penney, Moki   *4–5

SHACKLETON, ERNEST
Bixby, Impossible Journey of Sir Ernest Shackleton   5–6
Frank, Ice Island, p.41–45, 48–64, 121–38   6
Lansing, A., Shackleton's Valiant Voyage   6

SHADOW PLAYS
Mulac, Game Book, p.108–11   6
Severn, Let's Give a Show, p.85–92
     4–6

SHADOWS
Barr, Young Scientist Takes a Ride, p.104–5   5–6

SHAKESPEARE, WILLIAM
Coffman, Famous Authors for Young People, p.8–9   5–6

SHARING
Albee, Three Young Kings   *4–5
Bialk, Taffy's Foal   *4–5
Bishop, C. H., Pancakes—Paris   *4–6
Bothwell, Empty Tower   *4–5
Ceder, Ethan, the Shepherd Boy   *4–6
Clewes, Secret   *4–5
Enright, Gone-Away Lake   *4–6

Godden, Miss Happiness and Miss Flower   *4–5
Haywood, Betsy's Busy Summer   *4–5
Kingman, Best Christmas   *4–6
    ——— Magic Christmas Tree   *4–5
Osborne, C. G., First Lake Dwellers
     *4–6
Spyri, Heidi   *4–6
Steele, Winter Danger   *4–6
Vance, Star for Hansi   *4–5
Van Stockum, Cottage at Bantry Bay
     *6
    ——— Pegeen   *6
Wilde, Selfish Giant   *4–6

SHARKS
Knight, C. R., Life through the Ages, p.26–27   6
Knowlton, Let's Explore beneath the Sea, p.61–83   5–6
Robertson, G., Strange Sea Life, p.87–91   5–6

SHEEP: *see also* Bighorns; Great Plains; Meat Industry; Shepherd Life; Wool
Barr, Young Scientist Takes a Ride, p.124–25   5–6
Brown, V., How To Understand Animal Talk, p.31–34, 117   6
Buehr, Meat from Ranch to Table, p.76–80   4–6
Carlson, N. S., Sashes Red and Blue, p.92–107   *4–6
Coatsworth, Cave   *4–6
Comstock, Handbook of Nature Study, p.270–74   6
Dalgliesh, America Travels, p.15–23
     *4–6
Eberle, Basketful, p.71–76   4–6
Golden, Made in Iceland, p.71–75   6
Hazeltine, Easter Book of Legends and Stories, p.268–84   *5–6
Hogeboom, Familiar Animals and How To Draw Them, p.36–39   4–5
Hogner, Animal Book, p.100–102   6
    ——— Barnyard Family, p.37–42
     5–6
    ——— Farm Animals, p.67–86   6
Hollos, Story of Your Coat   4–5
Israel, About Sheep on the Ranch   4
Johnson, M. S., Gay: A Shetland Sheepdog   *4–6
McCracken, Sentinel of the Snow Peaks
     *5–6

Mason, G. F., Animal Tracks, p.78–79
(Rocky Mountain sheep)   4–6
Meigs, Covered Bridge, p.104–10   *4–6
Weil, Animal Families   4
Wilder, Farmer Boy, p.154–62   *4–6
Yates, E., Mountain Born   *5–6

SHELLFISH: *see also* Clams; Crustacea;
Cuttlefish; Oysters; Snails
Cavanna, First Book of Sea Shells   4–6
Cooper, E. K., Science on the Shores
and Banks, p.56–82   5–6
Dudley, Sea Shells   4–6
Earle, Octopus   4–6
Fenton, C. L., Life Long Ago, p.50–69,
76–81, 88–103   6
Hausman, Beginner's Guide to Fresh-
Water Life, p.92–99   6
Hylander, Out of Doors in Summer,
p.117–23   5–6
Jaeger, Easy Crafts, p.26–27   4–6
Morgan, A. H., Field Book of Animals
in Winter, p.286–318   6
———— Field Book of Ponds and
Streams, p.301–23   6
Reed, Earth for Sam, p.24–28, 66–67
6
———— Sea for Sam, p.165–79   6
Robertson, G., Strange Sea Life, p.67–
74   5–6

SHENANDOAH NATIONAL PARK
Melbo, Our Country's National Parks,
v.1, p.122–35   6

SHEPHERD LIFE: *see also* Herding;
Navaho Indians; Sheep
Petersham, David   4–5
Stinetorf, Children of North Africa,
p.129–43   *5–6

SHEPHERD LIFE—HUNGARY
Seredy, Good Master, p.70–78   *5–6

SHEPHERD LIFE—ICELAND
Arason, Smoky Bay, p.59–87   *5–6

SHEPHERD LIFE—PALESTINE
Ceder, Ethan, the Shepherd Boy   *4–6
Hewes, Boy of the Lost Crusade, p.50–
195   *6
Lillie, Book of Three Festivals, p.11–27
*5–6

SHEPHERD LIFE—UNITED STATES
Yates, E., Mountain Born   *5–6

SHEPHERD LIFE—YUGOSLAVIA
Gidal, My Village in Yugoslavia, p.56–
76   4–6

SHERIDAN, PHILIP HENRY
Garst, Buffalo Bill   6

SHETLAND ISLANDS
Hader, Spunky, p.7–18   *4–6

SHINTOISM
Fitch, Their Search for God, p.84–109
5–6

SHIPBUILDING: *see also* Boats; Ships;
Ships—Models; Steamboats; Warships
Batchelor, Sea Lady   *4–5
Buehr, Timber!, p.23–27   5–6
Holling, Seabird, p.34–35   4–6

SHIPS: *see also* Boats; Navigation; Ocean
Travel; Sailing; Shipbuilding; Ship-
wrecks; Steamboats; Submarines; Tug-
boats; United States—Coast Guard;
Warships; also names of special ships,
as Constitution (ship)
Bendick, First Book of Ships   4–6
Block, Real Book about Ships   5–6
Colby, Ships of Our Navy   5–6
Fermi, Story of Atomic Energy, p.152–
53   6
Mitchell, Ships That Made U.S. History
6
Pratt, Monitor and the Merrimac   5–6
Zaffo, Big Book of Real Boats and
Ships   4–6

SHIPS—MODELS
Jordan, Holiday Handicraft, p.140–48,
177–80   4–6
Leeming, Fun with Boxes, p.65–66, 77–
78, 100–101   4–6
Maginley, Historic Models of Early
America, p.3–7, 49–54, 75–78   6

SHIPWRECKS
Coatsworth, Littlest House, p.70–80
*4–6
De Angeli, Jared's Island, p.7–12 *4–6
Du Soe, Three without Fear, p.1–7
*4–6
Henry, M., Misty of Chincoteague,
p.11–22   *4–6
Holling, Paddle-to-the-Sea   *4–6
Williams, U. M., Island MacKenzie
*5–6
Wyss, Swiss Family Robinson   *6

SHOES: *see also* Indians of North America—Costume
De Angeli, Copper-toed Boots   *4–6
Lent, Men at Work in New England, p.18–21   4–6
Wilder, Farmer Boy, p.285–98   *4–6

SHOOTING: *see* Guns; Hunting

SHOOTING STARS: *see* Meteors

SHOPPING
Bothwell, Little Boat Boy, p.193–200   *4–5

SHREWS
Hogner, Animal Book, p.13–16   6
Kane, Tale of a Meadow, p.84–86   4–6
Mason, G. F., Animal Tracks, p.46–47   4–6
Ripper, Moles and Shrews, p.38–64   4–6

SIAM: *see* Thailand

SIBELIUS, JEAN
Burch, Modern Composers for Young People, p.93–107   5–6

SIBERIA
American Heritage, Discoverers of the New World, p.146–48   5–6
Nazaroff, Land of the Russian People, p.9–24   6

SIBERIA—FOLK TALES
Guillot, Grishka and the Bear   *5–6

SIBLINGS
Corbin, Golden Mare   *4–6
De Angeli, Elin's Amerika   *4–6
Enright, Four-Story Mistake   *5–6
———— Saturdays   *4–6
———— Then There Were Five   *5–6
———— Thimble Summer   *5–6
Frost, Windy Foot at the County Fair   *4–6
Lenski, Cotton in My Sack   *4–6
Moore, Snake That Went to School   *4
Rushmore, Shadow of Robbers Roost   *6
Seymour, Kaatje and the Christmas Compass   *4–6
Spykman, Terrible, Horrible Edie   *5–6

SICILY
Fletcher, D., Confetti for Cortorelli   *4–6

Joy, Young People of the Western Mediterranean, p.33–42   6

SIEGFRIED: *see also* Sigurd
Hazeltine, Hero Tales of Many Lands, p.253–68   5–6

SIGN LANGUAGE
Hofsinde, Indian Sign Language   4–6

SIGNALING: *see also* Flags; Heliograph; Lighthouses; Morse Code; Navigation; Radio; Railroads—Signaling; Semaphore Code; Sign Language; Smoke Signals; Telegraph
Beeler, Experiments with Electricity, p.88–92   5–6
Hamilton, R., First Book of Trains, p.35–45   4–5
Rogers, F., Heels, Wheels, and Wire, p.132–97   5–6

SIGURD: *see also* Siegfried
Colum, Children of Odin, p.207–82   4–5
Hazeltine, Hero Tales of Many Lands, p.270–77   5–6

SIKORSKY, IGOR
Lewellen, Helicopters, p.86–91, 96–105   6

SILHOUETTES
Leeming, Fun with Paper, p.82–83   4–6
Robinson, J., Things To Make from Odds & Ends, p.26   4–6

SILKWORMS
Lane, F. C., All about the Insect World, p.30–34   5–6
Spencer, C., Made in China, p.10–20   5–6

SILVER: *see also* Metals; Mining; Money; Silversmithing
Beeler, Experiments in Chemistry, p.78–83   5–6
Fenton, C. L., Riches from the Earth, p.129–31   5–6
Loomis, Field Book of Common Rocks and Minerals, p.32–37   6
Morgan, A. P., First Chemistry Book for Boys and Girls, p.156–63   5–6

SILVERSMITHING: *see also* Revere, Paul
Bailey, C. S., Pioneer Art in America, p.39–51   5–6

Bleeker, Navajo, p.113–29   4–6

SINGING GAMES: *see also* Dancing;
   Folk Songs
   Bancroft, Games, p.343–78   4–6
   Forbush, Book of Games, p.40–88   4–6
   Mulac, Game Book, p.80–88   6

SINKIANG
   Quinn, Picture Map Geography of Asia,
   p.95–96   4–6

SIOUAN INDIANS
   Fletcher, S. E., American Indian, p.75–
   88   5–6
   Garst, Sitting Bull   6
   Tavo, Buffalo Are Running   *6

SITTING BULL (Sioux Indian chief)
   Garst, Buffalo Bill   6
   ———— Sitting Bull   6

SKATING
   Association for Childhood Education,
   Told under the Stars and Stripes,
   p.218–38   *4–6
   Beeler, Experiments in Science, p.113–
   15   5–6
   Schneider, H., Everyday Machines and
   How They Work, p.40–41   5–6
   Scott, B. A., Skating for Beginners   6
   Woolley, Ginnie and Geneva, p.132–45,
   175–80   *4–5

SKIING
   Benary-Isbert, Shooting Star   *4–6
   Brown, C., Skiing for Beginners
                                                      4–6
   Burglon, Children of the Soil, p.173–90
                                                    *4–6
   Dahl, Cloud Shoes   *4–6
   Rothery, Scandinavian Roundabout, p.
   82–86   6

SKIMMERS
   Webb, Birds in Their Homes, p.59   4–6

SKIN
   Beauchamp, Discovering Our World,
   Bk.1, p.82   4
   Mason, G. F., Animal Clothing, p.53–60
                                                      5–6
   Zim, Our Senses and How They Work,
   p.87–96   4–6

SKITS
   Carlson, B. W., Do It Yourself!, p.115–
   56   4–6

SKRIABIN, ALEKSANDR NIKOLAE-
   VICH
   Burch, Modern Composers for Young
   People, p.111–20   5–6

SKUNKS
   Barker, Winter-sleeping Wildlife, p.53–
   58   5–6
   Buff, Big Tree, p.16–22   *5–6
   Carlson, N. S., Talking Cat, p.3–16
                                                    *4–6
   Comstock, Handbook of Nature Study,
   p.245–47   6
   De Jong, M., Smoke above the Lane
                                                    *4–5
   Hogner, Animal Book, p.124–28   6
   Kane, Tale of a Meadow, p.92–96 4–6
   Mason, G. F., Animal Tracks, p.54–55
                                                      4–6
   ———— Animal Weapons, p.66–70
                                                      5–6
   Moe, Animal Inn, p.129–38   4–6
   Ripper, Weasel Family, p.22–30   4–5
   Stoutenberg, Wild Animals of the Far
   West, p.33–36   4–6

SKYSCRAPERS
   Hillyer, Child's History of Art, p.420–
   26   5–6

SLAVERY: *see also* Civil War in the
   United States; Emancipation Day;
   Emancipation Proclamation; Negroes;
   South
   Bontemps, Frederick Douglass   4–6
   Commager, H. S., First Book of Amer-
   ican History, p.41–43   4–6
   Foster, G., Abraham Lincoln's World,
   p.150–53, 304–9   6
   Fritz, Brady   *5–6
   Holberg, John Greenleaf Whittier, p.51–
   57, 74–75   6
   Meadowcroft, By Secret Railway   *5–6

SLEDS
   Wilder, Farmer Boy, p.299–304   *4–6

SLEEP
   Batchelor, Superstitious? Here's Why!,
   p.100–105   6

SLEZAK, LEO
   Schwimmer, Great Musicians as Children, p.207–13   6

SLOTHS

Andrews, All about Strange Beasts of the Past, p.113–17   5–6

Fox, From Bones to Bodies, p.50–53   6

Knight, C. R., Life through the Ages, p.60–61   6

Robinson, W. W., Beasts of the Tar Pits, p.30–32   5–6

SLOVAKIA: *see* Czechoslovakia

SMELTING: *see* Metallurgy; also names of metals, as Copper; Iron

SMITH, JOHN

Aulaire, Pocahontas   4–5

Dalgliesh, America Builds Homes   4–5

Duvoisin, And There Was America, p.50–52   4–6

Foster, G., World of Captain John Smith   6

Lawson, M. A., Pocahontas and Captain John Smith   6

SMOKE

Barr, Young Scientist Takes a Ride, p.10–14   5–6

Parker, B. M., Fire, p.31   4–6

SMOKE PRINTING

Jaeger, Easy Crafts, p.2–3   4–6

SMOKE SIGNALS

Rogers, F., Heels, Wheels, and Wire, p.194–97   5–6

SMOKING: *see* Tobacco

SMOKY MOUNTAINS: *see* Great Smoky Mountains

SMOKY MOUNTAINS NATIONAL PARK: *see* Great Smoky Mountains National Park

SMYTH, ETHEL MARY

Schwimmer, Great Musicians as Children, p.186–93   6

SNAILS

Barker, Winter-sleeping Wildlife, p.126–29   5–6

Buck, M. W., In Ponds and Streams, p.18   4–6

———— Pets from the Pond, p.22–24, 26–27   4–6

Comstock, Handbook of Nature Study, p.416–22   6

Cooper, E. K., Science in Your Own Back Yard, p.106–10   5–6

———— Science on the Shores and Banks, p.63–71   5–6

Dudley, Sea Shells, p.86–96   4–6

Fenton, C. L., Life Long Ago, p.93–97   6

Hogner, Snails   4–6

Morgan, A. H., Field Book of Animals in Winter, p.286–318   6

Pels, Care of Winter Pets, p.36–40   4–6

SNAKES: *see also* Reptiles

Barker, Winter-sleeping Wildlife, p.65–69   5–6

Bevans, Book of Reptiles and Amphibians, p.9–32   4–6

Bridges, Zoo Pets, p.45–51   4–6

Brown, V., How To Understand Animal Talk, p.171–74   6

Buck, M. W., In Ponds and Streams, p.50   4–6

———— In Yards and Gardens, p.58–59   4–6

Comstock, Handbook of Nature Study, p.194–203   6

Fenton, C. L., Wild Folk in the Desert, p.52–58   4–6

Haywood, Eddie's Pay Dirt   *4–5

Hecht, All about Snakes   5–6

Hoke, First Book of Snakes   4–5

Huntington, Let's Go to the Desert, p.74–83   4–5

Hylander, Animals in Armor, p.123–95   6

———— Out of Doors in Summer, p.81–90   5–6

Kane, Tale of a Meadow, p.49–54   4–6

Kipling, Jungle Book, p.49–104, 187–217   *5–6

Lathrop, Let Them Live, p.58–60   4–6

McClung, Buzztail   4–6

Mason, G. F., Animal Weapons, p.60–65   5–6

Mason, M. E., Susannah, p.55–63   *4–5

May, Let's Read about Brazil, p.80–83   4–6

Moore, Snake That Went to School   *4

Morgan, A. H., Field Book of Animals in Winter, p.361–66   6

———— Field Book of Ponds and
Streams, p.404–6   6
Parker, B. M., Reptiles, p.23–33 4–6
Rothery, South American Roundabout,
p.168–70   5–6
Rounds, Swamp Life, p.12–16   5–6
Stinetorf, Children of North Africa,
p.38–43   *5–6
Zim, Snakes   5–6

SNOW: *see also* Avalanches
Bell, Snow   4–6
Graham, E. H., Water for America,
p.11   6

SNOWBIRDS: *see* Juncos

SOAP
Beeler, Experiments in Chemistry, p.18–
23, 117–21   5–6
Lent, Men at Work in the Great Lakes
States, p.58–61   4–6
Morgan, A. P., First Chemistry Book
for Boys and Girls, p.164–68   5–6
Schwartz, It's Fun To Know Why,
p.93–106   5–6

SOAP SCULPTURE
Haywood, Betsy's Winterhouse, p.109–
27   *4–5
Robinson, J., Things To Make from
Odds & Ends, p.50–51   4–6
Zarchy, Let's Make More Things, p.58–
61   5–6
———— Let's Make Something, p.66–
69   5–6

SOCCER
Bancroft, Games, p.605–20   4–6

SOCIAL ANIMALS: *see* Community Life
among the Animals and Insects; also
names of social animals and insects,
as Ants; Bees; Musk Oxen; Prairie
Dogs

SOCIAL POISE
Lee, Manners To Grow On   4–6

SOCIAL RESPONSIBILITY
Franklin, Monte   *4–6
McGinley, Plain Princess   *4–6
Sechrist, Heigh-Ho for Halloween!,
p.235–40   5–6
Turner, Town Meeting Means Me   4–6

SOCIAL SERVICE: *see* names of social
workers, as Addams, Jane

SOCIAL SETTLEMENTS
McNeer, Armed with Courage, p.61–68
5–6

SOCIETY ISLANDS
Quinn, Picture Map Geography of the
Pacific Islands, p.107–13   5–6

SOCRATES
Hartman, Builders of the Old World,
p.153–56   6

SODA WATER
Elting, Lollypop Factory and Lots of
Others, p.94–95   4–5

SOIL CONSERVATION: *see also* Con-
servation; Erosion
Adler, Dust, p.57–73   5–6
Comstock, Handbook of Nature Study,
p.770–75   6
Fenton, C. L., Land We Live On, p.36–
37, 68–77   4–6
Van Dersal, Land Renewed   6

SOILS: *see also* Agriculture; Fertilizers;
Gardening; Irrigation
Beeler, More Experiments in Science,
p.51–55   5–6
Comstock, Handbook of Nature Study,
p.760–75   6
Cooper, E. K., Science in Your Own
Back Yard   5–6
Fenton, C. L., Land We Live On, p.56–
59   4–6
Hogner, Earthworms, p.16–22   4–6

SOLAR BATTERY
Morgan, A. P., Boys' Book of Engines,
Motors & Turbines, p.164–67   6
Yates, R. F., Boy and a Battery, p.107–
13   5–6

SOLAR SYSTEM: *see* Astronomy

SOLOMON, KING
Bowie, Bible Story for Boys and Girls:
Old Testament, p.126–31   4–6
Falls, First 3000 Years, p.119, 121–23,
141   6
Hartman, In Bible Days, p.104–10 6

SOLOMON ISLANDS
Quinn, Picture Map Geography of the
Pacific Islands, p.52–56   5–6

SOMALILAND
Epstein, E., First Book of the United
Nations, p.67–81   4–6

SONAR
  Icenhower, First Book of Submarines,
    p.34–39   5–6

SONG SPARROWS
  Webb, Birds in Their Homes, p.30   4–6

SONGS: *see also* American Ballads and
    Songs; Ballads; Folk Songs; Lullabies;
    National Songs; Sea Songs; also
    names of composers of songs, as
    Foster, Stephen Collins; Schubert,
    Franz Peter
  Allstrom, Songs along the Way   4–6
  Buchanan, How Man Made Music,
    p.15–19, 147–48   6
  Justus, Surprise for Peter Pocket
                                      *4–6

SONGS—CANADA
  Bonner, Made in Canada, p.83–93
                                      5–6

SONGS—ENGLAND
  Buchanan, How Man Made Music,
    p.148–51   6

SONGS—GERMANY
  Buchanan, How Man Made Music,
    p.161–64   6

SONGS—IRELAND
  Buchanan, How Man Made Music,
    p.158–61   6

SONGS—JEWISH
  Buchanan, How Man Made Music,
    p.168–69   6

SONGS—MEXICO
  Buchanan, How Man Made Music,
    p.166–67   6

SONGS—PIONEER LIFE
  Brink, Caddie Woodlawn, p.166–70   *6
  Buchanan, How Man Made Music,
    p.186–87   6
  Carr, Children of the Covered Wagon
                                      *4–6
  Wilder, By the Shores of Silver Lake
                                      *5–6
  ———— Little House on the Prairie
                                      *4–6
  ———— Long Winter   *5–6

SONGS—SCANDINAVIA
  Buchanan, How Man Made Music,
    p.165–66   6

SONGS—SCOTLAND
  Buchanan, How Man Made Music,
    p.154–58   6

SONGS—SPAIN
  Buchanan, How Man Made Music,
    p.166–67   6

SONGS—SWEDEN
  Buchanan, How Man Made Music,
    p.165–66   6

SONGS—WALES
  Buchanan, How Man Made Music,
    p.151–54   6

SONIC BOOM
  Crouse, W. H., Understanding Science,
    p.167–69   6
  Irving, Sound and Ultrasonics, p.139–
    46   6
  Zarem, New Dimensions of Flight,
    p.19–20   6

SONS OF LIBERTY: *see* Revere, Paul;
    Revolutionary War in America

SOTO, HERNANDO DE: *see* De Soto,
    Hernando

SOUND: *see also* Music; Phonograph;
    Physics; Radio; Telephone
  Baer, Sound   4–6
  Baker, A. O., Your Science World,
    p.227–40   6
  Barnard, Macmillan Science-Life Series,
    Bk.6, p.80–111   6
  Barr, More Research Ideas for Young
    Scientists, p.127–32, 136–40   5–6
  ———— Research Ideas for Young
    Scientists, p.41–44   5–6
  Batchelor, Superstitious? Here's Why!,
    p.19–22   6
  Beeler, More Experiments in Science,
    p.5–7   5–6
  Freeman, M. B., Fun with Science,
    p.35–40   6
  Geralton, Story of Sound   5–6
  Huey, What Makes the Wheels Go
    Round, p.126–30   6
  Irving, Sound and Ultrasonics   6
  Kettelkamp, Magic of Sound   4–6
  Knight, D. C., First Book of Sound
                                      5–6
  Morgan, A. P., Boys' Book of Science
    and Construction, p.199–230   6
  Parker, B. M., Sound   5–6

Podendorf, 101 Science Experiments, p.88–93   4–5

Reed, And That's Why, p.95–104   4–5

Rogers, F., Heels, Wheels, and Wire, p.132–67   5–6

Schneider, H., Your Telephone and How It Works, p.12–20   5–6

Zim, Our Senses and How They Work, p.79–83   4–6

SOUND WAVES

Beeler, Experiments in Science, p.53–55   5–6

Geralton, Story of Sound, p.4–7   5–6

SOUTH: *see also* Cotton; Great Smoky Mountains; Mountain Life—South; Negroes; Plantation Life; Slavery; Southwest; also names of states and cities, as Florida; New Orleans

Banta, Life in America: The South   5–6

Barrows, American Continents, p.85–124   5

Field, Hitty, p.156–79   *5–6

Payne, Leprechaun of Bayou Luce   *4–5

Purdy, He Heard America Sing, p.200–213   6

SOUTH AMERICA: *see also* Amazon River; Amazon Valley; Andes Mountains; Animals—South America; Indians of South America; Latin America; also names of countries, as Brazil; and names of products, as Coffee

Epstein, S., All about the Desert, p.112–16   5–6

Goetz, Neighbors to the South, p.59–112   5–6

Hudson, Little Boy Lost   *5–6

Quinn, Picture Map Geography of South America   4–6

Rothery, South American Roundabout   5–6

Selsam, See through the Jungle   4–5

SOUTH AMERICA—ART; *see* Art—South America

SOUTH AMERICA—FOLK TALES

Harper, Ghosts and Goblins, p.37–51   4–6

SOUTH AMERICA—HISTORY: *see also* Bolívar, Simón; Miranda, Francisco de; O'Higgins, Bernardo; Pedro II, Emperor of Brazil; San Martín, José de

Foster, G., Abraham Lincoln's World, p.15–18, 32–35, 88–91, 108–11   6

Peck, Pageant of South American History   6

Rothery, South American Roundabout   5–6

SOUTH AMERICA—INDUSTRIES

Quinn, Picture Map Geography of South America   4–6

SOUTH ATLANTIC STATES: *see* Atlantic States

SOUTH CAROLINA

Banta, Life in America: The South, p.102–7   5–6

Lattimore, Junior   *4–5

Lenski, Judy's Journey, p.139–55   *4–6

Quinn, Picture Map Geography of the United States, p.56–59   4–6

SOUTH DAKOTA: *see also* Dakota Territory; Wind Cave National Park

Quinn, Picture Map Geography of the United States, p.112–15   4–6

Rounds, Stolen Pony   *5–6

SOUTH SEA ISLANDS: *see* Pacific Islands

SOUTHWEST: *see also* Carlsbad Caverns National Park; Navaho Indians; Pueblo Indians; Santa Fe Trail; also names of states, as Arizona

Bleeker, Apache Indians   4–6

Dorian, Hokahey!, p.42–52   5–6

Lauritzen, Glitter-eyed Wouser   *5–6

McGinley, Mince Pie and Mistletoe   4–6

McNeer, Story of the Southwest   4–6

SOVIET UNION: *see* Union of Soviet Socialist Republics

SPACE SHIPS

Hendrickson, Handbook for Space Travelers   5–6

SPACE STATIONS

Coggins, J., Rockets, Satellites, and Space Travel, p.34–40   6

Hendrickson, Handbook for Space Travelers, p.143–47, 161–67   5–6

SPACE TRAVEL: *see also* Astronauts;
  Astronomy; Science Fiction
Adler, Time in Your Life, p.112–16
                                    4–6
Asimov, Satellites in Outer Space, p.67–
  73   4–5
Baker, A. O., Your Science World,
  p.217–24   6
Barnard, Macmillan Science-Life Series,
  Bk.6, p.202–34   6
Beatty, Matthew Looney's Voyage to the
  Earth   *4–6
Bendick, First Book of Space Travel
                                    5–6
_____ How Much and How Many,
  p.115–18   5–6
Branley, Exploring by Satellite   6
_____ Guide to Outer Space   4–6
_____ Moon, p.88–95   6
Burt, Space Monkey   4–6
Coggins, J., Rockets, Satellites, and
  Space Travel, p.41–64   6
Coombs, Gateway to Space   6
_____ Rockets, Missiles, and Moons,
  p.229–43   6
Crouse, W. H., Understanding Science,
  p.117–18   6
Dietz, All about Satellites and Space
  Ships   5–6
Fisher, J., Wonderful World of the Air,
  p.64–69   5–6
Hendrickson, Handbook for Space Trav-
  elers   5–6
Hyde, Animal Clocks and Compasses,
  p.117–22   5–6
Kay, Space Volunteers   6
Lent, Man Alive in Outer Space   5–6
Leonard, Exploring Science, p.136–45
                                     6
Lewellen, Earth Satellite   4–6
MacGregor, Miss Pickerell Goes to
  Mars   *4–6
Munch, What Is a Rocket?, p.38–47
                                    4–5
Nephew, Beyond Mars   4–6
Schneider, L., Space in Your Future,
  p.203–45   6
Todd, Space Cat   *4–5
_____ Space Cat Meets Mars   *4–5
_____ Space Cat Visits Venus   *4–5
Wells, What Does an Astronaut Do?   6
Zarem, New Dimensions of Flight,
  p.172–247   6

SPAIN: *see also* Costume—Spain
Barrows, Old World Lands, p.93–95   6
_____ Our Big World, p.75–80   4
Buckley, Luis of Spain   *4–6
_____ Spanish Plateau   6
Carlson, N. S., Song of the Lop-eared
  Mule   *4–5
Joy, Young People of the Western Med-
  iterranean, p.107–23   6
Lamprey, All the Ways of Building,
  p.128–39   6

SPAIN—FOLK TALES
Fenner, Fools and Funny Fellows, p.18–
  25   4–6
Sawyer, Long Christmas, p.20–31, 85–
  96   4–6

SPAIN—HISTORY: *see also* Moors;
  Spanish-American War, 1898; Spanish Armada, 1588; also names of persons, as Columbus, Christopher
Baker, N. B., Juan Ponce de León 5–6
Hazeltine, Hero Tales of Many Lands,
  p.236–51   5–6
McGuire, Glimpses into the Long Ago,
  p.272–75   5–6

SPANIARDS IN AMERICA: *see also*
  names of persons, as Cortez, Hernando
Brindze, Gulf Stream, p.18–21   4–6
Dalgliesh, America Begins, p.19–31, 40–
  49, 52–54   4–5
Dawson, California   5–6
Duvoisin, And There Was America, p.7–
  14, 19–24   4–6

SPANISH AMERICA: *see* Central America; Latin America; Mexico; South
  America; West Indies

SPANISH-AMERICAN WAR, 1898
Judson, Theodore Roosevelt, p.118–49
                                    5–6
Pace, Juliette Low, p.92–99   5–6

SPANISH ARMADA, 1588: *see also*
  Drake, Francis; England—History;
  Spain—History
Trease, Sir Walter Raleigh, p.58–72
                                    5–6

SPANISH MISSIONS IN CALIFORNIA
Bleeker, Mission Indians of California,
  p.99–128   4–6

Dawson, California, p.49–72, 84–92
                                        5–6
Politi, Mission Bell   4–6

SPARROW HAWKS: *see* Hawks

SPARROWS: *see also* Chipping Sparrows;
    Field Sparrows; Juncos; Song Spar-
    rows; Vesper Sparrows
    Comstock, Handbook of Nature Study,
    p.83–91   6
    Earle, White Patch   4–6

SPATTER WORK
    Jaeger, Easy Crafts, p.6–7   4–6

SPAULDING, CHARLES CLINTON
    Shackelford, Child's Story of the Negro,
    p.194–200   4–5

SPECTOGRAPH
    Schneider, L., Space in Your Future,
    p.179–83   6

SPEEDOMETER
    Barr, Young Scientist Takes a Ride,
    p.94–95   5–6

SPHINX
    Benson, Stories of the Gods and Heroes,
    p.136–38   5–6
    Hillyer, Child's History of Art, p.164–
    66   5–6
    Meadowcroft, Gift of the River, p.44–
    46   5–6

SPICES
    Caldwell, Let's Visit India, p.21–23
                                        4–6
    ———— Let's Visit Pakistan, p.47–49
                                        4–6
    Duvoisin, They Put Out to Sea, p.44–46
                                        4–6
    Hewes, Spice Ho!   5–6

SPIDERS
    Barker, Winter-sleeping Wildlife, p.93–
    99   5–6
    Barr, More Research Ideas for Young
    Scientists, p.114–17   5–6
    Brown, V., How To Understand Animal
    Talk, p.188–90   6
    Buck, M. W., In Yards and Gardens,
    p.54–55   4–6
    ———— Small Pets from Woods and
    Fields, p.44–56   4–6
    Comstock, Handbook of Nature Study,
    p.435–50   6

Cooper, E. K., Science in Your Own
    Back Yard, p.123–32   5–6
Disney, Worlds of Nature, p.91–92,
    142–43   4–6
Disraeli, New Worlds through the Mi-
    croscope, p.71–74   6
Hogner, Spiders   4–5
Huntington, Let's Go to the Desert,
    p.60–63   4–5
Lutz, Field Book of Insects, p.27–33
                                        4–6
Mason, G. F., Animal Homes, p.63–67
                                        4–6
    ———— Animal Tools, p.73–78   5–6
Morgan, A. H., Field Book of Animals
    in Winter, p.279–85   6
Parker, B. M., Spiders   4–6
Shuttlesworth, Story of Spiders   6
White, E. B., Charlotte's Web   *4–6
Williamson, First Book of Bugs, p.24–
    28   4–5

SPIES: *see also* names of spies, as Hale,
    Nathan
    McSwigan, Snow Treasure, p.143–49
                                       *5–6
    Meadowcroft, Silver for General Wash-
    ington, p.78–89   *5–6

SPINNING: *see also* Textiles
    Hartman, Machines, p.1-13   6
    Hollos, Story of Your Coat   4–5
    Maginley, Historic Models of Early
    America, p.137–40   6

SPIRITUALS: *see* Negroes—Songs

SPONGE FISHERIES
    Bronson, Children of the Sea, p.220–64
                                        6
    Stinetorf, Children of North Africa,
    p.76–94   *5–6

SPONGES
    Disraeli, New Worlds through the Mi-
    croscope, p.75–78   6
    Fenton, C. L., Life Long Ago, p.34–40
                                        6
    Hausman, Beginner's Guide to Fresh-
    Water Life, p.110–11   6
    Morgan, A. H., Field Book of Animals
    in Winter, p.53–59   6
    ———— Field Book of Ponds and
    Streams, p.104–11   6
    Reed, Sea for Sam, p.121–29   6

Robertson, G., Strange Sea Life, p.50–53   5–6

SPONTANEOUS COMBUSTION: *see* Combustion

SPORTS: *see also* Amusements; Athletics; Ball; Fishing; Games; Hunting; Kites; Olympic Games; Sailing; Skating; Skiing; Swimming; also names of ball games, as Baseball
Jackson, C. P., Buzzy Plays Midget League Football   *4–5
———— Spice's Football   *4–5
Renick, M. L., Nicky's Football Team   *4–5
———— Pete's Home Run   *4–5
Rothery, Scandinavian Roundabout, p.82–88   6

SPORTSMANSHIP
Spencer, P. R., Finding New Trails, p.299–300   4
———— Traveling New Trails, p.387–92   6

SPOTSWOOD, ALEXANDER
Barksdale, That Country Called Virginia, p.57–65   6

SPRING: *see also* Proserpina; Seasons
Alden, Why the Chimes Rang, p.30–40   *4–6
Harrison, Outdoor Adventures, p.9–39   4–5
Hazeltine, Easter Book of Legends and Stories, p.191–98   *5–6
Hylander, Out of Doors in Spring   5–6
Kane, Tale of a Pond, p.9–18   5–6

SPRINGBUCK
Hyde, Animal Clocks and Compasses, p.104–5   5–6

SPRINGS: *see* Water Supply

SPRUCE TREES
Comstock, Handbook of Nature Study, p.675–78   6
Cormack, First Book of Trees, p.53–54   4–6

SQUIRRELS
Bailey, C. S., Miss Hickory   *4–6
Brown, V., How To Understand Animal Talk, p.131–35   6
Buck, F., Jungle Animals, p.9   5–6

Buck, M. W., In Yards and Gardens, p.64–65   4–6
Colby, First Hunt, p.8–9   5–6
Comstock, Handbook of Nature Study, p.233–38   6
Fisher, A. L., Summer of Little Rain   *4–6
Hogner, Animal Book, p.34–42   6
Lathrop, Let Them Live, p.68–70   4–6
Mason, G. F., Animal Homes, p.44–48   4–6
———— Animal Tracks, p.24–27   4–6
Moe, Animal Inn, p.89–108, 155–61   4–6
Stoutenberg, Wild Animals of the Far West, p.59–72   4–6
Weeks, Tales of a Common Pigeon, p.25–34   *4–6

SQUIRRELS—FLYING: *see* Flying Squirrels

STAGE—CONSTRUCTION: *see* Theater —Miniature

STAGECOACHES
Bulla, Riding the Pony Express, p.21–28   *4–5
Dalgliesh, America Travels, p.3–12   *4–6
Proudfit, River-Boy, p.151–61   6
Rogers, F., Heels, Wheels, and Wire, p.61–67   5–6
Tousey, Cowboy Tommy   *4–5

STAGECOACHES—MODELS
Maginley, Historic Models of Early America, p.34–45   6

STAGECRAFT: *see* Motion Pictures; Plays—Production

STAINED GLASS WINDOWS
Carlson, B. W., Make It Yourself!, p.19   4–6
Epstein, S., First Book of Glass, p.34–35   5–6

STALIN, JOSEPH
Nazaroff, Land of the Russian People, p.148–49   6

STAMP ACT, 1765: *see also* Colonial Period in America; Revolutionary War in America
Eaton, That Lively Man, Ben Franklin, p.149–57   6
Pace, Early American, p.18–25   5–6

STAMPS—POSTAGE: *see* Postage Stamps

STANDARD TIME
Adler, Time in Your Life, p.69–73
4–6
Bragdon, L. J., Tell Me the Time, Please
4–5
Freeman, M. B., Fun with Astronomy, p.11
4–6
Henry, R. S., Trains, p.74–76   5–6
Reck, Clocks Tell the Time, p.46–47
4–6
Tannenbaum, Understanding Time, p.108–27   6

STANLEY, HENRY MORTON
Hughes, First Book of Africa, p.15, 17–19, 23   5–6

STARCH
Beeler, Experiments in Chemistry, p.64–71   5–6
Disraeli, New Worlds through the Microscope, p.138–40   6

STARFISH
Cooper, E. K., Science on the Shores and Banks, p.83–90   5–6
Dudley, Sea Shells, p.108–17   4–6
Fenton, C. L., Life Long Ago, p.104–8
6
Neurath, Wonder World of the Seashore, p.18–19   4–6
Robertson, G., Strange Sea Life, p.18–23   5–6

STARLINGS
Bronson, Starlings   4–5

STARS: *see also* Astronomy; Meteors; Planets
Baker, R. H., When the Stars Come Out
6
Barr, Young Scientist Takes a Ride, p.105–6   5–6
Beauchamp, Discovering Our World, Bk.1, p.113–15   4
Cassell, Nature Games and Activities, p.66–68   4–6
Comstock, Handbook of Nature Study, p.815–33   6
Cooper, E. K., Science in Your Own Back Yard, p.179–87   5–6
Freeman, M. B., Fun with Astronomy, p.46–55   4–6

Hendrickson, Handbook for Space Travelers, p.246–50   5–6
Leeming, Fun with Paper, p.11–12
4–5
Meyer, Picture Book of Astronomy, p.31–36   4–5
Schealer, This Way to the Stars   6
Schneider, L., Space in Your Future, p.105–18   6
Tannenbaum, Understanding Maps, p.89–104   5–6

STATE TREES
Earle, State Trees   5–6

STATESMEN: *see* names of statesmen, as Franklin, Benjamin

STATIC ELECTRICITY: *see* Electrostatics

STATUES: *see* Sculpture; also names of special statues, as Liberty—Statue of

STEAM: *see also* Evaporation; Heating
Dalgliesh, America Travels, p.93–100
4–6
Scheib, What Happened?, p.21–27
5–6
Schneider, H., More Power to You, p.35–47   5–6

STEAM ENGINES: *see also* Locomotives
Adler, Fire in Your Life, p.92–94   4–6
Branley, Solar Energy, p.72–80   6
Crouse, W. H., Understanding Science, p.32–38   6
Darrow, Boys' Own Book of Great Inventions, p.128–36   6
Hartman, Machines, p.48–62   6
Henry, R. S., Trains, p.3–5   5–6
Morgan, A. P., Boys' Book of Engines, Motors & Turbines, p.1–26   6

STEAM TURBINES: *see* Turbines

STEAMBOATS: *see also* Clermont (ship); Fulton, Robert; Ocean Travel; Warships
Crawford, "Hello, the Boat!"   *6
Darrow, Boys' Own Book of Great Inventions, p.222–38   6
Hartman, Machines, p.63–71   6
Judson, Boat Builder, p.94–119   5–6
Lane, C. D., River Dragon   *4–6
Mitchell, Ships That Made U.S. History, p.30–34, 49–52   6

Shapiro, Steamboat Bill and the Captain's Top Hat   *5–6

STEEL: *see also* Iron; Pittsburgh; Tools
Adler, Fire in Your Life, p.86–90
                                      4–6
Darrow, Boys' Own Book of Great Inventions, p.379–407   6
Freeman, I. M., All about the Wonders of Chemistry, p.49–58   6
Hartman, Machines, p.108–20   6
Lent, Men at Work in the Great Lakes States, p.20–25   4–6
Writers Project, Story of Iron and Steel, no.34   5–6

STEMS
Selsam, Plants We Eat, p.31–43   4–6

STENCIL WORK
Hamilton, E. T., Handicraft for Girls, p.3–13   6
Ota, Printing for Fun, p.40–47   4–6
Weiss, H., Paper, Ink and Roller, p.30–39   4–6

STEPHENSON, GEORGE
Hartman, Machines, p.73–77   6

STEPPARENTS—ADJUSTMENT TO
Bialk, Taffy's Foal   *4–5
De Angeli, Jared's Island   *4–6
Gates, Blue Willow   *5–6

STEREOTYPE
Lent, "I Work on a Newspaper," p.56–61   6

STEVENSON, ROBERT LOUIS
Coffman, Famous Authors for Young People, p.125–30   5–6
Peare, Robert Louis Stevenson   4–6
Proudfit, Treasure Hunter   6

STICK INSECTS
Bronson, Grasshopper Book, p.118–23
                                      4–6

STOCK RAISING: *see* Cattle; Grasslands; Meat Industry; Ranch Life; Sheep

STOCKYARDS: *see* Meat Industry

STONE AGE: *see also* Archeology; Prehistoric Man
Writers Project, Aluminum, no.31, p.7–8   5–6
———— Cement, no.33, p.5–6   5–6

STONEHENGE
Hillyer, Child's History of Art, p.284–85   5–6

STONEMASONRY
Bleeker, Inca, p.30, 61, 63, 106–9
                                      5–6

STORAGE BATTERIES: *see* Electric Batteries

STORES: *see also* Business; Grocery Stores; Supermarkets; Window Decoration
Lenski, Blue Ridge Billy, p.104–19
                                      *5–6
Spencer, C., Land of the Chinese People, p.95–101   6

STORMS: *see also* Barometers; Rain; Snow; Weather; Winds
Adler, Weather in Your Life, p.43–44, 51–52, 85–88, 95–96   5–6
Arason, Smoky Bay, p.132–46   *5–6
Armer, Waterless Mountain, p.113–17
                                      *5–6
Barnes, Wonderful Year, p.105–12
                                      *4–6
Bronson, Children of the Sea, p.83–93
                                      6
Buff, Dancing Cloud, p.51–57   *4–5
Coatsworth, Away Goes Sally, p.90–98
                                      *4–6
———— Fair American, p.94–103
                                      *5–6
Crowley, Tor and Azor, p.67–71 (hurricane)   *4–6
Du Soe, Three without Fear, p.37–42
                                      *4–6
Gallant, R. A., Exploring the Weather, p.42–49   5–6
Hunt, M. L., Ladycake Farm, p.93–101 (cyclone)   *4–6
Irving, Hurricanes and Twisters   4–6
Ladd, Night of the Hurricane   *4–6
Lang, Strawberry Roan, p.45–51   *5–6
Lauber, Battle against the Sea, p.28–36
                                      5–6
Lawrence, Sand in Her Shoes, p.168–211 (hurricane)   *4–6
Leonard, Exploring Science, p.71–79, 88–97   6
McCloskey, Time of Wonder   *4–5
Parker, B. M., Clouds, Rain, and Snow, p.22–27   4–6

Reed, And That's Why, p.48–55   4–5

Schneider, H., Everyday Weather and How It Works, p.58–77   5–6

Sheehy, Molly and the Golden Wedding, p.13–42 (blizzard)   *4–5

Tannehill, All about the Weather, p.65–76   4–6

Weeks, Tales of a Common Pigeon, p.81–104 (hurricane)   *4–6

Wilder, Long Winter   *5–6

————— On the Banks of Plum Creek, p.282–334   *4–6

Wyler, First Book of Weather, p.28–30   5–6

STORYTELLING: *see also* Bards; Ghosts; Indians of North America—Folk Tales; Legends

Olcott, Good Stories for Great Holidays   4–6

Sawyer, Long Christmas   4–6

STOVES: *see also* Heating

Adler, Fire in Your Life, p.49–53   4–6

Schneider, H., Everyday Machines and How They Work, p.26, 125–27 (gas)   5–6

STOWE, HARRIET BEECHER

Foster, G., Abraham Lincoln's World, p.73–75, 152–53, 236–37   6

STRADIVARI, ANTONIO

Buchanan, How Man Made Music, p.69–71   6

STRATFORD ON AVON: *see* Shakespeare, William

STRATOSPHERE: *see* Space Travel; Weather

STRAUSS, JOHANN

Schwimmer, Great Musicians as Children, p.112–22   6

STRAUSS, RICHARD

Burch, Modern Composers for Young People, p.85–89   5–6

Schwimmer, Great Musicians as Children, p.123–30   6

STRAVINSKY, IGOR FĔDOROVICH

Burch, Modern Composers for Young People, p.169–75   5–6

STRAWBERRIES

Coatsworth, Five Bushel Farm, p.80–88   *4–5

Lenski, Strawberry Girl   *4–6

STREAMLINED TRAINS

Henry, R. S., Trains, p.97–106   5–6

Van Metre, Trains, Tracks and Travel, p.334–58   6

STREPTOMYCIN

Eberle, Modern Medical Discoveries, p.68–78   5–6

STRING: *see* Twine

STRINGED INSTRUMENTS

Balet, What Makes an Orchestra, p.3–9   5–6

Buchanan, How Man Made Music, p.59–71   6

Commins, Making an Orchestra, p.6–9   5–6

Huntington, Tune Up   4–6

Kettelkamp, Singing Strings   5–6

Lacey, Picture Book of Musical Instruments, p.1–9   5–6

Norman, First Book of Music, p.51   4–6

Posell, This Is an Orchestra, p.17–27   5–6

STUART, GILBERT

Chandler, Story-Lives of Master Artists, p.177–86   6

Hillyer, Child's History of Art, p.139–40   5–6

STUNTS

Bancroft, Games, p.328–34   4–6

Carlson, B. W., Act It Out, p.38–49   4–6

————— Do It Yourself!, p.51–114   4–6

Forbush, Book of Games, p.254–66   4–6

Mulac, Game Book, p.52–111, 211–20, 226–35   6

SUBMARINE CABLES: *see* Atlantic Cable; Cables; Field, Cyrus West

SUBMARINES

Anderson, W. R., First under the North Pole   4–6

Cooke, D. C., How Atomic Submarines Are Made   6

Darrow, Boys' Own Book of Great Inventions, p.239–58   6

Gilmore, Model Boats for Beginners, p.84–88   5–6

Icenhower, First Book of Submarines
5–6
Judson, Boat Builder, p.82–93   5–6
McCoy, Big Book of Real Submarines
4–6
MacGregor, Miss Pickerell Goes Undersea (atomic)   *4–6
Mitchell, Ships That Made U.S. History,
p.81–85   6

SUBWAYS
Bloch, Tunnels, p.84–87   5–6
Brenner, Barto Takes the Subway   *4

SUCRE, ANTONIO JOSÉ DE
Goetz, Neighbors to the South, p.144–
45   5–6
Spencer, P. R., Traveling New Trails,
p.317–23   6

SUEZ CANAL
Boardman, Canals, p.84–94   6
Epstein, E., First Book of the United
Nations, p.16–18   4–6
Foster, G., Abraham Lincoln's World,
p.139–42, 262–64   6

SUGAR: *see also* Beet Sugar; Candy; Maple Sugar
Eberle, Basketful, p.201–27   4–6
————— Grasses, p.40–43   4–6
Rothery, Central American Roundabout,
p.67–69   6
Scheib, First Book of Food, p.43–45
5–6
Tor, Getting To Know Puerto Rico,
p.36–39   4–6

SUKKOTH
Taylor, All-of-a-Kind Family, p.166–75
*4–6

SULFA DRUGS
Eberle, Modern Medical Discoveries,
p.50–67   5–6
Freeman, I. M., All about the Wonders
of Chemistry, p.85–90   6

SULFUR
Fenton, C. L., Riches from the Earth,
p.136–40   5–6
Loomis, Field Book of Common Rocks
and Minerals, p.166–67   6
Parker, B. M., Earth a Great Storehouse, p.13–14   4–6

SUMAC
Comstock, Handbook of Nature Study,
p.683–86   6

SUMATRA
Caldwell, Let's Visit Indonesia, p.20–22
4–6
Quinn, Picture Map Geography of the
Pacific Islands, p.37–40   5–6
Smith, D. C., Land and People of Indonesia   6

SUMERIANS
Falls, First 3000 Years, p.48–53   6

SUMMER: *see also* Seasons
Harrison, Outdoor Adventures, p.40–85
4–5
Hylander, Out of Doors in Summer
5–6
Kane, Tale of a Pond, p.18–28   5–6

SUN: *see also* Astronomy; Eclipses
Baker, R. H., When the Stars Come
Out, p.112–24   6
Branley, Solar Energy   6
Comstock, Handbook of Nature Study,
p.833–38   6
Freeman, M. B., Fun with Astronomy,
p.35–45   4–6
Gallant, R. A., Exploring the Sun
5–6
Goodwin, Real Book about Stars   4–6
Hazeltine, Easter Book of Legends and
Stories, p.130–45   *5–6
Hendrickson, Handbook for Space Travelers, p.197–99   5–6
Leonard, Exploring Science, p.98–106
6
Meyer, Picture Book of Astronomy,
p.7–10   4–5
Schealer, This Way to the Stars, p.81–
88   6
Schneider, L., Space in Your Future,
p.55–63   6
Writers Project, Light of the World,
no.12   5–6

SUN YAT-SEN
Caldwell, Let's Visit China, p.61–63
5–6

SUNDIALS
Adler, Time in Your Life, p.48–51
4–6

Comstock, Handbook of Nature Study, p.853–54   6

Reck, Clocks Tell the Time, p.10–11
                                                      4–6

Tannenbaum, Understanding Time, p. 16–32   6

Writers Project, Light of the World, no.12, p.23–26   5–6

SUNFISH
Cooper, E. K., Science on the Shores and Banks, p.147–48   5–6

SUNFLOWERS
Comstock, Handbook of Nature Study, p.574–78   6

SUPERIOR, LAKE: *see* Isle Royale National Park

SUPERMARKETS
Bendick, First Book of Supermarkets
                                                      4–5

Haywood, Betsy's Busy Summer, p.136–52   *4–5

SUPERSONICS: *see also* Sonic Boom
Beeler, More Experiments in Science, p.8–10   5–6

Knight, D. C., First Book of Sound, p.69–73   5–6

Zarem, New Dimensions of Flight, p.22–41   6

SUPERSTITION: *see also* Halloween
Batchelor, Superstitious? Here's Why!
                                                        6

Branley, Moon, p.96–109   6

Caldwell, Let's Visit Formosa, p.48–50
                                                      5–6

Gatti, Here Is the Veld, p.93–102   6

Leach, Thing at the Foot of the Bed
                                                     *4–6

Selsam, Plants That Heal, p.27–34   6

Stinetorf, Children of South Africa, p.80–94   *5–6

SURFACE TENSION
Beeler, Experiments in Science, p.30–32
                                                      5–6

Freeman, M. B., Fun with Science, p.25–28   6

Huey, What Makes the Wheels Go Round, p.99–105   6

SURPRISES
Agle, Three Boys and the Remarkable Cow   *4–5

SURVEYING
Bendick, How Much and How Many, p.137–46   5–6

SUTTER, JOHN AUGUSTUS
Bauer, California Gold Days, p.18–38
                                                      5–6

SWALLOWS: *see also* Cliff Swallows
Comstock, Handbook of Nature Study, p.109–15   6

Sears, Barn Swallow   4–6

Webb, Birds in Their Homes, p.14, 43
                                                      4–6

SWAMPS
Disney, Worlds of Nature, p.149–59
                                                      4–6

Rounds, Swamp Life   5–6

SWANS
Lathrop, Let Them Live, p.31–33
                                                      4–6

SWEATERS
Elting, Lollypop Factory and Lots of Others, p.69–80   4–5

SWEDEN: *see also* Costume—Sweden; Dancing—Sweden
Anckarsvard, Rider by Night   *5–6
——— Robber Ghost   *5–6
Bergaust, Rockets around the World, p.40–41   6

Burglon, Children of the Soil   *4–6

Jordan, Homemade Dolls in Foreign Dress, p.133–43   4–6

Lindgren, Rasmus and the Vagabond
                                                     *4–6

Rothery, Scandinavian Roundabout, p. 135–248   6

Seymour, Erik's Christmas Camera
                                                     *4–6

Unnerstad, Journey with Grandmother
                                                     *4–6
——— Little O   *4–6
——— Spettecake Holiday   *4–6

SWEDEN—FOLK TALES
Harper, Ghosts and Goblins, p.88–104
                                                      4–6

SWEDEN—INDUSTRIES
Rothery, Scandinavian Roundabout, p. 146–54   6

SWEDES IN AMERICA
Dalgliesh, America Builds Homes   4–5

De Angeli, Elin's Amerika   *4–6
Rich, First Book of the Early Settlers,
   p.63–76   4–6

SWEDES IN THE UNITED STATES
Association for Childhood Education,
   Told under the Stars and Stripes,
   p.150–58   *4–6
Brock, Here Comes Kristie   *4–5
Lindquist, J. D., Golden Name Day
                                      *4–6
———— Little Silver House   *4–6

SWEET PEAS
Comstock, Handbook of Nature Study,
   p.588–90   6

SWIFTS: see Chimney Swifts

SWIMMING
Beim, Just Plain Maggie   *4–6
Mulac, Game Book, p.298–320   6
Wilder, On the Banks of Plum Creek,
   p.22–27   *4–6

SWINE: see Pigs

SWITZERLAND: see also Alps; Costume
   —Switzerland; Dancing—Switzerland;
   St. Bernard Pass; Tell, William
Aulaire, Magic Meadow   *4–5
Barrows, Old World Lands, p.84–87   6
———— Our Big World, p.61–72   4
Benary-Isbert, Shooting Star   *4–6
Bergaust, Rockets around the World,
   p.38–39   6
Bragdon, L. J., Land and People of
   Switzerland   6
Buff, Apple and the Arrow   *4–6
Jordan, Homemade Dolls in Foreign
   Dress, p.157–72   4–6
Spyri, Heidi   *4–6

SWITZERLAND—FOLK TALES
Fenner, Fools and Funny Fellows, p.77–
   81   4–6

SWITZERLAND—GOVERNMENT
Bragdon, L. J., Land and People of
   Switzerland, p.109–13   6

SWITZERLAND—HISTORY
Bragdon, L. J., Land and People of
   Switzerland, p.30–40   6

SWITZERLAND—INDUSTRIES
Bragdon, L. J., Land and People of
   Switzerland, p.43–44   6

SYMBOLS
Epstein, S., First Book of Maps and
   Globes, p.33–35   4–6
Rogers, F., Heels, Wheels, and Wire,
   p.12–14   5–6

SYMPHONIES: see Beethoven, Ludwig
   van; Haydn, Franz Joseph

SYRIA
Quinn, Picture Map Geography of
   Asia, p.24–28   4–6

SYRIANS IN THE UNITED STATES
Association for Childhood Education,
   Told under the Stars and Stripes,
   p.102–14   *4–6

TABLE ETIQUETTE
Beery, Manners Made Easy, p.203–49
                                       6
Betz, Your Manners Are Showing, p.20–
   23   6
MacDonald, B., Mrs. Piggle-Wiggle's
   Magic, p.39–57   *4–5

TABLEWARE
Lent, Men at Work in New England,
   p.74–77   4–6

TADPOLES: see Frogs; Toads

TAFT, WILLIAM HOWARD
Beard, Presidents in American History,
   p.109–10, 173–74   6
Coy, First Book of Presidents, p.54
                                     4–6
Petersham, Story of the Presidents of
   the United States, p.61–62   4–6

TAHITI
Quinn, Picture Map Geography of the
   Pacific Islands, p.107–13   5–6

TAILORS: see Clothing

TAIWAN: see Formosa

TAJ MAHAL
Fitch, Allah, the God of Islam, p.120–
   23   6

TALKING PICTURES: see Motion Pictures

TALL TALES: see also Bunyan, Paul;
   John Henry
Du Bois, Great Geppy   4–5
———— Twenty-one Balloons   6
Fenner, Fools and Funny Fellows, p.96–
   103, 131–53   4–6

Shapiro, Steamboat Bill and the Captain's Top Hat   5–6
Steele, Daniel Boone's Echo   4–6
———— Davy Crockett's Earthquake   4–6
———— Spooky Thing   4–6

TANAGERS: *see* Scarlet Tanagers

TANGANYIKA
Stinetorf, Children of South Africa, p.11–23   *5–6

TANNER, HENRY OSSAWA
Shackelford, Child's Story of the Negro, p.146–49   4–5

TANNING
Salomon, Book of Indian Crafts & Indian Lore, p.102–6   6

TAOISM
Fitch, Their Search for God, p.66–83   5–6

TAPE RECORDERS
Buchanan, How Man Made Music, p.177–78   6

TAPESTRY
Tappan, When Knights Were Bold, p.85–96, 357–58   6

TAPIRS
Bridges, Zoo Babies, p.73–80   4–6
Buck, F., Jungle Animals, p.40–45   5–6

TARASCAN INDIANS
Bannon, Hat for a Hero   *4

TARLETON, BANASTRE
Barksdale, That Country Called Virginia, p.117–20   6

TARTARS
Duvoisin, They Put Out to Sea, p.58–61   4–6
Kent, He Went with Marco Polo, p.79–107   *6

TASMANIA
Chauncy, Devils' Hill   *6

TASTE
Zim, Our Senses and How They Work, p.97–107   4–6

TAYLOR, ZACHARY
Beard, Presidents in American History, p.53–54, 161–62   6

Coy, First Book of Presidents, p.38   4–6
Petersham, Story of the Presidents of the United States, p.34–35   4–6

TEA
Chrisman, Shen of the Sea, p.159-72   *5–6
Harper, Ghosts and Goblins, p.58–68   *4–6
Scheib, First Book of Food, p.47–49   5–6
Spencer, C., Made in China, p.58–66   5–6
Wiese, Chinese Ink Stick, p.117–20   *4–6

TEACHING: *see also* Education
Pace, Clara Barton, p.11–19   5–6

TEAMWORK: *see* Cooperation

TEASING—ADJUSTMENT TO
Aulaire, Nils   *4–5

TECUMSEH (Shawnee chief)
Foster, G., Abraham Lincoln's World, p.23–24   6

TEETH
Fox, From Bones to Bodies, p.22–35   6
Schloat, Your Wonderful Teeth   4–6

TELEGRAPH: *see also* Atlantic Cable; Cables; Morse, Samuel Finley Breese; Radio
Beeler, More Experiments in Science, p.23–28   5–6
Darrow, Boys' Own Book of Great Inventions, p.16–30   6
Driggs, Pony Express Goes Through, p.48–61   6
Freeman, I. M., All about Electricity, p.47–49   5–6
Hartman, Machines, p.137–58   6
Morgan, A. P., Boy Electrician, p.150–72   6
———— First Electrical Book for Boys, p.66–83, 202–9   6
Parker, B. M., Electricity, p.30–33   5–6
Rogers, F., Heels, Wheels, and Wire, p.94–120   5–6
Yates, R. F., Boys' Book of Communications   6
Zarchy, Let's Make Something, p.142–43   5–6

TELEPHONE: *see also* Bell, Alexander
Graham
Beeler, Experiments in Science, p.89–91
                               5–6
Crouse, W. H., Understanding Science,
p.80–86   6
Darrow, Boys' Own Book of Great In-
ventions, p.31–50   6
Freeman, I. M., All about Electricity,
p.78–87   5–6
Hartman, Machines, p.159–68   6
Huey, What Makes the Wheels Go
Round, p.131–34   6
Irving, Sound and Ultrasonics, p.109–12
                               6
Morgan, A. P., Boy Electrician, p.177–
94, 295–300   6
———— First Electrical Book for Boys,
p.113–31   6
Oakes, Bamboo Gate, p.1–20 .   *4–6
Rogers, F., Heels, Wheels, and Wire,
p.120–31   5–6
Schneider, H., Your Telephone and
How It Works   5–6
Yates, R. F., Boys' Book of Communi-
cations   6

TELEPHOTOGRAPHY
Yates, R. F., Boys' Book of Communications, p.79–98   6

TELESCOPES: *see also* Galileo; Observa-
tories
Branley, Exploring by Satellite, p.16–21
                               6
Darrow, Boys' Own Book of Great In-
ventions, p.320–30   6
Hendrickson, Handbook for Space Trav-
elers   5–6
Parker, B. M., Scientist and His Tools,
p.24–26   5–6
Schloat, Andy's Wonderful Telescope
                            4–5
Schneider, L., Space in Your Future,
p.131–53   6

TELEVISION
Barr, Young Scientist Takes a Ride,
p.106–7   5–6
Batchelor, Communication, p.93–97
                              4–6
Bendick, Electronics for Young People,
p.129–41   6

———— Television Works Like This
                               6
Butterworth, Trouble with Jenny's Ear
                           *4–6
Crouse, W. H., Understanding Science,
p.139–47   6
Darrow, Boys' Own Book of Great In-
ventions, p.354–75   6
Freeman, I. M., All about Electricity,
p.127–36   5–6
Gould, All about Radio and Television,
p.1–48, 84–105   5–6
Hendrickson, Handbook for Space Trav-
elers   5–6
Hogben, Wonderful World of Commu-
nication, p.54–55   6
Huey, What Makes the Wheels Go
Round, p.162–64   6
Meyer, Picture Book of Radio and Tele-
vision, p.26–40   5–6
Morgan, A. P., First Electrical Book for
Boys, p.230–35   6
Rogers, F., Heels, Wheels, and Wire,
p.233–36   5–6

TELL, WILLIAM
Aulaire, Magic Meadow, p.6–13   *4–5
Bragdon, L. J., Land and People of
Switzerland, p.35–37   6
Buff, Apple and the Arrow   *4–6

TELLING TIME: *see also* Clocks
Canfield, Understood Betsy, p.90–92
                             *5–6

TEMPERANCE
Benson, Stories of the Gods and Heroes,
p.188–97   5–6
Driggs, Pony Express Goes Through,
p.128–34   6

TEMPERATURE: *see* Climate; Heat;
Thermometers; Weather

TEMPTATION—RESISTANCE TO
Alden, Why the Chimes Rang   *4–6

TENNESSEE: *see also* Great Smoky
Mountains National Park
Association for Childhood Education,
Told under Spacious Skies, p.160–69
                             *4–6
Bailey, B. F., Picture Book of Tennessee
                               4–6
Banta, Life in America: The South,
p.144–49   5–6

Foster, G., Andrew Jackson   4–6
Judson, Andrew Jackson   5–6
Justus, Fiddlers' Fair   *4–5
———— Sammy   *4–5
Quinn, Picture Map Geography of the
    United States, p.76–79   4–6
Steele, Buffalo Knife   *4–6
———— Flaming Arrows   *4–6
Wilson, L., This Boy Cody   *4–6
———— This Boy Cody and His
    Friends   *4–6

TENNESSEE RIVER
Steele, Buffalo Knife   *4–6

TENNESSEE VALLEY AUTHORITY
Association for Childhood Education,
    Told under Spacious Skies, p.153–59
         *4–6
Banta, Life in America: The South,
    p.56–59   5–6
Elting, We Are the Government   6

TENNIS
Bancroft, Games, p.417–18, 512–14,
    548, 561–66, 578–79, 630–32   4–6
Gilbert, Champions Don't Cry   *5–6
Leeming, Fun with String, p.72–74
         4–6

TERMITES
Hylander, Insects on Parade, p.193–97
         6
Lane, F. C., All about the Insect World,
    p.100–105   5–6
Parker, B. M., Plant and Animal Part-
    nerships, p.8–10   5–6
Teale, Junior Book of Insects, p.107–13
         6

TERNS
Disney, Worlds of Nature, p.38–42 (arc-
    tic)   4–6
Gallup, Spinning Wings   5–6
Hyde, Animal Clocks and Compasses,
    p.9–10, 37, 40 (arctic)   5–6
Lavine, Strange Travelers, p.65–66
    (arctic)   5–6
Webb, Birds in Their Homes, p.56–58
         4–6

TERRA COTTA: *see* Pottery

TERRARIUMS
Bianco, All about Pets, p.119–34   5–6
Brown, V., How To Make a Miniature
    Zoo, p.108–17   5–6

Buck, M. W., Small Pets from Woods
    and Fields, p.10–11   4–6
Cooper, E. K., Science on the Shores
    and Banks, p.130, 135–36   5–6
Hylander, Out of Doors in Winter,
    p.139–46   5–6
Morgan, A. P., Aquarium Book, p.198–
    201   5–6
Parker, B. M., Garden Indoors, p.21–24
         5–6

TERRELL, MARY CHURCH
Shackelford, Child's Story of the Ne-
    gro, p.188–93   4–5

TESTING: *see* United States—Bureau of
    Standards

TEXAS
Association for Childhood Education,
    Told under Spacious Skies, p.230–42
         *4–6
Garst, Cowboys and Cattle Trails   4–6
Quinn, Picture Map Geography of the
    United States, p.140–43   4–6
Sayers, Tag-along Tooloo   *4
Waltrip, White Harvest   *4–6

TEXAS—HISTORY: *see also* Alamo—
    Siege of the; Crockett, David; Hous-
    ton, Samuel
Foster, G., Abraham Lincoln's World,
    p.158–62   6
Johnson, W. W., Birth of Texas   5–6

TEXTILES: *see also* Clothing; Cotton;
    Dyeing; Nylon; Rayon; Rugs; Spin-
    ning; Tapestry; Weaving; Wool
Beeler, Experiments in Science, p.107–9
         5–6
Disraeli, New Worlds through the Mi-
    croscope, p.159–63   6
Dudley, Our American Trees, p.80–83
         5–6
Freeman, I. M., All about the Wonders
    of Chemistry, p.102–16   6
Lent, Men at Work in New England,
    p.62–65   4–6

THAILAND
Ayer, Getting To Know Thailand   4–6
Quinn, Picture Map Geography of Asia,
    p.73–75   4–6

THANKSGIVING DAY
Bailey, C. S., Children of the Hand-
    crafts, p.146–55   *5–6

Barksdale, First Thanksgiving   *4–5

Brown, H. M., America Is My Country, p.202–3   5–6

Burnett, B., First Book of Holidays, p.46–49   4–5

Dalgliesh, America Builds Homes   4–5

Friedman, F., Dot for Short, p.190–207
                                   *4–5

Harper, Harvest Feast   4–6

Hays, Pilgrim Thanksgiving   4–5

Jordan, Holiday Handicraft, p.177–99
                                   4–6

Lillie, Book of Three Festivals, p.131–87   *5–6

McSpadden, Book of Holidays, p.168–73   6

Olcott, Good Stories for Great Holidays, p.269–95   *4–6

Pannell, Holiday Round Up, p.264–74
                                   4–6

Sechrist, Red Letter Days, p.196–204
                                   5–6

THANKSGIVING DAY—PILGRIM FA-
    THERS
Barksdale, First Thanksgiving   *4–5

Meadowcroft, First Year, p.136–40
                                   *4–6

THEATER: see also Costume; Miracle Plays; Motion Pictures; Operas; Plays; Puppet Shows
Bechdolt, Going Up, p.78–81   5–6

Lamprey, All the Ways of Building, p.265–75   6

THEATER—MINIATURE
Ackley, Marionettes   5–6

Ficklen, Handbook of Fist Puppets, p.119–30   4–6

THEATER—PIONEER LIFE
Crawford, "Hello, the Boat!," p.166–68
                                   *6

THERMOMETERS: see also Barometers
Comstock, Handbook of Nature Study, p.790   6

Huey, What Makes the Wheels Go Round, p.11–14   6

Parker, B. M., Scientist and His Tools, p.19–20   5–6

———— Thermometers, Heat, and Cold   5–6

Rothery, Scandinavian Roundabout, p. 191–92   6

Schneider, H., Everyday Machines and How They Work, p.147–50   5–6

Wyler, First Book of Weather, p.15–16
                                   5–6

THERMOPYLAE—BATTLE OF, 480
    B.C.
Hillyer, Child's History of the World, p.137–39   5–6

THERMOSTATS
Lent, Men at Work in the Great Lakes States, p.114–17   4–6

Schneider, H., Everyday Machines and How They Work, p.73–76, 136–39, 174, 179   5–6

THESEUS
Asimov, Words from the Myths, p.157–60   6

Benson, Stories of the Gods and Heroes, p.170–80   5–6

Kingsley, Heroes, p.251–320   6

THOREAU, HENRY DAVID
Bailey, C. S., Children of the Hand-crafts, p.126–35   5–6

THRESHING
Tousey, Cowboy Tommy   *4–5

Wilder, Farmer Boy, p.305–11   *4–6

THRUSHES: see also Wood Thrushes
Parker, B. M., Birds, p.8–9   4–6

THUNDERSTORMS: see Lightning; Storms

TIBET
Caldwell, Let's Visit India, p.92–93
                                   4–6

Hazeltine, Hero Tales from Many Lands, p.401–15   5–6

Quinn, Picture Map Geography of Asia, p.99–102   4–6

Rankin, L., Daughter of the Mountains, p.11–45   *5–6

TIDES: see also Astronomy; Moon; Ocean
Beaty, Baby Whale, p.22–23   4–6

Branley, Moon, p.83–87   5

Gallant, R. A., Exploring the Moon, p.56–57   4–6

Hinton, Exploring under the Sea, p.12–14   5–6

Kipling, Just So Stories, p.171–93
                                   *4–6

Lane, F. C., All about the Sea, p.33–40
4–6

Reed, Sea for Sam, p.40–56   6

TIE DYING
Robinson, J., Things To Make from Odds & Ends, p.32–34   4–6

TIGERS
Buck, F., Jungle Animals, p.26–28
5–6

Henry, J., Tiger's Chance   *4–6
Kipling, Jungle Book, p.107–42 *5–6
Knight, C. R., Life through the Ages, p.44–45   6
Mukerji, Hari, the Jungle Lad   *5–6
Perkins, Marlin Perkins' Zooparade, p.28–31   4–6
Singh, Gift of the Forest   *6
Stolz, Belling the Tiger   *4–5
Zim, Big Cats, p.35–40   5–6

TIGRIS-EUPHRATES VALLEY: *see* Babylonia; Iraq

TILES
Leeming, Fun with Clay, p.27–30 4–6
Zarchy, Let's Make a Lot of Things, p.106–11   5–6

TIMBER: *see* Forestry; Lumbering; Trees; Wood

TIME: *see also* Calendars; Clocks; Standard Time; Sundials; Telling Time
Adler, Time in Your Life   4–6
Barr, Research Ideas for Young Scientists, p.119–28   5–6
Bendick, How Much and How Many, p.103–14   5–6
Freeman, M. B., Fun with Astronomy, p.10–11   4–6
Hartman, Builders of the Old World, p.57–58   6
Holbrook, Golden Age of Railroads, p.157–61   5–6
Tannenbaum, Understanding Time 6

TIME ZONES: *see* Standard Time

TIN
Fenton, C. L., Riches from the Earth, p.143–46   5–6
Loomis, Field Book of Common Rocks and Minerals, p.92–93   6

TINWARE
Jaeger, Easy Crafts, p.28–29, 112–15
4–6

TOADS: *see also* Frogs
Barker, Winter-sleeping Wildlife, p.79–83   5–6
Bevans, Book of Reptiles and Amphibians, p.57–58   4–6
Brown, V., How To Understand Animal Talk, p.175–76   6
Buck, M. W., In Ponds and Streams, p.46   4–6
Comstock, Handbook of Nature Study, p.170–77, 184–85   6
Cooper, E. K., Science on the Shores and Banks, p.122–23   5–6
Gall, Wagtail, p.72–78   *4–6
Hogner, Frogs and Polliwogs, p.35–45
4–5
Hylander, Out of Doors in Spring, p.38–39, 49–57   5–6
Lavine, Strange Travelers, p.35, 38–39
5–6
Lawson, R., Edward, Hoppy, and Joe
*4–6
McClung, Bufo   4–5
Morgan, A. H., Field Book of Animals in Winter, p.348–52   6
———— Field Book of Ponds and Streams, p.368–88   6
Morgan, A. P., Aquarium Book, p.129–69   5–6
Parker, B. M., Toads and Frogs   4–6
Spencer, P. R., Finding New Trails, p.252–56   4
Zim, Frogs and Toads   4–6

TOADSTOOLS: *see* Fungi; Mushrooms

TOBACCO
Barnard, Macmillan Science-Life Series, Bk.6, p.317–18   6

TOLERANCE: *see* Brotherhood of Man; Religious Understanding

TOM THUMB (locomotive)
Maginley, Historic Models of Early America, p.66–74   6

TOMBS: *see also* Mound Builders; Pyramids; Taj Mahal; Tutankhamen
Hillyer, Child's History of the World, p.36–41   5–6

Meadowcroft, Gift of the River, p.4–7
5–6

TOMTIT
Bosiger, Bird Is Born, p.45–57   5–6

TONTI, HENRI DE: *see* La Salle, René Robert Cavelier, Sieur de

TOOLS: *see also* Agricultural Machinery; Carpentry; Machines; Screws
Adler, Tools in Your Life   5–6
———— Tools of Science   6
Bendick, First Book of How To Fix It, p.10–15   4–6
Burns, Man and His Tools   5–6
Epstein, S., First Book of Glass, p.2, 22–24   5–6
Holling, Book of Indians, p.99–100   4–6
Kirkus, First Book of Gardening, p.30–35   4–6
Leavitt, True Book of Tools for Building   4–6
Leonard, Exploring Science, p.162–71   6
Liberty, First Book of Tools   5–6
Schneider, H., Everyday Machines and How They Work   5–6
Tunis, Indians, p.30–32   6
Zarchy, Let's Make a Lot of Things, p.42–51   5–6
———— Let's Make More Things, p.18–27   5–6
———— Let's Make Something, p.18–29   5–6

TOPS
Adler, Things That Spin   5–6

TORNADOES: *see* Storms; Winds

TORTOISES: *see* Turtles

TOTEM POLES
Brindze, Story of the Totem Pole   4–6
Hunt, W. B., Golden Book of Indian Crafts and Lore, p.108–9   4–6

TOURIST TRADE—UNITED STATES
Lent, Men at Work in New England, p.56–61   4–6
———— Men at Work in the Great Lakes States, p.88–95   4–6

TOWHEES
Webb, Birds in Their Homes, p.26   4–6

TOWNS: *see* Cities and Towns

TOYS: *see also* Amusements; Dolls; Games; Kites; Paper Work
Carlson, B. W., Make It Yourself!   4–6
Chappell, Nutcracker   *4–5
Field, Hitty   *5–6
Jaeger, Easy Crafts, p.42–47, 72–77   4–6
Jordan, Holiday Handicraft, p.203–6   4–6
Leeming, Fun with Boxes   4–6
———— Fun with Paper   4–5
Maginley, Make It and Ride It   5–6
Milne, World of Pooh   *4–5
Robinson, J., Things To Make from Odds & Ends, p.71–78   4–6
Zarchy, Let's Make More Things   5–6

TRACK ATHLETICS
Bancroft, Games, p.657–66   4–6

TRACTORS: *see* Agricultural Machinery

TRADE: *see also* Advertising; Business; Canals; Caravans; Communication; Fairs; Freight; Hanseatic League; Harbors; Manufacturing; Markets; Meat Industry; Money; Pack Transportation; Phoenicia; Railroads; Rivers; Ships; Shopping; Trading Posts; Transportation; also names of articles of trade, as Cotton
Bendick, How Much and How Many, p.32–94   5–6
Bleeker, Inca, p.30–35   5–6
Crawford, "Hello, the Boat!"   *6
Dawson, California, p.109–17   5–6
Duvoisin, They Put Out to Sea   4–6
Hewes, Spice Ho!   5–6
Kent, He Went with Marco Polo   *6
Ritchie, B., Ramon Makes a Trade   *4–5
Watson, Golden History of the World, p.37–40   5–6

TRADE—COLONIAL PERIOD IN AMERICA
Bailey, C. S., Children of the Handcrafts, p.75–84   5–6

TRADE—MIDDLE AGES: *see also* Cities and Towns—Middle Ages; Fairs —Middle Ages; Hanseatic League
McGuire, Brave Young Land, p.10–49   5–6

Tappan, When Knights Were Bold, p.247–75   6

TRADE ROUTES: *see* Discoveries in Geography; Trade—Middle Ages

TRADING POSTS
Bleeker, Navajo, p.78–97   4–6
Buff, Dancing Cloud, p.76–80   4–5
Clark, A. N., Little Navajo Bluebird, p.7–17   4–6

TRAILERS: *see* Automobiles—Trailers

TRAILSIDE MUSEUM OF NATURAL HISTORY, THATCHER WOODS
Moe, Animal Inn   4–6

TRAINS: *see* Locomotives; Railroads

TRANSCONTINENTAL RAILWAY
Dawson, California, p.162–66   5–6
Henry, R. S., Trains, p.38–43, 52–56   5–6
Lawson, R., Watchwords of Liberty, p.76–78   4–6
Nathan, Building of the First Transcontinental Railroad   5–6
Rogers, F., Heels, Wheels, and Wire, p.77–84   5–6

TRANSISTORS
Crouse, W. H., Understanding Science, p.98–101   6

TRANSJORDAN
Quinn, Picture Map of Asia, p.32–33   4–6

TRANSPORTATION: *see also* various forms of transportation, as Airplanes; Automobiles; Boats; Railroads; Trucks
Barr, Research Ideas for Young Scientists, p.25–40   5–6
——— Young Scientist Takes a Ride   5–6
Bechdolt, Going Up   5–6
Bleeker, Eskimo, p.65–95   4–6
Bloch, Tunnels   5–6
Boardman, Roads   6
Bonner, Canada and Her Story, p.116–19   5–6
Bothwell, First Book of Roads   5–6
Brenner, Barto Takes the Subway   *4
Buehr, Story of the Wheel, p.6–15   4–6
——— Through the Locks   5–6
Bunce, Freight Train   4–6

Burns, Man and His Tools, p.94–107   5–6
Caldwell, Let's Visit Formosa, p.58–60   5–6
——— Let's Visit India, p.87–88   4–6
Dalgliesh, America Travels   4–6
Goetz, Neighbors to the South, p.113–18   5–6
Holling, Seabird   4–6
Hubbard, Train That Never Came Back   5–6
Icenhower, First Book of the Antarctic, p.41–47   4–6
Leonard, Exploring Science, p.208–32   6
Lewellen, You and American Life Lines   4–6
Mason, M. E., Young Mr. Meeker   *4–5
May, Let's Read about Brazil, p.103–9   4–6
Nathan, Famous Railroad Stations of the World   5–6
Neal, Story of the Kite   5–6
Olds, Riding the Rails   4–5
Peet, First Book of Bridges   5–6
Rogers, F., Heels, Wheels, and Wire   5–6
Rothery, South American Roundabout, p.120–26   5–6
Sasek, This Is New York, p.32–37   4–6
Stefansson, Here Is Alaska, p.16–21   6
Writers Project, Aluminum, no.31, p.39–41   5–6

TRANSPORTATION—COLONIAL LIFE IN AMERICA
Judson, Boat Builder   5–6
Maginley, Historic Models of Early America, p.10–86   6

TRANSPORTATION BY AIR: *see* Airplanes

TRANSPORTATION BY LAND: *see* Automobiles; Bicycles; Bridges; Carriages; Conestoga Wagons; Electric Railroads; Freight; Mail Service; Pack Transportation; Pony Express; Railroads; Roads; Stagecoaches; Subways; Travois; Wheels

TRANSPORTATION BY WATER: *see*
Boats; Canals; Ferries; Harbors;
Ocean Travel; Rivers; Ships; Steam-
boats

TRAPPING: *see also* Fur Trade; Hunting
Carr, Children of the Covered Wagon,
p.211–29   *4–6
Gall, Flat Tail, p.109–16   4–6
———— Ringtail, p.71–79   4–5
George, J. L., Vulpes, the Red Fox,
p.56–72   6

TRAVELING
Beery, Manners Made Easy, p.264–92
    6
Carroll, Tough Enough's Trip   *4–6
Daringer, Adopted Jane, p.21–38
    *4–6
Hale, Complete Peterkin Papers, p.41–
51 (The Peterkins' Summer Journey)
    *4–6
Hayes, Skid, p.62–81   *5–6

TRAVOIS
Maginley, Historic Models of Early
America, p.8–9   6

TREASURE HUNTS
Chase, V., Knight of the Golden Fleece,
p.46–96   6
De Angeli, Jared's Island, p.12–20, 85–
95   *4–6
Durell, Holly River Secret   *4–6
Payne, Leprechaun of Bayou Luce
    *4–5
Rushmore, Lost Treasure Box   *4–6

TREE HOUSES
Parker, B. M., Machines, p.2–7   5–6

TREE SWALLOWS: *see* Swallows

TREES: *see also* Arbor Day; Botany;
Evergreen Trees; Forestry; Fruit;
Fruit Culture; Grafting; Leaves; Lum-
bering; Maple Sugar; Nuts; Olives;
Plants; Wood; also names of trees, as
Oak Trees
Bancroft, Games, p.252–53   4–6
Barr, Young Scientist Takes a Ride,
p.110–22   5–6
Benson, Stories of the Gods and Heroes,
p.44–49   *5–6
Buck, M. W., In Yards and Gardens,
p.25–28   4–6
Buehr, Timber!   5–6

Cassell, Nature Games and Activities,
p.18–34   4–6
Comstock, Handbook of Nature Study,
p.618–92   6
Cormack, First Book of Trees   4–6
Doane, Book of Nature, p.24–25, 60–63,
96–97   5–6
Dudley, Our American Trees   5–6
Earle, State Trees   5–6
Faralla, Willow in the Attic   *4
Fenton, C. L., Trees and Their World
    5–6
George, J., Hole in the Tree   4–5
Holling, Tree in the Trail   *4–6
Hylander, Out of Doors in Spring, p.9–
27   5–6
———— Out of Doors in Winter, p.9–
67   5–6
McKenny, Trees of the Countryside
    4–6
Melbo, Our Country's National Parks,
v.1, v.2   6
Parker, B. M., Trees   4–6
Reed, Earth for Sam, p.133–35, 154–55
    6
Selsam, Play with Trees   4–6
Shannon, Dobry, p.75–77   *5–6
Sterling, Trees and Their Story   5–6
Webber, Thanks to Trees   4–5

TRICKS: *see also* Games; Magic; Puzzles;
Riddles
Adler, Magic House of Numbers, p.68–
89   6
Carlson, B. W., Do It Yourself!, p.13–50
    4–6
Leeming, Fun with Paper, p.133–52
    4–5
———— Fun with String, p.1–29
    4–6
Mulac, Game Book, p.52–71, 151–64
    6

TRILOBITES
Parker, B. M., Stories Read from the
Rocks, p.3–10   4–6

TRIPLETS
Agle, Three Boys and the Remarkable
Cow   *4–5

TRISTRAM, SIR
Hazeltine, Hero Tales from Many
Lands, p.120–34   5–6

TROJAN WAR: *see also* Aeneas; Menelaus; Ulysses
Asimov, Words from the Myths, p.177–211   6
Benson, Stories of the Gods and Heroes, p.217–24   5–6
Church, Iliad for Boys and Girls   5–6
Colum, Adventures of Odysseus   5–6
Farjeon, Mighty Men, p.1–20   4–6
Hartman, Builders of the Old World, p.137–40   6
Hazeltine, Hero Tales from Many Lands, p.27–34   5–6
Hillyer, Child's History of the World, p.64–69   5–6

TROPICS: *see also* Jungles; also names of tropical lands, as Brazil; Hawaiian Islands; Pacific Islands
Goetz, Tropical Rain Forests   4–6

TROUBADOURS: *see also* Minstrels
Buchanan, How Man Made Music, p.83–84   6
Tappan, When Knights Were Bold, p.304–8   6

TROUT
Comstock, Handbook of Nature Study, p.156–59   6

TRUCKS
Bendick, First Book of Automobiles, p.32–45   4–6
Colby, Earthmovers   5–6
Norling, Pogo's Truck Ride   4
Schneider, H., Science Fun with Milk Cartons, p.85–103   5–6
Todd, Trucks, Tractors, and Trailers
                                                      4–6

TRUMAN, HARRY S.
Beard, Presidents in American History, p.137–41, 179–80   6
Coy, First Book of Presidents, p.62
                                                      4–6
Petersham, Story of the Presidents of the United States, p.74–75   4–6

TRUMPETS
Buchanan, How Man Made Music, p.43–44   6
Huntington, Tune Up   4–6
Lacey, Picture Book of Musical Instruments, p.26–27   5–6

TRUSTWORTHINESS
Alden, Why the Chimes Rang   *4–6
Spencer, P. R., Traveling New Trails, p.379–85   6

TRUTHFULNESS
Alden, Why the Chimes Rang   *4–6
Collodi, Adventures of Pinocchio
                                                      *4–6

TSCHAIKOVSKY, PETER ILYITCH
Burch, Famous Composers for Young People, p.137–45   4–6
Schwimmer, Great Musicians as Children, p.163–71   6

TUBAS
Huntington, Tune Up   4–6
Lacey, Picture Book of Musical Instruments, p.32–33   5–6
Tripp, New Tuba   *4–5

TUGBOATS
Buehr, Harbors and Cargoes, p.26–27, 55–56   5–6
Gilmore, Model Boats for Beginners, p.54–58   5–6
Hogeboom, Boats and How To Draw Them, p.12–15   4–5

TULIPS: *see also* Netherlands
Comstock, Handbook of Nature Study, p.552–55   6

TUMBLEBUGS: *see* Beetles

TUNDRA
Goetz, Arctic Tundra   4–6
Lavine, Strange Travelers, p.31–32
                                                      5–6
Smith, J. R., Neighbors around the World, p.51–58   4

TUNGSTEN
Fenton, C. L., Riches from the Earth, p.147–50   5–6
Loomis, Field Book of Common Rocks and Minerals, p.87–89,   6
Schneider, H., Everyday Machines and How They Work, p.60–62, 64   5–6

TUNISIA
Joy, Young People of the Western Mediterranean, p.9–22   6
Stinetorf, Children of North Africa, p.76–94   *5–6

TUNNELS: *see also* Engineering; Mining; Subways

Bloch, Tunnels   5–6

Jackson, D., Wonderful World of Engineering, p.62–69   6

TURBINES

Beeler, More Experiments in Science, p.78–82   5–6

Crouse, W. H., Understanding Science, p.39–41   6

Darrow, Boys' Own Book of Inventions, p.136–40   6

Gottlieb, Jets and Rockets and How They Work, p.38–41   4–6

Huey, What Makes the Wheels Go Round, p.69–71   6

Morgan, A. P., Boys' Book of Engines, Motors & Turbines, p.38–46, 172–80, 201–7   6

Schneider, H., More Power to You, p.39–44   5–6

———— Science Fun with Milk Cartons, p.139–146, 154–55   5–6

TURKESTAN

Nazaroff, Land of the Russian People, p.59–66   6

TURKEY: *see also* Costume—Turkey

Barrows, Old World Lands, p.164–65   6

Nevil, Picture Story of the Middle East   4–6

Quinn, Picture Map Geography of Asia, p.18–23   4–6

TURKEY—FOLK TALES

Fenner, Fools and Funny Fellows, p.10–17   4–6

TURKEYS: *see also* Poultry; Thanksgiving Day

Brown, V., How To Understand Animal Talk, p.42–45   6

Comstock, Handbook of Nature Study, p.138–41   6

Eberle, Basketful, p.82–85   4–6

Hogeboom, Familiar Animals and How To Draw Them, p.24–27   4–5

Weil, Animal Families   4

TURNER, CHARLES HENRY

Shackelford, Child's Story of the Negro, p.146–49   4–5

TURNPIKES: *see* Roads

TURNSTONES

Webb, Birds in Their Homes, p.61   4–6

TURTLES

Barker, Winter-sleeping Wildlife, p.69–78   5–6

Bevans, Book of Reptiles and Amphibians, p.41–51   4–6

Brown, V., How To Understand Animal Talk, p.167–69   6

Buck, M. W., In Ponds and Streams, p.51–53   4–6

———— Pets from the Pond, p.58–63   4–6

Comstock, Handbook of Nature Study, p.204–9   6

Cooper, E. K., Science on the Shores and Banks, p.133–39   5–6

De Jong, M., Little Cow and the Turtle   *4–6

Fenton, C. L., Life Long Ago, p.198–200   6

———— Wild Folk in the Desert, p.30–34   4–6

Gall, Ringtail, p.59–62   *4–5

Holling, Minn of the Mississippi   5–6

Huntington, Let's Go to the Desert, p.84–89   4–5

Hyde, Animal Clocks and Compasses, p.123–25   5–6

Hylander, Animals in Armor, p.31–85   6

———— Out of Doors in Summer, p.75–81   5–6

Kane, Tale of a Meadow, p.54–56   4–6

———— Tale of a Pond   5–6

Moe, Animal Inn, p.60–66   4–6

Morgan, A. H., Field Book of Animals in Winter, p.366–69   6

———— Field Book of Ponds and Streams, p.389–404   6

Morgan, A. P., Aquarium Book, p.171–85   5–6

Parker, B. M., Reptiles, p.16–22   4–6

Pels, Care of Water Pets, p.30–35   4–6

Selsam, Underwater Zoos, p.74–75   4–6

TUTANKHAMEN

Friedman, E., Digging into Yesterday, p.36–51   5–6

Meadowcroft, Gift of the River, p.175–82   5–6

TWAIN, MARK: *see* Clemens, Samuel Langhorne

TWINE
Leeming, Fun with String   4–6

TYLER, JOHN
Beard, Presidents in American History,
p.45–46, 160   6
Coy, First Book of Presidents, p.36
                                  4–6
Petersham, Story of the Presidents of
the United States, p.30–31   4–6

TYPE
Foster, J., Pages, Pictures, and Print,
p.21, 25–34   6
Lent, "I Work on a Newspaper," p.22–
26, 40–41, 43–44   6

TYPEWRITERS
Darrow, Boys' Own Book of Great Inventions, p.13–15   6

TYPHOONS: see Storms

TYROL
Smith, E. S., Christmas Book of Legends & Stories, p.362–75   5–6

UKRAINE
Nazaroff, Land of the Russian People,
p.44–48   6

UKRAINIANS IN THE UNITED
STATES
Bloch, Marya of Clark Avenue   *4–6

UKULELES
Leeming, Fun with Boxes, p.109–11
                                  4–6

ULTRASONICS
Knight, D. C., First Book of Sound,
p.63–67   5–6

ULYSSES: see also Trojan War
Asimov, Words from the Myths, p.189–
92, 203–11   6
Benson, Stories of the Gods and Heroes,
p.225–56   5–6
Church, Odyssey for Boys and Girls
                                  4–6
Colum, Adventures of Odysseus   5–6
Farjeon, Mighty Men, p.22–27   4–6
Hazeltine, Hero Tales from Many
Lands, p.52–67   5–6

UMBRELLAS
Child Study Association of America,
Read to Yourself Storybook, p.70–
86   *4–5

UNANUE, HIPOLITO
Goetz, Neighbors to the South, p.147–
48   5–6

UNDERGROUND RAILROAD
Bontemps, Frederick Douglass   4–6
De Angeli, Thee, Hannah!   *4–6
Fritz, Brady   *5–6
Hunt, M. L., Lucinda, p.61–68, 98–111
                                  *5–6
Meadowcroft, By Secret Railway
                                  *5–6
Wriston, Susan's Secret   *4–5

UNEMPLOYMENT
Knight, E. M., Lassie Come-Home   *6
Langton, Majesty of Grace   *4–5

UNICORNS
Jacobson, First Book of Mythical Beasts,
p.28–32   4–6
Young, Unicorn with Silver Shoes, p.21–
42   *4–6

UNION OF SOUTH AFRICA
Barrows, Old World Lands, p.318–23
                                  6
Stinetorf, Children of South Africa,
p.50–66   *5–6

UNION OF SOVIET SOCIALIST RE-
PUBLICS: see also Christmas—
Union of Soviet Socialist Republics;
Costume—Union of Soviet Socialist
Republics; Dancing—Union of Soviet
Socialist Republics; Games—Union of
Soviet Socialist Republics; Mongolia;
Moscow; Siberia
Barrows, Old World Lands, p.118–52
                                  6
Bergaust, Rockets around the World,
p.12–21   6
Hazeltine, Easter Book of Legends and
Stories, p.319–21   *5–6
Hillyer, Child's History of the World,
p.488–93   5–6
Nazaroff, Land of the Russian People
                                  6
Parker, F., Russian Alphabet Book 6
Quinn, Picture Map Geography of Asia,
p.6–17   4–6
Snyder, First Book of the Soviet Union
                                  6
Unnerstad, Journey with Grandmother
                                  *4–6
Vandivert, Young Russia   4–5

UNION OF SOVIET SOCIALIST RE-
PUBLICS—FOLK TALES
Prokofieff, Peter and the Wolf   4–6

UNION OF SOVIET SOCIALIST RE-
PUBLICS—HISTORY
Nazaroff, Land of the Russian People,
p.67–147   6

UNITED NATIONS
Barrows, Old World Lands, p.333–34
                                      6
Epstein, E., First Book of the United
Nations   4–6
Fisher, L., You and the United Nations
                                    5–6
Galt, How the United Nations Works
                                    5–6
Hays, Freedom, p.53, 55 (charter)
                                    5–6
Wagner, Put Democracy to Work,
p.128–38   6

UNITED NATIONS DAY
Burnett, B., First Book of Holidays,
p.37   4–5

UNEF
Epstein, E., First Book of the United
Nations, p.17–18   4–6

UNICEF
Epstein, E., First Book of the United
Nations, p.53–54   4–6
Galt, How the United Nations Works,
p.72–74   5–6

UNITED STATES—AIR FORCE ACAD-
EMY
Engeman, U.S. Air Force Academy   6

UNITED   STATES—BUREAU   OF
STANDARDS: see also Standard
Time; Weights and Measures
Bendick, How Much and How Many,
p.168–76   5–6

UNITED STATES—CIVIL SERVICE
Elting, We Are the Government, p.84–
85   6

UNITED STATES—COAST GUARD
Spencer, P. R., Exploring New Trails,
p.47–54   5

UNITED   STATES—DECLARATION
OF INDEPENDENCE: see Declaration of Independence

UNITED STATES—ECONOMIC CON-
DITIONS: see Boom Towns; Business Depressions

UNITED   STATES—EXPLORATION:
see Discovery Period in America;
Lewis and Clark Expedition; also
names of explorers, as Frémont, John
Charles

UNITED STATES—FISH AND WILD-
LIFE SERVICE
Colby, Fish and Wildlife   5–6

UNITED STATES—FOLK TALES: see
also Indians of North America—Folk
Tales; Negroes—Folk Tales; also
names of folklore characters, as
Bunyan, Paul
Fenner, Fools and Funny Fellows,
p.131–53   4–6
Harper, Ghosts and Goblins, p.52–56,
194–96, 208–15   4–6
Shapiro, Steamboat Bill and the Captain's Top Hat   5–6

UNITED STATES—GEOGRAPHY: see
also Mount Vernon; National Parks;
also names of cities, states, and regions, as Boston; Tennessee; West
Quinn, Picture Map Geography of the
United States   4–6

UNITED   STATES—GOVERNMENT:
see also Citizenship; Conservation;
Constitution of the United States;
Food Laws; Mail Service; Presidents
—United States
Brown, H. M., America Is My Country,
p.70–77   5–6
Coy, First Book of Congress   6
Eaton, That Lively Man, Ben Franklin,
p.114–251   6
Elting, We Are the Government   6
Ross, G. E., Know Your Government
                                      6

UNITED STATES—HISTORY: see also
Civil War in the United States; Colo-
nial Period in America; Declaration of
Independence; Flags; Indians of North
America; National Songs; Pioneer
Life; Pony Express; Revolutionary
War in America; Spanish-American
War, 1898; War of 1812; Westward
Movement; also states and cities,

subhead History, as California— History; Boston—History; and names of persons, as Franklin, Benjamin
Adams, S. H., Pony Express   4–6
———— Santa Fe Trail   5–6
Bailey, C. S., Children of the Handcrafts   5–6
Commager, H. S., First Book of American History   4–6
Foster, G., Abraham Lincoln's World   6
———— George Washington's World   6
Hansen, Old Ironsides   5–6
Harper, Harvest Feast   *4–6
Hunt, G. P., Story of the U.S. Marines   5–6
Johnson, G. W., America Grows Up   5–6
———— America Is Born   5–6
———— America Moves Forward   5–6
Jordan, American Costume Dolls   5–6
Lawson, R., Watchwords of Liberty   4–6
Olcott, Good Stories for Great Birthdays   *4–6
Petersham, America's Stamps   5–6

UNITED STATES—INDUSTRIES
Gilchrist, Story of the Great Lakes   4–6
Lent, Men at Work in New England   4–6
———— Men at Work in the Great Lakes States   4–6
Quinn, Picture Map Geography of the United States   4–6
Writers Project, Cement, no.33, p.21–38   5–6

UNITED STATES—MARINE CORPS
Colby, Leatherneck   5–6
Hunt, G. P., Story of the U.S. Marines   5–6

UNITED STATES—NAVY
Colby, Ships of Our Navy   5–6
Pratt, Monitor and the Merrimac   5–6

UNITED STATES—PRESIDENTS: *see* Presidents—United States

UNITED STATES—SUPREME COURT
Brown, H. M., America Is My Country, p.77–80   5–6

Coy, First Book of the Supreme Court   5–6
Elting, We Are the Government, p.24–27   6

UNITED STATES—TREASURY DEPARTMENT: *see also* Hamilton, Alexander
Elting, We Are the Government, p.32–37   6

UNITED STATES—WEATHER BUREAU
Gaer, Everybody's Weather, p.86–96   5–6

UNIVERSAL DECLARATION OF HUMAN RIGHTS
Epstein, E., First Book of the United Nations, p.56–59   4–6

UNIVERSE: *see* Astronomy; Space Travel

UNSELFISHNESS
Alden, Why the Chimes Rang, p.123–35   *4–6
Harper, Easter Chimes, p.40–49   *4–6
McGinley, Plain Princess   *4–6
Ruskin, King of the Golden River   *4–6
Sawyer, This Way to Christmas   *4–6

URANIUM
Crouse, W. H., Understanding Science, p.183–87   6
Fenton, C. L., Riches from the Earth, p.151–53   5–6
Fermi, Story of Atomic Energy   6
Loomis, Field Book of Common Rocks and Minerals, p.89–90   6
MacGregor, Miss Pickerell and the Geiger Counter   *4–6

URANUS (planet)
Asimov, Words from the Myths, p.13–18   6
Branley, Nine Planets, p.60–65   6
Gallant, R. A., Exploring the Planets, p.102–7   5–6
Goodwin, Real Book about Stars, p.105–8   4–6

URBAN-RURAL CONTRASTS
Bialk, Taffy's Foal   *4–5
Lawrence, Homemade Year   *4–5
Lenski, Cotton in My Sack   *4–6

URUGUAY
Goetz, Neighbors to the South, p.101–5   5–6
Quinn, Picture Map Geography of South America, p.65–72   4–6
Rothery, South American Roundabout, p.158–63   5–6

U.S.S.R.: *see* Union of Soviet Socialist Republics

UTAH: *see also* Bryce Canyon National Park; Zion National Park
Association for Childhood Education, Told under Spacious Skies, p.271–86
                                                                *4–6
Burt, Cave of the Shouting Silence
                                                                *5–6
Quinn, Picture Map Geography of the United States, p.160–63   4–6

VACA, ÁLVAR NÚÑEZ CABEZA DE: *see* Cabeza de Vaca, Álvar Núñez

VACATIONS
Enright, Gone-Away Lake   *4–6
———— Saturdays, p.158–75   *4–6
———— Then There Were Five   *5–6
Haywood, Betsy's Busy Summer   *4–5

VALENTINE'S DAY
Association for Childhood Education, Told under Spacious Skies, p.160–69
                                                                *4–6
Burnett, B., First Book of Holidays, p.8–9   4–5
Jordan, Holiday Handicraft, p.50–65
                                                                4–6
Kohler, "Crazy As You Look!", p.85–102
                                                                *4–6
Lee, What To Do Now, p.86–87   4–6
Leeming, Fun with Greeting Cards, p.77–82   4–6
McSpadden, Book of Holidays, p.26–31
                                                                6
Olcott, Good Stories for Great Holidays, p.41–56   *4–6
Pannell, Holiday Round Up, p.63–71
                                                                4–6
Robinson, J., Things To Make from Odds & Ends, p.24–25   4–6
Sechrist, Red Letter Days, p.51–58
                                                                5–6

VALUE BUILDING
Alden, Why the Chimes Rang   *4–6

Aulaire, Benjamin Franklin   4–6
Bulla, Secret Valley   *4–5
Clark, A. N., Magic Money   *4–6
Daringer, Adopted Jane   *4–6
De Angeli, Elin's Amerika   *4–6
———— Thee, Hannah!   *4–6
Friedman, F., Dot for Short   *4–5
Gates, Sensible Kate   *4–6
Haywood, Eddie's Pay Dirt   *4–5
Knight, E. M., Lassie Come-Home   *6
Lawrence, Homemade Year   *4–5
Lenski, Boom Town Boy   *4–6
Sorensen, Plain Girl   *4–6
Steele, Flaming Arrows   *4–6
Stolz, Dog on Barkham Street   *5–6
Weaver, Poppy in the Corn   *6

VAN BUREN, MARTIN
Beard, Presidents in American History, p.37–38, 158–59   6
Coy, First Book of Presidents, p.34
                                                                4–6
Petersham, Story of the Presidents of the United States, p.27–28   4–6

VANDYKE, ANTHONY
Chandler, Story-Lives of Master Artists, p.110–21   6

VANITY
De Angeli, Thee, Hannah!   *4–6

VAPOR: *see* Evaporation; Steam

VASCO DA GAMA: *see* Gama, Vasco da

VASQUEZ DE CORONADO, FRANCISCO: *see* Coronado, Francisco Vasquez de

VAUGHAN-WILLIAMS, RALPH
Burch, Modern Composers for Young People, p.123–25   5–6

VEGETABLES: *see also* Cooking; Gardening; Markets; also names of vegetables, as Potatoes
Buck, M. W., In Yards and Gardens, p.35–37   4–6
Carlson, B. W., Make It Yourself!, p.97–104   4–6
Eberle, Basketful, p.154–80   4–6
Fenton, C. L., Plants That Feed Us
                                                                5–6
Kirkus, First Book of Gardening, p.17–24   4–6

Parker, B. M., Garden and Its Friends, p.10–17   4–6
Scheib, First Book of Food, p.36–39   5–6

VELASQUEZ
Chandler, Story-Lives of Master Artists, p.122–34   6
Hillyer, Child's History of Art, p.94–96   5–6

VENEZUELA: *see also* Bolívar, Simón; Miranda, Francisco de
Bailey, B. F., Venezuela   4–6
Barrows, American Continents, p.320–23   5
Goetz, Neighbors to the South, p.60–64   5–6
Land, M., Jungle Oil   5–6
Quinn, Picture Map Geography of South America, p.93–104   4–6
Rothery, South American Roundabout, p.202–15   5–6

VENICE: *see also* Art—Venice
Buehr, World of Marco Polo, p.13–16   5–6
Kent, He Went with Marco Polo   *6

VENTILATION: *see also* Air Circulation; Air Conditioning; Heating; Mining
Van Metre, Trains, Tracks and Travel, p.296–301   6

VENTRILOQUISM
Severn, Let's Give a Show, p.69–79   4–6

VENUS (planet)
Branley, Nine Planets, p.29–36   6
Gallant, R. A., Exploring the Planets, p.32–40   5–6
Goodwin, Real Book about Stars, p.79–82   4–6
Hendrickson, Handbook for Space Travelers, p.173–75, 205–12   5–6
Schealer, This Way to the Stars, p.94–99   6
Schneider, L., Space in Your Future, p.66–70   6
Todd, Space Cat Visits Venus   *4–5

VERDI, GIUSEPPE
Burch, Famous Composers for Young People, p.113–20   4–6
Schwimmer, Great Musicians as Children, p.54–58   6

VERMEER, JOHANNES
Chandler, Story-Lives of Master Artists, p.149–62   6
Hillyer, Child's History of Art, p.90–92   5–6

VERMONT: *see also* Allen, Ethan
Association for Childhood Education, Told under Spacious Skies, p.21–34   *4–6
Canfield, Understood Betsy, p.21–213   *5–6
Henry, M., Justin Morgan Had a Horse   *4–6
Meigs, Covered Bridge   *4–6
Quinn, Picture Map Geography of the United States, p.8–11   4–6
Wriston, Susan's Secret   *4–5

VERNE, JULES
Peare, Jules Verne   5–6

VESPER SPARROWS
Webb, Birds in Their Homes, p.31   4–6

VESPUCCI, AMERIGO
American Heritage, Discoverers of the New World, p.40–45   5–6
Baker, N. B., Amerigo Vespucci   5–6
Hartman, Builders of the Old World, p.442–44   6

VESUVIUS, MOUNT
Hall, J., Buried Cities, p.16–24   5–6

VETERANS DAY
Brown, H. M., America Is My Country, p.199–202   5–6
Burnett, B., First Book of Holidays, p.43   4–5
McSpadden, Book of Holidays, p.162–65   6
Pannell, Holiday Round Up, p.257–63   4–6
Sechrist, Red Letter Days, p.188–95   5–6

VETERINARIANS
Bridges, Zoo Doctor   4–6
Robertson, K., Ticktock and Jim, p.219–36   *4–6

VIBRATION
Beeler, Experiments in Science, p.89–91   5–6
Geralton, Story of Sound   5–6
Knight, D. C., First Book of Sound, p.15–17   5–6

Schneider, H., Everyday Machines and How They Work, p.97–120 (music)
5–6

VICTORIA, QUEEN OF ENGLAND
Foster, G., Abraham Lincoln's World, p.95, 99–101, 169–73, 180–81, 217–20, 243–46, 295–97
6

VIETNAM
O'Daniel, Nation That Refused To Starve
5–6

VIKING SHIPS
Maginley, Historic Models of Early America, p.3–7
6

VIKINGS: *see* Northmen

VILLAGE LIFE—ALASKA
Butler, Alaska, p.42–62, 108–41
6
Stefansson, Here Is Alaska, p.81–106
6

VILLAGE LIFE—CHINA
Lattimore, Willow Tree Village
*4–5

VILLAGE LIFE—INCA
Bleeker, Inca, p.45–46
5–6
Cavanna, Lucho of Peru
4–6

VILLAGE LIFE—INDIA
Batchelor, Cap for Mul Chand
*4–5
Hahn, First Book of India, p.33–36
5–6
Louden, Rain in the Winds
4–5
Singh, Gift of the Forest
*6

VILLAGE LIFE—JAPAN
Yashima, M., Plenty To Watch
4–5

VILLAGE LIFE—LAPLAND
Berry, Men, Moss, and Reindeer, p.48–65
5–6

VILLAGE LIFE—NEW GUINEA
Sperry, Rain Forest, p.162–81 (pygmy)
*6

VILLAGE LIFE—UNITED STATES
De Angeli, Copper-toed Boots
*4–6
Kingman, Village Band Mystery
*4–5
Lang, Strawberry Roan, p.116–45
*5–6
McCloskey, Homer Price
*5–6
Rankin, C. W., Dandelion Cottage
*5–6
Wilson, H. H., Owen Boys
*5–6

VILLAGE LIFE—YUGOSLAVIA
Gidal, My Village in Yugoslavia
4–6

VINEGAR FLIES
Hyde, Animal Clocks and Compasses, p.127–28, 139–43
5–6

VIOLINS
Association for Childhood Education, Told under the Stars and Stripes, p.196–217
*4–6
Huntington, Tune Up
4–6
Judson, Lost Violin
*5–6
Lacey, Picture Book of Musical Instruments, p.2–3
5–6
Paine, Arkansas Bear
*4–6
Wheeler, Paganini
4–6

VIREOS
Webb, Birds in Their Homes, p.51
4–6

VIRGIN ISLANDS
Hughes, First Book of the West Indies, p.26–30
5–6
Quinn, Picture Map Geography of Mexico, Central America and the West Indies, p.105–7
4–6

VIRGIN ISLANDS NATIONAL PARK
Melbo, Our Country's National Parks, v.1, p.189–202
6

VIRGINIA: *see also* Shenandoah National Park
Association for Childhood Education, Told under Spacious Skies, p.128–35
*4–6
Bailey, B. F., Picture Book of Virginia
4–6
Banta, Life in America: The South, p.90–95
5–6
Coatsworth, Golden Horseshoe
*6
Lenski, Judy's Journey, p.156–70
*4–6
———— Peanuts for Billy Ben
*4–5
Quinn, Picture Map Geography of the United States, p.44–47
4–6

VIRGINIA—HISTORY: *see also* Jamestown, Virginia; Mount Vernon; Smith, John; Williamsburg, Virginia
Barksdale, That Country Called Virginia
6
Coy, Americans
6
Dalgliesh, America Begins, p.58–59, 62–63
4–5
———— America Builds Homes
4–5

Duvoisin, And There Was America, p.42–57   4–6

McGinley, Mince Pie and Mistletoe
                                              4–6

VIRUSES

Lewis, L. Z., First Book of Microbes, p.45   5–6

VITAMINS: *see also* Nutrition

Beeler, Experiments in Science, p.33–35   5–6

Eberle, Modern Medical Discoveries, p.151–67   5–6

Freeman, I. M., All about the Wonders of Chemistry, p.74–80   6

VIVARIUMS

Buck, M. W., Small Pets from Woods and Fields, p.42–43   4–6

VOLCANOES: *see also* Crater Lake National Park; Earthquakes; Geology; Hawaii National Park; Lassen Volcanic National Park; Vesuvius, Mount

Adler, Fire in Your Life, p.13–15   4–6

Brown, A. F., In the Days of Giants, p.243–59   *4–6

Buck, P. S., Big Wave, p.14–26   *6

Disney, Worlds of Nature, p.100–101
                                              4–6

Galt, Volcano   5–6

Pough, All about Volcanoes and Earthquakes, p.3–102   4–6

Reed, Earth for Sam, p.45–50   6

Rothery, Central American Roundabout, p.69–73   6

Sevrey, First Book of the Earth, p.29–30
                                              5–6

Tennant, All the Proud Tribesmen   *6

White, A. T., All about Our Changing Rocks, p.36–43   5–6

Williams, H. L., Stories in Rocks, p.25–35   6

Wyckoff, Story of Geology, p.30–47
                                              5–6

VOLLEYBALL

Bancroft, Games, p.421–22, 638–46
                                              4–6

VOLSUNGA SAGA: *see* Nibelungenlied; Siegfried; Sigurd

VOLTAIRE, FRANÇOIS MARIE AROUET DE

Foster, G., George Washington's World, p.45–47, 102–4   6

VORTIGERN, KING OF THE BRITONS

Farjeon, Mighty Men, p.139–43   4–6

WAGNER, RICHARD: *see also* Nibelungenlied; Siegfried

Buchanan, How Man Made Music, p.139–43   6

Burch, Famous Composers for Young People, p.103–11   4–6

Schwimmer, Great Musicians as Children, p.152–62   6

Sechrist, It's Time for Easter, p.116–23   5–6

Wheeler, Robert Schumann and Mascot Ziff, p.111, 134   4–6

WAINAMOINEN

Hazeltine, Hero Tales from Many Lands, p.317–31   5–6

WALES: *see also* Songs—Wales

Banning, Pit Pony   *4–6

Hazeltine, Hero Tales from Many Lands, p.136–59   5–6

Weir, R., Robert's Rescued Railway
                                              *5–6

WALKER, MARY RICHARDSON

Ross, N. W., Heroines of the Early West, p.93–125   5–6

WALKING STICK: *see* Stick Insects

WALL OF CHINA

Boardman, Castles, p.21–22   6

WALLACE, ALFRED RUSSEL

Asimov, Breakthroughs in Science, p.149–53   5–6

WALRUSES

Bridges, Zoo Babies, p.65–72   4–6

Darling, L., Seals and Walruses   4–6

Disney, Worlds of Nature, p.21–23
                                              4–6

Hogner, Animal Book, p.165–66   6

McCracken, Son of the Walrus King   6

WAMPUM

Salomon, Book of Indian Crafts & Indian Lore, p.107–10   6

WAPITI: *see* Deer

WAR: *see also* Red Cross; also names of wars, as Civil War in the United States

Evans, All about Us, p.56–59   4–6

Jewett, God's Troubadour, p.13–23
5–6
Meadowcroft, Gift of the River, p.189–98
5–6
Orbaan, With Banners Flying
6

WAR OF 1812
Barksdale, That Country Called Virginia, p.133–36
6
Batchelor, Sea Lady
*4–5
Coy, Real Book about Andrew Jackson, p.92–110
5–6
Foster, G., Abraham Lincoln's World, p.28–55
6
——— Andrew Jackson, p.73–82
4–6
Grant, B., Zachary, the Governor's Pig
*4–6
Judson, Andrew Jackson, p.148–60
5–6

WARBLERS: *see also* names of warblers, as Bluebirds; Robins; Yellow Warblers; Yellowthroats
Hyde, Animal Clocks and Compasses, p.49–53
5–6

WARSHIPS: *see also* Constitution (ship); Submarines; United States—Navy
Writers Project, Warships, no.9
5–6

WASHING MACHINES—AUTOMATIC
Schneider, H., Everyday Machines and How They Work, p.178–86
5–6

WASHINGTON, BOOKER TALIAFERRO
Graham, S., Booker T. Washington
6
Lawson, R., Watchwords of Liberty, p.86–88
4–6
Shackelford, Child's Story of the Negro, p.129–36
4–5

WASHINGTON, GEORGE: *see also* Mount Vernon; Washington's Birthday
Bailey, C. S., Pioneer Art in America, p.78–89
5–6
Barksdale, That Country Called Virginia, p.91–95, 107–22
6
Beard, Presidents in American History, p.9–11, 152–53
6
Coy, First Book of Presidents, p.24–25
4–6
Eaton, Washington
4–6

Fisher, D. F. C., And Long Remember, p.20–25
6
Foster, G., George Washington's World
6
Judson, George Washington
5–7
Lawson, R., Watchwords of Liberty, p.26–29
4–6
Meadowcroft, By Wagon and Flatboat, p.27–34
*4–5
——— Silver for General Washington
*5–6
Meigs, Wind in the Chimney, p.60–66
*5–6
Petersham, Story of the Presidents of the United States, p.7–10
4–6

WASHINGTON, D.C.
Barrows, American Continents, p.64–68
5
Brown, H. M., America Is My Country, p.81–103
5–6
Elting, We Are the Government, p.86–89
6
Hillyer, Child's History of Art, p.408–12
5–6
Holland, They Built a City
4–6
Quinn, Picture Map Geography of the United States, p.43
4–6

WASHINGTON STATE: *see also* Mount Rainier National Park; Olympic National Park
Quinn, Picture Map Geography of the United States, p.188–91
4–6

WASHINGTON'S BIRTHDAY
Brown, H. M., America Is My Country, p.191–92
5–6
Burnett, B., First Book of Holidays, p.10
4–5
Jordan, Holiday Handicraft, p.66–77
4–6
McSpadden, Book of Holidays, p.34–41
6
Olcott, Good Stories for Great Birthdays, p.189–234
*4–6
——— Good Stories for Great Holidays, p.59–68
*4–6
Pannell, Holiday Round Up, p.72–85
4–6
Sechrist, Red Letter Days, p.59–66
5–6

WASPS
Comstock, Handbook of Nature Study, p.378–84
6

Disney, Worlds of Nature, p.91–92
4–6

Hyde, Animal Clocks and Compasses, p.71–75 5–6

Hylander, Insects on Parade, p.167–73
6

Lane, F. C., All about the Insect World, p.81–86 5–6

Rounds, Wildlife at Your Doorstep, p.35–56 5–6

Teale, Junior Book of Insects, p.121–30
6

Williamson, First Book of Bugs, p.39–41 4–5

WATCHES: *see* Clocks

WATER: *see also* Evaporation; Floods; Fog; Glaciers; Ocean; Rain; Rivers; Snow; Steam; Water Power; Water Supply

Barr, More Research Ideas for Young Scientists, p.77–89 5–6
———— Research Ideas for Young Scientists, p.74–82 5–6

Beauchamp, Discovering Our World, Bk.1, p.56–61 4

Comstock, Handbook of Nature Study, p.808–14 6

Cooper, E. K., Science in Your Own Back Yard, p.49–57 5–6

Graham, E. H., Water for America 6

Huey, What Makes the Wheels Go Round, p.99–105 6

Larrick, See for Yourself, p.38–47
4–5

Morgan, A. P., First Chemistry Book for Boys and Girls, p.21–28 5–6

Parker, B. M., Water 5–6

Podendorf, 101 Science Experiments, p.60–71 4–5

Reed, And That's Why 4–5

Riedman, Water for People 6

Schloat, Magic of Water 4–6

Smith, F. C., First Book of Water
4–6

Writers Project, Wind, Water, and Air, no.21 5–6

Wyckoff, Story of Geology, p.64–69
5–6

WATER ANIMALS: *see* Animals—Fresh-Water; Marine Animals; also names of animals, as Whales

WATER BIRDS: *see also* names of birds found in and near the water, as Cormorants; Ducks; Gulls; Sandpipers

Bronson, Children of the Sea, p.19–23, 74–75 6

Brown, V., How To Understand Animal Talk, p.145 6

Comstock, Handbook of Nature Study, p.142–43 6

Doane, Book of Nature, p.98–99 5–6

Hylander, Out of Doors in Summer, p.130–42 5–6

Lane, F. C., All about the Sea, p.111–18 4–6

Rothery, South American Roundabout, p.73–81 5–6

Webb, Birds in Their Homes, p.56
4–6

WATER BUGS: *see also* Insects—Aquatic

Parker, B. M., Insects and Their Ways, p.17 4–6

WATER CLOCKS

Adler, Time in Your Life, p.54–58
4–6

Reck, Clocks Tell the Time, p.12–15
4–6

Tannenbaum, Understanding Time, p. 36–40 6

WATER INSECTS: *see* Insects—Aquatic

WATER LILIES

Morgan, A. H., Field Book of Ponds and Streams, p.91–95 6

WATER MITES

Morgan, A. H., Field Book of Ponds and Streams, p.175–78 6

WATER POWER: *see also* Dams

Bechdolt, Going Up, p.52–60 5–6

Graham, E. H., Water for America, p.41–43 6

Morgan, A. P., Boys' Book of Engines, Motors & Turbines, p.59–63 6

Parker, B. M., Water, p.29–33 5–6

Riedman, Water for People, p.71–83
6

Schneider, H., More Power to You, p.19–33 5–6

Smith, F. C., First Book of Water, p.33–38 4–6

WATER PRESSURE
Beeler, More Experiments in Science, p.92–96   5–6

WATER SUPPLY: *see also* Canals; Dams; Irrigation; Rivers; Water; Wells
Dawson, California, p.182–94   5–6
Parker, B. M., Water, p.6–11   5–6
Riedman, Water for People, p.112–52   6
Schneider, H., Let's Look inside Your House, p.4–11   4–5
———— Rocks, Rivers & the Changing Earth, p.31–47   4–6
Tarshis, Village That Learned To Read, p.30–34   *4–6

WATER WHEELS
Bechdolt, Going Up, p.67–69   5–6
Morgan, A. P., Boys' Book of Engines, Motors & Turbines, p.64–77, 181–200   6
Schneider, H., More Power to You, p.21–24   5–6
———— Science Fun with Milk Cartons, p.146–53   5–6

WATERLOO—BATTLE OF, 1815; *see* Napoleon I, Emperor of the French

WATERMELONS
Liu, Little Wu and the Watermelons   *4–5

WATTS, JAMES
Asimov, Breakthroughs in Science, p.54–57   5–6
Cottler, Heroes of Civilization, p.138–45   6
Foster, G., George Washington's World, p.50–53, 113–15   6
Judson, Boat Builder, p.76–79   5–6

WAXWORKS
Bailey, C. S., Pioneer Art in America, p.25–38   *5–6

WEALTH: *see* Money

WEAPONS: *see also* Arms and Armor; Guns
Bleeker, Cherokee, p.44–51   4–6
Boardman, Castles, p.86–88, 91–95   6
Buehr, Knights and Castles and Feudal Life, p.34–39, 42–43   4–6
Colby, Leatherneck, p.24–38   5–6
Salomon, Book of Indian Crafts & Indian Lore, p.177–217   6

WEASELS: *see also* Badgers; Minks; Otters
Brown, V., How To Understand Animal Talk, p.49–64   6
Hogner, Animal Book, p.120–35   6
Mason, G. F., Animal Tracks, p.40–41   4–6
Ripper, Weasel Family   4–5
Stoutenberg, Wild Animals of the Far West, p.21–38   4–6

WEATHER: *see also* Air Pressure; Climate; Clouds; Evaporation; Fog; Rain; Rainbow; Seasons; Snow; Storms; Thermometers; United States —Weather Bureau; Winds
Adler, Dust, p.45–55   5–6
———— Weather in Your Life   5–6
Angelo, Nino, p.45–59   *6
Barr, More Research Ideas for Young Scientists, p.63–76   5–6
———— Research Ideas for Young Scientists, p.64–73   5–6
Bendick, How Much and How Many, p.130–36   5–6
Blough, Not Only for Ducks   *4–5
———— Wait for the Sunshine   4–5
Brindze, Gulf Stream, p.55–63   4–6
Comstock, Handbook of Nature Study, p.780–807   6
Cooper, E. K., Science in Your Own Back Yard, p.164–73   5–6
Gaer, Everybody's Weather   5–6
Gallant, R. A., Exploring the Weather   5–6
Icenhower, First Book of the Antarctic, p.16–17   4–6
Irving, Hurricanes and Twisters   4–6
Leonard, Exploring Science, p.56–97   6
McCloskey, Time of Wonder   *4–5
MacGregor, Miss Pickerell Goes to the Arctic   *4–6
Moon, Chi-Wee, p.119–31   *4–6
Parker, B. M., Clouds, Rain, and Snow   4–6
Riedman, Water for People, p.99–110   6
Scheib, What Happened?, p.1–7   5–6
Schneider, H., Everyday Weather and How It Works   5–6
Tannehill, All about the Weather   4–6
Tannenbaum, Understanding Maps, p.105–13   5–6

Wyler, First Book of Weather　5–6
Zim, Lightning and Thunder　4–5

WEATHER FORECASTING
Adler, Weather in Your Life, p.99–111
　5–6
Barnard, Macmillan Science-Life Series,
　Bk.6, p.46–77　6
Fisher, J., Wonderful World of the Air,
　p.9–14　5–6
Frank, Ice Island, p.158–62　6
Gallant, R. A., Exploring the Weather,
　p.57–59　5–6
Morgan, A. P., Boys' Book of Science
　and Construction, p.402–52　6
Spilhaus, Weathercraft　6
Tannehill, All about the Weather, p.77–
　144　4–6

WEATHER MAPS
Barnard, Macmillan Science-Life Series,
　Bk.6, p.72–75　6
Comstock, Handbook of Nature Study,
　p.799–807　6
Spilhaus, Weathercraft, p.57–64　6

WEATHER VANES
Dalgliesh, Adam and the Golden Cock
　*4–5

WEAVING: *see also* Basketry; Beadwork;
　Cotton; Paper Work; Rugs; Tapestry;
　Textiles
Bleeker, Inca, p.54–57, 59–61, 69　5–6
Bonner, Made in Canada, p.56–64
　5–6
Buff, Dancing Cloud, p.35–40　4–5
Burglon, Children of the Soil, p.165–72,
　207–37　*4–6
Hartman, Machines, p.1–13　6
Hollos, Story of Your Coat　4–5
Jaeger, Easy Crafts, p.92–99　4–6
Jordan, Holiday Handicraft, p.187–89
　4–6
Leeming, Fun with Boxes, p.79–81
　4–6
——— Fun with String, p.103–17
　4–6
Meigs, Wind in the Chimney　*5–6
Zarchy, Let's Make Something, p.138–
　39　5–6

WEBSTER, DANIEL
Lawson, R., Watchwords of Liberty,
　p.42–43　4–6

WEDGES
Meyer, Machines, p.57–64　4–6
Parker, B. M., Machines, p.22–23
　5–6
Schneider, H., Everyday Machines and
　How They Work, p.77–82　5–6

WEEDS: *see also* Gardening; Plants
Comstock, Handbook of Nature Study,
　p.512–45　6
Morgan, A. H., Field Book of Ponds
　and Streams　6

WEEMS, MASON LOCKE
Bailey, C. S., Pioneer Art in America,
　p.90–102　5–6

WEIGHTS AND MEASURES: *see also*
　Calendars; Flotation; Gravitation;
　Markets; Tools; United States—Bu-
　reau of Standards
Adler, Giant Golden Book of Math-
　ematics, p.14–15　6
Barr, More Research Ideas for Young
　Scientists, p.141–53　5–6
——— Research Ideas for Young
　Scientists, p.108–18　5–6
Beeler, Experiments in Science, p.119–
　24　5–6
Bendick, How Much and How Many
　5–6
Bleeker, Inca, p.86–87　5–6
Burns, Man and His Tools, p.145–55
　5–6
Morgan, A. P., First Electrical Book
　for Boys, p.91–100　6
Schneider, H., Everyday Machines and
　How They Work, p.146–56　5–6

WEINGARTNER, FELIX VON
Schwimmer, Great Musicians as Chil-
　dren, p.180–85　6

WELDING
Darrow, Boys' Own Book of Great In-
　ventions, p.401–7　6

WELLS: *see also* Water Supply
Maginley, Historic Models of Early
　America, p.145–47　6
Wilder, Little House on the Prairie,
　p.147–61　*4–6

WEST, BENJAMIN
Foster, G., George Washington's World,
　p.18–20　6

Henry, M., Benjamin West and His Cat Grimalkin 4–6
Hillyer, Child's History of Art, p.136–39 5–6
Judson, Boat Builder, p.66–73 5–6

WEST: *see also* Colorado River; Great Plains; Indians of North America; Lewis and Clark Expedition; National Parks; Oregon Trail; Pioneer Life; Pony Express; Prairies; Ranch Life; Santa Fe Trail; Southwest; also names of western states, as Colorado; and of national parks, as Yellowstone National Park
Aulaire, Buffalo Bill 4
Barrows, American Continents, p.181–226 5
Bleeker, Horsemen of the Western Plateaus 4–6
Garst, Jim Bridger 6
——— Kit Carson 6
Hooker, Star *5–6
Judson, Theodore Roosevelt 5–6
McGinley, Mince Pie and Mistletoe 4–6
Ross, N. W., Heroines of the Early West 5–6

WEST INDIES: *see also* Columbus, Christopher; Cuba; Haiti; Jamaica; Puerto Rico; Virgin Islands
Barrows, American Continents, p.308–12 5
Hughes, First Book of the West Indies 5–6
Quinn, Picture Map Geography of Mexico, Central America and the West Indies, p.78–114 4–6
Rothery, South American Roundabout, p.229–42 5–6

WEST VIRGINIA
Quinn, Picture Map Geography of the United States, p.48–51 4–6

WESTINGHOUSE, GEORGE: *see* Air Brakes

WESTWARD MOVEMENT: *see also* California Gold Rush; Covered Wagons; Oregon Trail; Pony Express; Santa Fe Trail; Stagecoaches; Transcontinental Railway; also names of leaders of the Westward Movement, as Boone, Daniel; Buffalo Bill

Brock, Drusilla *4–5
Commager, H. S., First Book of American History, p.29–39 4–6
Crawford, "Hello, the Boat!" *6
Dalgliesh, America Travels, p.107–11 4–6
Foster, G., Abraham Lincoln's World 6
Henry, R. S., Trains, p.21–56 5–6
Meadowcroft, By Wagon and Flatboat *4–5
Meigs, Wind in the Chimney *5–6
Olds, Riding the Rails 4–5
Orton, Treasure in the Little Trunk *4–6
Tousey, Jerry and the Pony Express *4–5
Wilder, Little House on the Prairie *4–6
——— On the Banks of Plum Creek *4–6

WHALES
Andrews, All about Whales 5–6
Beaty, Baby Whale 4–6
Disney, Worlds of Nature, p.18–21 4–6
Fenton, C. L., Life Long Ago, p.249–52 6
Hogner, Animal Book, p.181–85, 194–206 6
Hyde, Animal Clocks and Compasses, p.92–95 5–6
Icenhower, First Book of the Antarctic, p.57–60 4–6
Kipling, Just So Stories, p.1–12 *4–6
Knight, C. R., Life through the Ages, p.28–29 6
Lavine, Strange Travelers, p.106–12 5–6
Osmond, Animals of the World, v.2 4–6
Parker, B. M., Animals We Know, p.14–15 5–6
Zim, Great Whales 4–5

WHALING
American Heritage, Story of Yankee Whaling 5–6
Andrews, All about Whales, p.21–33 5–6
Fenner, Fools and Funny Fellows, p.131–53 *4–6
Field, Hitty, p.34–59 *5–6

Golden, Made in Iceland, p.88–96　6
Holling, Book of Indians, p.106–14
　　　　　　　　　　　　　　　*4–6
———— Seabird, p.16–30　　　*4–6
Icenhower, First Book of the Antarctic,
　p.22–24　　　　　　　　　　4–6
Mitchell, Ships That Made U.S. History, p.53–57　　　　　　　　6

WHARVES: *see* Harbors

WHEAT: *see also* Bread; Flour; Grain
Eberle, Basketful, p.9–24　　　4–6
———— Grasses, p.29–34　　　4–6
Shannon, Dobry, p.67–71　　　*5–6

WHEATLEY, PHILLIS
Shackelford, Child's Story of the Negro,
　p.78–82　　　　　　　　　　4–5

WHEELS: *see also* Bicycles; Machines;
　Water Wheels
Bechdolt, Going Up, p.19–22　5–6
Buehr, Story of the Wheel　　4–6
Liberty, First Book of Tools, p.31, 34–
　37　　　　　　　　　　　　5–6
Meyer, Machines, p.21–37　　4–6
Parker, B. M., Machines, p.20–21　5–6
Schneider, H., Everyday Machines and
　How They Work, p.38–47, 79–80,
　167–72　　　　　　　　　　5–6

WHIPPOORWILLS
Blough, After the Sun Goes Down,
　p.10–13　　　　　　　　　　4–5
Mason, G. F., Animal Sounds, p.29–30
　　　　　　　　　　　　　　5–6

WHISTLER, JAMES McNEILL
Chandler, Story-Lives of Master Artists,
　p.212–22　　　　　　　　　6
Hillyer, Child's History of Art, p.146–
　49　　　　　　　　　　　　5–6

WHISTLES
Buchanan, How Man Made Music,
　p.49–50 (ancient)　　　　　6
Jaeger, Easy Crafts, p.36–37　4–6

WHITMAN, NARCISSA
Ross, N. W., Heroines of the Early
　West, p.52–92　　　　　　　5–6

WHITNEY, ELI
Hartman, Machines, p.14–23　6

WHITTIER, JOHN GREENLEAF
Bailey, C. S., Pioneer Art in America,
　p.129–42　　　　　　　　　*5–6

Holberg, John Greenleaf Whittier　6

WHITTLING: *see also* Carpentry; Handicraft
Bailey, C. S., Children of the Handcrafts, p.23–32　　　　　　　5–6

WIGGIN, KATE DOUGLAS
Coffman, Famous Authors for Young
　People, p.133–38　　　　　　5–6

WILD ANIMALS: *see* Animals

WILD BOARS
Buck, F., Jungle Animals, p.36–37
　　　　　　　　　　　　　　5–6

WILD CATS
Zim, Big Cats　　　　　　　5–6

WILD FLOWERS: *see also* Botany; Flowers; Plants
Beeler, More Experiments in Science,
　p.64–67　　　　　　　　　　5–6
Comstock, Handbook of Nature Study,
　p.460–511　　　　　　　　　6
Hylander, Out of Doors in Autumn,
　p.9–42　　　　　　　　　　5–6
———— Out of Doors in Spring, p.58–
　83　　　　　　　　　　　　5–6
Parker, B. M., Saving Our Wild Life,
　p.24–25　　　　　　　　　　5–6

WILD LIFE CONSERVATION: *see also*
　Animals—Protection; Birds—Protection; National Parks
Franklin, Monte　　　　　　*4–6
Melbo, Our Country's National Parks,
　v.1, v.2　　　　　　　　　　6
Parker, B. M., Saving Our Wild Life
　　　　　　　　　　　　　　5–6

WILDERNESS ROAD
Meadowcroft, On Indian Trails with
　Daniel Boone　　　　　　　4–5

WILKES, CHARLES
Frank, Ice Island, p.19–24　　6

WILLIAM I, THE CONQUEROR, KING
　OF ENGLAND
Farjeon, Mighty Men, p.194–211　4–6
Hartman, Builders of the Old World,
　p.231–35　　　　　　　　　6

WILLIAM OF ORANGE
Barnouw, Land of William of Orange,
　p.28–38　　　　　　　　　　6

WILLIAMS, RALPH VAUGHAN: *see*
　Vaughan-Williams, Ralph

WILLIAMS, ROGER
  Duvoisin, And There Was America, p.67–69   4–6
  Olcott, Good Stories for Great Birthdays, p.347–55   *4–6

WILLIAMSBURG, VIRGINIA
  Barksdale, That Country Called Virginia, p.50   6
  Petersham, Silver Mace   4–5

WILLOW TREES
  Comstock, Handbook of Nature Study, p.651–55   6
  Cormack, First Book of Trees, p.85–86   4–6
  Faralla, Willow in the Attic   *4
  McKenny, Trees of the Countryside, p.34–35   4–6

WILSON, WOODROW
  Beard, Presidents in American History, p.113–15, 174–75   6
  Coy, First Book of Presidents, p.55–56   4–6
  Lawson, R., Watchwords of Liberty, p.102–3   4–6
  Petersham, Story of the Presidents of the United States, p.63–65   4–6

WIND CAVE NATIONAL PARK
  Melbo, Our Country's National Parks, v.1, p.82–90   6

WIND INSTRUMENTS
  Balet, What Makes an Orchestra, p.10–13, 16–21, 24–25   5–6
  Buchanan, How Man Made Music, p.36–58   6
  Commins, Making an Orchestra, p.10–17   5–6
  Huntington, Tune Up   4–6
  Lacey, Picture Book of Musical Instruments, p.11–13   5–6
  Norman, First Book of Music, p.52–55   4–6
  Posell, This Is an Orchestra, p.28–50   5–6

WIND POWER
  Branley, Solar Energy, p.104–9   6
  Schneider, H., More Power to You, p.4–17   5–6

WINDLASS
  Bechdolt, Going Up, p.23–24   5–6

WINDMILLS
  Schneider, H., More Power to You, p.8–14   5–6

WINDOW DECORATION
  Bechdolt, Going Up, p.74–77   5–6
  Schneider, H., Science Fun with Milk Cartons, p.129–30   5–6

WINDOWS: *see* Stained Glass Windows

WINDS
  Adler, Weather in Your Life, p.21–56   5–6
  Beeler, More Experiments in Science, p.124–27   5–6
  Brindze, Story of the Trade Winds   4–6
  Comstock, Handbook of Nature Study, p.791–98   6
  Irving, Hurricanes and Twisters   4–6
  Spilhaus, Weathercraft, p.18–28   6
  Writers Project, Wind, Water, and Air, no.21   5–6
  Wyler, First Book of Weather, p.22–27   5–6

WINDWARD ISLANDS
  Quinn, Picture Map Geography of Mexico, Central America and the West Indies, p.111–12   4–6

WINE
  Angelo, Nino, p.141–46   *6
  Writers Project, Grapes, no.37, p.40–44   5–6

WINGED HORSE: *see* Pegasus

WINTER: *see also* Animals—Migration; Animals in Winter; Birds—Migration; Hibernation; Plants in Winter; Seasons; Snow
  Harrison, Outdoor Adventures, p.106–25   4–5
  Hylander, Out of Doors in Winter   5–6
  Kane, Tale of a Pond, p.4–8   5–6
  Lawson, R., Tough Winter   *4–6
  Stong, Honk, the Moose   *4–5
  Wilder, Long Winter   *5–6

WINTER SPORTS
  Lattimore, Little Pear and His Friends, p.46–80   *4–5
  McSwigan, Snow Treasure   *5–6

WIRE
  Leeming, Fun with Wire   5–6

WIRELESS: *see also* Radio
Darrow, Boy's Own Book of Great Inventions, p.60–97   6
Freeman, I. M., All about Electricity, p.88–97   5–6

WISCONSIN
Bailey, B. F., Picture Book of Wisconsin   4–6
Brink, Caddie Woodlawn   *6
———— Magical Melons   *5–6
Enright, Thimble Summer   *5–6
Havighurst, Life in America: The Midwest, p.130–34   5–6
Lent, Men at Work in the Great Lakes States, p.66–69, 78–87, 110–13 4–6
Quinn, Picture Map Geography of the United States, p.100–103   4–6
Rietveld, Nicky's Bugle   *4–6
Wilder, Little House in the Big Woods   *4–6

WITCHCRAFT: *see also* names of countries, subhead Folk Tales, as Hungary —Folk Tales
Chase, V., Knight of the Golden Fleece   6
Coatsworth, Away Goes Sally, p.29–37   *4–6
Estes, Witch Family   *4–6
Gatti, Here Is the Veld, p.93–102   6
Laughlin, Little Left-over Witch *4–5
Leach, Thing at the Foot of the Bed, p.91–101   *4–6
Norton, Bed-Knob and Broomstick   *4–5
Sleigh, Carbonel   *4–6

WOLVERINES
Hogner, Animal Book, p.130–31   6
Mason, G. F., Animal Tracks, p.66–67   4–6
Ripper, Weasel Family, p.54–59   4–5
Stoutenberg, Wild Animals of the Far West, p.28–29   4–6

WOLVES: *see also* Coyotes
Comstock, Handbook of Nature Study, p.250–51   6
Franklin, Wild Animals of the Southwest, p.103–15   5–6
Hogner, Animal Book, p.140–44   6
Jewett, God's Troubadour, p.58–65   5–6
Kipling, Jungle Book, p.3–46   *5–6

Lippincott, Wilderness Champion   *5–6
McCracken, Sentinel of the Snow Peaks   5–6
Mason, G. F., Animal Homes, p.13–17   4–6
———— Animal Sounds, p.88–89 5–6
———— Animal Tracks, p.62–63 4–6
Orton, Treasure in the Little Trunk, p.133–41   *4–6
Robinson, W. W., Beasts of the Tar Pits, p.14–16   5–6
Stoutenberg, Wild Animals of the Far West, p.44–46   4–6
Wilder, Little House on the Prairie, p.80–98   *4–6

WOOD, GRANT
Bailey, C. S., Pioneer Art in America, p.208–21   *5–6

WOOD: *see also* Forestry; Lumbering; Trees
Buehr, Timber!   5–6

WOOD CARVING
Burglon, Children of the Soil, p.191–206   *4–6
Carlson, B. W., Make It and Use It, p.125–41   4–6
Coatsworth, Alice-All-By-Herself, p.135–44   *4–6
———— Five Bushel Farm, p.35–40   *4–5
Fry, Bell for Ringelblume   *4–5
Golden, Made in Iceland, p.97–108   6
Smith, E. S., Christmas Book of Legends & Stories, p.362–75   5–6

WOOD ENGRAVING: *see* Engraving

WOOD THRUSHES
Webb, Birds in Their Homes, p.13   4–6

WOODCHUCKS
Barker, Winter-sleeping Wildlife, p.10–18   5–6
Colby, First Hunt, p.6   5–6
Comstock, Handbook of Nature Study, p.229–32   6
Gall, Flat Tail, p.75–83   4–6
———— Wagtail, p.109–22 4–6
Hogner, Animal Book, p.52–55   6
Hyde, Animal Clocks and Compasses, p.110–12   5–6
Kane, Tale of a Meadow, p.90–92 4–6

Lathrop, Let Them Live, p.61–63 4–6
Mason, G. F., Animal Homes, p.25–27
  4–6

———— Animal Tracks, p.14 4–6
Moe, Animal Inn, p.7–18 4–6
Snow, Come, Chucky, Come *4–6

WOODCRAFT: *see also* Camping
Mason, B. S., Junior Book of Camping
  and Woodcraft 5–6

WOODLAND INDIANS
Tunis, Indians, p.30–57 6

WOODPECKERS: *see also* Flickers; Redheaded Woodpeckers
Comstock, Handbook of Nature Study,
  p.70–80 6
Disney, Worlds of Nature, p.140–41
  4–6
Parker, B. M., Birds, p.6–8 4–6

WOODSON, CARTER G.
Shackelford, Child's Story of the Negro,
  p.202–6 4–5

WOOL: *see also* Dyeing; Sheep; Textiles
Buff, Dancing Cloud, p.58–67 4–5
Freeman, I. M., All about the Wonders
  of Chemistry, p.102–6 6
Schwartz, It's Fun To Know Why,
  p.62–74 5–6

WORDS: *see also* Dictionaries; Language
Asimov, Words from the Myths 6
Brown, M. J., Peter Piper's Alphabet
  4–5
Epstein, S., First Book of Codes and
  Ciphers 4–6
———— First Book of Words 5–6
Frasconi, See and Say 4–6
Galt, Seven Days from Sunday 6
Hughes, First Book of Rhythms, p.34–
  36 4–6
Leeming, Fun with Puzzles, p.64–74
  6
Lobsenz, First Book of West Germany,
  p.59–63 4–6
McMeekin, Journey Cake, p.229–31
  *5–6
Mulac, Game Book, p.165–78 6
Parker, F., Russian Alphabet Book 6
Picturesque Word Origins 6
Rhoads, Corn Grows Ripe, p.85–88
  *4–6

WORK
Batchelor, Superstitious? Here's Why!,
  p.56–59 6

WORLD HEALTH ORGANIZATION
Epstein, E., First Book of the United
  Nations, p.63–64 4–6

WORLD UNDERSTANDING: *see*
  Brotherhood of Man

WORLD WAR, 1914–18: *see also* Submarines; Veterans Day
Hillyer, Child's History of the World,
  p.460–64 5–6
Hunt, G. P., Story of the U.S. Marines,
  p.117–32 5–6
Seredy, Singing Tree *6
Snyder, First Book of World War I
  5–6

WORLD WAR, 1939–45
Bishop, C. H., Pancakes—Paris *4–6
Bliven, Story of D–Day: June 6, 1944
  5–6
Flexner, Wishing Window *4
Hillyer, Child's History of the World,
  p.474–87 5–6
Hunt, G. P., Story of the U.S. Marines,
  p.134–63 5–6
Lattimore, Peachblossom *4–5
McSwigan, Snow Treasure *5–6
Rothery, Scandinavian Roundabout, p.
  120–31, 217–26 6
Shirer, Rise and Fall of Adolf Hitler
  5–6
Snyder, First Book of World War II
  5–6
Sowers, Swords and Sails in the Philip-
  pines *5–6
Street, Land of the English People,
  p.55–59, 110–22 6

WORLD'S FAIR: *see* Chicago—World's
  Columbian Exposition, 1893

WORMS: *see also* Caterpillars; Silkworms
Comstock, Handbook of Nature Study,
  p.422–25 6
Cooper, E. K., Science in Your Own
  Back Yard, p.100–105 5–6
Doane, Book of Nature, p.104–5 5–6
Fenton, C. L., Life Long Ago, p.46–49
  6
Hausman, Beginner's Guide to Fresh-
  Water Life, p.84–91, 102–7 6

Morgan, A. H., Field Book of Animals in Winter, p.69–78, 97–101　　6

———— Field Book of Ponds and Streams, p.119–26, 139–47　　6

Robertson, G., Strange Sea Life, p.35–39　　5–6

WREN, CHRISTOPHER
Hillyer, Child's History of Art, p.397–400　　5–6

WRENS
Webb, Birds in Their Homes, p.42　　4–6

WRIGHT, ORVILLE, AND WRIGHT, WILBUR
Bishop, R. W., From Kite to Kitty Hawk, p.161–74　　6
Cottler, Heroes of Civilization, p.239–48　　6
Haines, Wright Brothers　　4–5
Hartman, Machines, p.237–42　　6
Reynolds, Q. J., Wright Brothers　　4–6

WRITERS: *see* Authors; Poets; also names of authors and poets, as Hawthorne, Nathaniel; Whittier, John Greenleaf

WRITING: *see also* Alphabets; Authors; Books; Hieroglyphics; Ink; Language; Paper; Pens; Picture Writing; Typewriters
Kubie, First Book of Archaeology, p.38–42　　6
Pei, All about Language, p.22–29　　6
Spencer, P. R., Finding New Trails, p.187–94　　4

WRITING—ARABIC
Fitch, Allah, the God of Islam, p.108–9　　6

WRITING—CHINESE
Spencer, C., Made in China, p.73–78　　5–6

WYOMING: *see also* Grand Teton National Park; Yellowstone National Park
Association for Childhood Education, Told under Spacious Skies, p.257–70　　*4–6
Floethe, Triangle X　　*4
Larom, Mountain Pony　　*6
———— Mountain Pony and the Pinto Colt　　*6

Lippincott, Wilderness Champion, p.90–133　　*5–6
Quinn, Picture Map Geography of the United States, p.164–67　　4–6

X RAYS
Morgan, A. P., First Electrical Book for Boys, p.250–53　　6

XERXES THE GREAT, KING OF PERSIA
Falls, First 3000 Years, p.153–56, 165, 173　　6
Farjeon, Mighty Men, p.38–50　　4–6

YARN: *see* Cotton; Wool

YEAST
Buehr, Bread, p.14–16, 63–64　　4–6
Parker, B. M., Dependent Plants, p.22–24　　5–6

YELLOW WARBLERS
Webb, Birds in Their Homes, p.24　　4–6

YELLOWSTONE NATIONAL PARK
Holling, Book of Indians, p.70–72　　4–6
Melbo, Our Country's National Parks, v.1, p.3–44　　6

YELLOWTHROATS
Webb, Birds in Their Homes, p.23　　4–6

YOM KIPPUR
Taylor, S., More All-of-a-Kind Family, p.25–38　　*4–6

YOSEMITE NATIONAL PARK
Melbo, Our Country's National Parks, v.2, p.3–28　　6

YOSHITSUNE
Hazeltine, Hero Tales from Many Lands, p.429–46　　5–6

YOUNG, CHARLES
Shackelford, Child's Story of the Negro, p.168–71　　4–5

YUCATAN: *see also* Mayas
Rhoads, Corn Grows Ripe　　*4–6

YUCCA
Fox, From Bones to Bodies, p.52–53　　6
Parker, B. M., Plant and Animal Partnerships, p.30–31　　5–6

YUDHISTHIR
  Hazeltine, Hero Tales from Many
    Lands, p.363–80   5–6

YUGOSLAVIA: *see also* Costume—Yu-
  goslavia
  Barrows, Old World Lands, p.115–17
                                      6
  Gidal, My Village in Yugoslavia 4–6
  Kish, Yugoslavia   6

YUGOSLAVIA—FOLK TALES
  Fenner, Time To Laugh, p.85–107
                                    4–6

YUKON TERRITORY
  Lindquist, W., Alaska, p.36–46   5–6
  Quinn, Picture Map Geography of Can-
    ada and Alaska, p.86–92   4–6

ZANZIBAR
  Stinetorf, Children of South Africa,
    p.107–18   *5–6

ZEBRAS
  Buck, F., Jungle Animals, p.50–52
                                    5–6
  Disney, Worlds of Nature, p.167–69
                                    4–6
  Hogner, Horse Family, p.32–38   4–6
  Perkins, Marlin Perkins' Zooparade,
    p.48–49   4–6

ZEPPELINS: *see* Airships

ZICHY, GEZA
  Schwimmer, Great Musicians as Chil-
    dren, p.146–51   6

ZINC
  Fenton, C. L., Riches from the Earth,
    p.154–56   5–6
  Loomis, Field Book of Common Rocks
    and Minerals, p.63–70   6

ZION NATIONAL PARK
  Burt, Cave of the Shouting Silence
                                   *5–6
  Melbo, Our Country's National Parks,
    v.1, p.242–56   6

ZIPPERS
  Schneider, H., Everyday Machines and
    How They Work, p.162–63   5–6

ZOOLOGY: *see also* Animals; Animals—
  Domestic;   Animals—Fresh-Water;
  Animals—Habits and Behavior; Bac-
  teria; Birds; Crustacea; Evolution;
  Fishes; Fossils; Hibernation; Insects;
  Mammals; Marine Animals; Nature
  Study; Reptiles; Snakes; Worms; also
  names of animals, as Dogs; Reindeer
  Morgan, A. H., Field Book of Animals
    in Winter   6

ZOOS: *see also* names of zoo animals,
  as Pandas
  Blough, When You Go to the Zoo
                                    4–6
  Bridges, Zoo Babies   4–6
  ———— Zoo Doctor   4–6
  Brown, V., How To Make a Miniature
    Zoo   5–6
  Mason, G. F., Animal Sounds, p.92–94
                                    5–6
  Perkins, Marlin Perkins' Zooparade
                                    4–6
  Reynolds, B. L., Pepper   *4–6
  Selsam, Underwater Zoos   4–6

ZULUS
  Gatti, Here Is the Veld, p.67–76   6

ZUNI INDIANS
  Brewster, First Book of Indians, p.44–
    53   4–5